# SOCIAL POLICY

## Second Edition

**Hugh Bochel**
Department of Policy Studies, University of Lincoln

**Catherine Bochel**
Department of Policy Studies, University of Lincoln

**Robert Page**
Institute of Applied Social Studies, University of Birmingham

**Robert Sykes**
Faculty of Development and Society, Sheffield Hallam University

PEARSON
Prentice
Hall

Harlow, England • London • New York • Boston • San Francisco • Toronto • Sydney • Singapore • Hong Kong
Tokyo • Seoul • Taipei • New Delhi • Cape Town • Madrid • Mexico City • Amsterdam • Munich • Paris • Milan

**Pearson Education Limited**

Edinburgh Gate
Harlow
Essex CM20 2JE
England

and Associated Companies throughout the world

*Visit us on the World Wide Web at:*

www.pearsoned.co.uk

First published 2005
**Second edition published 2009**

© Pearson Education Limited 2005, 2009

ISBN: 978-1-4058-5836-6

**British Library Cataloguing-in-Publication Data**
A catalogue record for this book is available from the British Library.

**Library of Congress Cataloging-in-Publication Data**
Social policy : themes, issues and debates / Hugh Bochel . . . [et al.]. – 2nd ed.
    p. cm.
 Includes bibliographical references and index.
 ISBN 978-1-4058-5836-6 (pbk. : alk. paper) 1. Great Britain—Social policy.
I. Bochel, Hugh M.
 HV248.S264 2009
 320.60941–dc22

                                      2008052587

10 9 8 7 6 5 4 3 2
13 12 11

Typeset in 9.5/12.5 pt Stone Serif by 73
Printed and bound by *Ashford Colour Press, Gosport*

# Short contents

# Contents

## Supporting resources

Visit www.pearsoned.co.uk/bochel to find valuable
online resources

### Companion Website for students

- Annual updates
- Online glossary
- Extra weblinks
- Further information on social policy in the devolved administrations
  including Eire

For more information please contact your local Pearson Education sales
representative or visit www.pearsoned.co.uk/bochel

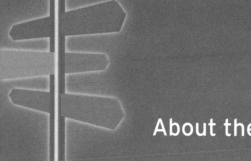

# About the contributors

**Sue Bond-Taylor** is Senior Lecturer in Criminology at the University of Lincoln.

**Paul Daniel** is Senior Lecturer in Childhood and Society at Roehampton University.

**Nick Ellison** is Professor of Sociology and Social Policy at the University of Leeds.

**Norman Ginsburg** is Professor of Social Policy at London Metropolitan University.

**Jon Glasby** is Professor of Health and Social Care at the University of Birmingham.

**Bernard Harris** is Professor of the History of Social Policy at the University of Southampton.

**Kelvin Jones** is Head of the Department of Policy Studies at the University of Lincoln.

**Brian Lund** is Principal Lecturer in Social Policy at Manchester Metropolitan University.

**Stephen McKay** is Professor of Social Research at the University of Birmingham.

**Lavinia Mitton** is Lecturer in Social Policy at the University of Kent.

**Karen Rowlingson** is Professor of Social Policy at the University of Birmingham.

**Gary Taylor** is Principal Lecturer in Applied Social Science at Sheffield Hallam University.

# Preface

The few years that have elapsed between the writing of the first and second editions of this book have only served to reinforce the view that social policy is of fundamental importance in contemporary societies, with debates over the appropriate direction of policies, and the relationship with politics and economics, having been key features of the period.

As we noted in the first edition, social policy affects all of us, featuring in our everyday lives effectively from the cradle to the grave, through our use of services, our payment for them, whether directly or through taxation, and our discussions about topics such as asylum seekers, employment and unemployment, housing, education, health care or pensions.

This, significantly expanded, second edition, is intended to support the study of social policy, providing a comprehensive picture from the early development of social policies to an exploration of contemporary policies, ideas and issues.

The book sets out to make its presentation of the subject thorough but accessible, through the use of text, boxed examples and tables, and cartoons. Each chapter begins by identifying the key issues with which it deals, and uses a variety of examples (labelled as 'spotlight on the issues' and 'briefings'), raises questions ('thought provokers') and ends with a chapter summary and conclusion, followed by review questions, suggestions for further reading and useful websites.

Each student will develop their own way to use the book: some may seek to read it through from start to finish, others will be concerned to develop more specific knowledge, and will therefore focus on certain chapters, or even parts of chapters. However, the nature of the subject is such that there will inevitably be links that can be made between the contents of different chapters, and these will strengthen your understanding of social policy. We hope that you find it useful.

*Catherine Bochel*
*Hugh Bochel*
*Robert Page*
*Robert Sykes*

# Guided tour

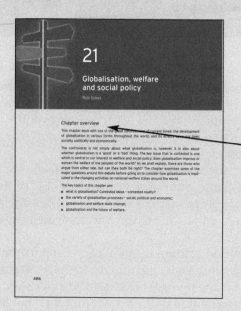

**Chapter overview** serves as a brief introduction to the themes of each chapter and quickly allows you to see the main points to be explored.

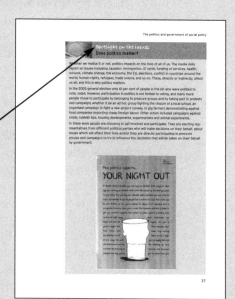

**Spotlight on the issues** brings social policy to life by demonstrating the relevance of the themes of each chapter to the real world.

**Controversy and debate** gives you a 'snapshot' of some of the most contentious and divisive issues in social policy today, and provides the opportunity to assess these debates and your own standpoint on them.

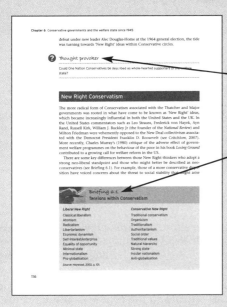

**Thought provoker** provides a chance to stop and reflect on what you've learned, and what you think of particular examples of social policy in action.

**Briefing** boxes condense key information within chapters, to help you get to grips with important facts and issues. They are also a highly-useful revision tool.

**Summary**, at the end of each chapter, reminds you of the key concepts you've covered, to consolidate your learning and aid revision.

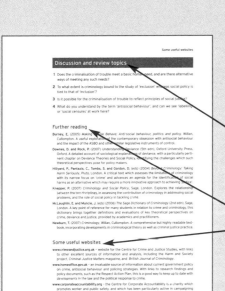

**Discussion and review topics** are an opportunity to apply what you've learned from each chapter, by providing challenging questions for group or individual consideration.

**Further reading** and **Some useful websites**, at the end of each chapter, help you to go further with your learning, and provide useful starting points for research and revision resources.

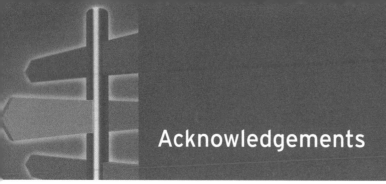

# Acknowledgements

## Authors' acknowledgement

We are grateful to Andrew Taylor, for suggesting a second edition of this book, and for seeing it through to completion, and his colleagues at Pearson, Catherine Morrissey and Sarah Busby, for their encouragement and support. They have been enormously important in helping ensure that the book was produced successfully. We would also like to thank Tim Parker, Colin Reed, Angela Hawksbee and Michelle Morgan for their excellent work on the production of the book.

## Publisher

The publishers would like to thank all the contributors for their efforts towards providing such excellent chapters for this new edition. We'd also like to extend our gratitude to all the editors for their dedication and expertise in pulling together this revision. Particular thanks to Hugh Bochel, for leading the project with such enthusiasm, generosity and helpfulness.

The publishers would also like to thank the panel of anonymous reviewers who generously offered so many useful ideas towards the preparation of a new edition. Particular thanks to the reviewers of the manuscript, who are listed below and provided expert assistance as the book was being written.

Hyun Bang Shin, University of Leeds

Michael Cahill, University of Brighton

John Richardson, Cardiff University

Phil Haynes, University of Brighton

Richard Parry, University of Edinburgh

Penny Bernstock, UEL

We are grateful to the following for permission to reproduce copyright material:

Figures 4.1 and 4.2 from Ethics: The Heart of Health Care, Copyright 1998 © John Wiley & Sons Limited, reproduced with permission (Seedhouse, D. 1988); Figure 15.2 from *Policies and strategies to promote social equity in health* with permission from Institute for Futures Studies, Stockholm, Sweden (Dahlgren, G. and Whitehead, M. (1991); Tables 19.1 and 19.2 from *The social situation in the European Union 2003*, with permission of OPOCE (European Commission/Eurostat 2003); Figure 21.1 redrawn from Koenig-Archibugi, M. (2002) 'Mapping global governance' in Governing Globalization edited by D. Held and A. McGrew, reprinted by permission of Polity Press Ltd; Chapter 11, text extract from 'Parents ready to move for good school' by Lucy Ward, The Guardian, 17/10/07 with permission, Copyright 2007, Guardian News & Media Ltd; Chapter 18 selected text extracts from 'Inequality is fattening' by Polly Toynbee, The Guardian, 28/05/04 with permission, Copyright 2004, Guardian News & Media Ltd. Chapter 20 text extract from 'The Awful Truth About Sweden' (J Wennström, 2005), First published by the Institute of Economic Affairs, London, December 2005.

We would like to thank the following for their kind permission to reproduce their photographs:

Page 75, CartoonStock Ltd: Canary Pete; Page 90, Corbis: Historical Picture Archive; Page 119, British Cartoon Archive, University of Kent, www.cartoons.ac.uk: Chris Duggan; Page 130, Getty Images: Max Mumby/Kelvin Bruce; Page 153, British Cartoon Archive, University of Kent, www.cartoons.ac.uk: David Simonds; Page 171, CartoonStock Ltd: Robert Thompson; Page 242, CartoonStock Ltd: Jackson Graham; Page 418, CartoonStock Ltd: Harley Schwadron.

In some instances we have been unable to trace the owners of copyright material, and we would appreciate any information that would enable us to do so.

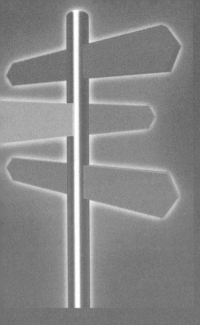

# Part I

## THE CONTEXT FOR SOCIAL POLICY

# 1

# Introducing social policy

Hugh Bochel

## Chapter overview

Social policy is one of the social sciences, along with subjects such as politics or sociology. It is sometimes studied on its own, sometimes jointly with another subject, and also is frequently delivered as part of another subject. It is often taken as part of professional training, such as in nursing or social work. This chapter seeks to provide a consideration of the subject of social policy, how it relates to other cognate subjects, and what it means to be studying it. It therefore:

● explores the nature of the subject, including the way in which it has developed as an academic discipline over time;
● outlines the structure of the remainder of the book.

# What is social policy?

The almost inevitable starting point for a book such as this is the question 'what is social policy?' Whilst this is perhaps equally likely for a book on other social sciences, there is perhaps a greater importance for social policy, in part because the subject itself has developed and changed direction considerably from the 1980s, in part because the actions of governments and others impact upon what might be considered as 'social policy' (see, for example, Chapter 18), and in part because these considerations continue to have significant resonance within the subject as it and its subject matter evolve further.

As an academic subject, social policy is clearly related to other social science disciplines, such as economics, politics or sociology, but it also has a resonance with many professional courses, such as those focusing on social work, housing or nursing. Given the connections, it is not surprising that the study of social policy often draws upon concepts and insights that come from all of these areas, but at the same time it brings its own distinctive approach to the understanding and analysis of the world. In the same way, a subject such as criminology, which has largely emerged in UK higher education since the 1990s, also draws upon a range of subjects, including social policy, but is itself developing and debating its boundaries (see, for example, Chapter 14).

Although it may draw upon a range of cognate areas, social policy as an academic discipline can be seen as differing from others in a number of ways. For example, it is different from sociology in its focus upon the formulation, implementation and delivery of policies that affect the circumstances of individuals, groups and society; it differs from politics in its focus upon welfare and well-being; and it is different from economics because it is less concerned with the production of goods and services, and because of its emphasis upon social or welfare policies and their outcomes. This is not to say that there are not sometimes closely related interests, and social policy academics and courses may be located in departments with a variety of labels in different higher education institutions, whilst social policy departments may in turn contain individuals who draw heavily upon or who originate from other subjects. There are also many institutions where social policy is in a department jointly with one or more other subjects, such as criminology, politics, social work or sociology. These all reflect the complexity and breadth of the subject.

Notwithstanding the discussion above, the nature of the subject has changed considerably over time. For much of the twentieth century 'social administration', as it was then called, was strongly associated with the **Fabian** tradition, itself linked to social democratic thought including the Labour Party (see Chapter 7). Many social administration academics were therefore seeking not merely to study social policy, but also to influence it in a direction that fitted generally with Fabian beliefs, often using their research and analysis to support their political arguments. These could roughly be characterised as a belief in the role of the state as a central pillar of welfare provision (the '**welfare state**'), generally located in a mixed economy, and a commitment to research and analysis that was concerned with the identification of needs and the impact of state welfare in attempting to meet those needs. However, in the second half of the twentieth century a more critical approach emerged within the subject, and by the 1970s and 1980s it was possible to identify a number of theoretical challenges to the association of Fabianism and the study of social administration and social policies linked to the welfare state. These included:

- The **New Right** and other 'anti-collectivists' – one of the most significant attacks on state provision of welfare (see Chapters 6 and 8) came from the right, and in particular from think tanks such as the Adam Smith Institute, the Centre for Policy Studies and the Institute for Economic Affairs. These critiques took a number of forms but could generally be seen as arguing that: the welfare state was a burden on the economy and that it demanded too high levels of public expenditure and an excessive tax burden upon entrepreneurs and citizens; that it damaged individual choice, in contrast to the market, which is seen from this perspective as promoting choice; and that it weakens the family and encourages dependency. The strategies which the New Right put forward as alternatives typically involved cuts in income tax, a shift away from state provision to individuals providing for themselves and their families through the private market, direct charging for services such as education and health, and the replacement of most of the benefits and services provided by the state with alternatives from the private and voluntary sectors.

- On the left there also emerged a number of criticisms – some began to accept that the role of the state remained problematic in the provision of welfare, and whilst in some instances state intervention had been valuable in changing social conditions, in others it had not always been so beneficial. Some argued that one answer was the injection of more resources to help tackle problems more successfully, whilst others favoured alternative approaches, such as the decentralisation of power and the encouragement of self-help for particular groups. One view, associated with a Marxist approach, suggested that in reality state welfare reflected the needs of capitalism for an educated, healthy workforce, and that this explained the failure of the welfare state to solve social problems.

- Critiques of the welfare state also emerged from centrist positions, often focusing upon the view that the large bureaucratic organisations that were often responsible for delivering welfare were inefficient and inflexible and were remote from the needs of consumers, and that they tended to be run in the interests of professionals and administrators rather than users or citizens; from this perspective proposed solutions generally involved a shift towards a pluralistic, decentralised and more participative pattern of provision, including a much greater role for the voluntary sector.

- Other critical perspectives (see Chapter 14) – for example, feminists pointed out that there were a number of assumptions behind the provision of many services, including education, healthcare and the personal social services, such as that it was 'natural' for women to provide care for children, disabled people and older people, and that they would often provide this care free at home whilst men went out to work and earn the household income. The state therefore could be seen as exploiting and encouraging the 'caring role' of women. Even when women did work (often in the 'caring services') there was a tendency for them to do so in the less-well paid jobs, whilst men dominated the higher status better-paid positions. In a similar manner, it could also be pointed out that many welfare services failed to recognise particular needs of minority ethnic groups, disabled people and others.

In addition there were other developments that encouraged reflection within the subject. These included other New Right critiques, in particular of bureaucracies, which have been important in the delivery of state welfare. New Right thinkers have argued that bureaucrats are primarily concerned with promoting their own interests, and that they do this at the expense of the public interest. In addition they suggest that political control of state bureaucracies is often ineffective. From the perspective of the New Right these combine to increase the pressure for higher levels of public expenditure, which itself is seen as problematic and a drain on the economy. Given the large bureaucracies often associated with state welfare provision, these arguments, if accepted, raise significant questions over the mechanisms used for delivering welfare.

It is also worth noting here that, whilst the academic subject of social policy, and indeed many social policies, has been concerned with improving the welfare of citizens, or leading to greater social justice, there is nothing necessary or inevitable about this. Social policies (and other measures, such as taxation (see Chapter 9)) can equally be designed to ignore or even to increase inequalities.

From the 1970s there also came to be a much greater awareness of the relevance of comparison to the study and understanding of social policy. In part this resulted from the United Kingdom's membership of the European Union, which inevitably focused greater attention upon Europe and other European states. However, increasingly this interest spread to other areas of the world, and in particular sought to learn from the experiences and policies of other states. For some, for example, the Scandinavian states provided models for state welfare founded in a social democratic approach. For others, the more market-oriented approach of the United States appeared to present a more appropriate path for the United Kingdom. Whatever the approach, it became apparent that there was a great diversity of forms of welfare provision, with very different mixes of provision by the public, private, voluntary and informal sectors. The comparative approach to social policy has developed greatly in recent years and is now a major strand within the subject (see Chapters 19 and 20), while concerns over international trends such as globalisation have been seen as having implications for the shape of social policies, and thus for the academic subject (see Chapter 21). In addition, there are many examples of **policy transfer**, with governments drawing upon ideas and policies from other countries, such as the establishment of the Child Support Agency by the Conservatives (see Dolowitz, 2000), and elements of Labour's New Deal, which drew on the experience of the United States.

The impact of all of these developments has inevitably affected the academic subject of social policy. Over a period of time it came to reflect and respond to these debates, arguably becoming broader and, in some respects at least, more critical. It is therefore not surprising that during the 1980s there was considerable debate about the nature of the discipline. However, the subject has not entirely lost its traditional links, with a number of university departments and awards continuing to use the term 'social administration', whilst the government bodies that fund and oversee much of higher education, such as the Higher Education Funding Council for England and the Quality Assurance Agency for Higher Education (QAA), often refer to social policy and administration. Indeed the QAA's subject benchmark statement (Briefing 1.1), which seeks to outline the nature and characteristics of the subject and the attributes and capabilities that an honours graduate in social policy should possess, is for social policy and administration. As illustrated elsewhere in this book (for example, Chapters 11 and 16), the boundaries and relevance of social policy and its insights continue to evolve.

Interestingly, consideration of the statement contained within Briefing 1.1 demonstrates both the academic and the applied nature of the subject, since the benchmark statement attempts to set out academic characteristics but is doing so in response to a policy imperative in the form of pressure from governments to measure and maintain standards in higher education (see Chapter 11).

### Briefing 1.1
### Social policy and administration subject benchmark: the nature and extent of the subject

Social policy and administration is about the study of the distribution and organisation of welfare and well-being within societies. Its focus is on the ways in which different societies understand and meet the needs of their populations. The discipline is characterised by the following principles:

- the rigorous linking of theoretical analysis with empirical enquiry
- the identification and understanding of different value positions
- a willingness to engage with a range of intellectual traditions and social science disciplines
- the belief that students should acquire the skills and qualities which enable them to become active and informed citizens.

Social policy is an interdisciplinary and applied discipline which is concerned with analysing the distribution and delivery of resources in response to social need. The subject draws on ideas and methods from sociology, political science and economics, while also using insights from a range of disciplines including social anthropology, human geography, social psychology and social work. As a discipline in its own right, social policy studies the ways in which societies provide for the social needs of their members through structures and systems of distribution, redistribution, regulation, provision and empowerment. It seeks to foster in its students a capacity to assess critically evidence from a range of social science disciplines and to appreciate how social policies are continuously reconstructed and changed. Students will understand the contribution to these processes from those who come from different value positions and different social, cultural and economic backgrounds. They will also appreciate the fact that some social groups are more able to protect, alter or advance their value positions more effectively than others.

*Source*: Quality Assurance Agency for Higher Education (2007) *Social Policy and Administration*, QAA, Gloucester, p. 2.

However, attempts to define the subject also need to recognise that social policy exists outside the academic world, and that much of what governments and other bodies do is social policy. Policies can be designed to help people, although even those that are intended to do so may not always achieve their aims, for a variety of reasons. Others may be 'technocratic' in nature – designed to improve a mechanism, perhaps to achieve something more efficiently or economically, or even to improve the nature of policy making itself. And social policies can be used to control people, as we have seen in recent years with demands to control or deter asylum seekers and migrants, or with regard to antisocial behaviour. One of the things that students and analysts of social policy need to do, therefore, is to examine policies critically – to look at their intentions and impacts and consider the extent to which they do actually achieve their goals, and the reasons why and why not this might be the case. As the QAA benchmark statement suggests, we must therefore sometimes try to set aside our personal views and opinions, and, in addition, it can be useful to try to see things from the perspectives of others. For example, we can seek to understand why some people feel strongly about individual choice and others favour collective provision, or why managers and health professionals in the National Health Service may clash over the best way to meet particular goals. We can try to put ourselves in the place of politicians who have to make sometimes difficult decisions about the level of resources that should be spent on welfare (and other areas of activity) and how the money for this should be raised, or the people who then have to deliver services, or those who are recipients. Each of these may provide us with very different perspectives on social policies. However, we also have to recognise that we all have our own values and attitudes, our own visions of what a good society should be like, and that the study of social policy is likely to involve us in both seeking to be objective and in maintaining our beliefs, and that at times there is likely to be a tension between the two.

## The structure of this book

Whilst the discussion above has outlined the complexity of the study of social policy, this book is written on the assumption that most students of social policy have little or no knowledge of the academic subject, even if all have inevitably come into contact with social policies. Given that social policy exists in a social, political and economic environment, the chapters in Part I set out the background, including social and economic changes and the political context, within which social policies are made and delivered.

Part II focuses upon the development of social policy, beginning with changes in the provision of welfare and changing attitudes to the role of the state, and then considering key influences upon social policy in the form of the ideas that have underpinned Conservative and Labour governments and their approaches. Chapter 8 then considers a number of alternative approaches and their implications for the understanding and development of social policy.

There then follows in Part III a series of chapters that can be broadly characterised as focusing primarily upon the delivery and impacts of social policy. Whilst inevitably reflecting the legacy of previous governments and policies, these examine the development of social policy under Labour from 1997. In many respects, therefore, these chapters are concerned not only with changes and priorities in social policy, but also with social policies as they affect individuals.

Reflecting the preceding discussion about the broader international scope of interests in social policy, Part IV examines European and international developments, including the European Union and its impact upon social policy development, comparisons between the UK and other states, and debates about globalisation and its implications for social policy.

Each chapter is designed to provide information and also to encourage you to think for yourself about its subject matter. Each also gives directions to additional sources of information, both written and via the Internet, to allow students to follow up areas in which they have a particular interest.

## Summary

This chapter has outlined the development of the subject of social policy and has shown that:

- the academic study of social policy has moved away from a focus upon the welfare state towards a much broader consideration of provision by the public, private, voluntary and informal sectors;

- theoretical debates have been and continue to be important, not only in increasing our ability to understand and explain social policy, but also in influencing the decisions of policy makers, as was reflected in the move away from the post-war consensus over the social democratic state towards a view that has been more influenced by New Right thinking;

- our understanding of social policy has been affected further by the growth of an international dimension which itself has been affected by the greater awareness of the range of modes of welfare provision (and different systems of payment for welfare) in different states, and by the United Kingdom's involvement in the European Union.

## Discussion and review topics

1 What is social policy?

2 In what ways do social policies affect your everyday life?

3 How useful is the concept of the 'welfare state'?

## Further reading

**Alcock, P., May, M. and Rowlingson, K.** (eds) (2008) *The Student's Companion to Social Policy,* Blackwell, Oxford. Contains a number of useful discussions including what social policy is, approaches to social policy, resources and careers.

**Alcock, P., Erskine, A. and May, M.** (eds) (2002) *The Blackwell Dictionary of Social Policy*, Blackwell, Oxford. A useful source of definitions of a range of ideas relevant to social policy.

**Fraser, D.** (2002) *The Evolution of the British Welfare State*, Palgrave Macmillan, Basingstoke. This book provides a comprehensive history of welfare policy in Britain.

## Some useful websites

**www.direct.gov.uk** – provides links to government departments and other organisations responsible for social policy and services throughout the United Kingdom.

**www.oecd.org** – the Organisation for Economic Cooperation and Development site contains considerable amounts of information relevant for comparisons across countries.

**www.qaa.ac.uk/academicinfrastructure/benchmark/statements/SocialPolicy07.pdf** – this is the QAA benchmark statement for 'Social Policy and Administration'.

## References

Dolowitz, D. (2000) *Policy Transfer and British Social Policy*, Open University Press, Buckingham.

Quality Assurance Agency for Higher Education (2007) *Social Policy and Administration*, QAA, Gloucester.

# 2

# The socio-economic context of social policy

Nick Ellison

## Chapter overview

Changing patterns of employment, the changing shape of families and family life, the impact of key demographic changes on national communities – each of these phenomena carries profound implications for how social policy is perceived and understood. Why should this be so? How is it that welfare policies are so closely connected to issues of employment and family life?

There is a constant 'dialogue' between social and economic phenomena that make up the context of social policy making and the organisation of social policy itself. So, briefly taking changes in employment patterns as an example, the majority of welfare systems in the mid to late twentieth century were constructed around particular assumptions about the nature of work and the respective roles of men and women in the labour market. Unfortunately (for policy makers at least) these assumptions quickly became outdated. What constituted 'work' and who did it changed rapidly and radically – and it is no exaggeration to say that the majority of welfare states have been playing catch-up ever since the 1960s when these changes first became visible.

This chapter demonstrates how rapidly things can change in the modern world and how relatively slowly welfare arrangements seem to respond to these changes. The result, of course, is that welfare states, despite having their roots in the radical, progressive politics of the first half of the twentieth century, can appear rather 'conservative' and unresponsive to social and economic change.

The chapter explores the following key issues:

- **Changing patterns of work in the UK and elsewhere.** Over the past fifty years the impact of employment changes on post-war assumptions about what constitutes 'work' and who does it have challenged the very basis of welfare state organisation in the developed economies.

- **The impact of employment changes on key social divisions.** One aspect of these changes has been the way in which they have reduced the salience of traditional social class divisions and substituted a more fragmented, overlapping series of divisions that include class, gender, 'race' and disability as key points of 'difference'.
- **Changing family structures.** Although the nature of work constitutes a key dimension of the socio-economic environment, changing perceptions of, and expectations about, the role of the family are equally significant because these too affect the organisation and delivery of welfare.
- **Demographic change.** The character and make-up of populations change over time – and this chapter examines the implications of migration and population ageing for the organisation of social policy.

## Spotlight on the issues
### Changing families

- The proportion of children living in lone-parent families in Great Britain more than tripled between 1972 and spring 2006 to 24 per cent.
- In 2005 the number of people living alone in Great Britain had more than doubled since 1971, from 3 million to 7 million.
- In the second quarter of 2006, 58 per cent of men and 39 per cent of women aged 20-24 in England lived with their parents, an increase of around 8 percentage points since 1991.
- There were 15,700 civil partnerships formed in the UK between December 2005 and September 2006. Of these, 93 per cent were in England and Wales, 6 per cent were in Scotland and 1 per cent were in Northern Ireland.
- In 2005, 24 per cent of non-married people aged under 60 were cohabiting in Great Britain, around twice the proportion recorded in 1986.
- The average age for mothers at first child-birth was 27.3 years in England and Wales in 2005, more than three years older than in 1971.

These 'headline' figures from the 'Households and families' chapter of the 2007 edition of *Social Trends* illustrate the type and pace of social change that has been occurring in the United Kingdom in recent years, and the consequent challenges facing policy makers in responding to such developments. Similar rapid change can be seen in relation to the economy, and in other policy areas. It is clearly difficult for governments to predict such changes, let alone their implications for the way that we live our lives. Yet such developments can be of crucial importance, including in relation to social policy. This chapter outlines some of the major changes that have taken place in the UK and considers what they may mean for social policy and the provision of welfare.

# Changing employment patterns

Work is absolutely central to social policy. Why? Because ensuring the availability of paid employment is the most obvious way of reducing the risk of poverty for individuals and their families. While this statement needs to be qualified in a number of ways – for example, it may not be possible for literally everyone to work, even if jobs are available, because some people are disabled, and women carry out a vast amount of unpaid domestic and caring work in the home – it is the case, nevertheless, that paid employment underpins social policy making in all the developed welfare states (see also Chapter 10, which explores the relationship between work and welfare in recent years in greater depth).

This stress on employment is as old as 'social policy' itself. In Britain, the Elizabethan Poor Law (1601) saw the appointment of overseers in each parish who were charged with the task of finding work for the able-bodied unemployed, while the 'New Poor Law' (1834) actively forced the able-bodied into the employment market by making conditions in the new 'workhouses' so bad that only the completely destitute would contemplate entering them (see Chapter 5). Poor Law arrangements of one kind or other existed in most parts of Europe into the twentieth century, only being gradually overtaken by organised welfare systems which aimed to produce full employment as part of a wider strategy of economic management. Certainly by the end of the Second World War governments in Northern and Western Europe, in addition to those in Australia, New Zealand, Canada and the USA, acknowledged that they had a major role in maintaining employment. Quite how they did this varied somewhat among the different countries, but between roughly the late 1940s and the late 1970s 'full employment' was a major policy goal in these states, with governments actively managing the '**demand side**' of their economies in efforts to achieve it.

The real issue, however, is what sort of 'employment' governments were attempting to sustain. In the early part of the post-war period, almost without exception, the (unstated) goal was full *male* employment and it is no great exaggeration to suggest that the welfare systems that developed in Europe and elsewhere took for granted the fact that men worked while married women remained at home. Consequently, income provision for unemployment, sickness and old age largely depended on the size and continuity of the male wage. In the majority of welfare states, the employed 'breadwinner' would pay insurance contributions from his wages either directly to the state or into special insurance funds to provide pensions and other benefits for both himself and his wife. Outside these arrangements, which were quite generous in countries like Germany and France, though less so in Britain, there were only means tested forms of 'social assistance' to support those who were not able to work or who had gaps in their employment record.

Whether or not this understanding of full employment is defensible in terms of the clear gender bias that characterises it is not the issue here – important though this matter is. In terms of the socio-economic context of social policy, the significant point is that, from the 1960s onwards, structural changes in the majority of the developed economies meant that full male employment became increasingly hard to maintain. These changes favoured new forms of work which were less dependent on the male industrial worker and, if anything, more disposed towards the employment of women.

The key shift concerned the dramatic decline of the '**Fordist**' manufacturing industry – characterised by the virtually all-male, unionised workforce engaged in production line assembly – and the rise of '**post-Fordist**' or 'post-industrial' forms of employment, usually based in the service industries (Amin, 1994). Although the causes of this change are complex and cannot be discussed in detail here, it is important to appreciate that a number of factors contributed to it. It is highly likely that rising global economic competition meant that many manufactured goods could be produced more cheaply in the developing economies; but it is also the case that 'post-industrial' changes *within* many advanced economies were also significant factors. The emergence of new labour-saving technologies reduced reliance on human labour, for example, while changes in patterns of consumption as incomes rose and consumers became more discerning meant that demand for mass-produced standardised goods gave way to a range of new 'wants' for ever more sophisticated 'niche' products and services. To meet these changing consumption patterns, producers had to become more 'flexible' – able to shift product lines and refocus workforce skills according to market demands. Underpinning these changes has been the extraordinary rise of the 'knowledge economy' which has entailed a need to move workforces away from the traditional skills associated with heavy industry and mass production towards a very different range of abilities concerned with knowledge exploitation, creativity and, above all, the capacity continually to 're-skill' in response to constantly shifting consumption patterns.

The following tables provide an insight into the nature and timing of this move from male-based manufacturing to service sector employment – a process that became visible around the early 1960s, developed throughout that decade and gathered speed across the 1980s and early 1990s. Table 2.1 provides data gathered by the Organisation for Economic Cooperation and Development (OECD) which demonstrates how employment in manufacturing fell in a number of countries between 1960 and 1994.

**Table 2.1** Employment in manufacturing as a percentage of civilian employment

| Country | 1960 | 1968 | 1974 | 1986 | 1990 | 1994 |
|---|---|---|---|---|---|---|
| United States | 26.5 | 27.5 | 24.2 | 19.1 | 18.0 | 16.0 |
| Japan | 21.3 | 26.1 | 27.2 | 24.7 | 24.1 | 23.2 |
| Germany | 34.3 | 35.7 | 35.8 | 32.2 | 30.2 | 25.6 |
| France | 27.3 | 26.8 | 28.3 | 22.7 | 19.8 | 19.0 |
| Italy | 24.2 | 27.0 | 28.0 | 22.9 | 22.4 | 22.9 |
| United Kingdom | 38.4 | 36.4 | 34.6 | 24.4 | 22.2 | 18.0 |
| Canada | 24.6 | 24.4 | 21.7 | 17.1 | 15.8 | 14.4 |
| Australia | 30.7 | 27.2 | 25.1 | 18.3 | 14.3 | 13.2 |
| Denmark | 25.1 | 22.2 | 21.4 | 21.6 | 21.6 | 20.8 |
| Sweden | 31.5 | 30.5 | 28.3 | 22.9 | 20.0 | 17.3 |

*Source*: OECD, 1996, Table 2.11.

With the exception of Japan (which is something of an anomaly in the table on manufacturing employment because, during the 1960s and 1970s, the country benefited from having a large and cheap workforce, but this advantage was lost during the late 1980s and 1990s as other Asian and South East Asian countries overtook Japan in their ability to produce cheap manufactured goods), all countries experienced a loss of manufacturing employment during the period, but it is worth acknowledging how serious the decline was in the United States, the United Kingdom, Canada and Australia. However, the rise in service sector employment over the same period is also very clear, as Table 2.2 illustrates.

**Table 2.2** Employment in services as a percentage of civilian employment

| Country | 1960 | 1968 | 1974 | 1986 | 1990 | 1994 |
| --- | --- | --- | --- | --- | --- | --- |
| United States | 56.2 | 59.4 | 63.4 | 69.3 | 70.9 | 73.1 |
| Japan | 41.3 | 45.7 | 50.1 | 57.1 | 58.7 | 60.2 |
| Germany | 39.1 | 43.0 | 46.3 | 54.8 | 56.7 | 59.1 |
| France | 39.9 | 45.8 | 49.9 | 61.3 | 64.4 | 68.4 |
| Italy | 33.5 | 39.3 | 43.2 | 56.0 | 58.5 | 59.7 |
| United Kingdom | 47.6 | 51.3 | 55.1 | 66.7 | 69.2 | 72.4 |
| Canada | 54.1 | 59.7 | 63.1 | 69.9 | 71.1 | 73.3 |
| Australia | 50.1 | 54.1 | 58.0 | 66.9 | 69.2 | 71.3 |
| Denmark | 44.8 | 49.9 | 58.0 | 65.9 | 66.9 | 68.1 |
| Sweden | 44.0 | 49.8 | 56.3 | 65.7 | 67.3 | 71.6 |

*Source*: OECD, 1996, Table 2.12.

So, employment in manufacturing industry plainly declined over the 1960–94 period in the major economies – and indeed this trend continues, although not at so dramatic a pace. In addition, service sector work, which includes a wide variety of employment ranging from the highly paid banking and legal sectors to low-paid jobs in catering, cleaning and leisure services, increased markedly in all cases and, again, continues to do so at a slower pace. Table 2.3 shows how the percentage of women in the workforce has risen as the nature of employment has changed.

In fairly simple terms, then, as male employment in the manufacturing sector declined, employment in the service sector increased and this shift allowed more women to enter the workforce. Although the change was by no means an unalloyed good for women, because many service sector jobs are non-unionised, part-time or casual, with the low wages that these working conditions often imply, it nevertheless had the effect of radically altering prevailing assumptions about the nature of work.

A final table (2.4) is necessary because it is important to see how the changes discussed here affected overall rates of employment. In essence, the numbers of unemployed rose in the majority of the advanced economies as manufacturing industry shed workers. Although the service sector certainly helped to stem resulting unemployment, the fact that work in this sector tends to be less secure and non-unionised has meant that service jobs have never fully offset the combined effects of the decline in manufacturing employment and (with more women coming into the labour market) the rising numbers of people seeking work.

Table 2.3 Female labour force as a percentage of the total labour force

| Country | 1970 | 1974 | 1990 | 1994 | 1996 | 2003 |
|---|---|---|---|---|---|---|
| United States | 37.2 | 38.7 | 44.9 | 45.6 | 45.9 | 46.8 |
| Japan | 39.3 | 37.6 | 40.6 | 40.5 | 40.5 | – |
| Germany | 35.9 | 37.5 | 40.4 | 42.4 | 42.8 | 45.3 |
| France | 35.7 | 37.0 | 43.4 | 44.5 | 44.7 | 46.4 |
| Italy | 28.8 | 29.7 | 36.8 | 36.2 | 37.0 | 38.3 |
| United Kingdom | 35.3 | 37.4 | 43.0 | 43.8 | 44.0 | 45.0 |
| Canada | 33.3 | 35.8 | 44.2 | 44.8 | 45.1 | – |
| Australia | 32.2 | 34.4 | 41.4 | 42.1 | 42.8 | 44.6 |
| Denmark | 38.6 | 40.9 | 46.1 | 46.0 | 45.8 | 46.5 |
| Sweden | 39.5 | 41.8 | 47.9 | 48.0 | 47.8 | 48.3 |

*Source*: OECD, 2001, Table 2.3; OECD, 2004.

Table 2.4 Standardised unemployment rates

| Country | 1960–64 | 1970 | 1974 | 1990 | 1994 | 2000 | 2005 |
|---|---|---|---|---|---|---|---|
| United States | 5.5 | 4.9 | 5.6 | 5.6 | 6.9 | 4.0 | 5.1 |
| Japan | 1.4 | 1.2 | 1.4 | 2.1 | 2.9 | 4.7 | 4.6 |
| Germany | 0.8 | – | – | 4.8 | 8.5 | 7.8 | 11.3 |
| France | 1.5 | – | – | 9.0 | 12.3 | 9.3 | 9.9 |
| Italy | 3.5 | – | – | 9.0 | 11.2 | 10.4 | 7.8 |
| United Kingdom | 2.6 | – | 2.6 | 7.1 | 9.6 | 5.4 | 4.6 |
| Canada | 5.5 | 5.7 | 5.3 | 8.1 | 10.4 | 6.8 | 6.8 |
| Australia | 2.5 | 1.7 | 2.7 | 6.9 | 9.7 | 6.3 | 5.2 |
| Denmark | 2.2 | – | – | 7.7 | 8.2 | 4.4 | 4.9 |
| Sweden | 1.2 | 1.5 | 2.0 | 1.7 | 9.4 | 5.6 | – |

*Source*: 1960–64 data reported in Nickell *et al.* (2005); 1970–94 data, OECD, 2001, Table 2.19; 2000 data, OECD, 2004, Table A; 2005 data, OECD, 2006, Table B.

## Changing social divisions

The above discussion suggests that the changing nature of work, including the rising incidence of unemployment, has had a clear impact on the social structures of the developed economies, but what changes have taken place and who has been most affected? These are complex questions and only fairly brief answers can be provided here. It is important, however, to appreciate how traditional class divisions have changed over the past thirty years or so, while the impact of post-industrial employment patterns on gender divisions, alluded to above, need to be explored in more detail.

Where 'social class' is concerned, there are many ways of defining the term (see Giddens, 2006) but for present purposes 'occupation' and particularly the division between manual and non-manual employment is the most useful. The decline in manufacturing employment implies a decline in manual work and the system of class-based industrial relations associated with it. In short, as 'working class' manual occupations based in manufacturing declined, the strength of organised labour was simultaneously reduced. This process was hastened and exacerbated in the UK in the 1980s by the Conservative governments' attacks on trade unions, the 1984–5 miners' strike being the most dramatic example of the assault on organised labour at a time when the days of the traditional, unionised, male working class were already numbered. The speed of the decline of trade union membership in the UK is marked. In 1979, membership stood at 13.3 million, with 55 per cent of employees belonging to a union. By 2005 these figures were 6.8 million and 29 per cent respectively. An indicative aspect of this process is that, as union strength has waned, those areas of employment that have remained relatively highly unionised have been the professions (such as lawyers, accountants and teachers), as opposed to what remains of the manufacturing sector. In addition, women are now more likely than men to be members of a trade union, the proportion of females in professional occupations being one and a half times more likely to be union members than their male counterparts.

Similar patterns of trade union decline can be detected in many – though not all – developed economies. The USA, for instance, has seen a marked reduction in union membership, from 36 per cent of the labour force in the 1950s to 16 per cent in the 1990s, with particularly steep declines in manufacturing and construction. Elsewhere union membership fell in Sweden and Germany – but actually increased in Denmark and The Netherlands. According to the Federation of European Employers (**http://www.fedee.com/tradeunions.html**), membership rates are generally falling across Europe, with a dramatic (if unsurprising) collapse in trade union membership in the latest countries to join the European Union from Eastern Europe. While this decline cannot be attributed solely to changing employment patterns – after all, political changes in Eastern Europe have clearly influenced matters in the post-Communist states – this dimension is crucial.

What, then, does the post-industrial socio-economic landscape look like in terms of social structure? With the old unionised class politics in abeyance, if by no means entirely absent, the picture is highly fragmented. The growth of flexible and casual work has meant that individuals across a range of areas and income groups have been affected by unemployment and insecurity. With the threat of unemployment ever-present for *all* sectors of the labour market, it has been easier for employers to demand more from their employees, with the result that the amount of hours spent at work has risen while the amount of work actually carried out during those hours has also gone up. This intensification of work has been accompanied by greater income inequalities. Although it is important to note, as does Hills (2004), that absolute living standards in the UK and other developed economies have risen for the majority of people over the past thirty years, the absence of strong labour movements to maintain income levels for the low paid has meant that income distribution has been increasingly 'stretched'. As Hills (2004) reports of the UK between 1979 and 1995:

> On average, real income grew by 40 per cent . . . or 42 per cent [depending on the measure used] . . . however, rates of growth were very different across the distribution. Incomes from the highest tenth rose by 60–68 per cent. At the median, incomes grew by about 30 per cent, and incomes for the poorest tenth rose by only 10 per cent before housing costs. After allowing for housing costs, incomes for the poorest tenth were 8 per cent lower in 1994/5 than in 1979.
>
> (2004, p. 21)

In place of the single most significant twentieth-century division between manual and non-manual occupations have come more fine-grained divisions among different income groups. While those in certain professions – law, financial services, medicine and the higher echelons of business – have seen their incomes rise markedly, others in the lower reaches of the service sector, where employment patterns tend to be more casual, have fared less well. Of course, many women work in these latter occupations, as do individuals from minority ethnic communities, with the result that income divisions tend to be gendered and racialised. As the recent edition of *Social Trends* makes clear:

> In 2004/5 in Great Britain, all ethnic minority groups had greater than average likelihood of being in the bottom quintile group, with the Pakistani/Bangladeshi group being particularly at risk. In addition, groups with greater than average risks of being in the bottom quintile in the UK were single parent families and families where one or more adults and one or more children were disabled.
>
> (2007, p. 65)

The only way in which this picture of more subtle income divisions needs to be qualified concerns not so much a divide between social classes as one between those who work (or have access to work) and those who do not. As Rowlingson has written, 'another fairly new phenomenon in the 1980s and 1990s was the *workless household*. Work has polarised across households as there has been a rise in the number of dual-earner households and the number of no-earner households' (2003, p. 15, original emphasis). Rowlingson goes on to note that 'there has been a substantial increase in worklessness among couples over the last 30 years' with about 'two-thirds . . . of the change [being] caused by variations in access to employment for different types of household'. Essentially, in better-off households women joined their partners in employment, whereas 'in worse-off households, men were joining their partners in the home'.

If lone parents, who are another group which suffers from high unemployment rates, are added to those in workless households, it is possible to portray the resulting divide between the 'work rich' and 'work poor' as a variation on more traditional class divides. In this case, the phraseology used by some commentators – particularly those like Charles Murray in the USA – is considered by others (Lister, 2004; Deacon, 2002), especially in the UK, to be pejorative. Murray (1994) refers to certain key segments of the workless poor (he particularly singles out African-Americans) as an '**underclass**', arguing that individuals in this 'class' are distinguished by high rates of single parenthood, high divorce rates, high crime rates, poor educational achievement and dependency on welfare benefits. One way of encouraging different behaviours, according to Murray, would be to remove all welfare support so that individuals had little choice but to find work – in other words, the important issue is to alter the behaviour of 'irresponsible individuals'. Others, the US sociologist William Julius Wilson (1987) for example, while accepting that an 'underclass' might exist, nevertheless do not ascribe its existence to individual behaviour but to key 'structural' factors associated with the decline of manufacturing employment and the associated rise of unemployment and casual, low-paid jobs. Wilson also acknowledges that, in the USA, additional difficulties have been created by the close association between 'race' and poverty, although he argues that these, too, owe more to structural failings of the economy than to the behaviours of African-American individuals and communities. Yet others (see Bagguley and Mann, 1992; Lister, 2004; Alcock, 2006; Deacon, 2002) argue that the use of the term 'underclass' is dangerous and should be avoided. For one thing, there is little empirical evidence to suggest that the 'underclass' is a coherent class at all but rather a series of different groups (lone parents, the unemployed) who may experience particular kinds of misfortune at different stages of the life cycle. Again, it is not clear that the apparent behaviours associated with the 'underclass' such as lone parenthood and high divorce rates differ much from those found in other sections of society. More importantly, perhaps, the tendency to use flimsy evidence to label vulnerable people as irresponsible and 'undeserving' itself separates and excludes them from the social mainstream – and this stigmatising process can hardly be expected to result in greater social inclusion or better understanding of the challenges facing the most deprived sections of society.

Debates of this kind, stimulated as they are by the ever-changing socioeconomic environment, are highly significant, and relate directly to social policy. In view of the sweeping changes that have occurred in the world of work over the past thirty years, how should governments respond? Is it really the case that the welfare states of the post-war era created a dependent 'underclass'? How should governments balance employers' demands for a 'flexible' workforce with the problems, particularly for women and minority ethnic communities, generated by unemployment and low pay? Is there a way for welfare provision both to support the 'new economy' *and* protect the interests of the most vulnerable?

 Controversy and debate

Charles Murray's 'underclass' thesis rests on the assertion that a distinct and separate class exists outside 'normal' society. This 'class' is distinguished by certain types of behaviour which Murray deems unacceptable. High rates of single parenthood, divorce, fatherless families, illegitimacy, crime and welfare dependency mean that this 'class' is both economically and culturally segregated. For further detail see Murray 1996a and 1996b. Other studies such as Buckingham's (1999) also argue that there is evidence of the existence of an 'underclass' in the UK. Buckingham's analysis of the National Child Development Study indicated that there is good reason to distinguish between a 'working class' and an 'underclass' in the UK – and evidence to suggest that there are distinct patterns of family formation, commitment to work and political allegiance between the two classes.

Many academics, especially in the UK, have challenged these views. They argue that there is no real evidence to support the conclusions advanced by Murray and Buckingham, pointing to the fact that rising rates of divorce, single parenthood and illegitimacy are by no means confined to an 'underclass' but characterise changes throughout society. They also argue that to stigmatise groups and individuals in this way is inherently counter-productive. For further details see Bagguley and Mann 1992, Lister 1996, 2004; Deacon 2002; Prideaux 2005; Alcock 2006.

Examine the evidence that Murray uses to argue for the existence of an 'underclass' and then assess the evidence discussed by Buckingham. Consider how accurate both accounts are by considering the arguments against the existence of an 'underclass' by the critics mentioned above.

## The changing nature of the welfare state

The changes discussed above have, over time, resulted in wide-ranging alterations to the role and purpose of social policies in the developed economies. What follows concentrates mainly on the UK because it constitutes one of the more marked examples of how welfare arrangements developed in the late 1940s have changed to accommodate the challenges posed by changing economic conditions and employment patterns. However, it is important to understand that the majority of welfare states in the developed economies have been confronted with the same difficulties and have responded in similar, though not identical, ways (see, for example, Chapter 20).

At the most general level of analysis, social policies in the UK and other welfare states have shifted from an orientation around 'social protection' to one that is more concerned with 'competition'. Commentators such as Jessop (1994, 2002) and Cerny (1990, 2000) have discussed the ways in which states, faced with the mounting costs of welfare support in the face of rising unemployment and falling economic growth, turned to forms of 'welfare' that would support the changing economic environment rather than compensate the victims of it. Jessop (1994) suggested that there has been a shift from what is frequently referred to as the 'Keynesian Welfare State' to the 'Schumpeterian Workfare State', while Cerny (1990) refers simply to the emergence of the 'competition state'. In both cases the point being made is that the role of the state in the newly competitive capitalist world economy is one of securing and maintaining the conditions for economic growth. In particular, the extension of the free market and retreat from direct state intervention in economic management has characterised state economic strategies in the developed economies, and the conduct of social policy has been a key aspect of – in fact almost a metaphor for – this change. As Evans and Cerny state:

The creation of the competition state involves a policy agenda which seeks to provide the conditions that will help the state to adapt state action to cope more effectively with what [are perceived] as global 'realities'. Particular types of policy change have thus risen to the top of the policy agenda . . . [including] a shift . . . in the focal point of party and governmental politics away from the general maximisation of welfare within a nation (full employment, redistributive transfer payments and social service provision) to the promotion of enterprise, innovation and profitability in both private and public sectors.                    (2003, p. 26)

In other words, where competition is becoming increasingly global, domestic economies 'post-industrial' and the nature of the workforce changing as a result, social policy is used to work with the grain of the new economy rather than to act as a countervailing force. It is in this way that those claiming unemployment benefit have been turned into 'job-seekers' and labour market policies have been reorientated to 'activate' the unemployed. In the UK, the Job-Seekers Allowance (1996) was the first sustained attempt to 'encourage' those claiming unemployment benefit to seek work. Under New Labour governments since 1997 this formula has been increasingly refined in the shape of various 'New Deals' (for the young unem-ployed, the long-term unemployed, lone parents and disabled people), which have required claimants to attend regular work-based interviews and take active respon-sibility for finding paid employment – with penalties being imposed on those who refused to attend interviews or accept job offers. Similar systems have developed in many other countries, including the USA and Australia (from which the UK learned a great deal) and more recently Germany and France. In each case, too, these policy changes have been accompanied by a political rhetoric that emphasises the dangers of welfare dependency and lack of individual responsibility, while stressing the benefits of work, the free market, low taxation and workforce flexibility.

On one reading, then, welfare has become more 'conditional' (Dwyer, 2000). Certain goods and services are not supplied as of right but according to acceptable behaviour and there is a greater awareness of how welfare support can create dependency. Do these changes mean that Murray's 'underclass' thesis has been vindicated? The short answer is 'not entirely'. Although New Labour governments in the UK have clearly endorsed elements of the 'underclass' analysis, it is too sim-plistic to argue that welfare reform over the past decade has been entirely driven by it. Ruth Levitas (2005), for example, is correct to argue that evidence of a 'moral underclass discourse' can be found in the New Labour governments' social policies – the stress on 'conditionality' stands as evidence of this tendency – but she also makes it clear that other 'discourses' are present in New Labour's approach to welfare. The emphasis on **social inclusion** has been a key feature of welfare debates, for instance, as the need to maintain social stability and cohesion in the face of increasing economic pressures has become clear.

The concept of social inclusion is important, not only because of what it says about the reform of welfare in the UK, but because it offers a further example of the ways in which the changing socio-economic context bears directly on percep-tions of social policy. As discussed earlier, twentieth-century welfare was origina-lly grounded in particular types of work that gave rise to specific kinds of welfare state organised around the fully employed male breadwinner. The collapse of this economic environment and the emergence of a more fractured employment land-scape effectively removed the prevailing assumption that people would be included in society simply by virtue of an inevitable association (direct or, in the case of women, indirect) with work. While the persistence of poverty indicated that inclusion could be precarious for some groups in any period of the twentieth century, awareness of what it means to be *excluded*, and of the multiple causes and effects of social exclusion, has increased in the past fifteen years or so. For example, the experiences of **social exclusion** among a range of overlapping populations – women, single parents, minority ethnic groups, older people, disabled people, unemployed people, young people and children – are perhaps better understood than they used to be and at least some attempts have been made to develop more 'inclusive' social policies. In the UK, initiatives such as Sure Start and (now) Children's Centres, education and health action zones, and a variety of urban regeneration schemes owe much to a desire to enhance social inclusion amongst the most vulnerable sections of society.

Even so, outside initiatives such as these, New Labour has made it abundantly clear that paid work remains the most direct path to greater inclusion, largely because of the income it brings. To this end, UK governments have followed their counterparts in the USA and Australia, and introduced tax credits to encourage parents (and others) to take low-paid work (see Chapter 9) – and it is in efforts such as these, which are designed to encourage opportunities for, and the take-up of, employment in post-industrial societies that the 'underclass' and 'inclusion' discourses clearly fuse. For many governments in Western Europe and beyond, paid employment, though no longer taken for granted as the foundation stone of the welfare state, is still regarded as essential both for economic competitiveness through the maintenance of a trained workforce, and also because it is thought to encourage the sense of individual responsibility and obligation to the wider community that underpins individual well-being and social inclusion. So the stress on work remains, even though the social and economic context in which governments emphasise its importance has fundamentally changed.

In concluding this section one key issue needs to be emphasised. As Levitas (2005) points out, one consequence of relying on social inclusion/exclusion as a core theme of social policy is that attention is diverted away from more forthright demands for a more equal distribution of income and wealth. It is important to remember that there is nothing necessarily egalitarian about social policies designed to combat exclusion – and in this sense something has perhaps been lost. For all their faults – and certainly their failure actually to create measurably greater social equality (Le Grand, 1982) – post-war welfare states were characterised by an egalitarian rhetoric that acted as a reminder, to paraphrase Tawney (quoted in Dean with Melrose, 1999), that 'what thoughtful rich people call the problem of poverty, thoughtful poor people call . . . a problem of riches'.

## Further challenges: social policy, family structures and demographic change

Whether in fact the stress on paid employment is really a panacea for the economic and social challenges posed by post-industrialism is unclear. Although the central objectives of welfare reform in the developed economies have undoubtedly been to improve access to work, it is evident that other changes in economy and society also have an impact on how social policy is understood and perceived –

and here it is not so obvious that paid work offers a solution to the difficulties that welfare states are currently facing. The discussion that follows explores two key changes. First, the changing structure of the family has forced policy makers to confront traditional assumptions about the role of women and the nature of 'care'. Second, certain demographic changes have led to the emergence of greater ethnic and cultural diversity, while other demographic shifts are beginning to impact upon the ability of post-war welfare systems to provide security in old age.

## The changing family

With the partial exceptions of the Scandinavian systems, post-war welfare states essentially allocated women to the private sphere of the home. The necessary corollary of the full-time, permanently employed **'male breadwinner'** is the unpaid female domestic worker who takes care of the children and other family members. In return, she receives certain types of support in the form of access to healthcare and an old age pension, although not in her own right, but as a function of contributions taken in the form of social insurance from her husband's income. Superficially, it could be argued that this system worked. Certainly for the first twenty years or so after the end of the Second World War, the breadwinner model was not explicitly challenged and welfare states in the UK, USA, Australia and the greater part of Western Europe established social insurance arrangements that essentially confined married women to the home. However, from approximately the mid 1960s onwards, changes began to occur that were to result in mounting criticism of both the model and the assumptions about the family and the role of women in society that underpinned it.

These assumptions about the structure of the family in the post-war world were largely based on quite recent perceptions of its role – family structures in previous eras being radically different (Steel and Kidd, 2000). So, for example, the ideal type of family unit was perceived to be the small 'nuclear family' comprising two adults and roughly two children. The relationship between the husband/father and wife/mother was typically portrayed as based on sexual attraction and romantic attachment, with responsibility for the family's economic well-being allocated to the male worker and for its emotional or 'affective' well-being to the wife and mother. A number of potentially problematic issues with this depiction of the family were taken for granted. Among these are that:

- all families in all cultures either are, or should be, based on the nuclear unit;
- women are essentially domestic creatures, content in their caring and nurturing roles;
- all families are based on primary (hetero)sexual attachments,
- (hetero)sexual attachments should be monogamous;
- the nuclear family is the most stable social unit yet to have evolved and, by virtue of its flexibility and capacity for mobility, is better-suited than other family types to the demands of industrial society.

There is no need to go into too much detail here to see how misplaced assumptions of this kind have turned out to be. Leaving aside the fact that the nuclear family is mainly a Western phenomenon – different family structures operate in different cultures and parts of the world – it has become clear over the past thirty years that the perception of gender roles that lies at the heart of the nuclear family is open to challenge. From the mid 1960s, with their increasing ability to control contraception as a result of the pill, and with the labour market beginning to offer greater opportunities than had existed hitherto, women began to speak out against the oppressive nature of 'a domestic life bound up with child care, domestic drudgery and a husband who only occasionally put in an appearance and with who, little emotional communication was possible' (Giddens, 2006, p. 211). This 'speaking out' took a number of forms. Certainly the emergence of feminism as a major social movement starting in the USA and spreading to the UK and the Western world served to crystallise and advance women's demands for greater equality both within the home and outside it. Betty Friedan's *The Feminine Mystique* (1963) and Germaine Greer's *The Female Eunuch* (1970) formed the intellectual basis for a range of increasingly radical demands for equality of opportunity and equal pay to an end to male patriarchy in the private and public spheres (Barrett and McIntosh, 1991). Radical feminists in particular (Firestone, 1970) not only challenged assumptions about the domestic orientation of women but also their predisposition to monogamous heterosexual attachments, while socialist feminists argued that the patriarchal nuclear family was essentially a creature of industrial capitalism, using female domestic labour to 'reproduce' the male workforce and so perpetuate the capitalist mode of production.

Looking specifically to the changing context for social policy, it is clear that the nuclear family, understood as a stable, monogamous, heterosexual unit comprising two married adults and their offspring, began a rapid decline from the 1970s onwards. The erosion of this institution is relatively easy to trace in the form of the rising incidence of divorce, single parenthood and cohabitation. In the UK, marriage rates have fallen from a peak of 480,000 in 1972 to 283,700 in 2005. Following the Civil Partnership Act of 2004, 15,700 same-sex couples formed civil partnerships between December 2005 and September 2006. Divorce rates have been on the rise since the low-point of 24,000 in 1958. By 1968 the figure had climbed to 50,000, rising steadily to a peak of 180,000 in 1993. Thereafter, the rate lessened a little, falling to 155,000 in 2000 – and the same figure was recorded for 2004. The incidence of divorce has been complemented by an associated rise in the numbers of people forming new relationships and either choosing to remarry or cohabit. Remarriages for one or both partners increased by a third between 1971 and 1972, to 120,000, and peaked at 141,000 in 1988. Since that time the figures have fallen somewhat – to 113,000 in 2005. Perhaps the most dramatic figures are those that chart the rise of cohabitation. The proportion of non-married men and women under the age of 60 who were cohabiting doubled from 11 per cent to 24 per cent between 1986 and 2005. Significantly, too, the percentage of births occurring outside marriage has risen from 12 per cent in 1980 to 43 per cent in 2005 – the fact that over 80 per cent of these births were registered by both parents giving the same address provides evidence that cohabitation is coming to be regarded by many people as a socially acceptable alternative to marriage. Finally, there has also been a steep rise in the numbers of people who form single-parent families. The proportion of children living in lone-parent families increased from 7 per cent in 1972 to 24 per cent in 2006 – with 90 per cent of these families being headed by lone mothers (above data taken from *Social Trends 37*, 2007, pp. 15–20).

Changes of the kind discussed here can also be observed elsewhere in the developed economies, although not always to such a marked extent. Thus, divorce rates have risen throughout Western Europe (about 22 per cent between 1960 and 2002), although the pattern is uneven, with Northern countries typically having higher rates of divorce than those in Catholic Southern Europe. The number of divorces has also risen in the USA but there is a distinct variation between the states and overall numbers are lower than those of the UK. Again, numbers of lone-parent families have increased in Europe with the UK, Ireland, Denmark and Finland leading the way. Rates are much lower in Southern Europe and a mixed picture can be observed in countries such as Belgium, Germany and Austria (Chambaz, 2001).

To this already complex picture should be added the important dimension of ethnic and cultural diversity. Certainly in Britain, but also in many other countries, populations have become increasingly diverse as those migrant groups that arrived in the early years of the post-war period become settled second- and third-generation communities. New waves of migration have added to these communities over the years while new migrant populations are emerging as a result of the expansion of the European Union into the former Communist countries of Eastern Europe, and rising numbers of 'economic refugees' and asylum seekers. Clearly attitudes to marriage and the family differ among different groups. Indian, Pakistani and Bangladeshi communities display higher rates of marriage than either white or mixed communities, and significantly lower rates of cohabiting and single parenthood. Conversely, black African and black Caribbean populations have lower rates of marriage and cohabiting and higher rates of lone parenthood – but these trends need to be understood in the cultural context of the extended family structures and kinship networks that characterise black Caribbean groups in particular. On a different note, in the more sexually tolerant climate of the later 1990s and early twenty-first century, gay and lesbian couples have begun to adopt children in greater numbers, while individuals who may have had children in heterosexual relationships are perhaps more likely to redefine their sexuality and move with their offspring into same-sex relationships.

 Thought provoker

## The changing nature of the family

Arguments that there has been a 'revolution' in the nature of the family and family life are not exaggerated – but why should social policies accommodate these changes?

Perhaps, as James Q. Wilson argues, the point of social policy is not to move with the grain of social and economic change but to protect 'core values' – including marriage and the traditional family. On this reading, social policies should aim to rebuild fragile relationships, encourage marriage and responsible fatherhood, and discourage divorce and the formation of 'non-traditional' families.

See J.Q. Wilson, 1985, 1997 and contrast this conservative approach with F. Williams, 2004 and the articles contained in the themed section of *Social Policy and Society*, 2004, Volume 3, Number 4.

Taking all these changes into account, it appears that the 'traditional' nuclear family is far from being the typical family form in many, if not all, of the developed economies. In fact, sociologists have been arguing for some time that this model – if it ever really was dominant – has now given way to very different types of family structure characterised not only by 'natural' parents and their offspring, but also by step-parents, half-brothers and half-sisters, and the grandparents and other family members associated with past marriages and cohabitations (Williams, 2004). The most important feature of contemporary family life, perhaps, is its innate 'flexibility'. When discussing changes of the kind considered here – and especially when categorising social groups in particular ways – it is easy to suppose that these groups are somehow 'fixed' and unchanging. Of course, nothing could be further from the truth. Rising divorce rates have to be set in the context of remarriage, cohabitation and changes in the shape of the families involved (Smart and Neale, 1999). While it continues to be true that, at any one time, the majority of families continue to be constituted as two-parent, heterosexual couples and their children, the point is that these 'families' are increasingly likely to be 'reconstituted' with step-children, ex-husbands/wives/partners participating – one way or another – in 'family life'. Where lone parents are concerned, rising overall numbers of lone-parent families say little about the key feature of lone parenthood – that it is a potentially fluid state. Depending on the reasons why women become lone parents – these covering a range of possibilities from widowhood, through divorce or separation to active choice – this type of family is the most likely to be reconstituted through (re)marriage or cohabitation.

Where social policy is concerned, the changes to the family examined here present serious challenges. Without doubt, the breadwinner model of welfare is not appropriate to family structures which have become so far removed from the two-parent, two-child structure of old. In its place, and over time, governments have begun (more or less reluctantly) to recognise that a more individualised system of welfare support is required if women are to have the recognition that they deserve as both paid workers and unpaid carers, and children are also to be properly supported. However, progress has been piecemeal at best, with social policy provision tending to lag behind the social and economic changes that have been the key subject of this chapter. As Rowlingson (2003) argues, the following features are necessary for an approach to social policy that would treat the individual, rather than the family, as the prime unit of welfare:

- Gender equality and justice in the welfare state and within the family.
- Work–life balance.
- Labour supply.
- Poverty alleviation.
- The value that should be attributed to care and caring by government on behalf of society as a whole.

With the exception of Sweden, which treats both men and women as individual citizens able to receive benefits, goods and services in their own right, the majority of welfare systems are some way from being able to make such a claim. Precisely how the welfare system operates in the UK will be discussed in later chapters, but suffice it to say here that much greater and more generous attention would need to be paid to the following matters if British social policy was to be moved permanently beyond the post-war breadwinner model:

- rights to maternity and paternity leave, with fathers in particular having the right to substantial periods of time for childcare duties;
- the availability and affordability of care for children under five years of age;
- more generous remuneration for those who undertake caring roles in the home;
- rules governing the payment of tax credits and other income-enhancing measures (which remain subject to *couple-based* assessment).

## Demographic change

The final area of crucial significance for an understanding of the socio-economic context of social policy concerns 'demography'. Demographic changes are particularly important 'because they alter the size and composition of the population who contribute to and use the services provided by welfare states' (Liddiard, 2007, p. 132). In short, in the context of (inevitably) scarce resources, the precise amount of spending on different services is partly dictated by the numbers of potential users involved. So, for example, numbers of schoolchildren will influence the amount and nature of expenditure on education, while a rise or fall in the numbers of retired people will impact upon health and pensions policies. Certain aspects of population change in the UK and other developed economies over the past fifty years or so have been dramatic – and two examples will be examined here. First, migration in and out of a country can result in the emergence (and in some cases the decline) of communities with different cultural assumptions and lifestyles, and movements of this kind are likely to influence social and political debates about the nature of welfare as well as the kinds of support that society may be expected to provide. Second, perhaps the most compelling issue in terms of its urgency is population ageing – and this will be discussed in some detail below.

UK migrations patterns altered considerably over the course of the twentieth century (see also Chapter 17). For much of the century more people left Britain than entered the country but this pattern had reversed by the 1990s. In 2005 about 185,000 more people entered the UK than left – approximately 380,000 people departed and 565,000 arrived (*Social Trends*, 2007). About 26 per cent of these new entrants came from the 25 countries of the European Union, with a further 21 per cent coming from New Commonwealth countries. This current increase in human migration, which stems in large part from the expansion of the European Union, greater awareness among those in developing countries of the relative wealth of Northern and Western economies, and consequences of (civil) war and political oppression in key parts of the world, is important because it has led to marked rises in demand for employment, education or healthcare. Rising demand for these goods and services can create short-term difficulties for service providers in those areas where new migrant populations settle – although it is also the case that immigration can also bring important benefits to destination countries (see the 'Thought provoker' below). Conversely, those groups which, over a period of time, move from first-generation 'immigrant' status to become settled second- and third-generation *citizens* present rather different issues. In the UK, for example, although individuals from different minority ethnic groups comprise about 8 per cent of the total population, the great majority have been born in the UK and enjoy full UK citizenship. Here, as initial phases of immigration give way to increasingly settled, permanent communities, the population as a whole comes to be characterised by greater ethnic and cultural diversity.

 Thought provoker

### A way forward for immigration

Statement from *Highly Skilled Migrants Under the Points Based System* (Home Office, 2007: 4):

In 2006, following an extensive public consultation, we published proposals to modernise and strengthen our immigration system by bringing in an Australian-style points system comprising five tiers:

**Tier 1**  Highly skilled individuals to contribute to growth and productivity.

**Tier 2**  Skilled workers with a job offer to fill gaps in the UK labour force.

**Tier 3**  Low skilled workers to fill specific temporary labour shortages.

**Tier 4**  Students.

**Tier 5**  Youth mobility and temporary workers: people coming to the UK to satisfy primarily non-economic objectives.

How necessary is a system of this type in the UK today?

Demographic changes of this kind raise a number of issues for social policy, not least because the needs of different minority ethnic groups need to be understood and accommodated differently. While there is no doubt that individuals from all established minority ethnic communities generally fare less well than their counterparts in the majority white population in terms of access to employment and welfare goods and services, differences of treatment among these communities, as well as between them and the white population, are marked. For example, although all minority ethnic groups suffer from higher levels of unemployment than the white population, Bangladeshi communities experience the highest incidence of worklessness (closely followed by the Pakistani and black Caribbean populations). Again, looking at educational attainment rates, large differences can be found among ethnic groups. At GCSE level African-Caribbean, Pakistani and Bangladeshi children do less well than white students – but Indian and Chinese students do better than any of these groups. Where the highest qualifications are concerned, in 2005, 34 per cent of Chinese men and 32 per cent of Indian men were likely to have a degree, compared to 9 per cent of black Caribbean and 13 per cent of Bangladeshi men – figures for women are similar (*Social Trends*, 2007). While it is certainly true that greater attention has been paid recently to how welfare institutions treat people from minority ethnic communities – much greater attention being paid to the incidence of '**institutional racism**', for example – the challenge is to ensure that social policies provide different communities with the resources and opportunities required to eradicate poverty and allow individuals to realise their full potential.

A different, and in some ways more challenging, demographic problem which now confronts the majority of the developed economies is population ageing. This phenomenon has two main causes. First, it is certainly the case that people in the developed economies of the West and North now live longer than their parents or grandparents did. However, second, fertility rates have been declining for some time; indeed, fertility fell for much of the twentieth century – with the marked exception of the post-war 'baby boom'. The combination of these two factors is expected to lead to a near doubling of the 'old age dependency ratio' (OADR) in many countries, which in simple terms means that there will be fewer and fewer people of working age to support increasing numbers of people in retirement and old age. Of course, now that the first cohorts of the baby boom generation are beginning to hit retirement, the potential difficulties are becoming easy to see. As Pierson writes:

> The key argument in relation to ageing societies is that at some point in the next fifty years in all developed societies and many developing countries the costs of supporting a growing elderly population out of the current production of a much smaller active workforce will place on the latter a burden which is either unsustainable or . . . politically unacceptable.
>
> (2001, p. 91)

Any examination of population ageing can quickly become highly technical and impenetrable – and it is important to point out that some commentators are more sceptical about its possible impact than others (Bonoli, 2000). Nevertheless, it is important to consider two particularly significant issues which impinge directly on social policy. First, in many countries – Australia and the USA as well as Northern and Western Europe – rising OADRs mean that the arrangements for old age pension provision put in place in the aftermath of the Second World War are likely to be inadequate. In short, the money produced by working populations through taxation and other surpluses from increased production will not be sufficient to pay the pensions and associated costs of health and social care for those either in or nearing retirement. However, second, to change arrangements that have been established for the best part of fifty years is exceedingly difficult. Any dramatic alteration in pensions policies can have a significant impact on those who, having contributed through taxation or social insurance contributions to preceding generations' pensions, see their own assumptions about their income in old age undermined. To do nothing, on the other hand, would impose equally unacceptable costs on younger generations who would be faced with much higher taxes and insurance contributions. In other words, national governments are caught between a rock and a hard place! Failure to act could lead to the disenchantment of economically active populations and the collapse of the unspoken intergenerational agreement about paying for old age, while to alter existing systems could provoke the wrath of those nearing retirement.

In the event – and unsurprisingly – governments appear to be opting for a mixture of policies that will certainly reduce state pension commitments over time, as greater reliance is placed upon occupational and private provision. So, in the UK for example, governments have discouraged over-reliance on the contributory state pension for the past twenty-five years, shifting away from an earnings-related system in the 1980s to a minimal (and declining, at least in real terms) basic state pension that can be enhanced by means-tested supplements for those without alternative sources of income in old age. Meanwhile UK governments have also attempted to persuade those in work to make provision for occupational pensions where employers offer them, or take out private pensions plans. Elsewhere governments have been more generous, although the principle that a pensions system should be arranged among a number of 'tiers' – state, occupational and private – rather than relying too heavily on any one of these is becoming universal. Australia, for example, alongside the basic 'Age Pension', has established a system of mandatory superannuation, with employers and employees contributing to approved private funds, which now cover the vast majority of Australians. After a lengthy consultation process that lasted throughout the latter part of the 1990s, Sweden radically reformed its pension system to cater for the difficulties posed by population ageing – although the full effects of the new system will not be felt for some years. Again, various tiers are involved, including a reorganised 'Guaranteed Pension' which sits alongside a contributory scheme that has both state- and privately-funded elements. Other policies being adopted – particularly in France, Italy and Germany – involve downward pressure on early retirement, an increase in the official retirement age (or encouragement to work past the official age of retirement) and the general encouragement of 'active ageing' (Ellison, 2006).

Generally speaking, the phenomenon of population ageing offers a particularly good example of how social policy constantly needs to be adjusted to take account of wider social and economic changes. In the case of pensions, it is important to understand that the pace of change is in fact quite slow – after all, the retirement of the baby boom generation will take over ten years to complete and the impact of changing OADRs will continue for at least another thirty years. However, this apparently gradual process has to be understood in the context of how long certain forms of social policy take to establish and properly embed. Once embedded, whole generations develop expectations about life in retirement based on the policies they have grown up with. It is not surprising, then, that decisions to alter social policies, although they may be deemed necessary by an analysis of the changing socio-economic environment, are intensely complex, involving significant political as well as economic calculations about the impact of new arrangements as well as an assessment of likely policy 'winners' and 'losers'.

## Conclusion

This chapter has examined some important dimensions of the changing socio-economic context of social policy. Looking back over the past thirty to fifty years, it is clear just how much societies in the economically developed world have altered. Indeed it is not an exaggeration to argue that assumptions about the nature of working life, the relationships between genders and generations, what is understood by the 'family' and family life – and even the character of entire national populations – have changed out of all recognition.

In conclusion, what does attention to the socio-economic environment say about the nature of social policy? For one thing, it points to an area of politics and policy making that is, of necessity, dynamic. Social policies are never 'settled' for long and, of course, in a world increasingly characterised by a range of global pressures (see Chapter 21) it is important that welfare systems remain able to respond flexibly to the needs of vulnerable populations even as policy makers struggle with inevitably scarce resources. Second, in contrast to the welfare pioneers of sixty years ago, who believed that welfare states were inherently progressive, providing welcome relief from the rigours of market solutions for vulnerable sections of the populations, it is possible to see now that this perception is not always accurate. Indeed, welfare systems can be highly conservative forces, depending on their institutional make-up. It is clear from the discussion of the changing nature of employment, or changing family structures, that social policies make assumptions about work and gender roles that turn out to be based on particular understandings of social needs and values that themselves are historically specific. Far from always being at the forefront of societal change, welfare arrangements can act as brakes upon it. Finally, it is important to be clear that welfare states are inherently *political* projects. If the socio-economic environment contributes significantly to establishing the overall framework within which discussion can take place, *how* this environment is 'interpreted', *who* does the 'interpreting' and the *priorities* subsequently established are decided through political argument and struggle. For this reason debates about the role and purpose of social policy should not be confined to the realm of representative politics but should extend into broader forms of 'social politics' because decisions about welfare affect such a vast range of populations, communities, interests and movements.

## Summary

This chapter has shown how a range of socio-economic factors create an overarching framework for political arguments about the role and nature of social policy. The discussion has also established how rapid social and economic changes can make welfare systems and the assumptions that informed their development appear outdated. The key issues explored here were:

● The changing nature of employment in many economically developed countries and particularly the decline of full male employment in manufacturing industry. This decline has been offset by a rise in service sector employment – the change also being accompanied by the increasing numbers of women in some form (full-time, part-time or casual) of work. Rising female and falling male employment has challenged the basis of the 'breadwinner model' of welfare – forcing national governments to develop social policies that are less dependent on the male earner.

- These changes were associated with others – specifically the emergence of a central division between 'work rich' and 'work poor' households. A key argument is whether the shift in employment patterns has led to the development of an 'underclass' as those most vulnerable to unemployment in the 'new economy' become increasingly dependent on welfare.

- While it is difficult to argue that a distinct 'underclass' has emerged, particularly in the UK and European societies, it is nevertheless clear that changing employment patterns have altered the nature of social policy and the shape of welfare states. Specifically, welfare systems have become less 'protective' and more 'competitive' – and in so doing it may be that neo-liberal and conservative critiques of the dangers of welfare dependency have at least partly influenced policy makers.

- Changing employment patterns are partly, but by no means wholly, responsible for changing family structures. Greater access to employment has encouraged women to leave the home in ever-increasing numbers, but a higher degree of economic independence has been accompanied by greater sexual freedom as a result of the universal availability of contraception in many countries. Both these factors contributed to nothing less than a revolution in women's perception of their roles and a 'cultural revolution' that saw the traditional model of the 'nuclear family' rapidly undermined in favour of a range of family types arising from the increasing incidence of divorce and remarriage, single parenthood, civil and same-sex partnerships.

- Demographic changes associated with the emergence of second- and third-generation minority ethnic communities stemming from initial periods of inward migration have contributed to greater ethnic and cultural diversity in many of the developed economies. The presence of settled ethnic communities raises issues about the nature of social policy and whether policies are sufficiently sensitive to minority ethnic needs.

- A further dimension of demographic change concerns population ageing. That the numbers of those either in or nearing retirement are rising is not in doubt – the real issue is how governments are responding to rising OADRs. Whether or not population ageing poses a 'real' threat to existing arrangements in the developed welfare states is not entirely the point. The issue is that governments *think* that ageing populations will create difficulties in time to come and are consequently taking measures to reduce their commitments to those nearing retirement while encouraging individuals to provide for themselves in old age by contributing to different 'tiers' of provision. In many countries, these developments have led to significant changes in traditional post-war pensions policies.

## Discussion and review topics

1 What have been the key changes in employment patterns over the past fifty years and how have these affected welfare state organisation in developed welfare systems?

2 In what ways have women's roles changed over the past fifty years and what factors in your view have been responsible for the changes?

3 To what extent have changing employment patterns contributed to the emergence of an 'underclass'?

4 Consider how family structures have changed since the 1960s. What implications does the changing structure of the family have for social policy?

5 Why might demographic changes such as the increasing size of minority ethnic communities or population ageing have an impact on perceptions of welfare and social policy making?

## Further reading

**Ellison, N.** (2006) *The Transformation of Welfare States?* Routledge, London. Provides a broad overview of the influence of global economic pressures on welfare states.

**Pierson, C.** (2001) *Hard Choices: Social Democracy in the 21st Century*, Polity, Cambridge. Within a consideration of social democracy, this book examines the challenges posed by demographic change and globalisation.

**Levitas, R.** (2005) *The Inclusive Society? Social Exclusion and New Labour*, Palgrave, Basingstoke. This book examines differing conceptions of social inclusion under the Labour governments since 1997 and the ways in which the government has responded to social exclusion.

**Murray, C.** (1996) 'The Emerging British Underclass', in R. Lister (ed.) *Charles Murray and the Underclass Debate*, IEA Health and Welfare Unit, London. Murray's work was influential in sparking debate about the 'underclass'.

**Williams, F.** (2004) *Rethinking Families*, Calouste Gulbenkian Foundation, London. Outlines the major trends around families, the effects of these, and their implications for social policy.

## Some useful websites

http://www.guardian.co.uk/ – this general reference to *The Guardian's* website (Guardian Unlimited) is included mainly because the easy search facilities provide swift access to news and commentary about key social policy issues. *Guardian Society*, published each Wednesday, also carries important news and information about social policy matters.

http://www.policyhub.gov.uk/news_item/social_trends07.asp – the Policy Hub website provides links to a wide range of material, much of which is helpful in outlining and understanding social change.

http://www.statistics.gov.uk/ – a more challenging website that provides access to the full range of UK government statistical information. The current issue of *Social Trends* can be downloaded free. It carries a wealth of detail about core areas of UK society and social policy.

## References

Alcock, P. (2006) *Understanding Poverty*, 3rd edn, Palgrave, Basingstoke.

Amin, A. (ed.) (1994) *Post-Fordism*, Blackwell, Oxford.

Bagguley, P. and Mann, K. (1992) 'Idle Thieving Bastards? Scholarly Representations of the "Underclass"', *Work, Employment and Society*, Vol. 6, pp. 113-26.

Barrett, M. and McIntosh, M. (1991) *The Anti-social Family*, Verso, London.

Bonoli, G. (2000) *The Politics of Pension Reform*, Cambridge University Press, Cambridge.

Buckingham, A. (1999) 'Is There An Underclass in Britain?' *British Journal of Sociology*, Vol. 50, No. 1, pp. 49-75.

Cerny, P. (1990) *The Changing Architecture of Politics*, Sage, London.

Cerny, P. (2000) 'Restructuring the Political Arena: Globalization and the Paradoxes of the Competition State', in R. Germain (ed.) *Globalization and its Critics*, Macmillan, Basingstoke.

Chambaz, C. (2001) 'Lone-parent Families in Europe: A Variety of Economic Circumstances', *Social Policy and Administration*, Vol. 35, No. 6. pp. 658-71.

Deacon, A. (2002) *Perspectives on Welfare*, Open University Press, Buckingham.

Dean, H. with Melrose, M. (1999) *Poverty, Riches and Social Citizenship*, Palgrave, Basingstoke.

Dwyer, P. (2000) *Welfare Rights and Responsibilities: Contesting Social Citizenship*, The Policy Press, Bristol.

Ellison, N. (2006) *The Transformation of Welfare States?* Routledge, London.

Evans, M. and Cerny, P. (2003) 'Globalization and Social Policy', in N. Ellison and C. Pierson (eds) *Developments in British Social Policy 2*, Palgrave, Basingstoke.

Firestone, S. (1970) *The Dialectic of Sex*, Bantam, New York.

Friedan, B. (1963) *The Feminine Mystique*, Penguin, Harmondsworth.

Giddens, A. (2006) *Sociology*, 5th edn, Polity, Cambridge.

Greer, G. (1970) *The Female Eunuch*, Flamingo, London.

Hills, J. (2004) *Inequality and the State*, Oxford University Press, Oxford.

Home Office (2007) *Highly Skilled Migrants Under the Points Based System*, Border and Immigration Agency Communications Directorate, London.

Jessop, B. (1994) 'The Schumpeterian Workfare State', in R. Burrows and I. Loader (eds) *Towards a Post-Fordist Welfare State?* Routledge, London.

Jessop, B. (2002) *The Future of the Capitalist State*, Polity, Cambridge.

Le Grand, J. (1982) *The Strategy of Equality*, George Allen & Unwin, London.

Levitas, R. (2005) *The Inclusive Society? Social Exclusion and New Labour*, Palgrave, Basingstoke.

Liddiard, M. (2007) 'Social Need and Patterns of Inequality', in J. Baldock, N. Manning and S. Vickerstaff (eds) *Social Policy*, Oxford, University Press, Oxford.

Lister, R. (ed.) (1996) *Charles Murray and the Underclass: The Developing Debate*, IEA Health and Welfare Unit, London.

Lister, R. (2004) *Poverty*, Polity, Cambridge.

Murray, C. (1994) *Losing Ground* (10th anniversary edition), Basic Books, New York.

Murray, C. (1996a) 'The Emerging British Underclass', in R. Lister (ed.) *Charles Murray and the Underclass: The Developing Debate*, IEA Health and Welfare Unit, London.

Murray, C. (1996b) 'Underclass: The Crisis Deepens', in R. Lister (ed.) *Charles Murray and the Underclass: The Developing Debate*, IEA Health and Welfare Unit, London.

Nickell, S., Nunziata, L. and Ochel, W. (2005) 'Unemployment in the OECD Since the 1960s: What Do We Know?' *The Economic Journal*, Vol. 115 (Jan), pp. 1-27.

OECD (1996) *Historical Statistics, 1960-1994*, OECD, Paris.

OECD (2001) *Historical Statistics, 1970-1999*, OECD, Paris.

OECD (2004) *Labour Market Statistics*, OECD, Paris.

OECD (2006) *Employment Outlook: Boosting Jobs and Incomes*, OECD, Paris.

Pierson, C. (2001) *Hard Choices: Social Democracy in the 21st Century*, Polity, Cambridge.

Prideaux, S. (2005) *Not So New Labour*, The Policy Press, Bristol.

Rowlingson, K. (2003) '"From Cradle to Grave": Social Security Over the Life Cycle', in J. Millar (ed.) *Understanding Social Security: Issues for Policy and Practice*, The Policy Press, Bristol.

Smart, C. and Neale, B. (1999) *Family Fragments?* Polity, Cambridge.

*Social Trends 37* (2007) Self, A. and Zealey, L. (eds), Office for National Statistics, London.

Steel, L. and Kidd, W. (2000) *The Family*, Palgrave, Basingstoke.

Williams, F. (2004) *Rethinking Families*, Calouste Gulbenkian Foundation, London.

Wilson, J.Q. (1985) 'The Rediscovery of Character', *Public Interest*, Vol. 81, pp. 3-17.

Wilson, J.Q. (1997) 'Paternalism, Democracy and Bureaucracy', in L. Mead (ed.) *The New Paternalism*, AEI Press, Washington DC.

Wilson, W.J. (1987) *The Truly Disadvantaged*, University of Chicago Press, Chicago/London.

# 3

# The politics and government of social policy

Catherine Bochel

## Chapter overview

Both social policy and politics are closely tied to decisions about the make-up of society and the distribution of resources (including income and wealth) within it. Each is therefore concerned with the appropriateness of social arrangements and the means by which these are determined. Within the political system there are a variety of forces that impact upon social policy – changes of government inevitably bring different policy priorities and approaches, pressure groups lobby governments to achieve their aims, the media also seek to influence government and to highlight issues and, as implied above, individuals and groups can also participate in different ways. In addition, recent years have seen significant changes in the mechanisms of social policy formulation and implementation, with devolution to Scotland, Northern Ireland and Wales being a clear instance of this, and these also have implications for social policy.

This chapter examines:

- the role of political parties, pressure groups and the media with regard to social policy;
- developments in approaches to the government of social policy under both Conservative and Labour governments.

## Does politics matter?

Whether we realise it or not, politics impacts on the lives of all of us. The media daily report on issues including: taxation, immigration, ID cards, funding of services, health, schools, climate change, the economy, the EU, elections, conflict in countries around the world, human rights, refugees, trade unions, and so on. These, directly or indirectly, affect us all, and this is why politics matters.

In the 2005 general election only 61 per cent of people in the UK who were entitled to vote, voted. However, participation in politics is not limited to voting, and many more people chose to participate by belonging to pressure groups and by taking part in protests and campaigns whether it be an ad hoc group fighting the closure of a local school, an organised campaign to fight a new airport runway, or pig farmers demonstrating against food companies importing cheap foreign bacon. Other action included campaigns against roads, rubbish tips, housing developments, supermarkets and animal experiments.

In these ways people are choosing to get involved and participate. They are electing representatives from different political parties who will make decisions on their behalf, about issues which will affect their lives and/or they are directly participating in pressure groups and campaigns to try to influence the decisions that will be taken on their behalf by government.

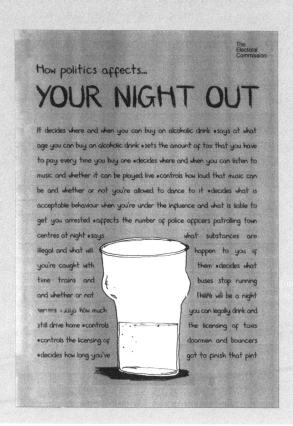

Over recent years there has been considerable evidence that many people, and particularly younger people, have been less engaged with 'politics', or at least with 'mainstream politics', than was previously the case. Yet, as the Electoral Commission poster highlights, politics, broadly defined, affects all of our lives.

Does it matter whether you vote? Does it matter which representatives are elected and which political party governs? In what ways might it make a difference to the policies that are implemented? How does this affect you and to what extent can pressure groups, protests and campaigns influence the decisions that are made and the policies that are implemented?

It is almost impossible to consider social policy divorced from 'politics', as social policy is concerned with, amongst other things, the distribution of goods, services and life chances, all of which are affected by 'political' decisions.

## Politics and social policy

Attempts to define 'politics' can develop into complicated debates in the same way as can occur with definitions of social policy. However, for present purposes we can adopt a simple view. Politics can be seen as the arena within which conflicts and differences are expressed and, to a greater or lesser extent, resolved. If politics is sometimes defined as 'who gets what, when and how', this illustrates well the inevitable link between politics and social policy. Similarly, given the centrality of social policy concerns in contemporary society, with issues such as education, employment, immigration, housing, health and pensions frequently at the core of political debate, this is clearly a two-way relationship.

There are, of course, many aspects of politics that could be considered in relation to social policy. For present purposes the concentration will be on political parties, pressure groups and the media, as these can be seen as having a direct impact on social policies. Later in this chapter some of the institutions and mechanisms of government will also be examined.

### Political parties

Perhaps surprisingly, there is a relative paucity of literature on political parties and social policy and in looking at this area students of social policy are therefore often reliant upon more general literature drawn from political science. However, Bochel and Defty's (2007) *Welfare Policy Under New Labour* provides a recent example of links between political parties and social policy, particularly at the parliamentary level, whilst Jones and MacGregor (1998), although more dated, provides an example of a linkage from the social policy perspective, focusing particularly on the 1997 general election. This section draws out some of the key characteristics of parties as they might be seen to relate to social policy.

## The functions of parties

The functions of political parties can be categorised in a number of different ways, many of which can be seen to have some relationship with social policy, although for some the connection is more apparent and perhaps more important. If we examine three of these, the nature of the links with social policy can be illustrated:

(a) **Representation** – political parties seek to organise within the electorate and to provide meaningful choices which enable voters to elect governments. In reality, most voters cast their vote for a party rather than for an individual candidate. These votes may encapsulate a number of reasons, such as judgements on their policies (including those that relate to social policy), the parties' likely effectiveness as governments and, perhaps increasingly, their leaders.

(b) **Participation** – parties also provide one significant form of participation, varying from voting at general elections to membership and working for a party through attending meetings, campaigning and even standing for election.

(c) **Elaboration of policies** – parties develop programmes and policies to present to the electorate as part of their attempts to achieve office. These may range from fairly general statements of intent to much more detailed policy proposals. Any examination of political debates or party manifestos over the post-war period demonstrates that social policies have been a fundamental part of this function.

## Ideology and political parties

The close relationship between politics and social policy is further illustrated by the importance of ideas to parties and the impact that these have had upon their policies. Chapters 6 and 7 examine this in some detail in relation to the Conservative and Labour Parties. However, if we examine the post-war period, whilst it is quite apparent that ideology has impacted upon social policy, it may not always do so as extensively as might be supposed.

The Labour government elected in 1945 is often depicted as creating the welfare state in the United Kingdom, or at least with doing so on the foundations laid by previous governments, and in particular the Liberal government of 1906–14. Whichever of these views is accepted, there can be little doubt that Clement Attlee's Labour government, itself influenced by the Beveridge Report of 1942, did fundamentally shape the welfare state as it developed in the post-war years. Importantly, however, whilst it was the Labour Party that became associated with the creation of the welfare state, the very idea appeared to have widespread support so that even when Labour were defeated at the general election of 1951 there followed a period that has often been described as one of 'consensus'. This implied a general acceptance of broadly **social democratic** ideals that included a commitment to the welfare state and to a continued expansion of state welfare provision as the economy grew as well as to the role of government in maintaining low levels of unemployment through **Keynesian** economic policies.

Whilst the extent and basis of this 'consensus' might be questioned, for the next thirty years the reality was that there was a maintenance and expansion of the role of the state in the provision of welfare. However, by the mid 1970s a number of challenges had emerged to the welfare state, including practical problems, such as reduced economic growth and oil price rises, and political and ideological questions about the extent to which the welfare state had been successful and whether it was the most appropriate way of meeting needs. From the mid 1970s the Conservative Party began to move more to the political right, influenced by 'New Right' ideas (see Chapter 6), and when it returned to power in 1979 under the leadership of Margaret Thatcher it had a commitment to the free market and the private sector and to reducing state intervention in society. The period from 1979 to 1997 therefore saw attempts to roll back and reshape the frontiers of the state, including welfare provision, using a variety of instruments such as privatisation (for example sales of council homes), increased use of **means-testing** (in social security), restructuring (including the NHS and local government), greater use of **performance measurement** (school and hospital 'league tables') and the introduction of **internal markets** (such as in health and social care).

Following the election of Tony Blair as leader of the Labour Party in 1994, many commentators have suggested that the Party shifted to the political right, and that the creation of 'New Labour' (see Chapter 7) included acceptance of some of the ideas that had emerged from New Right critiques of the state, and of the welfare state, and the continuation of policy trends that had originated under the Conservatives, such as means-testing and encouragement of private sector provision. However, it is also possible to argue that there have been some changes that contrast with the position under the Conservatives, with, for example, significant increases in public expenditure and some evidence of a general redistribution from the rich to the poor (see Chapter 9). Not surprisingly, the start of Gordon Brown's premiership from the summer of 2007 saw a continuation of many of the policies which had been put into place whilst Tony Blair was Prime Minister and over which Brown had been influential while Chancellor. These included a commitment to fiscal responsibility, an increased role for private and voluntary sectors in the provision of welfare services, and the encouragement of an active welfare state in which citizens accept that in return for certain rights to welfare, they have obligations to society. It is also possible to argue that following their election defeat in 2001 the Conservative Party in turn began to adapt its policies, seeking to develop itself as a more inclusivist party, with successive leaders at least paying lip-service to the recognition that the United Kingdom had changed and that some of the Party's perceived political excesses during the 1980s and 1990s were no longer appropriate. After another election defeat in 2005, David Cameron's leadership appeared to reinforce this with a shift towards a recognition that there is a significant role for the state in social welfare, breaking with the dominant stream of Conservative thinking in this area from the late 1970s.

## Party leaders

From the 1960s onwards it has frequently been argued that British government has been moving towards a 'prime ministerial' or even 'presidential' style of government, with the Prime Minister occupying an increasingly central and powerful position. This has arisen at least in part from the increasing emphasis on the party

## Controversy and debate

It is often difficult to be clear exactly what new policy directions different governments would take. The amount of taxation that different groups in society pay raises issues around equality, fairness and social responsibility, and affects the level of resources available for public expenditure, including welfare services such as health and education.

Tax evasion is illegal; however, tax avoidance is not. In recent years the government has sought to reduce levels of tax avoidance by individuals and companies, although at the same time it has sometimes used it to encourage what it sees as positive behaviour, such as paying money into pension schemes.

Visit the websites of the three major parties (**www.conservatives.com**; **www.libdems.org.uk**; **www.labour.org.uk**) and consider how each might address the issue of tax avoidance, why they might take different approaches to this, and what effects this might have on policy.

leaders in the media, and thus in the eyes of the public, not only at election time, but continuously as part of the political debate, a shift which has been intensified by the greater role of television as a means of communication. The apparent dominance of Prime Ministers such as Harold Wilson in the 1960s and 1970s, Margaret Thatcher in the 1980s, and Tony Blair in the late twentieth and early twenty-first century has helped reinforce this impression.

It is clear that Prime Ministers can bring significant influence to bear upon welfare policies. It was Margaret Thatcher's commitment to New Right ideas and her use of right-of-centre **think-tanks**, such as the Adam Smith Institute and the Institute for Economic Affairs, that encouraged the adoption of policies such as the 'right to buy' council houses, the creation of internal markets in health and social care and the use of league tables of performance in education. The example of Margaret Thatcher pushing the poll tax through Parliament against the wishes of her ministerial colleagues and many in her party illustrates the power that Prime Ministers can exert, but her removal from power in 1990 also serves to demonstrate that even dominant Prime Ministers rely upon the support of their Members of Parliament, and if they lose that they risk being removed from office by their own parties.

One of the characteristics of the first Blair government that was much commented upon was the strengthening of government within the Prime Minister's Office, and the role of key individuals, such as the chief of staff, Jonathan Powell, and the press secretary, Alistair Campbell. However, despite this apparent strengthening, and Blair's attempts to define and develop a 'Third Way' (see Chapter 7), in many respects the government was not dominated by the Prime Minister alone, but also by the Chancellor of the Exchequer, Gordon Brown. Whilst the Prime Minister did make occasional forays into the social policy arena, the government also saw the Treasury, under Gordon Brown, developing an almost unprecedented role in social policy, ranging from initiatives such as tax credits, largely designed to help the 'working poor', to **public service agreements** requiring other government departments to establish targets for delivery of services. When Brown took over as Prime Minister in 2007 the emphasis on social policy appeared set to continue, including attempts to improve the lives of children and families, to get more people into work as a way of lifting people out of poverty, and with the continued and perhaps greater use of a plurality of service providers and mechanisms such as collaboration and partnerships to help achieve these ends.

## Pressure groups

A central feature of liberal democracies such as the United Kingdom is that it is often argued that power is widely distributed among different groups (sometimes called **pluralism**) and that at any one time there are a variety of interests competing to influence decision making. Outside the party political arena there exists a huge number of pressure or interest groups. These can usually be differentiated from political parties by the fact that they generally seek to influence government, rather than to govern themselves. They can range in size from small, ad hoc groups, such as those which sometimes form to campaign against the closures of local schools or hospitals, or to fight for or against particular local forms of provision, to the large, well-known groups that feature regularly in the media (Briefing 3.1). Pressure groups are an alternative and important form of participation, with the membership of pressure groups far exceeding that of the political parties. They enable individuals to try to influence the decisions that are taken by government through more participatory methods, rather than through traditional representative means.

Whilst pressure groups can be characterised in a number of ways it is perhaps useful to consider them as 'cause' and 'sectional' groups, as illustrated in Briefing 3.1 on next page:

- **Cause groups** – those organisations that seek to promote causes which are based upon particular values or beliefs, such as Child Poverty Action Group, Age Concern, Fathers 4 Justice and Shelter. It is this category that would normally include the ad hoc groups mentioned above.

- **Sectional groups** – those bodies that represent the interests of particular groups in society, such as trade unions or professional organisations, such as the British Medical Association or the British Association of Social Workers.

Groups are also often described as 'insider' or 'outsider', a terminology that refers to their relationship with government. Insider groups are those that are seen by government as legitimate, are consulted with, and which are most likely to have their voices heard. An example here might be Child Poverty Action Group. Outsider groups do not have, or in some cases do not wish to have, a close relationship with officials and policy makers. The queer rights group OutRage might be an example of such a group.

In relation to social policy it is apparent that there are a whole host of pressure groups that campaign on a wide variety of issues at both central and sub-central government levels. Following the 1997 general election the emphasis on 'partnership' under Labour appeared to offer a greater prospect for consultation and partnership with regard to policy making and implementation for some groups, although the extent to which this occurred in practice was sometimes questionable. Indeed, it is

## Briefing 3.1
## Examples of pressure groups

### Cause groups

*Child Poverty Action Group (CPAG)* – campaigns for the abolition of poverty among children and young people in the UK and for the improvement of the lives of low-income families. Its membership consists of individuals and organisations. It is funded predominantly from membership subscriptions, sales of CPAG publications, and grants and donations. www.cpag.org.uk

*Amnesty International UK* – launched in 1961, with around 265,000 supporters in the UK. It works to improve human rights worldwide. It is funded predominantly through membership subscriptions, appeals and donations, events and community fundraising, and from legacies. www.amnesty.org.uk

*Voice For Choice* – an example of a national coalition of organisations including the British Pregnancy Advisory Service and the Family Planning Association, which campaigns for a woman's choice on abortion. It works alongside the All Party Parliamentary Pro-Choice and Sexual Health Group. www.vfc.org.uk

*Right to Life* – campaigns for 'respect for human life from conception to natural death', and is consequently hostile to abortion and to euthanasia. www.nrlc.org

### Sectional groups

*British Medical Association (BMA)* – founded in 1832, the BMA is a professional association of doctors, representing their interests and providing services for its 128,000 members. It is funded through membership subscriptions. www.bma.org.uk

*National Union of Teachers (NUT)* – organisation that represents teachers; the NUT has a membership of 232,000. It is represented on national education bodies and makes representations to government on all matters affecting teachers and schools, particularly education policy at national and local level. It is funded through membership subscriptions. www.teachers.org.uk

difficult to assess the impact of pressure groups in social policy as their influence may vary with a whole variety of factors including the proximity of their ideas to governments' policy proposals, the resources available to the group, the acceptability of their views to the media and the public, and the external economic and political environment. The cause group Action on Smoking and Health (ASH) might be seen as successful in working towards eliminating the harm caused by tobacco. It has campaigned to ban tobacco advertising, which is now illegal in the UK, and workplace smoking bans have been implemented in Scotland (March 2006), Wales and Northern Ireland (April 2007) and in England (July 2007). But despite the undoubted success of ASH in working towards this, other factors and pressure groups, for example the British Medical Association, will also have played a role in this achievement, serving to underline the difficulty in assessing the precise impact of particular factors and groups. Nevertheless, the continued existence and activity of pressure groups in the social policy field itself requires some consideration of their role.

## The media

The media has become a key part of British society. Whether newspapers, maga-zines, radio, television or the Internet for online news, there are myriad sources of information available to us. However, it is important to recognise that the role of the media is not confined to the provision of information; it also has the potential for influencing the way in which we interpret issues and debates, and perhaps even setting the agenda for decision makers and influencing decisions themselves.

Despite the potential importance of the media to social policy there has been relatively little research upon this relationship. Yet there remain a number of im-portant questions, including: What is the role of the media in setting the agenda? What influence does the media have upon those who make policies? What might this tell us about the exercise of power in contemporary society?

One of the best-known examples of media coverage of social issues is Cohen's (2002) study of Mods and Rockers in the 1960s, which highlighted the role of the media in creating and amplifying what he termed 'folk devils' and 'moral panics' (Briefing 3.2).

From roughly the same period, another well-known example of the role of the media is that of the television drama *Cathy Come Home*, which has frequently been credited with leading to the creation of the charity Shelter, and having a sub-stantial impact on the issue of homelessness and the introduction of legislation in the 1970s. More recent examples of media coverage and involvement range from portraying increased immigration to the UK as a threat to society (in respect of crime and jobs), the effects of designer drugs such as ecstasy, and campaigns to name and shame paedophiles. Given the variety of media and the complexity of their roles and influences, the remainder of this section seeks to provide some framework through which we can seek to analyse and understand the relation-ship with social policy.

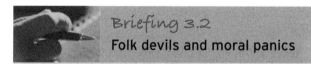

*Briefing 3.2*
### Folk devils and moral panics

Societies appear to be subject, every now and then, to periods of moral panic. A condi-tion, episode, person or group of persons emerges to become defined as a threat to socie-tal values and interests; its nature is presented in a stylised and stereotypical fashion by the mass media; the moral barricades are manned by editors, bishops, politicians and other right-thinking people; socially accredited experts pronounce their diagnoses and solutions . . . Sometimes the panic passes over and is forgotten, except in folklore and collective memory; at other times it has more serious and long-lasting repercussions and might produce such changes as those in legal and social policy or even in the way the society conceives itself.

*Source:* Cohen, S. (2002) *Folk Devils and Moral Panics*, Routledge, London, p. 1.

## The media and public opinion

There is perhaps a general assumption by both the media and by many commentators that the media is important in bringing issues to public attention, and that it is to some extent influential in changing attitudes and perceptions, and even in affecting policy. However, the extent to which this might be the case is not easy to gauge. For example, there are major differences, not just between, say, TV and the press, but also within the press (and with the advent of satellite and digital broadcasting increasingly within TV), for example between coverage in the tabloids and the broadsheets, or between left- and right-leaning papers. The same story can be portrayed in a variety of different ways, and differ not only in respect of the level of detail and accuracy of coverage, but also in terms of political perspectives, with some papers, such as the *Guardian* and the *Daily Mirror*, being seen as tending to favour the Labour Party, whilst others, such as the *Daily Mail* and *The Times*, tend to be seen as favouring the Conservative Party. The public also make distinctions, with the evidence suggesting that they are generally much more ready to say that they believe TV news reporting is more truthful than newspaper coverage.

The media are often accused of trivialising or distorting issues, either to make headlines or as a form of entertainment. Sometimes this may be positive, as a way of bringing an issue to public attention, but often it can create or reinforce misconceptions or stereotypes, or may personalise or individualise what could be seen as *social* issues or problems. However, this may not entirely be the media's fault – for example, many agencies view the media as being in a position of power, able to influence public opinion and policy making. They may thus seek to attract media interest and this in turn may mean accepting media agendas and a subsequent modification of their messages and concerns. Journalists may therefore use crude and stereotypical images of, say, homeless or disabled people as a way of making good copy, attracting attention or making a point; but importantly some agencies may collude with these images to attract coverage (or in the case of some charities, coverage and, potentially, funds).

In terms of seeking to assess the overall impact of the media upon public opinion there have been a number of perspectives upon this:

- **Direct effects** – the view that the media has a direct impact on public attitudes is now largely discredited – the public do not form a passive audience which unquestioningly absorbs and accepts whatever they are fed by the media.

- **Reinforcement** – this perspective argues that the media do not create or mould public opinion so much as reinforce pre-existing opinion. It is now widely accepted that the public select and interpret media messages in accordance with their existing viewpoints – in other words, we actively interpret the information that the media provides; in addition, it is mainly those media messages that reinforce what we already believe that we select. The same media coverage can therefore be interpreted very differently by different members of the public.

- **Agenda-setting** – the argument from this view is that the media do not determine what we think, but that they can influence what we think about. In general, this view accepts that the public has its own agenda, but that the media can influence its priorities, especially on matters about which the public knows relatively little.

- **Framing** – progressing from the agenda-setting standpoint, this view suggests that the media is able to affect political life (including social policy) and the way that people see and understand it. This may happen in different ways: *interpretation* – so that the same event may be presented in different ways to give it a completely different meaning, and the effect may be both unintentional and unconscious; *bad news* – the mass media concentrates on bad news, conflict and violence because these sell newspapers and attract TV audiences, but negative news can create cynicism, disillusion, distrust of politicians and professionals, and apathy; *the 'fast forward syndrome'* – news and reaction to it now spreads so rapidly that policies can be launched in the morning news, criticised at lunch time and buried by the evening, and at the same time there is so much 'news' that the public cannot cope with or understand such a flow of events; *personalisation and trivialisation* – the mass media concentrate not on problems, issues or policies but on personalities and appearances, so that politicians and others may sometimes be less concerned with policy options than with looking and sounding right.

Whichever interpretation we accept, for social policy one of the important abilities of the media is its potential to reach millions of people who may not otherwise be involved or interested in an issue.

### The media and policy making

So to what extent can the media impact upon policy makers? Does coverage of issues such as immigration, homelessness or hospital waiting lists influence either their agendas or decisions. Again, these are difficult questions to answer because it is hard to measure the extent of influence, since it is dependent on different factors. The type of issue – child abuse or cruelty to animals may gain the sympathy and support of the public to a greater extent than gay rights, for example – the intensity of coverage, and the extent to which the public and policy makers trust the source may all be factors. However, it is possible to consider a number of points:

- It is perhaps at the stage where issues may be coming on to the agenda (for example through pressure group activity) that the media may be most likely to have an impact; it is certainly the case that many pressure groups make great attempts to get the media on their side or depend on the media to get issues on to the public and politicians' agendas.

- Despite this, it is difficult to identify many concrete examples of the media having an impact on social policy; indeed, it is arguable that the media has most impact when the ideas that it is pushing are compatible with the general socio-economic and political environment; at the same time, and related to this, the transmission of ideas may not be a one-way process, so that government views and interpretations can themselves permeate into mass media accounts.

- The media may have only a limited impact upon policy making, but they can perhaps play a role in setting the parameters for policy debates and in framing policy discussions and in some cases media coverage and campaigning can be an important factor in attempts to change policy.

**?** *Thought provoker*

Different parts of the mass media portray topics in different ways. Look at the ways in which different newspapers have recently portrayed groups such as women, young people, migrant workers or asylum seekers.

What messages do these portrayals send to their readers and to policy makers?

## Ownership and regulation

Whilst freedom of the press is often presented as one of the central tenets of liberal democracy, at the same time, one of the major concerns of many academics and others has been the ownership and control of the media and the impact of this. Whilst initially concerns were often focused around the power of press barons to directly influence politics, for example through persuading people to vote for particular parties or candidates, others have argued that the major influence of newspapers has been their 'cumulative support for conservative values' (Curran and Seaton, 1991, p. 61) and the status quo. In addition, it is clear that newspapers are able to select particular issues for discussion and to marginalise or ignore others. This latter point is perhaps of significance to social policy as it is sometimes said that it is radical or progressive voices that receive least space in the press.

As with the press, the broadcasting media, and particularly television, have also seen a concentration of ownership, with News International's dominance of satellite broadcasting within the United Kingdom being seen as problematic by many (especially when combined with its strong press presence). One difference here is the existence of the state-funded BBC, with its responsibility to provide public service broadcasting, although it has been argued that this has been, and will continue to be, undermined by the pressure to maintain audiences and the increased choice available to viewers. In addition, at least for party politics, the terrestrial broadcasters have a statutory duty to provide 'balanced' coverage, although this does not necessarily apply to the satellite broadcasters, which it would clearly be difficult for a national government to control in any case.

For the written media, in reality, control and regulation has rested largely with the media themselves. Whilst there have been debates about the extent to which parts of their coverage are acceptable, for example in relation to privacy, particularly of public figures, or to coverage of some particular issues, as with the *Daily Mirror's* publication of photographs in 2004 (later accepted as fakes) alleged to be of British soldiers mistreating Iraqi prisoners, and there have been calls for greater regulation, the primary responsibility continues to lie with individual newspapers and with the Press Complaints Commission rather than through legal or statutory controls.

Recently the debate over the role and control of the media has become further complicated with the widespread availability of the Internet. This has created new opportunities for the collection and dissemination of ideas and information but raises new questions over the regulation of content. In addition, the Internet is already being used to campaign in both old and new manners, for example by anti-globalisation protesters (see Chapter 21). In other respects there is clearly potential for a whole range of individuals and groups to have much wider access to a great variety of information and potentially for more inputs into policy making; but at present much of this is speculation. However, there are already fears that existing inequalities might be reinforced by unequal access (see Chapter 18). Whilst the government therefore seeks to provide more and more of its services online, it will therefore be important to monitor the ability of different social groups to use this new facility.

## The government of social policy

Whilst the preceding section has demonstrated the importance of politics to social policy (by and large, *politics matters*), this section seeks to illustrate that the mechanisms by which policies are made and implemented can also be significant. If we reflect over the period since 1979 it is possible to identify not only major shifts in policy under Conservative and then Labour governments, but also changes in the way in which social policy is 'governed'.

The remainder of the chapter seeks to discuss the governance of social policy under the Conservatives from 1979 to 1997 and to consider the extent to which there is continuity or change under Labour and the implications of this for social policy in the future.

### Government under the Conservatives, 1979–1997

Butcher (1995) described the traditional mode of operation of government in the social policy arena before 1979 as 'the public administration model of welfare delivery . . . in which the five core social services . . . were delivered by a combination of national and local governmental organizations' (p. 155). However, from 1979 to 1997, styles of governance can be seen to have moved through two main phases. Up to 1988 the emphasis was largely on 'managerialism', reflected in the focus of initiatives which drew upon what the government perceived to be 'private sector values' and based upon the belief that business performance tools from the private sector could be transferred to the public sector to make it more efficient and effective at both central government and local government levels. From around 1988, there was a shift towards a style of governance based on 'the new institutional economics' (Hood, 1991) with concepts such as markets and consumer choice being central to this (Rhodes, 1997a). At the same time there were attempts by the government to encourage a greater range of service providers across public, private and voluntary sectors, making the organisation, implementation and delivery of services more complex and dependent on a much wider network of organisations. Many of these changes were encapsulated in the term 'the new public management', a concept that encompasses features such as devolution of responsibility towards lower-level agencies, budgetary limits, incentives to collaborate with the private sector, competition between providers, concentration on core services and privatisation of non-essential functions, use of performance measurement and greater consumer choice.

The programme of management reforms introduced by Margaret Thatcher in 1979 was to stretch for eighteeen years and resulted in significant change to both the structures and styles of governance over that period. These included the introduction of internal markets such as those in the NHS and education, privatisation, greater use of performance measures and standards, the increased use of arm's length government including **quangos** and Next Steps agencies, centralisation of power, reform and residualisation of local government and the introduction of a variety of mechanisms designed to give consumers a greater say in the operation and delivery of services.

An important feature of governance under the Conservatives, including social policy, was the use of structures of 'macro-governance' to devolve a variety of functions previously undertaken by local and central government to organisations such as quangos, non-departmental bodies and Next Steps agencies. Between 1979 and 1997 the Conservative governments created 109 agencies and increased the number of special purpose bodies to well over 5,000 involving 70,000 government appointments and the responsibility for £52 billion of public expenditure. Here the concept of 'governance' can be seen to involve the devolution of 'non-essential' functions such as policy implementation and service delivery, whilst allowing the centre to retain control over core functions such as policy formulation.

The very nature of 'governance' of social policy, particularly after the Conservatives' emphasis on the creation of a mixed economy of welfare, involves a broader range of organisations from all sectors, public, private and voluntary, becoming involved in service implementation and delivery. This creates multiple networks of organisations each of which need to form links with others. As a result highly complex networks of relationships develop and a key aspect of this is the extent to which they are dependent upon one another. Yet for much of the 1980s and 1990s the government's approach could be seen to equate much more to the traditional model of central–local government relations, with local government being viewed merely as the agent of central government and existing to carry out its wishes. For social policy such a model was arguably inappropriate, because the essence of governance in the field involves delegation and cooperation between a wide range of welfare agencies.

There are a variety of issues that arise from this approach. One of the most important is that the actual process of governing becomes more complex because of the number and variety of organisations involved and this raises issues such as: the extent to which these organisations are accountable to the state and the public; the relationship between the state and these organisations; and the interdependence and fragmentation created by the complexity of organisations and the structures of governance (see also the discussion of risk in Chapter 4).

## Government under New Labour

The changes to the mechanisms of policy making and implementation that took place under the Conservatives may have been substantial, but in the early years of the Labour government the pace accelerated further, with constitutional reforms, new emphases, such as on partnership and 'joined-up government', and continued use of measures such as performance 'league tables' that had been introduced under the Conservatives. Whilst some commentators characterised Labour's social policies as displaying a high degree of continuity from those of the Conservatives, a process which might be described as incremental in nature, since new policies differ little from previous ones, the same could not be said about the government's approach to the policy process.

The Labour government's commitment to improving the quality of policy making might be perceived as a rational approach (Briefing 3.3). Such an approach assumes that any policy will be tackled by progressing logically through a series of steps, eventually selecting the most appropriate outcome at the end of the process. The notion of 'joined-up' government – that each department is aware of what is going on within other departments and can take account of the work each is undertaking – served to reinforce this approach. The use of public and pressure group consultations and the incorporation into legislation (DETR, 1998) of a duty for local authorities to consult with local communities can be seen further dimensions of this inclusive approach.

## Briefing 3.3
### Professional policy making for the twenty-first century

A series of high level 'features' which, if adhered to, should produce fully effective policies:

- Three 'themes' – vision, effectiveness and continuous improvement;
- Nine core 'competencies':

  1 Forward looking – takes a long term view of the likely impact of policy.

  2 Outward looking – takes account of factors in the national, European and international situation and communicates policy effectively.

  3 Innovative and creative – questions established ways of dealing with things and encourages new ideas; open to comments and suggestions from others.

  4 Using evidence – uses best available evidence from a wide range of sources and involves key stakeholders from an early stage.

  5 Inclusive – takes account of the impact on the needs of all those directly or indirectly affected by the policy.

  6 Joined up – looks beyond institutional boundaries to the Government's strategic objectives; establishes the ethical and legal base for policy.

  7 Evaluates – builds systematic evaluation of early outcomes into the policy process.

  8 Reviews – keeps established policy under review to ensure it continues to deal with the problems it was designed to tackle, taking account of associated effects elsewhere.

  9 Learns lessons – learns from experience of what works and what does not.

*Source*: Cabinet Office Strategic Policy Making Team (1999) *Professional Policy Making for the Twenty-First Century*, Cabinet Office, London.

To take one aspect highlighted in *Professional Policy Making for the Twenty-First Century*, as part of the emphasis on 'inclusive' policy making, the use of consultations under the Labour Government was widespread, at both local and national levels. This was based upon a belief that by asking citizens and other stakeholders for their views, this would increase the likelihood that the policies developed and implemented would both reflect what people want and work better in practice. These 'consultations' took many different forms, ranging from traditional written consultation exercises such as questionnaires, through to public meetings and the use of citizens' panels or juries (Briefing 3.4). However, the extent to which this apparent commitment to different modes of decision making, evidence-based policy and participation was realised in practice remains a matter for debate.

More specifically there have been a number of other changes in policy making under Labour. One has been the greater role for the Treasury, which under Gordon Brown as Chancellor of the Exchequer played a significant part in directing social policy through the **Comprehensive Spending Reviews** and public service agreements, as well as the use of the tax system to deliver credits such as the Working Tax Credit (see Chapter 9).

Partnership has been seen by Labour as one of the key mechanisms for the implementation and delivery of policy and whilst this approach was used by the Conservatives, it was to a more limited extent. Under Labour there have been a wide range of attempts to encourage partnerships across the public, private and voluntary sectors in health, education, housing, crime prevention and so on. These were viewed by the government as appropriate for tackling particular social

### Briefing 3.4
### Welsh Assembly Government: Reaching 'hard to reach' groups

Making the Connections, the Welsh Assembly Government's public reform programme, includes a strong commitment to establish and uphold core customer service standards for public services in Wales. The development of five core principles in 2006 was supported by a programme of research to explore people's requirements of public services. The research programme, which included a literature review, household survey, citizen forums, focus groups and in-depth interviews, placed considerable emphasis on including groups who can face particular barriers in engaging with public services, such as people with learning, literacy and numeracy difficulties, people with physical and sensory disabilities and impairments, lesbian/gay/bisexual/transgender people and those using languages other than English.

The core principles developed as a result of this feedback address issues of access, personal experience, responsiveness, language options and redress.

*Source*: Welsh Assembly Government, July 2006.

problems and in improving the quality of public services. The **Private Finance Initiative** (PFI) is one of the more controversial initiatives, with the private sector building schools, which have then been leased to local authorities, and hospitals, which have been leased to the NHS, before these revert to the public sector after a set period. Critics have claimed that such initiatives have proved more costly than if they had been undertaken wholly by the public sector.

The revolution in ICT has also been seen by the government as opening up opportunities for electronic service delivery, and the government made a commitment to provide all government services electronically by 2008, in much the same manner as electronic banking services. Whilst this does appear to have a number of benefits for citizens there remain concerns about a number of issues, including equality of access (see Chapter 18). For example, 'the rate of [internet] connection among the D/E groups has remained around the 20 per cent level since 2001' (cited in Social Exclusion Unit, 2005, p. 20). In addition, 'Single parent households are . . . significantly less likely to have home Internet access than households with two adults' (cited in Social Exclusion Unit, 2005, p. 20).

Since 1997 there have also been other developments relevant to social policy. One of these was the increase in the numbers of women elected to the House of Commons and the devolved administrations. In Westminster the proportion of MPs who were women rose significantly from 9 per cent in 1992 to 18 per cent in 1997, remaining around that level for the 2001 and 2005 Parliaments. Within Parliament, in 2007 27 per cent of Labour MPs were female, compared with 14 per cent of Liberal Democrats and 9 per cent of Conservatives. The advent of devolution resulted in significant female representation in the Scottish Parliament (33 per cent in 2007) and the National Assembly for Wales (47 per cent in 2007). This led some to anticipate different approaches to decision making, with perhaps a more consensual and less adversarial approach, and different policy emphases, such as a greater stress on family-friendly policies.

Overall, many of the issues that can be identified with the Conservatives' approach to the governance of social policy are also applicable to Labour. The complexity of networks continues to pose questions about the mechanisms that governments seek to use to implement policy, as does the contradiction between centralising and devolving tendencies that have been particularly apparent under New Labour. And, despite the apparent commitment to improving the quality of policy making, questions remain over the extent to which this is being achieved in practice.

## Constitutional and structural change

Immediately after coming to office in 1997 Labour introduced or outlined a number of changes that had significant implications for the government of social policy. These included devolution, incorporation of the European Convention of Human Rights into UK law, and acceptance of the Agreement on Social Policy (originally signed at Maastricht in 1992 by the then other 11 members of the European Union). Shortly after becoming Prime Minister Gordon Brown signed the European Union Reform Treaty which was designed to replace the failed European Union Constitution, which was rejected by French and Dutch voters in 2005.

This section will consider the nature and impact of some these reforms; the Agreement on Social Policy is discussed (in part) in Chapter 19.

*Devolution*

It is important to note that the different constituent parts of the United Kingdom have always possessed some social, economic, legal and political features that have distinguished them from each other. These were to some extent recognised by the existence of the Northern Ireland Office, the Scottish Office and the Welsh Office as part of the governmental machinery, seeking to take account of at least some of these differences. However, until recently these differences were not reflected in terms of elected legislative bodies.

Following referendums in the autumn of 1997 the Scottish Parliament and the National Assembly for Wales came into being on 1 July 1999. In Northern Ireland, as part of the ongoing peace process, an Assembly came into existence on 2 December 1999, although it had a rather on–off existence for a period, reflecting the vagaries of the peace process. Devolution therefore played a major part in Labour's attempts to modernise government.

Each of the new devolved administrations possessed some powers over social policy (Briefing 3.5), arguably greatest in the case of the Scottish Parliament and least in the case of the Welsh Assembly. Whilst some have been critical of what

## Briefing 3.5
### Social policy and the devolved administrations

Responsibilities

| Scottish Parliament | National Assembly for Wales | Northern Ireland Assembly |
|---|---|---|
| Local government | Local government | Education |
| Education | Education | Health |
| Health | Health | Social services |
| Housing | Housing | Social development |
| Social work | Social services | |
| Transport | Transport | |
| Police and fire services | | |
| Prison and prosecution systems | | |
| Criminal law | | |

Powers

| | | |
|---|---|---|
| Primary legislative power and tax varying powers | Secondary legislative abilities but no tax varying powers | Primary legislative and executive authority for devolved matters |

they have seen as a lack of radicalism in the new bodies, and in general they could be seen as following the same path as Westminster (perhaps not surprisingly given that Labour were also in power in both Scotland and Wales at the time, and the on–off nature of the Northern Ireland Assembly), it is nevertheless possible to identify a number of areas where they could be seen to be diverging from the path taken at Westminster. In Scotland examples included the early repeal of 'Section 28', which banned the promotion of homosexuality, a decision in 2001, in contrast to the government at Westminster, to accept the recommendation of the Royal Commission on Long-Term Care of Older People that long-term care should be free, and the exemption of Scottish university students from top-up fees. In Wales, the Assembly took the decision to abolish prescription charges from April 2007, and announced the abolition of car parking charges at Welsh hospitals in March 2008.

As a consequence of devolution we now have an even greater variety of approaches to social policy across the United Kingdom including differences on foundation hospitals, funding of higher education, prescription charges, testing of school pupils and the use of tables of school performance. Following the 2007 elections to the devolved administrations in Scotland and Wales, political control of the Scottish Government passed from Labour to the Scottish National Party, while Plaid Cymru shared power with Labour in Wales. It seems likely that in future the diversity of policies and methods of policy implementation and delivery will continue, particularly as political control in the different administrations will be likely to change over time. Devolution will therefore provide different models and approaches to social policy within the United Kingdom.

### The Human Rights Act and the European Convention on Human Rights

Although the United Kingdom ratified the European Convention of Human Rights (ECHR) in 1951 successive governments refused to incorporate it into UK law. Citizens who felt that their human rights had been infringed were therefore not able to use the domestic courts although they were able to appeal to the European Court of Human Rights in Strasbourg, an expensive and time-consuming process. The Court found against the UK government on many occasions, on issues varying from censorship of prisoners' mail to different ages of consent for heterosexuals and homosexuals, and although the UK was not bound to comply with the decisions of the Court it consistently did so and UK law was changed to reflect the judgments. However, the Human Rights Act 1998 finally incorporated the ECHR into UK law, thus making it possible for individuals who believe that their human rights have been infringed to pursue this in the domestic courts, speeding up the timescale and reducing the costs. Whilst much of the early media coverage of the impact of the Act involved the rights (or otherwise) to privacy of often high-profile individuals, the effects of the Act have already been seen in a number of areas of social policy, including mental health, where patients detained under the Mental Health Act do not now have to demonstrate that they should no longer be detained, but it is now incumbent upon those detaining them to demonstrate that they have a case. Similarly, many public authorities have been forced to change some of the ways in which they operate and interact with the public because of the requirements of the Act and the ECHR.

*The European Union Reform Treaty 2007*

The EU represents 27 Member States and there is the prospect of this number increasing in the future. The European Union Reform Treaty 2007, which replaces the European Union Constitution, was signed by 27 European Union leaders including Gordon Brown. At the time of writing the treaty had still to be ratified by all EU parliaments. Those in favour of the Treaty believed that it will enable the EU's working practices and institutions to be reformed so that it can work effectively on behalf of citizens across Europe. This will include a larger role for national parliaments, more transparency of what the EU can and cannot do and a greater focus on global challenges. Critics said that there should have been a referendum in the UK and that it will transfer too many rights to Europe. The UK appeared to have agreed 'opt-outs' in relation to the treaty's social policy implications.

*Local government*

Many of New Labour's changes have also affected local government. Local government in the United Kingdom has always been subservient to central government. It has no independent right to exist and all of its functions and activities can be changed by Parliament. Despite this relative weakness, and constant reforms over recent decades, local government has retained a significant role in social policy. Even following eighteen years of Conservative government which saw large-scale restructuring of local government in England, Scotland and Wales, a reduction in its ability to raise its own income and a reduced responsibility for the direct provision of services, it retained a significant role in social policy. At its most basic it is possible to identify a number of services which clearly relate to social policy for which local authorities have a responsibility, including education, the personal social services, housing and planning. Whilst from the 1980s there has been a shift away from the direct provision of services by local government to a position where councils play a much greater role in the strategic planning of services and the enabling of provision, in many instances they continue to be significant providers. When these responsibilities are added to those for planning, highways and passenger transport, sport, environmental health and libraries, the continued importance of local government for social policy is clear.

Following Labour's return to power in 1997 the new government produced a plethora of policies and proposals which not only outlined potential reforms of local government but also dealt directly with many of the services for which it is responsible. Amongst the most important of the government reforms have been those which have sought to 'modernise' local government. These included:

- **New decision-making structures** – it was clear from the early days of the 1997 Labour Government that they wanted to see new political management and decision-making structures introduced into local government in an attempt to provide greater democratic accountability and more effective policy making. By the late 1990s many local authorities had shifted away from the traditional model of services overseen by committees of councillors towards a cabinet model, with in most cases a cabinet with a leader, and other councillors having primarily a responsibility for scrutinising the decisions of the cabinet. In a smaller number of instances authorities chose to go for a directly elected mayor and a cabinet. These changes were supposed to result in more efficient, transparent and accountable local government.

- **The creation of the GLA and the election of a Mayor of London** – whilst the Conservatives had abolished the Greater London Council in 1986, Labour recreated a London-wide tier of local government with an elected Mayor of London and a Greater London Authority. However, they had little power over social policy with the emphasis being primarily on strategic economic and to some extent transport policy. In common with other local authorities, the London boroughs retained responsibility for local government's social policy commitments.

- **Best Value** – from 2000 Labour replaced the system of Compulsory Competitive Tendering (CCT), which had been introduced under the Conservatives, with a new scheme called Best Value. Whilst critics suggested that there was little change, the government argued that, whilst CCT was concerned only with the cost of a service, emphases on quality, continuous improvement and public consultation made Best Value a very different and more comprehensive system. However, if a council is deemed to be failing in their duty to secure Best Value the Secretary of State has the power to intervene and even to impose an outside provider.

- **English regional assemblies** – these were initially proposed in a White Paper in May 2000 and delivered on Labour's election commitment to provide for directly elected regional assemblies. Where the government believed that there was sufficient interest in a region for an elected assembly a referendum would be held in order to give the people of that region choice. The north-east of England was felt to have the strongest pressure group for a regional assembly and a referendum was held. This was viewed as a test case for the remaining regions. However, it was rejected by the voters and all further plans for regional assemblies were abandoned.

In addition, local government was affected by many other initiatives emanating from central government, ranging from tackling social exclusion, through the use of testing of school pupils and performance measures for schools and the provision of accommodation for asylum seekers, to attempts to tackle antisocial behaviour and to reduce crime. Although these developments ranged across the spectrum of local government responsibilities, it is possible to identify a number of key features. First, they followed the approach of the previous Conservative governments in continuing to stress the role of local authorities as enablers of services rather than as providers. Second, as with other areas of social policy, there was an emphasis on 'partnerships' and collaboration across public, private and voluntary sectors as a way of tackling problems and meeting needs. Third, there was continued use of mechanisms of external audit and inspection as a major driver, from the government's perspective, of improving standards and quality. And fourth, a wider range of approaches to social policy as illustrated by different initiatives within the Scottish Parliament, Welsh and Northern Ireland Assemblies. Whilst there may have been a rather less critical view of local government than before 1997, nevertheless the government's attitude showed an unwillingness to trust local government to deliver improvements on its own.

Finally, it is worth noting that devolution and the European Union (Chapter 19) have a growing influence upon social policy, and therefore the concept of 'multi-level governance' is perhaps now appropriate in the United Kingdom, emphasising the number of levels of government and the overlapping networks across them.

## Conclusion

Whilst social policy as an academic subject may not always pay considerable direct attention to 'politics', or to the mechanisms by which policies are made and implemented, social policy and politics are inseparable. Politics inevitably affects social policy, but so too is it intimately concerned with social policy. Many key contemporary issues are social policy issues, and even those that may not on the face of it appear to be, such as climate change or the development of technology, may have significant social policy implications (see, for example, Chapter 18). This means that in order to fully comprehend what is going on in social policy, we need to have a broad understanding of the world of politics and government, and of the ways in which power and influence work.

## Summary

This chapter has outlined a variety of features of politics and government in the United Kingdom and related these to the making and implementation of social policy. It has suggested that:

- There are a variety of ways in which social policy can be affected by politics, not only directly through political parties and the process of governing, but also by influences such as pressure groups and the media.

- Under the Conservative Governments of 1979–97 there was an emphasis upon what were seen as the virtues of the private sector, and in particular markets and marketisation, with the 'consumer' at the centre, and this was reflected in social policy through initiatives such as privatisation, compulsory competitive tendering, attempts to create 'internal markets', greater managerialism, and use of quangos and 'Next Steps' agencies for the delivery of some services.

- The New Labour Government elected in 1997 demonstrated a significant degree of radicalism in its approach to the policy process, most notably through the introduction of devolution to Northern Ireland, Scotland and Wales, the passage of the Human Rights Act, and an emphasis on 'better' policy making and implementation, making terms such as 'joined-up government', 'evidence-based policy', 'partnership' and 'modernisation' part of the social policy lexicon.

- The role of the European Union (discussed in Chapter 19) in social policy should not be neglected here.

# Discussion and review topics

**1** How do political parties and pressure groups differ in their attempts to influence social policy?

**2** What is the role of sub-central government (the devolved administrations and local authorities) in the making and implementation of social policy?

**3** What are the principal differences between the Conservative Governments of 1979-1997 and the Labour Governments that followed in their approaches to the government of social policy?

## Further reading

Bochel, C. and Bochel, H. (2004) *The UK Social Policy Process*, Palgrave, Basingstoke. This book examines the policy process and social policy, drawing upon both theoretical and practical ideas and examples.

Bochel, H. and Duncan, S. (eds) (2007) *Making Policy in Theory and Practice*, The Policy Press, Bristol. Presents a range of academic and practitioner perspectives on policy analysis.

Budge, I., McKay, D., Bartle, J. and Newton, K. (2007) *The New British Politics*, Pearson, Harlow. One of the big current politics textbooks which provides a thorough introduction to British politics.

Hill, M. (1997) *The Policy Process in the Modern State*, Prentice Hall/Harvester Wheatsheaf, Hemel Hempstead. Provides a discussion and evaluation of the policy process and the exercise of power in contemporary society.

Newman, J. (2001) *Understanding Governance*, Sage, London. This book is a comprehensive exploration of the shifting agendas of governance under New Labour.

## Some useful websites

The main political parties throughout the UK each have their own websites, including: **www.conservatives.com**, **www.labour.org.uk**, **www.libdems.org.uk**, **www.snp.org**.

**www.direct.gov.uk** - this site provides access to a huge amount of information about government and services, with links to most central and local government sites, including those in the devolved administrations of Northern Ireland, Scotland and Wales.

The Electoral Commission ran a series of advertisements prior to the 2005 general election highlighting the ways in which politics affect our lives - **www.electoralcommission.org.uk/media-centre/dontdopolitics2005.cfm**.

**www.europa.eu.index_en.htm** - the gateway to the European Union - provides access to information on the institutions and policies of the EU.

**www.policyhub.gov.uk** - provides useful information on a wide range of policy areas.

# References

Bochel, C. and Bochel. H. (2004) *The UK Social Policy Process*, Palgrave Macmillan, Basingstoke.

Bochel, H. and Defty, A. (2007) *Welfare Policy Under New Labour*, Policy Press, Bristol.

Butcher (1995) *Delivering Welfare: The Governance of Social Services in the 1990s*, Open University Press, Buckingham.

Cabinet Office Strategic Policy Making Team (1999) *Professional Policy Making for the Twenty-First Century*, Cabinet Office, London.

Cabinet Office (1999) *Modernising Government*, Stationery Office, London.

Cohen, S. (2002) *Folk Devils and Moral Panics*, Routledge, London.

Curran, J. and Seaton, J. (1991) *Power Without Responsibility: The Press and Broadcasting in Britain*, Routledge, London.

Department of the Environment, Transport and the Regions (1998) *Modern Local Government: In Touch with the People*, Stationery Office, London.

Hood, C. (1991) 'A Public Management for All Seasons?' *Public Administration*, Vol. 69, pp. 3-19.

Jones, H. and MacGregor, S. (1998) *Social Issues and Party Politics*, Routledge, London.

Rhodes, R. (1997a) *Understanding Governance: Policy Networks, Governance, Reflexivity and Accountability*, Open University Press, Buckingham.

Rhodes, R. (1997b) *Good Governance*, Economic and Social Research Council, Bristol.

Social Exclusion Unit (2005) *Inclusion Through Innovation: Tackling Social Exclusion Through New Technologies*, ODPM, London.

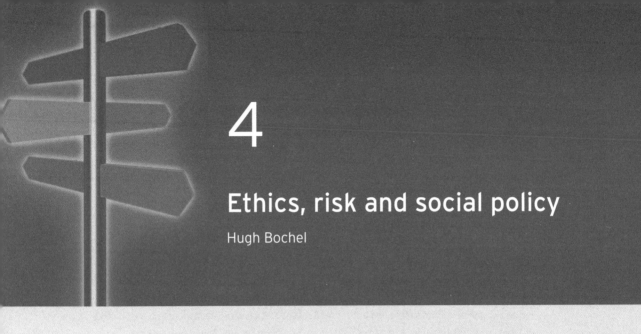

# 4

# Ethics, risk and social policy

Hugh Bochel

## Chapter overview

Whilst ethical considerations have always been a part of social policy, they have not always received overt consideration, including within the academic study of the subject. Yet the ways in which they can be seen to impinge upon people's lives, both as recipients and providers of services, have become increasingly apparent in recent years. This is perhaps most obvious with regard to the rationing and targeting of services, but includes the behaviour of professionals, and has also spread into new areas including reproductive technologies, ranging from topics such as in vitro fertilisation to cloning and genetic modification of crops.

Ethical concerns can be wide ranging in their relationship with social policy, from issues such as abortion, adoption and euthanasia to topics such as food and nutrition and more general questions such as the role and place of charging and rationing. In addition, increasingly, attention has also been paid to the importance of 'risk' and some of the implications that different interpretations of this have for social policy, whether in relation to fears about food safety, choices in healthcare, or the balance between public and private provision.

Seeking to outline some of the key considerations in relation to these matters, this chapter examines:

- different approaches to ethical theory;
- the implications of these for our understanding of issues;
- the application of ethical theory to practical issues;
- why the idea of 'risk' has become more important in social policy.

**Spotlight on the issues**
**The abortion debate – two different perspectives**

### bpas

bpas believes that:

- currently available methods of contraception cannot prevent all unintended pregnancies and that legal abortion is necessary if women are to regulate their fertility;

- contraception and legal abortion are an essential part of healthcare and should be freely available to all through publicly funded NHS;

- reproductive health services offered by specialist agencies such as bpas are an essential supplement to the NHS if all women with unwanted pregnancies are to have early access to affordable specialist care.

*Source:* **www.bpas.org/bpasknowledge.php?page=40,** accessed 2 June 2008.

### ProLife Alliance

The ProLife Alliance was established with the aim of securing the right to life of all human beings, from conception to natural death. We seek to achieve this by advancing the education of the public in all matters pertaining to the inviolability of human life.

Absolute respect for human life is the keystone of justice. A truly just society affirms the fundamental moral equality of all human beings and provides the full protection of the law for all its members, regardless of sex, race, creed, age, size, wealth or physical or mental attainments. It bestows special protection on the weak and vulnerable and makes generous provision for those in need. It proclaims human duties as well as human rights. It cherishes virtue.

The right to life is the most important right from which all others flow. Issues such as healthcare, housing, education, freedom of speech, the environment, foreign policy, and so on, are of little significance if one's life can be arbitrarily ended at various stages of its existence.

In a country where embryo destruction, abortion and euthanasia by omission are practised regularly, we choose to fight against these abuses and will address the lesser issues when the basic right to life is firmly re-instated in the political agenda.

*Source:* **www.prolife.org.uk/show?item=14,** accessed 2 June 2008.

Although in some respects rather obvious, the concerns and debates over abortion, as highlighted above, provide clear evidence of the importance of ethical debates in contemporary society.

Other difficult questions are frequently associated with the idea of 'risk' which has become more central in social policy in recent times, with events such as the emergence of BSE during the late 1980s and early 1990s and outbreaks of foot and mouth disease, such as that which occurred in 2001, highlighting some of the difficulties of assessing risk while at the same time adding to public uncertainties over the abilities of experts and politicians to anticipate risk and the likelihood of harm. Identifying, responding to and coping with such risks is rarely straightforward, but broader interpretations of risk raise even more difficult questions, including those relating to ethical debates, such as the distribution of risks within society, and the extent of trust in those who make key decisions.

This chapter therefore seeks to explore the nature of ethical theory and to consider its relevance to social policy, before moving on to a consideration of some of the interpretations of the concept of risk, and their implications for society.

# Ethics and social policy

Ethical issues in social policy can be examined from a number of perspectives. They can be grounded in some of the traditional key concepts of social policy, such as social needs and social problems, related to notions of rights, equality, social justice and choice, linked with concepts such as efficiency and effectiveness, or related to notions of altruism and reciprocity. They also emerge strongly from **applied philosophy**, for example with regard to the practitioner–patient relationship in healthcare.

'Being ethical' might be seen as always conforming to a particular view of what is right and what is wrong, so that two people with conflicting views over what is right and wrong would make different choices about what actions to take. This can easily be seen in debates over abortion, where one doctor might believe that it is wrong to destroy a group of cells that could become a human being, whilst another might believe that a pregnant woman has the right to make choices about her body. Here the very idea of applying ethical theory frequently seems to be difficult and fraught with problems, as it appears to be subject to interpretation, contestation and conflict. However, many moral philosophers argue that this is not the case, and that some decisions and actions can be seen as being of a higher ethical calibre than others. In social policy, there is perhaps a general acceptance that legitimate differences in views need to be recognised and, where possible, sympathetically accommodated. That requires an understanding of the basis of different views, and a consideration of whether there is any common ground between them.

However, debates about ethics can also be even more complicated than they may at first appear. To take the example of euthanasia, where there has been considerable debate about the rights and wrongs of such action, some people have argued that because disabled people's lives are sometimes perceived as less worthwhile, and more tragic and burdensome, there is a danger that additional pressures might be brought to bear upon them. This draws in part upon the view that the legalisation of 'assisted dying' (or assisted suicide) may bring further pressures to bear on some groups, including not only disabled people, but also older people, who fear becoming a burden; however, it also draws upon debates about whether all lives have equal value; and it raises questions about whether individuals' 'informed choice' might be the same if sufficient and appropriate support and resources were provided to enable people to live in a dignified manner.

# Ethical theory

Ethical theory draws heavily upon concepts of morality and explanations of how our behaviour affects others. Whilst some ethical 'choices' may appear relatively easy to make, such as whether a health or social care professional should report a case of child sexual abuse, in many cases it is not possible to reach a straightforward decision about whether an action is right or wrong, or good or bad (Briefing 4.1 provides the view of one thinker, Peter Singer, of what ethics is). Making difficult decisions is further complicated by the awareness that our own moral and ethical outlook and thinking is inevitably shaped and affected by others, including family, friends, community and society. Yet if individuals are to make their own decisions it is generally seen as desirable that they do so independently, and that they do not simply reflect the views of others. Whilst it may be possible, and sometimes appropriate, to learn from the views and experiences of others, it is equally the case that collective wisdom is not necessarily correct, as can be evidenced from examples such as slavery, genocide, or denying women the right to vote.

One way in which we can seek to analyse and evaluate our views more critically is through a more abstract consideration of issues. LaFollette (1997) suggests that we can make three principal mistakes in ethical deliberations:

- We can apply ethical principles inconsistently – for us to defend our views successfully it is essential that they are *consistent*; conversely, inconsistency is frequently seen as a weakness in the arguments of others. This is true whether the debate is over abortion, rationing of healthcare, or freedom of speech.

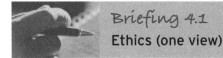

## Briefing 4.1
### Ethics (one view)

| *What ethics is not* | *What ethics is* |
| --- | --- |
| Prohibitions particularly concerned with sex – moral issues around sex are not unique | Living according to ethical standards so long as people believe that it is right to do as they are doing |
| An ideal system that does not work in practice – different perspectives on ethics can successfully argue that in ethics the failure of short, simple rules is not a failure of ethics as a whole | Takes a universal point of view – ethics requires a view that goes beyond 'I' or 'you' |
| Something intelligible only in the context of religion – ethical behaviour does not require a religious underpinning | Can draw on a variety of approaches, including utilitarianism/consequentialism and deontology |
| Relative or subjective – ethical reasoning is possible. | |

*Source*: Adapted from Singer, P. (1993) *Practical Ethics*, Cambridge University Press, Cambridge, Chapter 1.

Inconsistency can therefore often be a compelling reason to reject someone's ethical position.

● We can use inappropriate moral standards – not only is it important to be consistent; we must also base our arguments upon appropriate guidelines or standards (*correct principles*), and theorising about ethics is a good way of identifying the best standards or guidelines.

● We can apply moral standards inappropriately – even if we have identified what is morally relevant and seek to act consistently based upon that, we can still make moral mistakes, for example if we try to protect someone's feelings or to protect ourselves, or through lacking the personal and verbal skills to be honest in a way which will not harm others. *Correct application* of moral standards is therefore important.

## Are ethical judgements simply matters of opinion?

It is sometimes argued that ethical judgements are simply 'matters of opinion'. However, an implication of this would be that if ethical judgements are just opinions, all opinions may be equally good (or bad), and it would not therefore be possible to ethically scrutinise the judgements of ourselves or others. This is likely to be an undesirable situation, and it is generally accepted that not all opinions on ethical issues are in reality equally reliable. For instance, an opinion that is clearly based upon misinformation, lack of perception or understanding, or upon untenable assumptions, would be viewed by most people as inferior to one which is based upon full information, shrewd perception and consistent ethical principles that have been subject to and withstood the careful scrutiny of others. In addition, in some circumstances we are required to make an informed decision that will profoundly affect others, and that will require appropriate ethical choices.

Importantly, abiding by ethical principles should not be viewed as being the same as following the law. The law may be, and often is, informed by ethics, but at times it may oppose ethical principles, with one of the most commonly used examples of this being laws that existed in Nazi Germany. Individuals have frequently rebelled against laws on ethical grounds. It is also apparent that laws change over time, as has been the case with abortion.

## The role of theory

Even in cases where people agree that an issue should be evaluated, at least in part, by criteria based upon **ethical theory**, there is often disagreement about how this should be done. This is clear with regard to absolute and relative definitions of poverty, or whether long-term social care for older people should be free or paid for, as well as arguments such as those for and against abortion and capital punishment. However, people do not normally make arbitrary ethical judgements: they are usually prepared to explain and give reasons for their views. For example, anti-abortionists may claim that abortion is not justified as the foetus has the same right to life as other people, whilst pro-abortionists may argue that a woman has the right to decide what happens to and in her body. In such debates the protagonists are usually putting forward some feature of their view that is supposed to underpin their evaluation. Such arguments can be developed. To take the case of capital punishment, it may not be sufficient simply to argue over whether capital punishment deters crime (a consequentialist argument, as discussed below), but it may be necessary to discover exactly how important the deterrent is. Ethical theories are therefore concerned to undertake systematic discussions of theoretical questions; they seek to identify the relevant ethical criteria, to gauge the weight or significance of those criteria, and to provide a sense of how we can determine whether an action or decision satisfies those criteria. However, as is explored later in the chapter, ethical theories are rarely claimed to tell us how we should act in all situations. Rather, what they do is to offer different criteria of ethical relevance and to direct our attention to specific features of action.

Broadly speaking, there can be said to be two main classes of ethical theory: consequentialist and deontological. Whilst there are other moral theories it is these that shall be considered here. The consequentialist approach is that we should choose the available action with the best overall consequences, whilst deontological theory suggests that we should act in ways which are circumscribed by moral rules or rights that are defined, at least in part, independently of consequences.

However, while there are very different approaches to ethical theory, and to its relationship with decisions and actions, the idea of reflective equilibrium, associated with the philosopher John Rawls, suggests that a feeling of what is right, in terms of moral principles and intuitions, together with the exercise of reasoning, helps establish a link between ethical theory and actions.

## Consequentialism

Consequentialists argue that we should act in ways that produce the best consequences. In making a decision we would therefore seek to identify the available options, trace the likely moral consequences of each, and then select the option with the best outcome for all concerned. Yet, whilst this approach appears to have considerable appeal, for it is hard to argue against achieving the best outcome, it may be difficult to determine which consequences should be considered and how much weight should be given to each, for without that information it is not possible to know how to act. The best-known form of consequentialism is utilitarianism, often associated with the work of Jeremy Bentham and John Stuart Mill, and sometimes summarised as being about choosing 'the greatest happiness for the greatest number'. Again, however, this is not as simple as it may first appear; for example, there are differences between act utilitarians, who claim that we should determine the morality of each action by deciding which action is more likely to promote the greatest happiness of the greatest number, and rule utilitarians who argue that the concern should not be whether a *particular* action is likely to promote the greatest happiness of the greatest number, but whether a particular *type* of action would, if done by most people, promote the greatest happiness of the greatest number. An act utilitarian might therefore conclude that in a particular instance a lie would be justified as it maximises the happiness of all those concerned, whilst a rule utilitarian might argue that since the result of everyone lying would be a reduction in happiness it would be best to have a rule against lying, even if in a particular case lying would appear to give the greatest happiness of the greatest number (Briefing 4.2).

### Briefing 4.2
### An ethical dilemma

On whether to tell a client that his wife is sleeping with another woman in order to have the school fees for her son paid: Mma Ramotswe:

'It is unethical for a detective to lie to the client. You can't do it.'

'I can understand that,' said Mma Makutsi. 'But there are times, surely, when a lie is a good thing. What if a murderer came to your house and asked you where a certain person was? And what if you knew where that person was, would it be wrong to say: "I do not know anything about that person. I do not know where he is." Would that not be a lie?'

'Yes. But then you have no duty to tell the truth to that murderer. So you can lie to him. But you do have a duty to tell the truth to your client, or to your spouse, or to the police. That is all different.'

'Why? Surely if it is wrong to lie, then it is always wrong to lie. If people could lie when they thought it was the right thing to do, then we could never tell when they meant it.' Mma Makutsi, stopped, and pondered for a few moments before continuing. 'One person's idea of what is right may be quite different from another's. If each person can make up his own rule . . .' She shrugged, leaving the consequences unspoken.

*Source:* Alexander McCall Smith (2003) *Tears of the Giraffe*, Abacus, London, pp. 170–1.

 Thought provoker

There has been much debate about 'air miles' and imported food, particularly organic food, which may be flown thousands of miles.

Is it better to eat locally grown non-organic food or imported organic food?

Is it better to support farmers in developing countries, who may be more in need of economic support, or local farmers?

However, there are a number of criticisms of such approaches. Teichman (1996), for example, identifies a number of problems with consequentialism:

- it cannot be put into practice as short-term consequences cannot be predicted with certainty and long-term consequences cannot be predicted at all;

- it is not possible to weigh one person's happiness or pleasure against that of another, nor can a person's present happiness be weighed against their future potential happiness;

- consequentialism in practice would be likely to damage the rights of individuals and minority groups in favour of the happiness of majorities;

- there would be risks of politicians deciding what sort of results were the most important, potentially leading them to make decisions in the interests of themselves and their supporters at the expense of others;
- consequentialism would mean that justice could be overruled where an act of injustice might be thought likely to produce better results.

There are also questions over the scope of utilitarian analysis including, for example, whether it applies only to our own country or region, or to others as well, and whether it is limited to those currently alive, or should future generations be included?

There are also other problems with utilitarianism, including that not all utilitarian philosophers accept that happiness should be the measure of the greatest good, with possible alternative principal values including friendship, health, knowledge or personal autonomy.

## Deontological theory

Deontology is closely associated with the philosopher Immanuel Kant, who argued that principles should be based upon reason, and that nothing should be an ethical principle for one person that could not be a principle for everyone else. From such a perspective: each person has a duty to respect the autonomy of others; morality consists of performing the right actions; and ethical rights are universal and should therefore be respected by all.

In contrast to consequentialists, therefore, deontologists argue that our ethical choices can be seen as, to some extent, independent of consequences. For deontologists acts and decisions must not only be in accordance with, but also for the sake of duty or obligation. For example, obligations such as not to kill or steal are not justified simply on the grounds that following such rules will always produce the best consequences, but because they are underpinned by some other judgement, whether this emerges from abstract reasoning, intuitions, or some other form of principles. Whilst consequentialist approaches may be attractive for their apparent rationality, deontological ideas are appealing as they suggest that we can discover that some ways of acting are right, whilst others are wrong.

From a deontological perspective decisions should therefore be made by referring to considered principles, rather than on the basis of expedient calculation, and what is most important is not the outcome, but whether a person acts according to a perceived obligation, and intends that some good come about. If telling the truth is an ethical duty, then telling the truth is the right way to act even if the result is to cause more misery than happiness. For deontologists it is wrong to ignore these principles, as to do so allows us to choose decisions that are made on the basis of contingency, and, even more problematically, whilst breaking faith with principles may appear to be beneficial in the short term, in the longer term the consequences will not be better. Rule deontology in theory therefore gives predictability, with rules being recognised and respected. However, in the case of almost any rule there will be times when a judgement might be made that the outcome may be better if the rule is broken. There will also be times, perhaps even more awkwardly, particularly for many areas of social policy, when different rules come into conflict and it is necessary to choose between them. And in such situations, even if it is possible to choose one rule over another, the position that it may sometimes be better if a rule is broken would still be likely to apply.

Act deontology is a form of deontology that on the face of it is almost self-contradictory. Rather than following rules, act deontologists assume that each situation is different and that each individual must make their own judgement. The moral obligation for act deontologists is to be true to themselves. Whilst arguably being difficult or impossible to put into practice, act deontology does direct us towards a different consideration of moral rules, and in particular to recognise that simply because a rule has worked successfully in the past it may not do so in each subsequent situation, as each circumstance will have its own unique features. It also highlights the argument that a person should be true to themselves in each situation, and should not operate differently, for example in their 'professional' and 'ordinary' lives, a line of reasoning often of great relevance to many professionals involved with areas of social policy.

## Justice

The concept of 'justice' is widely used in social and political theory. It is also important in ethics. Whilst it is used in many different ways, these can perhaps be subdivided into two principal categories: concerns over 'fairness' and 'appropriate punishment for wrongdoing'. Whilst the latter is also clearly of importance to society it is the former category that is of concern here. However, even 'justice as fairness' is not a straightforward concept, as, for example, it could be interpreted as 'to each according to her/his need', 'to each according to what s/he deserves', or 'to each according to her/his rights'.

One approach that is frequently used in considering justice is that of the philosopher John Rawls (1973), through which he argues that unequal possession and distribution of qualities such as power, wealth and income are unacceptable in a society unless they actually work to benefit the worst-off members of society. Although this is a complex argument a simplified version is given here. Rawls uses the hypothetical situation of people as free, logical and disinterested beings, about to enter into a social contract with everyone else in order to form a just society; yet a key feature of this is that no one knows what or where they will be in the society, so that the social contract is to be made behind a 'veil of ignorance' – no one would know in advance whether they would be rich or poor, male or female, young or old, ill or healthy, employer or employee. He then asks us, as potential social contractors, to consider which principles should be adopted by the society in order to be just. Rawls' own answer is that there should be two main principles of justice, with the first taking precedence in the event of any conflict between them:

1 Each person should have an equal right to the maximum amount of liberty consistent with a similar liberty for others, so that each person has the same right to freedom as any other, unless that freedom works against the freedom of others. The basic liberties, for Rawls, are political liberty, the right to property, freedom from arbitrary arrest, and being within a system of law which deals impartially with those who fall under its remit.

2 Any social and economic inequalities should be arranged to ensure that they work to everyone's advantage, including the worst off in society. Inequalities may be inevitable, but if these work only to benefit those who are already privileged they should not be allowed. For Rawls a justifiable inequality would be a surgeon who is well-off, but only because their skills contribute to the well-being of all, so that a society without the services of the rich surgeon would be worse off.

Of course, Rawls' argument can be criticised: for example over whether equality should come after liberty, as the social contractors might feasibly conclude that the equal distribution of resources is the best way of ensuring justice within society; inequality might also legitimately increase if the position of the worst off improves by only a very small amount. However, whatever the rights and wrongs, or the nuances of the arguments, it is clear that Rawls' theory highlights the strong connection between morality and politics, and in particular suggests that if social structures do not allow all people the opportunity to achieve their potentials then morality is not being created to the greatest degree possible. Since most work related to social policy is arguably moral in nature, and often sits on basic principles of justice and fairness, then it is of moral concern because it itself can be directly responsible for increasing or decreasing the level or morality achieved.

## Feminist ethics and ethical relativism

It is possible to identify feminist critiques of traditional ethical approaches. Whilst these reflect the diversity of feminist approaches (see also Chapter 8), Porter (1999) suggests that there are three interrelated features of feminist ethics (personal experience; context, with an emphasis on the idea that context is important in informing morally appropriate choices; and nurturant relationships, with care, nurture and relationships being central to the consideration of ethics) which, whilst also important for other ethical perspectives, provide a distinctiveness for feminist ethics through being located in women's experiences, challenging gendered dualisms and enabling the development of alternatives.

These arguments can have an impact upon the way that we understand ethics. Many feminists would, for example, challenge Rawls' liberal justice perspective, arguing that people are not rational, disembodied individuals, and that instead it is important to recognise that identity is constituted and affected by a variety of ties, links with communities and social structures. Similarly, feminists may argue that it is necessary to recognise the existence of gendered moral perspectives, for example over the extent to which men and women display care, and that it may be appropriate to examine power relationships rather than simply suggesting that men and women have different moral perspectives.

Some argue that ethics are derived from the social and cultural environments in which we exist, so that the rightness or wrongness of an action depends upon where we live or were brought up; in other words, no opinions or actions are in themselves ethically right or wrong. However, whilst it is clear that cultural and social norms do have an impact on interpretations of right and wrong, and while an understanding of moral diversity may be valuable, an acceptance of a normative ethical relativism would not allow any criticism of the behaviour of others on ethical grounds, including practices such as torture or slavery.

# Applied ethics

Applied, or practical, ethics is clearly concerned with the application of ethical theory to practical issues. Part of the reason that ethics are so important to social policy is that many actions will involve intervention in the lives of others, whether this is in terms of healthcare, social care, housing or other areas of policy.

There are a number of areas where ethical debates are immediately apparent and can have a direct effect on policy, such as those around abortion, conception and euthanasia. In areas such as these there is considerable material available from groups campaigning for and against different position and from others with interests in those debates. For example, Singer, in *Practical Ethics* (1993), examines a variety of topics, some of which have a clear social policy dimension, including notions of equality, abortion, euthanasia and divisions between rich and poor countries. Although not seeking to provide a comprehensive consideration of the relevance of applied ethics to social policy, this section briefly considers two very different areas of concern where ethical debates have clear relevance to the development and implementation of policy: rationing and human genetics.

## Rationing

Rationing and targeting of resources has long been a significant feature in the discussion and delivery of public services. Arksey (2002) has pointed out that, in healthcare in particular, media coverage has at times been intense, whilst there has also been periodic concern over rationing in other fields, such as the provision of social care or social housing, as is evident from the chapters on these topics in this book. It is arguable that in areas such as these, decisions are increasingly being driven according to what is available, rather than what individuals need. Indeed, rationing is inevitably a major dilemma for social policy as resources are not limitless, and problems can rarely be solved simply through an ever-greater input of resources. It is therefore necessary to devise strategies for rationing, whether the provision is of education, healthcare or social security benefits (Briefing 4.3). Arksey argues that rationing is of itself not necessarily bad or undesirable, as, if based on the principle of 'equity-based-on-need', people with equal need could receive equal treatment and those with the greatest needs would receive top priority, although, of course, issues over the level of resourcing of each service would remain.

If the example of healthcare is followed here, one approach to rationing that received considerable attention during the 1980s and 1990s was suggestions for measures to allow the calculation of priorities through criteria such as the relief of symptoms, quality of life and likely survival time. Quality Adjusted Life Years (QALYs) were one such method proposed in the United Kingdom, whilst in the United States the state of Oregon devised and implemented a form of rationing based on a set of costs and benefits. In terms of the arguments outlined earlier in this chapter above, initiatives such as these can arguably be seen as representing a shift from a deontological approach to consequentialism, with the emphasis

## Briefing 4.3
### Forms of rationing

- **Rationing by denial** – turning people away on the grounds that they are not suitable or their needs are not urgent enough; the threshold of eligibility for a service is raised and lowered to match supply and demand.

- **Rationing by selection** – the converse of rationing by denial; providers of services select clients who are most likely to benefit from intervention, who are seen as deserving cases, or who are least likely to cause problems.

- **Rationing by deflection** – potential recipients are diverted towards another service, for example, with a social services problem being redefined as a health or housing problem.

- **Rationing by deterrence** – discouraging entry into the system, through barriers such as receptionists, lack of provision of information, queues, or costs.

- **Rationing by delay** – demand can be discouraged by delay, with appointments weeks or months ahead, or through waiting lists.

- **Rationing by dilution** – rather than reducing services, the scale and depth of them is reduced so that users are not excluded, but everyone receives less, for example through cutting appointment periods for doctors, or raising class sizes in schools.

- **Rationing by termination** – in some cases delivery of a service may be ended, with doctors discharging patients, or social workers closing cases.

*Source*: Adapted from Klein, R., Day, P. and Redmayne, S. (1996) *Managing Scarcity: Priority Setting and Rationing in the National Health Service*, Open University Press, Buckingham, pp. 11-12.

being upon the assessment of the consequences of human actions. They can also be criticised in a similar way as they tend to an approach whereby so long as there is more 'good' (in this case measured by 'cost-effective life') than 'bad' (expensive life) then particular actions could be said to be justified.

However, one of the strongest arguments for the adoption of measures such as QALYs is that they expose the often hidden rationing that already takes place and the injustice of some of the decisions that have existed within the NHS, and suggest that these might have been avoided had the structure and funding of the NHS been different. Supporters of QALYs produced a variety of arguments for their use including that they provide a way of making priorities explicit, to compare the costs and effectiveness of different treatments, and therefore to make the most cost-effective use of resources. Even some critics accept that they have a use in helping to remind us that decisions about rationing may not always result from a lack of overall resources, but because decisions are made to use resources for other purposes.

Whilst QALYs were not formally accepted as part of UK healthcare, the NHS does provide another example of the ways in which rationing has become more explicit. With the creation by the Labour Government of the National Institute for Clinical Excellence (NICE) in 1999, for the first time there was a statutory body responsible for advising professionals, patients and the public in England and Wales about the use of health technologies (medicines, medical devices, diagnostic techniques and procedures and the clinical management of specific conditions). NICE was also intended to help ensure that provision of drugs and services should become more even across different parts of England and Wales. Whilst NICE has a wide range of responsibilities, perhaps the most obvious to the public has been its decisions about which drugs and treatments should be available through the NHS. For example, in early 2002 NICE decided that access to the drug irinotecan, used for treating bowel cancer, should be heavily restricted, although it had become standard treatment for the condition in the United States and much of Europe. Critics have also argued that the denial of drugs on prescription, following decisions made by NICE, effectively leads to a two-tier service, with those who can afford to pay for treatment doing better than NHS patients, effectively failing to end the 'postcode prescribing' that NICE was established to prevent, and that rationing has therefore been shifted even further in the direction of class and ability to pay, so that it is only those patients who can afford private treatment who have access to some treatments.

It is clear from this brief consideration of rationing within the NHS that ethical analysis can have significant implications, and that the application of ideas based upon interpretations of consequentialist or deontological approaches, as well as notions of justice, could be used to explore many of the existing practices upon which rationing is based. A consequentialist, and particularly a utilitarian, view would emphasise an approach which produced collective benefit. Consequentialists might also favour decision making based on the use of more 'objective' measures rather than on considered moral principles that might arise from a deontological perspective that prioritised patients' right to treatment. Given this, even from the short discussion above, it is perhaps possible to suggest that the provision of healthcare has been moving towards a more consequentialist position than was previously the case.

## Science, human genetics and reproduction

Scientific advances in recent years have brought a series of major questions to the fore around **human genetics** and reproduction (as well as those around agriculture and food, bioethics more generally). In the context of this chapter it is possible only to highlight some of these challenges and examples of the dilemmas that they are introducing, so that two areas are outlined briefly below, 'saviour siblings' and genetic screening and insurance. However, it is safe to say that the issues and questions associated with these developments are both wide ranging and profound, and that many may have significant long-term implications for both individuals and societies. Some of those which have been most apparent have been around human fertilisation, with, for example, concerns over cloning, 'saviour siblings' (a form of 'designer baby') and the use of embryos in researching the understanding and treatment of disease having been widely raised in the media in recent years. The wider issues related to human genetics have also come more to the attention of the public, with the possible implications of genetic testing and genetic manipulation raising the prospect of further difficult ethical decisions in the future.

In the United Kingdom the response of governments to the emergence of these new challenges has largely involved the introduction of new regulatory and advisory bodies, such as the Human Fertilisation and Embryology Authority and the Human Genetics Commission, established in 1991 and 2000 respectively.

## Controversy and debate

### Zain Hashmi – ethics and the legal system

Zain Hashmi was born with a genetic blood disorder, beta thalassaemia, leaving him needing frequent blood transfusions and threatening his life. Having failed to find a donor with matching tissue, in December 2001 his parents, Raj and Shahana Hashmi were given permission by the Human Fertilisation and Embryology Authority to attempt to create a new sibling whose umbilical cord blood could be used to cure Zain. The proposal was that embryos would be screened and if one were to match Zain's tissue type and was also free of beta thalassaemia, it would be implanted in Shahana Hashmi's womb. This went one step beyond the HFEA's previous decisions, which had been limited to licensing pre-implementation genetic diagnoses, allowing parents at risk of having a child with genetic disorder to have their embryos screened and only those that were unaffected implanted. This was the first time that the HFEA had allowed such a move and although the Authority insisted that this was a one-off decision it was seen by others as setting an ethical precedent for the parents of other children who suffer from life-threatening disorders that can be cured only by bone marrow transplants and for whom no suitable donor can be found. A legal challenge to this was launched by Josephine Quintavalle of the group Comment on Reproductive Ethics (CORE), which believed that IVF techniques should not be used to help a sibling (a human being should not be used instrumentally), but only for the benefit of the baby concerned. CORE argued that the HFEA had no power to licence the new process and the High Court ruled in CORE's favour. However, in April 2003 the Appeal Court overturned this decision, allowing the Hashmis the possibility of proceeding with treatment.

The entire affair was made more complicated by the existence of the Human Rights Act, as the HFEA had earlier been concerned that if it had not given the Hashmis permission to go ahead, they might have challenged such a decision legally as violating Zain's right to life.

The Human Fertilisation and Embryology Authority was created following the Human Fertilisation and Embryology Act 1990 to regulate and advise upon infertility treatment and embryology research. Perhaps inevitably, in an area where there are major ethical dimensions and disagreements, and where laws made even a decade before are challenged by rapid scientific advances, there has been extensive use of the courts. The HFEA has been involved in a number of high-profile cases, including its attempts in the 1990s to prevent the widowed Diane Blood from using her dead husband's sperm to conceive children in the absence of his written consent, a battle which she ultimately won through using EU law to travel to Brussels for treatment, and that of Zain Hashmi (see the 'Controversy and debate' box, above). It is apparent here that there are a number of complex and interrelated issues. However, from one perspective a key ethical dimension could be seen as being that Zain's parents' intention was to use their unborn child to help their existing son. Blood was to be derived from the umbilical cord, and there should therefore be no risk to the younger sibling, and its birth would help Zain. But were they right to propose to use their new child as a means to an end? Clearly this is not an easy question to answer.

Where human genetics is concerned, the government created the Human Genetics Commission in 1999 to review the likely benefits and risks of advances and to address the ethical, legal and social implications arising from these advances. It sees a key element of its work as consulting with and informing the public and other stakeholders. One of the first areas to be affected by awareness of the potential implications of these advances in genetics has been the world of insurance, particularly over genetic screening and testing and their implications. In April 1997 the Council of Europe adopted a convention that stated that there should be no discrimination against a person on the grounds of their genetic heritage. Whilst the UK has not ratified that convention it does serve to indicate the levels of concern about the uses of genetic tests and the ways that they may create new or reinforce existing inequalities. In the UK in 2001 the Human Genetics Commission made a number of recommendations, including a three-year moratorium on the use of genetic test results by employers, and from October 2001 the insurance industry and the government agreed a five-year moratorium on the use of **predictive genetic tests** for most policies, with only those which might potentially pay out large sums of money being excluded. Daykin *et al.* (2003) have identified a number of philosophical considerations around this issue, each of which relate to traditional social policy concerns:

- **Solidarity and mutuality** – with insurance schemes operating on principles of solidarity and equality, there has been confusion between solidarity and mutuality.

- **Moral hazard** – where individuals may change their behaviour patterns because they have taken out insurance, perhaps exercising less caution because they are protected against particular risks, with insurers fearing that advances in genetic testing may increase the likelihood of moral hazard.

- **Concepts of fairness in insurance** – these change over time with, for example, distinctions between smokers and non-smokers now taken into account in risk categories in a way that would not have been seen as acceptable previously. It could be argued, for instance, that it is unfair to penalise people who inherit genetic 'conditions' as they can do nothing to affect that situation.

- **Adverse selection** – the situation where those seeking cover have more information about their true level of risk than does the insurer, which they can use to their advantage when buying insurance.

However, for some people the ethical concerns go much further, sometimes reflecting past concerns over **eugenics** (a view that society can be improved through the manipulation of genetic inheritance through reproduction). For example, Kerr (2003) notes that whilst there are significant differences, emphases such as those on personal responsibility and public education are similar. There have also been fears that because for the great majority of genetically identified conditions there are no new therapies, pre-natal screening can often lead to abortion of a foetus, and that this in turn may be seen as 'an attempt to get rid of disabled people' (BCODP, 2000). However, others seek to differentiate the two issues and argue that a woman's right to choose should not be used to imply a particular view of a condition that might lead to a disability.

Again, many of the arguments around genetics can be examined from either a consequentialist or a deontological perspective. For consequentialists it would obviously be the consequences that arise from any use of human genetics that would be important, rather than a pre-existing idea of the right or wrong of an action. A deontological perspective, on the other hand, would argue that in addition to the consequences the right or wrong of the type of action to be taken would be important, whether or not the outcome was to be good.

## Professional ethics

For social policy, additional obvious links with ethics come in relation to professional practice, and in the arenas of health and social care in particular, where social, political and technological changes have seen the development of ethical codes or guidelines for many professions. Many professions now have codes written for them, including doctors, nurses and clinical psychologists. Used in this sense 'profession' tends to mean a self-regulating organisation that controls entry into particular occupations through recognition of the achievement of the necessary knowledge and skills. Ethical codes for such groups tend to form part of the statement about the profession and its standards so that 'professional standards' are seen as distinct from those standards that may be imposed by other bodies, such as governments, even though there may be overlap between them. However, whilst such codes can provide valuable guidance they can be criticised for implying that a professional who meets the requirement of the code is fulfilling all their moral obligations. Similarly, the extent to which such codes are comprehensive and coherent can be debated and frequently there is a need for further clarification and guidance.

*Source*: www.CartoonStock.com.

Seedhouse (1988) raises two important questions, arising out of the debate about ethical theory as discussed earlier in this chapter, which, although he applies them to healthcare, are more generally applicable:

● How can we be ethical when we do not know for certain what it is to be ethical?

● How can we be ethical when we do not agree among ourselves what it is to be ethical?

He then seeks to help answer his own questions and to enable a more practical use of moral reasoning through the introduction of an 'ethical grid' (Figure 4.1), which he intended to be an instrument to help health workers reason morally, but which he argues could be used by others in society. His approach draws upon a social aspect to moral reasoning rather than some of the alternatives, such as that of

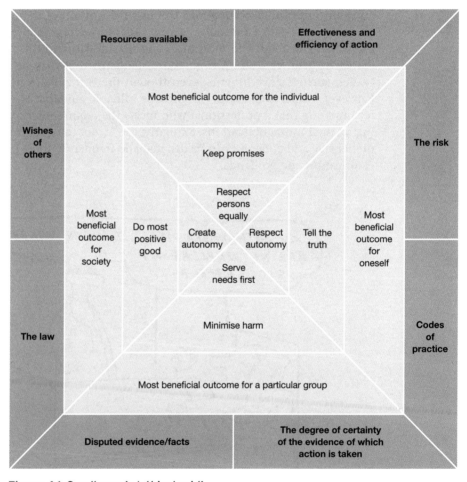

**Figure 4.1** Seedhouse's 'ethical grid'

*Source*: Seedhouse, D. (1988) *Ethics: The Heart of Health Care*, John Wiley & Sons, Chichester.

Beauchamp and Childress (1994), discussed below, which is founded more in the medical model. The grid consists of four layers: blue, which lies at the centre and provides the core rationale, consisting of boxes that 'present a rich and fruitful theory of health' (p. 129); red, which focuses upon duties and motives, corresponding largely with deontological theories, with boxes that 'are intimately related to the richest sense of health' (p. 135); green, drawing upon consequentialist approaches to 'focus attention on the necessity always to consider the consequences of any proposed intervention' (p. 137); and black, involving external considerations such as the law, professional codes of practice or the wishes of others. Seedhouse and others who favour the idea of the ethical grid argue that its use can clarify processes and complex situations and promote confidence in moral reasoning.

Seedhouse suggests that the ethical grid can be utilised in a variety of situations, ranging from reading of ethical issues in newspapers, or when watching television, through to use in practice by professionals. He suggests four steps in the use of the grid:

1 Consider the issue intuitively, without referring to the grid and attempt to consider the ramifications of possible actions, including the basic positives and negatives of the various options, to develop an initial position.

2 Consider the grid and a first layer (often the blue layer because of its centrality to the rationale of health work).

3 Consider all the other aspects of the grid and select those boxes that appear to offer the most appropriate solution, that is, those that appear to offer the highest degree of morality.

4 Apply the boxes to the mental picture of the proposed action. This will give both a course of action and a justification of it in moral terms.

It is important to note here that, as outlined earlier in this chapter, there may be no 'correct' answers and that two individuals using the grid to examine one situation may come up with different actions. As with ethical reasoning in general, it therefore remains the responsibility of individuals to justify their decisions and select that which produces the highest degree of morality; and it is this which Seedhouse argues that the grid can assist with.

In the second edition of his book (1998) Seedhouse introduced an additional device designed to help, in this instance, health workers, which he calls the 'rings of uncertainty' (Figure 4.2). Ring A might be no or very little uncertainty, Ring B, some uncertainty, C, considerable uncertainty and D, total uncertainty.

With the rings Seedhouse also notes a variety of concerns: technical competence, resources, law, communication and ethics. He suggests that the rings can be used to help with the consideration of possible actions, so that a health worker could subdivide the rings into appropriate sections. A doctor considering undertaking a minor operation might consider where in the rings their situation lies with regard to resources, technical competence, ethics and the law. Similarly, if a professional was concerned about whether child abuse had occurred, Ring C might suggest that it would be important to seek the involvement of others in making a decision. They would then be in a better position to decide whether to

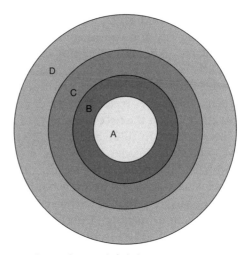

**Figure 4.2** Seedhouse's 'rings of uncertainty'
*Source*: Seedhouse, D. (1998) *Ethics: The Heart of Health Care*, John Wiley & Sons, Chichester.

proceed or not. However, Seedhouse is clear that if professionals find themselves standing outside the rings of uncertainty they ought not to intervene – if the potential action appears immoral, illegal, beyond communication, or lacks resources, or if the worker is not competent to undertake the action, then it should not be done. However, he also notes that there can be exceptional circumstances when action is still justified, so that just because an action is illegal does not necessarily mean that it should always not be taken, perhaps particularly where there is a strong ethical case for doing so. For some people the position regarding euthanasia would be an example of this, as was abortion before its legalisation.

A rather different and in many respects a more traditional approach to establishing professional guidance has been taken by Beauchamp and Childress (1994) who, drawing upon various approaches, including utilitarianism and deontology, set out four, effectively *prima facie*, principles for medical ethics:

1  **Respect for autonomy** – the obligation to respect the decision-making capacities of autonomous persons – actions that enhance autonomy are seen as desirable whilst those that diminish autonomy are seen as undesirable.
2  **Non-maleficence** – the obligation to avoid causing harm.
3  **Beneficence** – the obligation to provide benefits and balance benefits against risks.
4  **Justice** – obligations of fairness in the distribution of benefits and risks in terms of the consequences of an action.

Beauchamp and Childress argue that these four clusters of principles are central to biomedical ethics, although they note that whilst non-maleficence and beneficence have long been central to medical ethics the concepts of respect for autonomy and justice have only more recently been recognised as of importance.

Beauchamp and Childress recognise that different ethical principles can and do conflict, and that in some instances there may be no clear 'correct' decision, but argue that by using these principles, either on their own or in combination, medical professionals should be able to reason about what should be done, and generally, but not on every occasion, be able to resolve the ethical questions that they meet in their work.

Whilst this approach has the benefit of simplicity, it is equally possible to criticise it for the same reason – the 'principles' can be interpreted as a checklist of desirable values and do not relate closely to a theory that justifies their use together as a coherent set of rules; and as the principles can be accused of lacking detail, they could be utilised by different people to justify very different positions and actions. However, they have a clear value in providing a framework for discussion and consideration of difficult decisions.

Indeed, such an approach can be taken further. For example, in relation to bioethics, Mepham (2005) has developed an 'ethical matrix' which uses the three principles of 'respect for' each of well-being (reflecting Beauchamp and Childress' beneficence and non-maleficence), autonomy and fairness, but adds to these a concern for those groups who might have 'interests' in the outcomes, such as patients, consumers and professionals (or conceivably animals, for example in experimental or agricultural settings). Mepham suggests that the three principles and the interest groups can be arranged in a table to produce a grid, in the cells of which the relevance of the principles to each group can be set out to aid decision making.

From these examples it is apparent that seeking to provide ethical guidance for the decisions of professionals is not easy. There are a range of difficulties, including attempting to encapsulate what may be difficult and complex ethical arguments into fairly simple and straightforward guidelines whilst at the same time seeking to ensure that these are applicable to the range of choices that professionals can face and recognising that each situation can be unique. Tools such as those discussed here therefore generally aim to recognise that sincere differences of opinion can lead to different decisions, which it is the role of ethical deliberation to address and, if possible, resolve. They are therefore intended to facilitate deliberation but not to prescribe outcomes.

 ## Thought provoker

The duty of beneficence (see discussion above), to act in a way that benefits the patient, is an important ethical principle in healthcare. However, sometimes it can be difficult to know what is in a patient's best interests. For health professionals, decisions about treatment decisions at the end of life can depend upon the interpretation of this. Whilst in most circumstances it may be difficult to see how death could be in a patient's best interests, in some circumstances, for example where the quality of life is very poor, it might be argued that continuing treatment is not a benefit to the patient.

## Risk

In recent years the concept of 'risk' and its implications have come more to the fore in society, and there is now very considerable discussion of different aspects of 'risk' in many areas of social policy. It is possible to conceptualise 'risk' in many different ways, ranging from approaches that seek to provide 'objective' measures of probability and harm to those that see risks as entirely social or cultural constructions (Ball and Boehmer-Christiansen, 2002; Kemshall, 2002). These include:

- **The rational actor** – this has arguably been the approach that has dominated traditional, number-based methods of assessing risk, using probabilities (such as the risk of dying from smoking cigarettes), with both individuals and institutions seen as rational entities that seek to balance risks with benefits. Whilst it has historically formed the basis of risk assessments, it has come under increasing criticism, particularly for what critics see as its inappropriateness in the consideration of many social phenomena.

- **Reflexive modernity** – a view that recognises that expert-based and numerical risk assessment are no longer as widely accepted as they once were, and that science and technology alone no not provide sufficient justification for decisions. From this perspective traditional risk assessment can be criticised for shifting risk elsewhere (to others, to nature, or to the future) and instead it can be argued that there is a need to recognise and take account of different views and positions, rather than attempting to set rules for behaviour. As a result there will be a need for organisations to become reflexive entities which are able to respond to the changes and complexities of contemporary society.

- **Cultural theory** – emphasising the relationship between values and beliefs and perceptions of risks, this approach examines how risks are selected as being of concern and how they become legitimated for public attention. Risks can therefore be seen as being chosen for their usefulness to the social system, contributing to social cohesion and creating distinctions between insiders and outsiders.

- **Social constructivism** – a perspective that again rejects the traditional rational actor approach and tends to see risks and risk assessments as socially constructed and therefore amenable to criticism and deconstruction. Similarly, social processes are seen as contributing to the formulation of concerns and the way in which risks are perceived. Disputes over the levels or acceptability of risk can be seen as disputes over values and meaning.

Some of the major areas of debate in recent years have arisen as a result of scientific advances, and perhaps particularly in plant, animal and human genetics, such as genetic manipulation and cloning, and have been grounded in risk as uncertainty. For example, the introduction of genetically modified foods has generally been portrayed by government and by industry as matters of science, with clearly calculated probabilities that can be established through scientific trials, along the lines of the rational actor model outlined above. However, reflecting changing attitudes towards 'risk', with a move away from probabilistic measurements of the likelihood of harm towards a greater emphasis on institutional performance and trust, media, pressure group and public concern has tended to reflect the alternative perspectives, focusing upon the problems in calculating risks in such fields, the difficulty in being aware of the potential consequences until it is too late, and a lack of trust in the 'experts'. This suggests that it is necessary to be aware that 'risk' and the acceptability of risk, go beyond simple scientific calculation and are grounded in views that have their own logic and rationale to those making their own decisions.

For social policy these debates over risk have a number of implications. In particular, the development of social theories of risk, combined with a growing scepticism amongst the public, has raised questions about the creation of many policies. For example, in many policy areas, ranging from food safety through health and social care to the presence of paedophiles in the community, whilst governments may seek to develop actuarial approaches which govern access to services on a statistical calculation of risk, this may conflict with the range of perceptions of risk and the meanings that risk has in society.

It is also the case that economic and social change, as outlined in Chapter 2 and elsewhere, has contributed to the emergence of 'new' social risks. For example, Taylor-Gooby (2004) has suggested that more vulnerable groups are likely to experience new challenges in three areas:

- Family and gender roles:
  - balancing paid work and family responsibilities, particularly childcare;
  - caring for older relatives or themselves becoming frail and lacking family support.
- Labour market changes:
  - lacking the necessary skills to achieve adequately paid and secure employment;
  - being unable to access appropriate training to ensure the development of necessary new skills.
- Welfare state change:
  - using private provision that delivers unsatisfactory services or an insecure or inadequate pension.

Taken with other economic, social and political changes, these new risks can be argued to be placing additional strains on both individuals and the state, with the response of governments generally being in seeking to shift responsibilities away from the state and towards individuals, while encouraging labour market flexibility to increase economic competitiveness. The relationship between risk and social policy therefore becomes further complicated.

The concept of a 'risk society', where traditional certainties can no longer be taken for granted, and where the risks of anticipated events influence decision making (see Beck, 1992; Giddens, 1990, 1991), has potentially significant implications for social policy and for the welfare state, including such questions as whether state welfare can transform society, and whether traditional forms of welfare are able to respond to challenges such as exclusion, oppression, increasing costs and moral hazard. At the level of individuals, social policy has, over the past two decades, moved to a position where individuals are more responsible for their own risk management, both by shifting the burden of provision away from the state and through emphasising personal choice. To a considerable extent this has resulted in a move away from the state taking responsibility for risk and towards individuals being responsible for risk or, in cases of last resort, professionals of social welfare agencies. Some writers therefore argue that social policy is no longer principally about meeting the needs of individuals, or the pursuit of the collective good, but is now primarily concerned with the prevention of risk and the displacement of risk management responsibilities on to individuals (see, for example, the discussion of taxation and social security in Chapter 9). Kemshall notes that 'With the considerable benefit of hindsight the welfare recipient of the twentieth century has been recast as either risk-averse (preferring welfare dependency) or an imprudent risk taker (taking risks with self, health and future prosperity). The welfare recipient of the twenty-first century has been cast as a largely residual category replaced where possible by the responsible risk-taking citizen prudently exercising a range of risk choices' (2002, p. 130). In addition, there are many risks over which individuals have little or no control, so that 'Basing risk assessments on the broader ethical issues identified may thus be an inevitable feature of many people's worldview in the risk society' (Mepham, 2005, p. 317).

## Responding to risk

At the practical level the idea of 'risk' has been taken on board in relation to many welfare services. Attempts to address risk frequently involve:

- **Risk assessment** – seeking to determine both the likelihood that an event will occur and the size of the potential loss or harm.
- **Risk management** – with measures being taken to minimise risks, although there may be differences between voluntary risks, such as smoking or drinking alcohol, where the risks are well understood and generally accepted, and involuntary risks, where individuals may have little or no choice, and where governments may be expected to intervene to protect the public.
- **Risk communication** – with governments being increasingly aware of the need to communicate risks to the public effectively.

It is clearly not possible to achieve zero risk for all activities. Indeed, such a goal may not even be desirable. For example, in the personal social services some user groups have advocated the need for risk to challenge the practices of professionals that they have seen as serving to limit individual choice and maintain professional power. However, at the same time, risks have often been viewed negatively, so that many welfare services have worked towards risk avoidance, so that in areas such as mental health there has been an increased emphasis on compulsory treatment for some mentally ill people living in the community. In child protection, Munro (1999) has argued that the emphasis on risk has meant that professionals may overestimate risk of abuse, as the dangers to children and to themselves of making a mistake can be so great.

It is apparent therefore that whilst the idea of 'risk' has become a more central part of social policy than in the past, there is as yet little agreement on its implications, either at the individual or societal level. Nevertheless, an understanding of risk and its differing interpretations and meanings can add substantially to our understanding of social policy.

## Conclusion

This chapter differs from many in this book in dealing with topics that have not always been seen as central to the study of social policy. Nevertheless, it is apparent that the awareness of issues around both ethics and risk and how they relate to social policies and to practice is growing. Where risk is concerned, much of the recent interest has arisen out of perceptions that societies are becoming increasingly complex, while at the same time there have been growing doubts about the abilities of 'experts' to give adequate advice, and about the capacities of governments (and others) to anticipate and react to new challenges. This has led to questions about the responsibilities of individuals and the state in relation to meeting welfare needs and responding to risks.

Ethical concerns have long underpinned areas of theoretical debate about social policy, such as the 'fair' distribution of resources in society, or the rights and wrongs of particular courses of action. They have also been central to the codes of conduct of many professions for some time. However, the development of new technologies has brought ethical questions more to the attention of the media and to society as a whole, while many of the same concerns noted around 'risk' have meant that policy makers and individual citizens have been faced with additional decisions over appropriate courses of action.

## Summary

This chapter has introduced a general consideration of ethics and risk as they can relate to social policy. These are complex and almost constantly changing areas. Nevertheless the chapter has sought to:

● Provide an introduction to ethical theory, and in particular to consequentialist and deontological approaches, and the differing implications and interpretations of decisions that these can lead us to. Both of these have appeals, consequentialism in its apparent direction towards decisions that will create the greatest happiness, and deontologicalism in its suggestion that we can base decisions on considered principles and obligation.

▶

- Illustrate the application of ethical theory to practical issues and to demonstrate that historical social policy debates, such as rationing, and new issues, such as human genetics, can be examined using ethical theory, and that the use of ethical ideas does not necessarily provide us with a 'correct' answer to difficult decisions; they can encourage ethical reflection and reasoned and defensible explanations for particular choices.
- Consider different approaches to professional ethics and guidance to professionals in the social policy arena, noting again the emphasis on helping resolve ethical questions rather than necessarily reaching a 'right' decision.
- Examine the emergence of 'risk' as a significant factor in social policy debates, at the individual and collective levels, and the possible implications of this for the development of ideas of responsibility and forms of welfare provision whether by individuals or by the state.

# Discussion and review topics

1 Compare the strengths and weaknesses of QALYs in ethical terms compared with current forms of rationing of healthcare.

2 What ethical concerns might apply to a person who knows that they have a 50 per cent chance of carrying a disease that might lead to long-term chronic illness? Would these change if they decide to have a child who might inherit that disease?

3 What might Seedhouse's ethical grid and rings of uncertainty, and Beauchamp and Childress' four principles, suggest to a medical professional faced with a patient refusing, on religious grounds, a blood transfusion that might save her life?

4 Why have changing views of risk encouraged a shift from state to individual responsibility for welfare?

## Further reading

**Beauchamp, T. and Childress, J.** (2001) *Principles of Biomedical Ethics*, Oxford University Press, New York. The four principles discussed within this book have been one of the most widely used frameworks for medical ethics.

**Beckett, C. and Maynard, A.** (2005) *Values and Ethics in Social Work*, Sage, London. A good introductory text, aimed at social work, but providing discussion of values, ethics and their application.

**Klein, R., Day, P. and Redmayne, S.** (1996) *Managing Scarcity: Priority Setting and Rationing in the National Health Service*, Open University Press, Buckingham. A thorough consideration of the rationing of healthcare in the UK. Although now somewhat dated it continues to provide a good discussion of the topic.

**Mepham, B.** (2005) *Bioethics*, Oxford University Press, Oxford. Although aimed at students of the biosciences this book provides a readable introduction to ethical theory and covers topics such as reproductive choices, dietary futures and environmental sustainability.

**Seedhouse, D.** (1998) *Ethics: The Heart of Health Care*, John Wiley & Sons, Chichester. The second edition of this book expands considerably upon the first and introduces new 'tools' for decision making; Seedhouse provides a perspective on ethics that is markedly different from the more traditional approach of Beauchamp and Childress.

## Some useful websites

**www.basw.co.uk** – the British Association of Social Workers' site provides one example of a professional code of ethics.

**www.bbc.co.uk/religion/ethics** – a limited number of ethical issues are considered in some depth on the BBC's web pages.

**www.ethics-network.org.uk** – the UK Clinical Ethics Network provides case studies, guidance and other information primarily on healthcare ethics.

**www.hgc.gov.uk** – the website of the Human Genetics Commission provides information on the regulatory and advisory framework for human genetics in the United Kingdom including links to a number of other relevant organisations.

**www.nice.org.uk** – established under the Labour government in 1999 the National Institute for Health and Clinical Excellence aims to provide guidance on health technologies and the management of specific conditions. This site provides access to much of the Institute's work.

**www.nuffieldbioethics.org** – the Nuffield Council on Bioethics is a non-governmental body that aims to contribute to debates and policy making in bioethics. It demonstrates the range of work in this area from research involving animals through genetically modified crops to genetic screening and stem cell research.

## References

Arksey, H. (2002) 'Rationed Care: Assessing the Support Needs of Informal Carers in English Social Services Authorities', *Journal of Social Policy*, Vol. 31, pp. 81-101.

Ball, D.J. and Boehmer-Christiansen, S. (2002) *Understanding and responding to societal concerns*, Health and Safety Executive Research Report 34, Health and Safety Executive, London.

Beauchamp, T. and Childress, J. (1994) *Principles of Biomedical Ethics*, Oxford University Press, New York.

Beck, U. (1992) *Risk Society: Towards a New Modernity*, Sage, London.

British Council of Disabled People (2000) 'The New Genetics and Disabled People', BCODP, Derby.

Daykin, C.D., Akers, D.A., Macdonald, A.S., McGleenan, T., Paul, S. and Turvey, P.J. (2003) 'Genetics and Insurance – Some Social Policy Issues', presented to the Institute of Actuaries, 24 February 2003.

Giddens, A. (1990) *The Consequences of Modernity*, Polity, Cambridge.

Giddens, A. (1991) *Modernity and Self Identity*, Polity, Cambridge

Kemshall, H. (2002) *Risk, Social Policy and Welfare*, Open University Press, Buckingham.

Kerr, A. (2003) 'Rights and Responsibilities in the New Genetics Era', *Critical Social Policy*, Vol. 23, pp. 208-26.

Klein, R., Day, P. and Redmayne, S. (1996) *Managing Scarcity: Priority Setting and Rationing in the National Health Service*, Open University Press, Buckingham.

LaFollette, H. (1997) 'Theorizing about Ethics', in LaFollette, H. (ed.) *Ethics in Practice*, Blackwell, Cambridge, Massachusetts.

McCall Smith, A. (2003) *Tears of the Giraffe*, Abacus, London.

Mepham, B. (2005) *Bioethics*, Oxford University Press, Oxford.

Munro, E. (1999) 'Protecting children in an anxious society', *Health, Risk and Society*, Vol. 1, pp. 117–27.

Porter, E. (1999) *Feminist Perspectives on Ethics*, Longman, London.

Rawls, J. (1973) *A Theory of Justice*, Oxford University Press, Oxford.

Seedhouse, D. (1988) *Ethics: The Heart of Health Care*, John Wiley & Sons, Chichester.

Seedhouse, D. (1998) *Ethics: The Heart of Health Care*, John Wiley & Sons, Chichester.

Singer, P. (1993) *Practical Ethics*, Cambridge University Press, Cambridge.

Taylor-Gooby, P. (ed.) (2004) *New Risks, New Welfare: The Transformation of the European Welfare State*, Oxford University Press, Oxford.

Teichman, J. (1996) *Social Ethics: A Student's Guide*, Blackwell, Oxford.

# Part II

## THE DEVELOPMENT OF SOCIAL POLICY

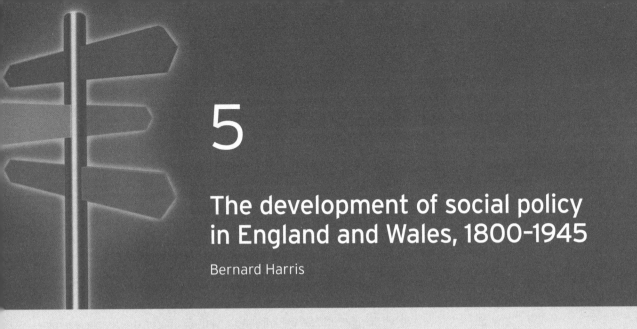

# 5

# The development of social policy in England and Wales, 1800-1945

Bernard Harris

## Chapter overview

The period between 1800 and 1945 saw many changes in welfare policy. At the start of this period, most people relied on their families and local communities for support in times of need, and central government played very little role in the provision of welfare services. However, by 1945 the state played a much larger role in the provision of a wide range of services, covering all the main areas of social policy.

This chapter provides an introduction to the development of public welfare policy during this period by examining the following issues:

- the initial growth of state welfare intervention before *circa* 1870;
- changing attitudes to welfare provision between 1870 and 1900;
- the Liberal welfare reforms of 1906-14;
- the development of social policy between 1914 and 1939;
- the impact of the Second World War on the development of the 'welfare state'.

## Spotlight on the issues
## Healthcare before the state

The early hospitals [most built between 1730 and 1850] were cold and dismal institutions; one feels that their benefactors were motivated less by genuine compassion than the need to justify themselves to their evangelical God, for even here the stigmas of pauperism were relentlessly insisted upon. Hospitals generally were centers of incredibly high mortality; on admission, patients were frequently asked to pay a deposit for funeral expenses. At most the early voluntary hospital provided a place where the infirm poor could obtain food and beer, a simple kind of nursing, and occasional access to such technical competence as the scientific development afforded; but it had about it the air both of the penal institution and the bawdy house. Great quantities of alcoholic drinks were surreptitiously consumed on the premises; patients 'escaped'; there was a great deal of unsavoury behaviour by the nursing staff.          Eckstein (1959, pp. 15-16)

The quotation above forms part of the background given by one of the first academic considerations of the NHS – Eckstein's *The English Health Service: Its Origins, Structure and Achievements*. The depressing picture painted of hospitals was reflected by many writers in the nineteenth century, including novelists such as Dickens and Disraeli, and helps explain why there were demands for change during this period. Indeed, it is the ways in which differing pressures for change have impacted upon social policies over the years, and in particular the role of the state in providing welfare services, that is in some respects the basis for this chapter.

Scene in Bedlam, from the series *A Rake's Progress* by William Hogarth
*Source*: © Historical Picture Archive/CORBIS.

# The development of social policy and the 'mixed economy of welfare'

During the last twenty years, the historiography of British welfare provision has been transformed by a growing emphasis on the provision of welfare outside the state. In 1994, the historian Geoffrey Finlayson (1994, p. 6) argued that Britain had always 'possessed what is now called a "mixed economy of welfare"' and that 'within that mixed economy, the state was only one element – and, arguably, for much of the nineteenth century, and even the twentieth century, it was not the most important element'. Other historians have echoed this view. Jane Lewis (1995, p. 3) claimed that Britain has 'always . . . had a mixed economy of welfare, in which the state, the voluntary sector, the family and the market have played different parts at different points in time' and Joanna Innes (1996, p. 140) concluded that 'a mixed economy of welfare' persisted throughout Western Europe from the sixteenth century onwards.

However, it is also important to recognise the extent to which the state's role within this mixed economy has developed and expanded since the end of the eighteenth century. At the beginning of this period, the majority of people relied on their families and their local communities for welfare support, and central government played a very limited role in the provision of welfare services (Brewer, 1989, p. 40). However, over the course of the next 150 years, the extent of state intervention increased dramatically. It included the introduction of measures to regulate conditions of work and establish minimum standards for the construction of new housing, as well as the provision of public services (such as public health and education) and the introduction of new forms of income support, such as unemployment insurance and health insurance. These developments meant that, despite their deficiencies, Britain still possessed a more comprehensive set of social services than almost any other democratic country on the eve of the Second World War (Stevenson and Cook, 1994, p. 83).

One of the ways in which we can 'measure' the growth of public welfare provision is by looking at the statistics on public expenditure. During the nineteenth century, the majority of the additional expenditure on social services was incurred by local authorities, but in the twentieth century a much larger share of the burden was borne by central government (see Table 5.1). In 1790, central government expenditure on social services probably amounted to no more than 1 per cent of the country's total national income, but this proportion more than doubled between 1790 and 1900, and by 1938 it had reached 10.7 per cent, before increasing still further after the Second World War. This expenditure reflected a degree of public intervention in welfare provision which would have been almost unthinkable at the end of the eighteenth century.

Table 5.1 Government expenditure on social, economic and environmental services in the United Kingdom, 1790-2000

| | As % of total expenditure | | As % of GDP | |
|---|---|---|---|---|
| | Social services | Economic and environmental services | Social services | Economic and environmental services |
| 1790 | 8.7 | 8.7 | 1.0 | 1.0 |
| 1840 | 9.4 | 9.4 | 1.0 | 1.0 |
| 1890 | 20.9 | 14.8 | 1.9 | 1.3 |
| 1900 | 18.0 | 17.3 | 2.5 | 2.4 |
| 1910 | 32.8 | 19.2 | 4.0 | 2.3 |
| 1920 | 25.9 | 14.4 | 6.9 | 3.8 |
| 1930 | 42.3 | 14.9 | 10.3 | 3.6 |
| 1938 | 37.6 | 12.7 | 10.7 | 3.6 |
| 1950 | 41.9 | 15.7 | 14.1 | 5.3 |
| 1960 | 46.1 | 15.1 | 16.9 | 5.5 |
| 1970 | 47.1 | 25.5 | 20.0 | 10.8 |
| 1980 | 54.3 | 16.2 | 25.4 | 7.6 |
| 1990 | 55.0 | 12.5 | 21.9 | 5.0 |
| 2000 | 60.3 | 9.8 | 22.9 | 3.7 |

Source: Harris, B. (2004) pp. 12–13.

## Victorian origins of the welfare state

Although it is conventional to assume that the 'welfare state' only came into being in Britain after 1945, some historians have argued that a form of welfare state existed much earlier. One historian of early-modern England, Paul Slack (1999), claimed that Britain (or rather England) already possessed a 'local welfare state' by the end of the eighteenth century, and the American historian David Roberts (1960) suggested that the foundations of a national welfare state were laid between 1833 and 1854.

However, other historians have rejected this view. Ursula Henriques (1979, p. 268) argued that it was difficult to apply the label 'Victorian origins of the welfare state' to the mid nineteenth century when 'the welfare state represents, at least in theory, the total reversal of nineteenth-century attitudes', and Pat Thane (1982, p. vii) claimed that it was only around 1870 'that important demands began to arise for the state . . . to take a permanent, as distinct from a temporary and residual, responsibility for the social and economic conditions experienced by its citizens'. However, despite these reservations, the period between 1800 and 1870 witnessed a number of developments which had profound implications for the role of the state in the provision of welfare services. These developments were particularly apparent in relation to the administration of the Poor Law, and to the identification of the state's responsibility for the promotion of education and protection of public health.

During the last twenty years, historians have shown renewed interest in the development of intellectual thought in the late eighteenth and early nineteenth centuries. At the end of the eighteenth century, Thomas Malthus (1970) argued that the poor laws removed one of the major incentives to population control and therefore encouraged the growth of the poverty which they were designed to alleviate, and these ideas were taken up by David Ricardo, who claimed that the poor laws 'deteriorate[d] the condition of both poor and rich' (Sraffa, 1951, pp. 105–6), and by the Evangelicals, who believed that personal misfortune was the result of people's failure to adjust their behaviour to the dictates of divine law (see Hilton, 1988). However, although both the political economists and the Evangelicals emphasised the extent to which individuals were responsible for their own fates, these ideas were not necessarily incompatible with some conception of an enhanced role for the state, and during the first half of the nineteenth century both the Benthamites and the Whigs argued that it was also necessary to extend the role played by central government in the development of welfare provision (Harris, 2004).

The different principles of all these groups were reflected in the debates which preceded the introduction of the New Poor Law in 1834. As Henriques argued, the underlying aim of the New Poor Law was to impose severe restrictions on the welfare entitlements of able-bodied men, and in this respect it is difficult to argue that the introduction of such a measure is readily compatible with the principles of a universalist welfare state, but in other respects the Poor Law Amendment Act did, nevertheless, represent an important beginning. From an administrative point of view, its most significant innovation was the reorganisation of the Poor Law's administrative structure, with the reorganisation of individual parishes into Poor Law Unions, the establishment of the central Poor Law Commission, and the appointment of Assistant Commissioners who were then able to exercise a significant influence over the development of local relief policies (Harling, 1992). Even though these measures were originally designed to curtail the growth of welfare expenditure, they also reflected the view that there ought to be a nationally agreed framework for the possession of welfare rights which could be applied across the entire country (in this instance, the whole of England and Wales; legislation to establish national systems of poor relief in Ireland and Scotland was only introduced in 1838 and 1845 respectively (Harris, 2004)).

## ? Thought provoker

The Poor Law Amendment Act has been described as 'one of the great watersheds in English social policy' (Jones, 1990, p. 13). One of its main aims was to establish a framework for the introduction of policies which would lead to a dramatic reduction in Poor Law expenditure. However, when the Poor Law Commissioners tried to introduce the new Act in the north of England, they encountered opposition from members of both the working and middle classes.

Why might middle-class ratepayers have been opposed to the changes the Commissioners wished to introduce?

The first half of the nineteenth century also witnessed a number of other developments which extended the role of the state in other ways. In 1802, Parliament passed the Health and Morals of Apprentices Act, which sought to limit the working hours of apprentices and prevent them from working through the night, and this was followed by a series of other measures, including the Factory Acts of 1819, 1825 and 1833 (Harris, 2004). The first state grant for public education was also introduced in 1833. Even though the size of the grant was very small (only £20,000), it marked the first official acceptance of the principle that it was in the state's interest for children to be educated, and that children might even be considered to have a right to some form of education, and both the extent and the scope of education grants increased significantly in the ensuing years. In 1839 Parliament established a Privy Council Committee on Education to supervise the expenditure of public funds, and after 1843 schools were permitted to request public support for the purchase of new equipment as well as the construction of new buildings (Harris, 2004).

Important as these developments were, it is arguable that the most important example of the growth of state intervention in this period lay in the sphere of **public health**. During the seventeenth and eighteenth centuries, local communities had taken a variety of steps to improve the quality of the built environment and avoid exposure to disease, but these measures had only a limited effect, across the country as a whole, on the reduction of mortality. However, the rapid pace of early nineteenth century urbanisation, combined with the increased visibility of diseases such as typhoid and cholera, led to a renewed interest in the question of sanitary reform, and this culminated in the passage of the Public Health Act in 1848, which established the first General Board of Health and granted it the power to conduct its own inspections in areas where the local death rate had exceeded 23 deaths per thousand living over a seven-year period. The Act was not passed without controversy and it would be easy to exaggerate its practical impact, but it nevertheless marked a crucial watershed in the national government's conception of the sphere of public responsibility (Harris, 2004).

## Welfare provision 1870-1906

At the beginning of the twenty-first century, Simon Szreter (2002b, p. 1) used the example of the growth of civic government between 1870 and 1914 to urge Tony Blair's Labour government to 'reinvigorate civil society and reduce poverty by devolving its own powers and resources to a revived elected local democracy'. Although Szreter may have exaggerated the extent of improvements in local government action in this period, the period as a whole certainly played an important part in the overall development of welfare provision, despite the occurrence at the start of the period of the Local Government Board's infamous 'crusade against outdoor relief'.

As we have already seen, the introduction of the Poor Law Amendment Act in 1834 led to a sharp reduction in the number of able-bodied men in receipt of **outdoor relief** and a significant decline in the overall level of Poor Law expenditure, but the number of paupers began to rise once more during the 1860s and this led to renewed calls for a return to the 'principles of 1834' and a further crackdown on relief payments (Harris, 2004, pp. 53–4). However, although the number of claimants fell by more than 300,000 (from 917,890 to 571,892) between 1871 and 1877, the late 1860s and 1870s also witnessed a number of other developments which may have been less eye-catching in themselves, but also betokened the emergence of a rather different attitude to the question of poor relief. Perhaps the most important of these was the gradual separation, in London at any rate, of the poor relief functions of the Poor Law from its medical functions, with the creation of the Metropolitan Asylums Board. This measure created a separate administrative authority for the organisation of hospital services, and marked the first stage in a process which gradually enabled an increasing number of people to receive medical assistance from the public authorities without suffering any loss of personal or civic status.

In addition to the gradual extension of medical rights under the Poor Law (reinforced by the decision to admit non-paupers to infectious disease hospitals after 1871 and the promulgation of the Medical Relief (Disqualifications Removal) Act of 1885), the last three decades of the nineteenth century also witnessed a series of other developments which bore directly on the question of poverty itself. In 1870, when Parliament introduced the Forster Education Act, it gave school boards the power to remit fees for children whose parents were unable to afford the cost of sending them to board schools, and after 1891 the vast majority of children became exempt from the payment of elementary school fees altogether. At the same time, new measures were also initiated to deal with the problems of unemployment and to investigate the incidence of poverty in old age. In 1886, Joseph Chamberlain issued the first of a series of Circulars authorising the establishment of public works schemes during periods of cyclical unemployment, and in 1894 Parliament appointed the Royal Commission on the Aged Poor, which was charged with investigating the problem of poverty in old age. Once again, it would be easy to exaggerate the practical importance of these initiatives, particularly in the short term, but they were nevertheless indicative of a growing awareness of the limitations of existing approaches to social policy (Harris, 2004).

The 1870s and 1880s also witnessed a number of other significant developments in the area of health policy. As we have just seen, the provision of therapeutic services by public authorities continued to be closely linked to the Poor Law, but many local authorities began to build their own infectious disease hospitals (which came under municipal rather than Poor Law control), and it became much easier to receive medical assistance without suffering the stigma or disabilities associated with pauperism. However, the most radical changes occurred in relation to the preventive or environmental medical services. In 1871, the powers of the Medical Department of the Privy Council (the successor to the second General Board of Health) were transferred to the newly established Local Government Board, and in 1872 Parliament compelled all county boroughs to appoint a Medical Officer of Health who would be responsible for advising the local authority on the discharge of its public health functions. The growing importance of public health was also underlined by the passage of the Public Health Act of 1875, which reinforced the compulsory clauses of the 1866 Sanitary Act, and by the increase in the value of the loans contracted by local authorities for public works, including the construction of new sewers (Harris, 2004).

Although Szreter's (2002b, p. 4) suggestion that the period between 1870 and 1914 witnessed 'colossal and ever-increasing investments' in the improvement of local housing stock may be a little misleading, the period was nevertheless notable for a series of legislative innovations. In 1868 and 1875 Parliament introduced the first slum clearance acts, but these had only a limited impact because of the failure to build substantial numbers of new properties to replace those which had been demolished. However, the Housing of the Working Classes Act of 1890 opened a new chapter in the history of municipal housing by giving local authorities the power to construct additional housing for more affluent workers in suburban areas in the hope that this would 'free up' housing at the bottom of the market for the more poorly paid. As in many other cases, the practical impact of this legislation was limited (only around 5 per cent of all the houses constructed between 1890 and 1914 were built by local authorities), but the legislation pointed the way for the much more significant expansion of local authority housing after 1919 (Harris, 2004).

Perhaps the most important policy innovation between 1870 and 1900 was the introduction of the Forster Education Act of 1870. This Act gave local ratepayers the power to establish school boards in areas where the existing level of elementary education was deemed inadequate, and allowed them to raise money for the support of these schools from local rates. The Act did not make elementary education compulsory or free, but it paved the way for both, and by 1900 more than half of all the children between the ages of five and twelve who were attending publicly supported schools in England and Wales were attending board schools, and many school boards were also providing voluntary classes for children above this age (Harris, 2004). It is not surprising, therefore, that observers such as A.V. Dicey (1962, p. iiii) should have regarded the passage of Forster's Act as the true beginning of what subsequently came to be seen as late-Victorian and Edwardian collectivism.

 Thought provoker

The Education Act of 1870 has often been regarded as one of the major landmarks in the history of state welfare intervention. It enabled school boards to establish their own public elementary schools and gave them the power to make education compulsory for children between the ages of five and ten in their areas. However, many parents resented the introduction of compulsory education and this led to several prosecutions for non-attendance.

Why might some parents have been reluctant to take advantage of the opportunities the Act provided?

## Liberal welfare and the 'social service state'

By the early twentieth century, there was a growing recognition of the problem faced by the Poor Law, coupled with an increasing awareness of the extent of working-class poverty and its implications for the country's ability to maintain social stability and protect its economic and military interests. However, despite these pressures, the main changes in welfare provision were not implemented within the structure of the Poor Law itself but alongside it, and this had profound implications for its longer-term future.

It is customary for historians to begin their accounts of the 'Liberal welfare reforms' with the Education (Provision of Meals) Act of 1906. This was a relatively brief measure (containing only three clauses) which was designed primarily to encourage greater cooperation between local authorities and voluntary agencies, and its main aim was not so much to provide free school meals as to facilitate the provision of meals to paying children which could be provided at cost price. However, the third clause of the Act recognised that there was also a minority of children who were 'unable by reason of lack of food to profit from the education provided for them', and whose parents were unable to pay, and for this reason the Act also allowed the local education authority to raise a small amount of money (not more than the yield of a halfpenny rate) to feed these children without charge. The Act did not lead to any huge increase in the number of children who received free meals at school, but it did represent a marked break with Poor Law orthodoxy, since meals were being provided to the children without any penalty to the parents, and this undoubtedly enraged many conservative commentators. As Dicey observed in 1914:

> No-one can deny that a starving boy will hardly profit from the attempt to teach him the rules of arithmetic. But it does not necessarily follow that a local authority must therefore provide every hungry child at school with a meal . . . [or] that a father who first lets his child starve, and then fails to pay the price legally due from him for a meal . . . should, under the Act of 1906, retain the right of voting for a Member of Parliament. Why a man who first neglects his duty as a father and then defrauds the state should retain his full political rights is a question easier to ask than to answer.
>
> Dicey (1962, p. i)

Although the Liberals also introduced a number of other measures affecting children (including the establishment of a national system of school medical inspection, the introduction of free places in secondary schools and the Children Act of 1908), these measures were probably rather less important than the introduction of old age pensions in 1908. As is well known, the new Act provided a non-contributory pension of five shillings a week to pensioners who were over the age of seventy and whose annual income was less than £21, with a sliding scale of payments for individuals whose annual income was between £21 and £31 10s. When the scheme was first introduced, it was limited to individuals who met a small number of 'character' tests and who had not recently been in receipt of poor relief, although these measures were subsequently rescinded over the next few years (Harris, 2004, pp. 158–60). Although the Act was still quite a limited measure, providing a comparatively small pension to approximately 500,000 elderly individuals ('a pension for the very poor, the very respectable and the very old', in Pat Thane's (1982, p. 83) evocative if slightly exaggerated phrase), it was nevertheless a further breach in the wall of traditional Poor Law thinking and it prompted the Prime Minister, Herbert Asquith, to insist that it was not a final destination but a 'new departure' on an 'unmeasured road of future social progress' (Parliamentary Debates, 1908, cols. 828–9).

Following the passage of the Old Age Pensions Bill, the government was able to turn its attention to a range of issues connected with the labour market. In 1909, Parliament approved legislation covering the establishment of labour exchanges, a Development Fund for the promotion of public works programmes during periods of cyclical unemployment, and trade boards, with the power to set minimum wages in a range of 'sweated industries'. The government also introduced a major new housing Act, the Housing and Town Planning Act. This Act reinforced many of the provisions introduced by earlier Acts, such as the Housing of the Working Classes Acts of 1890, 1900 and 1903, but it broke new ground by giving official encouragement to the principle of town planning, and also sought to strengthen the local administration of public health services by preventing newly appointed Medical Officers of Health from engaging in private practice and granting them greater security of tenure (Harris, 2004).

Although each of these measures was undoubtedly important, none was more so than the Finance Bill which the Chancellor, David Lloyd George, presented to Parliament in the same year. During the nineteenth century, the government had derived the bulk of its revenue from indirect taxation, but the growth of new obligations forced politicians of all parties to consider new ways of generating the revenue on which public expenditure depended. In 1903, Joseph Chamberlain had persuaded the Conservative party to abandon its historic support for free trade in favour of tariff reform, but the Liberals believed that new revenue could best be raised by introducing a more graduated form of income tax and increasing death duties. The new proposals, which were finally approved in 1910, led to a significant increase in the proportion of all revenue which was derived from income tax, and in the proportion of income tax revenue derived from higher earners (Harris, 2004).

The long-drawn-out passage of what became known as the 'People's Budget' enabled the government to proceed with its plans for the creation of a new system of national insurance. During the nineteenth century, a growing proportion of working-class men (together with a much smaller number of working-class women) had sought to protect themselves against the financial hazards of sickness and old age (and, to a much lesser extent, unemployment) by taking out voluntary insurance through friendly societies or trade union benefit schemes and these schemes formed the basis – to some extent, at least – of the national scheme which the government introduced in 1911. As is well known, Part I of the National Insurance Act established a national health insurance scheme which was financed by contributions from workers, employers and the state, and which offered a range of health-related benefits, including free accommodation in a tuberculosis sanatorium, general practitioner treatment, a maternity allowance for insured women and the wives of insured men, and, most importantly, cash benefits of ten shillings a week for men and 7s 6d a week for women for the first twenty-six weeks of any incapacitating illness. Part II of the Act introduced a much more limited scheme, covering approximately 2.25 million workers, to deal with the problem of unemployment. This scheme was also financed by contributions from workers, employers and the state, and offered a flat-rate benefit of seven shillings a week for up to fifteen weeks in any 52-week period.

Although national insurance has long been regarded as the flagship of the Liberal welfare reforms, it has not been without its critics. In 1913, a Treasury official pointed out that the flat-rate nature of the employees' contributions meant that the cost of insurance bore most heavily on those with the lowest incomes (Harris, 1972), and Paul Johnson (1996) has complained that the introduction of national insurance substituted an 'individualistic' system of social protection for the more 'solidaristic' nature of the Poor Law. However, whilst neither of these criticisms should be treated lightly, it is also important to remember that the Poor Law was only able to preserve its 'solidaristic' features by imposing a highly deterrent framework on the administration of poor relief and by stigmatising the recipients of poor relief. In view of this, it is perhaps less surprising that so many people should have been willing to accept the principle of national insurance as a welcome and worthwhile alternative to traditional Poor Law policies.

 Controversy and debate

## Working-class attitudes and the Liberal welfare reforms

In a famous article, Henry Pelling (1968, pp. 1–2) once argued that 'the extension of the power of the state at the beginning of . . . [the twentieth] century . . . was by no means welcomed by members of the working class' and may even have been undertaken 'over the critical hostility of many of them, perhaps of most of them'. He claimed that this hostility was rooted in 'working class attitudes of suspicion or dislike towards existing institutions' – such as the Poor Law and the public vaccination service – 'which were the expression of national social policy'.

One of the major limitations of this debate is that it is often very difficult to find direct evidence of working-class views. Pelling's account was largely dependent on evidence obtained from official enquiries, such as the Royal Commission on the Poor Laws and the Interdepartmental Committee on Partial Exemption from School Attendance, observations by middle-class observers, such as the District Nurse Margaret Loane, and from his analysis of the main topics discussed during general elections between 1886 and 1914. However, other authors have been able to move beyond this, using evidence from oral historians, working-class autobiographies, and surveys carried out among the members of trade unions and friendly societies, and their investigations have yielded a rather more nuanced view. Pat Thane (1984, pp. 879, 882–92) concluded that 'many poorer people . . . were grateful for any amelioration of their hard lives', and that it was the leaders of trade unions who tended to be most sceptical of the motives of those advocating reform. However, even those who were hostile to state intervention were forced to recognise that some form of state welfare provision may be necessary to improve the conditions of the very poor, and during the 1890s and 1900s trade unionists and friendly society members played an increasingly important role in campaigns for the introduction of such measures as school meals and school medical inspection, old-age pensions, the abolition of the Poor Law, the establishment of trade boards, and measures to reduce unemployment (Harris, 2004, p. 154).

▶

However, although it seems clear that working-class pressure was *one* of the reasons for the introduction of the Liberal welfare reforms, it was not the only one, and Thane (1984, p. 896) also pointed out that the reforms themselves 'were far from being complete victories for Labour; they were granted very much on Liberal terms'. It is also important to recognise the extent to which they were designed to fend off calls for more fundamental change, as Winston Churchill explained in relation to the introduction of unemployment insurance in 1909:

The idea is to increase the stability of our institutions by giving the mass of industrial workers a direct interest in maintaining them . . . This scheme . . . will help to remove the dangerous element of uncertainty from the existence of the industrial worker. It will give him an assurance that his home, got together through long years and with affectionate sacrifice, will not be broken up, sent bit by bit to the pawnshop, just because . . . he falls out of work. It will make him a better citizen, a more efficient worker, [and] a happier man. Quoted in Harris (1972, pp. 365–6)

# Welfare between the wars

Although the Liberal welfare reforms represented a major shift in the history of British social policy, their impact was almost immediately overshadowed by the outbreak of the First World War. The war severely disrupted many welfare services and forced the government to take a number of emergency measures, but it also generated a new sense of entitlement on the part of many working-class people and fuelled a wide-ranging debate on the future of welfare provision.

One of the most important changes (if not the most important change) in the infrastructure of welfare provision after 1918 was the expansion of the unemployment insurance scheme. As we have already seen, the original unemployment insurance scheme was set up under Part II of the National Insurance Act of 1911, and was designed to provide a short-term flat-rate benefit for a limited number of workers employed in a selected range of industries, but during the course of 1920 and 1921 this scheme was transformed by a series of changes which meant that by the end of 1921 it covered approximately 75 per cent of the employed workforce, and provided benefits which were intended not only to cover both short- and long-term periods of unemployment, but also to cater for the needs of both unemployed workers *and* their dependants. During the remainder of the 1920s and 1930s, the government introduced a number of other changes, many of which were designed to restrict access to the unemployment insurance fund and reduce overall levels of expenditure, but in spite of this the basic principle which had been established by the reforms of 1920 and 1921 remained intact, and by the end of the interwar period the overwhelming majority of unemployed workers were receiving benefits under the statutory unemployment insurance scheme (Harris, 2004, pp. 204–7).

Although the expansion of unemployment insurance represented the most dramatic change in the state's response to the problem of poverty, the period also witnessed important developments in other areas of anti-poverty policy. During the interwar period, the number of workers covered by national health insurance increased from 15.9 million in 1918 to 21.6 million in 1938, and there were also some significant (though by no means universal) improvements in the provision of municipal welfare benefits, such as school meals and the distribution of nutritional supplements at maternity and child welfare centres. One of the most significant innovations was the development of a contributory pension scheme for those between the ages of 65 and 70. This scheme was grafted on to the existing health insurance scheme and provided a basic pension of ten shillings a week for insured workers, the wives of insured men (where the man was over the age of 65 and his wife was aged between 65 and 70), and the widows of insured men, with additional allowances for widows' children and orphans.

These changes in the overall framework of welfare support had profound implications for the oldest form of statutory welfare provision, the Poor Law. As we have already seen, the main aim of the New Poor Law after 1834 had been one of deterrence, but this attitude came under growing attack during the 1890s and early 1900s, and became increasingly difficult to sustain in many parts of the country after the end of the First World War. The role of the Poor Law (or public assistance, as it became known after 1930) was also affected by the development of alternative welfare systems. During the nineteenth century, the Poor Law had formed the bedrock of statutory welfare support, but during the interwar period acted more as a back-up, providing supplementary benefits to individuals who received the majority of their support from one of the contributory schemes, but still required additional support to 'make ends meet'. In this respect, then, it is at least arguable that there was rather more continuity between the public assistance scheme of the late 1930s and the national assistance scheme of the 1940s and 1950s than post-war welfare rhetoric might suggest.

The interwar years also witnessed important developments in the provision of hospital services. Although the number of publicly controlled hospital beds remained largely unchanged, an increasing proportion of these hospitals began to develop acute medical services, with the result that the number of patients treated in public hospitals increased substantially. There were also important changes in the administrative structure of public hospital provision. During the nineteenth and early twentieth centuries, the majority of public sector hospitals had been under the control of Poor Law authorities, but in 1929 these were transferred to the local county and county borough councils, and these authorities were also given the power to transfer responsibility for hospital administration from their public assistance committees to their public health committees. There has been some debate over the extent and pace of the process of transfer, or 'appropriation', but by the end of the 1930s more than half the public sector hospital beds in England and Wales were under public health control.

These changes in the development and administration of the public sector hospital service were matched by equally significant changes in the voluntary hospital sector. As is well known, the voluntary hospitals originated during the eighteenth and nineteenth centuries as privately controlled institutions supported by voluntary contributions, but during the interwar years they began to see themselves not so much as charitable institutions for the deserving poor, but rather as general medical institutions for the population at large. This change in the character of the voluntary hospitals encouraged new demands for better coordination between the public and voluntary hospital sectors and also for the management of voluntary hospitals to become more accountable to the populations they served, and these twin demands for coordination and accountability both played an important part in the debates over the plans for a national health service during the Second World War (Harris, 2004).

In legislative terms, some of the most dramatic changes in welfare policy affected the area of housing. Although local authorities had enjoyed at least the theoretical power to construct their own houses since the mid nineteenth century, only around one-quarter of 1 per cent of all householders lived in municipally owned accommodation on the eve of the First World War. However, in 1919 Parliament passed two Acts, the Housing and Town Planning, etc. Act and the Housing (Additional Powers) Act, which provided central government subsidies to local authorities and private builders to enable them to build new homes for working-class use, and in 1930 the second Labour government introduced the Greenwood Housing Act, which earmarked separate subsidies for the construction of replacement housing for individuals who were to be evicted from their existing properties under slum clearance schemes. During the period as a whole, more than 1.1 million homes were built by local authorities between 1 January 1919 and 31 March 1939, and more than 2.8 million homes were built by private builders, of which approximately 430,000 were constructed with the aid of government subsidies.

Historians of social policy have often seen the interwar period as a wasted period in terms of educational development. The reduction in the birth rate should have enabled interwar governments to achieve significant improvements in educational provision, but the process of 'Hadow reorganistion' proceeded only slowly, there was only a small increase in the number of pupils attending selective secondary schools, and the school-leaving age remained fixed at fourteen despite a series of attempts to raise it. However, the period did see a number of improvements in the experience of education and the development of educational facilities. Although very few new schools were constructed during the immediate postwar period, education authorities were able to embark on a substantial new building programme from the mid 1920s onwards, and by the middle of the following decade a substantial proportion of children were being educated in schools which had either been newly constructed or significantly refurbished since the end of the First World War. These developments were central to such reorganisation as did occur, and they played an important role in helping to reduce class sizes and facilitate the introduction of more modern methods of teaching. In 1925, more than 14 per cent of elementary schoolchildren attended classes containing more than 50 pupils, but by 1938 this proportion had fallen to less than 1.5 per cent, and the number of 'black-listed' schools which were still awaiting replacement had fallen by more than 70 per cent (from 2,827 to 844) (Harris, 2004).

## The Second World War and after

By 1939 it was clear that the structure of the British welfare services had expanded considerably, but there were still large numbers of people who lived in squalid and overcrowded accommodation, who were unable to obtain adequate medical care, or who continued to depend on means-tested public assistance benefits. The outbreak of war heightened public awareness of the implications of many of these issues and led to the publication of a series of reports with proposals for change.

Of all the reports issued during the war, none is more famous that the Beveridge Report of 1942. William Beveridge was one of the architects of the Labour Exchanges Act of 1909, and had been summoned out of retirement to advise the wartime Minister of Labour, Ernest Bevin, in 1940. However, in June 1941 he was invited by Arthur Greenwood, the Minister-without-Portfolio, to chair an enquiry into the development of a consolidated scheme of social insurance. According to his biographer, José Harris (1977), Beveridge was initially quite reluctant to take on this role, but he soon realised that it offered him a unique opportunity to develop proposals for a much more fundamental reform of welfare provision.

As we have just seen, the primary aim of the Beveridge Committee was to frame proposals for the development of a more consolidated scheme of social insurance. He argued that there ought to be a single scheme providing insurance against sickness, unemployment and old age, and that it should provide benefits to the entire population, and not just manual workers. He also argued that these benefits should be sufficient to meet the recipients' subsistence needs, and this became the focus of particular controversy during the remainder of the war years.

In addition to recommending the establishment of a more comprehensive and more generous insurance scheme, Beveridge also included two other sets of recommendations – one implicit and one explicit – which had major implications for the government's welfare role. In the first place, he argued that the new scheme of social insurance would only work if it was supported by action in three other sets of areas: the provision of family allowances for all families with children, whether they were in work or not; the development of a comprehensive health and rehabilitation service to enable every individual to maintain themselves in good health and obtain adequate medical care when they needed it; and the prevention of mass unemployment. Second, he also argued that 'Want' was only one of the 'five giants' on the road to social reconstruction, and that the government's attack on Want had to be accompanied by a parallel assault on the giants of Ignorance, Disease, Idleness and Squalor.

The attack on Idleness was one of the most important 'Assumptions' on which the Beveridge Report was based. During the 1920s and 1930s, unemployment had been a major cause of hardship and the cost of supporting unemployed people and their families had been a significant drain on the government's finances, but the Treasury argued that there was very little which governments could do to reduce unemployment, other than by seeking to restore normal trading conditions. However, in June 1944 the government published a White Paper on Employment Policy which represented a major departure from the 'Treasury view'. It marked the first official acceptance of the idea that governments had a legitimate role to play in maintaining a high and stable level of employment under normal peacetime conditions.

After Idleness and Want came Ignorance. As we have already seen, the interwar period witnessed a number of important change in the organisation of public education but the process of 'Hadow reorganisation' remained incomplete and the school-leaving age had still not been raised since 1918. However, in 1943 the government published a White Paper on Educational Reconstruction, and this formed the basis of the Education Act which the President of the Board of Education, 'Rab' Butler, introduced in the following year. Although the new Act was not short of critics – it ignored the position of the country's private fee-paying schools and sidestepped the controversial question of the structure of secondary education beyond the age of eleven – it also introduced a number of important changes. It removed one of the major barriers to the coordination of primary and secondary education by placing responsibility for both forms of education in the hands of a single education authority in each area; it insisted that all children should move from primary schools to some form of secondary school at the age of eleven; and it raised the status of education at the level of central government by converting the Board of Education into a fully-fledged Ministry. It also introduced some major changes in the organisation of the schools themselves. It abolished the payment of fees in all state secondary schools, and raised the school-leaving age from fourteen to fifteen. It also gave the Minister of Education the power to raise the school-leaving age to sixteen as soon as circumstances permitted (the school-leaving age was eventually raised to sixteen in 1972 (Harris, 2004)).

Although some historians have suggested that the politics of educational reform were comparatively straightforward, the reform of health service provision was much less so. This was partly the result of the attitude of the medical profession itself. During the 1930s, there was a growing consensus that the existing system of national health insurance needed to be extended to provide better access to medical care for those sections of the population – principally women and children – who were not already covered by it, but it was also assumed that there would continue to be significant scope for the continuation of private medical practice. However, when Beveridge published his report in 1942, he argued that the new social insurance scheme should cover the entire population, in which case the whole population would become entitled to free medical care under it. This proposal attracted fierce opposition within the medical profession, because they believed that it would lead to the erosion of private practice and pose a significant threat to medical independence.

This was not the only way in which the Beveridge Report affected the debate over healthcare. During the interwar period, the voluntary hospitals had begun to derive an increasing proportion of their income from patients' payments and contributory insurance schemes, but Beveridge's proposals threatened to undermine these sources of income by suggesting that everyone would be covered by the government's social insurance scheme. The British Medical Association also believed that people would be much less inclined to support the voluntary hospitals as charitable institutions in the atmosphere created by what it called 'the government's "free-for-all" propaganda'.

In view of these difficulties, it is perhaps not surprising that the development of concrete plans for the reform of the country's health services should have proceeded more slowly than the development of plans for educational reform, but it is still important to recognise the importance of the changes which did occur. In February 1944 the Ministry of Health and the Department of Health for Scotland published a joint White Paper in which they set out their initial proposals for the development of a comprehensive system of healthcare. Although many of the details of these proposals were subsequently changed, the White Paper nevertheless established the basic principles on which the National Health Service would develop after 1948. Its opening paragraph read as follows:

> The Government have announced that they intend to establish a comprehensive health service for everybody in this country. They want to ensure that in future every man and woman and child can rely on getting all the advice and treatment and care which they may need in matters of personal health; that what they get shall be the best medical and other facilities available; that their getting these shall not depend on whether they can pay for them, or on any other factor irrelevant to the real need - the real need being to bring the country's full resources to bear upon reducing ill-health and promoting good health in all its citizens.
>
> Ministry of Health/Department of Health for Scotland (1944, p. 1)

The last of Beveridge's five giants was Squalor. Although significant progress had been made before 1939, many people continued to live in insanitary and overcrowded conditions on the eve of the Second World War, and these problems were exacerbated by the outbreak of hostilities. The war diverted resources from the construction of new housing and it has been estimated that approximately 475,000 homes (out of a total of approximately 11.5 million) were either destroyed or rendered uninhabitable by enemy action. In 1944, the Prime Minister, Winston Churchill, announced plans for the immediate construction of 500,000 prefabricated houses and promised to build 2–300,000 permanent homes during the first two years of peace, but the Labour Party promised to build between 4 and 5 million new homes, the majority of which would supplied by local authorities. This marked a reversion to an earlier view of the role of council houses, in which local authorities would build homes for general needs, and not just for the poorest sections of the population.

 *Controversy and debate*

### Consensus and social policy during the Second World War

In 1950, one of the pioneering figures of academic social policy in Britain, Richard Titmuss, published a magisterial survey of the history of social policy during the Second World War. In it, he not only provided a vivid account of the social challenges posed by the war, but also attempted to draw a connection between the events of war and the development of the postwar welfare state. He was particularly impressed by the importance of three critical events in the first year of war: the evacuation of mothers and children in September 1939; the evacuation of British soldiers from Dunkirk; and the Blitz. He claimed that the popular reaction to these three events generated what he called 'the war-warmed impulse of people for a more generous society' (Titmuss, 1950).

In addition to exploring the specific effect of the Second World War on the development of social policy, Titmuss also attempted to develop a more general theory, based on the ideas of the sociologist Stanislaw Andrzejewski (1954), about the relationship between war and social policy more generally. In a lecture originally delivered in 1955, he wrote that:

The aims and content of social policy, both in peace and in war, are thus determined - at least to a substantial extent - by how far the cooperation of the masses is essential to the successful prosecution of war. If this cooperation is thought to be essential, then inequalities must be reduced, and the pyramid of social stratification must be flattened.                    Titmuss (1987, p. 111)

Whilst few historians would deny that the war saw some changes in social policy, many have questioned the extent to which all classes and all sections of the population shared Titmuss's concept of a 'war-warmed impulse to a more generous society' (see, for example, Harris, 1981; Macnicol, 1986; Jefferys, 1987). At the same time, it is also clear that the war did have some effect in helping to alert official minds to the extent of existing social problems. As authors of a London County Council survey explained in 1943:

The experience of evacuation has - in advance of the Beveridge Report - brought home to social workers, and indeed to the nation at large, how real and formidable are the giants of Want, Ignorance and Squalor, and how sadly they are hindering, in town and country alike, the wellbeing of the rising generation.          Quoted in Welshman (1997, p. 53); see also Harris (2004, p. 286)

In 1990, Rodney Lowe attempted to reconcile these conflicting accounts by examining the extent of consensus at three different levels: among politicians, within the civil service, and among the public at large. He concluded that 'at all levels of society and in each area of welfare policy, consensus - defined as an historically-unusual degree of agreement - was not a mirage in the 1940s' (1990, p. 180). However, he also argued that this was an increasingly passive consensus, and that the failure to develop a more active consensus after 1945 lay at the heart of Britain's problems in the post-war era (1990).

## Conclusion

As noted in this chapter, the development of state welfare provision has taken place over a long period of time, for different reasons and with different outcomes. However, when, at the end of the Second World War, Britain emerged victorious but shattered from six years of hostilities, despite these difficulties it also possessed a series of plans for the reform of social policy and the development of what came to be known as the 'welfare state' (Lowe, 2005). These plans provided the initial starting point for many of the policies that are discussed in the following chapters of this book.

## Summary

This chapter has examined the history of social welfare provision in Britain from the beginning of the nineteenth century to the end of the Second World War. Although the chapter has recognised the importance of the 'mixed economy of welfare' and the contributions made by the different elements within this mixed economy, including the informal and voluntary sectors, the family and the market, the main focus has been on the role of the state. This has been reflected in a number of ways, including the following:

- The acknowledgement of a basic level of responsibility for welfare provision under the Poor Laws of 1597 and 1601.

- The regulation of living and working conditions through such measures as the Factory Acts of 1819, 1825 and 1833, and the introduction of building bye-laws under successive Public Health Acts.

- The provision of public services, such as the development of public education and the expansion of public health service provision.

- The introduction of new forms of income support and other changes in welfare policy as part of the Liberal welfare reforms of 1906–14.

- The introduction of publicly subsidised local authority housing and the gradual expansion of other forms of public welfare provision between 1914 and 1939.

- The emergence of plans for the establishment of a more comprehensive 'welfare state' between 1939 and 1945.

## Discussion and review topics

1 In what sense, if any, is it appropriate to talk about the 'Victorian origins of the welfare state' in Britain between *circa* 1800 and 1870?

2 Did the period between 1870 and 1906 witness any important changes in attitudes to the relief of poverty or other aspects of social policy?

3 In what ways did the introduction of the Liberal welfare reforms of 1906–14 represent a significant change in the relationship between the state and the individual?

4 Why did public expenditure on the social services increase in Britain between 1914 and 1939?

5 To what extent did the Beveridge Report and the 'White Paper chase' of 1943-4 lay the foundations of Britain's postwar welfare state?

## Further reading

Finlayson, G. (1994) *Citizen, state and social welfare in Britain 1830-1990*, Oxford University Press, Oxford. The current chapter has focused on the growth of state welfare provision between 1800 and 1945; this book explores the same issues from the point of view of changes in the voluntary sector.

Fraser, D. (2003) *The evolution of the British welfare state: A history of social policy since the Industrial Revolution*, Palgrave, Basingstoke (3rd edn). This is the third edition of a text which was first published in 1973, and it continues to provide a highly accessible and readable introduction to the history of British social policy.

Harris, B. (2004) *The origins of the British welfare state: Social welfare in England and Wales, 1800-1945*, Palgrave, Basingstoke. This book is designed to provide a comprehensive account of the development of all aspects of British welfare policy. It includes much of the detailed evidence which forms the basis of this chapter.

**Lowe, R.** (2003) *The welfare state in Britain since 1945*, Macmillan, Basingstoke (3rd edn). This book has become the standard academic work on the history of the welfare state in Britain after 1945.

**Thane, P.** (1996) *Foundations of the welfare state*, Longman, London (2nd edn). The first edition of this book was published in 1982. The second edition was thoroughly revised, with the introduction of new material on the relationship between women and welfare and the contribution of the voluntary sector. A distinguishing feature of both editions was the inclusion of international comparisons.

## Some useful websites

www.workhouses.org.uk – for much of the nineteenth and early twentieth centuries, the workhouse was one of the central institutions of British social policy. This website provides a fascinating guide to its buildings, inmates, staff and administrators, even its poets.

http://medphoto.wellcome.ac.uk – this website provides access to a range of historical photographs illustrating aspects of nineteenth and early twentieth century hospitals.

www.nationalarchives.gov.uk – this is the website of the UK's National Archives. The Archives include administrative records covering all aspects of welfare history. An increasing number of records are now being made available online.

www.nationalarchives.gov.uk – History and Policy was founded by a group of historians in 2002 with the explicit aim of using history to address current issues in public policy. This website provides access to a wide range of papers, covering all aspects of welfare policy.

## References

Andrzejewski, S. (1954) *Military organisation and society*, Routledge and Kegan Paul, London.

Brewer, J. (1989) *The sinews of power: war, money and the English state, 1688-1783*, Unwin Hyman, London.

Dicey, A.V. (1962) *Lectures on the relation between law and public opinion in England during the nineteenth century*, Macmillan, London (1st edn, 1905; 2nd edn first published in 1914).

Eckstein, H. (1959) *The English Health Service: Its Origins, Structure and Achievements*, Harvard University Press, Cambridge, Massachusetts.

Harling, P. (1992) 'The power of persuasion: Central authority, local bureaucracy and the New Poor Law', *English Historical Review*, Vol. 107, pp. 30–53.

Harris, B. (2004) *The origins of the British welfare state: Social welfare in England and Wales, 1800-1945*, Palgrave Macmillan, Basingstoke.

Harris, J. (1972) *Unemployment and politics: A study in English social policy 1886-1914*, Clarendon Press, Oxford.

Harris, J. (1977) *William Beveridge: A biography*, Clarendon Press, Oxford.

Harris, J. (1981) 'Some aspects of social policy in Britain during the Second World War', in W.J. Mommsen (ed.) *The emergence of the welfare state in Britain and Germany, 1850-1950*, Croom Helm, London, pp. 247–62.

Henriques, U. (1979) *Before the welfare state: Social administration in early industrial Britain*, Longman, London.

Hilton, B. (1988) *The age of atonement: The influence of Evangelicalism on social and economic thought, 1795-1865*, Clarendon, Oxford.

Jefferys, K. (1987) 'British politics and social policy during the Second World War', *Historical Journal*, Vol. 30, pp. 123–44.

Johnson, P. (1996) 'Risk, redistribution and social welfare in Britain from the Poor Law to Beveridge', in M. Danton (ed.) *Charity, self-interest and welfare in the English past*, UCL Press, London, pp. 225–48.

Jones, K. (1990) *The making of social policy in Britain, 1830-1990*, Athlone, London.

Lewis, J. (1995) *The Voluntary Sector, the State and Social Work in Britain*, Edward Elgar, Aldershot.

Lowe, R. (1990) 'The Second World War, consensus and the foundation of the welfare state', *Twentieth Century British History*, Vol. 1, pp. 152–82.

Lowe, R. (2005) *The Welfare State in Britain Since 1945*, Macmillan, Basingstoke (3rd edn).

Macnicol, J. (1986) 'The effect of the evacuation of schoolchildren on official attitudes to state intervention', in H.L. Smith (ed.) *War and social change: British society in the Second World War*, Manchester University Press, Manchester, pp. 3–31.

Malthus, T. (1970) *An essay on the principle of population* (edited with an introduction by Anthony Flew), Penguin, Harmondsworth (1st edn published 1798). Ministry of Health/Department of Health for Scotland (1944), *A National Health Service*, HMSO, London.

Parliamentary Debates (1908) *Parliamentary Debates*, 4th series, Vol. 190.

Pelling, H. (1968) 'The working class and the origins of the welfare state', in H. Pelling, *Popular politics and society in late-Victorian Britain*, Macmillan, London and Basingstoke, pp. 1–18.

Roberts, D. (1960) *Victorian origins of the British welfare state*, Yale University Press, New Haven.

Roberts, E. (2000) 'The recipients' view of welfare', in J. Bornat, R. Perks, P. Thompson and J. Walmsley (eds) *Oral history, health and welfare*, Routledge, London, pp. 203-26.

Slack, P. (1999) *From Reformation to improvement: Public welfare in early-modern England*, Clarendon Press, Oxford.

Sraffa, P. (ed.) (1951) *The works and correspondence of David Ricardo, edited by Piero Sraffa, with the collaboration of M.H. Dobb. Vol. I. On the principles of political economy and taxation*, Cambridge University Press, Cambridge.

Stevenson, S. and Cook, C. (1994) *Britain in the Depression*, Longman, London.

Szreter, S. (2002a) 'Health, class, place and politics: Social capital and collective provision in Britain', *Contemporary British History*, Vol. 16, No. 3, pp. 27-57.

Szreter, S. (2002b) 'A central role for local government? The example of late-Victorian Britain', *History and Policy*, Policy Paper No. 1. URL: **www.historyandpolicy.org/archive/pol-paper-print01.html**.

Thane, P. (1982) *The foundations of the welfare state*, Longman, London (1st edn).

Thane, P. (1984) 'The working class and state "welfare" in Britain 1880-1914', *Historical Journal*, Vol. 27, pp. 877-900.

Thane, P. (1996) *Foundations of the welfare state*, Longman, London, (2nd edn).

Titmuss, R.M. (1950) *Problems of social policy*, HMSO, London.

Titmuss, R.M. (1987) 'War and social policy', in B. Abel-Smith and K. Titmuss (eds) *The philosophy of welfare: Selected writings of Richard M. Titmuss*, Allen & Unwin, London, pp. 102-12.

Welshman, A.J. (1997) 'Evacuation and social policy during the Second World War: Myth and reality', *Twentieth Century British History*, Vol. 9, pp. 28-53.

# 6

# Conservative governments and the welfare state since 1945

Robert Page

## Chapter overview

The Conservative Party dominated British government for much of the second half of the twentieth century, and whilst the most significant welfare reforms are often associated with the post-war Labour government, it is important to consider the attitudes and impact of Conservative thinking over the years.

The chapter will look at the rise, and fall, of the One Nation Conservative approach to the welfare state during the second half of the twentieth century. It will also explore the growing influence of New Right ideas in the social policy strategies pursued by both the Thatcher and Major governments.

This chapter provides:

- a brief introduction to key elements of Conservative political and social thought;
- a review of One Nation Conservatism;
- illustrations of the One Nation approach to social policy;
- the emergence of a radical New Right Conservatism;
- New Right social policy during the Thatcher and Major eras.

## Spotlight on the issues
### A chip off the old block?

I think we've been through a period when too many people have been given to understand that if they have a problem, it's the government's job to cope with it. 'I have a problem, I'll get a grant.' 'I'm homeless the government must house me.' They're casting their problems on society. And you know, there is no such thing as society. There are individual men and women, and there are families. And no government can do anything except through people, and people must look to themselves first. It's our duty to look after ourselves and then, also to look after our neighbour. People have got the entitlements too much in mind without the obligations. There's no such thing as entitlement, unless someone has first met an obligation.

Margaret Thatcher, interview for *Women's Own*, 31 October 1987

We will never get to the heart of the big problems we face, whether it's crime, antisocial behaviour, welfare dependency or anything else, if we go on pretending that government can pull levers and find the answers. Real, lasting, long-term change means backing parents, backing commitment and helping the best institution in our country – the family – to do the vital work it does.

David Cameron, speech to the Conservative Party's spring Forum, 15 March 2008

For most people under 40 their experiences of governments have been dominated by the eighteen years of Conservative governments from 1979 to 1997 and the Labour governments that followed. However, the policies and priorities of political parties change considerably over time, and, as Chapter 5 has shown, many of the key areas of social policy have been shaped by a much longer history.

This chapter explores the approach that Conservative governments have adopted towards the welfare state since the Second World War. In the introductory section attention will be directed towards the defining features of British Conservatism. Given that British Conservatism has often been thought of as a pragmatic doctrine with a limited ideological base, is it possible to identify any enduring values, ideas and policies? The second part of the chapter will look at the emergence of 'One Nation' Conservatism after the Second World War which subsequently held sway within the Party during the 1950s and 60s. The third part of the chapter will examine the emergence of what might be described as a more radical 'New Right' form of Conservatism which came to full prominence in the late 1970s and which continues to have an impact on contemporary social policy.

# The British Conservative Party

Sir Robert Peel founded the modern Conservative Party in 1834, although its philosophical roots can be traced back to late seventeenth century **Toryism** (see Blake, 1998). Since its formation the Conservative Party has been guided by a desire to maintain the existing social and political order and has, in consequence, been highly sceptical of radical as opposed to gradual forms of change. Not surprisingly, perhaps, this doctrine has been seen by some as little more 'than a veil for the selfishness of the possessing classes' (O'Sullivan, 1999, p. 51). Conservatives have attempted to counter this 'caricature' by highlighting the advantages that can accrue to *all* citizens by supporting evolutionary rather than radical forms of change, by relying on tradition rather than untested rationalism, by acknowledging human imperfectability, by upholding the need for order and authority, by defending private property and by recognising the inevitability of economic and social inequalities. Indeed, one of the achievements of the modern Conservative Party has been its ability to persuade significant numbers of working-class voters to support the maintenance of an ordered, unequal and deferential society.

Conservative support for private ownership has not, however, resulted in unconditional support for the doctrine of laissez-faire. Indeed, there is a strong paternalistic tradition in British Conservatism in which those with wealth and power are seen as having obligations to help the less fortunate. Although strongly committed to informal and voluntary forms of welfare, the Conservatives have supported state intervention, particularly when this has been deemed necessary to protect vital economic interests or promote industrial development. State intervention has also been used to ameliorate adverse social conditions and other forms of disadvantage. During the Second World War, for example, Churchill's Conservative-led coalition government introduced a new Education Act (1944) that was intended to enhance educational opportunity for all, legislated for the introduction of family allowances and published plans for major improvements in the areas of social security and healthcare.

In contrast to their pre-war position, the Conservatives adopted a more positive approach to social and economic interventionism during the general election campaign of 1945. This was intended to demonstrate their commitment to enhancing the well-being and security of all citizens. They promised to maintain 'a high and stable level of employment', 'build at least 222,000 permanent new homes' in their first two years in office, develop a 'nation-wide and compulsory scheme of National Insurance' and ensure that healthcare would 'be made available to all citizens' on the basis of need' (Dale, 2000, p. 63). As it turned out, however, the public proved reluctant to place their trust in a party that had failed to respond adequately to high levels of unemployment and social deprivation in the pre-war period. The Conservative cause was not helped by what many regarded as an ill-conceived election broadcast by Churchill in June 1945 in which he claimed that the election of a 'socialist' government would lead to totalitarian rule requiring 'some form of Gestapo' (quoted in Kramnick and Sheerman, 1993, p. 481).

This hostility towards Labour's collectivist programme is likely to have raised doubts in the minds of some voters about the depth of the Conservatives' commitment to the welfare state.

# One Nation Conservatism

Labour's landslide victory in the 1945 general election led to calls from more progressive Conservatives for a clearer statement of the principles and aims that the Party would adhere to in the post-war era. In particular they believed that the 'One Nation' vision of 'an ordered society of mutual dependence, where privilege entailed obligations to those less fortunate and where social divisions and class conflict did not exist' (Dale, 2000, p. 60), a viewpoint first articulated by Disraeli in the late nineteenth century, represented the way forward.

Churchill responded to these calls for change by setting up an 'industrial' committee under the chairmanship of R.A. Butler, who had been the guiding force behind the 1944 Education Act. Following their deliberations, the Committee published *The Industrial Charter* in 1947. The Charter reaffirmed the Party's traditional commitment to free enterprise and the need for a 'light' regulatory framework for industry. Importantly, however, it also declared that the Party would seek to maintain cordial relations with the trade unions and maintain a level of demand which would 'offer jobs to all who are willing to work' (Conservative and Unionist Central Office, 1947, p. 16). Workers were also to have 'a reasonable expectation of industrial security' (p. 29), improved education and training opportunities, and enhanced status in the workplace. In a subsequent document published in the run-up to the general election of 1950, *The Right Road for Britain* (Conservative and Unionist Central Office, 1949), the Party declared that it was sympathetic to Labour's post-war welfare reforms, stating that they would continue to 'maintain the range and scope of these Services, and the rates of benefit' (p. 42).

While supportive of the welfare state, the Conservative's One Nation approach was not intended to imitate the egalitarian strategy pursued by Labour. Concern was expressed, for example, about the unaffordable growth in the cost of the NHS, as well as Labour's desire to create 'enormous and unwieldy multilateral [comprehensive] schools' (p. 44).

## The One Nation Group

Despite their more inclusive rhetoric (Conservative and Unionist Central Office, 1950), the Conservatives narrowly lost the 1950 general election. This prompted nine newly elected backbench MPs, including Iain Macleod, Enoch Powell and Edward Heath, to form a One Nation Group (ONG), which aimed to set out a clearer vision for post-war Conservative economic and social policy. In an influential pamphlet, entitled *One Nation: A Tory Approach to Social Problems*, published shortly before the Party's first post-election Party conference in the autumn of

1950 (Macleod and Maude (eds) 1950), the group set out a distinctive 'forward looking' Conservative approach to social policy. As the opening paragraph of the pamphlet made clear:

> There is a fundamental disagreement between Conservatives and Socialists on the question of social policy. Socialists would give the same benefits to everyone, whether or not the help is needed, and indeed whether or not the country's resources are adequate. We believe that we must first help those in need. Socialists believe that the State should provide an average standard. We believe that it should provide a minimum standard, above which people should be free to rise as far as their industry, their thrift, their ability or their genius may take them.
>
> Macleod and Maude (eds) (1950, p. 9)

For the ONG, then, the Conservative Party would, in contrast to Labour, accord priority to economic stability, *not* egalitarian forms of social expenditure, opt for selectivity rather than universalism, and aim to deliver minimum rather than optimal levels of service.

In their *One Nation* pamphlet, the ONG provided a number of examples of their distinctive approach to social policy. In the case of housing, for example, the private sector was accorded a key role to play in supplying homes for rent or purchase. Local authorities, on the other hand, were to focus more on slum clearance and the problem of overcrowding. In healthcare, the need to rein in expenditure by means of more rigorous need assessments and the imposition of charging was highlighted.

The ONG's support for the welfare state did not reflect any desire to abandon traditional Conservative concerns such as a stable currency, greater efficiency, low taxation, thrift, self-reliance, voluntarism and charitable activity. Rather, in keeping with the Conservative Party maxim of conserving 'what is best in the old while adapting constantly to the new' (quoted Lowe, 2005, p. 25), the ONG sought to persuade Party members that positive support for state intervention would *complement*, not *challenge*, the progressive potential of the market (Green, 2002).

It is difficult to judge how far the ideas of the ONG had been absorbed by the Conservative leadership in the run-up to the general election of 1951. Although the manifesto committed the Party to building 300,000 houses a year if elected, and promised better targeted education and health spending, there was only limited focus on welfare issues. Instead emphasis was placed on 'setting the people free' from Labour's bureaucratic controls and putting an end to rationing and shortages.

## One Nation Conservatism in practice

The depth of the Conservative commitment to the welfare state was quickly tested following their narrow election victory in 1951, which left them with an overall majority of just seventeen seats. Faced with a substantial balance of payments deficit that had triggered international speculation against the pound, the incoming Chancellor, R.A. Butler, decided to cut imports, tighten monetary policy and review public expenditure commitments. Although a number of cost containment measures were introduced, such as the introduction of NHS charges and a reduction in the school building programme, Butler's commitment to One Nation Conservatism dissuaded him from making any draconian cuts in the welfare budget.

The appointment of more 'progressive' ministers in areas such as health (Macleod, 1952–55) and education (Eccles, 1954–57) served to establish One Nation Conservatism within the Party at this time. Certainly, a distinct One Nation approach towards the welfare state, involving targeting, tighter spending controls and increased reliance on charging, was beginning to take shape. The establishment of the Phillips Committee (1953) on the Economic and Financial Problems of Provision for Old Age and the Guillebaud enquiry (1953) into the costs of the NHS were, for example, indicative of the government's desire to distance themselves from Labour's egalitarian approach to the welfare state. This challenge to Labour's approach to social policy did not, however, reflect any covert desire to dismantle the welfare state, as was evidenced by Butler's decision to opt for a review of NHS expenditure, rather than a more wide-ranging examination of welfare spending.

By the time of the 1955 general election, there was a much clearer indication that Party leaders had firmly embraced the One Nation approach to the welfare state. As the manifesto declared:

> We denounce the Labour Party's desire to use the social services, which we all helped to create, as an instrument for levelling down. We regard social security, not as a substitute for family thrift, but as a necessary basis or supplement to it. We think of the National Health Service as a means, not of preventing anyone from paying anything for any service, but of ensuring that proper attention and treatment are denied to no one. We believe that equality of opportunity is to be achieved, not by sending every boy and girl to exactly the same kind of school, but by seeing that every child gets the schooling most suited to his or her aptitudes. We see a sensible housing policy in terms, not of one hopeless Council waiting list, but of adequate and appropriate provision both for letting and for sale.
>
> *United for Peace and Progress, the Conservative and Unionist Party's General Election Manifesto 1955*, reprinted in Dale (ed.), 2000a, p. 119

Election victories in 1955 and 1959 enabled successive Conservative governments under the leadership of Eden (1955–57), Macmillan (1957–63) and Douglas-Home (1963–4) to pursue a One Nation strategy which involved balancing traditional economic concerns, such as low taxes and price stability, with 'social' imperatives such as the maintenance of full employment and support for the welfare state. This proved no easy task, not least because of persistent Treasury concerns about the growing cost of the welfare state. Matters came to a head in 1958 when the then Chancellor, Peter Thorneycroft, resigned from office along with two of his junior cabinet colleagues (Enoch Powell and Nigel Birch) after the Cabinet vetoed his request for welfare cuts of £153 million in order to stem the growth in inflation and restore international confidence in the pound. Three years later a further sterling crisis led the Treasury to again demand cuts in welfare expenditure. An internal Party review entitled *The Future of the Social Services* (1961–63) suggested that withdrawing the universal state pension and introducing fees in state schools could ease the growth in spending. Although these proposals were regarded as too radical for a One Nation administration, alternative more modest cost-cutting measures were introduced, including increased health and social security contributions and higher rents for council house tenants.

When Macmillan resigned as Prime Minister on health grounds in 1963 the One Nation approach to social policy had reached its apex. Following the Party's defeat under new leader Alec Douglas-Home at the 1964 general election, the tide was turning towards 'New Right' ideas within Conservative circles.

 **Thought provoker**

Could One Nation Conservatives be described as whole-hearted supporters of the welfare state?

## New Right Conservatism

The more radical form of Conservatism associated with the Thatcher and Major governments was rooted in what have come to be known as 'New Right' ideas, which became increasingly influential in both the United States and the UK. In the United States commentators such as Leo Strauss, Frederick von Hayek, Ayn Rand, Russell Kirk, William J. Buckley Jr (the founder of the *National Review*) and Milton Friedman were vehemently opposed to the New Deal collectivism associated with the Democrat President Franklin D. Roosevelt (see Critchlow, 2007). More recently, Charles Murray's (1980) critique of the adverse effect of government welfare programmes on the behaviour of the poor in his book *Losing Ground* contributed to a growing call for welfare reform in the US.

There are some key differences between those New Right thinkers who adopt a strong neo-liberal standpoint and those who might better be described as neo-conservatives (see Briefing 6.1). For example, those of a more conservative disposition have voiced concerns about the threat to social stability that might arise

**Briefing 6.1**
**Tensions within Conservatism**

| *Liberal New Right* | *Conservative New Right* |
|---|---|
| Classical liberalism | Traditional conservatism |
| Atomism | Organicism |
| Radicalism | Traditionalism |
| Libertarianism | Authoritarianism |
| Economic dynamism | Social order |
| Self-interest/enterprise | Traditional values |
| Equality of opportunity | Natural hierarchy |
| Minimal state | Strong state |
| Internationalism | Insular nationalism |
| Pro-globalisation | Anti-globalisation |

*Source*: Heywood, 2003, p. 101.

if the free market approach favoured by economic liberals such as Hayek were adopted. According to the neo-conservatives, the rampant individualism unleashed by the free market could spill over into civil society thereby undermining self-restraint, obligation and a sense of community. However, the differences between neo-liberals and neo-conservatives should not be exaggerated. Indeed the emergence of the term 'the New Right' serves to confirm the underlying compatibility of these two traditions (see Gamble, 1988). As Heywood (2003) points out, 'neoliberal and neoconservative views usually do coincide, and it is this attempt to fuse economic liberalism with social conservatism that gives the New Right its distinctive character' (pp. 100–101). Importantly, in terms of this discussion, both economic liberals and social conservatives are united in their opposition to the welfare state.

According to New Right commentators, the welfare state poses a threat to personal freedom by compelling citizens to contribute to the cost of welfare provision regardless of whether they are willing or able to use such services. The welfare state is also deemed to have economic shortcomings. They argue that the lack of both competitive pressures and market signals in tax-financed, need-based, producer-dominated welfare systems leads to inefficient and costly services which are unresponsive to consumer preferences (see Tullock, 1965; Buchanan, 1986). The New Right also maintain that the welfare state has undesirable social consequences. 'Unconditional' welfare services based on citizenship are deemed to have given rise to a situation in which citizens become reluctant to take responsibility for their own needs and those of their dependants (see Marsland, 1996). Indeed, Murray (1990) has argued that the growth of lone parenthood in the United States can be attributed to the provision of ever more generous forms of state support. Finally, it is contended that the monolithic state welfare sector has 'crowded out' more responsive forms of familial, voluntary and private welfare (Green, 1996).

Although New Right organisations in Britain, such as the Institute of Economic Affairs (IEA), have been raising objections to interventionist One Nation Conservatism since the mid 1950s, their impact on Conservative Party politicians was insignificant until the early 1960s, when Enoch Powell, Keith Joseph and Geoffrey Howe became attracted to the merits of less interventionist forms of economic and social policy. While the IEA accepted that the government still had an important role to play in areas such as upholding the rule of law and providing a limited range of 'public' goods, such as policing or defence, they believed that the more extensive forms of post-war state intervention, particularly in the area of welfare, was having a detrimental effect on the economy and the wider society.

## Testing the water

The first clear indication that the Conservative Party was becoming more receptive to New Right ideas came at a pre-election Party conference held at the Selsdon Park Hotel in south-east London in 1970. A range of New Right measures were considered including tax cuts, curbs on trade union powers, reduced government support for failing industries and the ending of prices and incomes policies. On the welfare front, the need for increased targeting of resources was suggested, as was the imposition of charges for non-medical NHS provision such as food and accommodation. This prospective change of direction led the Labour leader of the time, Harold Wilson, to coin the phrase 'Selsdon man' in an effort to portray the Conservatives as the hard-hearted enemies of full employment, the welfare state and economic interventionism.

The first opportunity to put these New Right ideas into practice came after the Conservative victory in the 1970 general election. Early examples included the decision by the new Minister of Trade and Industry in the Heath government, John Davies, to put a stop to the use of taxpayers' money to bail out 'lame-duck' industries. An Industrial Relations Bill was also introduced, giving industrial relations courts the power to enforce strike ballots and impose cooling-off periods in an effort to tackle 'excessive' trade union power. However, rising levels of inflation (which had been fuelled in part by the Conservatives' expansionist budget in 1971) and unemployment, as well as the threat of bankruptcy at both Rolls Royce and the Upper Clyde Shipbuilders, tested the resolve of the Heath government. Unlike the future Conservative Prime Minister Margaret Thatcher, who famously declared that she was 'not for turning', Heath did perform a U-turn and reverted to the interventionist policies characteristic of One Nation Conservatism.

Heath's U-turn did not, however, resolve the severe economic difficulties he faced during his remaining period in office, a failure which only served to strengthen the hand of his New Right critics following consecutive general elections defeats in February and October 1974. One key figure in the vanguard of New Right Conservatism was Keith Joseph, who had hitherto been regarded as a 'One Nation' Heath loyalist. Persuaded by critics, such as Alfred Sherman, Peter Bauer, Ralph Harris and Alan Walters, of the flaws in the One Nation interventionist strategy that the Heath government had come to rely on, Joseph (who had been a high-spending minister at the Department of Health and Social Security) now argued that the Conservative Party must embrace New Right ideas if the pressing problems of the age such as rising inflation and the growing welfare budgets were to be rectified.

The Centre for Policy Studies, which had been established by Joseph and Thatcher in 1974, provided the institutional base for a concerted 'New Right' challenge to One Nation Conservatism (see Sherman, 2007). In a series of well-publicised speeches, Joseph argued that the rising inflation that occurred during the Heath era should have been tackled by curbs on the money supply even if this had resulted in higher levels of unemployment. He also bemoaned the negative impact of the post-war state welfare state, arguing that over-generous state welfare provision was creating a **dependency culture**.

When Heath decided to seek re-election as leader of the Conservative Party in 1975, Joseph was expected to stand against him on a radical New Right platform. However, adverse publicity surrounding a speech in Birmingham, in which Joseph appeared to condone the compulsory sterilisation of poor, adolescent, working-class mothers, coupled with personal doubts about his suitability to lead the Party, led him to stand aside, leaving the way clear for his 'acolyte' Margaret Thatcher to take up the mantle. After defeating Heath in the first leadership ballot for the Conservative leadership, Thatcher saw off challenges from Whitelaw, Howe, Prior and Peyton in the second round of the contest to become leader of the Conservative Party.

## Radical New Right Conservatism takes hold

Thatcher had to endure a baptism of fire during the initial period of her leadership of the Party and was forced to battle against sceptics in her own Party who believed that she was little more than a 'narrow minded dogmatist' with 'simple minded remedies' (Campbell, 2003, p. 2). Indeed, in the months leading up to the 1979 general election, Thatcher was still being written off by many of her critics as 'too suburban, strident, right-wing and inexperienced' to enter Downing Street (Campbell, 2000, p. 319). The Labour Prime Minister Callaghan's reluctance to call a snap election in the autumn of 1978, coupled with the negative public response to industrial unrest during the so-called 'Winter of Discontent' (in which there were a series of public sector strikes over pay), led to an upturn in Thatcher's fortunes. She emerged victorious in the May 1979 general election with 43.9 per cent of the popular vote and a 43-seat majority.

## Thatcher's first Conservative government 1979–1983

New Right rather than One Nation ideas were at the heart of the Conservative Party's general election manifesto of 1979. In her foreword to the manifesto, Thatcher reiterated her belief that individual rather than state action was the key to 'the recovery of our country' (Conservative Party, 1979, p. 5). The manifesto committed the newly elected government to bring inflation under control through

*Source*: Chris Duggan, New Statesman 1987, The British Cartoon Archive, University of Kent, www.cartoons.ac.uk

'proper monetary discipline', reduce state spending as a proportion of national income and tackling waste. Trade union powers and privileges were to be curbed and income taxes were to be reduced. The fight against crime was to be prioritised and immigration controls tightened. Home ownership was to be encouraged by a 'right to buy' scheme, under which tenants were given the opportunity to buy their council property. An assisted places scheme was proposed whereby 'bright children from modest backgrounds' were to be given the opportunity to study in independent (private) schools on a subsidised basis. Private healthcare was to be boosted by restoring tax relief for occupational medical insurance schemes and by allowing pay beds in NHS hospitals 'where there is a demand for them'.

Despite her resounding success in the 1979 general election, Thatcher did not embark on what many thought would be an all-out attack on the welfare state. This was, however, due more to the problem of devising practical policies than any lack of reforming zeal. As Timmins (2001) has observed, 'It was one thing for the IEA to say student loans or health vouchers were needed, quite another to devise them' (p. 359). Moreover, many of the ministers appointed to Thatcher's first cabinet, such as Ian Gilmour, Francis Pym, James Prior and Peter Walker, were far from convinced that root and branch welfare reform was necessary. Indeed, it was not until the subsequent appointment of 'anti-collectivist' ministers such as Cecil Parkinson, Norman Tebbit and Nigel Lawson that the prospects for radical reform improved. It was not, however, until Thatcher's third term in government that major structural changes were introduced. During the first term the new government gave priority to the control of inflation, the lowering of personal taxes and further curbs on trade union powers.

The future direction of change became ever clearer in the first term. The government's desire to reduce public spending presented a real threat to the long-term future of the welfare state (HM Treasury, 1979). Following some initial increases in certain social security benefits (which had been promised in the manifesto), the new government embarked on a series of cost-cutting measures, including the abolition of the earnings-related elements of unemployment and sickness benefits as well as reducing benefit payments to those on strike. Substantial spending cuts were also made in the areas of housing and education.

The limited structural welfare reforms that the first Thatcher government undertook demonstrated a clear desire to shift away from One Nation Conservatism. The sale of council housing reflected a strong desire to reverse the postwar collectivist advance. Under the 1980 Housing Act, council house tenants of at least three years' standing were given the right to buy their home at a discounted price, which varied according to length of tenure. This scheme proved extremely popular. By 1983, some 500,000 tenants had bought their own homes. The government's New Right stance was also reflected in their decision to introduce an Assisted Places Scheme, which provided financial support for children from lower-income families to study at independent schools and the abolition of the Health Services Board, which the previous Labour government had established to phase out NHS pay beds and regulate private hospitals.

Vociferous opposition to Thatcher's plans for welfare reform, coupled with rising unemployment and inner-city disturbances in areas such as Brixton, Toxteth and Moss Side did not bode well for a government seeking a further term in office. However, buoyed up by a recovery in the world economy, a successful military campaign in the Falklands in 1982, and a divided opposition, the Conservatives emerged triumphant in the 1983 general election, increasing their overall majority to 144 seats.

## Thatcher's second Conservative government 1983–1987

Economic reform remained the main focus of the second Thatcher government. Building on a 'successful' first-term privatisation programme, the new government launched an even more ambitious sales programme. British Telecom was sold for £4 billion in 1984 while £5.4 billion was raised from the sale of British Gas in 1986. British Coal proved to be a more difficult challenge. However, after the government's 'victory' in the bitter national coal strike of 1984–5, which represented a significant setback for the National Union of Mineworkers and the wider trade union movement, plans for the eventual privatisation of the coal mining industry were put in place.

Although the Conservatives once again exhibited caution in relation to structural welfare reform, New Right ideas continued to be applied. Further steps were taken, for example, to curb welfare state expenditure. In the area of social security, the then Minister Norman Fowler instigated a wide-ranging review in four key areas of activity – pensions, housing benefit, supplementary benefits and provision for children and young people – to ensure that spending was targeted on those in greatest need. Although this review, and the legislation that followed (the 1986 Social Security Act), did not generate any short-term economies for the Treasury, the changes (such as the introduction of a less generous State Earnings Related Pension Scheme) succeeded in slowing the rate of expenditure growth.

Private sector-style efficiency savings was also sought in relation to NHS spending. Health authorities were given annual efficiency savings targets. Performance indicators were introduced so that comparisons could be made between health authorities in terms of length of hospital stays, treatment costs and waiting times. Spending on some non-medical services such as cleaning, catering and laundry was to be 'contested' by the introduction of tendering processes which led to £110 million worth of 'savings' during their first year of operation. Private sector-style management structures were also introduced following an enquiry by Roy Griffiths (the managing director of the Sainsbury's supermarket chain) into the operation of the service in 1983. **New public management** of this kind was intended to ensure that welfare providers focused more sharply on the needs of service users.

In education, expenditure constraints proved rather controversial. Keith Joseph's plan to secure savings of £39 million by requiring higher-earning parents to contribute towards the university tuition fees of their children had to be withdrawn in the face of vociferous parental and backbench opposition. In addition, teaching unions took industrial action for fifteen months from February 1985 over a pay claim which eventually led to a more generous settlement (Timmins, 2001).

In the area of housing, cost reductions were achieved by continuing with the sale of council housing and pressurising local authorities to raise rents to market levels for remaining tenants by the withdrawal of central government subsidies (Hills, 1998).

**Thought provoker**

On the basis of US evidence, which shows that applications for 'social assistance' have fallen markedly since the introduction of more stringent 'work first' welfare reforms in 1996 (Haskins, 2006), are New Right commentators right to conclude that over-generous state welfare provision leads to the creation of an antisocial dependency culture?

## Thatcher's 'third' Conservative government (1987–1990)

Although Thatcher (1995) considered the general election manifesto of 1987 to be the finest her Party had ever produced, it only hinted at the more radical welfare agenda that would actually be pursued during the third term. The one major exception was education, where the government outlined plans for improving educational standards and reductions in local authority control. In other areas of social policy, though, 'gradualism' held sway. The manifesto contained promises to improve the NHS by means of greater emphasis on prevention, the promotion of community care, support for NHS staff, more modern facilities and improved management. In social security, the Conservatives promised to maintain the value of the state retirement pension and to encourage the 'ten million employees who do not yet have their own occupational scheme to have a pension of their own'. They also pledged to provide additional help for low-income families. In housing, the Conservatives sought to increase owner-occupation, regenerate the privately rented sector, enhance 'landlord' choice for council tenants and transform the worst housing estates through the creation of Housing Action Trusts.

Once back in government, though, the pace of change along New Right lines quickened, most notably in the areas of health and community care. Constant criticism about ward closures and cancelled operations in the National Health Service led Thatcher to set up a small NHS review team consisting of herself, four other Ministers, three deputy secretaries and a number of policy unit advisers. The idea that the service should be dismantled was rejected, not least because the NHS was seen to be highly effective in terms of containing healthcare costs. Instead it was decided to create an **internal market** within the NHS which would help to keep costs under control by means of competitive pressures. In future, providers such as hospitals would have to deliver competitively priced, high-quality services if they wanted to secure contracts from purchasers such as District Health Authorities and GP fund holders. Although these proposals were opposed by both the Labour opposition and the British Medical Association, the Health Secretary, Kenneth Clarke, succeeded in implementing the *National Health Service and Community Care Act* in 1990 without having to make any significant concessions.

The reform of community care outlined in the 1990 Act proved to be another significant development, again demonstrating the government's belief that the welfare state could be reformed along anti-collectivist lines. The government had been concerned about the growing social security bill for residential care that had risen from £10 million in 1979 to some £2 billion by 1991. Following influential reports from the Audit Commission (1986) and Roy Griffiths (1988), it was decided to transfer budgetary responsibility for the care of elderly people from the social security system to local authorities in the hope that this might help to contain costs. The provider role of local authorities was, however, to be supplanted by non-state providers. The Act stipulated that while local authorities would be expected to assess the needs of elderly people and prepare community care plans, they were to contract out the provision of services to private and voluntary organisations. As Glennerster (2007) points out, 'the reform of community care thus fitted into what was now emerging as the common pattern of social policy reforms in the Thatcher period – continued state funding but a variety of forms of private and public providers' (p. 191).

The education reforms outlined in the manifesto of 1987 were implemented with the passage of the *Education Reform Act* in 1988. One of the main rationales of this change was to improve educational outcomes for children and shift power away from local authorities and teachers towards parents. A ten-subject National Curriculum was introduced for all state schools. In addition, national testing for all pupils aged seven, eleven, fourteen and sixteen was introduced to determine the extent to which designated attainment levels (knowledge, skills and understanding) had been achieved. These test results were to be made available to parents so that they could compare the performance of individual schools. The Act also enabled schools to apply for so-called grant-maintained (GM) status. These new GM schools could opt out of local authority control (after a parental ballot) and receive their funds directly from the Department of Education. Non-GM schools were also given a greater degree of autonomy. Under a local management of schools initiative (LMS), headteachers and governors were granted greater control over expenditure and staff appointments. Privately sponsored (but largely state funded) City Technology Colleges were also to be established in an effort to create centres of educational excellence in educationally disadvantaged neighbourhoods.

Given that many of the previous reforms in social security introduced by Norman Fowler during the second term needed time to take root, there were few major developments in this area of social policy during the third term. There was, however, a clear New Right underpinning to those policy initiatives enacted by the new Minister, John Moore. He attacked the growth of the 'dependency' culture by compelling 16- and 17-year-olds to undertake youth training rather than subsist on Income Support. His preference for selectivity rather than universalism was reflected in his decision to freeze the level of Child Benefit (a universal benefit) for three consecutive years (1988–91).

The influence of New Right ideas was also evident in the area of housing. Reducing the state's role in the construction, ownership, administration and regulation of housing and reviving the privately rented sector remained the order of the day. Under the 1988 Housing Act, private landlords or housing associations were permitted to take over the running of council housing in a given locality if this was supported by existing tenants by means of a ballot. Housing Action Trusts were encouraged, rent controls were abolished and landlords were able to let property on an 'assured' or shorthold basis. Those tenants who were ineligible for housing benefit faced steep rises in rent levels as a result of the withdrawal of central government subsidies and the prohibition of local authority rent subsidies. In practice these reforms had limited success. Only five Housing Action Trusts had been established by 1994, and although some council stock passed from local authorities to alternative landlords, this was rarely the result of so-called 'Tenants' Choice'. Transfers tended to be instigated by Conservative-controlled local authorities in the south of England who wanted to dispose of their housing stock. By 1994 some 3.7 million homes still remained in the council sector compared to 4.2 million in 1988 (Timmins, 2001).

## From Thatcher to Major

Margaret Thatcher's position as leader of the Conservative Party appeared unassailable at the time of the 1987 general election. Within three years, however, she had been forced out of office by members of her own party. Various events led to her downfall. The economic climate deteriorated as the post-election boom proved short-lived and a recession had taken hold by 1989. The replacement of the household rating system by a community charge or poll tax (which was levied on each adult in a household) proved highly unpopular because it was seen as imposing an unfair burden on those with low or moderate incomes. In response, a highly-effective, broad-based anti-poll tax campaign was launched culminating in extensive media coverage of a mass demonstration in Trafalgar Square in March 1990 which portrayed the government in a poor light. The Prime Minister was also weakened by a series of ministerial resignations including Michael Heseltine, Leon Brittan, Norman Tebbit, Nigel Lawson, Norman Fowler, Peter Walker and Nicholas Ridley. The final straw came in November 1990 when Thatcher's longest-serving Minister, Geoffrey Howe, left the government after the Prime Minister had made another anti-European speech of the type for which she was becoming renowned. Although Thatcher managed to see off a leadership challenge from Sir Anthony Meyer in 1989, a more serious challenge was subsequently mounted by Michael Heseltine. Although Thatcher polled 204 votes to Heseltine's 152, the margin of victory proved insufficient to prevent a second ballot. Although Thatcher may well have won that ballot, she decided to leave office, recognising that her 'friends and allies' no longer regarded her as an electoral asset (Thatcher, 1995, p. 855).

## The Major years 1990–1997

John Major, the favoured candidate of Margaret Thatcher, was elected leader of the Conservative Party in November 1990. Faced with the task of securing an election victory within two years, Major focused on three key issues – replacing the much despised poll tax, reviving the ailing British economy, and placating those within his party who remained implacably opposed to closer social and political integration with Europe (the eurosceptics). The new environment secretary, Michael Heseltine, was charged with the first of these tasks. A new, 'fairer', eight-banded property-based tax was drawn up for introduction in 1993. In the interim the adverse impact of the Community Charge on the public was to be softened by means of a £4.5 billion injection of Treasury funds. Improving the economic outlook proved to be a stiffer challenge. Although the new Chancellor Norman Lamont presided over falls in inflation and interest rates, unemployment remained persistently high. On the European front, Major was able to placate backbench eurosceptics by securing an 'opt out' for Britain in relation to European Union jurisdiction in some areas of social policy (the Social Chapter), minimum wage regulation and the Exchange Rate Mechanism.

During his first period of office (1990–92) Major also attempted to improve the quality of public services through the introduction of the Citizens' Charter in 1991. Major's determination to drive through change in this sphere was prompted in part by his own family experiences of trying to access public services (Major, 2000). Under this initiative, service providers were required to devise performance targets which would be scrutinised by independent monitors, deal with user complaints more responsively and provide redress where appropriate (see Lowe, 2005).

Although Major had succeeded in steadying the Conservative ship by the time of the general election of 1992, it had not been deemed necessary to make any decisive shift away from the radical Conservative agenda of the previous Thatcher governments. Indeed, the party's general election manifesto was highly 'Thatcherite' in tone. The manifesto promised renewed commitment to the pursuit of price stability, public expenditure restraint, prudent tax reductions, balanced budgets, and unequivocal support for the free market (Conservative Party, 1992, p. 5). Plans for the privatisation of British Coal, local authority bus companies and airports were unveiled, deregulation was to continue and the numbers of home owners and shareholders expanded. The Citizens' Charter (which would now be the personal responsibility of a Minister of Cabinet rank) was to be developed further and public services were to be exposed to greater competition and accountability.

The Party's commitment to the reformed NHS was reaffirmed with promises of increased funding, enhanced patient rights and a greater emphasis on preventative services. In terms of social security, the manifesto committed the Party to making further improvements in provision (especially in the sphere of disability benefits) and to the retention of Child Benefit payments for all families. In housing, the reform process was to be continued by giving council tenants increased rights including an option to take a part-share in their home prior to full ownership under a new 'rents to mortgages' scheme. The need to ensure that 'the most important and wide-ranging reforms since the 1940s' (p. 17) were embedded was highlighted in relation to education.

Despite widespread predictions that the Conservatives would lose the 1992 general election, Major confounded his sceptics by polling more votes than any party had previously achieved, even though this only gave him an overall majority of 21 seats.

The main objective of the new Major administration was to consolidate the third-term reforms. This proved difficult given the gloomy economic outlook. The Chancellor, Norman Lamont, had to grapple with the fallout from the humiliating decision to withdraw from the **Exchange Rate Mechanism** on what came to be known as 'Black Wednesday' (16 September 1992), when costly but ultimately futile attempts were made to protect the value of the pound. Lamont was also faced with a projected budgetary deficit of £50 billion in 1993.

The deteriorating state of the public finance led to significant changes in social security. The Chief Secretary to the Treasury, Michael Portillo, conducted a fundamental review of welfare spending in February 1993 which aimed to ident-ify those areas where resources could be targeted more effectively or even where the state might withdraw funding completely. The Social Security secretary, Peter Lilley, a close ally of Portillo, introduced a number of reforms that were intended to bring spending under control. The eligibility criteria for a number of benefits were tightened or changed. For example, a new Incapacity Benefit was introduced in 1993. It included a more stringent 'work test', which, it was hoped, would secure a 7 per cent reduction in claimant numbers. Tougher benefit rules were in-troduced for asylum seekers and a less generous housing benefit scheme was de-veloped. The value of the State Earnings Related Pension Scheme (SERPS) was further reduced whilst plans were put into effect to raise the pension age for women to sixty-five with effect from 2010. Lone-parent benefit rates were also frozen in 1996 (Timmins, 2001, pp. 525–6).

Arguably, the most significant change made by Lilley was the introduction of the Jobseeker's Allowance in 1996, which 'halved the entitlement to non-means-tested benefit from twelve months to six and merged it with income support for the unemployed' (ibid., p. 528). In order to encourage more rapid returns to the job market, those seeking this form of assistance were required to demonstrate that they were actively seeking work.

Major's emphasis on consolidation proved far from straightforward. For exam-ple, the Education Reform Act of 1988 had given rise to 'a dual process of change, with moves towards both decentralisation and centralisation' (Ball, 1998, pp. 146–7). In terms of the former, schools were encouraged to become 'more innovative, risk-taking and entrepreneurial than their LEA counterparts' (ibid., p. 147) by opting for grant-maintained status. Those that decided to remain under local education authority control were also given greater budgetary discretion under the Local Management of Schools (LMS) initiative. The most significant cen-tralising measures were the introduction of a National Curriculum, the systematic testing of pupils, league tables of performance and increased inspection. During his tenure as Education Secretary, John Patten experienced considerable difficulties in persuading teachers of the merits of either the National Curriculum or the new testing regime. Indeed, his hasty decision to introduce national testing in English for 14-year-olds in 1993 led to a national teachers' boycott of testing for all age groups. This issue was eventually resolved when the new head of a School Curricu-lum and Assessment Authority, Sir Ron Dearing, recommended paring back the National Curriculum and limiting national testing to just three subjects.

A new external inspection regime for schools also met with resistance from teachers' unions after the head of the newly formed Office for Standards in Educa-tion (Ofsted), Chris Woodhead, stated that improved standards were required in 50 per cent of primary and 40 per cent of secondary schools. The grant-maintained scheme for primary and secondary schools also proved problematic. Despite financial incentives, only around 4 per cent of all schools had acquired GM status by the time of the 1997 general election.

There were fewer 'consolidation' problems in the sphere of housing. A further 300,000 council houses were sold off in this period, while some 170,000 tenants acquired a new landlord under the large-scale voluntary transfer of council housing (Ginsburg, 2005). Housing Associations became firmly established as the largest providers of new 'social' housing whilst 'deregulation' appeared to boost the supply of privately rented housing. By 1996 around 2.1 million households were renting privately compared to 1.7 million in 1988 (Timmins, 2001).

In October 1993 the Prime Minister launched a so-called 'back to basics' campaign based on a populist approach to issues such as crime, health, education and social work. The idea was to challenge the received wisdom of 'out of touch' welfare professionals. Although Major (2000) insisted that his back to basics campaign was 'not about bashing single mothers or preaching sexual fidelity at private citizens' (p. 555), the media took a different line, highlighting what they regarded as the improper personal conduct of a number of Ministers and MPs. Major's ill-conceived campaign only served to highlight his inability to control the news agenda or his parliamentary colleagues, particularly those of a eurosceptic persuasion. Faced with constant attacks on his leadership, Major voluntarily stood for re-election as Party leader in June 1995. Although he secured a comfortable victory over his only rival, John Redwood, this did little to bolster his standing. Faced with a vibrant 'New' Labour leader and a reputation for economic incompetence following the Black Wednesday debacle, it was now clear that the long period of Conservative government was coming to an end.

Major fought the 1997 general election on a New Right platform (Conservative Party, 1997). The virtues of the free market, low taxes, privatisation, deregulation, shareholding, restrained public spending, low inflation, trade union reform and tough law and order measures were much in evidence. In terms of social policy, the vision of 'a smaller state doing fewer things and doing them better' (p. 29) remained the paramount goal. Unfortunately, from Major's perspective, the British public was no longer willing to place their trust in the Conservatives. In a dramatic change of fortune the Conservatives lost 182 seats, mustering just under 31 per cent of the popular vote. 'New Labour', under the youthful leadership of Tony Blair, swept to power with a 179-seat majority (43.2 per cent of the popular vote) on the largest swing to an opposition party since 1945.

## Controversy and debate

Were there more similarities than differences between the One Nation and New Right Conservative approaches to the welfare state?

*United for Peace and Progress: The Conservative and Unionist Party's Policy* - the Conservative Party's 1955 general election manifesto stated:

We denounce the Labour Party's desire to use the social services, which we all helped to create, as an instrument for levelling down. We regard social security, not as a substitute for family thrift, but as a necessary basis or supplement to it. We think of the National Health Service as a means, not of preventing anyone from paying anything for any service, but of ensuring that proper attention and treatment are denied to no-one. We believe that equality of opportunity is to be achieved, not by sending every boy and girl to exactly the same sort of school, but by seeing that every child gets the schooling most suited to his or her aptitudes. We see a sensible housing policy in terms, not of one hopeless Council waiting list, but of adequate and appropriate provision both for letting and for sale.

*The Next Moves Forward* – the Conservative Party's 1983 general election manifesto stated:

Freedom and responsibility go together. The Conservative Party believes in encouraging people to take responsibility for their own decisions. We shall continue to return more choice to individuals and their families. That is the way to increase personal freedom. It is also the way to improve standards in the state services.

Conservatives believe strongly in the duty of government to help those who are least able to help themselves. We have more than carried out our pledges to protect pensioners against price rises and to maintain standards in the National Health Services. This rebuts the totally unfavourable charge that we would 'dismantle the Welfare State'. We are determined that our public services should provide the best possible value both for people they seek to help and for the taxpayer who pays the bill. We will give groups of tenants the right to form tenant co-operatives, owning and running their management and budget for themselves. They will also have the right to ask other institutions to take over their housing.

## Social policy under Thatcher and Major: a Conservative welfare revolution?

Some commentators have argued that the adoption of New Right ideas by both the Thatcher and Major governments represented a departure from what might be described as 'traditional' Conservatism (Gilmour, 1992). This is questionable. Although both Thatcher and Major moved away from One Nation Conservatism they remained committed to mainstream Conservative thinking in relation to the importance of the nation state, the family, social order, the market, voluntarism, property rights and differential rewards and status. The key issue is whether the 'New Right' measures employed in support of these values between 1979 and 1997 actually served to undermine these core Conservative principles. While it can be argued that the Conservatives' economic remedies contributed to family instability, increased social disorder and a more divisive society, it can be argued that the Conservatives have always been willing to pursue unpopular policies in the short term if they adjudge them to be for the long-term benefit of the nation. The means employed by Thatcher and Major were certainly harsher than in the eras of Macmillan or Heath, but the radical New Right approach pursued in the 1980s and 90s was deemed to be the more appropriate form of Conservatism given the economic and social circumstances of the age (Green, 2006).

Although the welfare state was not, in fact, dismantled during the Thatcher and Major eras, it had been transformed in significant ways. The injection of a private sector ethos into the delivery of public services, improved targeting, cost containment measures and greater 'consumer' choice ensured that the welfare state was operating along New Right lines. Arguably, the transformation was most successful in cultural terms. By challenging commonly held assumptions about the 'selflessness' of state welfare providers and their ability to make effective use of taxpayer funds, as well as by championing service users, the Conservatives succeeded in promoting the idea that the 'good' citizen should approach state welfare provision with the same level of discernment as they would as a private consumer. By the end of the 1990s the welfare state was no longer being regarded as a vehicle for social solidarity or redistribution (though see Park *et al.*, 2008). Rather, it was being portrayed as a means to provide consumers with tailored, cost-effective services. The success of this cultural onslaught can be gauged by the fact that New Labour did not attempt to turn back the clock when they were elected in 1997. As Ferguson, Lavalette and Mooney (2002) conclude, the Thatcher and Major governments 'did succeed to a significant extent in securing legitimation for the role of the market in the delivery of heartland social and welfare services, and in the role of management in securing cost effectiveness. More significantly perhaps, they also created a new culture around welfare that New Labour was quick to embrace' (p. 165).

## Conclusion

Following John Major's defeat in the general election of 1997, the Conservatives have spent more than a decade in the political 'wilderness'. The Party's unwillingness to jettison the New Right inheritance of Thatcher and, to a lesser extent, Major, coupled with New Labour's policy shifts to the 'centre', led to general election defeats in 1997, 2001 and 2005 as well as a brisk trade in Party leaders (William Hague, Iain Duncan Smith and Michael Howard).

However, under the leadership of David Cameron, there are signs of a Conservative revival. Cameron has abandoned the confrontational form of Conservatism associated with leaders such as Thatcher and Howard. Adopting a more emollient 'One Nation' tone, Cameron has attempted to reconnect the Conservative Party with 'moderate' middle income voters who are economically, socially and, to some extent, culturally conservative (see Park *et al.*, 2008). Importantly, though, targeting support of this kind is not seen as incompatible with reaching out to other groups of voters. Portraying himself as a compassionate Conservative, Cameron has made strenuous efforts to ensure that his Party is no longer associated with negative attacks on minority groups such as lone parents or immigrants. Moreover, Cameron has adopted a 'greener' stance on environmental issues and has attempted to appeal to younger voters by making use of new media such as Facebook.

Cameron has also indicated that a future Conservative government will not only match New Labour's existing spending plans in the area of social policy, but also will ensure that any proceeds from economic growth will be divided equally between public spending and tax cuts. However, Cameron's reservations about the effectiveness of state-provided welfare has led him to advocate the use of state funds to support alternative providers, particularly from the voluntary sector. He believes that this sector is much better able to tackle long-standing problems such as drug misuse or poor parenting. Cameron has been supportive of those New

Labour programmes such as Academy schools which present a challenge to traditional forms of state education. His only criticism has been the slow pace of change. A rapid expansion of the Academy programme is deemed necessary to improve the educational performance of children from disadvantaged backgrounds. Cameron has also promised to abandon the centralised target culture of New Labour which he believes has undermined the morale and professionalism of groups such as doctors, nurses and teachers. He is seeking to ensure that decisions about priorities or investment are taken by professionals working at the local level rather than by remote officials at the centre.

It remains to be seen whether this 'rebranding' exercise will restore the electoral fortunes of the Conservative Party. However, New Labour's unwillingness and inability to secure a deep 'ideological' bond with the electorate, preferring to rely on the appeal of 'competence' has left them vulnerable to a challenge from a re-energised Conservative Party. In the event of adverse economic and social conditions it seems entirely possible that 'disenchanted' swing voters might switch their allegiance to Cameron's 'modern' form of Conservatism.

*Source*: Getty Images/Max Mumby/Kelvin Bruce

# Summary

Building on the discussions in Chapter 5, this chapter has examined the changing approaches of the Conservative Party to social policy since 1945. It has shown that:

- Following the Second World War, and Labour's 1945 general election victory, One Nation Conservatism emerged as a major influence within the Party.
- During the 1950s and 1960s successive Conservative governments embraced a One Nation approach to the welfare state.
- By the early 1970s 'New Right' ideas became more influential in the Conservative Party. As a result, the welfare state came to be viewed as a threat to individual freedom and a drain on the economy.
- Although all of the Thatcher governments were committed to a radical overhaul of the welfare state, it was not until her third term that a concerted welfare reform programme took shape.
- During the eighteen years of Conservative government from 1979 to 1997 there were significant changes in the welfare state. The 'cultural' changes proved to be the most significant legacy.
- Following their 1997 election defeat the Conservatives made little headway in developing a post-Thatcher approach to social policy. Under David Cameron there has been an attempt to adopt a more positive approach to the welfare state. It remains to be seen whether this represents a return to the One Nation Conservatism of the past or merely a tactical modification of New Right ideals.

# Discussion and review topics

1 What are the distinguishing features of One Nation Conservative social policy?

2 Did the Thatcher and Major governments adopt a 'full-bloodied' 'New Right' welfare agenda?

3 Have there been significant shifts in Conservative approaches to the welfare state since 1945?

## Further reading

Blake, R. (1998) *The Conservative Party From Peel to Major*, Arrow, London. A useful introduction to developments within the Conservative Party over time.

Hickson, K. (ed.) (2005) *The Political Thought of the Conservative Party Since 1945*, Palgrave Macmillan, Basingstoke. An impressive collection of essays which outline the changing political, social and economic ideas within the Conservative Party since the Second World War.

Ludlam, S. and Smith, M.J. (eds) (1996) *Contemporary British Conservatism*, Macmillan, Basingstoke. This edited volume examines the impact of Thatcherism on the Conservative Party in relation to ideology and policies.

**Raison, T.** (1990) *Tories and the Welfare State*, Macmillan, London. Although now out of print, Raison's book provided an excellent overview of the Conservative Party's approach to the welfare state over the first four decades of the post-war era.

## Some useful websites

www.conservatives.com – the website of the Conservative Party provides a range of information, including access to speeches and policy documents.

In addition, there are a number of right-leaning think-tanks whose websites make available a variety of information and publications. These include **www.adamsmith.org** – the Adam Smith Institute; **www.centreforsocialjustice.org.uk** – the Centre for Social Justice, established by the former Conservative leader Iain Duncan Smith; **www.civitas.org.uk** – Civitas; **www.cps.org.uk** – the Centre for Policy Studies; and **www.iea.org.uk** – the Institute for Economic Affairs.

## References

Audit Commission (1986) *Making a Reality of Community Care*, HMSO, London.

Ball, S.J. (1998) 'Education policy', in N. Ellison and C. Pierson (eds) *Developments in British Social Policy*, Macmillan, Basingstoke, pp. 146-59.

Blake, R. (1998) *The Conservative Party From Peel to Major*, Arrow, London.

Buchanan, J. (1986) *Liberty, Market and the State*, Harvester-Wheatsheaf, Hemel Hempstead.

Campbell, J. (2000) *Margaret Thatcher, Volume One: The Grocer's Daughter*, Jonathan Cape, London.

Campbell, J. (2003) *Margaret Thatcher, Volume Two: The Iron Lady*, Jonathan Cape, London.

Conservative and Unionist Central Office (1947) *The Industrial Charter*, Conservative and Unionist Central Office, London.

Conservative and Unionist Central Office (1949) *The Right Road for Britain*, Conservative and Unionist Central Office, London.

Conservative and Unionist Central Office (1950) *This is the Road, the Conservative and Unionist Party's Policy for the General Election 1950*, Conservative and Unionist Central Office, London.

Conservative Party (1979) *The Conservative Manifesto 1979*, Conservative central Office, London.

Conservative Party (1992) *The Best Future for Britain: The Conservative Manifesto 1992*, Conservative Central Office, London.

Conservative Party (1997) *You Can Only Be Sure With The Conservatives: The Conservative Manifesto 1997*, Conservative Central Office, London.

Critchlow, D.T. (2007) The *Conservative Ascendancy*, Harvard University Press, Cambridge, MA.

Dale, I. (ed.) (2000) *Conservative Party General Election Manifestos, 1900-1997*, Routledge, London.

Ferguson, I., Lavalette, M. and Mooney, G. (2002) *Rethinking Welfare: A Critical Perspective*, Sage, London.

Gamble, A. (1988) *The Free Economy and the Strong State*, Palgrave Macmillan, Basingstoke.

Gilmour, I. (1992) *Dancing With Dogma*, Simon & Schuster, London.

Ginsburg, N. (2005) 'The privatisation of council housing', *Critical Social Policy*, Vol. 25, No. 1, pp. 115-35.

Glennerster, H. (2007) *British Social Policy Since 1945* (3rd edn), Blackwell, Oxford.

Green, D.G. (1996) *Community Without Politics*, IEA Health and Welfare Unit, London.

Green, E.H. (2002) *Ideologies of Conservatism*, Oxford University Press, Oxford.

Green, E.H. (2006) *Thatcher*, Hodder Arnold, London.

Griffiths, R. (1988) *Community Care: Agenda for Action*, HMSO, London.

Guillebaud Committee (1956) *Report of the Committee into the Cost of the National Health Service*, HMSO, London.

Haskins, R. (2006) Work Over Welfare: *The Inside Story of the 1996 Welfare Reform Law*, The Brookings Institution, Washington DC.

Heywood, A. (2003) *Political Ideologies* (3rd edn), Palgrave, Basingstoke.

Hills, J. (1998) *The State of Welfare: The Economics of Social Spending*, Oxford University Press, Oxford.

HM Treasury (1979) *The Government's Expenditure Plans, 1980-81*, HMSO, London.

Kramnick, I. and Sheerman, B. (1993) *Harold Laski: A Life on the Left*, Hamish Hamilton, London.

Lowe, R. (2005) *The Welfare State in Britain Since 1945* (3rd edn), Macmillan, Basingstoke.

Macleod, I. and Maude, A. (eds) (1950) *One Nation: A Tory Approach to Social Problems*, Conservative Political Centre, London.

Major, J. (2000) *John Major: The Autobiography*, HarperCollins, London.

Marsland, D. (1996) *Welfare or Welfare State?* Macmillan, Basingstoke.

Murray, C. (1980) *Losing Ground*, Basic Books, New York.

Murray, C. (1990) *The Emerging British Underclass*, IEA Health and Welfare Unit, London.

O'Sullivan, N. (1999) 'Conservatism', in R. Eatwell and A. Wright (eds) (1999) *Contemporary Political Ideologies*, Pinter, London, pp. 51-79.

Park, A., Curtice, J., Thomson, K., Phillips, M., Johnson, M. and Clery, F. (eds) (2008) *British Social Attitudes, the 24th Report*, Sage, London.

Phillips Committee (1953) *Report of the Phillips Committee on the Economic and Financial Provision for Old Age*, HMSO, London.

Sherman, A. (2007) *Paradoxes of Power*, Imprint, Exeter.

Thatcher, M. (1995) *The Path to Power*, HarperCollins, London.

Timmins, N. (2001) *The Five Giants* (Revised and updated edition), HarperCollins, London.

Tullock, G. (1965) *The Politics of Bureaucracy*, Public Affairs Press, Washington DC.

# 7

# Labour governments and the welfare state since 1945

Robert Page

## Chapter overview

This chapter begins by looking at the creation of the welfare state by the post-1945 Labour government, highlighting the way in which this programme of reform formed part of a broader strategy to create a socialist commonwealth. Subsequently it explores the revisionist democratic socialist stance of the Wilson and Callaghan governments in the 1960s and 70s where the welfare state was seen as having a key role to play in the pursuit of greater social equality. Finally, attention is turned to the New Labour governments from 1997 to the present day, and a consideration of the extent to which the welfare strategy pursued by New Labour represents a significant departure from previous post-1945 Labour governments.

This chapter provides:

- a guide to the key elements of the welfare strategy pursued by the Attlee governments from 1945 to 1951;
- a review of the revisionist democratic socialist strategy of the Wilson and Callaghan governments in the 1960s and 70s;
- the emergence of New Labour;
- a review of New Labour's approach to the welfare state.

## Spotlight on the issues
## War and social change

The Second World War provides the backdrop to Labour's victory in the 1945 general election. According to one official wartime historian, Richard Titmuss, the bombing raids on major towns and cities coupled with the prospect of enemy invasion led to an upsurge in community spirit amongst the British public and a call for a more egalitarian, less divided society. This public's appetite for fundamental economic and social change was reflected in their positive response to the publication of the Beveridge Report on social insurance in 1942, which promised to tackle the five giants of want, idleness, squalor, disease and ignorance. Over one hundred thousand copies of the Report were sold within a month of its publication. Although Churchill believed that plans for post-war reconstruction were premature at a time when hostilities were continuing, the Beveridge Report served to energise those seeking immediate reforms in areas such as social security, health and education. Although Labour members of the coalition did manage to reach pragmatic accords with Conservative members of the government in a number of social policy areas, both they and their grass-roots members wanted to press ahead with more ambitious reforms. It was only after their overwhelming election victory in 1945 that the Party committed to 'fair shares for all' was finally in a position to push ahead with their plans to transform British society.

For many people it was the 1945 Labour government that was seen as creating the post-war welfare state, building on the Beveridge Report and the proposals contained within it. However, Labour's aims for, commitment to, and use of different aspects of the welfare state has varied considerably over the period since the Attlee government.

This chapter explores the approach that Labour governments have adopted towards the welfare state since the Second World War. In the first section, attention will be given to the democratic socialist welfare strategy adopted by the Attlee governments between 1945 and 1951. The 'revisionist' democratic socialist strategy followed by both the Wilson (1964-70) and the Wilson/Callaghan governments (1974-79) in the 1960s and 70s will be the focus of the second part of the chapter. Both of these administrations remained committed to the creation of a fairer society but, unlike the Attlee governments, they believed that it was possible to secure such a transformation through expansive state welfare provision rather than through increased forms of public ownership. In the final section of the chapter, the New Labour governments of Tony Blair (1997-2007) and Gordon Brown (2007-present) are considered. It is argued that New Labour's approach to the welfare state represents a significant departure in ideology and practice from previous post-war Labour governments.

## The Attlee governments 1945–1951: Establishing a democratic socialist welfare state

After sweeping to power in the 1945 general election, securing 393 seats out of a possible 604, the post-war Labour government was provided with an opportunity to fulfil its manifesto pledge of creating a 'Socialist Commonwealth of Great Britain – free, democratic, efficient, progressive, public-spirited, its material resources organised in the service of the British people' (Labour Party, 1945, p. 6). For Labour, democratic socialism was not to be equated with the establishment of a more humane form of capitalist society. Instead, the new government sought to create an egalitarian and solidaristic society, albeit through gradual, constitutional means. The first phase of this transformation would involve the nationalisation of key industries, state regulation of the economy, progressive taxation and the introduction of an egalitarian welfare state. The focus here will be on Labour's democratic socialist welfare strategy.

### Creating a democratic socialist welfare state

There is an ongoing debate as to whether the incoming Labour government 'created' the welfare state or merely built on the foundations already laid down by both pre-war governments and Churchill's coalition administration. While there were a number of state welfare initiatives prior to 1945, the Attlee government's reforms were more comprehensive and based on distinctive democratic socialist ideals (Jefferys, 1992). The most significant transformative reforms undertaken by these governments were in the areas of social security and healthcare.

#### Social security

Although there was no explicit reference to the problem of poverty or want in Labour's 1945 general election manifesto, *Let Us Face The Future* (Labour Party, 1945), there was little doubt that the new government would move quickly to tackle poverty and establish a comprehensive social security system. Indeed, at the Party's conference in 1942 'a comprehensive scheme of social security' had been endorsed prior to the publication of the Beveridge Report in the same year (Pearce, 1994, p. 48).

In practice, the post-war Labour government followed the broad parameters of the social security scheme laid out in William Beveridge's (1942) influential wartime *Report on Social Insurance and Allied Services*. Under the Industrial Injuries Act of 1946, the state, rather than employers and private insurers, would in future take responsibility for compensating those injured at work. The National Insurance Act of 1946, the cornerstone of Labour's social security programme, entitled all insured workers 'from the barrow boy to the field marshal' (Griffiths, 1969, p. 84) to claim a range of flat-rate benefits (unemployment benefit, sickness benefit, dependants' allowances, maternity payments, retirement pensions and a death grant) at time of need. The third element in Labour's social security programme was the National Assistance Act of 1948, which provided means-tested payments for those who did not qualify for National Insurance benefits. These safety net benefits were to be administered by a newly established National Assistance Board rather than local authority Public Assistance Committees.

Labour's decision to pursue a Beveridge-style social insurance scheme despite its limited egalitarian potential seemed somewhat surprising. However, as Jackson (2007) points out, 'an egalitarian critique [of social insurance] was prevented from gathering support by a myriad of factors, such as the apparently overwhelming public support for Beveridge; the symbolic importance of the insurance metaphor; and all-important perceptions of affordability' (p. 139). The adoption of this less egalitarian social insurance scheme based on low level, 'affordable' flat-rate contributions made it extremely difficult to resolve the problem of poverty. Indeed, when Labour announced their National Insurance benefit rates in 1946 (42/- [£2.10] for a couple and 26/- [£1.30] for a single person), doubts were expressed as to whether those having to subsist on such payments would be able to avoid 'poverty' without additional forms of income. While Attlee's first Minister for National Insurance, James Griffiths, was confident that the scale rates would provide for a **subsistence** living standard in the vast majority of cases, not least if the period of dependency was short term, he acknowledged that the decision to use a standardised, rather than variable, rent allowance would result in hardship for those with above average housing costs (Deacon, 1982). Indeed, by 1948 some 675,000 recipients of National Insurance were claiming additional means-tested National Assistance benefits (which included a full rent allowance) in order to maintain a basic living standard.

Labour's decision to continue with a **means-tested** safety net benefit for the very poorest could be interpreted as a failure to remove the stigma of the Poor Law (see Chapter 5). However, Labour believed that the wartime coalition government's abolition of both the workhouse and the household means test in 1941 (under which the financial circumstances of the individual claimant as well as of all those living in the same household including children and lodgers were taken into account to determine eligibility) were sufficient to resolve the problem of stigma. Accordingly, they believed that the retention of a residual *individual* means-tested scheme, administered in a humane way, would not stigmatise claimants, not least because a more solidaristic public would recognise that such claims on the public purse were entirely legitimate.

In providing citizens with protection against the 'most abject destitution of the 1930s' (Jefferys, 1992, p. 21), Labour's social security reforms represented a major step forward. Of course, further modifications in both the design and operation of the system would be needed before a fully-fledged democratic socialist social security could be said to have been established, including less rigid eligibility criteria, higher benefit levels and more comprehensive support for all those outside the labour market.

It should also be noted that Labour's new social security measures formed part of a broader anti-poverty strategy which included the introduction of Family Allowances (which had been brought on to the statute book by the wartime coalition government) and full employment. As Brooke (1992) reminds us, 'Between 1945 and 1951, unemployment averaged 310,000 a year, compared to 1,716,000 for the period 1935–9. Only once, during the fuel crisis of 1947, did unemployment briefly approach the levels of the interwar period' (p. 16).

## The National Health Service

The National Health Service has come to be seen as the most notable achievement of the Attlee governments (Webster, 2002). Prior to the 1946 Act, medical care had been restricted to the better off and those covered by the National Insurance scheme of 1911 or by virtue of trade union or friendly society membership. Around 20 million workers (though, importantly, not their dependants) were covered by the National Insurance scheme which provided basic financial protection during periods of ill health, the services of a general practitioner (GP) selected from a designated list (the panel system) and a limited degree of specialist provision. However, there was no unified hospital system which meant that 'the privately run voluntary and publicly run municipal institutions operated side by side, with no semblance of co-ordination' (Brooke, 1992, p. 134).

Labour's new Minister of Health, Aneurin Bevan, was determined to establish a National Health Service in which high-standard comprehensive care was to be made freely available to all citizens. His decision to nationalise the hospitals represented a major departure from the coalition government's health strategy. In order to achieve this objective, Bevan acknowledged that he would have to secure the cooperation of hospital consultants. He achieved this by offering them generous salaries, thereby freeing 'them from the necessity to drum up business from GPs and rich clients to pay for their basic income' (Glennerster, 2000, p. 47), as well as additional merit awards in recognition of their loss of private earnings and their high levels of expertise. Bevan also upheld their right to engage in private work (pay beds were to be permitted in NHS hospitals) and ensured that they were properly represented within the new NHS administrative structures. Separate governance arrangements were also introduced to maintain a degree of autonomy for the teaching hospitals.

GPs, who were highly influential within the British Medical Association, were less persuaded by Bevan's proposals. They objected to the possibility that they might become salaried state employees rather than independent contractors and voiced concerns about the prohibition on the sale of medical practices. They were also uneasy about the 'oppressive' administrative arrangements of the new service that would permit medical personnel to be 'directed' to work in 'under-doctored' localities. Although Bevan's health legislation came on to the statute book in 1946, it was not until a few weeks before the service was due to become operational on the 'appointed day' (5 July 1948) that the GPs finally agreed, after long and protracted negotiations, to join the new service.

The concessions that Bevan made regarding a salaried service, medical centres and pay beds have been seen by some as a high price to pay for the establishment of a National Health Service. There are good grounds, however, for contending that the compromises Bevan made were necessary to secure a major improvement in healthcare provision, not least for the poorer members of society. As Francis (1997) concludes, the 'new medical service which Bevan had helped to establish had been moulded in accordance with a number of priorities which he understood to be distinctly socialist. The NHS fulfilled the principles of universalism, comprehensiveness, and funding from central taxation. It had also sought to establish that health care should be seen as an inalienable right, rather than a commodity whose provision was dependent on the vagaries of the market' (pp. 113–14).

## Housing

In their 1945 general election manifesto, Labour declared that they would seek to ensure that 'every family in this island has a good standard of accommodation' (Labour Party, 1945, p. 8). This proved to be an ambitious goal. In the first place, the post-war housing stock was in a poor state. It was estimated that some 200,000 houses had been destroyed during the war, whilst a further 250,000 had been made uninhabitable. Moreover, many of the habitable homes required urgent repairs of various kinds. Second, there was an upsurge in the demand for housing as millions of servicemen and women returned home, many of whom were keen to marry and start families. Third, there was a shortage of both building materials (much of which had to be imported) and skilled construction workers.

Bevan (whose ministerial responsibilities included housing as well as health) believed that centrally subsidised, local authority house building for rent represented the best way to meet the growing demand for housing in post-war Britain. Although Bevan recognised the importance of maximising the supply of new homes, he was not prepared to sacrifice quality for quantity. As Francis (1997) notes, Bevan 'insisted that new council homes should be buildings of a much higher standard than had previously been postulated for municipal housing. He was unapologetic in his belief that the working class had as much right to live in quality housing as the middle class' (p. 127). For Bevan the construction of spacious, albeit more costly, council houses that would stand the test of time, was preferable to building more homes of a lower standard. Bevan justified his preference for a Treasury-subsidised, local authority-led housing drive on the grounds that it would best meet the needs of those on low incomes who could not afford to take out a mortgage or pay high private sector rents.

Bevan has been criticised for his 'ideological' opposition to the construction of private homes for sale (Campbell, 1994; though see Francis, 1997), neglect of the privately rented sector (Glennerster, 2000, p. 62), administrative failures, 'over-reliance on privately owned building firms to deliver production' (Malpass, 2003, p. 600) and insufficient house completions (only 1 million houses had been built by 1951 instead of a projected 4 or 5 million). However, as Campbell (1994) notes, 'There was in truth no way that any Minister, in the economic conditions prevailing after 1945, could have met in full either the real housing need which the war had left behind or the inflated expectations which Labour had aroused during the General Election' (p. 153).

Labour's transformative vision was not limited solely to the construction of high-quality homes. An ambitious New Town programme, which was to become 'one of the great successes of post-war planning' (Timmins, 2001, p. 147) was introduced in 1946. Fourteen new town development corporations were to be established across the nation from Crawley in Sussex to East Kilbride in Scotland.

While it is difficult to take issue with Morgan's (1984) overall assessment that Labour's housing policy was 'competent' rather than 'outstanding' (p. 169), it is important to recognise Bevan's achievements in this sphere. As Jefferys (1992) notes, 'Bevan's house-building programme meant that affordable, decent accommodation was, as never before, within the reach of thousands of lower-income families' (p. 61).

## Education

Labour members of Churchill's coalition, most notably Chuter-Ede, had played a significant role in securing the passage of the 1944 Education Act. This Act was regarded by the post-war Labour government as a significant step forward and there was deemed to be no need to create a more 'distinctive' democratic socialist education policy at this time. Indeed, both of Attlee's education ministers, Ellen Wilkinson (1945–47) and George Tomlinson (1947–51), believed that adherence to the principle of 'equality of educational opportunity' and the introduction of 'free secondary education for all' (Francis, 1997, p. 149) were the key components of a democratic socialist education policy. Accordingly, they did not object, for example, to the competitive academic selection procedures favoured by the grammar schools, provided that working-class children had the same chance of success as their middle- and upper-class counterparts. Similarly, they supported the tripartite schooling system (grammar, technical and modern), provided that pupils were allocated to such schools on the basis of their skills and aptitude, *not* their social background. Although pupils would receive different types of education, there was to be no difference of esteem between the three kinds of school. In the more integrated society that Labour was seeking to create, it was envisaged that the technician and the craftsman would eventually enjoy equal status with the doctor or lawyer.

Implementing the provisions of the 1944 Education Act and raising the school-leaving age from fourteen to fifteen proved no easy task for either Wilkinson or Tomlinson. Wilkinson had, for example, to battle hard with Cabinet colleagues such as Cripps and Morrison to obtain the resources for the additional teachers and new buildings required to extend the school-leaving age to fifteen by 1947.

While the Labour government's efforts to ensure that all children, regardless of means, should be able to continue in full-time education until the age of fifteen was widely supported within the Party, they have been criticised for failing to grasp the deep-rooted impact of class factors in determining the type of school that pupils would attend and the socially divisive impact of a tripartite system of schooling. There were two main ways in which Labour could have pursued a more overtly democratic socialist approach. First, they could have given more support to the establishment of multilateral or **comprehensive** schools, not least in the light of growing criticisms about middle-class capture of the grammar schools and the deficiencies in secondary modern education, where pupils were denied the opportunity of sitting external examinations. Although both Wilkinson and Tomlinson were willing to see the setting up of experimental comprehensive *schools*, they had no desire to press for a 'national comprehensive *system*' (Francis, 1997, pp. 144–5). Second, Labour had proved reluctant to tackle the privileged position of the independent (private) school sector. The fact that a number of influential Cabinet Ministers were enthusiastic former pupils of these elitist institutions was one reason why reform was not initiated in this area. In addition, it was believed that any direct attempt to abolish private schools would prove counter-productive given limited public appetite for such reform. Rapid improvement in the quality of state education was seen as the best way to challenge the pre-eminence of the private schools.

Thought provoker

Does the democratic socialist approach to social policy have any contemporary relevance?

## The end of the Attlee era

The unity which had been such a feature of Labour's first term in office began to evaporate during their second term in government (1950–51), most notably when Bevan, Wilson and Freeman resigned following Attlee's decision to support the recommendation of his then Chancellor, Gaitskell, to cut welfare expenditure in order to finance hefty defence commitments following the Korean War. Although, as the Party's 1951 general election manifesto made clear, there was still much to be done to create a fairer society, there seemed to be little idea as to how this was to be achieved (Labour Party, 1951). Whilst Labour obtained a higher proportion of the popular vote than the Conservatives, they still lost the 1951 election.

Labour's success in establishing the post-war welfare state was a remarkable achievement not least because of the perilous state of the post-war economy. Britain had incurred wartime debts of £3,000 million and was heavily dependent on US financial support in the form of **Lease Lend**, which ended abruptly following the Japanese surrender in 1945. Exports stood at just one-third of their pre-war level and 40 per cent of overseas markets had been lost. Although Labour was forced to introduce a more 'austere' welfare programme than they would have wished, this still represented a significant advance in terms of both security and opportunity for British citizens.

## A revisionist democratic socialist era: Labour governments in the 1960s and 1970s

During Labour's thirteen years in opposition (1951–64), the transformative economic and social vision of the Attlee era was modified. Following the Party's electoral defeat in 1951 a battle raged between 'fundamentalists' and 'consolidators'. Those in the former camp, such as Bevan, favoured a continuation of the transformative economic and social programme begun under Attlee including more extensive forms of **nationalisation**. In contrast, consolidators such as Morrison and Gaitskell believed that Labour should be more cautious with regard to issues such as nationalisation, workers control and increased taxation of the rich on the grounds that such measures might prove unpopular with middle-class voters. Subsequently, a 'revisionist' democratic socialist doctrine took root within the Party. Anthony Crosland's (1956) book, *The Future of Socialism*, came to be seen as the key revisionist text within Labour circles. According to Crosland, Britain could no longer be regarded as an unreconstructed capitalist society, given the advance of democracy, increasing degrees of state intervention, growing trade union influence and the emergence of a more autonomous, socially responsive managerial class. These developments led Crosland to argue that Labour could now use different means to create a more egalitarian society. Importantly, Crosland believed that extensive forms of public ownership were no longer needed for the creation of an egalitarian post-war society. As he made clear, 'state ownership of all industrial capital is not now a condition of creating a socialist society, establishing social equality, increasing social welfare, or eliminating class distinctions' (Crosland, 1956, p. 497). Although Crosland acknowledged that greater economic equality was still required, especially in the distribution of wealth, he contended that modern socialism should focus on *social* equality. 'The socialist seeks a distribution of rewards, status, and privileges egalitarian enough to minimise social resentment, to secure justice between individuals, and to equalise opportunities; and he seeks to weaken the existing deep-seated class stratification, with its concomitant feelings of envy and inferiority, and its barriers to uninhibited mingling between the classes' (p. 113). For Crosland, high-quality state welfare provision in healthcare, housing and education was to play a vital role in his strategy of equality.

Crosland's emphasis on *social* rather than *economic* equality was based on the belief that any further redistribution of income would have limited impact on the well-being of the poor and would do little to address family–cultural disadvantage, which could only be addressed through state-provided services (particularly in education). For Crosland, the attainment of socialism was best achieved by *mechanical* rather than *moral* means. Unlike the moral reformer who seeks to create an egalitarian social culture in which the better off are persuaded by ethical arguments to support their less advantaged neighbours, the mechanical reformer believes that there are 'political, social and economic strategies available which would produce the desired results, without necessarily having to transform the underlying moral culture of citizens' (Plant, 2002, pp. 128–9). Crucially though, Crosland's 'mechanical' welfare strategy was dependent on sustained economic growth that provides 'a fiscal dividend for government to invest in public services which will have an egalitarian effect (at least in terms of social if not income inequality) and will allow the absolute position of the better-off to be sustained while incrementally improving the relative position of the worst-off' (ibid., p. 130).

Not surprisingly, Crosland's revisionist strategy, with its optimistic assumptions about the transformed nature of capitalism, found little favour with 'fundamentalists', who believed that this approach represented little more than a dilution of Labour's commitment to change. They were also concerned about Crosland's call for 'a greater emphasis on private life, on freedom and dissent, on culture, beauty, leisure, and even frivolity' (ibid., p. 524), fearing that this would give undue emphasis to individual as opposed to collective well-being.

Labour's third consecutive electoral defeat in 1959 convinced the new Labour leader Hugh Gaitskell, who had succeeded Attlee in 1955, that the Party was losing touch with influential 'swing voters'. In response to this setback, Gaitskell pursued a more explicit revisionist political strategy including a controversial, though ultimately unsuccessful, attempt to redraft Clause Four of the Party's constitution relating to public ownership, believing that more sceptical voters would be reassured that Labour's commitment to public ownership was selective and strategic rather than doctrinaire.

The debate about 'Clause Four' served to highlight the continuing division between the fundamentalist and revisionist wings of the Party. There were signs, however, that this rift was beginning to heal at the beginning of the 1960s. According to Pimlott (1992), two key Party publications, *Labour in the Sixties* (Labour Party, 1960) and *Signposts for the Sixties* (Labour Party, 1961) served to bridge 'the gap between right and centre-left and demonstrated the lack of distance between them' (p. 272). These documents made it clear that the Party's continued support for the mixed economy was now to be combined with a growth-oriented scientific revolution that would necessitate increased reliance on both public ownership and planning.

This emphasis on scientific and technological change intensified under Harold Wilson, who was elected as Labour's leader following Gaitskell's sudden death in 1963. As Jones (1996) notes, Wilson's insistence that 'a future Labour government would ensure that new developments in science and technology would be introduced in a purposeful way through economic planning rather than through the haphazard interplay of unregulated market forces' served 'to redefine Labour's socialist purpose in contemporary terms' (p. 77). This strategy also enabled Labour to reach out to aspiring middle-class voters such as 'scientists, technicians, managers and skilled workers – whose advance was held to be blocked by a privileged, complacent and amateurish Establishment' (ibid., p. 78).

The ascendency of revisionism resulted in social policy taking centre stage in the pursuit of a more equal and just society. However the success of this 'social' strategy was tied to the performance of the economy. Faltering economic performance would hinder progress on the social front.

## The Wilson governments 1964–70

The Wilson governments embraced the growth-led revisionist welfare strategy outlined by Crosland. Labour aimed to boost the economy by means of a scientific and technologically informed industrial policy, overseen by a new Ministry of Technology. A Department of Economic Affairs was created with the aim of devising a plan for increased growth. When the national plan was finally published in the autumn of 1965, an ambitious GDP growth target of 25 per cent over the period from 1964 to 1970 was set. In addition, an Industrial Reorganisation Corporation was established, which was 'designed to direct state investment into corporate enterprises, to gain greater governmental control over the private sector, and to change the structure of private industry' (Jones, 1996, pp. 78–9).

This economic platform was to provide the basis for the 'drastic reforms' that were deemed necessary if the major social services were to be made fit for the 1960s and 1970s. As the Party's general election manifesto of 1964, *Let's Go With Labour for the New Britain,* made clear, 'This will not be achieved all at once: but, as economic expansion increases our national wealth we shall see to it that the needs of the community are increasingly met. *For the children*, this will mean better education; *for the family* decent houses at prices that people can afford; *for the sick*, the care of a modernised health service; *for the old people and widows*, a guaranteed share in rising national prosperity' (Labour Party, 1964, p. 13).

A number of specific welfare pledges were put forward. In education, Labour promised to reduce class sizes, reorganise secondary education 'on comprehensive lines', increase the school-leaving age to sixteen and expand 'higher, further and university education' in accordance with its ambitious plans for technological and scientific advance (ibid., pp. 13–14). Labour also vowed to 'reconstruct the social security system' by increasing National Insurance benefits (and subsequently linking them with the rise in average earnings) and introducing a non-stigmatised Income Guarantee for pensioners and widows. In healthcare, prescription charges were to be abolished as a first step towards the restoration of 'a completely free Health Service' (ibid., p. 17). A properly funded hospital plan was to be put in place and the numbers of qualified medical staff increased.

Labour's narrow victory in the 1964 general election followed by a more impressive success in 1966 provided an opportunity for Labour to pursue its ambitious welfare agenda. Once in government, however, Labour was confronted with serious economic difficulties. It proved problematic to stimulate growth and investment, maintain the value of sterling, avoid deflation, control wages, modernise the economy, avoid 'stop-go' economic policies and retain international confidence in the harsher climate of the time. Moreover, various 'white heat' innovations such as the Department of Economic Affairs and the Ministry of Technology failed to ignite the economy.

Significantly, protecting the value of the pound in order to 'preserve Britain's role as a world banker and to keep sterling as a major reserve currency' (Morgan, 1992, p. 269) was given priority over the maintenance of high employment levels, growth and social expenditure. Accordingly, public expenditure cuts and wage and price controls provided some short-term economic respite for the government before they finally agreed to a devaluation of the currency in November 1967. In the event, it took two years before the new Chancellor, Roy Jenkins, could justifiably claim to have restored the fortunes of the economy at least in terms of currency stability and the balance of payments.

## Social policy in the Wilson era

Not surprisingly, Labour found it difficult to meet some of its welfare objectives because of these economic difficulties. For example, prescription charges, which had been abolished in 1964 in fulfilment of a manifesto commitment, were restored in 1968 as part of a round of expenditure cuts. The decision to delay the raising of the school-leaving age from fifteen to sixteen and the failure to publish details of a national superannuation scheme until 1969 can also be linked to the need to constrain public expenditure. In addition, although some 2 million new homes were built under Labour's housing drive (1965–70), the quality (system built) and design (high-rise) of these dwellings was the subject of much criticism.

Despite these economic problems, Labour made progress in a number of areas of social policy. Although they could not deliver on their promise to provide pensioners with a non-means-tested income guarantee, efforts were made to ensure that the incomes of the elderly poor were improved. Structural reform (the creation of the Supplementary Benefits Commission), more sensitive benefit procedures (a less stigmatised 'rights based' service), and a more generous and flexible payment system led to real improvements in the living standards of many poorer pensioners. The government also introduced earnings related unemployment and sickness benefits, increased National Insurance benefit levels and abolished the earnings rule for widows. Other initiatives included the introduction of means-tested rate and rent rebate system and a redundancy pay scheme.

## Controversy and debate

In a short pamphlet for the Fabian Society in 1966, Richard Titmuss used the example of blood transfusion services to illustrate the advantages of the decommodified, collectivist system operating in the United Kingdom over the market-based system in the United States.

The question I have raised whether human blood is a trading commodity, a market good like aspirins or cars, or a service rendered by the community for the community, is no idle academic question asked in a philosophical mood . . . I find no support here for the model of choice in the private market; on criteria of efficiency, of efficacy, of quality, or of safety. No consumer can estimate, in advance, the nature of these and other hazards; few, in any event, will know that they are to be the recipient of someone else's blood. In this private market . . . the consumer is not sovereign. He has less choice; he is simultaneously exposed to greater hazards; he pays a far higher price for a more hazardous service . . . The characteristics of uncertainty and unpredictability are the dominating ones in this particular component of medical care. They are the product of scientific advances accentuated . . . by the application of inapplicable economic theories to the procurement and distribution of human blood.                    Titmuss (1966, pp. 15-16)

How convincing is Titmuss' view that blood should not be a market commodity? Are there other welfare areas where the market should not be allowed to operate?

Significant developments also occurred in the area of state education. Under arguably the most famous and effective advisory circular in the history of social policy (10/65), local authorities were requested to submit plans to the Department of Education for the development of non-selective secondary schooling. As Timmins (2001) notes, 'by 1970 the proportion of pupils in schools that at least in name were comprehensive had risen from 10 to 32 per cent, and by the time Labour left office only eight authorities were actively refusing to submit plans' (p. 242). Labour also built on previous Conservative attempts to increase the number of places available in higher education. This was achieved by allowing Colleges of Advanced Technology to become universities and by the expansion of separate, though nominally equal, local authority-controlled polytechnics, which would specialise in more vocationally oriented programmes to better meet the needs of industry. The needs of non-traditional students such as those 'already in work' or 'at home bringing up children' (Glennerster, 2000, p. 127) were to be met by the introduction of the Open University's distance learning courses (Hall, 1975).

The Wilson years had also seen a concerted attempt to extent personal liberty in areas such as penal reform, homosexuality, divorce, censorship and capital punishment. Although a number of these measures came on to the statute book as a result of Private Members' Bills, few would take issue with Marquand's (2004) assessment that it was 'the courageous and buoyant liberalism' of Home Secretary Roy Jenkins (1965–67) that proved decisive in smoothing the passage of this legislation. Labour also sought to improve 'race relations' through legislative change in 1965 and 1968 and the establishment of the Community Relations Commission in 1968. However, its 'two-pronged policy' (Marwick, 2003, p. 133) under which increased protection for migrants who were legally settled in Britain was counter-balanced by restrictions on those seeking residence such as the Commonwealth Immigrants Act of 1968 (which was hurriedly introduced to prevent the sizeable migration of the Asian community from East Africa) proved controversial.

Although Labour's record on both public spending and redistribution (of income if not wealth) was creditable during its period of office, it failed to capture the hearts and minds of its own supporters or the general public in the way that the Attlee government had. In terms of equality, it was noticeable how some members of the so-called 'Titmuss group' (Ellison, 1994) at the London School of Economics were beginning to express doubts about the limited egalitarian impact of Labour's social policy. Such was the level of scepticism that the Labour government even had to counter the claim made by the Child Poverty Action Group during the general election campaign of 1970 that the poor were actually becoming poorer under Labour (McCarthy, 1986; see Tomlinson, 2004, on the validity of this claim). As Ellison (2000) sums up, 'the abiding image' of the 1964–70 Labour government was 'of a party beset by criticism from within and without, in many ways doing its best to maintain the welfare state that it had created but, owing to constant economic difficulties, failing to live up to the egalitarian hopes of its supporters' (p. 435). The 1970s were to prove no less troubling.

## The Wilson and Callaghan governments 1974-79

Labour's defeat in the 1970 general election led to renewed questioning about the revisionist democratic socialist approach which the party had been pursuing. Concerns were raised, for example, about the ability of government to exercise economic control in an era characterised by the rise of the multinational corporation (Holland, 1976). Critics of Labour's revisionist approach contended that 'the private sector of the economy was no longer responsive to persuasion and incentives offered by government, and that a major extension of public ownership into the private manufacturing sector was required if a reforming government was to deliver its economic policy objectives' (Tomlinson, 2000, p. 63). The establishment of a National Enterprise Board, which would take a stake in some leading companies in order to promote improved levels of performance, was seen as a key way of overcoming this difficulty. It was also recognised that a new concordat with the trade unions was required. A Social Contract was proposed which would commit the trade unions to wage restraint in exchange for government commitments to pursue full employment policies, high levels of public spending and the repeal of Conservative industrial relations legislation.

Although Labour's February 1974 manifesto was 'appreciably more left-wing than in 1964' (Timmins, 2001, p. 314), including as it did a promise to 'bring about a fundamental and irreversible shift in the balance of power and wealth in favour of working people and their families' (Labour Party, 1974, p. 15), this did not signify the jettisoning of a revisionist democratic socialist approach. Following their narrow victory, Wilson's minority government was unwilling to adopt the radical economic programme favoured in particular by the new Industry Secretary, Tony Benn (who was moved to the Department of Energy in 1975), and his deputy Eric Heffer. Indeed, both the Wilson (1974–76) and Callaghan administrations (1976–79) were unable even to pursue a moderate revisionist democratic socialist approach. Sluggish growth, high inflation and rising unemployment continued to dominate the political agenda. As early as the spring of 1975 the then Chancellor, Dennis Healey, was seeking Cabinet approval for social expenditure cuts in order to stabilise the economy. Further cuts were agreed to by the Cabinet in 1976 as part of an International Monetary Fund rescue package. These measures proved to be something of a turning point. Growing North Sea oil revenues and an upturn in international trade bolstered the British economy to such an extent that the possibility of winning a further term in office was beginning to take hold by 1978. Such optimism proved short-lived however as the latest phase of Labour's pay policy unravelled. As Tomlinson (2000) notes, the decision to 'enforce a five per cent pay norm when inflation was several points higher was too much for workers and unions' (p. 67). Although the impact of the 'winter of discontent' which followed was not as extreme as has often been asserted (see Tomlinson, 2000), it undoubtedly contributed to Labour's electoral defeat in 1979.

## Social policy in the Wilson/Callaghan era (1974–79)

The economic challenges faced by the 1974–79 Labour government restricted its room for manoeuvre in the area of social policy. Nevertheless, a number of initiatives were implemented. In the case of social security, the government fulfilled its manifesto commitment by increasing the level of pensions and uprating the value of this and other long-term benefits (except those for the unemployed) according to the annual growth in prices or earnings (whichever was the higher). This latter measure ensured that pensioners would be able to share in any growing prosperity. The government also introduced a State Earnings Related Pension Scheme (SERPS) in 1975 based on an individual's best twenty years of earnings. This was particularly beneficial to those whose earnings peaked at the beginning of their career, female carers and those with interrupted work records. A number of other benefits were also introduced including Child Benefit (albeit after protracted debate; see Field, 1982), mobility allowance, invalid care allowance and a non-contributory invalidity pension.

In addition, it was decided to abolish direct grant schools in October 1975 and phase out pay beds in the NHS. The impact of both these measures proved disappointing for many egalitarians as they actually resulted in an *expansion* of private provision. The vast majority of direct grant schools opted to rejoin the private sector rather than accept comprehensive status, while the lengthy phasing out period for pay beds did little damage to the long-term prospects of private medicine. As Timmins (2001) notes 'Just as abolishing direct grant schools had expanded the private education sector, so phasing out pay beds . . . helped the private medical sector to grow. By an awful irony, Barbara Castle had become the patron saint of private medicine' (p. 338).

Although there was less progress in the area of housing, Labour did freeze council rents on its return to office and introduced a Housing (Homeless Person's) Act in 1977 which underlined the importance of improving the housing rights of vulnerable groups such as lone parents and victims of domestic violence.

Persistent economic difficulties during this period led to more wide-ranging critiques of Keynesian-styled forms of economic interventionism and to suggestions that the welfare state was approaching a crisis point. Certainly, greater credence was being given to the idea that growing welfare expenditure might be having an adverse impact on Britain's economic performance (see Bacon and Eltis, 1978; Hickson, 2004). It was not just the rising cost of 'welfare' that was seen as problematic, but also the 'rationale' for such spending. In the case of state education, for example, it was suggested that too great an emphasis was being placed on the inculcation of citizenship values rather than on those competencies and skills that were more likely to have a beneficial impact on future economic prosperity.

When a general election was called in 1979 there were few (including Prime Minister Callaghan; see Donoughue, 2003) who thought that Labour would remain in office. As Seldon and Hickson (2004) note, the 1974–79 Labour government had been constantly criticised for 'mishandling of the economy, symbolised by the 1976 IMF crisis, for its failure to manage relations with the trade unions, culminating in the "winter of discontent" and for its failure to implement major changes in social policy' (p. 1). In contrast, the Conservatives under the new leadership of Margaret Thatcher were now viewed by the electorate as potential saviours of the nation with their heady combination of strong and effective government and greater reliance on the free market (Gamble, 1988).

Although Labour lost the 1979 general election they did not experience any dramatic loss of support (securing 36.9 per cent of the vote compared to 39.2 per cent in October 1974). However, their defeat led to growing concern about the viability of a revisionist democratic socialist welfare strategy. On the economic front the longer-term limitations of **Keynesian** demand management were readily acknowledged. Indeed, from 1975 onwards there had been a decided shift towards a more monetarist economic policy. As Timmins (2001) explains, 'the magic prescription of growth, public expenditure and full employment, paid for by higher taxation and perhaps slightly higher inflation, had ceased to work. Labour was discovering . . . that you could have the inflation and taxation, but without the growth and full employment' (pp. 313–14). Moreover, the downward pressure on welfare spending from 1975 led to increased scepticism about the possibilities of a redistributive welfare strategy.

Following their electoral defeat there was a concerted attempt to take the Party in a more 'fundamental' democratic socialist direction. A range of internal party reforms ensured that the parliamentary party and the leadership were no longer able to thwart the more radical policy agenda emerging from the Party conference and from activists. This leftward shift led a number of 'revisionists', such as Jenkins, Owen, Williams and Rodgers to desert Labour's ranks and form the Social Democratic Party in 1981, an organisation that later merged with the Liberal Party to create the Liberal Democrats.

The ascendancy of the left within Labour's ranks was reflected in the 1983 general election manifesto in which the Party committed itself to large-scale public ownership, protectionism, unilateral nuclear disarmament and withdrawal from the European Community. However, this move to the left proved short-lived. Labour's catastrophic performance in the 1983 general election, in which their share of the popular vote fell to just 27.6 per cent led to a renewed burst of revisionism (Jones, 1996). Under the leadership of Kinnock (1983–92) and subsequently Smith (1992–94), the party made a concerted attempt to change the organisation, image and policies of the party in an effort to improve its electoral prospects. Although these changes led to a steady improvement in Labour's electoral performance (30.8 per cent of the popular vote in 1987 and 34.4 per cent in 1992), the extent of Labour support proved insufficient to challenge Conservative dominance. It was only with the emergence of New Labour that an electoral breakthrough was finally achieved.

## The emergence of New Labour

Under the leadership of Neil Kinnock (1983–1992) and, subsequently, John Smith (1992–94), Labour repositioned itself in an attempt to persuade the public that the party was 'fit' to return to office for the first time since 1979. According to Shaw (1996), this reorientation involved substantial policy revisions including a retreat from public ownership, a 'rapprochement with industry', a firm commitment to 'fiscal and monetary orthodoxy', the retention of Conservative curbs on trade unionism, the abandonment of nuclear unilateralism and a revamped welfare state (pp. 184–5). This was complemented by organisational reforms which gave the party's parliamentary leadership rather than the trade unions greater power and control.

The revisionism of Kinnock, and to a lesser extent Smith, provided the platform for the creation of New Labour. Following Smith's sudden death in 1994, the Labour Party elected its first 'non-socialist' leader – Tony Blair (Morgan, 2004). In order to maximise the Party's electoral appeal, Blair and other influential 'modernisers', such as Jonathan Powell and Philip Gould, took their lead from the 'New' Democrats in the United States (Deacon, 2000; Greenberg, 2005) and sought to rebrand Labour as a non-sectarian 'progressive' Party that would appeal to 'middle' England. In practical terms this involved embracing the virtues of the market, the deregulation of financial markets, and reliance on service sector employment growth. It was also argued that the Party needed to sever any lingering attachment to public ownership, planning and deficit financing. A more circumspect approach to state intervention and public spending was also deemed necessary.

Blair's pro-market message was endorsed by the Labour Party at a special conference in April 1995 when Clause Four (section four) of the Party's constitution (which had 'committed' the Party, in theory though rarely in practice, to the common ownership of the means of production) was replaced by a broader statement of aims. New Labour's support for the market led them to adopt a more relaxed approach to disparities of income and wealth. Accepting that 'substantial personal incentives and rewards are necessary in order to encourage risk-taking and entrepreneurialism' (Mandelson and Liddle, 1996, p. 22), New Labour sought to avoid the criticism that it would govern in a way that penalised economic success.

New Labour's economic reappraisal had important implications for its welfare strategy. It was seen as necessary to move away from the position taken by former advisers in the 1950s and 1960s such as Abel-Smith, Titmuss and Townsend that the aim of social policy was to challenge market imperatives. For New Labour, the task was 'to develop an approach whereby welfare policy supports rather than obstructs the operation of a market system, and contributes to the economic goal of competitiveness in a more open economy' (Taylor-Gooby *et al.*, 2004, p. 574). Certainly, New Labour was fully supportive of what the Commission on Social Justice (1994) termed an 'investors' approach to the welfare state. From this perspective, a modern welfare state should operate in ways which helped working-aged adults avoid long-term dependency on benefits. Such claimants were to be encouraged to seek paid work, if necessary by means of compulsion. The 'modernisation' of the welfare state was to become a cornerstone of the New Labour 'project'. Although the policy prescriptions of the post-war Attlee governments were acknowledged as having helped to ameliorate the 'five giants' identified by Beveridge (Blair, 1995), more innovative welfare arrangements were now deemed necessary to respond to changes in the labour market, family formations and the growth of consumerism. It was argued that the inherent design faults in the 'classic' welfare state, such as 'dependency, moral hazard, bureaucracy, interest-group formation and fraud' had to be remedied (Giddens, 2000, p. 33).

The notion of a 'Third Way', which had been used by the New Democrats in the United States, and subsequently developed by the sociologist Anthony Giddens (1994, 1998), was employed by New Labour in an attempt to describe their distinctive approach to economic and social policy. According to Giddens, the demise of communism, the growth of global markets, changing family and work patterns and more diverse forms of personal and cultural identity had made the left/right distinction in politics increasingly irrelevant. His view was echoed by Tony Blair (1997) in his foreword to Labour's manifesto for the 1997 general election. 'We aim to put behind us the bitter political struggles of left and right that have torn our country apart for too many decades. Many of those conflicts have no relevance whatsoever to the modern world – public versus private, bosses versus workers, middle class versus working class' (p. 2). In a subsequent Fabian pamphlet, Blair identified four distinctive Third Way values. Equal worth was the *first* such value. 'Social justice must be founded on the equal worth of each individual, whatever their background, capability, creed or race. Talent and effort should be encouraged to flourish in all quarters, and governments must act decisively to end discrimination and prejudice' (Blair, 1998, p. 3). Opportunity for all was the *second* core Third Way value. According to Blair, this particular value had 'too often been neglected or distorted' by both the right, who had focused too narrowly on freeing individuals from coercive forms of state intervention, and the left, who had 'too readily downplayed [the state's] duty to promote a wide range of responsibilities for individuals to advance themselves and their families' (ibid., p. 3). Responsibility was the *third* key value identified by Blair. Contending that this value had for too long become the 'preserve of the Right' (ibid., p. 3), Blair stressed the importance of a Third Way reconnection between rights and responsibilities. 'The rights we enjoy reflect the duties we owe: rights and opportunity without responsibility are engines of selfishness and greed' (ibid., p. 4).

The fourth Third Way value is community. For Blair, an acceptance of the need for strong government to promote freedom does not mean that the community and voluntary activity should be marginalised as it was by those on the left in the twentieth century. 'A key challenge of progressive politics is to use the state as an enabling force, protecting effective communities and voluntary organisations and encouraging their growth to tackle new needs, in partnership as appropriate' (ibid., p. 4).

In response to some initial criticism that the Third Way was little more than a softer variant of the radical New Right Conservatism of the Thatcher years, both Blair and Giddens sought to highlight the 'social democratic' nature of the Third Way. In an article in *Prospect* in 2001, Blair declared that New Labour's approach is 'not a third way between conservative and social democratic philosophy. It is social democracy renewed. It is firmly anchored in the tradition of progressive politics and the values which have motivated the democratic left for more than a century' (p. 10). Similarly, Giddens (2002) argued that 'the new social democracy seeks to preserve the basic values of the left' such as 'a commitment to combating inequality and protecting the vulnerable. It asserts that active government, coupled with strong public institutions and a developed welfare state, have an indispensable role to play in furthering these objectives. But it holds that many traditional leftist perspectives or policies either no longer do so, or have become directly counterproductive' (p. 10).

Although this 'clarification' did not signify a retreat from the central tenets of the Third Way thesis that had been previously outlined, it did represent a desire to position New Labour as a progressive 'left' of centre political movement that wanted to combine the insights of earlier twentieth-century liberal thinkers such as T.H. Green, Beveridge and Keynes with some of the more traditional elements of social democracy. 'In the last century, the tradition of social liberalism emphasised individual freedom in a market economy. Social democracy used the power of government to advance social justice. The third way works to combine their commitments in a relevant way for the 21st century' (Blair, 2001, p. 10).

## New Labour, the 'Third Way' and the welfare state under Blair and Brown

In turning to New Labour's Third Way welfare strategy, six overarching and interconnected themes can be identified, the impact of which is reflected in many of the following chapters in this book. First, it is contended that a modern welfare state should be *active* rather than *passive*. For example, benefit recipients of working age deemed capable of undertaking paid work were to be encouraged to return to the labour market in order to avoid the 'debilitating' effects of long-term dependency on state benefits. To this end, New Labour introduced a 'welfare-to-work' programme shortly after their election victory in 1997. Funded by a windfall tax on the profits of the privatised utility companies, a 'flagship' New Deal scheme for young people under the age of 25 was introduced in 1998. Under this initiative, young people were first provided with assistance to help them find work. Those unable to secure a job after this initial stage were then provided with subsidised employment, full-time education or training, voluntary work or work with the Environmental Task Force. All young 'New Dealers' were denied the 'fifth option' of non-participation. Additional New Deal programmes were subsequently introduced. Most of these schemes such as the New Deal for Lone Parents (1997), the New Deal for Disabled People (1998) and the New Deal 50+ (1999, for those over the age of 50) were voluntary in the first instance. Those covered by these schemes were offered advice and information about opportunities for paid work. Other adults who came within the remit of New Deal for the long-term unemployed such as those in their twenties and thirties were *required* to receive advice and participate in job searches and training. This more stringent approach has gradually been extended to other groups. The Welfare Reform and Pensions Act in 1999 paved the way for the introduction of compulsory, work-focused yearly interviews for lone parents (April 2001) and disabled people. By 2006, lone parents who had been claiming Income Support for over a year, and whose youngest child was of secondary school age, were required to attend a work-focused interview every three months (DWP, 2005a).

New Labour recognised that a number of complementary measures were needed to smooth the transition from welfare to work and to provide clear financial incentives to return to the labour market. These included the introduction of a statutory minimum wage (1999), tax credits (a Working Families Tax Credit was introduced in October 1999 and was eventually superseded by two separate tax credits, the Working Tax Credit and the Child Tax Credit in April 2003), and a National Childcare Strategy designed to increase the supply of affordable substitute care for children up to the age of fourteen.

Welfare to Work has been an enduring feature of New Labour's 'active' welfare strategy since 1997. By the time of the 2005 general election, for example, New Labour was highlighting the need to reform Incapacity Benefit and enhance its Access to Work support scheme so that more people with disabilities could be encouraged to return to the labour market.

 Thought provoker

Is it possible to detect any elements of democratic socialist ideals in the welfare policies pursued by the New Labour governments since 1997?

The second of New Labour's themes relates to the *delivery* of publicly funded services. New Labour has rejected the Party's long-standing ideological preference for publicly provided welfare services. For New Labour the choice of provider should be based on what best promotes the public interest (Brown, 2003). As Giddens (2002) points out, the common good may be advanced by the increased involvement of 'mutuals, social enterprises, not-for-profit trusts and public benefit corporations' (p. 65).

New Labour's desire to encourage the private sector and voluntary bodies to provide publicly funded services has been particularly noticeable in the areas of health and education. In both of these spheres, New Labour has expanded the **Private**

**Finance Initiative** introduced by the previous Conservative government in order to finance its hospital and school building programme through Public–Private Partnerships. Under this scheme, a private sector contractor finances and builds a new hospital or school which is then leased back to the public sector. In addition to the defrayed costs of such projects, the government also benefits from the fact that these schemes have been 'designed to transfer risk for construction delays and cost over-runs away from the taxpayer and towards private sector companies who have strong incentives as well as specialist skills to manage those risks' (Giddens, 2002, p. 14).

New Labour's enthusiasm for private sector involvement has also extended to direct service provision. In the case of healthcare, Alan Milburn, the then Health Secretary, agreed a 'concordat' with the Independent Health Care Association in 2000 guaranteeing private health providers a share of NHS funding for routine procedures. Private sector companies have also taken on the role previously performed by local education authorities in a number of locations.

New Labour has also encouraged the expansion of 'independent', state-funded, faith-based schools 'on the grounds that they have achieved high attainment levels for their pupils' (Labour Party, 2005, p. 37). Under the Education Act of 2006, steps were taken to ensure that the subsidies for faith schools in the public sector were extended to more faith groups. New Labour also paved the way for the development of 'independent' City Academy schools in deprived areas of the country under the Learning and Skills Act of 2000.

Even those publicly funded schools and hospitals that remain in the state sector have been encouraged to adopt a more 'individualised' ethos. New Labour

*Source*: David Simonds, Observer 03 Aug 2003, The British Cartoon Archive, University of Kent, www.cartoons.ac.uk

wants all secondary schools, for example, to become independent specialist schools 'with a strong ethos, high-quality leadership, good discipline (including school uniforms) setting by ability and high-quality facilities as the norm' (Labour Party, 2005, p. 35). Although all of these schools will follow the National Curriculum, they will also have distinctive Centres of Excellence in one or two subjects.

In the case of health, all NHS hospitals and Primary Care Trusts can, following the passage of the Health and Social Care Act of 2003, now apply to an independent regulator to be granted foundation status. Although these Trusts remain formally within the NHS and will not be able to impose charges on NHS patients or exceed the existing resource share derived from private patients, they are to 'be free to set their own pay scales, borrow on the private market, enter into contracts with private providers, and determine their own priorities' (Pollock, 2004, p. 71).

New Labour's enthusiasm for diverse forms of provision has also been evident in the area of housing. It has shown little inclination to return to the traditional provider role of local authorities favouring instead a diverse mix of social landlords. Councils with a 'good' record of housing management have also been allowed to set up arm's length management organisations (ALMO) under which a board comprising tenants, councillors and community representatives manages the housing stock.

Prioritising the needs and preferences of service users is the third element in New Labour's welfare strategy. It is argued that although the public still want services such as education and health to be state funded, they also want individually tailored services that meet their needs and aspirations rather than the uniform and undifferentiated services of the past (see Blair, 2002). New providers or new configurations of existing services are seen as necessary to fulfil this goal.

In education, New Labour has, for example, responded to parental concerns about the inadequacies of teaching in some state schools by introducing the School Standards and Education Act in 1998, which empowered the government to close poorly performing schools and to dispatch 'improvement' teams to 'under achieving' LEA's. A 'Fresh Start' scheme was introduced under which a 'failing' school could be closed and then reopened under the direction of a new head-teacher and governors. New Labour has continued to publish school performance league tables on the grounds that parents will be unable to make informed choices about their child's prospective schooling without such information. The best-performing schools have been awarded 'Beacon' status to signify their capacity both to deliver high-quality education and to offer help and support to less successful schools. The establishment of a General Teaching Council in 2000 was an attempt to raise teaching standards, which were also to be enhanced by the introduction of performance-related pay.

In the area of healthcare, New Labour has endeavoured to cut waiting times for NHS outpatient and inpatient appointments. In its general election manifesto of 2005 the government claimed that inpatient appointment times had been cut from 18 months to 9 months since 1997 and promised to ensure that eventually no patient would wait for more than 18 weeks 'from the time they are referred for a hospital operation by their GP until the time they have that operation' (Labour Party, 2005, p. 58). By the end of 2008 patients requiring non-urgent hospital treatments were to be given the right to choose any approved healthcare provider for their operation. Under an Expert Patients Programme, many patients with chronic conditions will also be provided with an opportunity to 'take control of their own care plans' (ibid., p. 64).

New Labour has also attempted to make the NHS more responsive to the needs of the consumer by introducing a number of innovative services. These include NHS Direct (a telephone advice service that was dealing with 6.4 million calls in 2004), NHS Online (a website that had 6.5 million 'hits' in the same year) and over 40 NHS walk-in centres. These are due to be complemented in the future by the development of 'new specialised diagnostic and testing services; comprehensive out of hours services; high street drop-in centres for chiropody, physiotherapy and check-ups' (Labour Party, 2005, p. 61).

New Labour's fourth theme relates to opportunity. They believe that a modern welfare strategy should extend opportunity in society by tackling socially constructed barriers to advancement such as poor schooling or inadequate health provision. Improving opportunities, particularly for labour market participation, has been seen as a vital means of enhancing both individual and collective well-being. Policy has focused in particular on ensuring that every child has the opportunity to develop their potential. Poverty and sub-standard education have been identified as two central barriers to the achievement of this goal.

In response to evidence that a third of all children were living in poverty in 1999/2001 compared to just 12.6 per cent in 1979 (Department of Social Security, 1997, 2001), Tony Blair (1999) promised to abolish child poverty within 20 years. This was to be achieved in various ways including the various generic measures designed to improve parental income levels such as Welfare to Work and tax credits. The Working Families Tax Credit scheme, which included a childcare element, increased the average income of recipients by £30 a week more than the Family Credit scheme it replaced in 2000/2001 (McKay, 2002). Child Benefit (which can be claimed by all families with dependent children) and children's allowances for those receiving income support were also increased substantially during the first three terms of the Labour government. Although New Labour has failed to meet its interim benchmark target of reducing child poverty by a quarter by 2005 and seems unlikely to meet its 2010 target (a 50 per cent reduction), it has not abandoned its overall policy goal, as witnessed by a £1.7 billion package of support to lift 250,000 children out of poverty in the 2008 budget.

Other measures designed to improve the position of children include a national parenting helpline and the Sure Start programme. Introduced in April 1999, around 250 Sure Start schemes have been established in the most deprived neighbourhoods in the UK, providing health and support services such as day centres for the under fours and their parents. Like the earlier pioneering Head Start programme in the US, it was hoped that this scheme would enable poorer children to flourish once they started their mainstream schooling.

Many of New Labour's educational reforms have been designed to ensure that *all* children have opportunities to develop their academic potential. These have included a guaranteed, free part-time nursery place for all three- (2004) and four-year-olds (2000). Compulsory one-hour daily teaching periods devoted to literacy (1998) and numeracy (1999) have also been introduced.

New Labour has also endeavoured to increase the numbers of young people in higher education, where a participation rate of 50 per cent by 2010 remains the long-term goal (Labour Party, 2005). In order to help meet the rising costs of higher student numbers New Labour, in line with one of the recommendations of the Dearing Report on *Higher Education in the Learning Society* in 1997, decided to introduce student tuition fees under The Teacher and Higher Education Act of 1998. The initial method of collecting fee income has been modified from an unpopular up-front system to a post-graduation repayment scheme. Under the 2004 Higher Education Act, students from poorer families are eligible for reduced fees and a maintenance grant of an initial minimum value of £2,700 per annum.

In addition, New Labour has introduced what has been described as 'an entirely new "pillar" of welfare policy in the form of asset based welfare' (Harker, 2005, p. 267). A Child Trust scheme was introduced in the autumn of 2002 to provide all children with a 'nest egg' when they reach adulthood. Each child receives a lump sum payment, which can be topped up by relatives or (in the case of poorer children) by the state. The fund can be accessed at the age of eighteen and used for a designated purpose such as helping to fund continuing education or training.

New Labour's fifth value relates to the increased role they believe that individuals should play in advancing their own welfare and the level of well-being in their local community. In terms of the former, New Labour lays great stress on the need for individuals to understand that their rights to various forms of state support must be matched by a responsibility to use such assistance effectively. From this perspective various government initiatives in the shape of work, educational and other services and opportunities should be reciprocated by citizens endeavouring to remain in full-time education, acquire new skills, follow a healthy lifestyle and make appropriate financial arrangements for old age. In some instances such reciprocity has been codified. Under The School Standards and Framework Act of 1998, for example, the parents of school-age children are expected to sign a home–school agreement under which they promise to ensure that their child attends school regularly and to support the school's homework policy.

This emphasis on personal responsibility has been particularly evident in New Labour's approach to antisocial behaviour and criminal justice. While it remains committed to tackling the underlying causes of crime and helping communities deal with crime, New Labour has distanced itself from the 'Labour approach of the past' by refusing to excuse criminal or antisocial acts on the grounds of material or other forms of disadvantage (Labour Party, 1997). New Labour has reformed the juvenile justice system, introduced antisocial behaviour orders and legislated for the imposition of curfews for young people in designated areas. The parents of young offenders can now be issued with a parenting order, under which they are provided with guidance and counselling.

Influenced by the ideas of American academics such as Etzioni (1997) and Putnam (2000), New Labour has also emphasised the need for increased neighbourly and civic activity. This reflects New Labour's belief that the government is no longer able, if it ever could, to provide citizens with a guaranteed level of security and well-being. It has encouraged local councils to offer residents the chance to engage in their local neighbourhood so that 'social inclusion and mutual support' can flourish (DWP, 2005b, p. 51).

A focus on outcomes is the sixth and final theme of New Labour's welfare strategy. It is contended that the quality *and* performance of publicly funded welfare services can only be improved if rigorous targets are set for service providers and effective audit and inspection regimes established. The notion that welfare professionals, motivated by a public service ethic, can be relied upon to develop high-quality, cost-efficient services without such external monitoring is rejected. To this end Public Service Agreements with accompanying 'SMART' (specific, measurable, achievable, relevant, timed) targets were put in place. Some of New Labour's targets relate to highly specific objectives such as reducing deaths from cancer and heart disease, raising literacy and numeracy levels or cutting street crime and rough sleeping. Others, in contrast, have been devised to monitor the overall performance of public bodies such as local authorities. The Audit Commission has played a key role in formulating appropriate performance indicators and reporting on the extent to which local councils in England and Wales meet these exacting standards.

Although New Labour's commitment to targets and performance management has not waivered during the Blair/Brown era, there has been a willingness to refine these measures in the light of experience. Local Public Service Agreements and Local Area Agreements were introduced, for example, in recognition of the fact that the achievement of national targets often requires collaboration between councils, health authorities, businesses and the voluntary sector at the local level.

## Conclusion

Given that many of New Labour's welfare reforms are designed to bring about improvements over the medium to longer term, it is premature to offer any definitive assessment of the 'effectiveness' of their initiatives in this area (though see Hills and Stewart, 2005; Pearce and Paxton, 2005; Toynbee and Walker, 2001 and 2005 for interim reviews). However, New Labour's 'ideological' approach to the welfare state is sufficiently well established to enable comparisons to be drawn with previous post-1945 Labour administrations.

As was noted previously, the creation of the post-1945 welfare state by the Attlee governments was a key part of a broader strategy to create a socialist commonwealth. Innovations in social policy such as comprehensive social security and health provision were to be complemented by more radical forms of economic interventionism such as public ownership and planning. In addition, it was hoped that the upsurge in wartime solidarity would continue during peacetime, thereby breaking down class barriers between citizens. Although Labour's welfare provision was of a basic rather than optimal kind as a result of the parlous state of the post-war economy, the fact that the government made so much progress in this sphere is a credit to the tenacity and drive of the various Ministers concerned.

Although Labour enjoyed considerable popular support, it is important to note that its determination to transform society was somewhat in advance of public opinion at the time. Indeed, Labour's inability to devise a longer-term transformative strategy in the early 1950s after their initial burst of activity owed much to the realisation that their socialist vision was not yet shared by the majority of the British public. As Pearce (1994) notes, it could be said that while the Attlee governments proved successful in 'remedying the evils of the past', they found it more difficult to devise 'a challenging agenda for the future' (p. 77).

Although Labour's commitment to the creation of a more equal society did not diminish in the 1960s and 70s, both the Wilson and Callaghan governments pursued a 'revisionist' democratic socialist approach. Unlike the Attlee government, the revisionists believed that a socialist society could be created without the extensive forms of public ownership that had been deemed pivotal by the Attlee governments. The Wilson and Callaghan governments placed greater emphasis on enhancing social equality through redistributive forms of welfare provision rather than through what they adjudged to be 'ineffective' forms of income redistribution. Critically, though, the success of this new 'social' strategy was predicated on economic growth. Poor economic performance in both the 1960s and 70s served to undermine the revisionist approach. Indeed, by the end of the 1970s the long-term sustainability of an egalitarian welfare strategy was being questioned.

New Labour has turned away from both the transformative welfare strategy of the Attlee governments and the revisionist democratic socialist approach pursued by the Wilson and Callaghan governments. For New Labour it is no longer possible or desirable to transform society along socialist lines in an era in which free market ideas and practice have achieved global hegemonic status. Its approach towards the welfare state has been adapted to reflect 'new times'. For New Labour, a modern welfare state must work with, not against, the grain of market imperatives. For adults of working age, the welfare state should, according to New Labour, come to be regarded *not* as a permanent place of refuge or sanctuary from the vicissitudes of the market, but *rather* a staging post for catching one's breath before returning to the economic fray. Over-generous forms of welfare entitlements will, it is maintained, only serve to undermine endeavour and stifle the risk taking and entrepreneurial activity deemed necessary for economic advance. New Labour has also distanced itself from the principle of universalism, which it believes is ill-suited to a more individualistic age in which choice and competition are the order of the day.

Although New Labour contends that their welfare reforms form part of a modernised, left of centre, social democratic strategy, others detect greater similarities with the radical 'new right' Conservatism of the Thatcher and Major years. Given that New Labour has shown no desire to challenge embedded class inequalities or create an egalitarian society preferring, instead, to focus on the removal of opportunity barriers, it is difficult to conclude that New Labour is pursuing a social democratic agenda. If anything New Labour has allied itself with earlier forms of British New Liberalism and American progressivism which sought to create a 'harmonious' society by tackling inequalities of opportunity whilst accepting, or even embracing, significant inequalities of outcome.

## Summary

This chapter traces the welfare policies and approaches adopted towards the welfare state by Labour governments in the post-1945 era. It is argued that:

- The Attlee governments of 1945–51 created the post-war welfare state on the basis of democratic socialist ideas which emphasised equality and a major role for the state in both the economy and the provision of welfare.

- From the end of the Attlee era and through a subsequent thirteen-year period of Conservative governments, and during the thirteen years of Conservative government from 1951 to 1964, a 'revisionist' approach took hold within the Labour Party. This was grounded in the belief that a reformed capitalism could operate in the interests of the whole community and that socialists should focus on the achievement of social equality.

- As a result of serious economic difficulties, the Labour governments of 1964 to 1970 and 1974 to 1979, found it difficult to fulfil their promises in social policy, although they did introduce a number of significant reforms to advance personal freedom.

- Following a series of electoral defeats from 1979 to 1992 attempts were made by leaders such as Neil Kinnock and John Smith to 'modernise' the Party. The transformation in Labour's electoral fortune occurred after Tony Blair rebranded the Party as New Labour. The Party adopted a 'progressive', non-socialist economic and social policy that was modelled on the New Democrats in the US.

## Discussion and review topics

1  What are the distinctive features of democratic socialist social policy?

2  Did the revisionist democratic socialist governments of Wilson and Callaghan place too great an emphasis on *social* rather than *economic* equality?

3  To what extent has New Labour followed the welfare agenda of the Thatcher and Major governments?

## Further reading

Ellison, N. (1994) *Egalitarian Thought and Labour Politics*, Routledge, London. This book examines the different understandings of equality that have impacted upon the Labour Party from the 1930s.

Francis, M. (1997) *Ideas and Policies Under Labour 1945–1951*, Manchester University Press, Manchester. A lively analysis of the relationship between political ideas and policies under the Attlee governments.

Shaw, E. (2007) *Losing Labour's Soul?* Routledge, London. Shaw's book looks at the ideological underpinnings and tensions within the Labour Party during its period in government from 1997, with case studies of five policy areas.

**Thorpe, A.** (2008) *A History of the British Labour Party*, Palgrave Macmillan, Basingstoke. This book considers the history of the Labour Party from its creation to the end of the Blair era in 2007.

## Some useful websites

**www.labour.org.uk** – the Labour Party's website provides information on the party and its policies, and access to a variety of other materials (see also www.scottishlabour.org.uk – the Scottish Labour Party – and www.welshlabour.org.uk – the Welsh Labour Party).

**www.fabian-society.org.uk** – an influence on thinking from before the Labour Party's creation, the Fabian Society's web pages give access to its research and publications.

**www.ippr.org** – the Institute for Public Policy Research, founded in 1986, has been a major source of ideas for the Labour governments since 1997. Information about the work of the IPPR, its research and publications are available here.

**www.compassonline.org.uk** – Compass is a left-leaning organisation that emphasises the goals of democracy and equality.

**www.smith-institute.org.uk** – named after the former Labour leader John Smith, much of the work of the Smith Institute focuses on policy implications arising from the interactions of equality, enterprise and equity.

## References

Bacon, R. and Eltis, W. (1976) *Britain's Economic Problems: Too Few Producers*, Macmillan, London.

Bacon, R. and Eltis, W. (1978) *Britain's Economic Problem: Too Few Producers*, Macmillan, London.

Beveridge, W. (1942) *Social Insurance and Allied Services* (the Beveridge Report), HMSO, London.

Blair, T. (1995) 'Let Us Face the Future: the 1945 anniversary lecture', in P. Richards (ed.) (2004) *Tony Blair in His Own Words*, Politico's, London, pp. 97–117.

Blair, T. (1997) 'Britain will be better with New Labour', foreword to Labour Party (1997), op. cit, pp. 1–5.

Blair, T. (1998) *The Third Way*, Fabian Pamphlet 588, Fabian Society, London.

Blair, T. (1999) 'Beveridge revisited: a welfare state for the 21st century', in R. Walker (ed.) *Ending Child Poverty*, Policy, Bristol, pp. 7–18.

Blair. T. (2001) 'Third Way, phase two', *Prospect*, Vol. 61, March, pp. 10–13.

Blair, T. (2002) *The Courage of our Convictions: Why Reform of the Public Services is the Route to Social Justice*, Fabian Society, London.

Brooke, S. (1992) *Labour's War: The Labour Party During the Second World War*, Clarendon, Oxford.

Brown, G. (2003) 'State and market: Towards a public interest test', *The Political Quarterly*, Vol. 7, No. 3, pp. 266–84.

Campbell, J. (1994) *Nye Bevan: A Biography*, Hodder & Stoughton, London.

Commission on Social Justice (1994) *Social Justice: Strategies for National Renewal*, Vantage, London.

Crosland, C.A.R. (1956) *The Future of Socialism*, Jonathan Cape, London.

Deacon, A. (1982) 'An end to the means test? Social security and the Attlee government', *Journal of Social Policy*, Vol. 11, No. 1, pp. 289–306.

Deacon, A. (2000) 'Learning from the US? The influence of American ideas upon 'New Labour' thinking on welfare reform', *Policy and Politics*, Vol. 28, No. 1, pp. 5-18.

Department for Work and Pensions (2005a) *A New Deal for Welfare: Empowering People to Work*, The Stationery Office, London.

Department for Work and Pensions (2005b) *Opportunity for all*, Seventh Annual Report 2005, The Stationery Office, London.

Department of Social Security (1997) *Households Below Average Incomes*, The Stationery Office, London.

Department of Social Security (2001) *Households Below Average Incomes*, The Stationery Office, London.

Donoughue, B. (2003) *The Heat of the Kitchen*, Politico's, London.

Ellison, N. (1994) *Egalitarian Thought and Labour Politics*, Routledge, London.

Ellison, N. (2000) 'Labour and welfare politics', in B. Brivati and R. Heffernan (eds) *The Labour Party: A Centenary History*, Macmillan, Basingstoke, pp. 422-48.

Etzioni, A. (1997) *The New Golden Rule*, New York, Basic.

Field, F. (1982) *Poverty and Politics: The Inside Story of the Child Poverty Action Group's Campaigns in the 1970s*, Heinemann, London.

Francis, M. (1997) *Ideas and Policies Under Labour 1945-1951*, Manchester University Press, Manchester.

Gamble, A. (1988) *The Free Economy and the Strong State*, Macmillan, London.

Giddens, A. (1994) *Beyond Left and Right*, Polity, Cambridge.

Giddens, A, (1998) *The Third Way*, Polity, Cambridge.

Giddens, A. (2000) *The Third Way and Its Critics*, Polity, Cambridge.

Giddens, A. (2002) *Where Now for New Labour?* Polity, Cambridge.

Glennerster, H. (2000) *British Social Policy Since 1945* (2nd edn), Blackwell, Oxford.

Greenberg, S.B. (2005) The *Two Americas*, St Martins Griffin, New York.

Griffiths, J. (1969) *Pages From Memory*, Dent, London.

Hall, P. (1975) 'Creating the Open University', in P. Hall, H. Land, R. Parker and A. Webb, *Change, Choice and Conflict in Social Policy*, Heinemann, London, pp. 231-76.

Harker, L. (2005) 'A 21st century welfare state', in N. Pearce and W. Paxton (eds) *Social Justice: Building a Fairer Britain*, Politico's, London, pp. 263-81.

Hickson, K. (2004) 'Economic thought', in A. Seldon and K. Hickson (eds) (2004) *New Labour, Old Labour*, Routledge, London, pp. 34-51.

Hills, J. and Stewart, K. (eds) (2005) *A More Equal Society? New Labour, poverty, inequality and exclusion*, Policy, Bristol.

Holland, S. (1976) *Capital Versus the Regions*, Macmillan, London.

Jackson, B. (2007) *Equality and the British Left*, Manchester University Press, Manchester.

Jefferys, K. (1992) *The Attlee Governments 1945-1951*, Longman, London.

Jones, T. (1996) *Remaking the Labour Party: From Gaitskell to Blair*, Routledge, London.

Labour Party (1945) *Let Us Face The Future: A Declaration of Labour Policy for the Consideration of the Nation*, Labour Party, London.

Labour Party (1951) *Labour Party Election Manifesto*, Labour Party, London.

Labour Party (1960) *Labour in the Sixties*, Labour Party, London.

Labour Party (1961) *Signposts for the Sixties*, Labour Party, London.

Labour Party (1964) *Let's Go With Labour for the New Britain: The Labour Party's Manifesto for the 1964 General Election*, Labour Party, London.

Labour Party (1997) *New Labour Because Britain Deserves Better, The Labour Party Manifesto for the 1997 General Election*, Labour Party, London.

Labour Party (2005) *Britain forward not back, The Labour Party Manifesto for the 2005 General Election*, Labour Party, London.

McCarthy, M. (1986) *Campaigning for the Poor*, Croom Helm, Beckenham.

Malpass, P. (2003) 'The wobbly pillar? Housing and the British postwar welfare state', *Journal of Social Policy*, Vol. 32, No. 4, pp. 589-606.

Mandelson, P. and Liddle, R. (1996) *The Blair Revolution*, Faber, London.

Marquand, D. (2004) 'The Welsh wrecker', in A. Adonis and K. Thomas (eds) *Roy Jenkins: A Retrospective*, Oxford University Press, Oxford, pp. 109-38.

Marwick, A. (2003) *British Society Since 1945* (4th edn), Penguin, London.

McKay, S. (2002) *Low/moderate-income families in Britain: Work, Working, Families' Tax Credit and Childcare in 2000*, DWP, Leeds.

Morgan, K.O. (1984) *Labour in Power 1945-1951*, Clarendon, Oxford.

Morgan, K.O. (1992) *The People's Peace*, Oxford University Press, Oxford.

Morgan, K.O. (2004) 'United Kingdom: A comparative case study of Labour Prime Ministers Attlee, Wilson, Callaghan and Blair', *Journal of Legislative Studies*, Vol. 10, No. 2&3, pp. 38-52.

Pearce, N. and Paxton, W. (2005) *Social Justice: Building a Fairer Britain*, Politico's, London.

Pearce, R. (1994) *Attlee's Labour Governments 1945-51*, Routledge, London.

Pimlott, B. (1992) *Harold Wilson*, HarperCollins, London.

Plant, R. (2002) 'Tony Crosland', in K. Jefferys, (ed.) *Labour Forces*, I.B. Tauris, London, pp. 119-33.

Pollock, A.M. (2004) *NHS plc*, Verso, London.

Putnam, R.D. (2000) *Bowling Alone*, Simon & Schuster, London.

Seldon, A. and Hickson, K. (2004) 'Introduction', in A. Seldon and K. Hickson (eds) *New Labour, Old Labour*, Routledge, London, pp. 1-2.

Shaw, E. (1996) *The Labour Party Since 1945*, Blackwell, Oxford.

Taylor-Gooby, P., Larsen, T. and Kananen, J. (2004) 'Market means and welfare ends: The UK welfare state experiment', *Journal of Social Policy*, Vol. 33, No. 4, pp. 573-92.

Timmins, N. (2001) *The Five Giants* (Revised edition), HarperCollins, London.

Titmuss, R. (1966) *Choice and the Welfare State*, Fabian Society, London.

Tomlinson, J. (2000) 'Labour and the economy', in D. Tanner, P. Thane and N. Tiratsoo (eds) *Labour's First Century*, Cambridge University Press, Cambridge, pp. 46-79.

Tomlinson, J. (2004) *The Labour Governments 1964-1970, Volume 3, Economic Policy*, Manchester University Press, Manchester.

Toynbee, P. and Walker, D. (2001) *Did Things Get Better?* Penguin, Harmondsworth.

Toynbee, P. and Walker, D. (2005) *Better or Worse? Has Labour Delivered?* Bloomsbury, London.

Webster, C. (2002) *The National Health Service* (2nd edn), Oxford University Press, Oxford.

# 8

# Alternative approaches to social policy

Gary Taylor

## Chapter overview

The aim of this chapter is to investigate alternative approaches to social policy. It is argued in the chapter that mainstream approaches to social policy attempt to utilise the state to remedy at least some social ills and that they are concerned primarily with operating in the context of the capitalist system. The alternative approaches to social policy contained in this chapter are those that look for alternatives to state provision and ask us to reassess our place in the economic and social systems. It concentrates on the theoretical perspectives developed by Marxists, feminists and the Greens, and contrasts these perspectives with the political mainstream.

This chapter examines:

- a range of views on the benefits and problems of capitalism;
- the arguments for and against a welfare state;
- different perspectives on the benefits system, housing, health and healthcare;
- alternatives to the state provision of welfare services.

It could be argued that the current system provides us with everything we need. In large parts of Northern Europe and the United States, the economy is reasonably stable and vibrant. The state intervenes to varying degrees to provide its citizens with healthcare, education and a range of welfare benefits. What more could we ask for? The answer to this question depends upon what we value. Consider the following:

The assumption that capitalism is a major force developing the 'productive forces' overlooks the massive destructive role of capitalism throughout the twentieth century: two world wars and probably close to 10 million killed in numerous imperial interventions throughout the Third World. Moreover, the magnitude of social regression throughout the 1980s and 1990s in most of the capitalist world makes this a particularly inappropriate moment to hoist the banner of capitalist dynamism.
Petras and Vieux (1996, pp. 3-4)

Although the claim of universal patriarchy no longer enjoys the kind of credibility it once did, the notion of a generally shared conception of 'women', the corollary to that framework, has been much more difficult to displace. Certainly, there have been plenty of debates: Is there some commonality among 'women' that pre-exists their oppression, or do 'women' have a bond by virtue of their oppression alone?
Butler (1998, p. 276)

The Green Party knows that we are all interdependent and that many people need support at some stage in their lives. The basic aim is that all people should be able to lead an empowered and fulfilled life. We believe that every individual in society has an equal right to food, water, warmth and housing.
Green Party (2007a, p. 1)

It is apparent from the examples above that there is clearly not universal agreement that current forms of welfare provision are ideal. Indeed, for some of those who are critical of the existing foundations of the economic and social system, traditional approaches to social policy can only ever make matters worse by protecting an unjust system. But what are the alternatives? This chapter seeks to explore some of the variety of approaches that are sometimes advocated, considering in particular their perspectives on and criticisms of the existing system, and what these might mean for the way that we see and understand the provision of welfare.

## The 'mainstream'

When attempting to understand the development of social policy, we should remember that policies tend to be shaped by those who attain sufficient power and influence in the political system. It might sometimes be tempting to believe that at any given time there are two alternative approaches to social policy. If we concentrate solely upon the ideas advanced in Party manifestos and hurled at opponents in parliament, it might seem that the only opinions that matter are those put forward by the government and to a lesser extent by the opposition. This view of the political process would clearly ignore the opinions of minority groups and the myriad views expressed in society. It appears to be increasingly the case that young people, in particular, are turning against the current political system. Rather than join or vote for political parties, young people are far more likely to campaign for causes that are considered 'marginal' by the mainstream political parties. As one response, some politicians have argued that young people need to be taught about the principles and obligations of citizenship. According to this world-view, it is important to re-engage young people with the current system and to show them the benefits of working towards piecemeal reform (and even the conservation) of the current system (see Crick, 1998; Todd and Taylor, 2004). Such moves could be seen from some perspectives as a deliberate attempt to undermine political protest and the apparent popularity of radical views. It could instead be argued indeed that young people gain an interest in politics not because of slick electioneering and the political messages released by mainstream political parties, but because radical world-views (however bizarre they might seem) ask us to think about our futures in a variety of ways rather than to accept the status quo and to choose between political parties that sometimes seem to have more in common with each other than with significant sections of the British population.

The political mainstream is fairly safe. People with mainstream political views generally attempt to conserve and to protect society from radical views and move-ments. Mainstream views are of course culturally specific. What is mainstream in Britain will be considerably different from what is mainstream in Africa or in the Middle East. We must also recognise differences between the groups that inhabit the mainstream. In Britain we have a number of parties and ideologies that have been dominant throughout the modern democratic era. Mainstream political parties in Britain include the Labour Party, the Conservative Party and the Liberal Democrat Party (formerly the Liberal Party and the Social Democratic Party), each of which has enjoyed periods of office over the past two hundred years (see Chapters 6 and 7 for more in-depth analyses of Conservative and Labour govern-ments' approaches to social policy since 1945). Each party is associated with a range of ideas. These ideas are set out in Briefing 8.1.

What these ideologies and political parties share is a willingness to compete for power within the parliamentary system and to use this power to determine, amongst other things, the extent to which the state should intervene in the econ-omy and in social provision. We should recognise, however, that when ideologies are applied they are often adapted and diluted to fit the needs of the day and that the lessons learned from applying these ideas will in turn help to shape future de-velopments in the ideologies. The social democratic ideas of the **Fabian Society**, for example, influenced the policies of the Labour Party, which in turn impacted upon the development of social democratic ideas. Ideologies influence but rarely determine policy. They provide general guidance on what is possible and/or desir-able for the state to do.

For many in the political mainstream, the state should have a role in social pro-vision. Since the Second World War, we have become accustomed in Britain to see the state having some role in the provision of welfare benefits, housing, healthcare and education. The extent of this role has of course changed over time. As Chap-ters 6 and 7 make clear, both Labour and Conservative governments were willing to use the state for social reform from the end of the Second World War until the

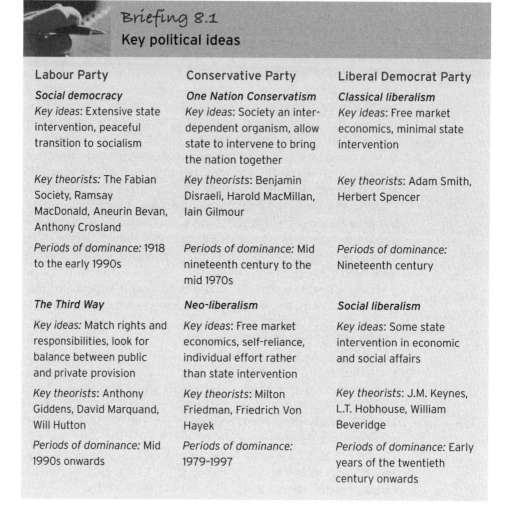

*Briefing 8.1*
**Key political ideas**

| Labour Party | Conservative Party | Liberal Democrat Party |
|---|---|---|
| *Social democracy* | *One Nation Conservatism* | *Classical liberalism* |
| *Key ideas*: Extensive state intervention, peaceful transition to socialism | *Key ideas*: Society an interdependent organism, allow state to intervene to bring the nation together | *Key ideas*: Free market economics, minimal state intervention |
| *Key theorists:* The Fabian Society, Ramsay MacDonald, Aneurin Bevan, Anthony Crosland | *Key theorists*: Benjamin Disraeli, Harold MacMillan, Iain Gilmour | *Key theorists*: Adam Smith, Herbert Spencer |
| *Periods of dominance:* 1918 to the early 1990s | *Periods of dominance:* Mid nineteenth century to the mid 1970s | *Periods of dominance:* Nineteenth century |
| *The Third Way* | *Neo-liberalism* | *Social liberalism* |
| *Key ideas:* Match rights and responsibilities, look for balance between public and private provision | *Key ideas:* Free market economics, self-reliance, individual effort rather than state intervention | *Key ideas:* Some state intervention in economic and social affairs |
| *Key theorists*: Anthony Giddens, David Marquand, Will Hutton | *Key theorists*: Milton Friedman, Friedrich Von Hayek | *Key theorists*: J.M. Keynes, L.T. Hobhouse, William Beveridge |
| *Periods of dominance:* Mid 1990s onwards | *Periods of dominance:* 1979–1997 | *Periods of dominance:* Early years of the twentieth century onwards |

mid 1970s. Since then, both Conservative and Labour governments have been far more sceptical of giving the state too great a role in the economic and social life of the nation. The old nationalised industries have been dismantled or privatised, the welfare state has given way to a welfare society and more room has been given to private and voluntary sector groups in social provision. But social policy does not merely have to operate within a framework set by existing elites. Social policies can and do make life more bearable in an unstable economic system, but social policies can also be couched within a broader programme for economic, social and political emancipation. For some theorists and movements, it is necessary to search for a new scale of values and to fight for a radical transformation of the economic, social and political system. As part of such programmes, social policies would aim to emancipate marginalised sections of the community. This aspiration can be seen clearly in the ideas of Marxists, feminists and the Greens. This chapter aims to make use of these ideas to show some alternative ways to view social policies and different ways to view the role and responsibilities of the state.

# The economy

If we are to appreciate a variety of perspectives on social policy, it is important that we recognise the ways in which our views on the economy influence what we expect from the state. The economic system is clearly an important framework for the development of social policies. Apart from anything else, it would be impossible for the state to finance an extensive social agenda without the resources generated through economic activity. It could be argued, however, that we need the state to play a part in coordinating or delivering social policies because the capitalist system is unable to deal adequately with our social needs. The capitalist system relies upon the buying and selling of labour power. There is little room within the capitalist system itself for justice, fairness, compassion or even decency. These are things that some people would wish to bolt on the capitalist system but the capitalist system, if unrestrained in any way, obeys market mechanisms. Employers will produce for profit and hire labour to maximise this profit. Failure to do so could put a business at a disadvantage compared with its main competitors. If the demand for a product increases, the employer might spend more on technology or on labour in order to increase production. If the demand declines, employers will cut back on investment on technology or perhaps spend less on labour. But before we get sucked into this and resign ourselves to this mechanism, we need to ask some questions. What happens to those workers who are made unemployed? Is there a benefits system? If not, how would these people live? Are the unemployed still eligible for healthcare? Will their children still be educated? If you were expected to pay directly for healthcare and education, you would have no access to healthcare or education unless you could afford to pay. The impact upon society would be dramatic. It is for this reason, amongst others, that social policies have been devised to compensate for some of the instabilities and inadequacies of the capitalist system.

Clearly, there are things that can be done to stabilise the capitalist system. State intervention to enhance the demand for goods and services and thereby assist in the maintenance of high levels of employment was a particularly popular method in the post-war period in Britain until it was largely overturned by the free market ethos championed by the Thatcher governments (Dorey, 1995). It is debatable, however, whether capitalism should be stabilised. It could be argued that instability is necessary for capitalism to flourish. Classical and neo-liberals argue with some force that individuals are motivated by self-interest and that individuals should be allowed as much freedom as possible to pursue their own economic interests. These types of liberals have argued that the state must keep out of economic affairs and leave the fate of the economy to the energy and vision of entrepreneurs and workings of the free market. Many social reformers argue that this view of life fails to acknowledge that we are all members of society and that our interests and responsibilities overlap and interconnect. For these reformers, found more commonly in the Liberal Party, the Labour Party and in the 'One Nation' wing of the Conservative Party, it makes sense for the state to intervene to stabilise the economy and to redistribute some resources to the poorer sections of the community by providing a range of social services. This is one of the ways in which the political mainstream can be seen as attempting to protect capitalism. If resources can be redistributed to ensure that all citizens have access to some basic economic and social goods, then the argument that capitalism serves only the interests of the minority is to some extent undermined.

The temptation to patch an unsound economic system with a package of economic and social policies is rejected by many radicals as a futile gesture that will do little to eradicate any of the serious systemic problems apparent under capitalism. Marxists in particular have been extremely critical of reformist measures. Marxists argue that the capitalist system is exploitative and that the long-term welfare of the workers cannot be improved through the state intervening to bring stability to the capitalist system. Because of this, measures designed to establish full employment or to control levels of inflation are viewed with suspicion. It is believed that such measures only prolong the enslavement of working class and con the workers that the capitalist system can tend to their economic needs (see, for example, Miliband, 1977). For many Marxists, the only long-term solution to the exploitation of the working class lies in the abolition of capitalism and in the development of a socialist economy where the private ownership of the means of production gives way to some form of communal ownership. Under these conditions, production for profit would be replaced by production for use in which all citizens would receive what they need rather than what they can afford. There are clearly ambiguities surrounding Marxist alternatives to capitalism. The point to note, however, is that Marxists reject reformist measures for ignoring the real problems created by capitalism.

Capitalism has also been criticised for serving the interests of men at the expense of women. Although **liberal feminists** are generally happy to operate within the confines of the capitalist system and work towards the expansion of opportunities for women, **socialist feminists** in particular argue that the subordination of women stems from the capitalist system and that the emancipation of women can only take place under socialism. If indeed the subordination of women serves the interests of the capitalist system by providing care for the young and elderly and a cheap source of labour that can be used during times of economic boom, then it could be argued that the interests of capitalism and those of women are diametrically opposed (Jardine and Swindells, 1989). For at least some feminists, attempts to stabilise the capitalist system will do little in the long term to serve the interests of women.

For some critics of capitalism, the current economic system not only marginalises sections of the population but also elevates human comfort over the long-term health of the planet. For the Greens, Marxist and feminist critiques of capitalism miss the point. Whereas Marxists and feminists believe that capitalism is flawed because it creates unjust inequalities and fails to serve the common good, the Greens argue that capitalism is positively dangerous because it encourages the use of destructive technologies and perpetuates rampant consumerism. The Greens believe that capitalism and industrialism are unsustainable. They destroy not only the planet but also the human spirit and our sense of community (Daly, 1977; Ryle, 1988; Dobson, 1990). It is therefore argued that if capitalism operates in accordance with such a warped sense of priorities, attempts to prolong its existence should be rejected.

The way we view the economy in general, and capitalism in particular, will have a significant effect upon the way we approach social policy. Those who are active supporters of capitalism are unlikely to want the state do anything that would interrupt the natural ebbs and flows of the capitalist economy. For those who wish to defend capitalism through reforms, it makes sense to look to the state to intervene to some degree in economic and social affairs. For critics of capitalism, it would appear that it might be better to leave the capitalist system to self-destruct rather than save it from the problems it creates. As we will see, the way we view capitalism tends to have a significant effect upon the way we approach social policy.

## The welfare state

The willingness to use the state to advance social welfare has become one of the distinctive features of mainstream politics in Britain and elsewhere. Once again there is plenty of room for disagreements over just how far the state should intervene in welfare provision. Classical liberals and neo-liberals believe that the social functions of the state should be limited to providing some support for those who could not tend to their own welfare. For others, the welfare state is seen as a way to tackle the injustices of capitalism. Modern liberals, One Nation Conservatives and much of the Labour Party would argue that the state should have a significant role in improving the welfare of all. Taking the argument further, many social democrats would argue that the welfare state provides a way to introduce socialist policies in a gradual way (Taylor, 2007). It should be noted that those who believe that the state should have a role in taming or regulating the capitalist economy will also tend to believe that the state should be involved in the provision of welfare services. For those who are positively convinced of the benefits of capitalism, the social functions of the state should be kept to a minimum. It is clear that for others these social functions need to be increased to compensate for the instabilities and injustices of capitalism. As we shall see, however, those who are critical of the capitalist system itself (not only its social side-effects) tend to be less convinced of the value of the welfare state.

Marxists believe that the welfare state is used to stabilise the capitalist system by helping to create the illusion that capitalism will see to the economic and social needs of the working class. Although many Marxists recognise that the welfare state can do a great deal to alleviate suffering and promote the well-being of the working class, it is viewed as dealing with the symptoms rather than the causes of the problem. Inequality is a necessary part of the capitalist system. Left without economic or social regulation, our well-being would rise and fall according to rhythms of the economic cycle. During times of economic depression, for example, many would sink into poverty and be forced to make the best of it. According to the logic of free market economics, this would be necessary to force us to overcome our own deprivation either by becoming more entrepreneurial or by taking poorly paid work. Marxists are quick to point out that although the welfare state might help to alleviate such problems, it also deprives capitalism of the slumps it needs to advance and regenerate. Given this, the state could find itself managing a stagnant economic system (Offe, 1984; Pfaller and Gough, 1991). Marxists cast doubt upon the value of the welfare state and even argue that capitalism should be left to its own devices. This is not because they want to support or defend capitalism but because they believe that the welfare state postpones the final destruction of the capitalist system.

The welfare state is also of questionable value to women. Liberal feminists are well aware that the welfare state can assist women in providing help with childcare and intervening to secure improvements in the employment rights for women. For these feminists, welfare states have a particularly important role in redistributing resources not only between classes but also between genders. Welfare states in Scandinavia are often held up as examples of what can be done to improve the social rights of women (Pateman, 1989). Influential sections of the women's movement have pointed out, however, that right wing governments in particular are apt to attack welfare provision for women. The George W. Bush administration in the United States, for example, was criticised for cutting Medicaid, Medicare, the budget for the Office of Women's Health and a range of other services that have a dramatic impact upon the health and welfare of women (see NWLC, 2007). Socialist and radical feminists, however, argue that the welfare state does too little to redress the imbalance in power between men and women. Pateman (1989), for example, argued that welfare states give rights to men and only concessions to women. If the welfare state is merely another means by which men exert their influence over women, then alternatives need to be found. **Radical feminists** would prefer to see women rely upon their own efforts and to cooperate with other women to tend to at least some of their needs (Charles, 2000). Feminist scholars in particular have been instrumental in showing how traditional approaches to social policy and accounts of the welfare state concentrated upon the interests of men, and how women were often relegated to positions of wives and mothers. It has been argued that social policy makers were invariably men who acted as 'social ventriloquists' who appeared to give themselves the right to speak for women. This makes the feminist challenge particularly important (see Bessant, Watts, Dalton and Smyth, 2006). By cooperating with other women, feminists hope that women can free themselves from both dependence upon men and dependence upon the patriarchal state.

The Greens are also critical of the welfare state. They argue that it is far too bureaucratic and intrusive in what it does and that it can only provide the current range of services because of the financial wealth generated by the industrial system. If the economy is to shrink and our priorities are to change, then it is clear that we will no longer be able to afford the welfare state as we know it currently. For the Greens, this would not necessarily be a bad thing. The Greens are convinced, like many on the right and centre-left of the political spectrum, that the welfare state does too much for the citizen and deprives us of power over ourselves (Green Party, 1997; Cahill, 1998). The Greens want to find alternatives to the centralised welfare state. In their view, power should be decentralised as far as possible and we should give more thought to developing social capital and broader social responsibilities within our own communities. This would provide greater scope for local democratic associations and it is believed that these associations could in time replace the industrial capitalist state (Achterberg, 1996; Fitzpatrick, 2001). It is clear that for many Greens the welfare state is dangerous because it is polluted with the interests of industrial capitalism. As the Greens are ardent critics of industrial capitalism, they show little regard for using the state to protect this system.

"Damn!!! Nobody's female, who's
going to go out & get the sandwiches?"

*Source*: www.CartoonStock.com.

For Marxists, some feminists and the Greens, the welfare state props up a repugnant economic, social and political order. For those who believe that capitalism harms significant sections of the population and/or the natural environment, attempts to humanise its operations or minimise its side-effects are viewed fairly cynically as the work of a minority eager to maintain its dominance. For these critics, the welfare state is seen as consisting in a series of concessions given to protect the interests of the existing elite. By attacking the welfare state, however, Marxists, feminists and the Greens often minimise the importance of social policies for the groups or entities they represent. Feminists attack the welfare state even though it provides maternity benefits. Marxists seem unmoved by the argument that the welfare state has a reasonable track record of protecting sizeable sections of the working class from poverty and destitution. The state would also seem to be important in protecting the environment. Radical critics of the welfare state, however, point out that such measures are only made necessary because of the imbalance of power within the existing system and that if anything of significance is to be done to improve the lives of the working class, women and/or the environment, this will require a more far-reaching programme of economic, social and political change.

## The benefits system

Many Western states provide a range of benefits including unemployment benefits, retirement pensions and family allowances (see, for example, Chapter 9). A basic system of benefits has been seen as an essential part of the capitalist system for many years. Such benefits were introduced in Britain during the early years of the twentieth century and in the United States in an incremental way since the 1930s. For the most vociferous defenders of capitalism, the benefits system is seen as pandering to the weak and depriving the recipients of unemployment benefits in particular of the will to compete and succeed. Classical liberals and neo-liberals in particular are apt to argue that access to benefits should be limited and that people should be encouraged to provide for themselves and their own families. For those willing to use the state to reform and/or humanise capitalism, the benefits system is seen as a way to assist people during times of need and to ensure that all members of the social organism are provided for. Social democrats and social liberals in particular have regarded having access to benefits as a social right. In recent years, Third Way theorists and practitioners have argued that the rights we have must be matched by responsibilities. Because of this, it is sometimes felt that access to the benefits system must be made contingent upon us taking some responsibility for our own welfare and (in the case of unemployment benefit) being willing to take advantage of opportunities for employment and/or training (Taylor, 2007). For those who frequent the political mainstream, opinions differ significantly on whether benefits should be seen as a right or as a concession. For those who see access to the benefits system as a social right, state activity is seen as a way to enhance the freedom and the security of the population. For those who believe that benefits are concessions granted by the state, it is argued that attempts should be made to curtail state activity and promote greater levels of self-reliance. In both cases, it is believed that the benefits system assists the poor in particular, even if it is regarded as something of a regrettable necessity.

It could be said, however, that the benefits system does not improve the long-term prospects of the poorer sections of the community. For Marxists, the benefits system provides a mechanism by which the responsibility for maintaining workers passes from the capitalist to the state. The provision of state benefits means that the capitalist can dispense with workers during downturns in the market in the knowledge that the state will maintain them until needed. The capitalists need not feel any great sense of responsibility for their workers. These workers can be hired and fired at the will of the employer. Whereas Marx (1867) believed that forced unemployment would undermine capitalism by reducing the market for what is produced and by instilling the workers with the revolutionary consciousness necessary to take on the system, the benefits system helps to keep the system buoyant. In order to be effective, however, ways must be found to prevent the development and abuse of a benefits culture. So that workers do not look at the provision of benefits as a long-term alternative to work, Marxists have noted how the state has stigmatised the receipt of benefits. In so doing, the capitalist is exonerated and those who receive benefits are effectively blamed for their circumstances (Ginsburg, 1979). For Marxists, it makes more sense for workers to find alternative ways to live in a capitalist system than to rely upon the capitalist state. For Offe (1984) finding ways to work with others in worker cooperatives might alleviate some of the problems faced by many workers. But even this is short-term. For Marxists, there would appear to be little by way of a halfway house between capitalism and socialism.

The benefits system can also be seen to discriminate against women. Feminists recognise that the benefits system is often set up in the interests of men. They have argued that it gives men rights to benefits but leaves 'dependent women' with little more than means-tested benefits. This has a particularly detrimental effect on those women who operate primarily in the domestic sphere, where the work they do is not seen as giving them the right to access a range of benefits (Oakley, 1981; Williams, 1989; Lewis, 1992). The solution to this, however, depends upon fundamental social change. Whereas liberal feminists might be content to fight for an extended benefits system (and one which does not discriminate against women), socialist and radical feminists are often faced with the dilemma of whether to use the state to advance their programmes or to join with others who renounce the use of the current state. Given the choice between dependence on men and dependence on the state, feminists may well argue that dependence on the state is preferable even if this is far from ideal.

For the Greens, the existing benefits system is fundamentally flawed. They believe that it has created a benefits trap that dissuades the unemployed from taking low-paid jobs (for fear of losing their right to benefits) and those in insecure work from saving in case it disqualifies them from receiving benefits at a later date (Green Party, 2000a; Elkins, 1986). Rather than cut back on benefits, the Greens have argued that a basic income should be given to all people as an unconditional right. This income would be paid regardless of whether we were in paid employment or involved in caring for our families. It is hoped the money necessary to finance this system could be raised by increasing taxation, reducing expenditure on the military and withdrawing subsidies available for corporations. From a Green point of view, access to benefits should be a right rather than a concession. Giving everybody the right to a basic income is seen as a way to encourage people to take on a variety of roles, some of which could be outside of paid employment. With the guarantee of a basic income, it is possible that some people would choose to spend their time doing voluntary work or caring for others in their family or community. Whereas the existing benefits system can dissuade people from working and from community activity, it is believed that a guaranteed basic income could be liberating in a variety of ways.

Mainstream views on the benefits system tend to focus upon the need to set access to benefits in a way so as not to undermine the will to work and sense of individual responsibility of the recipient. This might involve setting benefits at a low level or attaching a stigma to those who are dependent on the receipt of benefits. Radical critics of this system attempt to show how the benefits system operates to preserve capitalism and how it gives the capitalist state considerable powers to intrude upon and effectively police the poorer sections of the community. They show, in a variety of ways, how the existing benefits system is demoralising and how it undermines self-respect and the willingness of people to participate in the life of the community. Although it could be conceded that cooperative or mutual aid ventures could help to alleviate the situation, it should be noted that such schemes operate within capitalism and address (in a fairly piecemeal way) problems that stem from capitalism itself. As always, radical critics insist that only radical or revolutionary change in the economic and social system can provide a solution to this problem.

Thought provoker

The benefits system is probably the most unpopular feature of the welfare state. For those who are in receipt of benefits, it might be seen an overly bureaucratic and intrusive system. For those who believe that they will never have to rely on benefits, it might be regarded as pandering to the 'weak' and as an unnecessary addition to their tax burden.

If you had the power to change the benefits system, what would you do?

In addressing this question, it would be useful if you considered who would benefit from the changes you propose.

## Housing

Capitalism is based on the private ownership of the means of production and places a positive value upon private property. Defenders of capitalism claim that capitalism allows room for individual freedom and for the accumulation of wealth by those with sufficient talent. The capitalist system also allows individuals to accumulate property and to make money in the form of rents. Defenders of capitalism will point out that the public ownership of property deprives individuals of freedom and that we should aspire to own our own homes. Whereas some social reformers are willing to allow the state to intervene in the housing market and provide subsidised housing, neo-liberals argue that the public provision of housing is against the natural order of things and undermines the development of individual responsibility (Taylor, 2007). For many in the mainstream, the current mixed economy of housing is the best that can be hoped for. This mixed economy consists in extensive private ownership alongside pockets of state or housing association property. This allows for those who can afford it to own their own homes and those who cannot to choose from a variety of providers.

Radicals tend to be sceptical of the motives behind state involvement in housing. Whilst acknowledging that social housing can benefit the poor, Marxists point out that this form of housing was developed to relieve pressure on employers for higher wages and that it provides the state with another weapon of social control which it can use against the working class (Ginsburg, 1979). Although the long-term solution to housing problems might for Marxists involve the state control of housing and the distribution of housing according to social need, housing cooperatives could provide an immediate alternative to social housing or renting from the private sector.

Feminists are likewise unimpressed by the current shape of housing policy. Feminists have argued that housing policies tend to favour fairly traditional family structures and that women often face severe housing problems, especially if the woman is a single parent and on a low income (Woods, 1996). Women have been particularly active in establishing women-only cooperatives and in providing suitable accommodation for women who are fleeing from domestic violence (Charles, 2000). These ventures allow women to remain relatively free in their housing from the intrusive powers of both men and of the welfare state.

For the Greens, corporate interests have hijacked housing policy to a large extent. The Greens believe that the planning priorities of local councils do little to address the urgent housing needs of the poor. Local authorities have been criticised for concentrating far too much on attracting the business sector and on building developments to attract wealthy foreign clients (Spretnak and Capra, 1985; Monbiot, 2001). Whilst the Greens are generally supportive of social housing, they are far more interested in seeing the further development of housing associations and housing cooperatives. They believe that the state could assist in these developments by helping with set-up costs and with financing architectural and planning services (Kemp and Wall, 1990; Ferris, 1995). For the Greens, as for some Marxists and Feminists, the alternative to state and private sector housing lies in people joining together in cooperative ventures.

Although consistently sceptical of the capitalist state, Marxists, feminists and the Greens are far from supporters of the private sector in housing. They recognise that those who are unable to afford their own property can be at the mercy of unscrupulous property owners. State provision offers an alternative but this is often at a cost. Everything that strengthens the surveillance powers of the capitalist state poses a potential danger. Radicals are aware that the state provides welfare services in part to keep the socially excluded in a welfare comfort zone. For radicals, it is important to find alternatives to both state and private provision. Housing cooperatives provide an interesting alternative and one that allows people to join with others who embrace alternative world-views.

 Thought provoker

It could be argued that by providing social housing, the state has done all it needs to attend to the housing needs of the less privileged sections of the community. Radical critics, however, have shown that the state has used social housing to monitor and control behaviour.

Should the state have such powers and what are the implications for civil rights?

In addressing this question, it would be useful to consider the rights of the tenant, the neighbours and the state.

## Healthcare

The state has an important role in providing and coordinating healthcare in Britain and in many other Western countries. This state provision usually exists alongside private practice and often aims to provide all people with at least some basic healthcare. Social liberals and social democrats generally support this system of public provision but neo-liberals and the New Right often view it less enthusiastically. It could be argued that health is a social product and that the state should therefore have an active role in providing free or subsidised healthcare. The Labour Party and the Liberal Party in Britain have put forward this argument consistently since the Second World War. The Democratic Party in the United

States has voiced similar arguments since the 1960s. Conservatives on the right of the Conservative Party in Britain and in the Republican Party in the United States tend to be less convinced of the importance of state intervention in the provision of healthcare. It is clear that, for some, health is a personal possession. If this is the case, then we are responsible for our own health and should not look to the state to tend to our health needs.

Although it might be tempting to believe that the state provides healthcare out of compassion or in the interests of social justice, radicals have pointed out that the state provision and coordination of healthcare serves the interests of the capitalist system. Marxists in particular have criticised the state provision of healthcare in the belief that it serves the interests of the capitalist class by keeping workers fit for exploitation (Navarro, 1978). It is, however, difficult for Marxists to find an alternative to the state provision of healthcare, especially when this might mean reliance on the private sector. This does not necessarily take anything away from their conviction that state activity in healthcare should be seen (alongside other areas of social provision) in its economic context.

The radical critique of the state provision of healthcare also has a gender dimension. Feminists have argued that men use the state healthcare system to exert control over women. Feminists are deeply suspicious of the ways in which men attempt to exert control over reproduction and of the over-representation of women patients in psychiatric units. They point out that men control the state health system in Britain and run it in the interests of men (Lewis, 1992; Baggott, 1998). If the patriarchal control of healthcare is to be undermined, it is argued that attempts should be made to increase the role and prominence of women in healthcare. This could include improving the profile and responsibilities of women in the state healthcare system, perhaps by transferring some power from doctors (an occupation dominated by men) to nurses (traditionally dominated by women). Self-help groups could also be important, especially where women run these groups (Baggott, 1998). In this way, power relations within the health system could be altered.

Even if such inequalities could be eradicated, it might be that the state healthcare system fails to address important aspects of health. The Greens have argued that the National Health Service in Britain dedicates too many resources to treating the symptoms (rather than the causes) of poor health. It is argued that environmental factors are generally ignored and that not enough is made of the responsibility we have as individuals for our own state of health. For the Greens, the health system repairs us when needed rather than empower us to live healthy lives (Kemp and Wall, 1990; Green Party, 2000b). As an alternative, the Greens are in favour of tackling the environmental causes of poor health and on relying less upon conventional medicine. It is believed that conventional medicines (and medical practice) will only ever treat the symptoms of poor health and that a more holistic approach needs to be taken. Such alternative therapies as acupuncture, herbalism and homeopathy are favoured because of their patient-centred approach and the Greens have argued that far more resources need to be put into health promotion programmes (Green Party, 2000b; George and Wilding, 1994). For the Greens, the type of healthcare we get is far more important than who delivers this care.

For many of the mainstream political parties, maintaining a state-funded National Health Service has been one of the top priorities since the end of the Second World War. Even the Thatcher governments, which attacked significant sections of the welfare state, stopped short of privatising the National Health Service (see Chapter 6). For many radicals, the state provision of healthcare is something of a mixed blessing and there is a greater tendency to embrace alternative approaches to healthcare. This is seen in the support given by feminists for self-help groups and in the Greens' praise for alternative therapies. Rather than provide a uniform system of healthcare, radicals are more likely to call upon the state to subsidise or finance a range of self-governing alternatives. This could help to make alternative healthcare more affordable for a greater number of people.

# Education

As with other areas of social policy, the state has taken an increasing role in the provision and coordination of education. Indeed, state involvement in schooling precedes many of the areas of social policy dealt with in this chapter. It was recognised in the early stages of industrialism that people needed some education to function in the new world of work. Education reformers were keen to point out that state investment in education would benefit the capitalist system and that an uneducated workforce would be inefficient and extremely difficult to manage. State involvement in the provision of education tends to appeal to a broad range of political persuasions. For social reformers, education provides a means to liberate people and to create greater levels of equality. For conservatives, public provision of education is valued because it can be used to transmit important social values and to protect the fundamentals of the existing system (Taylor, 2007). Given this, debates are more likely to take place over the content rather than the existence of public education.

It is clear that for radicals the education system poses a potential threat to alternative world-views. Marxists have often found it difficult to reconcile the benefits of education with the ways in which it is used to maintain the capitalist system. The state education system has been criticised by Marxists because it provides the state with an effective way to transmit capitalist values to society (Offe, 1976). Once again, it would be difficult for Marxists to find alternatives to this. It is clear that Marxists would not wish to support private education, given that such education has traditionally been used by privileged sections of society to maintain their position. Organisations like the **Workers' Education Association** could be particularly important in challenging the dominance of capitalist values by providing an alternative system of adult education, but by then the damage could have been done by a narrowly focused school curriculum.

Whilst recognising that education has an important part to play in the advancement of women, feminists are likewise suspicious of the existing education system. Feminists have criticised the education system in Britain and in America for attempting to perpetuate inequalities between boys and girls by pushing girls into 'softer' subjects and thereby keeping them out of the corridors of power

(Frieden, 1971). They have consistently challenged these inequalities and pushed for reform in the education system. Feminists were at the forefront of arguing for the development of part-time provision in further and higher education. It was believed that such education would be particularly beneficial for women who wanted to return to education, especially where the woman was attempting to combine education with a busy home life and career (Frieden, 1971; Firestone, 1979). Feminists are adamant that the education system has to be adapted to suit the needs of all citizens.

The Greens are also critical of modern state education. They point out, like Marxists, that the modern education system was developed to equip people with the skills necessary to work in the industrial system. The system serves capitalism by offering a limited curriculum and by encouraging a hierarchal world-view (Bookchin, 1990; Green Party, 2000c). The Greens are willing to give far more support to private and alternative schools, especially those that concentrate on the holistic development of the individual rather than conventional academic attainment. For the Greens, it is important that we learn social skills, the importance of questioning and scrutinising the information we receive and how to advance our abilities as self-directed learners (Kemp and Wall, 1990; Green Party, 2000c). From a Green point of view, education is far more about personal development than about learning to function in the industrial world.

That the education system provides us with the opportunities to gain the skills and knowledge necessary to function well and even thrive in the current economic system could be seen as a good thing. If this education is financed by public money, then perhaps it should serve the public good. By equipping the workforce with relevant skills, the education system can help to build a prosperous economy. But surely there is more to education than this and those who reject capitalism and yearn for a radically different economic, social and political system are quick to point out that state education under capitalism helps to perpetuate inequalities and injustices. For these radicals, it is important to look for alternative ways to educate our young and assist in the development of our citizens.

## Controversy and debate

Education can be seen as one of the key mechanisms used to enable individuals to prosper and to compete well in a capitalist society. This view of education sees education primarily as an individual possession. Consider the position of the Conservative Party:

Conservative education policy is driven by a moral imperative - the need to make the most of every individual talent. We believe in raising the bar for achievement in Britain, helping every child to acquire a more comprehensive array of skills and providing them with the knowledge to become authors of their own life stories. We believe that ensuring every child has an excellent education is the principal role the state can play in making opportunity more equal. We plan to raise the standards of the worst-performing schools so they can catch up with the best. We will reverse the trend in Britain's schools which has those from disadvantaged backgrounds falling further and further behind with each year that passes. We will ensure those whom the state has failed most badly are given fresh hope by making our state education system excellent for all. And we will ensure that coasting schools face searching new scrutiny to guarantee improved standards for everyone. Our education reform plan, outlined in these pages, is driven by our commitment to social justice – a society made more equal by dispersing opportunity both more widely, and more fairly. We believe that education is the most powerful means by which individuals can be given the opportunity to shape their own futures. And we think there is a moral duty to secure change as quickly as possible before the gap between the fortunate and the forgotten grows wider.

Conservative Party (2007, p. 10)

State control of the education system can be seen a dangerous weapon. According to radicals, it can be used to indoctrinate the young and make us into the kind of citizens needed to serve the capitalist system. For many radicals, it is important to look beyond serving capitalism and to appreciate the wider benefits of education. This is what the Greens have to say:

Learning is a natural human activity which takes place from birth to death in an untold variety of situations, planned and unplanned, alone or with others. An education system should enhance, rather than inhibit, this natural activity, offering resources, teachers, opportunities, structures and challenges. In a Green society the education system will not be geared towards economic dominance, but towards co-operation, enlightenment, emancipation, and the nurturing of each individual.

Green Party (2007b, p. 1)

Does the education system promote capitalist values?

In addressing this question, you should begin by listing what you take to mean by capitalist values and then reflect upon your own experience of formal education.

## Conclusion

Whilst the degree of conflict and consensus within the political mainstream on social policy and the welfare state may be a matter for debate (see Chapters 3, 6 and 7), this chapter has outlined the views of some more radical perspectives. Here there are clearly major divisions, with Marxists believing that the use of state welfare works in the interests of capitalism and that what is needed is the destruction of the capitalist system itself, while Greens are concerned over both the cost and financing of a welfare state, which is dependent upon economic growth incompatible with the interests of the planet, and the bureaucratic and intrusive nature of state welfare. Feminists tend to be divided in their views of the welfare state, aware of its role in the oppression of women but also of its potential to reduce women's dependency.

## Summary

This chapter has identified a variety of ideas on economic and social affairs and in so doing provides a framework to view mainstream and alternative approaches to social policy. A number of arguments have been put forward:

- The way we view the benefits or problems of capitalism has an effect upon our expectations of social policy. Defenders of capitalism will often point out that capitalism can regulate itself and that there is little need for extensive state intervention in economic and social affairs. Whilst social reformers believe that capitalism needs to be tamed and regulated for the common good, radicals often argue that capitalism should be abolished and replaced by an alternative economic system.

- Defenders of capitalism view the welfare state as obstructing the free flow of market forces and a drain upon the nation's wealth. Social reformers will tend to believe that the welfare state can compensate for some of the instabilities of capitalism and provide all citizens with some basic social services. Radicals reject both of these perspectives and argue that the welfare state serves the interests of capitalism and will therefore doubt its long-term value.

- By using the examples of the benefits system, housing, healthcare and education we can see that defenders of capitalism want minimal state involvement in these areas, social reformers want the state to play an active role and radicals want us to look for alternatives to state provision.

- Alternative approaches to social policy, as exemplified in the radical ideas of Marxists, feminists and the Greens, call upon to fight for far-reaching economic, social and political change. In the interim, they suggest that we look for new ways to cooperate with others in our community to reduce (wherever possible) dependence on the capitalist state.

- Even if their immediate policy recommendations are a little vague, Marxists, feminists and the Greens alert us to some of the flaws within the current economic and social system and remind us that there are alternatives to the political mainstream.

# Discussion and review topics

1 Does the modern capitalist system serve the common good?

2 What might social policy (for example the provision of benefits, education, health and housing) look like in a Green world?

3 What evidence might you use to support the view that state provision of welfare is oppressive to women?

## Further reading

Deacon, A. (2002) *Perspectives on Welfare*, Open University Press, Buckingham. Provides a useful discussion of debates about welfare reform in both the United Kingdom and the United States.

Drake, R. (2001) *The Principles of Social Policy*, Palgrave Macmillan, Basingstoke. This book examines some of the key beliefs and values that have underpinned the development of social policy in Western democracies.

Fitzpatrick, T. (2001) *Welfare Theory*, Palgrave Macmillan, Basingstoke. Analyses key concepts relevant to welfare and draws upon a variety of perspectives, including gender, 'race' and disability.

Fitzpatrick, T. (2005) *New Theories of Welfare*, Palgrave Macmillan, Basingstoke. This book both outlines recent developments in welfare theory and examines a range of topics such as genetics, surveillance and the media.

O'Brien, M. and Penna, S. (1998) *Theorising Welfare*, Sage, London. Uses seven theoretical perspectives to explain how each contributes to differing interpretations and possible directions for welfare.

## Some useful websites

www.marxists.org/history/etol/writers/wright/1949/06/welfare.htm – in this article, John G. Wright advances a Marxist critique of social reformism and the use of the state to tame capitalism.

www.marxist.com/capitalism-unleashed-finance-globalisation050107-4.htm – here is an example of a Marxist campaigning organisation. This site, developed by the International Marxist Tendency, contains views on a variety of issues including the welfare state.

http://socialistregister.com/socialistregister.com/files/SR_1990_Gordon.pdf – this is an example of a socialist feminist critique of the welfare state.

www.nwlc.org – the National Women's Law Centre is a campaigning organisation in the United States that promotes the rights of women in a variety of areas. This site contains some interesting material on benefits, health and education.

http://policy.greenparty.org.uk/mfss – the website for the Green Party UK contains a range of sections on social policy.

http://environment.independent.co.uk/green_living – *The Independent* has a series of articles on green issues.

## References

Achterberg, W. (1996) 'Sustainability, community and democracy', in B. Docherty and M. de Geus (eds) *Democracy and Green Political Thought*, Routledge, New York, pp. 170–87.

Baggott, R. (1998) *Health and Health Care in Britain*, Macmillan, Basingstoke.

Bessant, J., Watts, R., Dalton, T. and Smyth, P. (2006) *Talking Policy: How Social Policy is Made*, Allen & Unwin, Crows Nest, NSW.

Bookchin, M. (1990) *Remaking Society: Pathways to a Green Future*, South End Press, Boston, MA.

Butler, J. (1998) 'Subjects of sex/gender/desire', in A. Phillips (ed.) *Feminism and Politics*, Oxford University Press, Oxford.

Cahill, M. (1998) 'The green perspective', in P. Alcock, A. Erskine and M. May (eds) *The Student's Companion to Social Policy*, Blackwell, Oxford, pp. 98–103.

Charles, N. (2000) *Feminism, the State and Social Policy*, Macmillan, Basingstoke.

Conservative Party (2007) 'Opportunity Agenda: Raising the bar, closing the gap' http://www.conservatives.com/pdf/New%20opportunity_proof.pdf.

Crick, B. (1998) *Education for citizenship and the teaching of democracy in schools: Final report of the advisory group on citizenship*, Qualifications and Curriculum Authority, London.

Daly, H. (1977) 'The Steady-State Economy', in A. Dobson (ed.) *The Green Reader*, Andre Deutsch, London, 1991, pp. 145–51.

Dobson, A. (1990) *Green Political Thought*, Unwin Hyman, London.

Dorey, P. (1995) *British Politics since 1945*, Blackwell, Oxford.

Elkins, P. (1986) 'The Basic Income Scheme', in A. Dobson (ed.) *The Green Political Reader*, Andre Deutsch, London, 1991, pp. 152–5.

Ferris, J. (1995) 'Ecological versus social rationality: Can there be green social policies?' in A. Dobson and P. Lucardie (eds) *The Politics of Nature*, Routledge, New York, 1995, pp. 145–60.

Firestone, S. (1979) *The Dialectic of Sex*, The Women's Press, London.

Fitzpatrick, T. (2001) *Welfare Theory*, Palgrave, Basingstoke.

Frieden, B. (1971) *The Feminine Mystique*, Victor Gollancz, London.

George, G. and Wilding, P. (1994) *Welfare and Ideology*, Harvester, Hemel Hempstead.

Ginsburg, N. (1979) *Class, Capital and Social Policy*, Macmillan, London.

Green Party (1997) *Manifesto for a Sustainable Society: Social Welfare*, **www.greenparty.org.uk/policy/mfss/welfare.html** (last accessed 6.06.2001).

Green Party (2000a) *Manifesto for a Sustainable Society: Economy* **www.greenparty.org.uk/policy/mfss/economy.html** (last accessed 6.06.2001).

Green Party (2000b) *Manifesto for a Sustainable Society: Health* **www.greenparty.org.uk/policy/mfss/health.html** (last accessed 6.06.2001).

Green Party (2000c) *Manifesto for a Sustainable Society: Education* **www.greenparty.org.uk/policy/mfss/education.html** (last accessed 6.06.2001).

Green Party (2007) *Manifesto for a Sustainable Society*, **http://policy.greenparty.org.uk/mfss/mfsssw.html** (accessed 14.08.08).

Green Party (2007a) *Manifesto for a Sustainable Society: Social Welfare*, **http://policy.greenparty.org.uk/mfss/msw.html** (last accessed 24.10.2008).

Green Party (2007b) *Manifesto for a Sustainable Society: Education*, **http://policy.greenparty.org.uk/mfss/mfssed.html** (last accessed 24.10.2008).

Heywood, A. (1992) *Political Ideologies*, Macmillan, London.

Jardine, L. and Swindells, J. (1989) *What's Left?* Routledge, London.

Kemp, P. and Wall, D. (1990) *Green Manifesto for the 1990s*, Penguin, London.

Lewis, J. (1992) *Women in Britain since 1945*, Blackwell, Oxford.

Marx, K. (1867) *Capital: Volume 1*, Lawrence and Wishart, London, 1954.

Miliband, R. (1977) *Marxism and Politics*, Oxford University Press, Oxford, 1977.

Monbiot, G. (2001) *Captive State*, Pan Books, London.

Navarro, V. (1978) *Class Struggle, the State and Medicine*, Martin Robinson, Oxford.

NWLC (2007) 'Increasing Inequality, increasing insecurity for women and their families: An Analysis of the Presdident's FY 2008 budget', **www.nwlc.org/pdf/NWLC%20Budget%20Analysis.pdf**.

Oakley, A. (1981) *Subject Women*, Martin Robertson, Oxford.

Offe, C. (1976) *Industry and Inequality*, Edward Arnold, London.

Offe, C. (1984) *Contradictions of the Welfare State*, Hutchinson, London.

Pateman, C. (1989) 'The Patriarchal Welfare State', in C. Pierson and F. Castles (eds) *The Welfare State Reader*, Polity, Cambridge, 2000, pp. 133-50.

Petras, J. and Vieux, S. (1996) 'Bosnia and the revival of US hegemony', *New Left Review*, Vol. 218, pp. 3-25.

Pfaller, A. and Gough, I. (1991) 'The competitiveness of industrialised welfare states: A cross country survey', in A. Pfaller, I. Gough and G. Therborn (eds) *Can the welfare state compete?* Macmillan, Basingstoke, pp. 15-43.

Ryle, M. (1988) 'Ecosocialism', in A. Dobson (ed.) *The Green Reader*, Andre Deutsch, London, 1991, pp. 138-41.

Spretnak, C. and Capra, F. (1985) *Green Politics: The Global Promise*, Paladin, London.

Taylor, G. (2007) *Ideology and Welfare*, Palgrave Macmillan, Basingstoke.

Todd, M. and Taylor, G. (eds) (2004) *Democracy and Participation*, Merlin, London.

Williams, F. (1989) *Social Policy: A Critical Introduction*, Polity, Cambridge.

Woods, R. (1996) 'Women and housing', in C. Hallett (ed.) *Women and Social Policy: An Introduction*, Harvester Wheatsheaf, Hemel Hempstead, 1996, pp. 65-83.

# Part III

## ISSUES AND DEVELOPMENTS

# 9

# Income maintenance and taxation

Karen Rowlingson and Stephen McKay

## Chapter overview

This chapter summarises the roles of the taxation and social security systems in the United Kingdom. These are the main – but not the only – ways in which money is redistributed between individuals, via the state. Both are fundamental parts of the role of the state in contemporary society, and crucial tools in relation to social policy.

The chapter will cover:

- the size and role of social security spending;
- the size and role of taxation;
- public attitudes towards both systems;
- how these systems have recently developed, and current plans for reform.

## Spotlight on the issues
### Tax and benefits

We will all spend most of our lives either receiving or paying for social security – frequently doing both at the same time. However, the systems themselves are far from simple and most of us understand very little about what they aim to do, how they operate and what their effects are. A number of facts illustrate the importance of these systems in Britain:

- Total public spending is forecast to increase from £589 billion in 2007–08 to £678 billion in 2010–11 (HM Treasury, 2007 – the main source for recent figures). Spending in 2007–08 equates to close to £10,000 for every man, woman and child in the UK.

- Government spending on social protection (principally social security benefits) takes up around £159 billion, well over one-quarter of all public spending and more than the total raised in income tax (£154 billion).

- The Department for Work and Pensions, which delivers most benefits, costs close to £6 billion to run.

- The total cost of the higher political priorities of health is around £105 billion whilst £78 billion is spent on education. Spending on defence occupies £32 billion.

- State support is received by 70 per cent of households in the UK, with 30 per cent receiving at least half their income from this source (FRS, 2005-6, Table 3.9).

- Some 59 per cent of households with a pensioner receive at least half their total income from state sources (FRS, 2005-6, Table 3.9).

The figures outlined above clearly illustrate the vast sums of money gathered in and passed out through taxation and social security. The social security and tax systems can, to some extent, be seen as two sides of the same coin. One collects in money for government, the other distributes it to people – sometimes straight back to the same people, sometimes to the same people at a later time, and quite often to other people. Virtually all of us, at one time or another, will receive money from the social security system and pay money in the form of taxes.

This chapter compares and contrasts the social security and tax systems. It begins by setting out the dominant – but by no means the only – discourse on social security and taxation. Within this neo-liberal discourse, taxation is seen as a burden and social security as a waste of money, a price paid for failure. In his 1996 Labour Party conference speech, Tony Blair was committed to reducing 'the welfare bills of social failure' (cited in Brewer et al., 2002, p. 8). The dominance of this discourse explains why governments of all political persuasions have, in recent decades, tried to maintain or reduce levels of taxation and social security expenditure. **Neo-liberalist** discourse also explains why 'tax expenditures' (tax breaks) have generally received such little attention and why benefit fraud is treated far more severely than tax fraud. We, however, put forward a more collectivist discourse, arguing that the tax and social security systems can be seen as a means of securing social justice by reducing levels of inequality. Within this overarching framework, we define the social security and tax systems, discuss their aims, describe the size and structure of the two systems and speculate on how the two systems are likely to change in the future.

# Cultural assumptions about tax and social security

Debates about each major political party's commitments to tax levels have figured strongly in recent elections, from allegations of 'tax bombshells' and gaps in funding tax cuts, to commitments not to raise income tax levels, to the concept of '**stealth taxes**'. The increase in National Insurance rates announced in the 2002 Budget – mostly to pay for additional spending on the National Health Service – represented a watershed to the extent that direct tax rises were used to fund public spending (Taylor-Gooby and Hastie, 2002). But they represented political business as usual to the extent that income tax levels were regarded as sacrosanct. More recently, debates over inheritance tax have ensured that even fewer families may expect to pay it. Despite the few who are liable for this tax, measures to reduce its scope have been seen to be extremely popular.

 *Controversy and debate*

### The political significance of inheritance tax?

Between June 2007 (when Gordon Brown became Labour PM) and October 2007 (Party conferences) the Conservatives' average poll rating was 34 per cent. After the conferences, featuring a proposed significant increase in the allowance for inheritance tax by the Conservative Party, their poll rating averaged 40 per cent between October and December 2007 (see **www.populus.co.uk/december/December_2007.pdf**). Other factors also changed, but this may have been a significant moment in tax policy and underlines the potential popularity of an agenda to cut inheritance taxes.

The main political discussions over social security would appear to concern how punitive the government should be in tackling fraud and reducing spending on the unemployed. Tony Blair consistently referred to social security spending as representing economic failure elsewhere, declaring in 2001 that Labour were 'cutting the costs of economic failure; with real terms social security spending falling for the first time in decades' (speech to the Confederation of British Industry, 5 November 2001).

Cultural assumptions form a crucial underpinning of the current systems of social security and taxation. These assumptions play a powerful role in setting the political agenda for the reform of social security and taxation. It is all too easy to portray spending on benefits as a 'burden', and to regard tax cuts are giving back people 'their money'. Only rarely does the system of tax exemptions figure in discussion.

Public attitudes to government spending and taxation are complex and often ambiguous, with people generally supporting higher taxes (so long as someone else is paying them) and also supporting higher spending on 'deserving' groups such as pensioners (Orton and Rowlingson, 2007). Hedges and Bromley (2001) found that people's responses to the tax system were based on both ignorance about the system along with strong emotions. The public generally believed that

Thought provoker

## The effects of poverty

Sometimes it is suggested that poverty is 'only relative' and is really about lifestyles rather than being unable to meet basic needs. However, government figures show an important link between living in a deprived area and life expectancy. According to *Health Statistics Quarterly* for winter 2006: 'The death rate for men aged 15–64 in the most deprived wards was 2.8 times the rate in the least deprived wards. For women the rate was 2.1 times higher' (Office for National Statistics, 2006, p. 1).

the level of taxation in the UK was constantly increasing and was far heavier than that in the rest of Europe. The vision of the tax system as a 'burden', or even 'highway robbery' as one respondent termed it (p. 8), illustrates the deeply negative attitudes towards taxation. People generally saw tax as a penalty rather than a payment for services. They did not feel that they gained value for money from their payment of taxes and they were generally very confused by the complexity of the system.

When respondents were told that most tax revenue was spent on social security benefits they were particularly annoyed and felt that this confirmed their view that much of 'their' money was being wasted – on 'scroungers' and the 'workshy'. Respondents assumed that most social security expenditure went on the unemployed, but when they were informed that most of the social security budget was spent on pensioners, they were happier to have 'their' money spent on pensioners than other groups. This attitude towards social security expenditure is confirmed by successive waves of the **British Social Attitudes Survey** which have asked respondents about the acceptability of spending more on different groups of social security recipients (Bryson, 1997). Pensioners are generally seen as far more 'deserving' than other groups. This notion of 'deserving' and 'undeserving' groups is another prevailing cultural assumption surrounding the benefit system.

The idea that taxation is a burden, and that social security is a waste of money, fits in with a free market or neo-liberal economic philosophy. This philosophy, stemming from the work of the eighteenth-century thinker Adam Smith (1976) and championed in the twentieth-century by Hayek (1976) and Nozick (1974), among others, is that state intervention should be minimal. Nozick (1974, p. 169) famously declared that 'Taxation of earnings from labor is on a par with forced labor'. It is argued that taxes and benefits should be kept very low because if they are set too high people will face disincentives to work. Underlying this philosophy is the idea that people who engage in paid work are 'independent' while those who receive social security benefits are 'dependent'. Wages from paid work constitute an individual's own money, to which they have an inalienable right. Such a philosophy suggests that those who put individual effort into earning wages should therefore be able to keep as much of 'their' money as possible.

These cultural assumptions are very strong in the United States. They are also very strong in the UK. The Conservative governments from 1979 to 1997 broke the tentative post-war consensus over the welfare state. **Thatcherism** sought to 'roll back the frontiers of the state' and allow the market to flourish unhindered by regulation and taxation. After successive defeats at the ballot box, 'New' Labour distinguished itself from 'Old' Labour precisely on this point of philosophy.

An alternative way of looking at tax and social security stems from what might be called a social solidarity or collectivist philosophy. Underpinning this philosophy is the idea that the role of the state is a positive one as it creates the conditions under which people can flourish and social justice can be achieved. People are not divided into those who are 'dependent' and those who are 'independent'; all are seen as interdependent on each other. This emphasis on **social inclusion**, interdependency and solidarity rather than individual freedom is the main difference between this philosophy and that of free market neo-liberalism. This broad philosophical approach encompasses elements of socialism and social democracy (see, for example, Tawney, 1921 and 1931; Crosland, 1956; Miliband, 1994).

Although neo-liberalism appears the most common way of seeing tax and social security, evidence from the *British Social Attitudes Surveys* has shown high, if variable, support for higher taxes to pay for higher public spending (see Figure 9.1). In 1983 the balance of opinion was to maintain levels of tax and spending. In each subsequent year the policy of taxing and spending more (on particular social areas) has proved the more popular view. There was a sizeable dip (to 50 per cent) in 2000 and a decline over much of Labour's first term, rising to 59 per cent by the 2001 survey. More recent data on public attitudes suggest that, if anything, attitudes towards state spending on welfare hardened between 2002 and 2006 (Orton and Rowlingson, 2007; Taylor-Gooby and Martin, 2007).

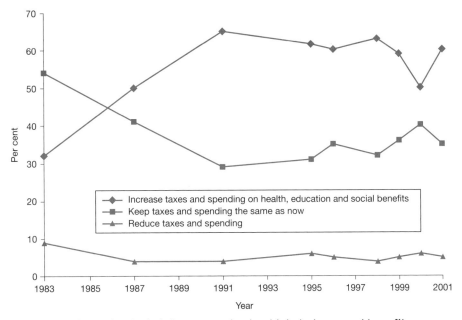

**Figure 9.1 Views about what Governments should do to taxes and benefits**
*Source*: Taylor-Gooby and Hastie (2002, Table 4.1).

Despite all this, Labour remain committed to maintaining rates of income tax, leading to charges of having introduced or increased so-called 'stealth taxes' instead. This has included such changes as increases in stamp duty, extension of employer National Insurance contributions to all benefits in kind, increases in insurance premium tax, and so on.

## The importance of social security and taxation

Since the Second World War, spending on social security has risen almost continuously. There has been a tenfold increase over the period, with only occasional dips generally associated with times of falling unemployment. This illustrated the manner in which social security has come to take on roles not anticipated in the post-war Beveridge plan such as growing levels of economic inactivity (such as rising spending on disability benefits), increases in life expectancy (affecting pensions spending) and changes in family forms (such as more lone parents receiving benefits in their own right). Until the 1980s, benefit rates also tended to increase more rapidly than price inflation, more closely matching growth in the economy as a whole.

Over the same time period, the number of people paying direct taxation has also increased to some 30 million, compared with fewer than 5 million before the Second World War (see Figure 9.2). Income tax used to be paid by higher earners, but is now paid by most people working (whether as employees or as self-employed).

The combined effects of taxes and benefits include providing some degree of equalisation of income between rich and poor in any given year. The incomes from employment, self-employment and investments of the best-off 10 per cent were nearly 30 times as great as those of the worst-off 10 per cent in 2005–6 (Jones,

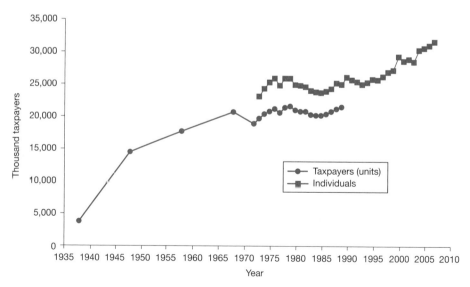

**Figure 9.2 Number of income tax payers, 1938–2007/8**

*Source*: HMRC tax receipt statistics, updated April 2007, www.hmrc.gov.uk/stats/tax_receipts/table1-4.pdf.

2007). After taking into account taxes and benefits, they were 'merely' 12 times better off. If we also include the benefits provided by the state in kind (health, education, housing subsidies) then the disparity falls to five-to-one (see Figure 9.3).

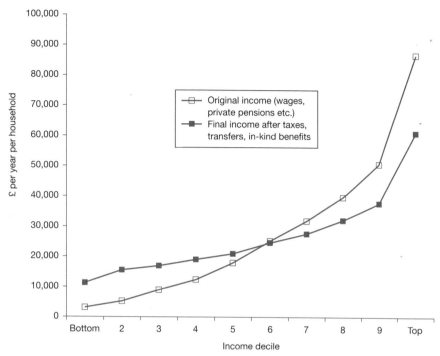

**Figure 9.3** Final incomes compared with original incomes
*Source*: Jones (2007, Table 14).

## Socio-economic inequality

The social security and tax systems should also be considered within the context of the dramatic increases in inequality which took place in the late 1980s (see Figure 9.4). Between 1979 and 1994/95, incomes for the richest tenth of the population grew by between 60 and 68 per cent. Those of the poorest tenth showed only a 10 per cent increase before housing costs, or a fall of 8 per cent when housing costs were taken into account (Hills, 1998). Families with children were much more likely to be poor at the end of the 1980s than they had been at the beginning. By 1990, roughly one child in three was living in poverty.

There are a number of explanations for the rising inequality that occurred over the 1980s. For example, tax cuts in the 1980s favoured those on higher incomes, with the result that the taxation system did not restrain rising inequality in the way that it did in other countries. A decision to link social security to the index of changes in prices, not earnings, meant that those who stayed on benefit fell behind as earnings grew. There was a rise in the number of people out of work (either unemployed or economically inactive) and for those in work, there was

191

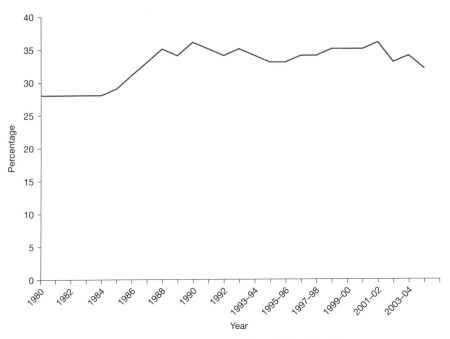

**Figure 9.4** Changes in overall income inequality 1980-2004/5

*Note*: This graph uses the **Gini coefficient** (a widely recognised measure of equality and inequality) for equivalised disposable income for the United Kingdom, www.statistics.gov.uk.

an increasing division between those in well-paid jobs and those in low-paid jobs. Inequality grew faster in Britain between the mid 1980s and the early 1990s than in any Western nation for which comparable data is available.

Britain became a little more equal in terms of incomes by the mid 1990s. Falling unemployment and abolition of the **Community Charge** (poll tax) were among the factors that helped those with the lowest incomes to make up some of the lost ground. But the divide between rich and poor that widened so dramatically during the 1980s was only narrowed to a limited extent and income inequality has remained much greater than in any previous decade since the Second World War (Hills, 1998).

## Defining 'social security' and taxation

Social security and taxation clearly play a central role in people's lives. But what is meant by these terms? There is no universally accepted neat definition of 'social security' or 'taxation', and this section discusses possible definitions.

### Social security

Starting with the very widest definition, it is sometimes used to refer to all the ways by which people organise their lives in order to ensure access to an adequate income. This wide concept includes securing income from all sources such as earnings from employers and self-employment, financial help from charities, money from a family member and cash benefits from the state. So in the area of welfare related to maintaining income there are different means by which this may be achieved. Of foremost importance is the private sector, for example earnings from employment and profits from self-employment are the chief source of income for most people of working age, and pensions in retirement are often based on such earnings.

A slightly narrower definition of social security would include all types of financial support, except those provide by the market system. In this way, reliance on the immediate or extended family would still be classed as helping to achieve social security. However, it is increasingly usual to adopt an even narrower definition, and to regard social security as those sources of immediate financial support provided by the state.

The definition of 'social security' as the system of cash benefits paid by the government to different individuals appears to be fairly simple and unproblematic. But it is inadequate or, at least, does not include the same range of activities that most people would regard as being social security. This is because some 'benefits' are not paid for by the state, or need not be. Statutory sick pay used to be paid by government but, whilst it remains a legal entitlement, it is now mostly a cost met by employers. There are also occupational schemes for sickness, widowhood and retirement that are similar to state benefits, and which have a similar function, but which are organised by employers. One could also envisage the government finding ways to 'privatise' what are currently state benefits, or instigating new compulsory private provision, perhaps for pensions. So, both voluntary employer schemes, and some programmes mandated by government, may also be classed as social security – neither of which neatly fit the above definition.

## Taxation

Taxation can be defined as the different sources of government revenue. This definition is quite wide and includes not only those sources known specifically as 'taxes' but also those sources known as insurance 'contributions' as well as 'duties', 'royalties', 'levies' and so on. Revenue from interest and dividends can also be included in a very wide definition of taxation and we employ such a definition for this chapter.

The British tax system is an individualised system whereby people within a couple are treated independently (for example in having their own personal allowances and not having their income combined for tax purposes). The social security system, however, treats couples as couples, operating a couple-based **means test** for income-related benefits and allowing additions for 'dependants' in the case of contributory benefits. In general, income tax liabilities are based on annual gross incomes. What payments are due depends on income over the whole tax year, whatever increases or decreases in weekly amounts takes place over the year. By contrast, many means-tested benefits are based on income over a relatively short period – if you have no money in a particular week, it is important you receive payment promptly. Income tax bills – and rebates – may be considered at a more leisurely pace.

A relatively new and growing feature of the tax system are '**tax credits**'. They started their life, however, as part of the social security system. Working Families Tax Credit (WFTC) was introduced in 1999 to replace Family Credit, a benefit to top up the wages of low-paid families. Although WFTC was termed a 'tax credit' it was very similar to the benefit it replaced, as it acted to top up people's wages. But the government generally prefers to see tax credits as standing apart from social security benefits – in particular, because they are received by those in work, rather than those not in work.

There are also reasons related to national accounting practices for preferring to treat tax credits as part of the tax system. A tax credit is treated as negative taxation rather than a positive expenditure on social security benefits. When WFTC was removed from the social security budget and placed, instead, within the taxation system, it looked as though social security spending had reduced overnight. This sits well with a free market neo-liberal philosophy where social security spending is seen as a waste and taxation should be kept as low as possible. What better than negative taxation!

Some tax credits are, however, more properly counted as part of the tax system. Child Tax Credit and Working Tax Credit were introduced in April 2003. They have some features that make them align more closely with the tax system. The amounts are based on gross incomes over the whole year – like income tax. However, amounts are based on family incomes, whereas income tax is an individual system. Moreover, Child Tax Credit is paid directly to the person most responsible for childcare in a way akin to Child Benefit, rather than first reducing any tax liability – which resembles more closely the benefits system. Amounts are also designed to be paid into bank accounts, rather than being collected in cash, or being credited to payslips. So, whilst the new tax credits take financial support more closely into the tax system – and are being delivered by the Inland Revenue – there are still good reasons for seeing some of the new tax credits as very similar to social security benefits.

The new state Pension Credit for pensioners, by contrast, is very clearly a renamed social security benefit with no closer linkage to taxation than the benefit it replaced.

## Tax expenditures

Most forms of taxation have systems of allowances, reliefs, credits, deductions and so on, which comprise exemptions from the general applicability of the tax. For example, some income is exempt from taxation – such as gross income spent on private pension contributions, and interest received on special savings accounts, currently called Individual Savings Accounts. It may be argued that tax allowances are similar to subsidies and so should properly be seen as public expenditure, rather than deductions from tax (McDaniel and Surrey, 1985). Why should direct payments to pensioners appear as a cost whilst tax concessions for private pensions shows up – if at all – simply as lower tax? For this reason, the term 'tax expenditures' has been coined for such exemptions, although in popular parlance the term 'loophole' might be equally apt. The existence of such exemptions is one means of pursuing tax avoidance – legal ways of reducing tax liability.

The value of tax expenditures seems to vary widely across OECD countries (Greve, 1994; Wood, 1988) and often to the benefit of better-off families. Many poorer families are not subject to tax measures attracting such exemptions, and hence cannot gain from certain tax expenditures. Conversely, some specific tax expenditures are said to be targeted at poorer households – such as a lower rate of value added tax (VAT) on domestic fuel and on children's clothes than on most other goods and services. However, since richer families spend more on these items than poorer households, the cash gain is actually smaller for poorer families than for the rich – although the proportionate gain for poorer households may be greater.

Tax expenditures remain an important part of government policy, although the value of some of them has been reduced, including removal of income tax reliefs for married couples and for mortgage interest payments. The costs of tax allowances and exemptions are only periodically subject to close scrutiny, although regular figures on their size are produced in government reports – if one gets through enough of the annexes! The cost of a tax exemption is inevitably an estimate, since people might behave differently if the exemption were removed. The estimated value of tax expenditures is vast. However, Her Majesty's Revenue and Customs estimates of the value of some particular tax exemptions are shown in Table 9.1 (the most up-to-date estimates are available from **www.hmrc.gov.uk/ stats/tax_expenditures/menu.htm**).

**Table 9.1** Value of selected tax expenditures in 2006–2007

| Tax expenditure | Value |
| --- | --- |
| Tax relief for approved pension schemes | £16.3 billion |
| Capital gains tax: exemption of gains from main residence | £15 billion |
| National Insurance contracted-out rebate for occupational schemes | £7.5 billion |
| VAT zero-rating of domestic passenger transport | £2.25 billion |
| National Insurance contracted-out rebate for personal and stakeholder pensions | £2.2 billion |
| Inheritance tax: exemption of transfers on death to surviving spouses | £2.2 billion |
| Individual Savings Accounts | £1.6 billion |
| Exemption of first £30,000 of payments on termination of employment | £800 million |
| Foreign service allowance paid to Crown Servants abroad | £95 million |

Source: HMRC.

# The aims of social security and taxation

Having defined taxation and social security we now ask what are the aims of these systems? The answer is complex. Like elsewhere, the system in Britain has evolved over time and so is not necessarily what would be designed if policy makers were now starting from scratch. Furthermore, different parts of the system have different aims and so it is not possible to identify one aim and it is even arguable as to what the main aim of the system is. With these reservations in mind, Briefing 9.1 lists some of the possible objectives of social security.

*Briefing 9.1*
## Possible aims of social security

- Insuring against the risks of particular events in life, such as unemployment and short-term sickness.
- Relieving poverty or low income.
- Redistributing resources across people's life cycles, especially from working age to retirement.
- Redistributing resources from rich to poor.
- 'Compensating' for some types of extra cost (such as children, disability).
- Providing financial support when 'traditional' families break down.

Within these general aims, the British social security system has been designed to achieve the following:

- To maintain incentives for self-provision (such as through earning and saving).
- To keep non-take-up of benefits low.
- To counter possible fraud.
- To ensure that administrative costs are low.

The aims of the British system have traditionally been more limited than those of systems in Europe, if wider than in some parts of the rest of the English-speaking world. The importance of relieving poverty in the British system explains the considerable reliance on means testing in Britain. Receipt of means-tested benefits depends on a person or family having resources (typically income, and perhaps savings) below a certain level in order to receive benefits. Means testing is also common in America, New Zealand and Australia but much less common elsewhere, especially in Continental Europe, where social security tends to be less centralised and more concerned with income maintenance and compensation.

Throughout history, one of the main reasons for taxation was to raise money for war (see Briefing 9.2). Indeed, this was the rationale for the introduction of income tax during the Napoleonic Wars (Field *et al.*, 1977). With the growth of the welfare state, however, the tax system has taken on rather different aims, such as enabling/compelling people to save money in case they experience unemployment, sickness or retirement. Taxes are also used to pay money to people who do not have sufficient to live on. The tax system also aims to raise money for local and central government services such as health and education. A rather different possible aim of the tax system might be to reduce people's consumption of particular goods. For example, tobacco is generally considered to be harmful and so it is argued that high taxes on tobacco will reduce people's consumption of this substance. Similarly, taxes on petrol may reduce car journeys which are detrimental to the environment.

A final possible aim of the tax system is to redistribute income and/or wealth from rich to poor. If the rich are most heavily taxed and most of the money then

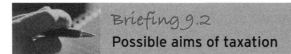

**Briefing 9.2**
## Possible aims of taxation

- To raise money for war and defence.
- To enable people to save against future risks.
- To pay money to people on very low incomes.
- To pay for local or central services.
- To reduce people's consumption of certain goods.
- To redistribute income/wealth.

given out either in cash or services to poorer groups, then the tax system is performing a 'Robin Hood' function. But the extent to which this occurs in practice is debatable as the poor pay a large proportion of their income in taxes (such as VAT) and wealthier groups actually take a great deal of advantage of welfare state services (for example, education and pensions – because they stay in education for longer and they live longer, thus receiving more in pensions).

As we shall see below, a distinction is generally made between direct taxes (such as on income) and indirect taxes (such as on personal spending). A tax system which takes a higher proportion of tax from the income of richer than poorer people is known as a progressive system. Under a regressive system, the poor pay a higher proportion of their income in taxes than do the rich. Generally speaking, direct taxes on income tend to be progressive, whilst indirect taxes tend to be regressive – partly because poorer groups spend a higher proportion of their incomes, partly because spending on some taxed goods does not rise much with income. Those who argue for greater emphasis on direct taxation are often doing so from a collectivist perspective since direct taxation tends to be more progressive than indirect taxation.

# An overview of the current systems

## Social security

The social security system today is highly complex, having evolved over time. Very few people understand it in all its detail. For every possible generalisation about the system there are myriad caveats. It is therefore difficult to give a brief overview without over-simplifying the system and therefore possibly misleading (see Millar, 2003, and McKay and Rowlingson, 1999, for further details). Nevertheless, this section attempts to provide such an overview. There are various ways of classifying the different benefits in the UK system. For example, benefits can be categorised into two dichotomies: universal versus means tested; contributory versus non-contributory. If we use the rules of entitlement as our yardstick, social security can be divided into three main components: contributory benefits (benefits which rely upon having paid contributions); means-tested benefits and tax credits (benefits which depend upon income); and contingent benefits (benefits which depend upon your position or category), as follows.

## Contributory benefits

The root for the current social security system lies in the Beveridge Report published in the early 1940s (see Chapter 5), although insurance-based and other benefits had been introduced well before this time. At the heart of the Beveridge approach – of contributory benefits or 'social insurance' – is the idea that people face a range of risks that might lead to severe reductions in living standards. These include the risk of unemployment, or being incapacitated and unable to work, or retiring, or losing the main income-earner in a family. Some risks are rather uncommon, and relatively unrelated to economic circumstances, such as widowhood. Other risks, such as retirement, are much more widespread and predictable.

The main issues that arise with social insurance include:

- Why should the state provide this service, rather than private insurance? What relationship should there then be between state and private insurance?
- What risks should be covered?
- On what basis should contributions be made, or be deemed to be made?

Social insurance benefits have entitlement based on having paid National Insurance contributions, and being in a risk covered by these benefits (such as unemployment or retirement). These benefits are individualised in that the earnings of a partner do not generally affect entitlement. The main benefit in this group is the State Retirement Pension. Other benefits are the contributory parts of Incapacity Benefit and contribution-based Jobseeker's Allowance.

## Means-tested benefits/tax credits

Entitlement to means-tested benefits depends on the level of 'family' resources, particularly income and savings. The four main examples in the British system are Income Support, Working Families Tax Credit, Housing Benefit and Council Tax Benefit.

The system of benefits based on means testing, particularly for those on low incomes, is sometimes known as 'social assistance'. In Britain, social assistance is almost synonymous with the benefit Income Support, and income-based Jobseeker's Allowance for unemployed people. These benefits are paid to those whose income and savings are below defined levels, taking into account the size and type of family.

Countries differ a great deal in the extent of this type of provision. In Australia and New Zealand, almost all benefits include an element of 'means testing' This does not mean that only the poorest may receive benefits – in some instances the aim is to exclude the richest rather than to include only the poorest. In much of Northern Europe, social assistance plays a much smaller role, picking up those not covered by the main social insurance system. In addition they are often administered locally, with local organisations having some discretion about the precise rules of entitlement.

Additional conditions are often attached to receiving social assistance. People of working age, without sole responsibility for caring for children or disabled adults, must be able to work, available for work and actively seeking work. In past times, they may have had to enter a workhouse to qualify.

### Contingent benefits

These are sometimes referred to as categorical benefits or as non means-tested and non-contributory. Entitlement depends on the existence of certain circumstances (or contingencies) such as having a child (Child Benefit) being disabled (Disability Living Allowance, Severe Disablement Allowance) or, at least until recent changes, being a lone parent (One Parent Benefit).

In the British social security system, some benefits effectively recognise that certain groups of people face extra costs which the state will share. The clearest example is benefits for dependent children and Child Benefit. There is no test of contributions, and the family's level of income is not taken into consideration (at the present time). There are, however, certain tests of residence that must be satisfied. Disability benefits provide another example, where some elements are purely contingent and reflect neither means nor previous contributions.

It is worth emphasising that this division into three groups is something of a simplification of differences between benefits. Means-tested benefits do not just depend on financial resources; they tend to also rely on some combination of being in a particular situation or a particular family type. For example, able-bodied single people may only claim Income Support if they meet conditions relating to being unemployed. And it is possible for certain sources of income to affect contributory benefits, for example Jobseeker's Allowance and Incapacity Benefit (both contribution-based) can be reduced if a person receives income from a personal or occupational pension.

## Taxation

The tax system is often divided into 'direct taxes' such as income tax and National Insurance contributions and 'indirect taxes' such as value added tax (VAT) that applies to most goods and service, and duties on petrol, alcohol and tobacco, and so on. But government revenue is more complex than that and we offer a different categorisation, as follows:

- Direct taxes on income
- Capital taxes
- Other indirect taxes
- Corporation taxes
- Council tax
- Other sources of revenue

Table 9.2 shows that income tax is the largest single source of government revenue but this most prominent form of tax still only accounts for just over a quarter of revenue. National Insurance contributions are the second most important source of government income followed by VAT and then corporation taxes.

Table 9.2 Main sources of government revenue in 2007-8 (forecasts)

|  | Forecast 2007–8 (£bn) | Percentage of total |
|---|---|---|
| Income tax (net of tax credits) | 154 | 28% |
| National Insurance contributions | 97 | 18% |
| Value added tax | 81 | 15% |
| Corporation taxes | 47 | 9% |
| Excise duties | 41 | 7% |
| Council tax | 24 | 4% |
| Business rates | 22 | 4% |
| Other sources of revenue | 86 | 16% |
| Total revenue | 551 | 100 |

Source: HM Treasury, Pre-Budget Report, 2007.

## Direct taxes on income

'Direct taxes' include both income tax and National Insurance contributions. Income tax is, perhaps, the most politically sensitive tax and the Labour Party committed itself to maintaining (or reducing) levels of income tax during the 1997, 2001 and 2005 election campaigns.

Not all income is subject to income tax. The main sources of income which are taxed include earnings from employment and self-employment, pension payments during retirement and some social security benefits (such as Incapacity Benefit). People do not pay tax on all of their income from these sources. They each have a personal allowance and if their income (from taxable sources) falls below this personal allowance, they pay no income tax at all. The level of personal allowance depends on age with, in 2007–8, those aged 75 and over having the most generous level (at £7,420 in 2006–7) and those aged 65–74 having a personal allowance of £7,280. Those under 65 had a personal allowance of £5,035.

Until April 2000, married couples had an extra allowance. This was often used by the man in the couple, particularly if the woman stayed at home to look after children. The Labour government abolished this married couples' allowance for all but those born before 1935. This reform was criticised by the Conservative opposition as penalising marriage, although the Labour government's main aim was to redistribute from married couples (who may or may not have children) to people with children (who may or may not be married). There also remains within the system a blind person's allowance, which amounted to £1,730 in 2007–8.

For those with taxable income above their personal allowance, there are different rates of tax depending on their level of income. Table 9.3 shows these different rates of tax and the current levels of the tax bands.

In the 2007 Budget, however, it was announced that the 10p starting rate was being abolished, and this was paid for by reducing the standard rate from 22p down to 20p. This took effect from April 2008.

This all looks relatively simple compared with the social security system. But people nevertheless get confused about how the tax system works in practice. For

**Table 9.3 Income tax rates 2006–7** (though see text for 2008)

| Gross income | Rate of income tax (%) |
| --- | --- |
| Less than personal allowance | 0 |
| Personal allowance plus £2,150 (lower-rate band) | 10 |
| From lower-rate band to £33,300 + personal allowance (basic-rate band) | 22 |
| Higher-rate band (gross income above £33,300 + personal allowance) | 40 |

example, people earning over £33,300 do not pay 40 per cent tax on the whole of their income. The 40 per cent tax rate is only paid on the income over £33,300 plus the personal allowance. So in practice, someone of working age would have to earn above £38,000 to come into the higher-rate band. And they would only pay 40 per cent tax on their income above this amount (or a tax rate of about 22 per cent of total gross income).

National Insurance contributions (NICs) may be considered as another form of direct taxation. They were initially introduced in the early part of the twentieth century to pay for unemployment insurance (and for health), before being extended to their main current purpose, retirement pensions, during the 1920s. NICs are sometimes portrayed as different from taxation because they are supposed to be contributions to one's own pension or other insurance benefits. However, the revenue from this source has never been invested in the way that private pension contributions are invested. Instead, today's national insurance contributors are paying towards the benefits of today's recipients.

The vast majority of revenue from NICs comes from 'Class 1' contributions. These are paid by employees as a tax on their earnings and employers as secondary contributions on those they employ. Employees pay NICs at a rate of 11 per cent on any earnings between the primary threshold (£97 per week in 2006–7) and an upper earnings limit (£645 a week in 2006–7), and at 1 per cent on earnings above the upper level. Employers pay contributions at a rate of 12.8 per cent on all earnings above a threshold (£97 a week in 2005–6). The existence of an upper limit on NICs – at least for employees, excepting the additional 1 per cent contribution – reduces the 'progressive' aspect of this tax.

## Capital taxes

There are three main capital taxes: capital gains tax; inheritance tax; and stamp duties of various kind. Capital gains tax is levied on gains from selling assets by individuals or trustees. The first £8,800 of an individual's gain is exempt currently. The amount of tax paid depends on how long the asset has been held and whether or not it is a business asset. The taxable rate was generally 40 per cent, but is being changed to be 18 per cent (2007 *Pre-Budget Report*) following the removal of various exemptions.

Inheritance tax is paid when people receive an asset on or shortly before someone's death. Asset transfers below £300,000 in 2007–8 are exempt from inheritance tax. If the asset is transferred on death then the rate of tax above the exempt amount is 40 per cent. However, the 2007 *Pre-Budget Report* announced a doubling of this exemption for legally married couples (and those in civil partnerships). This followed the announcement at the Conservative Party conference of a new policy of a £1 million threshold.

Stamp duty is paid on transfers of stocks and shares, land and property. All transfers of stocks and shares are taxed at 0.5 per cent, but there are different rates depending on the value of land/property, and exemptions for properties in some deprived areas.

### Value added tax

VAT can be divided into four categories, as follows (Adam and Browne, 2006):

- A standard rate of 17.5 per cent on most goods and services.
- A reduced rate of 5 per cent on a range of products including domestic fuel and power, women's sanitary products, and children's car seats (accounting for 3 per cent of consumers' expenditure).
- Exempt goods have no VAT levied on the final good sold to the consumer but firms cannot reclaim VAT paid on inputs.
- Zero-rated goods (including food, construction of new homes, public transport, children's clothing, books, medicines on prescription etc.) have no VAT levied upon the final good or upon the inputs used in its creation.

During the 1980s VAT was raised from 8 to 15 per cent and the money raised enabled the government to reduce the basic and higher rates of income tax. The rate was increased again in 1991 to pay for a reduction in the poll tax/community charge. The Conservative government at the time would have argued that a shift from direct (income) tax to indirect tax (VAT) would reduce tax-induced disincentives to work but, as argued above, this is not necessarily the case.

### Other indirect taxes

Duty on petrol sparked an explosive protest in the late 1990s, when the movement of petrol was blockaded by protestors and the pumps began to dry up. In 2001–2, almost 80 per cent of the cost of petrol and diesel went in taxation. A similarly high percentage of the price of cigarettes goes straight to the government. Wine is taxed less heavily than cigarettes and beer even less (about 29 per cent of the cost going in taxes) (Adam and Frayne, 2001).

The existence of high duties on petrol, alcohol and tobacco can provide incentives to evade taxes. For example, in 2002, it was claimed that there was a significant incidence of people illegally using sunflower oil to run their cars on rather than buying diesel. Similarly, people may cross the channel to stock up on tobacco and alcohol – perfectly legal for personal consumption but it is illegal to buy such goods with the intention of selling them on.

Vehicle excise duty (often referred to as road tax) is another indirect tax in this category. So too are insurance premium tax, air passenger duty, landfill tax, climate change levy and betting and gaming duties etc.

### Corporation taxes

Corporation taxes are charges on profits made by UK companies. The standard corporation tax is currently 30 per cent, with a reduced rate of 19 per cent for companies with profits less than £300,000.

### Council tax

The system of local taxation was a major problem area for government in the 1980s, leading to the introduction of the hated poll tax (or community charge as it was officially known). In 1993, the council tax was introduced, based on property price levels rather than on individuals. Properties are put into one of eight bands depending on their value and then individual councils set the amount of council tax to be paid by people living in each of the properties. Council tax provides about 20 per cent of local authority revenue (Adam and Frayne, 2001).

### Other sources of revenue

Other sources of revenue include the taxation of income from saving. Certain forms of saving have received more favourable treatment under the tax system than others. For example, personal and occupational pensions received tax relief on contributions and no tax on fund income. These reliefs were introduced to encourage people to save in such schemes but wealthier groups were much more likely to take advantage of these schemes than poorer people and so the tax system had an in-built advantage towards better-off groups. In recent years, various tax-privileged schemes have been introduced (such as Individual Savings Accounts) to benefit people with varying levels of income. These ISAs however, have still been mostly taken up by wealthy people and so government is piloting new schemes such as the Saving Gateway, which will only be available to working-age people on relatively low incomes.

## Tackling fraud in social security and taxation

A key issue in relation to the administration of tax and benefits is the extent and nature of fraud. Cook (1989) was one of the first to point to the considerable differences between the treatment of benefit fraud and tax fraud. Benefit fraud has traditionally received much more attention from the state and those suspected of committing benefit fraud have been treated much more harshly by investigators, prosecutors and sentencers. These differences relate back to the prevailing assumptions about tax and social security. For example, those committing tax fraud are generally seen to be merely trying to keep hold of 'their' money whereas benefit fraudsters are seen as receiving even more money than they should be entitled to. A collectivist perspective might be more sympathetic to benefit fraudsters as it would consider the very low incomes of people on benefit (and most benefit fraudsters) compared with the very high incomes of tax fraudsters.

Grabiner's (2000) report on the **informal economy** discusses both of these types of fraud but, in common with previous work, devotes far more of the discussion to benefit fraud. The report, however, pointed to the harsher penalties for benefit fraud and so recommended that new legislation be introduced to bring in a new statutory offence of fraudulently evading income tax, to be tried in magistrates' courts.

## Recent reforms and future prospects

In the field of social security, the government's main focus has been to increase employment rates as a mechanism for reducing poverty among children and those of working age. For those over state pension age, the initial mechanism for reducing poverty was through a more sophisticated means-tested benefit (Pension Credit) though recent reforms have sought to reduce the use of means testing through increases in social insurance and private saving. In the field of taxation, reforms have been redistributive in practice even if the government has not announced its intention to channel resources from rich to poor, nor trumpeted some reforms that have done just that. Major changes from 1997 to 2007 are shown in Table 9.4.

In general, the reforms have been redistributive, with people in the bottom half of the income distribution gaining more than those in the top half. If we add in the effects of the social security reforms to this calculation, we find an even more progressive effect. Those in the poorest 10 per cent of incomes have seen their incomes rise by 18.5 per cent due to the reforms whereas those in the wealthiest 10 per cent have seen their incomes drop slightly (Brewer, Clark and Wakefield, 2002). There has also been redistribution between different family types, with the main 'winners' being people with children and pensioners. Among people with children, the main 'winners' have been those with no earners in the household. However, levels of inequality remain high and poverty rates have not been reduced sufficiently to meet the government's own targets.

Despite the failure of employment-focused reforms to meet the government's own poverty-reduction targets, the government is continuing with the same overall

Table 9.4 Major reforms between 1997–2007

| Social security changes | Tax changes |
| --- | --- |
| Various New Deal programmes (e.g. for young people, lone parents etc.) | Married couple's allowance abolished for people born after 1935 |
| Work-focused interviews for all benefit claimants (the ONE programme) | Introduction of 10 per cent starting income tax rate, subsequently abolished, funding reduction in basic rate to 20% |
| Substantial increases in levels of child benefit and child components of Income Support | |
| Tax Credits introduced | Primary earnings threshold on NI raised Upper earnings limit for NI raised from £525 to £575 per week |
| Pension Credit introduced | |
| Raising state pension age | Extra 1% National Insurance payable beyond the upper limit (for NHS spending) |
| Restoring the link between state pension and earning (in future, subject to caveats) | Married couples and civil partners able to transfer their liability for inheritance tax to each other |
| Personal accounts introduced | Introduction of insurance premium tax |
| Winter fuel payments introduced | |

strategy. It now aims to increase employment rates further (to a target of 80 per cent). The 2007 Green Paper, *In Work, Better Off*, refers to: 'stubborn barriers to our goal of full employment in our generation. There are over three million people of working age who have been on benefit for over a year, many on incapacity benefits' (p. 5). The implication is that these 'stubborn barriers' are the incapacity benefit recipients them- selves, alongside other groups such as lone parents. The government aims to tackle these 'stubborn barriers' through replacing Incapacity Benefit with a new Employ- ment and Support Allowance alongside a Personal Capability Assessment. The Green Paper also proposes that lone parents with a youngest child aged under 12 should no longer be entitled to income support on the grounds of being a lone parent from October 2008 (and from October 2010 this age would be reduced to 7 years old).

Various reforms to the pension system have been introduced such as: increas- ing the state pension age for future cohorts; restoring the link between pensions and earning; and introducing new 'opt-out' personal accounts for those without private pensions. The effects of these will take many years to discern.

As far as the tax system goes, the government is still on its seemingly endless quest to simplify the system, though some commentators view Gordon Brown's time at the Treasury as one of increasing complication and regulation. Following the Lyons' Inquiry (2007), the government appeared to be dithering about reform of council tax and revaluing of property. Cuts in inheritance tax under Gordon Brown's administration, with Alistair Darling as Chancellor, also suggest that tax reforms are primarily motivated by political point-scoring and the pursuit of pop- ularity rather than any overarching ideological vision.

Despite the substantial increases in spending on health and education, social security remains by far the largest area of spending on the 'five giants' of social welfare. It also retains something of a reputation of a complex area, with limited public knowledge and discussion. Tax remains a key political battleground. After a decade of New Labour which has failed to argue the case for redistribution through higher taxes – instead preferring quieter modes of redistribution – selective reductions in tax (such as inheritance tax) remain popular and neither main party seems prepared to give up the mantle of the tax-cutter.

## Conclusion

Most of what government does is funded by taxation. Commitments to spend must generally be backed by tax revenue. This places an onus on government on finding ways to raise taxes that have the least effect on behaviour, unless behaviour change is an objective as with 'green taxes', and to ensure a 'fair' apportionment of who pays tax. The largest area of spending remains social security benefits, despite the negative connotations (of 'failure', according to Tony Blair) that such spending now often has. Rapid rises in spending on health and education have not changed the situation with expenditure on benefits remaining much more significant in money terms.

Both tax and social security benefits play an important role in reducing the in- equality generated through market incomes. Before looking at transfers, the best-off 10 per cent have incomes about 30 times greater than the poorest 10 per cent. After transfers the remaining inequality is still very high – a ratio of 12 to 1 – but clearly much reduced. It is an important social policy question as to just how much redistribution is politically feasible. Social security benefits are quite effective at redistributing income from rich to poor; many aspects of the tax system are progressive in this way (such as income tax) but other aspects are regressive (such as taxes on spending). The more hidden world of 'tax expenditures' generally acts to favour the better-off.

Policy within social security has been changed under New Labour to give even greater emphasis to returning people to work. It has become a work-based system, for most adults of working age. Moreover, many of the anti-poverty objectives are now shared with the 'tax credits' operated by the tax-collecting authority. This means an even greater relationship between the two arms of fiscal policy.

## Summary

This chapter has highlighted that the social security and tax systems can be seen as two sides of the same coin, and that there are a range of possible aims for both. It has also demonstrated the complexity of the systems. Examining the development of the tax and social security systems it is possible to say that:

- Much political discourse, including that of Tony Blair while Prime Minister, associates social security spending with economic and social failure.
- Notions of 'deserving' and 'undeserving' poor continue to affect attitudes towards the benefits system.
- Evidence, such as that from the British Social Attitudes Surveys, generally shows support for higher taxes to pay for higher public spending. However, recent data on public attitudes suggest that, if anything, attitudes towards state spending on welfare hardened between 2002 and 2006.
- At one time income tax used to be paid by only higher earners, but is now paid by most people in paid work.
- The incomes of the best-off 10 per cent are nearly 30 times as great as those of the worst-off. After taking into account taxes and benefits, they are 'merely' 12 times better off.
- 'Tax credits' are a relatively new and growing feature of the tax system, taking on functions traditionally performed by social security benefits.
- Tax expenditures ('tax breaks') are also important, but their costs are only periodically subject to close scrutiny.
- There are three main types of social security benefit: contributory; means-tested benefits and contingent. The importance of relieving poverty in the British system explains a strong reliance on means testing in Britain.
- Taxes are generally divided into 'direct taxes' such as income tax and National Insurance contributions and 'indirect taxes' such as value added tax (VAT) that applies to most goods and services.
- In social security, New Labour's main focus has been to increase employment rates as a mechanism for reducing poverty among children and those of working age.

## Discussion and review topics

**1** What are the main challenges currently facing the social security system? Is it well placed to meet those challenges?

**2** Only a small minority (under 10 per cent) of estates pay inheritance tax. So, why are proposals to abolish it (or make it affect even fewer people) so popular compared to other taxes?

**3** How much of the role of social security is now delivered through the tax system? What are the implications of using the tax system to achieve the aims of social security?

**4** Why is the social security system in the UK so complex? Is this complexity justified?

## Further reading

**Adam, S. and Browne, J.** (2006) *A survey of the UK tax system*, Institute for Fiscal Studies Briefing Note No. 9, IFS, London. This paper provides a useful overview of the tax system, describing each of the main taxes, how they work, and estimating the amount of revenue that they raise.

**McKay, S. and Rowlingson, K.** (1999) *Social Security in Britain*, Macmillan, Basingstoke. The authors provide a comprehensive coverage of the social security system whilst maintaining a generally clear approach.

**Millar, J.** (ed.) (2003) *Understanding Social Security*, the Policy Press, Bristol. This book provides a relatively recent review which takes account of reforms to the social security system.

**O'Dea, C., Phillips, D. and Vink, A.** (2007) *A survey of the UK benefit system*, IFS Briefing Note No. 13, IFS, London. This paper looks at the benefits system, considering both overall expenditure and examining each benefit in turn.

## Some useful websites

**www.policypress.org.uk/journals/benefits** – those wanting to keep up to date should read the journal *Benefits: The Journal of Poverty and Social Justice*.

**www.dwp.gov.uk** – the Department for Work and Pensions publishes regular research reports, and press releases.

**www.hmrc.gov.uk** – the website of HM Revenue and Customs provides a range of information, including figures on tax credits.

**www.ifs.org.uk** – the Institute for Fiscal Studies produces timely commentaries on tax and benefit reform, from an economic perspective.

## References

Adam, S. and Browne, J. (2006) *A survey of the UK tax system*, Institute for Fiscal Studies Briefing Note No. 9, IFS, London.

Adam, S. and Frayne, C. (2001) *A survey of the UK tax system*, Institute for Fiscal Studies Briefing Note No. 9, IFS, London.

Alcock, P., Erskine, A. and May, M. (1998) *The student's companion to social policy*, Blackwell, Oxford.

Brewer, M., Clark, T. and Wakefield, M. (2002) *Five years of social security reforms in the UK,* Institute for Fiscal Studies Working Paper W02/12, London.

Bryson, C. (1997) 'Benefit claimants: victims or villains?' in R. Jowell, J. Curtice, A. Park, L. Brook, K. Thomson, and C. Bryson (eds) *British Social Attitudes: The 14th Report*, Dartmouth, Aldershot.

Clark, T., Myck, M. and Smith, Z. (2001) *Fiscal reform affecting households, 1997-2001*, Institute for Fiscal Studies, London, **www.ifs.org.uk/election/index.shtml**.

Cook, D. (1989) *Rich law, poor law, different responses to tax and supplementary benefit fraud*, Open University Press, Milton Keynes.

Crosland, A. (1956) *The Future of Socialism,* Jonathan Cape, London.

DWP (2002) *Spending Review 2002: Benefit expenditure tables*, **www.dwp.gov.uk**.

Ditch, J. (ed.) (1999) *Introduction to Social Security*, Routledge, London (a collection of chapters on poverty and social security by different authors).

Family Resources Survey (2005-6) available at **www.dwp.gov.uk/asd/frs/2005_06/index.asp**.

Field, F., Meacher, M. and Pond, C. (1977) *To him who hath: A study of poverty and taxation*, Penguin, Harmondsworth.

George, V. and Wilding, P. (1985) *Ideology and Social Welfare*, Routledge and Kegan Paul, London.

Grabiner, Lord (2000) *The Informal Economy*, The Stationery Office, London.

Greve, B. (1994) 'The hidden welfare state, tax expenditure and social policy', *Scandinavian Journal of Social Welfare*, Vol. 3, No. 4, pp. 203-11.

Hayek, F. (1976) *The Constitution of Liberty*, Routledge and Kegan Paul, London.

Hedges, A. and Bromley, C. (2001) *Public Attitudes Towards Taxation: the Research Conducted for the Fabian Commission on Taxation and Citizenship*, Fabian Society, London.

Hills, J. (1998) *Income and wealth: The latest evidence*, York Publishing Services, York.

HM Treasury (1998) *The modernisation of Britain's tax and benefit system, Number 2: Work incentives, a report by Martin Taylor*, HM Treasury, London (available online at **www.hm-treasury.gov.uk/mediastore/otherfiles/taylor.pdf**).

HM Treasury (2000) *The informal economy: A report by Lord Grabiner QC*, HM Treasury, London.

HM Treasury (2007) *Meeting the aspirations of the British people: 2007 Pre-Budget Report and Comprehensive Spending Review* (October 2007), HM Treasury, London.

Jones, F. (2007) *The effects of taxes and benefits on household income, 2005-06*, online version at **www.statistics.gov.uk/downloads/theme_social/Taxes_Benefits_2005-2006/Taxes_Benefits_2005_06.pdf** (accessed 1 October 2007).

Lyons, M. (2007) *Lyons Inquiry into Local Government*, The Stationery Office, London.

McDaniel, S. and Surrey, P. (1985) *Tax Expenditures*, Harvard University Press, Cambridge MA.

McKay, S. and Rowlingson, K. (1999) *Social Security in Britain,* Macmillan (now Palgrave), London.

Miliband, R. (1994) *Socialism for a sceptical age*, Polity Press, Cambridge.

Millar, J. (ed.) (2003) *Understanding social security,* Policy Press, Bristol.

Nozick, R. (1974) *Anarchy, State and Utopia,* Basil Blackwell, Oxford.

Office for National Statistics (2006) *Health Statistics Quarterly - Winter 2006*, Office for National Statistics, London.

Orton, M. and Rowlingson, K. (2007) *Public attitudes to economic inequality*, Joseph Rowntree Foundation, York.

Phillips, D. and Sibieta, L. (2006) *A survey of the UK benefit system*, IFS Briefing Note No. 13, London.

Smith, A. (1976) *The Theory of Modern Sentiments*, Liberty Fund, Indianapolis.

Tawney, R. (1921) *The Acquisitive Society,* Allen & Unwin, London.

Tawney, R. (1931) *Equality*, Allen & Unwin, London.

Taylor-Gooby, P. and Hastie, C. (2002) 'Support for state spending: Has New Labour got it right?' in A. Park, J. Curtice, K. Thomson, L. Jarvis, and C. Bromley (eds) *British Social Attitudes: The 19th Report,* Sage Publications, London, pp. 75-96.

Taylor-Gooby, P. and Martin, R. (2007) 'Trends in sympathy for the poor', in *British Social Attitudes,* Sage Publications, London, pp. 59-88.

Wood, G. (1988) 'Housing tax expenditures in OECD countries economic impacts and prospects for reform', *Policy and Politics*, Vol. 16, No. 4, pp. 235-50.

# 10

# Work and welfare

Lavinia Mitton

## Chapter overview

In 2005 New Labour was elected a third time on a manifesto that referred to a huge and high-profile commitment to employment policy:

Our goal is employment opportunity for all – the modern definition of full employment. Britain has more people in work than ever before, with the highest employment rate in the G7. Our long-term aim is to raise the employment rate to 80 per cent . . . We will make work pay. . . . We will help people who can work into rehabilitation and eventually into employment.

Labour Party (2005, pp. 17-18)

This chapter will examine how the government has tried to meet these aims through discussion of:

- the important changes taking place in the labour market, and why there do not seem to be enough jobs to go round;
- wages and working hours;
- the implications of how unemployment is measured;
- groups that are disadvantaged in the labour market;
- different explanations of unemployment;
- unemployment and social policy;
- regulation of employment and workers' rights.

## Spotlight on the issues
## Welfare reform and New Labour

In its 2007 Green Paper, setting out its vision for welfare reform, the Labour government sought to present arguments for a continued shift from what it saw as a system of passive benefits to one of active support for unemployed people. It highlighted five design principles, arguing that:

We believe that, following the implementation of the Employment and Support Allowance, we need to ensure that the rest of the working-age benefits system is in line with clear principles:

*Promote work* – the system should be geared to actively promote work as the best route out of poverty for all those who can work. Financial gains from work must be clear, with simple and consistent messages.

*Value for money* – the system must be affordable, secure and cost-effective.

*Clear obligations* – people should be in no doubt as to what they need to do to get benefits. Conditions and requirements should be reasonable and proportionate.

*Straightforward rules* – the system should be easy for people to understand and access. Staff should be able to advise people with confidence and certainty.

*Fair treatment* – a presumption in favour of common rules for common situations, while recognising genuine differences in need.

Source: Department for Work and Pensions (2007) *Ready for work: Full employment in our generation*, London: The Stationery Office, p. 99.

These principles help highlight some of the issues facing policy makers in the area of work and welfare, including the pressure to deliver savings in public expenditure; the extent to which it is acceptable to expect or even require individuals to work, and the desire for clear and simple rules. However, as this chapter makes clear, the relationships between work and welfare are often problematic.

# Work as welfare?

Work is an important source of welfare – for most people paid employment is their main source of income. The government promotes 'work as the best form of welfare' (DWP, n.d.). This is not just because of the income that people get by earning, but because work also gives us other benefits. Some employers offer company cars, subsidised travel, or subsidised meals in the work canteen. Occupational pensions are an important extra benefit – the employer pays money into the employee's pension fund to top up their own savings. Work is also important because it is linked to better mental and physical health and a better sense of well-being and fulfilment. This is partly to do with having more money for social and leisure activities. However, some people like to work even if the financial gain to them is small, or do voluntary work, because it brings them higher self-esteem and they enjoy the social environment of the workplace. Work can bring us a sense of purpose in life, a structure to our day, and a sense of pride and is a key element of **social inclusion**. It has also been identified by the government as forming part of a solution to child poverty and as improving **social mobility**.

These are all compelling reasons why employment policy should be central to any government's social policy. The key policy issues are: What is the best way to get people into work? What should be the roles of individuals, business and the state in solving unemployment? What should be expected from recipients of benefits for the unemployed?

## Work: past and present

In drafting his report, Beveridge (see Chapter 5) assumed that the government would intervene in the economy to ensure that there was full employment (for men), thereby stamping out idleness – one of his 'five giants' of social evil. At that time, the public memory of the terrible unemployment in the interwar period was still very much alive. As it happened, governments' commitment to this ideal never had to be tested in the 1950s and 1960s because economic growth was strong without the need for state intervention.

However, unemployment started to rise during the economic recessions of the 1970s and governments' attempts to cut unemployment failed. In 1979, the Conservative Margaret Thatcher became Prime Minister. Her government's approach was first and foremost to get the economy back on track, by bringing down the inflation rate. Unfortunately this was achieved at the cost of high unemployment. Long-term employment, in particular, grew. Drawing on market-based **New Right** economics, Thatcher believed that the reason for unemployment was that wages were too high, which was holding down employers' willingness to employ more workers. She also believed that there was a high level of **welfare dependency** because the level of social security benefits compared to wages was too high (the so-called '**replacement ratio**') and so the unemployed would prefer to stay at home living on benefits rather than go out and get a job. In line with this belief, social security benefits were cut. She also believed that collective wage bargaining by the trades unions, organisations of workers which aim to protect the interests of their members, was keeping wages too high, again causing employers to be unable to afford to take on more workers. The problem with a highly regulated employment protection model, it is argued, is that it increases pay and reduces the number of dismissals, but at the expense of restricting the number of jobs. It also encourages employers to hire on the basis of temporary contracts with low protection, to get around the regulations that protect permanent staff. The labour market becomes segmented into those who cannot be sacked and a marginal workforce who will not be offered permanent jobs. In response, she curtailed the power of the trade unions. Famously she quashed the miners in their long-running strike.

The 1980s was a period of deindustrialisation. Industries such as car manufacturing, steel and mining went into decline, and Britain entered a post-industrial era as other countries were able to produce these goods at a cheaper price. The numbers of manual jobs declined and office jobs and the service sector increased. This shift has fundamentally changed the nature of the labour market.

Thought provoker

Work is the best route out of poverty for all groups in society. People who work are better off finan-cially. They are better off in terms of their health and well-being, their self-esteem and the future prospects for themselves and their families.

Peter Hain, Secretary of State for Work and Pensions (2008)

Is helping individuals into work the best way to lift them out of poverty?

In the twenty-first century the UK is in a global labour market. As Brazil, the Russian Federation, India and China have become more developed, goods can be manufactured much cheaper there than in the UK. There is a danger that Britain's low-skilled workers will fare worse and worse as **globalisation** intensifies low-wage competition. For example, new communications technology allows telephone call centres to be off-shored to India. The government's policy therefore is for the UK to be a 'knowledge economy', that is to say being superior in service industries which require a high level of skills and which cannot be substituted for technology. Examples are banking and other financial services, and creative industries such as design, TV production and music.

In reality, employment in low-skilled, low-waged service sector jobs which can-not be done overseas has also increased with globalisation. Examples are cleaning, catering, leisure and retail jobs. Increasing labour market segmentation has led to parallel labour markets for high-skilled and low-skilled workers, with little chance for low-skilled workers to climb the career ladder. Consequently, there has been growth in the numbers of working poor.

 Controversy and debate

A relatively recent development has been the influx of workers from the Eastern European countries which entered the EU in 2004, especially Poles. The employment of migrant workers is one of the most controversial policy issues in the UK. On average, the migrants are highly skilled – 45 per cent have degrees (RBS Royal Bank of Scotland Group, 2007). And they do the jobs least attractive to the British. Contrary to the stereo-type of the Polish plumber, they often do low-skill, low-wage jobs, many of them physically arduous, requiring long or anti-social hours, or in uncomfortable working conditions, such as meat-packing. More than half of Eastern European migrants work as process opera-tives, warehouse operatives or packers (Home Office *et al.*, 2006). Migrants go after this work in order to improve their English, because they can earn money to send to family back home, or because they see it as only temporary. Employers say that they like the migrants' work ethic, contrasting it favourably to the low motivation and poorer 'soft skills' they see in their British peers (Anderson *et al.*, 2006).

Why were migrants from Eastern Europe able to find jobs, when there were 1.65 million British people who are unemployed?

Another important change has been the appearance of a flexible labour market, and a decline in the number of jobs which are permanent and full time. In its place we have witnessed a growth in self-employment, freelancing, part-time, flexitime, and short-term contracts, fixed-term contracts, overtime, term-time-only working, and casual and agency work. There are some people, such as seasonal workers, who cycle between the low-paid jobs and unemployment. This change has been driven by employers trying to cut their labour costs, by hiring staff only when needed. The move to the flexible labour market has disadvantaged insecure low-paid workers, although some people, such as women with children, appreciate flexible work as a means to achieve a better work–life balance. There are also people with skills in high demand who have real career choices open to them and turn the flexible labour market to their advantage, choosing to work for a number of employers, maybe as a consultant. They have 'clients' and 'customers', rather than jobs and employers. The result can be a less secure but more fulfilling career. The concept of a 'job for life' no longer exists. Its disappearance has led to the need for 'lifelong learning', as workers need increasingly to be able to swiftly move from one job to another, rather than becoming stuck in an industry which has no future.

Two developments could cause major problems in the future, leading to fewer workers supporting those who are not working, thus worsening the **dependency ratio**. First, young people spend longer in education than in the past, with many more staying on into higher education today. Second, life expectancy is increasing, as is the popularity of retiring early. While this may increase the quality of life for the individual, it is a trend which will increase pension costs.

In summary, the jobs available and the skills that they require have changed enormously since the 1960s.

## Wage inequality

As work is most people's main source of income, analysis of the impact of the welfare state must take account of the role of paid work in welfare. It is inevitable that some people are able to earn more than others. The state intervenes to ameliorate the worst aspects of unequal wage distribution. In particular, there is redistribution through the system of tax and social security benefits (see Chapter 9). For example, the well-off have a larger proportion of their income taken away in tax, a system called progressive taxation. On the other hand, tax credits and social security benefits are given to people whose incomes from the labour market are lower.

Some service sector jobs require a higher level of skill than in the past. However, there are other service sector jobs which are poorly paid and require few skills. Examples are cleaning, call centre jobs, care work and work in fast-food restaurants, dubbed 'McJobs' (for a discussion of this phenomenon see Ritzer, 1993). These are less well paid than the manual occupations which disappeared in the 1980s. In effect, the middle ground of relatively well-paid semi-skilled or manual work has all but disappeared (for a discussion of this see Gallie, 1991; Bradley *et al.*, 2000). There are also reduced opportunities in non-manufacturing routine

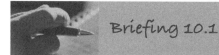

jobs that require only moderate skills. This so-called **labour market segmentation** has been driven by globalisation and technological change. For example, phone and internet banking and cash machines mean fewer bank counter staff are needed. On the other hand, these changes have increased the wages of the most highly skilled and talented: international firms now compete globally for talent, driving 'fat cat' pay up.

People tend to partner with someone of the same standing in the labour market as themselves. There has also been an increase in single people who are not working. These trends contribute to the phenomenon of 'dual-earner' and 'no-earner' households (Berthoud, 2007). Along with wage and income inequality, there has been widening inequality in the number of hours people work (Green, 2001). Some workers are working longer hours than their predecessors, including working Sundays and serving the 24-hour service sector. Professionals may choose to work longer hours to advance their career. Lower-paid workers may find themselves doing overtime or juggling two jobs. This has led to a common perception that Britain has a long-hours culture. On the other hand, more workers than in the past prefer to work part time or are being offered fewer hours than they would have been before, as employers respond to the needs of business. This pattern is obscured in the figures on average hours worked. When people work is also changing: some jobs which were traditionally nine-to-five are no longer. At the same time, many employees in both the public and private sectors feel they are working harder – they have experienced **labour intensification** (Green, 2001).

Arguably policy should aim not only for more jobs, but better jobs. The importance of the quality of jobs should not be underestimated: satisfactory working conditions matter, as well as pay, in increasing worker motivation. Labour intensification and longer hours can have a negative impact on the work–life balance, raising people's level of stress, and having a detrimental effect on their health and their family life. Other aspects of job quality include employee benefits (such as health club membership or pension scheme), job security, autonomy, occupational safety, and the opportunity for progression.

## Briefing 10.2

There are two broad political positions towards employment policy:

**1** The Conservative governments of the 1980s and early 1990s drew on the theories of the New Right, a position influenced by the theories of **neo-liberalism**. The belief is that state-run services are inefficient and therefore lead to economic problems. Instead, the argument goes, government intervention in the economy should be de-emphasised and market forces, private initiative and fewer restrictions on business be promoted. Underlying such policy ideas is the assumption that there are jobs available to all who want one.

**2** The other strand of thought which has influenced employment policy in the last three decades is **social democracy**, in which social objectives are held to be of importance as well as economic objectives. Policy making from this standpoint is more in favour of government intervention in the labour market and industrial relations and of promoting workers' rights. This position combines employment protection with social protection for those out of the labour market. New Labour is influenced by social democratic thought. The problem with this approach is that it is expensive.

## Measuring unemployment

Are jobless persons who want work but are not actively searching unemployed? No, according to the government's preferred measure, so-called 'ILO (International-al Labour Organisation) unemployment' (see Figure 10.1). This refers to people without a job who:

- want a job;
- are available to start work in the next two weeks;
- and who have looked for work in the previous four weeks;
- or who are out of work and waiting to start a job they have already obtained in the next two weeks.

On the other hand, the number of people on unemployment-related benefits – the 'claimant count' – will be lower than this, because some unemployed people are not eligible to receive benefits. Their savings may be too high or they may have resigned their previous job and therefore be deemed voluntarily unemployed. The difference between the two measures is wider for women than for men. Currently fewer than half of unemployed women claim unemployment-related benefits compared with around three quarters of men. This is partly because with having lower pay or being at home, fewer build up an entitlement to the benefits which are not means tested. It also means that the claimant count can be a misleading measure of unemployment.

When employment is high the gap between unemployment and the claimant count tends to widen, as some jobless people who were not previously looking for work start to do so. By actively looking for work they may become classified as unemployed under the ILO definition. However they do not feature in the claimant

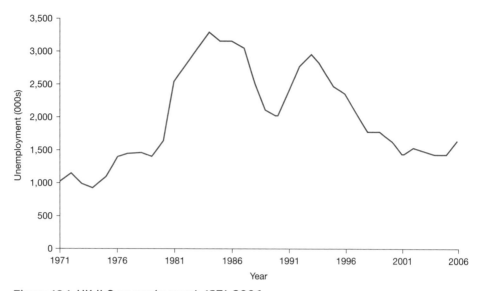

**Figure 10.1** UK ILO unemployment, 1971–2006

*Source*: Office for National Statistics, based on *Labour Force Survey* summary data.

count unless they also begin to claim benefits. Long-term unemployment is often defined as being out of work for 12 months or more.

The peak in the overall unemployment rate corresponds to the recessions in the 1980s and early 1990s. The peak in 1984 was equivalent to an unemployment rate of 11.9 per cent. Unemployment has gradually decreased between 1993 and 2008.

**Economic inactivity** is different from unemployment: it also includes people who are not looking for work. A related concept is the participation rate, the percentage of working-age people economically active – that is, people who are either in work or actively looking for work – compared to the total number of people of working age. The working-age population comprises men aged 16–64 and women aged 16–59.

The economically inactive may be at home with their children or be caring for another relative, be retired early, be students, or be unable to work because of long-term sickness or disability (Table 10.1). They may also be 'discouraged workers'. This effect occurs when, because of high unemployment, some people are discouraged from looking for work and withdraw from the labour force, thus reducing participation rates. Some of the economically inactive may think of themselves as unemployed, even though they do not fall within the definition of ILO unemployment.

The number of unemployed is relatively low. The numbers of people of working age who are not working because of sickness or disability is far higher than those unemployed. In late 2007, for example, the ILO unemployment rate was 5.4 per cent, but the inactivity rate of working-age people was 21.2 per cent (DWP, 2007b). The appropriate concept of unemployment to use depends on the purposes to which the resulting measure will be put, and different measures suggest different policy responses. For example, ILO unemployment is extremely useful for making international comparisons but, as the data shows, it can overlook those who would search for work if they believed that suitable opportunities were out there.

**Table 10.1** Reasons for economic inactivity: by sex and age, 2006, United Kingdom (%)

|  | 16–24 | 25–34 | 35–49 | 50–59/64 | All aged 16–59/64 |
|---|---|---|---|---|---|
| **Men** |  |  |  |  |  |
| Long-term sick or disabled | 5 | 39 | 62 | 49 | 36 |
| Looking after family or home | 1 | 11 | 16 | 5 | 6 |
| Student | 81 | 25 | 5 | – | 30 |
| Retired | 0 | * | * | 33 | 14 |
| Other | 13 | 25 | 18 | 12 | 14 |
| All men | 100 | 100 | 100 | 100 | 100 |
| **Women** |  |  |  |  |  |
| Long-term sick or disabled | 4 | 10 | 23 | 41 | 20 |
| Looking after family or home | 22 | 71 | 61 | 27 | 45 |
| Student | 66 | 11 | 4 | 1 | 21 |
| Retired | 0 | 0 | – | 13 | 3 |
| Other | 9 | 8 | 11 | 18 | 11 |
| All women | 100 | 100 | 100 | 100 | 100 |

*Source*: *Labour Force Survey,* Office for National Statistics, 2007.

## Access to work

In this section we look at the extent to which the patterns of work and unemployment vary according to gender, ethnicity, disability and age. In addition there are regions where worklessness is concentrated (see the section on explanations of unemployment).

### Gender and work

Fifty years ago, generally speaking, the male head of the household was in work, and his wife was dependent on him. It was taken for granted that most women would stay at home and look after the children, doing unpaid work (which traditionally has been accorded lower status than work outside the home). This is called the **male breadwinner** model (for more on this see Warren, 2007). It was assumed that the male wage, typically from a relatively well-paid manual job in industry, would support all his family. The social security system was based on this model. For example, it was assumed that relationships would last, and that the husband would support his wife in retirement with the pension he had built up during his working life. These days there are more divorces and women can find themselves without entitlement to a decent pension. It is also more common for the female partner to take the breadwinner role.

Women's access to work was restricted by their domestic responsibilities, the lack of childcare, and assumptions about which jobs were suitable for women, such as nursing, teaching and light industrial work. These are jobs that require supposedly feminine qualities, such as caring, childcare and manual dexterity. Statistics show that three-quarters of working women are still found in just five occupational groups: the five C's – cleaning, catering, caring, cashiering and clerical (Equal Opportunities Commission, 2005).

Since the 1950s there has been an enormous increase in the number of women working outside the home. These days the male breadwinner model no longer matches reality (see, for example, discussion in Charles and Harris, 2007). For example, more mothers return to work after having a baby. Some women now earn more than their partners. Better qualified women are those most likely to return to work after starting a family (see, for example, the discussion in Smeaton, 2006). Women whose partners are out of work are the least likely to work. If they do return to work, women with fewer qualifications often take part-time jobs once their children reach school age. As the number of women in work has increased, so the level of unemployment among men has grown. Those whose chances have deteriorated most are disabled men with poor educational qualifications and no working partner (Berthoud, 2007). This has occurred partly because the growth in the low-skilled service sector has changed the nature of the jobs which are available to ones less attractive to men, because the new unskilled jobs are in spheres traditionally viewed as women's work.

Figure 10.2 shows the proportion of the working-age population in the UK who were in employment between 1971 and 2007. Before 1993 there were strikingly different trends in the employment rate between the sexes: the male employment rate fell, while that for women rose. Since 1993 the employment rates for men and women have followed a similar pattern.

Women, on average, earn less then men. The gender pay gap is the difference between men's and women's median full-time hourly earnings. It stood at 12.6 per cent in 2007. This means that women working full time are paid, on average, 87.4 per cent of men's hourly pay. The part-time gender pay gap is worse: for 2007 it was 39.1 per cent. Since 1975, when the Equal Pay Act came into effect, the full-time pay gap has closed considerably, but there remains progress to be

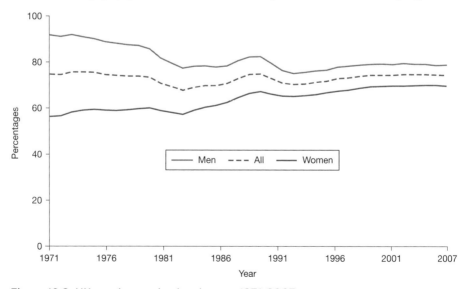

**Figure 10.2 UK employment rates, by sex, 1971–2007**
*Source*: Office for National Statistics, *Social Trends 38* (2008).

made. The Equal Pay Act addresses one aspect of the gender pay gap – that of unequal pay, but there are wider, complex and interconnected causes of the pay gap, such as job segregation and differences in work experience. Key factors include (Women & Equality Unit, 2006):

- **Human capital differences:** this refers to differences in educational levels and work experience. Historical differences in the levels of qualifications held by men and women have contributed to the pay gap. Women are also more likely than men to have breaks from paid work to care for children and other family members. These breaks impact on women's level of work experience, which in turn impacts on their pay rates.

- **Part-time working:** women are more likely than men to want part-time work which they can fit around their family commitments, but the kind of work available part time is often low paid.

- **Occupational segregation:** women's employment is highly concentrated in certain occupations. Those occupations which are female dominated and often part time, such as the unskilled service sector, are often the lowest paid and are low status. In addition, women are still under-represented in sectors such as engineering, ICT and the skilled trades.

- **Workplace segregation:** women are under-represented in the higher paid jobs within occupational career structures (such as management). This is sometimes called the 'glass ceiling' effect.

- **Travel patterns:** on average, women spend less time commuting than men. This may be because of time constraints due to balancing work and caring responsibilities. This can impact on women's pay in two ways: a smaller pool of jobs to choose from or lots of women wanting work in the same location (i.e. near to where they live), leading to lower wages for those jobs.

 Thought provoker

Women's typical work patterns have financial implications for them throughout their life course. Why might this be?

### Ethnicity and work

Different ethnic groups fare differently in the labour market (see also Chapter 17). The expression 'ethnic penalty' refers to all the sources of disadvantage that might lead an ethnic group to fare less well in the labour market than do similarly qualified whites. In other words, it is a broader concept than that of discrimination. While some groups are improving their labour market position relative to white people, substantial disadvantage remains, both in accessing jobs and in earnings once in employment (Clark and Drinkwater, 2007). There are substantial employment gaps for black African, black Caribbean, Pakistani and Bangladeshi men compared to white men. Among women, the employment rates of Pakistani and Bangladeshi women are particularly low, at less than 30 per cent (Clark and

Drinkwater, 2007). Table 10.2 shows unemployment rates by ethnic group and sex while Figure 10.3 illustrates the varying levels of economic inactivity between ethnic groups.

There is a high proportion of self-employment among Pakistanis, Bangladeshis, Indians and Chinese, perhaps because of disadvantage in employment. These family businesses are highly concentrated in retailing, restaurants, takeaways and taxi-driving, all sectors involving working long and anti-social hours.

Individuals from all ethnic minorities earn less on average than white people. Whilst the concentration of particular ethnic groups in particular occupations explains some of these earnings penalties, this is not the whole story. Even within occupations, earnings gaps are substantial, particularly so for men in professional and managerial occupations (Clark and Drinkwater, 2007).

Religion is a further source of diversity and being Muslim is associated with lower employment rates after ethnicity is taken into account. For example, the probability of white British Muslims gaining employment is 16–20 percentage

Table 10.2  UK unemployment rates,[1] by ethnic group and sex, 2001/2 (%)

| | ILO unemployment | |
| --- | --- | --- |
| | Men 16–64 | Women 16–59 |
| White | 5 | 4 |
| Mixed | 14 | 11 |
| Indian | 7 | 7 |
| Pakistani | 16 | 16 |
| Bangladeshi | 20 | 24 |
| Other Asian | 12 | 9 |
| Black Caribbean | 14 | 9 |
| Black African | 15 | 13 |
| Other[2] | 11 | 9 |
| *Unweighted bases* | | |
| White | 4452 | 3070 |
| Mixed | 57 | 44 |
| Indian | 108 | 82 |
| Pakistani | 127 | 57 |
| Bangladeshi | 59 | 25 |
| Other Asian | 39 | 24 |
| Black Caribbean | 95 | 69 |
| Black African | 78 | 64 |
| Other[2] | 41 | 30 |

[1]Unemployment based on the ILO definition as a percentage of all economically active.
[2]Other Black and Chinese were omitted because sample sizes were too small for reliable estimates.

Source: Office for National Statistics, *Annual Local Area Labour Force Survey*, 2001/2.

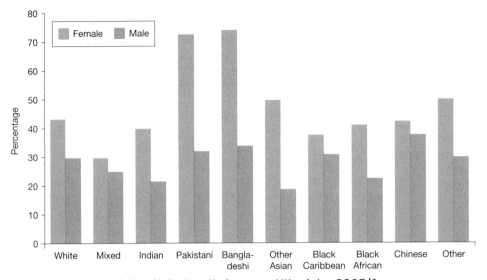

**Figure 10.3** Economic inactivity by ethnic group, UK, winter 2005/6

*Source*: Office for National Statistics, *Labour Force Survey*, 2005/06.

points lower than those with no religion (Clark and Drinkwater, 2007). This may reflect a number of factors including discrimination on the grounds of religious belief, attitudes to certain forms of employment or lack of access to employment opportunities.

### Disability and work

Another factor which keeps people out of work is long-term sickness or disability. This is despite government concerns about the numbers of long-term sick and disabled people leaving the labour market (see below). It is not just a concern because of social security costs: the absence of disabled people from the labour market contributes to their wider social exclusion.

Employment rates among disabled people are low, at around 40 per cent, but many more would like to work if suitable opportunities were available. Employed disabled people are disproportionately found in manual occupations. They also earn less – they have lower average hourly earnings than their non-disabled peers, even after taking account of differences in age, education and occupation (Burchardt, 2000). The general condition of the regional economy is also important for disabled people's employment: employers are more likely to hire a disabled person when the pool of prospective employers is smaller (Berthoud, 2007).

Under the 1995 Disability Discrimination Act (DDA) an employer must make 'reasonable adjustments' to the physical workplace or to working arrangements (for example, the pattern of hours worked) to ensure that a disabled person is not put at a 'substantial disadvantage'. The definition of disability under the DDA refers to a person's physical or mental impairment that has 'a long term effect on his ability to carry out day to day activities'. Yet disabled people continue to experience discrimination in employment and there are persistent problems with the character of legislation and its implementation (Foster, 2007). Outcomes in terms of adjustments made have been found to be almost entirely contingent upon the knowledge, attitudes and goodwill of poorly trained line managers, who frequently are ignorant of the law. Research has found that this often leads to instances of bullying by managers, resulting in stress and ill health among employees (Foster, 2007).

Other than the DDA, the policy has been to make individual disabled people 'more employable' by giving them training and skills as individuals, rather than making the workplace more accessible (see below on the New Deal for Disabled People).

### Ageing and work

As we have seen, the declining dependency ratio is a policy concern. It is not just that people are living longer, but more people are out of work below the state retirement age (60 for women and 65 for men). For instance, once older workers become unemployed, there is a high likelihood that they will become permanently unemployed, even if they want to work (Ashdown, 2000). In response, government is seeking to persuade people to delay retirement and work longer.

Early retirement was popular in the 1980s and 1990s, and is still used as a means of making redundancies. On the whole, those who have retired early are likely to be those with a generous **occupational pension** who can afford the luxury of doing so. On the other hand, there is pressure from government for people to carry on working to retirement age and beyond, and research has shown that most employees in fact prefer the idea of abolishing normal retirement ages in favour of retirement decisions being made on an individual basis, taking into account the needs of both the organisation and the employee (Vickerstaff *et al.*, 2004).

A large proportion of managers and employees like the idea of reducing workloads in the run-up to retirement (Vickerstaff *et al.*, 2004). Many are also in favour of a 'flexible' retirement, with employees drawing some pension while continuing to work reduced hours, in contrast to 'cliff-edge retirement'. Some people are able to benefit from drawing a pension and a salary at the same time by returning to work as a contractor after retirement – so-called double-dipping. The ability to take up such options, however, is affected by an individual's personal and financial

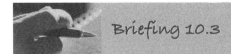

Briefing 10.3

The 2006 age discrimination legislation in Britain, prompted by new EU legal protections which forced the issue, is a development that, it is hoped, will extend working lives. The law maintains a default normal retirement age of 65. However, it has imposed some constraints on employer management of the older workforce. It is not legal to retire someone before they are 65 unless it is by agreement or for a reason with 'objective justification', and there is a duty on employers to consider requests from employees to stay on after 65. If the correct procedures are not followed, an older worker can make an unfair dismissal claim.

circumstances. In addition, workers may have little personal discretion over the timing and manner of their departure from work. Research has concluded that government urges for individuals to work longer will not be successful unless employers reappraise their management of older workers (Vickerstaff *et al.*, 2004).

## Explanations of unemployment

There are several types of unemployment, which can occur in combination. Understanding the causes of unemployment is important because it points to the most effective policy responses. Cyclical unemployment varies with how well the economy as a whole is doing. When the economy is booming, there will be lots of demand for goods and services and so firms will be employing large numbers of workers. If the economy slows down into a recession, firms will begin to lay workers off. The response to this since the 1980s has been for the government to use its economic policies to seek to ensure a consistent and stable economy, without prices or wages rising too fast. However, it is difficult to distinguish the success of employment policies from the effect of a healthy economy. For more than a decade (since 1997) governments had not had their employment policy seriously tested as the country enjoyed strong economic growth.

Structural unemployment occurs when the types of industry which are thriving and declining have changed. For example, in the UK, manufacturing industry has hugely decreased in its importance. One cause of structural unemployment is when the introduction of new technology reduces the number of workers required in an industry. The new jobs created in other industries, such as the service sector, may not be in sufficient numbers to compensate for those lost. If the industries that are dying are heavily concentrated in one part of the country, then this makes it much more difficult for people to find new jobs. For example, the shipbuilding and mining industries were heavily concentrated in the north of England, Scotland and Wales, but it is south-east England which has seen the most growth in jobs. Another cause of structural unemployment is when the growth industries demand skills which the unemployed do not have. Some other people may not be prepared to take a different type of work. Unfortunately, some former industrial areas have taken many years to adapt and reduce the level of structural unemployment. Structural unemployment carries the danger of becoming long term. This is a particular policy concern, because the longer a person is out of work, the harder it is for them to find a job because they may lose morale and work-related skills, and employers prefer to recruit people without a history of unemployment. One response could be to shore up the industry facing decline. However, since the 1980s governments have refused to subsidise struggling industries. Instead, policy now focuses on giving individuals education, training and support to help them get a job in another industry, a supply-side approach.

Some industries suffer particularly from seasonal unemployment, such as the hotel and tourism trades and agriculture. The effects of seasonal unemployment are often highly regionalised. Areas such as seaside resorts are very vulnerable to this type of unemployment.

Briefing 10.4

There are two broad approaches to employment policy:

1 Demand-side employment policies involve job creation, in other words, stimulating demand for workers.

2 Supply-side employment policies involve giving individuals the skills to get a job, in other words, improving the quality of the supply of workers.

The policy balance has shifted towards the supply side in the last thirty years following the failure of demand-side measures to cope with the unemployment of the 1970s.

Frictional or search unemployment occurs because when somebody loses their job they have a period of time out of work while they have to look for another one. The policy response to this is to make it easier for people to find another job, for example by maintaining the Jobcentre Plus website and digital TV service, and encouraging employers to notify the Jobcentre of their vacancies.

## Unemployment and social policy

The responsibility for employment policy lies with the Department for Work and Pensions (DWP). Administration of policy designed to help people back into work is carried out and coordinated by Jobcentres Plus. As well as a national network of Jobcentres Plus offices, which serve as the gateway to financial support and provide personal face-to-face advisory services, they have a network of telephone Contact Centres, a website for jobseekers, and a digital TV service which enables viewers to search for job vacancies. The DWP also works jointly with the Department for Innovation, Universities and Skills (DIUS), Jobcentre Plus and the Learning and Skills Council (LSC) to provide training in numeracy, literacy and language skills to increase the chances of the unemployed finding a job.

As we have seen, one response to unemployment is to pay social security benefits at a reasonable level, but also improve people's employability through education and training. Another response is to pay social security benefits which provide a minimal safety net to make sure there is a strong incentive to get a job. The key policy question is: what should be the balance between rights and responsibilities? In other words, to what extent should there be a right to welfare benefits and to what extent should there be a responsibility to retrain and try hard to find work? Currently the emphasis is on the latter, a system that offers 'a hand up, not a hand out' (Blair, 1999), in a bid to cut expenditure on social security and out of a belief that the best way to improve someone's welfare is to get them into work. This involves moving people from passive benefit recipients with little expected of them, to so-called **activation policies**, direct assistance designed to make people more employable. A 'something for something' principle is embodied in current policy. This involves support in return for individuals taking more responsibility to do what they can to return to work. The main benefit for the unemployed – Job-seeker's Allowance (JSA) – is so called to make clear the responsibilities of recipients to look for work.

In practice this has had three broad elements. First, 'making work pay'; second, welfare-to-work; and third, extending childcare. We will look at each of these, concentrating on policies towards the long-term sick, disabled and lone parents, some of the most disadvantaged groups in the jobs market.

## Making work pay

The first strand of New Labour employment policy is to 'make work pay', that is, to ensure that people are better off in work than out of work, avoiding the 'unem-ployment trap'. First, social security benefits are set relatively low, to encourage people to find a low-paid job. In April 2007 the rate of JSA for a single person was £59.15 (plus help with housing costs and council tax). The rate is lower for under 25s because of particular concerns about creating disincentives to work among younger people, as they have a lower earning capacity than prime-age adults.

Second, there is the national minimum wage (NMW). This gives a floor to wages. There are different levels of NMW, depending on the age of the worker. In October 2007 the rates were:

- Adults (people aged 22 and over) received the full rate of £5.52 an hour.
- A 'development rate' of £4.60 an hour was paid to workers aged 18 to 21 inclusive.
- Young people received £3.40 an hour. Young people are defined as those older than school-leaving age and younger than 18 (you are under school-leaving age until the end of summer term of the school year in which you turn 16).

As with JSA, the argument used to justify a lower minimum wage for young people is that they can command lower wages because they have less work experience, so a higher minimum wage would price them out of a job. The NMW particularly helps women, who, as we have seen, are concentrated in low-paid jobs. The key policy issue here is: what should be the rate of the NMW? The argument goes that if it is too low, it will not protect the most vulnerable workers. On the other hand, if it is too high, some people may not be able to find a job at all as employers cannot afford to hire them.

Third, there is the Working Tax Credit, not in fact a tax, but a top-up to the wages of those in low-paid work. The amount of Working Tax Credit a person can receive varies according to household income and circumstances and number of children.

Despite these policies, more needs to be done to ensure that moving into work really does pay, particularly for parents. There are problems with finding childcare places, in addition to the issue of whether they are affordable. Working Tax Credit currently pays 80 per cent of childcare costs for those in work, leaving working parents to find the other 20 per cent, which is hard for the low paid, especially for those with more than one child.

## Welfare-to-work

The current approach, called '**welfare-to-work**', has been influenced by the '**workfare**' system in the United States. These policies are intended to move those reliant on social security benefits (i.e. on welfare) into paid work. The policy consists of adequate benefits hand-in-hand with 'activation policies', which increase re-employment chances. Such policies include assistance with job hunting, job trials and work-related training programmes, with the threat that benefit may be cut for those who do not show willing.

Central to New Labour employment policy is the New Deal, introduced in 1998. It was a big change in policy towards the unemployed and 2.88 million people had taken part in a New Deal programme by mid 2007 (DWP, 2007a). Its aim is to increase a person's employability, but those groups for whom it is compulsory can have benefit sanctions imposed on them if they do not take part. This means that their benefit could be temporarily suspended or be disallowed. So far the government has been cautious about imposing sanctions, especially on lone parents and disabled people, fearing a backlash, because the children of lone parents could suffer and disabled people command a great deal of public sympathy.

In recent debates it has been suggested that the New Deal schemes could evolve into a system of individualised, tailored support, bringing in those groups who do not fall under any of the existing New Deal programmes or who are multiply disadvantaged. Increasingly, services to help people on the New Deal, such as Job Brokers, are delivered by private and voluntary sector partners, an example of public–private partnership – contracting out delivery of publicly-funded services. In the words of the 2005 Labour manifesto: 'We will continue to welcome new independent and voluntary sector partners to provide job-seeking services' (Labour Party, 2005, pp. 17–18). The government particularly encourages local providers to become more involved in the delivery of services because they can draw on their expert knowledge of their local area (GNN/DWP, 2007). They also work with smaller providers which have expertise in giving targeted help to some of the 'hard to reach'. The providers are given incentives (usually in the form of target outcomes) to deliver the best possible services. Another example of partnership with the private sector is Local Employment Partnerships (LEPs), in which employers work in partnership with Jobcentre Plus, the Learning and Skills Council, and other bodies, to help long-term benefit claimants into work. This might involve: work trials, which allow people to remain on benefits while they try out a job; giving employers a wage subsidy; work experience opportunities; guaranteed interviews; reviewing employers' application processes to ensure there are opportunities for all applicants to be considered; existing employees acting as mentors to Jobcentre Plus customers. These were first introduced in 2007 and there are ambitious plans for the extension of LEPs.

Proponents argue that the New Deal has been successful at getting people back into work. They say that the help with job-search can improve the suitability of the jobs the unemployed find, resulting in better career prospects and job stability. Critics say that many of those who have found jobs would have done so anyway because they are the most easily employable, and that performance management by targets encourages this. They also say that the people often become unemployed again once a job placement has ended, so it does not produce new stable jobs, and instead participants face the problem of the 'revolving-door'. Moreover, the jobs people move into are frequently poor-quality jobs with little prospect of advancement. Success also depends on the quality of the relationship a person has with their personal advisor. Further, they say that one of the reasons why the numbers on benefit has gone down is because the prospect of having to participate in these activation schemes means that some people drop a benefit claim, or never apply for benefit in the first place.

Next we focus on policy responses to unemployment among young people, disabled people and lone parents, as these are the most controversial.

## Youth unemployment

Young people have attracted particular policy attention because a difficult transition from school into work can seriously disadvantage a young person's long-term career prospects. Of particular concern are the 10 per cent of young people aged 16–18 not in employment, education or training (termed NEET). This is a heterogeneous group with different characteristics and needs (for a discussion of this see Furlong, 2006). It includes:

- The unemployed, either for the long term or short term
- Young parents
- Disabled and sick young people, either temporarily or long term
- Young carers
- Aspiring musicians, actors and artists
- Those taking a break from education and employment, travelling, or developing skills through voluntary work.

Some in the diverse NEET group have made an active choice not to take paid work, and would not be considered vulnerable or disadvantaged, so the 10 per cent figure is rather more than the number who are facing severe and persistent difficulties (Furlong, 2006). There have been suggestions that young people should continue to work towards qualifications until the age of 18, to ensure that they have the skills necessary to get a job. Every young person who has not been in employment, education or training for at least 26 weeks by their 18th birthday will be fast-tracked to an intensive support and sanctions regime. They will have to prove that they are actively looking for work and engaging in work-related activity – if they do not, their benefits will be stopped. But the focus on the concept of NEET draws attention away from the pressing problems of young people churning between short-term jobs with little prospects (Furlong, 2006), those who 'have work, but not jobs'.

## Long-term sick and disabled people

The number of people of working age out of work and receiving the sickness or disability benefits has risen significantly since 1979. Table 10.3 shows how it dwarfs the numbers of unemployed and lone parents on benefits. Many recipients never move back into work – they become 'detached' from the labour market. Not

**Table 10.3** Main out-of-work benefits, number of recipients, in thousands

| Date | JSA (claimant count) | Incapacity benefits | Lone Parents on Income Support | Other |
|---|---|---|---|---|
| May-97 | 1,619.6 | 2,616.3 | 1,014.2 | 256.2 |
| Feb-07 | 920.0 | 2,662.2 | 771.4 | 163.2 |

*Note:* This table includes the main out-of-work client group categories, with the exception of carers who are not subject to activation policies in the same way as other groups.
*Source:* DWP, 2007b.

surprisingly, the government has been trying to reduce that number. One of their current policies is to replace the former Incapacity Benefit with a new benefit, re-badged Employment and Support Allowance. The aim is quite simple: to increase the requirements for 'work-related activity'.

Incapacity Benefit came to be perceived as a passive benefit which people got fixed on. There were concerns that it was acting as a hindrance to moving into work. For example, some recipients were wary of taking up training or voluntary work in case it made them appear capable of work, and of later being denied a reinstatement of Incapacity Benefit if the job did not work out as hoped. Being unemployed of itself can lead to health problems, so it was not uncommon for people to move from JSA to Incapacity Benefit. Another problem was that little was done to prevent people coming on to incapacity benefits in the first place – addressing this would involve working with GPs. At the same time, many disabled people said that they would like to work if suitable employment was available.

Under the new system, there is an Employment Allowance for those deemed able to work again, at a lower amount than the former Incapacity Benefit. There will be financial sanctions for those in this group who do not cooperate in looking for work. The Support Allowance is a higher level of benefit for those assessed as unable to work. It is expected to be a relatively small group. In the words of 2005 Labour Party manifesto:

> The majority of claimants with more manageable conditions will be required to engage in both work-focused interviews and in activity to help them prepare for a return to work. Those with the most severe conditions will also be encouraged to engage in activity and should receive more money than now.                      Labour Party (2005, p. 18)

The success of the new system depends partly on the quality of the personal advisor and the jobs available. The test of capability for work which will be applied should take account of the complexity and reality of disabled people's lives and the social implications of their disability. For the new allowances system to achieve its aim, in-work support is needed, as is a better understanding of employers' barriers to hiring disabled people.

## Lone parents

The government is concerned that despite the progress in increasing the employment rate for lone parents, it remains the lowest of any major European country. This means that they are more likely to be dependent on state benefits. The existence of benefit is thought to have reduced the incentive to work and to have a new partner. Some have argued that the existence of benefits is therefore contributing to welfare dependency and family breakdown.

The response to this has been to require more of lone parents: the requirement to look for work when the youngest child reaches 16 has been dropped to when they reach 12. Of course, the ability of lone parents to work depends on being able to find nearby affordable childcare and jobs which match their skills and can be fitted around caring for their child.

 ## Thought provoker

A policy challenge is that some lone parents feel it is important to stay at home with their children, and so are prepared to accept a lower standard of living than they would otherwise enjoy.

Should lone parents be expected to work?

## Childcare strategy

Affordable, local childcare can benefit parents by helping them to balance their working lives with family commitments. Childcare is also seen as a route out of poverty for families, enabling parents to increase their income by working. The New Labour government has aimed to increase the availability of childcare, to expand early years education and has promoted after-school clubs. Tax credits to off-set the costs of registered childcare have been extended. All 3- and 4-year-olds are now offered a free, part-time early education place. These are delivered free in any of the maintained, private, voluntary and independent sectors. The **Sure Start** scheme (in England) incorporates a wide range of childcare programmes including some targeted on particular local areas or disadvantaged groups. New Labour have also introduced entitlement to four weeks' paid holiday; increased maternity pay and leave; paid paternity leave; the right to take time off to deal with family emergencies; the right for parents with young or disabled children to request flexible working; and extended the right to request flexible working for carers. Issues still remain in finding care for older children after school and during school holidays which is acceptable to them as well as their parents. It can also be hard to find childcare for disabled children. A policy debate to be had is whether this package of early childhood measures is driven by the needs of young children, by the desire to improve children's educational attainment, or by the desire to raise employment levels.

## Employment protection and regulation

Policies for rights at work seek to ensure that the jobs people go into have good working conditions. As we have already seen, there is legislation in place relating to the national minimum wage, discrimination in employment and the rights of parents and carers. European Union legislation has proved influential in shaping employment law in the UK. The election of a Labour government in 1997 was a turning point in UK industrial relations: the trades unions had always had a close relationship with the Labour Party, traditionally making large donations to the party. Although New Labour distanced itself from them to some extent, the trades unions still held greater influence in policy making than they had done for the preceding two decades. One of the government's first acts on taking office was to sign up to the Social Chapter of the Maastricht Treaty, which lays down EU policies on workers' rights. Also, the implementation of the EU Working Time Directive introduced a limit of, on average, 48 hours of work a week; a legal entitlement to paid leave; and new laws on rest breaks, night work and shift patterns (however, employers can vary the terms of implementation by agreement with employees). In addition, part-time workers now have the same rights as full-time staff, including equal pro-rata pay, pension and holiday entitlement. Although New Labour has tried to shake off its anti-business image, British industry continues to view employment legislation under New Labour as having the potential to undermine the labour market reforms started by Thatcher.

Workers' rights are protected through Employment Tribunals. These are special courts of law established to resolve disputes between employers and employees over employment rights, for example claims of unfair dismissal and issues to do with discrimination and redundancy payments. ACAS (the Advisory, Conciliation and Arbitration Service) is a publicly funded service which can help people involved in a complaint about their employment rights reach a solution that both sides find acceptable without having to go through a court hearing. This process is known as conciliation. In addition to this, the Health and Safety Executive ensures that people are protected against risks to health or safety arising out of work activities, and enforces occupational health and safety law.

## Conclusion

In the context of greater globalisation (see Chapter 21) the government will most likely continue to try to enhance the UK's economic competitiveness by improving the education and skills of the workforce, rather than trying to compete by lowering wages. Therefore, policies to increase people's employability, such as those outlined in this chapter, are likely to play a greater role in the future and the effectiveness of employment policies and their interaction with the social security system will remain a crucial issue.

## Summary

This chapter has covered recent developments in employment policy and several debates relevant to policy in this area:

● The world of work has changed hugely in the last 50 years. Many more women are in work. The patterns of work and the types of work available have changed. Globalisation has led to a decline in semi-skilled manual jobs and a more flexible labour market.

- There are several measures of unemployment and the concept most useful to use depends on the purposes to which the resulting measure will be put.
- There are different types of unemployment and they invite different policy responses.
- Debates remain current about the balance to be struck between rights to benefit, on the one hand, and responsibilities to take steps to prepare for work on the other.
- A problem for policy is not just to create more jobs, but also to increase the quality of those jobs. It is important that the jobs the unemployed move into are sustainable ones.

## Discussion and review topics

1  Who are the gainers and losers from the changes in the world of work which have taken place in the last 30 years?

2  What should be the goals of employment policy?

3  What are the best ways to ensure equality in the workplace?

4  What types of policy would be most effective at encouraging older people to continue working up to state pension age and beyond?

## Further reading

**Brewer, M. and Shephard, A.** (2005) *Employment and the Labour Market*, Institute for Fiscal Studies, London. Reviews the operation of welfare-to-work programmes under the 1997 and 2001 Labour governments.

**Hudson, J. and Lowe, S.** (2004) 'Changes in the World of Work', in J. Hudson and S. Lowe *Understanding the Policy Process: Analysing Welfare Policy and Practice*, Policy Press, Bristol. This chapter considers the consequences of economic restructuring on the way in which work is divided between men and women, the geographical shift of population and industry and the implications of this for the welfare state.

**McKnight, A.** (2005) 'Employment: tackling poverty through "work for those who can",' in J. Hills and K. Stewart (eds) *A More Equal Society? New Labour, poverty, inequality and social exclusion*, Policy Press, Bristol. This chapter in an edited collection provides an overview of New Labour employment policy.

**Noon, M. and Blyton, P.** (2007) *The Realities of Work: Experiencing Work and Employment in Contemporary Society* (3rd edn), Palgrave Macmillan, Basingstoke. Offers a sociological approach to the experience of work, including coverage of topical issues such as emotion work, skill change, work-life balance, and discrimination.

# Some useful websites

**www.tuc.org.uk** – the Trades Unions Congress (TUC) website is a good source of information about worker's rights.

**www.hm-treasury.gov.uk** – the Treasury has an area of its site containing its publications relating to employment and welfare policy.

**www.dwp.gov.uk/resourcecentre** – government policy publications and research reports can be found on the website of the Department for Work and Pensions (DWP).

**www.berr.gov.uk/employment** – the Department for Business, Enterprise and Regulatory Reform (BERR) has responsibility for business relations and its website has information on employment rights and responsibilities.

**www.lowpay.gov.uk** – the Low Pay Commission (LPC) advises the government about the national minimum wage. Its website contains relevant research reports.

**www.employment-studies.co.uk** – the Institute for Employment Studies has publications available on its website.

**www.theworkfoundation.com** – the Work Foundation website has a number of relevant publications.

**www.jrf.org.uk** – the Joseph Rowntree Foundation regularly funds research on employment issues and recent reports can be downloaded from their website.

# References

Anderson, B., *et al.* (2006) *Fair enough? Central and East European migrants in low-wage employment in the UK*, Joseph Rowntree Foundation, York.

Ashdown, C. (2000) 'The Position of Older Workers in the Labour Market', *Labour Market Trends* (September), pp. 397–400.

Berthoud, R. (2007) *Work-rich and work-poor: Three decades of change*, Policy Press, Bristol.

Blair, T. (1999) *Beveridge Lecture*, Toynbee Hall, London.

Bradley, H., *et al.* (2000) *Myths at Work*, Polity Press, Cambridge.

Burchardt, T. (2000) *Enduring economic exclusion: Disabled people, income and work*, York Publishing Services for the Joseph Rowntree Foundation, York.

Charles, N. and Harris, C. (2007) 'Continuity and change in work-life balance choices', *The British Journal of Sociology,* Vol. 58, No. 2, pp. 277–95.

Clark, K. and Drinkwater, S. (2007) *Ethnic minorities in the labour market: Dynamics and diversity*, Policy Press, Bristol.

DWP (Department for Work and Pensions) (2007a) *DWP Quarterly Statistical Summary,* available from: **www.gnn.gov.uk/Content/Detail.asp?ReleaseID=307683&NewsAreaID=2** (accessed 16 September 2007).

DWP (Department for Work and Pensions) (2007b) *Flint: Record numbers in work mark another step towards full employment*, available from: **www.gnn.gov.uk/Content/Detail.asp?ReleaseID= 313891&NewsAreaID=2** (accessed 16 September 2007).

DWP (Department for Work and Pensions) (n.d.). *About the Department*, available from: **www.dwp.gov.uk/aboutus** (accessed 16 September 2007).

Equal Opportunities Commission (2005) *Investigation: Free to Choose – tackling gender barriers to better jobs: Great Britain Summary Report*.

Foster, D. (2007) 'Legal obligation or personal lottery? Employee experiences of disability and the negotiation of adjustments in the public sector workplace', *Work, Employment and Society*, Vol. 21, No. 1, pp. 67–84.

Furlong, A. (2006) 'Not a very NEET solution: Representing problematic labour market transitions among early school-leavers', *Work, Employment and Society*, Vol. 20, No. 3, pp. 553–69.

Gallie, D. (1991) 'Patterns of skill change: Upskilling, deskilling or the polarisation of skills?' *Work, Employment and Society*, Vol. 5, No. 3, pp. 319–51.

GNN/DWP (2007) *City strategy pathfinders launched with access to £65 million deprived areas fund*, available from: **www.gnn.gov.uk/Content/Detail.asp?ReleaseID=293353&NewsAreaID=2** (accessed 27 June 2007).

Green, D. (2001) 'It's been a hard day's night: The concentration and intensification of work in late twentieth-century Britain', *British Journal of Inndustrial Relations*, Vol. 39, No. 1, pp. 53–80.

Home Office *et al.* (2006) *Accession Monitoring Report May 2004–June 2006.*

Labour Party (2005) *Labour Party Manifesto 2005: Britain Forward, Not Back.*

National Statistics (2007) *Labour Market Statistics, September 2007, First Release*, National Statistics, London.

ONS (Office for National Statistics) (2007) *Social Trends 37*, Palgrave Macmillan, Basingstoke.

RBS Royal Bank of Scotland Group (2007) *Polish Plumbers: Mending your pipes and keeping your mortgage down.*

Ritzer, G. (1993) *The McDonaldization of Society*, Pine Forge Press, Nerwbury Oark, CA.

Smeaton, D. (2006) 'Work return rates after childbirth in the UK - trends, determinants and implications: A comparison of cohorts born in 1958 and 1970,' *Work, Employment and Society*, Vol. 20, No. 1, pp. 5–25.

Vickerstaff, S., *et al.* (2004) *Happy retirement? The impact of employers' policies and practice on the process of retirement*, Policy Press, Bristol.

Warren, T. (2007) 'Conceptualizing breadwinning work,' *Work, Employment and Society*, Vol. 21, No. 2, pp. 317–36.

Women & Equality Unit (2006) *What is the Pay Gap and why does it exist?* Available from: **www.womenandequalityunit.gov.uk/pay/pay_facts.htm** (accessed 12 August 2007).

# 11

# Education

Hugh Bochel

## Chapter overview

Education has for long been viewed as a key feature of social policy, whether for its role in enabling individuals to fulfil their potential, as an influence on equality and inequality, or through its importance in providing an appropriate workforce to meet the economic and other needs of the country.

Before the 1997 general election New Labour placed education at the centre of its agenda, a position perhaps best summed up in Tony Blair's statement of priorities for his first government: 'Education, education, education'. However, education has always raised difficult questions for governments and, as this chapter makes clear, this has continued through the Blair and Brown governments with debates focusing on issues including:

- the level of resources available to schools, colleges and universities, including how higher education in particular should be funded;
- how to measure and improve levels of performance, both of educational institutions and of individuals;
- the best means of providing education and the relative roles of governmental organisations and individuals in creating frameworks and exercising choice;
- questions over the relationship between inequality and education and the role of education in reducing or mitigating inequality.

## Spotlight on the issues
### Choosing schools?

#### Parents ready to move for good school

Over half of parents would be prepared to move house to get their child into a good school, and one in seven is willing to lie to do so, according to a survey published today.

The poll, commissioned by the Children's Society as part of a two-year inquiry into childhood in Britain, suggests that a perceived education 'postcode lottery' is now having a significant effect on most parents' schooling decisions.

The phenomenon of school selection by postcode, in which only those families able to afford house prices artificially inflated by proximity to good schools are able to attend those schools, has been well documented anecdotally, but the Children's Society survey reveals willingness to move is now the norm.

A total of 51% of more than 1,250 people surveyed said they would be willing to move to get their child into a good school, and 14% said they would go as far as giving false information, such as lying about their faith or where they live. The proportion prepared to lie rose to 23% in London, where competition for places in good state schools is particularly cut-throat.

The demand for places in desirable schools has persuaded some authorities, including Brighton, to introduce admissions lotteries to deal with over-subscription, but the policy predictably leaves parents divided.

Bob Reitemeier, Children's Society chief executive, said: 'The lengths that parents are prepared to go to clearly indicate that there are huge variations in school standards. But for many parents the costly exercise of moving house to get their child into a good school is simply not an option.

'The current system is in danger of embedding inequality by making a child's social class and economic circumstances the key influencer in their educational success.' He added: 'Unless we create a system where all children have equal access to a good education millions of children will be denied a fair start in life.'

*Source*: Lucy Ward, *The Guardian*, 17 October 2007.

The example above highlights the potential importance of education in contemporary society. If many parents are prepared to go to the extent of moving house, or even lying, to get their children into a particular school, and if schools are deemed to be important in influencing children's future lives, then clearly education is likely to be central to the concerns of social policy. Other debates in recent years, such as those over the creation of faith schools, and about the role of evangelical Christian sponsors of schools such as academies, serve to reinforce our perceptions of the importance of education. One of the concerns of this chapter is to identify some of the reasons why education has been such a major topic in social policy and to outline governments' policies from pre-school to tertiary levels.

Attempts to reshape and reform the education system have been one of the major and recurring features of social policy during the New Labour years. Yet such attention to education is not new, with governments frequently having sought to adapt the education system to meet their perceptions of priorities at particular times. This apparently constant desire for reform is perhaps a result of education generally being seen as providing a variety of benefits – individual, social and economic – which governments seek to interpret and affect as part of their wider goals, as well as the costs to the state, with education accounting for around five per cent of GDP. For each individual, education can be portrayed as offering opportunities for personal development and the realisation of potential; at a social level it has frequently been viewed as having the potential for reducing social inequality and for contributing to social unity and development; and for the economy its purpose can be argued to lie in providing a skilled workforce ready to enter employment, as well as in encouraging other attributes, such as flexibility, self-responsibility and time-keeping, relevant to the world of work. The importance of education is therefore such that the temptations for governments to 'reform' education may therefore be almost overwhelming.

This chapter begins by outlining the development of the education system, and in particular the ways in which during the post-war period it has been affected by the differing concerns of governments, including its perceived importance to the United Kingdom's economic competitiveness. It moves on to examine the reforms introduced by the Conservative governments of 1979 to 1997. The chapter then considers the further changes to education, from pre-school to higher education, under the Labour governments since 1997. The focus of much of this chapter is on education in England and Wales, and it is important to recognise that this is one area of social policy where there have long been significant variations across the constituent elements of the United Kingdom; some of these are highlighted in the following discussion.

## Education up to 1979

Chapter 5 sets out the broad context and developments in social policy, including education, during the nineteenth and the first half or the twentieth century, but it is worth paying some further consideration to education here. Up to 1870 education was largely limited to those sections of the middle and upper classes who were able and willing to pay for the limited provision that was available through church, private and voluntary schools, although there was some education for poor children in schools associated with workhouses. However, in 1870 the Elementary Education Act was passed which created elected School Boards to establish non-compulsory education provision for 5- to 13-year-olds, funded from the rates, where existing provision was inadequate (in Scotland, where by the mid nineteenth century a considerable proportion of population was literate, through the provision of schools by large towns, individuals and societies, the Education (Scotland) Act of 1872 similarly made education the responsibility of School Boards). The next fifty years saw a series of extensions of the state's role in education. Compulsory education up to 10 was introduced in 1880. Fees for elementary education for most children were abolished in 1891 and the school-leaving age was raised to 11 in 1893 and 12 in 1899. In 1902 the Education Act made local authorities responsible for schools, including church schools, a position which laid the basis for the organisation of education for the remainder of the century. Then in 1918 the school-leaving age was raised to 14 (this had occurred in 1901 in Scotland). However, whilst the role of the state was developing gradually, private education, in the form of the independent **public schools**, was left largely untouched.

The next significant developments in education came with the appointment of R.A. (Rab) Butler as Minister for Education in 1941. At that time most children left school at the age of 14, with the majority leaving with no formal qualifications. Whilst there had been proposals for reform from the end of the First World War, economic recession during the 1920s and 1930s meant that the status quo had remained, despite a widespread recognition that the education system served largely to reinforce privilege and did not meet many of the nation's needs.

Butler proposed a radical review of the education system and the Education Act of 1944 saw the creation of a tripartite settlement:

- Grammar schools, to cater for academic 'high-fliers', who might be expected to progress to university or enter professional careers, business or management.
- Technical schools, for children who might go on to work in engineering or crafts.
- Secondary modern schools, which would take those children who did not appear to fall into either the 'academic' or 'applied' categories.

Entry into each of these schools would be through one common examination, the eleven-plus. This tripartite structure would cater from children aged from 11 to the new school-leaving age of 15. Although the Act proposed that the leaving age be raised to 16 as soon as practicable, this did not actually happen until 1972.

The Education Act made central government (the Ministry of Education and the Treasury) responsible for the provision of financial support for local authorities, whilst the latter were given responsibility for managing the schools and for the strategic planning of education in their areas (including **primary**, **secondary** and **further** education, to which part of **higher education** was added when polytechnics were created in the 1960s). In relation to this, the Act also reinforced the pre-existing divisions within education between primary education, secondary education up to 16, tertiary education from 16, and university education. The role given to local authorities allowed them to make different decisions about which elements they sought to develop, with some emphasising the primary sector whilst others placed greater stress on expenditure at secondary level.

The Act ensured, for the first time, the provision of free education for all children, and, through the abolition of fees, combined with the eleven-plus, gave bright working-class children the opportunity to progress to grammar schools. Butler also intended that the creation of technical schools would ensure that Britain did not lag behind its economic competitors in technical education, a desire that was to be followed up by the Labour governments of the 1960s with the expansion of vocational education and the establishment of polytechnics.

However, despite its radical nature and the administrative, structural and educational changes that it introduced, the Butler Act has been criticised for failing to tackle a number of issues. In particular it left the private 'public schools' untouched, and, according to some, actually further institutionalised the ethos of privilege through the creation of state grammar schools and the use of the eleven-plus as a means of selection. The Act also institutionalised the role of religion and the Church within state education, a development which has periodically been an area of tension, and which rose to the fore again in the late 1990s and early 2000s through the increasing multi-faith identity of the United Kingdom and in particular the issue of the establishment of Muslim and other faith schools. Despite Butler's hopes, the Act also failed to raise the profile of technical education in Britain, as local education authorities tended to focus on the provision of academic education through grammar schools and 'practical' education through secondary moderns, often seeing the question of technical education as primarily for employers to address through the system of apprenticeships.

Following the 1944 Act there was a period of relative consolidation of the education system. The primary area of conflict was over the eleven-plus examination, which increasingly was seen as serving to distinguish between those who 'passed' and progressed to grammar schools, and those who 'failed' and went to the secondary modern, a view given greater credence by the lack of development of the third type of school, the technical school, in many areas, and by the higher levels of funding given to the grammar schools. For many children and parents, attendance at secondary moderns was viewed as failure. In contrast, supporters of the system argued that grammar schools gave able working-class children the potential to progress to grammar schools on merit, and that the higher level of resourcing for those schools was appropriate in order to allow the most able to be able to develop their full potential. However, evidence tended to show that there was a significant relationship between social class and success in the test. This became an important part of the debate over equality and inequality during the 1960s and 1970s.

The Labour Party increasingly took the view that a move towards a system of **comprehensive** schooling, already adopted by some local authorities, would help reduce inequalities, and in 1965 the Secretary of State for Education, Tony Crosland, requested all local authorities to submit proposals to move towards local secondary schooling on a comprehensive basis. However, this was not a requirement supported by an Act of Parliament, and it was not until the 1976 Education Act that the government sought to use legislation to ensure the reorganisation of education on comprehensive lines. This Act also restricted the ability of local authorities to continue to fund grammar school places. However, like the Butler Act before it, the 1976 Act did not really address the role and position of private education. Table 11.1 provides an illustration of the changes in pupil numbers arising from attempts to introduce comprehensive education. In contrast, Scotland took quite a different direction and all state schools had become comprehensive by the mid 1970s and, albeit over a longer period of time, the same was true for Wales, where there was a gradual shift to entirely comprehensive state education.

Within higher education, during the 1950s the Conservatives established a number of new universities, creating some from scratch and upgrading others from university college to university status. In 1963 they also established the Robbins Committee on Higher Education, which recommended a doubling of student numbers. With the election of the Labour governments of the 1960s, concern over higher education was reinforced by anxiety over Britain's perceived failure to keep up with the rest of the world in industry and innovation. The government sought to develop a new, more vocational and technologically oriented form of higher education delivered through new 'polytechnics', which were intended to provide degree-level programmes in practical and technical subjects, rather than the arts subjects which had previously dominated university education. As with schools and **further education** colleges, the polytechnics were placed under the control of local education authorities, which then had a strategic overview from **nursery**, through primary and secondary schools, to higher education within their areas. The other major development in higher education under Labour in the 1960s was the creation of the Open University, aiming to provide degree-level education to adults who had missed that opportunity earlier in life. This education was radically different from the existing model, being delivered primarily through distance learning techniques supported by well-resourced, good-quality teaching materials and supplemented by television and radio programmes. In this way delivery in classrooms was to be much reduced, although some level of classroom support was maintained and supplemented through 'summer schools'.

By the mid 1970s education had returned to the policy agenda as a significant issue, in part again due to concern over the UK lagging behind its competitors in terms of economic performance, with the technical expansion of the previous decade seeming to have had little effect, but also with the emergence of a new issue, evidence of high levels of illiteracy and innumeracy amongst school leavers. Some critics sought to blame this on the creation of comprehensive schools and the bias against grammar school education, and argued that these had driven down standards of education for all children.

## Education 1979–1997

The Thatcher governments of the 1980s placed at least part of the blame for Britain's economic ills on 'trendy' educators who they perceived as having emphasised equality and new teaching methods at the expense of providing a solid educational foundation for children. In line with their emphasis on individual choice and the role of the market they sought to use these mechanisms to raise academic standards. The Education Act 1980 removed the requirement for local authorities to pursue comprehensive education and introduced the Assisted Places Scheme to allow 'high ability' children of poorer parents to attend fee-paying private schools.

However, it was not until the 1988 Education Reform Act that the Conservatives undertook radical reform of education. This piece of legislation allowed for the creation of **grant-maintained** schools, for local management of schools, the introduction of the **National Curriculum** and standardised testing in England and Wales. The Conservatives argued that allowing grant-maintained schools to opt out of local education authority control would enable them to develop their own policies, including on entry and selection. These schools would be funded directly by the then Department of Education and Science and would be managed by their head and deputy headteachers together with the school's governing body. Other schools would also be able to become locally managed, controlling the bulk of their budgets, including teachers' salaries and other staffing costs, equipment, books and internal maintenance, although local authorities would remain responsible for capital costs and providing services such as careers advice.

The 1988 Act therefore offered schools the choice of remaining under LEA 'control' with their budgets being 'top-sliced' for central administrative and service costs, or becoming grant maintained and receiving their entire budget directly from the Funding Agency for Schools, thus having no formal relationship with the LEA. Schools were able to move to grant-maintained status through a vote by governors followed by a vote by parents, with a simple majority of those voting being needed for acceptance. Using grant-maintained schools and locally managed schools the Conservatives hoped to create a 'market' with schools competing for pupil numbers. As resources would be allocated on the basis of the number of children enrolled in a school it was argued that schools would have an incentive to perform well to attract pupils, whilst those that performed badly would lose income and, ultimately, risk closure. By 1997 680 secondary schools (15 per cent of the total) had grant-maintained status, along with 514 primary schools (2 per cent of the total), overwhelmingly in England.

In order to further develop market mechanisms and to allow parents to make decisions about which school to choose, the government encouraged the production of 'league tables' of school performance which would allow parents to make comparisons of schools in their area. However, despite being widely publicised in the media, critics argued that in reality these league tables largely reflected the class backgrounds of children attending different schools and said little or nothing about the extent to which the schools themselves made a difference to their pupils' achievements.

As another part of the response to the criticism that standards of basic literacy and numeracy were falling and that children were leaving school unable to read, write and do basic arithmetic, the government introduced the National Curriculum in an attempt to emphasis the teaching of basic skills across England and Wales. This provided a standard syllabus and gave the Secretary of State the power to determine how much time each week would be spent on particular subjects. The Secretary of State was also given power over the content of the curriculum, although in practice this was largely allocated to the National Curriculum Council. There were a variety of criticisms of this innovation, including the danger of reducing time available for children to learn subjects such as drama, music and even sports and games (the latter sometimes combined with concern over the impact on children's health of a reduction in the time available for these). Other criticisms were centred around the idea of a 'national curriculum' in a multi-cultural and multi-faith society with children of a wide variety of backgrounds and abilities. Indeed, the first version of the National Curriculum was revised in 1995, allowing greater discretion for schools over non-core subjects, reducing the level of targets and monitoring, and giving greater flexibility of options for 14- to 16-year-olds to encourage more vocational routes for some students.

In order to measure educational standards the Education Reform Act also introduced **standardised attainment tests** (SATs), to be applied across a range of subjects at various stages in a child's school life (the original suggestion was for testing at 7, 11, 14 and 16 although the latter proposal was dropped). Supporters argued that the National Curriculum and SATs would place a new emphasis on

" OF COURSE WE CAN'T READ – WE'RE
ONLY ELEVEN. "

*Source*: www.CartoonStock.com.

traditional values and help make parents aware of the information that they needed to choose a school for their children. Critics feared that this was a return to selection and that children might be labelled as 'failures' at an early age.

The 1988 Act also introduced significant change to the realm of higher education, allowing polytechnics to leave LEA control and become free-standing corporations. One of the aims of this was to end the 'binary divide' between the polytechnics and the more traditional universities, a division which was arguably already in the process of diminishing as there was increasing commonality of courses taught between the two notionally different types of institution. Shortly after, the status of polytechnics was changed and they became universities, which, together with colleges of higher education, received funding from the Higher Education Funding Councils. Finally, under the Act, local planning and funding of vocational training was transferred to employer-led Training and Enterprise Councils.

One other significant feature of higher education under the Conservatives was the growth in the numbers of students, with an increase from 473,000 in full-time undergraduate education in 1980–81 to 664,000 in 1990–91 and 1,052,000 in 1997–98, although this was accompanied by a significant reduction in the level of resources paid to institutions for each student.

Under Margaret Thatcher's successor as Prime Minister, John Major, the Conservatives continued to seek to develop both consumerist and quality control approaches to education. The 1992 Education (Schools) Act abolished Her Majesty's Inspectors of Schools and created the Office for Standards in Education (OFSTED) with the remit of improving standards and achievement through regular inspection, public reporting and advice. OFSTED became a major, if often controversial, force in monitoring and influencing school-age education. The Act also legislated for the annual publication of school performance tables, with the intention of informing parents' choice of schools for their children. Also, from 1992 Further Education Colleges followed the path of incorporation previously undertaken by polytechnics and became independent of LEAs and responsible for their own management and finance.

However, despite the Conservatives' claims to be undertaking change to improve education and to raise standards, a rather different interpretation can be put on many of the educational reforms of the late 1980s and early 1990s, based upon the arguments that they were as concerned with reducing the power of local authorities as with improving educational standards, and that the attempts to create markets in education were as much for ideological as for educational reasons. This view is buttressed by the fact that many of the government's actions in education mirrored those in other areas of public services, such as health and social care, with the emphasis on the consumer and accountability through the market rather than the traditional pattern of services accountable to the public through elected representatives in local government.

## Education since 1997

New Labour were famously elected in 1997 to the echoes of Tony Blair's commitment to 'Education, education, education'. This emphasis was not limited to education on its own, but the role of education was seen as important for other flagship policy areas, such as the New Deal, which aimed to provide every adult with the opportunity to find employment, and Sure Start, which sought to improve outcomes for children in disadvantaged areas. Education was also portrayed as vital to tackling social exclusion and creating an opportunity society. The government therefore sought to emphasise the provision of basic skills, including literacy and numeracy.

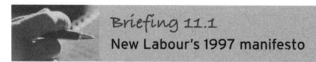

### Briefing 11.1
### New Labour's 1997 manifesto

New Labour's 1997 general election manifesto contained a number of education commitments including to:

- cut class sizes for 5-, 6- and 7-year-olds to 30 or under;
- guarantee nursery places for 4-year-olds;
- set targets for literacy and numeracy for primary school children;
- link schools and colleges to the internet;
- encourage lifelong learning through the University for Industry and Individual Learning Accounts;
- raise the proportion of national income spent on education over a five-year period.

This concern with education continued into the second and third Labour terms and following the party's second general election victory in June 2001 a new Department for Education and Skills was established, although this itself was superseded in 2007 by two new Departments: the Department for Innovation, Universities and Skills, and the Department for Children, Schools and Families. Where expenditure on education was concerned, after a period of fluctuation and then decline under the Conservatives, falling to 4.5 per cent of GDP in 1996–97, levels of spending began to grow again, reaching 5.5 per cent of GDP in 2005–6.

## Nursery places and pre-school education

Britain has often been differentiated from many other countries by the commencement of compulsory education at five years of age, compared with six or seven in some other countries, and by the perceived lack of development of public pre-school provision, so that for example in 1970–71 only 21 per cent of three- and four-year-olds were in such settings. There was a growing level of provision during the 1990s so that by 1999–2000 64 per cent of three- and four-year-olds were spending at least some time in pre-school education (Central Statistical Office, 2001) and shortly before their general election defeat in 1997 the Conservatives had introduced a voucher system which parents could use to purchase provision from the private or public sector. However, the new Labour government scrapped this scheme and instead sought a significant increase in the number of places to meet its promise of places for all four-year-olds and two-thirds of three-year-olds. Together with a significant increase in the level of resources for such provision it required LEAs to establish plans for early years development and childcare, including the provision of places for all four-year-olds. During their second term Labour undertook to provide free nursery places for all who wanted one by September 2004. As a result, by 2000–1 63 per cent of three- and four-year-olds were making use of pre-school provision, rising slightly to 65 per cent in 2004–5. Reflecting the government's continuing concerns for ensuring quality in education, from September 2001 OFSTED became responsible for inspecting all early-years childcare and education in England.

Reflecting the frequent complexity of social policy, and the government's attempts to encourage 'joined-up' policy, the Sure Start programme was introduced as part of Labour's attempts to tackle social exclusion, seeking to work across government departments to ensure that children and families in disadvantaged areas had access to services, opportunities and help for young children. As such it formed a significant part of the government's ambitious drive to eradicate child poverty in 20 years and to halve it in 10. It was intended to involve both parents and a range of agencies in a variety of initiatives designed to give children in disadvantaged areas a better start in life, including increasing the number of childcare places available and a number of other programmes associated with education. However, early evaluations were inconclusive about whether Sure Start was making a difference, leaving critics able to highlight the high levels of expenditure on the programme (around £500 million per year by

2003–4) while supporters were able to point out that the benefits from a programme aimed primarily at pre-school children were likely to take many years
to become evident.

## Primary and secondary education

From 1997 to 2005 education policy under the Labour governments was frequently characterised as dominated by flows of initiatives from central government,
some of which are outlined below. Indeed, there were frequent accusations from
teachers and others that the sheer volume of initiatives emerging from central
government was such that it was adding substantially to the workload and stres-
ses of teachers and itself undermining the prospects for achieving significant
change and quality education. Whilst not exhaustive, the developments outlined
below illustrate the pressures for reform of school-age education from the Labour
governments.

### Education Action Zones and Excellence in Cities

One of the features of the first Labour government was an attempt to focus on key
areas through a series of geographically oriented initiatives such as Health Action
Zones and Education Action Zones. Education Action Zones (EAZs) were established in the School Standards and Framework Act 1998, and were intended to
raise educational standards and tackle social exclusion in some of the worst-
performing areas of the country. Initially 25 EAZs were established with a further
48 following in the second round from September 1999 to April 2000. They were
initially established for three years but all of the first round zones were extended
to the maximum of five years. However, evaluations suggested some weaknesses
in the EAZs, including a lack of progress in raising standards in secondary schools
and a failure to innovate, as well as some problems with financial management.
In addition, in 1999 the government launched the Excellence in Cities initiative,
incorporating Education Action Zones, designed to bring additional resources to
some urban areas in order to tackle the problems of low expectations and achievement, as well as weaknesses in schools in inner cities. The programme was gradually expanded and developed over the next few years, and whilst evidence on its
achievements was mixed, it was praised by OFSTED in 2005 for contributing to a
steady increase in GCSE results in some of England's poorest areas. From 2006
however, the programme ended with funding going to local authorities as part of
their School Development Grant.

### Class sizes

The demand for schooling in terms of the number of pupils clearly changes over
time, reflecting demographic patterns, whilst government policies on the levels of
resourcing and the types of schools also change significantly (Table 11.1). Each of
these ultimately has an impact on class sizes, which were widely seen as too large
by the mid 1990s, based at least in part upon a view that larger class hinder pupils'

Table 11.1 School pupils (thousands): by type of school, United Kingdom

| | 1970/71 | 1980/81 | 1990/91 | 2000/1 | 2005/6 |
|---|---|---|---|---|---|
| **Public sector schools** | | | | | |
| Nursery | 50 | 89 | 105 | 152 | 151 |
| Primary | 5,902 | 5,171 | 4,955 | 5,298 | 4,975 |
| Secondary | | | | | |
| Comprehensive | 1,313 | 3,730 | 2,925 | 3,340 | 3,453 |
| Grammar | 673 | 149 | 156 | 205 | 218 |
| Modern | 1,164 | 233 | 94 | 112 | 102 |
| Other | 403 | 434 | 298 | 260 | 214 |
| *All public sector schools* | 9,507 | 9,806 | 8,533 | 9,367 | 9,113 |
| **Non-maintained schools** | 621 | 619 | 613 | 626 | 659 |
| **Special schools** | 103 | 148 | 114 | 113 | 106 |
| **Pupil referral units** | | | | 10 | 16 |
| **All schools** | 10,230 | 10,572 | 9,260 | 10,116 | 9,894 |

*Source: Social Trends 37*, The Stationery Office, London, 2007 (Table 3.3).

learning, although research evidence on this appears mixed, in part because it is difficult to separate out the impact of class size from that of other factors, such as the performance of teachers (see, for example, Pedder, 2006). One of Labour's main pledges prior to coming to power was to reduce class sizes for 5- to 7-year-olds to give a maximum class size of 30, using money freed up by the scrapping of the Conservatives' assisted places scheme to do this. Whilst there were disagreements over the value of such a policy, this was fairly rapidly achieved allowing the government to claim a significant manifesto success. By 2005–6 the average class size for Key Stage 1 (age 5 to 7) was 25, and for Key Stage 2 (age 7 to 11) was 27, although nearly one in five Key Stage 2 pupils was in a class of more than 31.

## Standards and the National Curriculum

Despite the changes under the Conservatives, including the introduction of the National Curriculum and standard national assessments using SATs, there remained a widespread belief that educational standards were continuing to fall, although evidence on this remained very unclear (see Thought provoker, below). Labour therefore maintained and even increased the emphasis on 'standards' and 'performance' from the Conservative years, including the use of testing. For example, by 2002 new, higher targets had been set for performance in English and maths at Key Stage 2 of 85 per cent of pupils achieving level 4 or higher in English and mathematics with 35 per cent achieving level 5 or higher in both subjects (see Table 11.2). Like the Conservatives, the Labour government used OFSTED to exercise pressure for much of this activity, including identifying schools and even local education authorities that were 'failing' and setting targets for national as well as schools' educational performance.

**Table 11.2** Pupils reaching or exceeding expected standards through teacher assessment: by Key Stage and sex, England

|  | 1997 | | 2007 | |
| --- | --- | --- | --- | --- |
|  | Boys (%) | Girls (%) | Boys (%) | Girls (%) |
| **Key stage 1** | | | | |
| English | | | | |
|   Reading | 75 | 85 | 80 | 88 |
|   Writing | 72 | 83 | 75 | 86 |
| Mathematics | 82 | 86 | 88 | 91 |
| Science | 84 | 86 | 87 | 90 |
| **Key stage 2** | | | | |
| English | 57 | 70 | 73 | 83 |
| Mathematics | 63 | 65 | 78 | 78 |
| Science | 68 | 70 | 84 | 85 |
| **Key stage 3** | | | | |
| English | 52 | 70 | 68 | 81 |
| Mathematics | 62 | 65 | 78 | 80 |
| Science | 60 | 63 | 73 | 76 |

Source: *Social Trends 38*, The Stationery Office, London, 2008 (Table 3.12).

## ? Thought provoker

Why might it be felt that GCSEs and A levels have become easier than in the past? What evidence would be needed to demonstrate that this is or is not the case? Why might it be argued that rather than GCSEs and A levels becoming easier, student performance has improved?

What does this tell us about debates over standards in education?

There have also been significant differences in the performance of boys and girls wth 52.2 per cent of boys gaining 5 or more GCSE grades A to C in 2005–6, compared with 61.9 per cent of girls, although there has been little agreement on the reasons for this gap (see also Table 11.2).

'Race', too, has emerged as a major issue in relation to education with big differences in educational attainment across different minority ethnic groups. While pupils of Indian and Chinese origin have tended to perform well in assessments, gypsy/traveller children, and black Caribbean pupils, and particularly boys, have had higher levels of 'underachievement' and of exclusion from schools. Some of the reasons for this 'underachievement' of black pupils are discussed in Chapter 17. However, despite the concerns over 'race' and gender inequalities in education, Ball (2008) notes that class (and poverty) remain important: '. . . in terms of educational performance the "class gap" remains greater, but receives far less attention in policy . . .' (p. 173).

The debate about standards and performance under both Conservative and Labour governments has frequently encompassed the publication of information on individual schools. Perhaps inevitably, there has been much debate about the value of 'school league tables', and in particular about what information they actually usefully provide: they apparently provide data on the achievements of individual schools, but since much educational attainment is determined by factors outside the control of schools they can be misleading – for example, some schools may be adding little value to the performance of students who might be expected to perform well largely arising from their socio-economic backgrounds (for instance, in 2000, 74 per cent of children of parents classified as 'higher professional' received 5 or more GCSE grades A to C, compared with 61 per cent of those from 'lower professional backgrounds', 51 per cent 'intermediate', 36 per cent 'lower supervisory', and 29 per cent of those whose parents were in 'routine' groups), whilst others might be adding considerable value to pupils who might be expected to perform less well, and such achievements do not generally emerge in 'league tables'. Critics have also noted that there is an incentive here for schools to try to attract pupils who might do well and that, for example, 'Filling up a school with "able" children and keeping children with SEN [special educational needs] to a minimum is the cheapest and most labour-efficient way of enhancing league-table performance' (Gewirtz et al., 1995, p. 186). In Wales, school league tables were abolished by the Labour-controlled Assembly in 2001 as they were seen as divisive and as placing an unnecessary burden on schools.

One of the apparent contradictions much noted under the Conservatives was the contrast between the devolution of some powers to schools through local management, and the unprecedented centralisation of overall control of education through the National Curriculum, standardised assessments, the publication of 'league tables' of school performance and the expansion of school inspection through OFSTED. Similarly, Labour showed a willingness to exercise control from the centre. This included the introduction of the literacy and numeracy hours, which some critics argued not only reflected a low level of trust of the teaching profession, but also through going beyond prescribing not only the time that should be spent to how it should be used, added a further dimension to central control. Another example of the government's willingness to become more directly involved in school age education came with the passage of the School Standards and Framework Act 1998 which gave the government the power to intervene where it considers that a local authority has failed to carry out its duties correctly, whether this is at the level of an individual school or a whole LEA. The first use of these powers was seen in 1999 when parts of the work of Hackney LEA were given to private contractors, and in 2000 there was further use of private sector contractors in Leeds, Rotherham and Sheffield.

Under Labour there were also a number of changes and adjustments to the National Curriculum, one of which not only reflected the governments' multifaceted approaches to education, but is also particularly apposite to social policy: citizenship was introduced as part of the secondary curriculum from September 2002 to encourage political literacy and understanding of topical issues, to help young people to learn about rights and responsibilities, and to encourage active involvement both in school and in the wider community. Other changes included revised syllabi across a range of subjects including English, history, mathematics and science. In 2007 the curriculum was revised again, this time with the intention of providing teachers with greater flexibility, for example through cross-curricular learning.

## Diversification

Perhaps somewhat ironically, given that one of the problems identified by some critics of the Conservatives' attempts to develop a market in education was the lack of diversity of provision, Labour's approach to secondary education has largely been to accept the diversification of educational institutions that took place under the Conservatives and the open enrolment approach of allowing parents to choose the most appropriate school for their children. Notably, in contrast with the Labour governments of the 1970s, selection by state schools was not opposed by the Labour governments, the status of the remaining grammar schools could be changed following ballots of parents in feeder schools, and the public schools have been left alone. The Green Paper *Schools Building on Success* (Department for Education and Employment, 2001) focused on secondary schools and set out Labour's proposals for extending diversity through the creation of more specialist schools (in areas such as technology, language, arts, business and enterprise, science and sport), faith-based schools, Academies and enabling external sponsors to take over 'underperforming' schools on fixed-term contracts. It also set further targets for performance for 14-year-olds.

The subsequent White Paper *Schools Achieving Success* (Department for Education and Skills, 2001) reiterated much of New Labour's aims including diversity of schooling, the role of standards and targets and flexibility of the education system and qualifications. It also re-emphasised the commitment to vocational education and attempts to raise the status of the vocational route through secondary school. It was followed by the Education Act 2002 which again promoted the government's vision of flexibility and innovation including a degree of deregulation, further possibilities for the creation of new state-funded schools with sponsorship

### Briefing 11.2
### Academies

One of the most controversial aspects of Labour's approaches to school age education has been the creation of Academies (originally City Academies). These are schools which are sponsored (for example, by businesses, charities, churches or universities) but where the government pays the bulk of the start-up costs, usually involving the provision of new buildings. They often replace existing schools. While Academies have some of the same constraints as other schools, such as following the National Curriculum, they are able to opt out of national pay agreements and to employ staff who are not registered with the General Teaching Council. Even more problematically for many, sponsors are given a majority of seats on the board of governors, and some critics have expressed concern about the implications of this when, for example, schools are sponsored by evangelical Christians.

from private, voluntary or faith groups, continued pressure to tackle 'failing' schools, and greater freedom for the best-performing schools. In addition the Act also allowed for the fairly widespread reform of existing legislation, for example to reduce the necessity for education matters to be dealt with by Parliamentary Bills. The 2005 White Paper, *Higher Standards, Better Schools for All*, included a proposal for the establishment of 'trust schools' which are self-governing, able to employ their own staff, manage their own land and assets, and make their own admissions arrangements, as well as being supported by external partners. Unlike the grant-maintained schools of the 1980s and 1990s, however, they are funded on the same basis as other local authority-maintained schools.

The impact of some of these changes was rapid, with a rapid expansion of specialist schools, so that by the summer of 2007, of around 3,300 state secondary schools in England, only around 3 (now about 10) per cent were still non-specialist comprehensives, while 164 were grammar schools (DCSF, 2007, **www.dfes.gov. uk/pns/DisplayPN.cgi?pn_id=2007_0121**).

In another form of diversification, *Higher Standards, Better Schools for All* contained proposals for the creation of 'trust schools', supported by a charitable foundation or trust, which would have greater independence from LEAs, including owning their own assets, being able to employ their own staff and having greater power to make their own admissions arrangements.

In 2000 the government also set out its view of the role of local education authorities (DfEE, 2000), making clear that 'schools that are good schools manage themselves' (p. 7) and that LEAs should only intervene in schools where there were problems, particularly 'failing' schools. It saw the remainder of the role of LEAs as being concerned with functions unsuitable for individual schools, such as planning the supply of places across the authority, ensuring that all children have access to a school place or suitable alternative provision.

However, the diminution of the powers of LEAs and the increasing fragmentation of the school system arguably made it harder to share good practice, so that in addition to initiatives such as Excellence in Cities, the government has introduced other initiatives designed to encourage cooperation across schools and improved management within schools.

## Relations with teachers

The Labour governments' relations with teachers were dogged by criticisms relating to the teaching profession, whether these related to difficulties of recruitment and retention, the administrative workloads created by the many initiatives emanating from central government, or critical remarks about the teaching profession, including from the Chief Inspector for Schools up to 2002, Chris Woodhead, and from some Ministers. The role of teaching assistants has also been debated following the huge increase in their numbers over the past decade and the need for training and qualifications for this group. The General Teaching Council for England and the General Teaching Council for Wales were established in September 2000 following the Teaching and Higher Education Act 1998 and became responsible for the regulation of the profession from 2001 when the registers of teachers were established, although they have no role in determining pay and conditions. These developments were intended to help raise the status of the profession and to ensure and improve the standards of teaching. In Scotland a General Teaching Council had been established in the 1960s.

In terms of the management of teaching it is quite clear that from the 1980s there has been a significant shift away from a position where management provided the framework, with teachers as professionals determining the nature of their teaching, through an attempt to manage through markets, to a position where there has largely been management by targets and performance, a situation which has arguably been mirrored in others areas of social policy, such as healthcare and social care. The changes to the National Curriculum introduced in 2007 were intended to provide greater freedom for teachers to make decisions based upon their professional judgement and the needs of their pupils, but at the same time the pressures of national tests and league tables remained as a potential constraint upon teachers' ability and willingness to make use of this potential freedom.

 ## Thought provoker

What do league tables of school performance tell us? Do they demonstrate the 'added value' from the schools' input, the performance of students, or do they primarily reflect the socio-economic backgrounds of the intakes?

How would you measure school performance?

### Other changes

Although outside school education, the government made further reforms affecting the secondary age group. These included the creation of the Connexions Service which draws on the work of a number of government departments to provide advice and guidance for 13- to 19-year-olds on topics ranging from careers to homelessness and drug abuse, and the establishment of the Learning and Skills Council in April 2001 which sought to develop greater links between education for 14- to 19-year-olds and employers. It also brought responsibility for all post-16 learning to one body for the first time. Also in 2001 the role of OFSTED was expanded further when it took over responsibility for inspecting all 16–19 education in sixth form and further education colleges.

In 2004, *Every Child Matters: Change for Children* (DfES, 2004) set out a new framework for policy (see also Chapter 13) which emphasised a holistic and joined-up approach to children and young people. Subsequently the Every Child Matters agenda continued to stress the importance of schools working together with other services to support children.

### Lifelong learning

Under Labour there has also been emphasis on 'lifelong learning', reflecting the perceived requirements of a flexible, skilled labour force able to adapt to the needs of the information age and the changing demands of employers. Labour made much of the commitment to lifelong learning, perhaps reflecting both the party's traditional concern with social justice and opportunity and New Labour's particular concern with economic efficiency and a skilled and flexible labour force. Education and training can be seen as central to both of these through removing barriers to employability (and hence potentially lessening some aspects of social exclusion), through investing in human capital, and thus creating greater flexibility. Making the link from school education the White Paper *Excellence in Schools* (DfEE, 1997) made clear the government's aim of broadening A levels and giving greater status to vocational qualifications while at the same time seeking to ensure the achievement of key skills and high standards.

Whilst higher education had already seen a great expansion in the age participation rate under the Conservatives, Labour's key target was that 50 per cent of young people should progress to higher education by the age of 30 by 2010. Among the tools intended to achieve this were Education Action Zones and Excellence in Cities initiatives outlined above, focused on areas where participation rates were often very low, and strands of targeted funding for HE institutions to encourage them to meet targets for widening participation.

However, progress was arguably slower than the government would have wished in relation to both lifelong learning and widening participation. In addition, critics have pointed out that the very aim of lifelong learning contrasts with the ending of free tuition, the introduction of fees for students in higher education and the phasing out of student grants.

In terms of lifelong learning two of the government's early initiatives were far from successful – the University for Industry (UfI) and Individual Learning Accounts (ILAs). The UfI was seen as a way of making education and training more widely available through acting as a broker for the delivery of high-quality, flexibly delivered learning with a target for initial operation of autumn 2000. By 2001 it was offering education in England and Wales through the learndirect network. However, early evaluations, whilst recognising that there were real gains to learners also questioned the extent to which learndirect was achieving some of its objectives, such as engaging with employers and enhancing productivity. An even more problematic area, which has arguably been one of Labour's greatest policy failures, was the introduction of Individual Learning Accounts. These were intended to make a government contribution of up to £200 for some courses for individuals in England seeking to develop their knowledge and skills, which it was hoped would be topped-up by employers and employees. However, whilst coming into effect on 1 September 2000 and reaching the initial target of 1 million ILAs by May 2001, almost a year ahead of schedule, ILAs were closed by 23 November 2001 following a perception that their growth had outstripped their anticipated cost to public funds and suspicions of widespread fraud and abuse of the scheme. A highly critical report by the House of Commons Education and Skills Select Committee identified a whole series of weaknesses with the approach taken by the government (Education and Skills Select Committee, 2002).

Another key aspect of the government's attempts to encourage lifelong learning in England has been the use of the Learning and Skills Council (with other more local Learning and Skills Councils) to plan and fund the provision of education and training for those outside universities.

## Higher education

Reflecting the emphasis on standards in school-age education, higher education has also seen attempts to measure and ensure quality, encompassing both teaching and research. From the 1990s higher education institutions have been subject to a number of external judgements including assessments of the quality of teaching in individual subjects, and research assessment exercises to judge the quality of research undertaken. From the 1990s, however, it has been the Research Assessment Exercise that has had the most significant influence upon the level of funding received by institutions, as well as often being an important factor in the construction of 'league tables', leading some critics to claim that it has tipped the balance away from a concern with teaching towards research. During Labour's second term there were significant debates over the extent to which research funds should be concentrated on a relatively small number of 'elite' institutions, rather than being dispersed more generally across the sector. In the run-up to the 2008 RAE, in many institutions the importance of the exercise, in terms of potential gains or losses in income, and in status, was arguably a key driver of decision making. In contrast, other key strands of HE policy, such as widening participation, tended to have a much lower profile, and developments such as Foundation Degrees, widely trumpeted when they were first introduced, did not immediately find favour in much of higher education. That said, the government has continued to push forward with its agenda for widening participation and combating the lack of participation by particular groups, such as those from lower socio-economic backgrounds and those who live in more deprived areas. Nevertheless, the failure to make significant progress has led some to suggest that 'If the government is to make real progress on widening participation (and the statistics suggest that they are not doing this), they need to be more courageous in the policies they adopt' (Greenbank, 2006, p. 161).

However, during the second Labour term in office much greater consideration was given to the funding of higher education, and particularly how to meet the government's aspirations of Britain possessing world-class universities and of achieving 50 per cent participation rates in higher education. Although in Scotland the Scottish parliament had already made a decision to abolish tuition fees, the calls from some universities to be allowed to charge 'top-up fees', with costs of up to £15,000 per year being mentioned in some cases, made this a national issue. By mid 2003 the debate had moved on to the point where the government was proposing that universities be able to charge 'top-up' fees of £3,000 per year, and despite significant opposition to this in universities and in Parliament these were introduced in England from 2006. During the third Labour term attention was shifting to whether the limit on fees would be lifted when the system was reviewed in 2009, with many institutions calling for at least £6,000 a year to cover teaching costs. However, evidence was also emerging which suggested that children from poorer backgrounds were more likely to be put off going to universities because of fears of debt, raising further questions about the appropriateness and impact of increases in fees. Whilst the debate on fees took place in England, Labour-led administrations in Scotland and Wales had both reversed some parts of this policy by 2002, and in 2007 the SNP-led Scottish government proposed abolishing the Graduate Endowment Fee which Scottish students had been required to pay on completing their course (a sum of around £2,300 in 2006/7).

## Private education

Although the bulk of this chapter has been concerned with the role of the state, it is important to recognise that the private sector is also involved in the provision of education at every level from pre-school to higher education. At the pre-school level, the expansion of places under Labour, noted earlier in this chapter, has been founded on a mixed economy, with providers from the public, private and not-for-profit sectors. There is also a significant role played by the private sector in school age education, with so-called 'public schools' operating, taking pupils largely on the basis of their own selection criteria and the ability to pay the requisite fees. Around 7 per cent of pupils attend private schools. Many of these schools have shown high levels of pupil attainment in examinations, although there is disagreement over the reasons for this. The requirement to pay fees mean that they take the bulk of their pupils from the upper and middle classes, and their higher levels of funding than state schools allow them to have smaller classes and to pay higher salaries to teachers. The examination performance of private schools also feeds into controversy over entry to universities, with evidence the acceptance rate for 'elite' universities, including Oxford and Cambridge, being much higher for pupils from private schools than it is for those who attend state schools.

There is also one private university in the United Kingdom, the University of Buckingham, which was created in the 1970s, but which remains the only example of its type. However, although there have been no additional private universities, in England and Wales degree-awarding powers can be granted to private organisations, with the approval of the Quality Assurance Agency, and in 2007 the government awarded BPP College, part of the company BPP Professional Education, the power to award honours and masters degrees in law.

## Controversy and debate

### Bennett backs private school ban

**Alan Bennett, author of award-winning play *The History Boys*, has called for private schools to be banned.**

He said abolishing private education would be unpopular, but it was worth it because the schools cause 'a fissure running through British society'.

He added: 'Buying advantages for your children over and above their abilities is wrong.'

The Independent Schools Council rejected his stance, saying private education was a 'human right'.

The row comes as arguments continue over the charitable status of public schools – which some critics say amounts to a state subsidy for rich fee-paying parents

*Source*: BBC news, 24 January 2008, **http://news.bbc.co.uk/1/hi/uk/7207070.stm.**

What do you think of the role of private schools in the British education system? What impact might banning them have?

## Education and devolution

As noted at the start of this chapter, historically there have always been some differences in the education systems of England, Northern Ireland, Wales and particularly Scotland, and these have been accentuated in the past 20 years. As with some other areas of social policy, responsibility for education has become even more fragmented with the introduction of devolution under Labour, with the devolved administrations in Northern Ireland, Scotland and Wales having responsibility for their some or all parts of their own systems, whilst in England it is under the remit of the Department for Education and Skills.

Amongst the differences that have previously existed between Scotland and England, for example, have been that Scotland took a different approach to comprehensive schools in the 1970s with a much more uniform move towards comprehensive education. Similarly the examination system has historically been based upon the system of 'Highers', with school students having typically taken five subjects at that level at the age of 17, although recent years have seen a shift towards greater depth of study. In addition, in Scotland a General Teaching Council came into being in 1966, 35 years before those for England and Wales. At degree level Scotland has awarded honours degrees after four years, with students potentially being admitted at 17 years of age. Even under four successive Conservative governments in the 1980s and 1990s Scotland retained significant differences, with no National Curriculum and no development of specialist schools.

The period since 1999 has seen further differences emerging across the United Kingdom, with among the most significant divergences being the decisions by the devolved administrations of Scotland and Wales to abolish tuition fees for undergraduate students, whilst in Northern Ireland publication of league tables of school examination performance has been ceased. Given the degree of diversity emerging so soon in the life of the devolved governments, it seems likely that education systems will demonstrate further diversity as political control of both Westminster and the devolved administrations changes and develops.

## Conclusion

This chapter has outlined the historical development and some of the most significant recent changes in education in the United Kingdom. There are clearly a number of tensions within Labour's education policy, both in terms of aims, such as promoting choice and diversity while also seeking to achieve social justice, and in terms of approach, with a top-down, interventionist approach seen by some as conflicting with attempts to improve schools in disadvantaged areas.

In another example of the difficulties that governments face in relation to education, Gordon Brown's creation in 2007 of the Department for Children, Schools and Families and the Department for Innovation, Universities and Skills arguably sent different and somewhat conflicting messages about the government's education agenda. On the one hand, the bringing together of many strands of children and family policy together with school-age education fitted well with the mantra of 'joined-up government' and the aims associated with Every Child Matters (see Chapter 13), and whilst some in universities might have been pleased to see representation in Cabinet, the separation of university education from schooling was rather less than joined-up, and some expressed concern that universities would increasingly be expected to serve the perceived needs of the economy, while further education was left in an uncertain position.

## Summary

Reflecting over the period since 1979 it is possible to identify a number of themes in education policy:

- There has been a steady shift towards the marketisation and diversification of school-age education, with Labour largely accepting the reforms made by the Conservatives in terms of open enrolment and variation among schools; indeed, some have viewed Labour as taking unprecedented steps towards the use of markets and the involvement of the private sector, whilst the introduction of trust schools was also seen as giving greater powers to the governing bodies of such schools and potentially reducing further the power of LEAs.

- The issue of 'standards' has been at the fore of governments' attempts to reform education, resulting in a range of proposals designed to maintain and raise standards including the National Curriculum, OFSTED, testing of children at set stages in their school careers, the introduction of the literacy and numeracy hours and the use of performance measures for schools.

- One of the significant criticisms of Labour's approach to education, particularly for primary and secondary schools, has been the sheer volume of initiatives and guidance directed at schools and teachers, leading the government to be accused of both increasing central direction and prescription and of overloading those responsible for implementing policies.

- Overall, there has been a movement towards a position where in general schools are responsible for their budgets and performance, where the role of LEAs is generally about strategic management, and where central government has enhanced its control through a range of mechanisms including central direction and performance measurement.

- The profile of 'lifelong learning' has been raised by governments, particularly in relation to the creation of a flexible labour force and the needs of the economy. However, attempts to increase the levels of involvement, whether through the University for Industry and Individual Learning Accounts, or through widening participation in higher education, have demonstrated that governments can face considerable difficulties in implementing policies in this area.

- Reforms to higher education from the 1980s onwards saw increasing pressure on the level of resources available to universities and colleges which, together with attempts to increase the level of participation in higher education, led to major debates about the way it should be funded and who should pay. The introduction of tuition fees in England from 2006 was one response to this, but universities continued to complain of a shortage of funds, whilst the different approaches of the devolved administrations further illustrated the difficulties of reaching consensus on such issues.

● Despite the attention paid to education by both Labour and Conservative governments, private education, and particularly private schools, have largely remained unaffected.

## Discussion and review topics

1 What role should the private sector play in the provision of education?

2 How successful have Conservative and Labour governments been in raising standards in school-age education since 1979?

3 Discuss the principal arguments for and against selectivity in education.

4 To what extent do changes to education under Conservatives and Labour mirror governments' approaches to social policy more generally?

## Further reading

Ball, S.J. (2008) *Education*, the Policy Press, Bristol. This book provides a relatively brief discussion of the development of education policy and considers a variety of policy models.

Department for Education and Skills (2005) *Higher Standards, Better Schools for All*, The Stationery Office, London. One of the series of Green and White Papers dealing with education that have emerged from the Labour government, it set out plans for further reform of the schools system.

Tomlinson, S. (2001) *Education in a Post-Welfare Society*, Open University Press, Buckingham. This book provides a thorough coverage of the development of education since the 1944 Education Act, including the different philosophical perspectives that have impacted on education.

Trowler, P. (2002) *Education Policy*, Routledge, London. Taking a rather different approach, the second edition of this book examines education policy from a perspective grounded more in the policy process.

## Some useful websites

www.dcsf.gov.uk and www.dius.gov.uk – the sites of the Department for Children, Schools and Families and the Department for Innovation, Universities and Skills contain and have links to a great deal of government information including publications and statistics from pre-school provision to higher education.

www.education.guardian.co.uk – *Education Guardian* – together with the two *Times* sites below, this provided ready access to contemporary debates and an archive of past articles.

www.tes.co.uk – *Times Education Supplement* – concerned with school-age and further education, this site contains much to interest students including news and analysis.

www.thes.co.uk – *Times Higher Education Supplement* – covers higher education in a fashion similar to its sister site above.

www.ofsted.gov.uk – Office for Standards in Education – this site provides information about the role and activities of OFSTED together with access to reports and other publications.

www.scotland.gov.uk – Scottish Executive – makes available a significant amount of information on current developments in education in Scotland, together with some useful historical background.

www.wales.gov.uk – National Assembly for Wales – through this site it is possible to access information on education and training in Wales.

www.northernireland.gov.uk – Northern Ireland Executive – through this site it is possible to access information on the education system in Northern Ireland.

## References

Ball, S.J. (2008) *Education*, the Policy Press, Bristol.

Central Statistical Office (2001) *Social Trends 31*, The Stationery Office, London.

Central Statistical Office (2003) *Social Trends 33*, The Stationery Office, London.

Central Statistical Office (2007) *Social Trends 37*, The Stationery Office, London.

Department for Education and Skills (2001) *Schools Achieving Success*, The Stationery Office, London.

Department for Education and Skills (2001) *Higher Standards, Better Schools for All*, The Stationery Office, London.

Department for Education and Skills (2004) *Every Child Matters: Change for Children*, DfES, London.

Department for Education and Skills (2005) *Every Child Matters: Change for Children*, DfES, London.

Department for Education and Employment (1997) *Excellence in Schools*, The Stationery Office, London.

Department for Education and Employment (2000) *The Role of the Local Education Authority in School Education*, DFEE, London.

Department for Education and Employment (2001) *Schools Building on Success*, The Stationery Office, London.

Education and Skills Select Committee (2002) *Third Report – Individual Learning Accounts*, House of Commons, London.

Gewirtz, S., Ball, S.J. and Bowe, R. (1995) *Markets, Choice and Equity in Education*, Open University Press, Buckingham.

Greenbank, P. (2006) 'The Evolution of Government Policy on Widening Participation', *Higher Education Quarterly*, Vol. 60, No. 2, pp. 141–66.

Pedder, D. (2006) 'Are Small Classes Better? Understanding Relationships Between Class Size, Classroom Processes and Pupils' Learning', *Oxford Review of Education*, Vol. 32, No. 2, pp. 213–34.

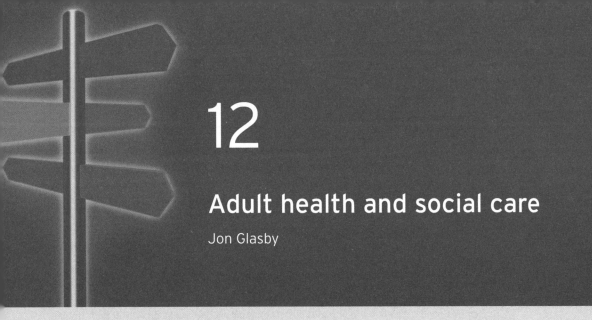

# 12

# Adult health and social care

Jon Glasby

## Chapter overview

It is clear that adult health and social care can have enormous implications for people's lives, both in helping to support people, or sometimes in a negative way when they fail to meet people's needs (see Spotlight on the issues, below). It is not surprising therefore that governments have been concerned to reform services, with a number of major changes having been introduced in the last two decades.

This chapter will discuss:

- the nature, scale and complexity of adult health and social services available to support people in the community;
- recent policy changes;
- key issues facing services;
- key tensions underlying current policy debates.

*Spotlight on the issues*
## The reality of caring

In the summer of 2007, a controversial documentary, *Love's Farewell*, told the story of a couple (Malcolm and Barbara Pointon) affected by dementia. Once a talented pianist and lecturer, Malcolm Pointon acquired dementia at the age of 51. Film-maker Paul Watson spent 11 years with the family making the documentary, with filming continuing up until shortly before Malcolm's death in February 2007. At the time, the documentary was controversial because of claims that it had filmed Malcolm's actual death (when in fact filming stopped several days before). However, critics and members of the public alike were united in their praise for such a hard-hitting and frank documentary:

The film was tender but unflinching. Watching, you could not but wince to see a grown man in nappies, beating up a teddy bear, throwing his drink on the floor. Finally he was in a hoist, a parody of a child's cradle, a bag of bones, a skull on a pillow. Barbara said, 'Do you want to film the bitter end, Paul?' and he agreed. 
Nancy Banks-Smith, *The Guardian*

At no point does the film-maker Paul Watson pull his punches. We see everything; from the trousers round the ankles in the bathroom to the gin bottles piling up by the back door – the progression to the literal end. Barbara's honesty, also, is total. She misses sex, she misses her husband loving her, she misses loving him. There's no redemption and no Hollywood moment of holding hands in the sunshine. For families unlucky enough to have first-hand experience of dementia, as mine does, it will make for either a terrifying vision of the future, or a bleak reminder of the past. Many, I suspect, won't last the full hour and a half. It makes you want to go and find somebody you love, and cry, and hug them, and be grateful that they still recognise you enough to hug back. 
Hugo Rifkind, *The Times*

Unbeknownst to many viewers, however, the Pointons are also well known in health and social care circles for other reasons. In 2003, they were the subject of a high-profile NHS Ombudsman judgement, with the Ombudsman ruling that they had been inappropriately assessed for NHS continuing healthcare (and may therefore have paid for means-tested long-term care that should perhaps have been provided free of charge by the NHS). In the process, health and social services found a new way of working together across agency boundaries, which involved using the direct payments (cash payments in lieu of directly provided services) common in social care to fund a package provided by the NHS (where direct payments are not currently available).

In many ways, this harrowing story was a microcosm of so many of the issues facing current adult health and social care, including: an ageing population and growing numbers of older people with mental health problems; the terrible impact that services can have on people's lives when they fail to work well together, or when they seem to be operating in the interests of the system rather than in the interests of the people they are there to serve; changing public expectations, with people more prepared to question expert opinion in order to achieve their rights; and new and innovative ways of working (such as direct payments) that may need to become more widespread if the current system is to respond to the challenges it faces.

By their very nature, adult health and social care tend to work with people at their most vulnerable and distressed. Accidents, injuries, death and bereavement are all everyday occurrences – with all the human emotions and complexities that these entail. Anyone who has celebrated the birth of a new baby, had a serious car accident, been diagnosed with a terminal illness, visited a loved one in hospital, looked after an older parent, or mourned the death of a family member, has probably had ongoing and intimate contact with services. As a result, the quality and responsiveness of such services is paramount and of fundamental importance to the individuals concerned. Because of the work they do, adult health and social care are also key issues in the media and in national and local politics. With such large sums of public money invested in public health and social services, politicians, the public and the media alike all have a strong interest in how well such services perform. In social care in particular, many of the groups supported – for example, people with mental health problems or people with learning difficulties – often experience considerable stigma, and can be the recipients of negative publicity and commentary.

This chapter provides a brief overview of current adult health and social care, summarising previous policy and highlighting some of the key debates and issues. In particular, it focuses on developments since the implementation of the landmark 1990 NHS and Community Care Act, and, in more detail, upon policy since the election of New Labour in 1997. Wherever specific organisational structures and policies are mentioned, these typically relate to the current system in England, although key differences following devolution are also signposted whenever possible. Until recently, such a chapter would have focused on *either* health *or* social care, with the latter including input on services for adults and on services for children and young people. However, recent changes (see below for further discussion) have sought to promote more effective inter-agency collaboration between health and social care, with an increased separation between services for adults and for children (at least in England). As a result, any current and future discussion of health and social care will need to be equally inter-agency in nature – exploring issues and appealing to an audience from both health *and* social care. It is for this reason that the current book has separate chapters on adult services and on children and families, acknowledging the growing divide that is developing in front-line services and national policy. The book also contains a separate chapter on health, although there are substantial areas of synergy with the areas covered here.

## Overview of adult health and social care

Like other sectors of the welfare state, adult health and social care provide support to many millions of people each year, employ many millions of workers and spend many billions of public money – often in the media spotlight and in response to public expectations that frequently exceed the resources available to deliver. Following major funding increases from 2002, the NHS spends around £90 billion, absorbing some 15 per cent of tax and national insurance (making it the second biggest single item of public expenditure after social security) (see NHS Confederation, 2006, for all NHS statistics in this paragraph). More than 600 NHS organisations employ about 1.3 million people (in England) with around 120,000 doctors and over 400,000 nurses, midwives, health visitors and practice nurses. In social care, moreover, there are more than 1.6 million service users and a workforce of 1.4 million in England alone, with social care workers making up around 4 per cent of the national working population and 15 per cent of the public service workforce

(Commission for Social Care Inspection/General Social Care Council/Social Care Institute for Excellence (CSCI, GSCC, SCIE), n.d.). Unlike the NHS, the social care workforce tends to be spread over a much larger number of public, private and voluntary organisations, and there is no sense of social care as being a single 'family' or organisation in the same way that the NHS is often seen as a single entity.

As suggested above, adult health and social care form a key part of many people's lives, and touch all of us at one stage or another. On a typical day in the NHS alone (Department of Health, 2000a, p. 23), almost 1 million people visit their family doctor, 33,000 people are treated in accident and emergency (A&E), 8,000 people are carried in NHS ambulances and district nurses make 100,000 visits. One in four people also seek help for a mental health problem at some stage in their life, there are some 5.2 million carers providing support to a family member, friend or neighbour, there are 11 million disabled people and the number of people aged 80 and over will nearly triple by 2031 (see Glasby, 2007, for a summary of all statistics quoted in this paragraph). With rising life expectancy and advances in medicine and technology, moreover, the focus of services is increasingly shifting away from the infectious diseases of the nineteenth century (for example, tuberculosis) and the big killers of the late twentieth century (for example, cancer and coronary heart disease) to the needs of people with long-term conditions. While the NHS in particular has traditionally focused on acute and episodic care, policy makers and front-line health and social care organisations have become increasingly aware of the ongoing and multifaceted needs of people with multiple chronic diseases. Indeed, evidence suggests that 80 per cent of GP consultations and two-thirds of hospital admissions relate to people with 'long-term conditions', and current policy is increasingly seeking ways of providing more coordinated and more proactive support to enable people to take much greater control of their own health before a major crisis occurs and they need emergency care (Department of Health, 2004a, 2004b, 2005a, 2005b).

At the time of writing, adult and social care are largely the responsibility of two main players – the NHS and local authority adult social services. From the beginning, the 1940s legislation that established the welfare state enshrined the ongoing assumption that it is possible to distinguish between people who are *sick* (who were defined as having *health needs* and who receive NHS services *free at the point of delivery*) and people who are *frail or disabled* (who are seen as having *social care needs* that fall under the remit of *means-tested social services* provided via the local authority). Out of this division has arisen a complex and divided system, with different organisations and professions responsible for different parts of people's care and support (see Figure 12.1 for a summary of key differences). In 1998, this was described by the then Health Secretary in terms of a 'Berlin Wall', and the phrase rapidly entered the policy literature as a visual image of a powerful and imposing barrier, artificially dividing two territories that ought naturally to be one. As many commentators have suggested (see, for example, Means and Smith, 1998; Glasby and Littlechild, 2004), such a divide has changed constantly over time, and rarely makes sense when viewed in terms of the lived experience of people who use services. However, the fact remains that any attempt to promote more joined-up working is likely to face a series of legal, financial, organisational and cultural barriers. While services have got much better at blurring the boundary between health and social care (see below for further discussion), the 'Berlin Wall' is still very much in evidence.

| | Healthcare | Social care |
|---|---|---|
| *Accountability* | National (to Secretary of State) | Local (to elected councillors) |
| *Policy* | Overseen by Department of Health (also responsible for social care policy) | Local government is overseen by the Department for Communities and Local Government |
| *Charges* | Free at the point of delivery | Means-tested and subject to charging |
| *Boundaries* | Based on GP registration | Based on geography and council boundaries |
| *Focus* | Individual (medical) cure | Individual in his/her wider context |
| *Culture and training* | Strongly influenced by medicine and science | Strongly influenced by social sciences |

**Figure 12.1 The health and social care divide**
*Source*: Glasby, 2007, p. 69.

The majority (over 85 per cent) of the NHS budget in England is held by Primary Care Trusts, who are responsible for commissioning community and hospital-based services for their local populations. The subsequent services have tended to be provided by NHS trusts (providing a range of hospital, mental health, learning disability and ambulance services) or by PCTs themselves (although this may change – see below). However, more recently, there has been a growing role for new Foundation Trusts (hospital or mental health trusts with greater freedom from Whitehall control) and a potentially expanding role for a range of new providers (including **Independent Sector Treatment Centres**, social enterprises and joint health and social care providers). Quality is ensured by a large number of national targets, inspections by national regulators (currently the Healthcare Commission and Monitor) and national guidance provided by the National Institute for Health and Clinical Excellence.

In social care, each local authority has a lead elected member for adult social care (an elected local politician) and a Director of Adult Social Services (DASS) (an appointed officer), responsible for social care services and for promoting social inclusion. The exact structure of departments varies considerably, but many now combine adult social care with other functions, such as housing, trading standards, adult education or leisure. In place of traditional 'Social Services Departments', therefore, local authorities are now creating 'Adults and Communities' or 'Social Inclusion and Health' departments that have a broader remit than traditional adult social care alone. In social care, too, there is a growing emphasis on commissioning, with social workers and social work assistants responsible for assessing individual needs and arranging a package of care to meet these needs. For some time now, such services – for example, home care, day care, residential care – may come from a mix of public, private or voluntary sector organisations, and local authorities tend to have a clear division between the commissioning and the provision of services (in much the same way as the NHS is trying to achieve).

In addition, a further option available in social care is a direct payment, with people assessed as needing support able to choose the cash equivalent to a directly provided service in order to hire their own staff, commission their own services and design their own care. More recently, this way of working has been supplemented by the concept of an individual budget, with individuals in pilot sites now told how much money is available to meet their needs and able to exercise much greater control over how such money is spent on their behalf. While the legal framework that governs adult social care remains complex and fragmented, local authorities are essentially responsible for providing practical support with the activities of daily living to a range of community care user groups (including older people, people with mental health problems, people with physical impairments and people with learning difficulties), as well as for supporting those who care for such people.

### Briefing 12.1
### Key terms, roles and responsibilities

In the NHS, services have traditionally been separated into hospital or acute care and primary and community services. Typically, it is primary care (GPs and other members of the primary healthcare team) that act as gatekeepers to the rest of the system, referring patients with more serious or ongoing needs through to more specialist hospital-based services. As a result, a series of reforms have tried to give GPs greater power and greater incentives to develop new, more community-based services to keep people healthy in their own homes (and thus avoiding the need for more costly hospital care). While different structures have existed over time to achieve this, the latest version (in England and at the time of writing) is the Primary Care Trust, which is often a provider of community health services (such as district nursing and health visiting etc.), as well as the local organisation that pays for hospital care on behalf of local people. More recently, there has been an attempt to focus PCTs more on designing and buying the overall services needed for the local area (known as commissioning), rather than on providing services directly themselves. Much more financial flexibility has also been devolved to GP practices (again to give them greater incentives to change services and reduce costs).

In social care, locally elected councils (local authorities) have traditionally run social services departments to support both children and adults. Key tasks have included ensuring that children are safe from harm (child protection or safeguarding) as well as providing practical support to older people, disabled people, people with mental health problems and people with learning difficulties (for example, via care homes, day centres, home care etc.). The lead professional in such settings has often been a qualified **social worker**, although the bulk of the workforce has always been made up of less or non-qualified workers (and services more generally can sometimes be referred to as **social care** to distinguish this from the input of qualified social workers). Since the early twenty-first century, former social services departments have tended to be split into separate children's services (working more with colleagues in education and children's healthcare) and adult services (working more with adult healthcare colleagues). Since 1993, moreover, the role of social workers (often now called care managers) has increasingly been to focus on assessing individual need, designing a subsequent care package to help meet these needs (which could include services from the public, private or voluntary sectors).

# Recent policy

From the beginning of the welfare state, both health and social care have tended to be dominated by (and spend most of their resources on) institutional forms of care – such as hospitals, care homes and day centres. Due to funding limitations and the age of many of the services concerned (which were often inherited from the old Victorian Poor Law), these buildings quickly became increasingly out of date and in need of repair. Over time, advances in technology and changes in public expectations have also resulted in a situation where services are much more able to support people in their own homes, and where people who use services frequently expect services to fit around their lives (rather than the other way round). As a result, current health and social care policy is very much focused upon trying to reform a post-war system from an approach based on acute care and on providing support to people in a crisis, to a more community-based and proactive system that tries to keep people healthy at home and to give them more control over their own services (Glasby, 2007). This is captured in a range of different phases from official reports – 'seamless services', 'modernisation', 'person-centred care', 'promoting health and well-being' – but is essentially an attempt to respond to the same social and demographic changes.

From the early 1990s, a key mechanism for trying to achieve such change has been the introduction of market-based approaches into both health and social care. Over time, this has taken a number of forms, including the development of general management in healthcare and the creation of an internal market (with health authorities purchasing services from self-governing NHS trusts) and GP-fund-holding (with GP practices holding more and more of their own funds with which to purchase services for their patients directly). Although such approaches were partially rejected following the election of New Labour in 1997, more recent policy has several similar features (including the emphasis on PCTs commissioning services from a more mixed economy of care, a greater role for the independent sector and the advent of practice-based commissioning – with GPs becoming more involved in decisions about care provision via 'indicative' practice budgets). In social care, too, the 1990 NHS and Community Care Act turned social workers into 'care managers' and gave them responsibility for commissioning 'care packages' to meet assessed need. Going even further than NHS reform, local authorities were given additional funding to meet their new responsibilities, but only if 85 per cent of the new money was spent in the voluntary or private sectors. Even now, with the debate about the role of the private sector in delivering healthcare, the NHS remains a publicly funded organisation with the bulk of services provided by public sector organisations and a minimal (albeit growing) role for private provision.

Another key way in which services have sought to become more responsive and person-centred is through more effective inter-agency working. While this has long been an ambition of successive governments, the partnership agenda has acquired increasing significance and impetus since the 1997 election of a New Labour government, stating its commitment to achieving 'joined-up solutions to joined-up problems'. From initial measures to bring down the 'Berlin Wall' between health and social care by greater cooperation and collaboration (see

Briefing 12.2 for some examples), the emphasis has gradually shifted to structural change as a means of improving joint working (with a series of organisational re-structurings) and, more recently, to the use of competition and markets to improve quality. Whether it is possible to collaborate and compete at the same time remains a key question, and the extent to which markets can promote more joined-up thinking by innovative health and social care providers, or will encourage greater fragmentation, remains to be seen. However, as outlined above, an early result of current policy has been the creation of much more inter-agency services for adults and separate children's services – with very real risks that the divide between children and adult's services could become just as problematic in future as the divide between health and social care. In the words of a well-known commentary on the 'five laws of integration': 'your integration is my fragmentation' (Leutz, 1999). Interestingly, the situation in England is currently very different to Wales and Scotland (where there is a similar emphasis on collaboration, but more of a rejection of the role of the market) and in Northern Ireland (where health and social services have traditionally been integrated at a strategic level – although arguably much less so in practice at ground level).

## Briefing 12.2
## Key policies promoting inter-agency working – some examples

In 1999, the Health Act introduced three new 'flexibilities' or powers for health and social care to work across agency boundaries – pooled budgets, lead commissioning and integrated provision (Glendinning et al., 2002b).

In 2000, The NHS Plan (Department of Health, 2000a) called for the creation of new Care Trusts to provide and/or commission integrated health and social care (Glasby and Peck, 2003). To date, there remain very few such organisations.

From 2003, the government's Every Child Matters policy (HM Treasury, 2003) has called for new Children's Trusts to provide and/or commission joined-up children's services. Much more flexible and less prescriptive than the Care Trust model, this has led to much greater interest from the front line, and has been accompanied by other policies promoting the co-location of services, a common assessment framework and lead professionals to coordinate care.

In 2007, legislation introduced a statutory duty to collaborate and to conduct a Joint Strategic Needs Assessment (that is, to work together to assess the current and long-term needs of the local population, using this information to plan future services).

On a more practical level, a further tool for 'modernising' services has been the advent (in social care) of direct payments and individual budgets. Rather than receiving directly provided services, a direct payment enables those individuals who wish to do so to commission their own services from an independent sector agency and/or to hire their own staff. Essentially, direct payment recipients become their own care managers, and the available evidence suggests that this can lead to greater choice and control, greater satisfaction, greater continuity of care and fewer unmet needs – all for the same amount of money (see Glasby and

Littlechild, 2002; Bornat and Leece, 2006 for a summary). In many areas of the country where this way of working has been most successful, there has either been a senior social care leader who has been very committed to direct payments and/or a service user-led Centre for Independent Living providing practical and peer support to people considering direct payments as an option.

Despite positive results, there remain very few direct payment recipients compared to the number of people receiving directly provided services, and this initial concept has since been developed by the advent of individual budgets. Currently being piloted with a view to being rolled out nationally, individual budgets (at their most simple) involve being clear with the individual service user from the beginning how much money is available to spend on meeting their needs and allowing them to choose how much control they wish to exert over this funding (ranging from a direct payment to the local authority managing the budget on the person's behalf). This way of working is being promoted both by government and by a national social enterprise – in Control – which was responsible for pioneering and testing out the original concept (see **www.in-control.org.uk**). To date, emerging evidence is very positive, although it remains very early days. However, deep down both direct payments and individual budgets share some key underlying principles and assumptions which contrast strongly with some directly provided services:

1 People using services often know best what will work for them in the context of their own lives and aspirations. While social care practitioners have expert knowledge of the law and of current services, it is the person using services who is often an expert in their own lives – a partnership between user and professional is therefore essential.

2 People with social care needs have a vested interest (and potentially more of a vested interest than the local authority) in making sure that each pound available to meet their needs is spent as effectively as possible.

3 With support, people can increase their confidence and self-esteem, design innovative and creative services and become much more in control of their own lives.

While these principles remain very powerful and appealing, they have not won over all in adult social care, and considerable resistance still exists from those who see direct payments and individual budgets as a form of privatisation or as a dereliction of the state's duty of care to vulnerable groups of people.

A final approach – only relatively recently being developed – is the emphasis being placed on outcomes-based approaches to health and social care. Historically, public services have tended to think about the world in terms of professional roles and in terms of processes and structures. To explain this in more detail, there has been a tendency for a nurse, for example, to see their contribution in terms of 'being a nurse' and 'doing nursing', without necessarily questioning what it is about the skills nurses have and the jobs they do that might contribute to better outcomes for people who use services. In the same way, the focus has often been on the type and nature of the service provided (and how it is organised), rather than on what it actually achieves for users. Thus, many previous government targets have tended to focus on counting the number or intensity of services provided, rather than on the impact that such services have.

In more recent years, this has started to change, with a much greater emphasis on the outcomes that services should be trying to achieve in key policy documents on children's services (HM Treasury, 2003) and on adult health and social care (Department of Health, 2006). As Briefing 12.3 suggests, future services should increasingly be judged not on what they do, but on how effective they are in delivering desired outcomes. Were this to happen, the results could potentially be extremely profound, with services and practitioners increasingly challenged to demonstrate the benefits of what they do rather than simply focusing on what they have always done. However, at the time of writing, the jury remains out on the extent to which such policy rhetoric will become reality, and it remains to be seen if future governments have sufficient courage and commitment to reform everything they do – from the policies they develop and the targets they set to the way in which services are inspected and evaluated – in line with an outcomes-based approach.

### Briefing 12.3
### Outcomes for children and for adults

In **children's services**, partners are tasked with ensuring that children and young people (HM Treasury, 2003):

- are healthy;
- stay safe;
- are able to enjoy and achieve;
- make a positive contribution;
- experience economic well-being.

In **adult services**, proposed outcomes include (Department of Health, 2006):

- improved health and emotional well-being;
- improved quality of life;
- making a positive contribution;
- choice and control;
- freedom from discrimination;
- economic well-being;
- personal dignity.

## Key issues

Despite all of the previous policies summarised above, there remains an ongoing need to promote more effective inter-agency collaboration between adult health and social care. While legislation such as the Health Act provides an opportunity for closer joint working, the 'Berlin Wall' is still very much in evidence (even if we have found ways to blur the boundaries a little more). A classic example of this is the funding of long-term care (see Controversy and debate, below, as well as Spotlight on the issues at the start of this chapter), with people's needs still divided into 'health' and 'social care' for the purposes of charging. Nor is this merely an academic exercise – with healthcare free at the point of delivery and social care means tested, whether or not an individual is assessed as having health or social care needs makes a significant financial difference to who pays and to the income and savings of the individual concerned. It is partly for this reason that the funding of long-term care has become so controversial in recent years, with a series of legal challenges and ombudsman rulings (see Glasby and Littlechild, 2004 for a summary). While the government has issued a string of circulars, guidance and criteria, the approach to date remains focused on finding ever more sophisticated ways of distinguishing between health and social care needs (rather than acknowledging that this is rarely a meaningful distinction from the perspective of the service user).

## Controversy and debate

## The funding of long-term care

In 1999, the government-appointed Royal Commission on Long Term Care produced its long-awaited recommendations on the future funding of long-term care for older people and younger disabled people. Instead of the current distinction between free NHS care and means-tested social care, the Commission recommended a new distinction, with people in care homes paying a financial contribution towards their living and hotel costs, but receiving all personal care (that is, the additional cost of being looked after arising from frailty or disability) free of charge. This was based in part on the allegation that the present system discriminates against people with long-term conditions for which there are currently no medical cures – thus, a person with cancer in hospital may have just the same personal care needs as someone with dementia in a care home, yet the former receives free treatment and the latter is often asked to pay.

immediately rejected in England, they were rapidly continues to rage as to whether this was a brave tem of long-term care, or a politically motivated to be seen to be different from Whitehall in an era d Bowes, 2006; Dickinson and Glasby, 2006).

the current health and social care divide, a p existing inter-agency relationships so that te health and well-being. With demand and ng the resources available, health and social e in crisis, cutting back on lower level services sive forms of support to retain their independ- their health. This is addressed in more detail t adult health and social care face a dual chal- s support whilst also starting to rebalance the current system towards a more proactive and preventative approach (Glasby, 2007). With the financial situation predicted to get even tighter over the coming years (see, for example, Wanless, 2006), reconciling this tension seems a major issue, and one with few easy answers. Indeed, focusing on the personalisation agenda more generally, services are arguably faced with a situation where they have to deliver higher-quality, more person-centred and more individually-tailored support to more and more people, with greater and greater needs, and with higher and higher expectations – all in difficult financial circumstances.

Against this background, it will be interesting to see whether such pressures force health and social care back into defensive positions in which each guards its own budget jealously from its partners, or whether necessity becomes the mother of invention (with the need to respond to such complex problems prompting a genuine reassessment of current ways of working and a willingness to do things radically differently in future). Put simply, when resources are tight, it can either force us to do more of the same, or it can make us realise that it was 'more of the same' that got us here in the first place, and that we need to do something different.

 Thought provoker

### Developing a preventative approach

How can adult health and social care know if they have prevented something (which would have happened had a preventative approach not been taken)?

Is it more equitable and appropriate for services to focus scarce resources on those with the most needs, or to prioritise low-level support to keep people as healthy and independent as possible before a major health crisis occurs?

To what extent is it possible to do both (that is, to meet the needs of people in crisis whilst also developing a more preventative approach) at the same time?

How can policy makers best achieve short-term improvements in health and social care (to satisfy the legitimate demands of the electorate and the media for better services) whilst also planning for long-term change?

While a preventative approach seems sensible at face value, what evidence exists to help health and social care services understand how best to put prevention into practice?

So far, this chapter has focused almost entirely on people receiving adult health and social care. However, since the mid 1990s, there has been growing recognition of the needs and the contribution of carers. With around 5.2 million carers providing support worth an estimated £57 billion per year (Carers UK, 2002 and 2005), there is substantial evidence to suggest that many people find themselves with little choice over whether or not to become carers and often feel unsupported and unvalued by health and social care (see, for example, Henwood, 1998; Department of Health, 2000b; see also the opening case study at the start of this chapter). This can have an impact on every aspect of life, from family relationships and friendships to social life, leisure, work, income and health. While health and social care have gradually been given greater statutory responsibilities for assessing and responding to the needs of carers, this has often been a slow process, and the availability of practical support remains inconsistent and patchy. Moreover, many services remain confused as to whether they are there to help the 'carer' (in their own right) or whether their main role should be to focus on the 'service user' (only supporting 'the carer' insofar as this improves outcomes for the user) (Glasby, 2007).

 ## Thought provoker

### The needs of carers

Imagine that a sudden accident or the onset of disease puts you into the position where you become a carer for a loved one (perhaps a spouse, a parent, a sibling or a disabled child):

How would this change your current relationship with the person concerned?

What impact might it have on your current quality of life (including your career, your income and your social life)?

Would you know where to go for help and what sort of support is available?

What sort of services might you want from health and social care services?

What kind of personal qualities would you want in the practitioners that worked with you?

Finally, implicit or explicit in much recent policy and debate has been the extent to which health and social care should be adopting an approach based on citizenship and on human rights. With many of the developments and approaches discussed so far in this chapter, it is possible to see people who use services as customers (who can take their 'business' elsewhere if they are not satisfied) and to see recent policy as an attempt to preserve current commitment to public services by making them more responsive and more cost-effective. With ongoing social and demographic changes, moreover, many of the above policies are arguably necessary if current services are to continue to meet the demands being made of them. At the same time, however, it is also possible to see recent policy as being much more about transforming public services in order to give people what they are entitled to as taxpayers and as citizens of this country. Thus, a government could adopt a policy of direct payments because it thinks this will increase competition and make services more efficient, or it could pursue the same policy because it thinks that disabled people deserve the same choice and control over their lives as non-disabled citizens. In both cases, the policy might be the same, but the reason for making this change and the underlying value base may be very different. While this is explored in more detail elsewhere (see Glasby, 2007), it has been argued that current adult health and social care face a series of tensions and dilemmas that may be potentially incompatible. Key examples include:

- Whether services achieve the best results by competing or by collaborating (and the extent to which it is possible to do both at the same time).
- Whether to support people with long-term conditions because they are citizens with a right to independent living, or simply as a means of reducing reliance on expensive hospital services.

- Whether to involve people with experience of using services because they are 'customers' who can help improve the 'product' or because they are citizens with a right to greater choice and control.

- Whether to support carers because they deserve the same access to a meaningful and stimulating life as everyone else, or whether to focus on the needs of carers as a means of helping the 'service user' and reducing demands on formal services.

In the short term, it may be that current adult health and social care can keep these tensions in check. In the long run, however, there may well need to be much more of a national debate about what health and social care services are for and about what we can expect from the state as citizens if services are to continue to evolve in response to changing social need.

## Conclusion

Health and social care are essential features of the UK welfare system, providing practical, crisis and ongoing support to millions of people each year. However, perhaps because they are so important, they are frequently a subject of discussion, debate and controversy, for politicians, the media and members of the public alike. From the early 1990s a series of attempts have been made to reform health and social care, particularly through the introduction of market-based principles. However, other key changes have included the desire to develop more of a preventive and personalised approach, based on a greater separation of commissioning and provision and on a more outcomes-focused approach. During these changes there have been ongoing difficulties and frequent discussion of particular issues, such as how best to support carers or to fund long-term care. However, underlying many of these debates is a deeper and often unspoken issue about the basis on which health and social care should be provided and reformed – through a consumerist or a citizen model.

## Summary

This chapter has outlined the structure, role and functions of adult health and social care, together with recent policy developments. It has also highlighted some of the key issues central to debates about provision in this area. From this discussion it is apparent that:

- Health and social care in the UK consume significant public resources and provide support to many millions of people facing potentially traumatic life events.

- They do so in a challenging policy and financial context, in which the resources available always seem to be outstripped by public and media expectations.

- Whereas health and social care have traditionally operated in relative isolation from each other, there is now much greater emphasis on joint working across agency boundaries.

- Faced with a series of social and demographic changes, adult health and social care have also been challenged with giving service users greater choice and control, and with delivering more person-centred, responsive and preventative support.

- Since the early 1990s, there has been fluctuating but growing emphasis on the market and on competition in a more mixed economy of care as a means of making services more responsive to the needs of individuals and achieving greater cost-efficiency.

- Despite significant change, there are ongoing tensions as to how best to achieve more effective joint working, how best to promote health and well-being, how best to support family carers and how best to fund long-term care.

- In several cases, it has been possible to pursue similar policies for different reasons, and future adult health and social care may well need to resolve the tension between citizenship on the one hand and consumerism/cost-efficiency on the other before further progress can be made.

## Discussion and review topics

1 In recent years, English policy has moved from a system based on a relatively rigid divide between health and social care to one based more on a growing separation between inter-agency adult services and inter-agency children's services. This is not the case in other parts of the UK, which have not to date distinguished between services for children and services for adults to such an extent. What are the advantages and disadvantages of each approach? (In particular, you might reflect on the needs of specific user groups who might be adversely affected by a growing separation between children's and adult services – an example here might be disabled parents (who may have personal care needs for themselves but also need support with aspects of their parenting role).)

2 The NHS is often seen as a symbol of 'Britishness', with strong national commitment to its founding principles of services based on clinical need and free at the point of delivery. However, social care has never enjoyed the same status or the same level of understanding, and its image remains much more ambiguous. What sort of support should be available free of charge to citizens of this country, and what preparations should individuals be expected to make and fund for themselves and their families in case of illness, frailty or disability? With the Scottish system of 'free personal care' in mind, how should services for older people with ongoing needs be organised and funded?

3 Irrespective of the structure and the nature of the services available, what interpersonal skills and values would you like to see in health and social care practitioners? If you were a senior manager in health or social care, how would you seek to ensure that such skills and values were embedded in the culture of front-line service delivery?

4 If you were Health Secretary, what practical measures would you introduce to enable adult health and social care to respond to the challenges set out in this chapter?

## Further reading

Balloch, S. and Taylor, M. (eds) (2001) *Partnership Working: Policy and Practice*, Policy Press, Bristol. The book provides an analysis of the development of partnership working in public services.

Glasby, J. (2007) *Understanding Health and Social Care*, Policy Press, Bristol. This book explores many of the themes from this chapter in more detail.

Glendinning, C., Powell, M. and Rummery, K. (eds) (2002) *Partnerships, New Labour and the Governance of Welfare*, Policy Press, Bristol. Examines partnerships and partnership working, drawing on evidence from a number of policy areas.

Lymbery, M. (2005) *Social Work with Older People*, Sage, London. This book provides an authoritative overview of social work and older people, drawing on both theory and practice.

Means, R., Richards, S. and Smith, R. (2003) *Community Care: Policy and Practice*, Palgrave Macmillan, Basingstoke. This book provides a comprehensive coverage of community care from its historical development to contemporary issues.

Sharkey, P. (2006) *The Essentials of Community Care*, Palgrave Macmillan, Basingstoke. This book gives an oversight of community care, with chapters focusing on key issues.

## Some useful websites

www.communitycare.co.uk - *Community Care* and www.hsj.co.uk the *Health Service Journal* are two of the main weekly trade publications in health and social care, with a mix of news, features and practice-focused articles.

www.dh.gov.uk - official policy is available via the Department of Health whilst the devolved administrations have their own sites - www.scotland.gov.uk for Scotland, www.new.wales. gov.uk for Wales, and www.dhsspsni.gov.uk for Northern Ireland. Good practice guidance in health and social care is also available via the National Institute for Health and Clinical Excellence (www.nice.org.uk) and the Social Care Institute for Excellence (www.scie.org.uk). The latter website includes free access to the social care database 'Social Care Online'.

www.in-control.org.uk - the in Control website (i.e. the national organisation that developed and is now supporting the implementation of individual budgets).

Various health and social care professional associations and membership organisations provide helpful information on current policy and practice, including, for example, Association of Directors of Adult Social Services (www.adass.org.uk), British Association of Social Workers (www.basw.co.uk), NHS Alliance (www.nhsalliance.org), NHS Confederation (www. nhsconfed. org). Leading national voluntary organisations also offer up-to-date information on key community care issues, including, for example, Age Concern (www.ace.org.uk), Carers UK (www.carersuk.org/Home) and Turning Point (www.turning-point.co.uk).

## References

Alakeson, V. (2007) *Putting patients in control: The case for extending self-direction into the NHS*, Social Market Foundation, London.

Balloch, S. and Taylor, M. (eds) (2001) *Partnership working: Policy and practice*, Policy Press, Bristol.

Bell, D. and Bowes, A. (2006) *Financial care models in Scotland and the UK: A review of the introduction of free personal care for older people in Scotland*, Joseph Rowntree Foundation, York.

Bornat, J. and Leece, J. (eds) (2006) *Developments in direct payments*, Policy Press, Bristol.

Carers UK (2002) *Without us . . .? Calculating the value of carers' support*, Carers UK, London.

Carers UK (2005) *Facts about carers*, Carers UK, London.

Commission for Social Care Inspection (2006) *The state of social care in England 2005-06*, CSCI, London.

Commission for Social Care Inspection (CSCI) General Social Care Council (GSCC) and Social Care Institute for Excellence (SCIE) (n.d.) *Facing the facts: Social care in England*, CSCI/GSCC/SCIE, London.

Department of Health (2000a) *The NHS plan: A plan for investment, a plan for reform*, The Stationery Office (TSO), London.

Department of Health (2000b) *Caring about carers: A national strategy for carers* (2nd edn; first published 1999), Department of Health, London.

Department of Health (2004a) *Chronic disease management: A compendium of information*, Department of Health, London.

Department of Health (2004b) *The NHS improvement plan*, Department of Health, London.

Department of Health (2005a) *The national service framework for long-term conditions*, Department of Health, London.

Department of Health (2005b) *Supporting people with long-term conditions: An NHS and social care model to support local innovation and integration*, Department of Health, London.

Department of Health (2006) *Our health, our care, our say: A new direction for community services*, TSO, London.

Dickinson, H. and Glasby, J. (2006) *Free personal care in Scotland* (Discussion paper commissioned by the Wanless Social Care Review), King's Fund, London.

Glasby, J. (2007) *Understanding health and social care*, Policy Press, Bristol.

Glasby, J. and Duffy, S. (2007) *'Our Health, Our Care, Our Say' – What could the NHS learn from individual budgets and direct payments?* Health Services Management Centre/In Control, Birmingham.

Glasby, J. and Littlechild, R. (2002) *Social work and direct payments*, Policy Press, Bristol.

Glasby, J. and Littlechild, R. (2004) *The health and social care divide: The experiences of older people* (2nd edn), Policy Press, Bristol.

Glasby, J. and Peck, E. (eds) (2003) *Care trusts: Partnership working in action*, Radcliffe Medical Press, Abingdon.

Glendinning, C., Hudson, B., Hardy, B. and Young, R. (2002a) *National evaluation of notifications for the use of the Section 31 partnership flexibilities in the Health Act 1999: Final project report*, Leeds/Manchester, Nuffield Institute for Health/National Primary Care Research and Development Centre.

Glendinning, C., Powell, M. and Rummery, K. (2002b) *Partnerships, New Labour and the governance of welfare*, Policy Press, Bristol.

Henwood, M. (1998) *Ignored and invisible? Carers' experience of the NHS*, Carers National Association (now Carers UK), London.

HM Treasury (2003) *Every child matters*, TSO, London.

Leutz, W. (1999) 'Five laws for integrating medical and social services: lessons from the United States and the United Kingdom', *Milbank Memorial Fund Quarterly*, Vol. 77, pp. 77-110.

Lymbery, M. (2005) *Social work with older people: Context, policy and practice*, Sage, London.

Means, R., Richards, S. and Smith, R. (2003) *Community care: Policy and practice* (3rd edn), Palgrave, Basingstoke.

Means, R. and Smith, R. (1998) *From poor law to community care*, Macmillan, Basingstoke.

NHS Confederation (2006) *The NHS in the UK 2006/07: A pocket guide*, NHS Confederation, London.

Parliamentary and Health Service Ombudsman (2003) *Case no. E.22/02-03. Complaint against: the former Cambridgeshire Health Authority and South Cambridgeshire Primary Care Trust – the Pointon case*, Parliamentary and Health Service Ombudsman, London.

Royal Commission on Long Term Care (1999) *With respect to old age: Long term care – rights and responsibilities*, TSO, London.

Sharkey, P. (2007) *The essentials of community care* (2nd edn), Palgrave Macmillan, Basingstoke.

Sullivan, H. and Skelcher, C. (2002) *Working across boundaries: Collaboration in public services*, Palgrave, Basingstoke.

The Guardian (2007) *Malcolm and Barbara: Love's Farewell*, 9 August. Online discussion available via **http://blogs.guardian.co.uk/organgrinder/2007/08/malcolm_and_barbara_loves_fare.html** (accessed 20.08.2007).

Wanless, D. (2006) *Securing good care for older people: Taking a long term view*, King's Fund, London.

# 13

# Children and families

Paul Daniel

## Chapter overview

New Labour's concern to tackle social exclusion and child poverty has placed the family at the heart of social policy as never before. In practice, however, this is an area of social policy which raises many issues and questions. Perhaps the most fundamental debate has centred on where to draw the line between state intervention on the one hand and respect for family privacy and autonomy on the other. Equally contentious is the question as to what we mean by family. More specifically, does support for the family translate into support for marriage?

Also, if policy is based around families, how does it weigh up the interests of parents against children, mothers against fathers? Then too, if we are concerned to improve parenting, what should be the balance between coercion and support - a point raised in the newspaper report, below? Finally, to the extent that family policy is primarily driven by the state's interest in children, what is the model of childhood upon which policy is based? Are children viewed as an investment in the future or as individuals in their own right?

These issues and debates, among others, are addressed in this chapter during which we will discuss:

- the extent of demographic change and family diversity;
- UK ambivalence over state involvement in family;
- the ways in which policy initiatives in relation to parenting impact unequally on mothers and fathers;
- contrasting perspectives on childhood and the implications for UK family policy.

## Spotlight on the issues
### 'Policing' families

A teenager whose mother was jailed because of his failure to attend school pleaded for her release yesterday, saying he was the one to blame. The mother of the 14-year-old, who cannot be named for legal reasons, was sentenced to 28 days in prison on Monday after he did not attend lessons for three months. The child's father said he and his ex-wife had been taking the teenager to school every day, only for him to leave by another door.

*Source: Independent,* 17 April 2003

Families are at the heart of our society. Most of us live in families and we value them because they provide love and support and care . . . Our future depends on their success in bringing up children. That is why we are committed to strengthening family life.

Home Office (1998, p. 1)

On the surface, this passage from Labour's Green Paper *Supporting Families: A Consultation Document* would command a fair degree of consensus. British political parties of all persuasion have been keen to brand themselves as 'the party of the family'. The reality, however, is that UK governments since the Second World War have been ambivalent in their approach to social policy in relation to the family. Indeed, in their comprehensive review of family policy in fourteen countries, Kamerman and Kahn (1978) classified the UK amongst a small group who lacked a comprehensive family policy and whose approach to supporting the family was deemed to be reluctant.

This chapter considers some of the difficulties associated with family policy in the United Kingdom, outlining a variety of developments under the Labour government, and discusses ideas developed from the notions of childrens' rights.

## Which family?

Arguably, since 1997 New Labour has given much higher priority to this area of social policy and the creation of a new government department of Children, Schools and Families in 2007 now enables a much more holistic 'joined-up' approach to policy. However, before we proceed to look in detail at UK family policy, we need to spend some time considering what we mean by 'family'.

Much of the post-Second World War welfare state reform, and in particular the Beveridge reforms of social security, were designed around a specific model of the family. This was the married couple with a **male breadwinner** and a mother whose job it was to stay at home and 'ensure the adequate continuance of the British Race' (Beveridge, 1942, para. 114). This was disputed as an accurate portrayal of family life even in the 1940s (see Abbott and Bompas, 1943). Subsequently, it has become further and further from the reality – although the repercussions of this assumption continue to be felt in terms of women's unequal entitlement to pensions.

Few areas of social life have changed so quickly and substantially in the last thirty years or so as our domestic living arrangements. Indeed there is now such diversity that, as Jane Millar has suggested, 'to talk about "the family" is to fail to reflect the range of "families" that people actually live in' (Millar, 1998, p. 122) (see Table 13.1).

**Table 13.1** Dependent children: by family type, 2004, UK

|  | *Thousands* | *Percentages* |
|---|---|---|
| Married couple | 8,585 | 66 |
| Cohabiting couple | 1,412 | 11 |
| Lone-mother | 2,829 | 22 |
| Lone-father | 254 | 2 |
| All dependent children in families | 13,080 | 100 |

*Source*: ONS, 2007.

Whilst there would be little argument that a married couple, or lone parent, with children, constitute a family, other arrangements would command much less consensus. Consider, for example, the following scenarios:

- a cohabiting couple (a) with children or (b) without children;
- a couple living with their divorced daughter and her children;
- a gay couple (a) with children or (b) without children;
- a divorced father whose children live with him at weekends;
- an elderly person with their adult child;
- a childless married couple.

It is probable that there would be considerable disagreement over some or all these examples. Yet this is not simply an academic debate. It is critical to the design of social policy since, as we saw above, the way in which 'family' is defined may well mean that certain types of living arrangement are privileged over others. The official definition of family, used in government surveys, is as follows;

A family: is a married or cohabiting couple, either with or without their never-married child or children (of any age), including couples with no children or a lone parent together with his or her never-married child or children provided they have no children of their own. A family could also consist of a grandparent(s) with their grandchild or grandchildren if the parents of the grandchild or grandchildren are not usually resident in the household.

Office for National Statistics (2007, p. 202)

In many respects this is a relatively broad and inclusive definition – although it is arguably based around a nuclear model of the family and does not encompass the three-generation or other extended family arrangements. It does not, though, draw any distinction between married and unmarried or even heterosexual and same-sex couples and, significantly, it also includes lone parents.

When it comes to policy, these issues have aroused more controversy. This reached its zenith, perhaps, in the 1980s and early 1990s during the governments of Margaret Thatcher and John Major. Concerns at the demographic and social changes that were leading to increasing numbers of children being brought up outside of marriage led to a number of moral crusades promoting 'family values' and '**back to basics**'. Although this provoked a number of policy initiatives such as Section 28 of the Local Government Act 1988, which made it illegal for local authorities and schools to promote homosexuality, and cuts in lone-parent benefit, the overall picture for family policy was more mixed. The reality was that families with children fared badly under the Conservative governments of the 1980s and 1990s relative to single people or childless couples (Bradshaw, 1990).

Arguably, the growth of child poverty was the single most notable family policy legacy of this period (see Table 13.2).

Table 13.2 Percentage of children in poverty
(below 60% of median income after housing costs)

| Year | Children |
|------|----------|
| 1979 | 14 |
| 1987 | 25 |
| 90/91 | 31 |
| 92/93 | 33 |
| 94/95 | 31 |
| 96/97 | 33 |
| 98/99 | 33 |

Indeed, for all the rhetoric about family values, there was an inherent contradiction within the New Right in both the UK and USA, between their traditional conservatism on social and moral issues, and their commitment to economic freedom and liberal autonomy. It was difficult to square an authoritarian or interventionist approach to family policy with the general philosophy of rolling back the state which was fundamental to New Right ideology. One aspect of policy where this caused particular problems, as Fawcett *et al.* (2004) have argued, was in the employment of mothers of young children. Traditional family values required that young mothers should stay at home to look after their children. Free market economics and individual choice, on the other hand, supported their right to enter paid employment. The result, as Fawcett *et al.* point out, was an unprecedented increase in young mothers working outside the home without any corresponding social policy support, whether through childcare or family-friendly employment legislation.

New Labour, by contrast, has taken a rather more pragmatic and less moralistic stance on family diversity. Both in its rhetoric and in its actual policy it has put children above any belief in a particular family form. This has not stopped it from promoting marriage as the ideal. In its Green Paper *Supporting Families* (Home Office, 1998), for example, it set out 'strengthening marriage' as one of its policy objectives. Proposals included pre-nuptial agreements, giving registrars more of a role in helping couples prepare for marriage as well as expanded counselling services for both married and cohabiting couples. However, this aspect of the Green Paper attracted more criticism than any other, and in the event the government retreated to the extent that it repealed Part 11 of the 1996 Family Law Act which made it compulsory for divorcing couples to attend 'information meetings'. Instead, Labour has taken a softer line, introducing a number of voluntary schemes and a new 'marriage and relationship support grant' administered by the Lord Chancellor's department.

## Briefing 13.1
### Demographic change and the family

The changes in family structure over the past thirty or forty years have been wide ranging and far reaching. The following are a few key points based upon data from *Social Trends*, 2007:

### Household composition

- The average size of households declined between 1971 and 2006 from 2.9 persons to 2.4. This was due principally to an increase in lone-parent families (from 3 per cent to 7 per cent), smaller families and an increase in single-person households (from 18% to 29%).

- The proportion of households comprising a couple with 1 or 2 children fell from 26 per cent to 18 per cent between 1971 and 2006.

- In 2006, 76 per cent of children were living in a family unit headed by a couple compared to 92 per cent in 1971.

- A more recent change in family life has been the increase in the number of grown-up children living with their parents (between 1991 and 2006 the proportion of 20–24-year-old males living with parents increased from 50 per cent to 58 per cent and for females the rise was from 32 per cent to 39 per cent).

### Partnerships

- Since the early 1970s the number of people marrying has decreased. Despite this, married couples are still the main type of partnership for men and women. In 2006 there were 17.1 million families in the UK and around 7 in 10 contained a married couple.

- The average age at which people get married for the first time has risen. Between 1971 and 2006 the average age for men increased from 25 to 32 and for women from 23 to 29.

- During the first year of the Civil Partnership Act there were 15,700 same sex partnerships formed.

### Divorce and cohabitation

- The rate of divorce climbed from 2.1 per 1,000 of the married population in 1961 to around 13 per 1,000 in 2005.

- The number of children under 16 who experienced divorce of their parents peaked at 176,000 in 1993. One-fifth of children whose parents divorced were under 5 and nearly two-thirds were ten or under.

- Two-fifths of all marriages in 2005 were remarriages.

- The proportion of non-married people under 60 cohabiting increased between 1986 (the first year for which data is available) and 2005 from 11 per cent to 24 per cent for men and 13 per cent to 24 per cent for women.

- As a consequence, children live in an increasing variety of family structures. Parents separating can result in lone-parent families, and new relationships can create step-families. More than 10 per cent of all families with dependent children in 2005 were stepfamilies.

## Family formation

- Women are having children later – 34 per cent of women born in 1940 were still child-less at age 25: this increased to 64 per cent among women born in 1980. The average age at which women give birth for the first time has increased from 24 in 1971 to 30 in 2005.

- Although most children are born to married couples the proportion of all births which were outside marriage rose to 43 per cent in 2005 – though 84 per cent of these were jointly registered by both parents, indicating an increase in cohabitation rather than lone parenthood.

## The ageing population

- For the first time in history people 60 and over form a larger part of the UK population than children under 16: 21 per cent compared to 20 per cent.

- Although the population grew by 8 per cent in the last thirty-five years, from 55.9 million in 1971 to 60.6 million in mid 2006, this change has not occurred evenly across all age groups. The population aged over 65 grew by 31 per cent, from 7.4 to 9.7 million, whilst the population aged under 16 declined by 19 per cent, from 14.2 to 11.5 million.

- Multi-generational families, with as many as four or even five generations alive at the same time, are becoming more common.

By the time it came to publish its policy review, *Building on Progress: Families*, the Labour government was much clearer that it did not see the role of govern-ment as promoting marriage:

> Families themselves are generally best placed to judge how to manage their affairs, and govern-ments should neither limit their choices nor make value judgements about private decisions.
>
> Cabinet Office (2007, p. 14)

In the intervening ten years Labour introduced a number of policy measures reflecting this move away from an emphasis on marriage in favour of support for family diversity, with children as the primary concern. For example, the married couples' tax allowance was abolished and resources redistributed to families with children. The Adoption and Children Act 2002 extended parental responsibility to unmarried fathers who register the child's birth (previously it was only auto-matically granted to married fathers). The same legislation granted cohabiting and same-sex couples the right to apply to adopt children. And the Civil Partner-ship Act 2004 gave same-sex couples parity with married couples in terms of legal and financial rights.

This acceptance of family diversity is not without its critics (for example, Centre for Social Justice, 2007). There is a growing body of evidence of a statistical correlation between marriage and children's well-being. Children who have married parents, irrespective of their social background, are more likely to be in full-time education at 17 than those living in any other type of household. Similarly, children suffer less long-term illness within married-couple households (ONS, 2007). It should be pointed out, however, that although this relationship is a clear and statistically significant one, it is not necessarily causal. As Kiernan points out 'in both the UK and the US a disproportionate number of cohabiting families are drawn from the poor and ill-educated. So comparisons between cohabiting and married couples are comparing apples and pears, not like with like' (*The Observer*, 7 July 2002).

## Controversy and debate

Britain is almost the only country in Europe that doesn't recognise marriage in the tax system. And the benefits system actively discourages parents from living together . . . We have the highest rate of family breakdown in Europe. Don't tell me these things aren't connected.

David Cameron, BBC News, 10 July 2007

● Does the tax/benefit system in the UK discourage marriage?
● The Conservative party has proposed the introduction of a **transferable married persons allowance** and changes to the tax credit system to reward marriage at a cost of £3 billion. Is this a good idea?

## Briefing 13.2
### The decline of the traditional family?

Contemporary trends benefit from being placed in a longer term perspective. It is worth remembering before we consider the most recent British changes, that the 'traditional' nuclear family is something of a misnomer. Its origins are relatively recent and its existence has coincided, to a great extent, with unusual social circumstances in the form of world wars. The most salient features of this 'modern' family arose in Britain in the twentieth century and, for many, not until after the Second World War . . . Pre-twentieth century marriage break up rates paralleled modern ones but were due to death rather than divorce . . . Also the proportion of children living outside a 'traditional' two parent family was almost the same in 1851 as it has been recently.

Clarke, (1996, p. 67)

## The balance between the state and the family in UK social policy

Kamerman and Kahn's claim that the UK has historically lacked an overt and comprehensive policy on the family should not distract us from the fact that there has been a multitude of policies which affect the family, nor indeed that there have been implicit assumptions about the family built into social policy. On the contrary, the post-1945 welfare reforms and the Beveridge Report in particular contained a number of very specific – and in the latter case also quite explicit – views about families and the role of social policy. We have already referred to one such assumption about families, which formed the cornerstone of the reform of social security in the 1940s – the male breadwinner model. A second important theme in the Beveridge Report was the need to invest in the next generation through state financial support. Thus he justified the introduction of Family Allowances (the predecessor of Child Benefit) as follows:

> These proposals are based on two principles, first that nothing should be done to remove from parents the responsibility of maintaining their children, and second that it is in the national interest for the state to help parents discharge that responsibility properly.
>
> Beveridge (1942, p. 14)

Here we see two pervasive themes which have continued to characterise UK social policy in relation to families: first, children are seen in terms of being an investment in the future of the nation; and, second, the responsibility for their upbringing is primarily that of their parents. Indeed on this latter point, Gillian Pascall has suggested that in UK policy discourse 'the real meaning of supporting the family is supporting family responsibility, as distinct from state responsibility' (Pascall, 1986, p. 38). It could also add that for family responsibility we should read maternal responsibility – a point we will expand upon later.

As a result, aside from education – which has been seen as a clear responsibility of the state – UK social policy has demonstrated a strongly residual approach when it comes to family support. This is perhaps best illustrated by the contrast in levels of childcare provision in the UK compared to most other European countries (see David, 1993).

Beyond the minimal levels of universal support for families provided by Family Allowances/Child Benefit, intervention has been limited to those cases deemed to be 'at risk' or 'in need' under the terms of child welfare legislation (the 1989 Children Act and its predecessors). Such support has not only been limited but it has also been accompanied by stigma, surveillance and potential sanction.

Ambivalence towards state support for the family in the UK has been underpinned by two beliefs. The first is that the family is a private sphere outside the public realm of the state. This has proved a powerful and, as David Archard has suggested, a self-perpetuating ideology: 'For what the state will not intrude upon is defined as "private", and the "privacy" of the private is what then serves as the principal ground for non-intervention' (Archard, 1993, p. 113). This is well illustrated by the issue of smacking. On this issue the Labour government experienced mounting pressure in the early years of the twenty-first century to bring UK policy in line with its obligations under the 1989 United Nations Convention on the Rights of the Child and grant children the same rights to protection from being hit as adults possess. This pressure came externally from the United Nations Committee on the Rights of the Child and internally from a powerful coalition of children's charities and came to a head when the UK government was defeated on this issue in the European Court on Human Rights (see Newell, 2002, for details). Yet the government effectively closed off debate, and delayed what is surely an inevitable reform, on the basis that discipline within the family is a private matter and not one in which government should intervene. This example is a clear differentiation on the subject of state involvement in the family between attitudes in the UK and the growing number of countries that have already made smacking illegal.

Controversy and debate

Children and young people should have the same right to protection under the law on common assault as that afforded to adults. There is no good reason why children are the only people in the UK who can still be lawfully hit . . . By not changing the legislation, we continue to send out confusing messages to parents about the acceptable use of violence across society.

Children's Commissioner for England, Al Aynsley-Green, *Guardian*, 25 October 2007

The second belief which has underpinned UK policy towards the family is that excessive social policy intervention will undermine family responsibility. This theme was particularly current during the 1980s and early 1990s, inspired by a number of New Right publications from both sides of the Atlantic. From the US the work of Charles Murray (1984) and Lawrence Mead (1986) argued that welfare support had contributed to an erosion of family responsibilities. Similar arguments were put forward in the UK by Dennis and Erdos (1993) and Morgan (1995). Much of the debate focused on the role of welfare benefits in fuelling the rise in the number of lone parents. There followed a 'moral crusade' driven by politicians and the media which only ran out of steam as a result of a series of family scandals involving Conservative MPs. This was not, however, before a significant policy change aimed at shifting responsibility for financial support of children in lone-parent families away from the state and back to what was termed the 'absent parent' – generally the father. Although this clearly had the aim of cutting expenditure on social security (see Garnham and Knights, 1994) it was also intended to send out a strong message about 'family responsibility'. Other policy changes in the 1980s included the new concept of 'parental responsibility'. This replaced 'parental rights' in the 1989 Children Act and reinforced the idea that the main responsibility for the care of children was that of the parents and not the state. Moreover, at the same time that the Conservative government was expanding parental responsibility towards children it was reducing state support to families by cutting services and freezing Child Benefit.

## Family policy under New Labour

Motivated by its two key policy objectives of eliminating child poverty and tackling antisocial behaviour, Labour has placed the family at the centre of its social policy agenda in a way never before seen in the UK. This has been reflected not only in the level of resources and the range of initiatives aimed at supporting the family (see Briefing 13.3), but also in a reorganisation of government to bring about a more coordinated approach to policy in England and Wales. Historically, the fact that services for children have been scattered over a number of government departments has been a major barrier to effective planning. The creation, in 2007, of the Department for Children, Schools and Families at central government level, and the move towards Children's Trusts (bringing together education, health and social services provision) at local level, is intended to bring about a

# Briefing 13.3

The following lists a selection of the more significant Labour policy measures relating to children and families.

## 1998

*Meeting the Childcare Challenge* – sets out the first ever UK national childcare strategy – free part-time early-education places for all four-year-olds announced.

Sure Start initiative launched – a comprehensive community-based programme of early intervention and family support.

New Deal for Lone Parents – a welfare-to-work programme.

*Supporting Families* Green Paper published; proposals included a National Family and Parenting Institute.

## 1999

Beveridge Lecture – Tony Blair's historic commitment to end child poverty within a generation.

Working Families Tax Credit announced.

Parental Leave introduced.

## 2000

Abolition of Married Couple's Allowance.

Children's Fund established to fund services to children at risk of social exclusion.

Work-life balance campaign launched.

## 2001

Children's Tax Credit introduced.

Marriage and Relationship Support Grant set up.

## 2002

Education Act 2002 – introduced extended school service.

Employment Act 2002 – increased statutory maternity leave to 6 months paid and a further 6 months unpaid, also 2 weeks paid paternity leave and the right to request flexible working for parents of children under 6 (18 for a disabled child).

## 2003

Child Tax Credit and Working Tax Credit introduced.

*Every Child Matters* – Green Paper response to Victoria Climbié Inquiry report.

Children's Trusts launched – 35 Pathfinder projects bringing together children's health, social services and education.

Antisocial Behaviour Act 2003 – extends use of parental responsibility orders.

Minister for Children – Margaret Hodge appointed as first ever post-holder.

## 2004

Children Act 2004 – implements main elements of *Every Child Matters*.

Choice for Parents, the Best Start for Children: A Ten Year Strategy for Childcare – including recommendations for 3,500 children's centres by 2010.

Extended entitlement to free early-years place (12.5 hours) to all three-year-olds.

**2005**

Commission on Families and the Well-Being of Children set up.

*Youth Matters*, Green Paper.

Children's Commissioner for England – Al Aynsley-Green appointed as first post-holder.

**2006**

Publication of Respect Action Plan – including recommendations for a network of 'family support schemes'.

Family Intervention Projects to be launched.

Childcare Act 2006.

**2007**

Maternity leave extended to 9 months.

*Every Parent Matters* launched – all local authorities required to have a parenting support strategy.

Department for Children, Schools and Families formed.

Ten Year Plan for Children produced.

much more 'joined-up' approach to policy. It should be noted here that even before devolution Scotland and Northern Ireland had their own separate legislative and administrative arrangements for education and child welfare services. Consequently, although policy in relation to children and families has run very much in parallel across the four countries which make up the UK, the specific detail in this chapter refers primarily to England and Wales.

Much of Labour's rhetoric echoes the familiar themes in UK policy towards the family. Consider this passage from its review of its policies on the family, for example: 'The success of families is first and foremost down to the commitment and behaviour of the individuals within them . . . It is right to be wary of state interference in family life' (Cabinet Office, 2007, p. 7). The reality, however, has been that Labour has redrawn the boundaries between the state and the family to a significant extent. This has come about through a much more explicit focus on the role of the state in supporting children. Indeed, it is probably more accurate to describe Labour's approach as a 'child policy' rather than a 'family policy' – there are many aspects of family life, such as the care of the elderly and dependent adults, which have received limited attention.

There is no one document which sets out Labour's family policy priorities or the values and principles upon which their policy is based. The independent Commission on Families and the Well-being of Children has, however produced a summary of key values which could serve as a fair approximation to those which underpin Labour's family policy (Briefing 13.4).

## Briefing 13.4

The Commission on Families and the Well-being of Children was established in April 2004 to consider the relationship between the state and the family in providing children with a humane and caring upbringing in the twenty-first century.

The Commission's recommendations have been informed by these values:

- A recognition of the importance of families in all their various forms as the environment in which most children are brought up and cared for.

- A recognition that families, as well as having the potential to offer a caring environment, can also be a place where people experience violence and abuse, and may not, in certain circumstances, serve the best interests of the children living in them.

- A recognition that families mediate between people as individuals and the wider community, and have an influence on society as a whole. Following from the above, an acceptance that the state has a role to play in supporting and regulating families, in respect of their impact on both society and individual family members, and children in particular because of their vulnerability.

- A recognition that, notwithstanding the above, many changes and static features in family social and demographic trends are not and should not be subject to significant influence by the state.

- A recognition that, because of their vulnerability, the well-being of children should be the paramount consideration in constructing family policy. This entails the adoption of an 'ethic of care' in the development of family policy.

- A recognition of the need to reduce inequities within society and to address discrimination associated with, *inter alia*, ethnic, cultural and social background, disability, gender and sexual orientation. In determining the dividing line between family autonomy and legitimate state intervention, and the scope of the state's obligations to support families, the Commission has been guided by two internationally accepted instruments establishing the dimensions of human and children's rights – the Human Rights Act 1998 and the United Nations Convention on the Rights of the Child 1989.

In terms of Labour's policy priorities, there were five pledges relating to the family in Labour's 1997 manifesto:

1  to help lone parents into employment;

2  to establish National Childcare Strategy;

3  to grant parental leave and other employment rights;

4  to retain universal Child Benefit;

5  to introduce parental responsibility orders.

The defining moment for Labour's family policy, however, arguably came with Tony Blair's Beveridge lecture in 1999 when he announced: 'Our historic aim will be for ours to be the first generation to end child poverty, and it will take a generation. It is a 20-year mission but I believe it can be done' (Blair, 1999).

It was this remarkable commitment which required the radical shift in the scale of state support for families which subsequently followed. This support has taken two forms. First, there have been a wide range of initiatives targeted at low-income families – schemes such as the **Children's Fund**, launched in 2001, which is intended to provide preventive services for 5- to 13-year-olds who show early signs of difficulty, with the aim of avoiding the risk of social exclusion. There is nothing new in this selective, targeted approach, and indeed much of Labour's social exclusion discourse is heavily reminiscent of its 1970s '**cycle of deprivation**' predecessor. What does mark out Labour's record from any previous government, though, is the sheer volume of initiatives and scale of spending. It also should be said that its flagship project, Sure Start, which began initially with 250 projects in the most disadvantaged areas (in England only) in 1999 and was later expanded to the point where the government announced plans in 2007 to fund 3,500 centres by 2010, was designed to provide a range of family support services targeted on a geographical basis rather than on grounds of individual disadvantage. It thus seeks to avoid the stigma attached to other selective services.

The more radical strand of Labour's family support, however, comes in the level of universal provision. The restoration of the value of ntroduction of the new tax credits were designed to redress the incomes of families with children during the Thatcher Labour's general stance on social security, the main anti- on welfare-to-work measures. The manifesto commitment ck to work, in 2000 became a firm target of 70 per cent by To support this, Labour acted on two more of its manifesto d the National Childcare Strategy and it implemented iendly employment policies. The former, as Lister (2003) ime that a UK government has accepted that childcare is a te responsibility and, as such, it marks a watershed in fam- isms, such as that of Land (2002), that the government has e private, for profit sector to deliver the expansion in child- e hard to dispute that, by the time of the publication of per, *Choice for Parents, the best start for children*, in 2004, the d been dramatically transformed.

ressed a number of serious reservations about this expan- suggests that in moving from a 'male breadwinner' to a del of the family, insufficient attention has been given to nen and children. In terms of its impact on women, Lister the government has taken on board growing demands to a bigger role in the care of young children, it has shown the traditional gendered division of labour' (p. 318). She the balance of parental leave away from mothers towards dic countries have attempted to do (see Andersson, 2005). ling to Lister, is for policy to balance the 'universal bread- 'universal caregiver' model 'in which men combine paid work and care responsibilities in the same way that women do' (p. 319).

As for children, Lister goes on, 'childcare and education policies are more oriented towards employment priorities – current and future – than towards children's well being' (p. 321). She cites Norman Glass, the civil servant who helped devise the Sure Start programme, as warning that it was in danger of 'becoming a New Deal for toddlers captured by the employability agenda' (Glass, 2005, p. 2, cited in Lister, 2006, p. 322). We have argued elsewhere (Daniel and Ivatts, 1998) that early-years policy in the UK has been driven more by adult concerns than the welfare of children, and in particular have questioned the rationale for the early admission to formal schooling in the UK. This trend towards children starting school at four (compared to six or seven in most other European countries) is one that has continued under this government along with a more general utilitarian and results-driven approach to education (see Figure 13.1).

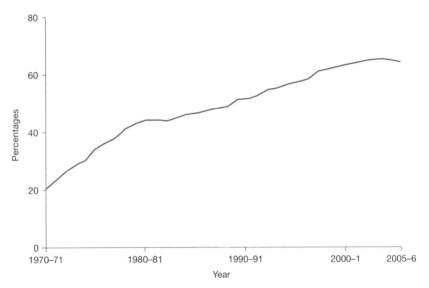

**Figure 13.1** Early-years education: children under five in schools, UK
*Source*: ONS, 2007.

**?** Thought provoker

Is there any justification for the fact that children in the UK start school at 4 or 5 when in most other developed countries the starting age is 6 or 7?

It is fair to say that there continues to be relatively little interest in, and discussion about, the impact that the privileging of the parental 'work ethic' over the 'care ethic' might have on children. Although the government does recognise the pressure that the current emphasis on parental employment is placing on family life, the concern is focused on the stress caused to parents (see, for example, Cabinet Office, 2007). Increasing government interest in the promotion of family-friendly employment practices and flexible working is justified in terms of improved employee relations, recruitment and retention of employees and in-creased productivity (op. cit). Meanwhile the effect of long parental working hours on children is glossed over. Yet we do know from the relatively few studies where children have been consulted, that they are unhappy with long hours worked by parents (see, for example, Ghazi, 2003).

## Briefing 13.5
## Choice for parents, the best start for children, 2004

The Government's vision is to ensure that every child gets the best start in life and to give parents more choice about how to balance work and family life.

**Choice and flexibility** - parents to have greater choice about balancing work and family life:

- a goal of twelve months paid maternity leave by the end of the next Parliament. As a first step this Pre-Budget Report announces the extension of the entitlement to nine months from April 2007;

- legislation to give mothers the right to transfer a proportion of this paid leave to the child's father by the end of the next Parliament; and every family to have easy access to integrated services through Children's Centres in their local community, offering in-formation, health, family support, childcare and other services for parents and children. 2,500 Children's Centres will be in place by 2008 and 3,500 by 2010.

**Availability** - for all families with children aged up to 14 who need it, an affordable, flexi-ble, high-quality childcare place that meets their circumstances:

- legislation for a new duty on local authorities in place by 2008 so that over time they will secure sufficient supply to meet the needs of families;

- a goal of 20 hours a week of free high-quality care for 38 weeks for all 3 and 4 year olds with this Pre-Budget Report announcing a first step of 15 hours a week for 38 weeks a year reaching all children by 2010; and

- an out of school childcare place for all children aged 3-14 between the hours of 8am to 6pm each weekday by 2010.

**Quality** - high-quality provision with a highly skilled childcare and early years workforce, among the best in the world:

- all full daycare settings to be professionally led;

- this Pre-Budget Report announces a Transformation Fund of £125 million each year from April 2006 to invest in high-quality, sustainable, affordable provision;

- radical reform of the workforce, with the Children's Workforce Development Council consulting on a new qualification and career structure in 2005; and

- reform of the regulation and inspection regime to improve standards and to give parents better information.

▶

**Affordability** - families to be able to afford flexible, high quality childcare that is appropriate for their needs:

- this Pre-Budget Report announces an increase in the limits of the childcare element of the Working Tax Credit to £300 a week (£175 for one child) from April 2005, and an increase in the maximum proportion of costs that can be claimed from 70 per cent to 80 per cent from April 2006;

- for a couple-family on £34,000 a year with both parents working and typical childcare costs for two young children, these reforms reduce the proportion of childcare costs they pay from 85 per cent to 75 per cent, a saving to them of £700 per year. Building on this first step, the Government's long-term ambition is to reduce further the proportion of childcare costs paid by such families, making childcare increasingly affordable; and

- this Pre-Budget Report also announces £5 million from April 2006 for a pilot to work with the Greater London Authority to address childcare affordability issues in London.

## Parental responsibilities

If the focus on child poverty has been the principal driver of Labour's family policy, then concern with antisocial behaviour has also played a part in the rapid growth in policy initiatives relating to parenting since 1997. It is by no means a new phenomenon that the government feels it necessary to take a close interest in the way parents rear their children. For all the rhetoric about family privacy, there has always been an element of state intervention in parent–child relationships. In the main, though, this has been confined to cases where parenting has been deemed to be so poor that the child is at risk. What is different about Labour's approach is the scale and range of initiatives aimed at raising parenting standards. When the National Family and Parenting Institute (itself a Labour creation) carried out a mapping exercise in 2001 it discovered that 40 per cent of parenting support services had been established within the previous five years.

Alongside the expansion of services to support parents in their role, there has also been a strong authoritarian streak in Labour's approach, with an amplification of parental responsibilities. We have already seen that the previous Conservative government shifted the balance from parental rights to parental responsibilities with the introduction of the 1989 Children Act. However the Act was not prescriptive about the extent of responsibilities which parents were expected to assume, and although the Scottish equivalent, the Children (Scotland) Act 1995, was a little more specific, it too remains rather general. Labour has spelled out parents' responsibilities, backed with sanctions, in controlling their children's behaviour. The Crime and Disorder Act 1998 introduced new powers to impose Parenting Orders on the parents of young offenders. The Anti-Social Behaviour Act 2003 went a step further in requiring the court to impose a Parenting Order in all cases where young people are made the subject of an Ant-Social Behaviour Order (ASBO) (see also Chapter 14). The substance of the Parenting Order is a requirement that parents attend some form of guidance or counselling. The significance, though, is that parents are made responsible for their teenage (up to age 17) children's behaviour to an extent which goes beyond previous obligations.

A similar expansion of parental responsibilities has occurred in the field of education. New contracts have been introduced, specifying parents' obligations over a range of behaviour and homework issues, but specifically in relation to attendance. This has led Henricson (2003) to comment that 'While on the one hand we have seen enhancement of parental choices in education, improved access to information and more widespread consultation, on the other we have witnessed the pendulum between parental autonomy and governmental intervention swing to some degree in the direction of the state' (p. 70).

The Labour government's preoccupation with enforcing, through the courts if necessary, parental responsibilities in relation to education and juvenile justice has come in for a number of criticisms. Two, in particular, raise important points. First, it has been suggested that the Parenting Order overstates the degree of control that parents can reasonably be expected to exert over children in their mid to late teens. By the same token it underestimates children's agency (see Morrow, 1999). In this respect, there is a clear inconsistency in the criminal justice system, for whereas Parenting Orders appears to minimise children's responsibility for their own actions, the fact that the age of criminal responsibility is set at 10 (8 in Scotland) – considerably lower than in most other countries – leans the other way.

 Thought provoker

Is Morrow right to suggest that punishing parents for their teenage children's failure to attend school overestimates the control that parents have in this situation?

The second major criticism of the increased emphasis in current policy on parental responsibility is that it is not gender neutral. For 'parents' we should read 'mothers'. It is clear from research that the majority of Parenting Orders are made against mothers (Ghate and Ramalla, 2002; Coleman et al., 1999). Equally, parent contracts within education might more accurately be termed 'mother contracts'. Similarly, support services for parents have continued to ignore, or fail to reach, fathers. For example, the National Mapping of Family Service (Henricson et al., 2001) estimated that less than 1 per cent of services were specifically targeted at fathers. Even where services were gender neutral, fathers were not well catered for, with programmes being held at unsuitable times. Until 2004 the exclusion of fathers was supported by legislation, since unmarried fathers did not have automatic entitlement to parental responsibility under the terms of the 1989 Children Act. Although the Adoption and Children Act 2002 extended this status to unmarried fathers who jointly register the child's birth, this still leaves a significant number who are excluded. In order to address this, the government proposed in *Building on Progress: Families* (Cabinet Office, 2007) that fathers should be legally required to register their child's birth.

Changing entrenched gender inequalities in caring for children is likely to require much more concerted state intervention than has so far been shown. We have already referred to the timid approach to parental leave compared to the Nordic countries. There is also a clear gender divide in requesting flexible working (women with children under six are three and a half times more likely to make a request than fathers) and a bias towards the acceptance of requests by mothers over those of fathers (men are two and a half times more likely to have their request rejected). Although this was highlighted in the government's review of its record on family policy (Cabinet Office, 2007) no proposals were made to bring about change. As Lister concludes, 'this reluctance to use policy to change behaviour in the "private" sphere of the family contrasts with New Labour's willingness to do so where the behaviour has more obvious "public" consequences' (Lister, 2006, p. 319).

## Children and childhood in UK social policy

We have established that children are at the heart of UK family policy. We have so far, though, only touched obliquely on the particular approach to children and childhood upon which UK social policy is based. Following the work of James and Prout (1997), it is generally accepted that childhood is not simply a biological fact. Different societies view or 'construct' childhood in different ways. Two contrasting views of childhood are, first, to see children as 'the future' or 'not yet adult' and, second, to view them as individuals in their own right in the here and now. In this section we will examine how childhood is 'constructed' within contemporary UK policy. We have elsewhere argued (Daniel and Ivatts, 1998) that the dominant view of children in post-1945 social policy has been as 'investment in the future'. We saw earlier in this chapter how the Beveridge Report, for example, saw children as the key to post-war social and economic renewal. Fifty years on, the Commission on Social Justice, established by Blair's predecessor as leader of the Labour Party, John Smith, put forward a similar view: 'Children are not a private pleasure or a personal burden they are a 100% of a nation's future . . . the best indicator of the capacity of our economy tomorrow is the quality of our children today' (Commission on Social Justice, 1994, p. 311).

So this view of children is by no means new within UK social policy. New Labour, though, has taken it to a different level. Key to their whole economic and social strategy is 'investment in human capital' – the skills of its workforce – in order to compete in a global market which is increasingly based around the knowledge economy rather than traditional industry. As a result, as Hendrick observes, the Labour governments have rarely mentioned 'child welfare' as such, generally speak in terms of children as 'investment', 'the future', 'our future' and so on (Hendrick, 2003).

Early childhood education and care is seen as a particularly important stage in the process of turning out productive adults and the language of 'investment' is given full rein in this area of policy – see, for example, *Children and Early Years Education: Investing in All our Futures* (DfES/LGA, 2001). But even the anti-child-poverty stance of New Labour is framed less in terms of its immediate impact on children's lives, and more in terms of its social investment potential: 'support for today's disadvantaged children will therefore help to ensure a more flexible economy tomorrow' (HM Treasury, 2003, para. 5.4). The fact that the lead government department on tackling child poverty is the Treasury is another indication of the importance given to child poverty within the government's economic strategy. There is little or no reference to 'Old Labour' priorities such as social justice or equality amidst all the emphasis on human capital and social investment (see Chapter 7).

## Children's rights

If the dominant view of childhood within UK social policy is that of 'becoming' (future adult, citizen, worker), an alternative view, which is associated with the sociological study of childhood from the 1980s onwards, starts from the premise that children are beings (in the present) in their own right. This view finds its political expression in the Children's Rights movement. We will now consider how far this has influenced UK policy on children and families. In particular, we will look at the impact of the 1989 United Nations Convention on the Rights of the Child which was ratified by the UK in 1991.

International interest in children's rights is not recent. In 1924 the League of Nations (the UN's predecessor) drew up the first declaration of the rights of the child. This was a limited document – of only five clauses – which focused entirely on children's right to welfare, including the rights to the means for normal development, food and medicine, relief in times of distress, protection against exploitation, and socialisation to serve others. This was followed in 1959 by the UN Declaration of the Rights of the Child which was slightly more detailed – with ten clauses – but still purely concerned with welfare rights. It is fair to say that, although symbolically important, neither Declaration made a significant impact in terms of promoting children's rights within signatory states.

The 1989 Convention takes children's rights to a new level. It was the result of ten years of painstaking negotiation and debate amongst both governmental and non-governmental representatives and incorporates a comprehensive set of economic, social, cultural, civil and political rights for children (defined as those aged 17 and under). In over forty substantive articles, the 1989 Convention recognises children's rights to participation in addition to the previously acknowledged rights of protection and welfare provision. Above all, it treats children as persons who are entitled to respect in their own right, and not simply because of their importance as future adults. The other significant development in the 1989 Convention compared to the earlier Declarations is that it included mechanisms to monitor individual governments' compliance. By ratifying the Convention (which all but two countries – the USA and Somalia – have done) states commit themselves to its implementation and are required to report at regular intervals to the United Nations Committee on the Rights of the Child (an elected panel of 18 international experts).

The UK ratified the Convention in 1991 and reported to the Committee in 1995, 2002 and 2007. Its record, though, on implementing key articles of the Convention has not been impressive. Certainly, both the Major and Blair governments came in for sharp criticism by the UNCRC. Arguably the initial ratification was lukewarm. There was no attempt to publicise the Convention or to inform children of their rights – as required by the terms of the ratification. Indeed, the Conservatives gave a strong impression that they viewed the Convention as relevant to developing countries perhaps but largely redundant in the case of the UK. The UK's first report in 1995 could be described as complacent in the extreme – there was no mention of child poverty at a time when over 4 million children were living below 60 per cent of the median income. Perhaps even more indicative of the Conservative government's attitude towards the Convention was its failure to involve children in any way in the production of the report.

Not surprisingly, the United Nations Committee on the Rights of the Child was highly critical of the UK's record in implementing the Convention (UNCRC, 1995), as was an independent report produced by the Children's Rights Development Unit – a coalition of children's organisations in the UK (CRDU, 1994). Labour's first report, submitted in 1999 and considered by the UNCRC in 2002, was more self-critical and did make some limited attempts to consult children's organisations in its compilation. A number of significant developments were noted, not least the measures introduced to tackle child poverty. Nevertheless, despite its stronger record on child welfare, there is very little evidence of a commitment to children's rights. Again the UNCRC was critical of the UK for breeching a number of fundamental rights of children in relation to corporal punishment by parents, youth justice, where the UK's policy on locking up children was noted, and the treatment of a number of minority groups, such as asylum-seeking children. In addition, the UK was criticised again for its failure to give children a voice in the policy-making process. Hendrick has suggested that children's rights have proved an uncomfortable concept for New Labour, with the government being suspicious of rights with respect to children, which it sees as potentially threatening conventional family life, undermining discipline in schools, and promoting a focus on the self (Hendrick, 2003). Labour's view of children as key to the future economic success of the nation has meant that responsibilities – both children's and their parents – are more likely to be stressed than rights. Children continue to be seen more as objects of concern than as subjects with a voice of their own.

Since the UK's second report in 2002, however, there have been a number of significant developments, notably in terms of children's participation and the extent to which their voices are being heard within public policy. Much of this progress, undoubtedly, results from the Convention on the Rights of the Child itself and from the work of the children's organisations which have used it in their campaigning activities. In part though, it can be traced also – as so often in the history of social policy in relation to children – to a child abuse inquiry. In this case it was the death of Victoria Climbié in 2000, and the subsequent inquiry by Lord Laming, which was the catalyst. The White Paper, *Every Child Matters: Change for Children* (DfES, 2004), which followed was produced after consultation that included young people. As a future framework for policy, it set out the following outcomes for children:

- Be healthy
- Stay safe
- Enjoy and be active
- Make a positive contribution
- Achieve economic well-being

This is a much more holistic view of childhood than had hitherto characterised government thinking. In particular the emphasis on children being active and making a positive contribution is a departure from the view of childhood as investment.

The publication of the handbook *Building a Culture of Participation* (DfES, 2003) and the rapid mushrooming of initiatives to involve children and young people across all government departments was a further reflection of this new attitude.

By the time the government came to compile the third report to the UNCRC in 2007 the participation of children was firmly established. The report was also able to point to the appointment of Al Aynsley-Green as the first **Children's Commissioner** for England in 2004 (Scotland, Wales and Northern Ireland already had their own Commissioners) – although the government fought hard to resist any reference to children's rights in his title. For all its progress on promoting children's participation, therefore, Labour arguably remains ambivalent on children's rights. Prout has suggested that in late modern societies generally: 'On the one hand, there is an increasing tendency to see children as individuals, with a capacity for self realisation and, within the limits of social interdependency, autonomous action; on the other, there are practices directed at a greater surveillance, control and regulation of children' (Prout, 2000, p. 304). This is a good summary of Labour's policy towards children, where the increasing awareness of the rights of children to participate in public policy making is balanced by a much more authoritarian approach when it comes to education and criminal justice.

## Conclusion

### Children's well-being in the UK in the first decade of the twenty-first century

Since 1997, as we have seen, children and families have enjoyed a higher profile than ever before within UK social policy. There have been some real achievements. Following its historic pledge to abolish child poverty by 2020, the Labour government did succeed in reversing the tide on this issue. However, having just failed to achieve its target of a reduction of 25 per cent by 2004/5, the numbers started creeping up again in 2005/6 (Brewer et al., 2007). The evidence suggests that the focus on 'welfare-to-work' may have run its course and more radical and redistributive tax/benefit changes will be required if the final target is to be achieved (Palmer et al., 2007).

Progress has been made too in the expansion of childcare provision from the very low base that Labour inherited. Here again, though, plaudits should be qualified; first, by the evidence emerging from the initial evaluation of the Sure Start scheme which suggests that the most disadvantaged children and families may not have benefited as much as had been hoped (NESS, 2005); and, second, from the growing disquiet among a number of early-years specialists about what they perceive to be a shift away from play based towards more structured and formal emphasis within early-years settings.

Certainly, when compared to other developed countries, the UK does not appear to be a particularly child-friendly society. When UNICEF produced their report on child well-being in rich countries in 2007 they compared children in 21 countries, using a series of indicators to measure well-being under the following headings:

- Material well-being
- Health and safety

- Educational well-being
- Family and peer relationships
- Behaviour and risks
- Subjective well-being

The UK scored badly on almost every single indicator and came last on a composite total of all six dimensions of well-being (UNICEF, 2007).

## Summary

This chapter has explored the increasing importance given to family policy since 1997. It has shown that, from being an implicit and reluctant aspect of UK policy, it has become central to New Labour's social and economic priorities. The importance given to children in terms of Labour's strategy of social investment has meant that the relationship between the state and the family has been reassessed. The chapter has considered a number of issues involved in this reassessment including:

- The extent to which demographic change and increasing family diversity challenge a model of family policy which is built around heterosexual marriage, leading to a more pragmatic support for children rather than for the 'traditional family'.
- The shift to a 'dual breadwinner' model of the family and the implications for women and children in the absence of a corresponding increase in the caring responsibilities of fathers.
- An ongoing tension between greater intervention in parenting on the one hand and a continuing belief in the privacy of the family on the other, as shown by the reluctance of the government to intervene to ban smacking.
- The ambivalent nature of government intervention in the family which has seen both more support for parents (for example, through expanded childcare provision) as well as more emphasis on parental responsibilities (such as Parenting Orders).
- The dominance of an 'investment' model of childhood and the challenge to this from the children's rights movement.

## Discussion and review topics

1 Discuss the ways in which the 'dual breadwinner' model of the family might have adverse consequences for women and children.

2 Has the Labour government found the right balance between 'carrot' and 'stick' in its policies on parenting?

3 Is it fair to claim that the UK has an indifferent record on implementing the 1989 United Nations Convention on the Rights of the Child?

# Further reading

**Bradshaw, J. and Mayhew, E.** (2005) *The Well being of Children in the UK*, Save the Children, London. This volume provides a useful collection of information about the position of children in the UK.

**Daniel, P. and Ivatts, J.** (1998) *Children and Social Policy*, Palgrave Macmillan, London. Using the UN Convention on the Rights of the Child this book examines British social policy since the Second World War, focusing on a variety of policy areas.

**Fawcett, B., Featherstone, B. and Goddard, J.** (2004) *Contemporary Child Care Policy and Practice*, London, Palgrave Macmillan. Examining recent developments in childcare, this includes coverage of a range of key topics.

**Franklin, B.** (ed.) (2002) *The New Handbook of Children's Rights*, Routledge, London. Covers debates about, and the development of, children's rights from the 1980s, including some comparative elements.

**Hendrick, H.** (2003) *Child Welfare: Historical Dimensions, Contemporary Debate*, the Policy Press, Bristol. This book provides a critical appraisal of policy towards children, including the approach taken by New Labour from 1997.

# Some useful websites

**www.dcsf.gov.uk** – the website of the Department for Children, Schools and Families gives access to a variety of information, including government publications.

**www.crae.org.uk** – the Children's Rights Alliance for England is an alliance of voluntary and statutory organisations that are committed to the full implementation of the Convention on the Rights of the Child.

**www.jrf.org.uk** – the Joseph Rowntree Foundation makes the results of the research that it funds available through its web pages.

**www.everychildmatters.gov.uk** – Every Child Matters is arguably key to the government's approach to the well-being of children. This website provides a wide range of information on Every Child Matters and access to a variety of resources.

**www.familyandparenting.org** – the Family and Parenting Institute is a charity which undertakes research and policy analysis on the well-being of children and families.

**www.statistics.gov.uk** – the Office of National Statistics website is a gateway to a wide range of official statistics and publications, including *Social Trends*.

# References

Abbott, E. and Bompas, K. (1943) *The Woman Citizen and Social Security*, Bompas, London.

Andersson, M. (2005) 'Why Gender Equality?' in A. Giddens and P. Diamond (eds) *The New Egalitarianism*, Polity, Cambridge.

Archard, D. (1993) *Children, Rights and Childhood*, Routledge, London.

Beveridge, W. (1942) *Social Security and Allied Services*, HMSO, London.

Blair, T. (1999) 'Beveridge Revisited', lecture delivered at Toynbee Hall (reprinted in R. Walker (ed.) *Ending Child Poverty: Popular Welfare for the 21st Century*, Bristol, the Policy Press).

Bradshaw, J. (1990) *Child Poverty and Deprivation in the UK*, Children's Bureau, London.

Brewer, M. *et al*. (2007) *Poverty and Inequality in the UK: 2007*, Institute for Fiscal Studies, London.

Cabinet Office (2007) *Building on Progress: Families*, The Stationery Office, London.

Centre for Social Justice (2007) *Breakthrough Britain: Ending the Costs of Social Breakdown*, Centre for Social Justice, London.

Children's Rights Development Unit (1994) *UK Agenda for Children*, CRDU, London.

Clarke, L. (1996) 'Demographic Change and the Family Situation of Children', in J. Brannen and M. O'Brien (eds) *Children in Families: Research and Policy*, Falmer Press, London.

Coleman, J. *et al.* (1999) *Parenting in the Youth Justice Context*, Youth Justice Board, London.

Commission on Social Justice (1994) *Social Justice: Strategies for National Renewal*, Vintage, London.

David, T. (1993) *Educational Provision for Our Youngest Children: European Perspectives*, Paul Chapman, London.

Dennis, N. and Erdos, G. (1993) *Families without Fatherhood*, IEA, London.

DfEE (1997) *Excellence in Schools*, The Stationery Office, London.

DfES/LGA (2001) *Children and Early Years Education: Investing in All Our Futures*, The Stationery Office, London.

DfES (2003) *Building a Culture of Participation*, HMSO, London.

DfES (2004) *Every Child Matters: Change for Children*, DfES, London.

Fawcett, B., Featherstone, B. and Goddard, J. (2004) *Contemporary Child Care Policy and Practice*, Palgrave Macmillan, Basingstoke.

Garnham, A. and Knights, E. (1994) *Putting the Treasury First: The Truth about Child Support*, Child Poverty Action Group, London.

Ghate, D. and Ramalla, M. (2002) *Positive Parenting: The National Evaluation of the Youth Justice Board's Parenting Programme*, Youth Justice Board, London.

Ghazi, P. (2003) *The 24hr Family: A Parent's Guide to the Work-Life Balance*, Women's Press, London.

Hendrick, H. (2003) *Child Welfare: Historical Dimensions, Contemporary Debates*, the Policy Press, Bristol.

Henricson, C. and Bainham, A. (2005) *The Child and Family Policy Divide*, Joseph Rowntree Foundation, York.

Henricson, C. *et al.* (2001) *National Mapping of Family Services in England and Wales*, National Family and Parenting Institute, London.

Henricson, C. (2003) *Government and Parenting*, Joseph Rowntree Foundation, York.

HM Treasury (2003) *Budget Report 2003*, The Stationery Office, London.

Home Office (1998) *Supporting Families: A Consultation Document*, The Stationery Office, London.

James, A. and Prout, A. (1997) *Constructing and Reconstructing Childhood: Contemporary Issues in the Sociological Study of Childhood*, Routledge, London.

Kamerman, S. and Kahn, A. (eds) (1978) *Family Policy in Fourteen Countries*, University of Columbia Press, New York.

Kiernan, K. (2002) *Observer*, 7 July 2007, (**http://education.guardian.co.uk/higher/socialsciences/story/0,751370,00.html**).

Laming, H. (2004) *Every Child Matters*, The Stationery Office, London.

Land, H. (1999) 'New Labour, New Families', in H. Dean and R. Woods (eds) *Social Policy Review 11*, Social Policy Association, Luton.

Land, H. (2002) *Building on Sand: Facing the Future: Policy Papers*, Daycare Trust, London.

Lister, R. (2006) 'Children (but not Women) First: New Labour, Child Welfare and Gender', *Critical Social Policy*, Vol. 26, No. 2, pp. 315-35.

Mead, L. (1986) *Beyond Entitlement*, Free Press, New York.

Millar, J. (1998) 'Family Policy', in P. Alcock, M. May and A. Erskine (eds) *The Student's Companion to Social Policy*, Blackwell, Oxford.

Morgan, P. (1995) *Farewell to the Family*, Institute for Economic Affairs, London.

Morrow, V. (1999) 'Conceptualising Social Capital in Relation to the Well Being of Children and Young People: A Critical Review', *The Sociological Review*, Vol. 74, No. 4, pp. 744-65.

Murray, C. (1984) *Losing Ground*, Basic Books, New York.

National Evaluation of Sure Start (2005) *Early Impact of Sure Start Local Programmes on Children and Families*, NESS, London.

Newell, P. (2002) 'Global progress towards giving up the habit of hitting children', in B. Franklin (ed.) *The New Handbook of Children's Rights*, Routledge, London.

Office for National Statistics (2007) *Social Trends*, The Stationery Office, London.

Palmer, G. *et al.* (2007) *Monitoring Poverty and Social Exclusion, 2006*, Joseph Rowntree Foundation, York.

Pascall, G. (1986) *Social Policy: A Feminist Analysis*, Tavistock, London.

Prout, A. (2000) 'Children's Participation: Control and Self-Realisation in British Late Modernity', *Children and Society*, Vol. 14, No. 4, pp. 304-15.

United Nations Committee on the Rights of the Child (1995) *Final Observations on UK Government's First Periodic Report on the Convention on the Rights of the Child*, Geneva, UN.

UNICEF (2007) *Children's Well Being in Rich Countries*, UNICEF, Florence.

# 14

# Crime, criminalisation and criminology: policing trouble?

Sue Bond-Taylor and Kelvin Jones

## Chapter overview

Over the last two or three decades there has been the development of an academic subject of 'criminology', which has arguably emerged in a similar way to that of 'social policy', drawing on a variety of other areas. This chapter is concerned with the relationship between crime, criminology and social policy, and between parallel problems and proposed solutions driven by the perceived need for a distinctly 'criminal justice' approach on one side, and those inspired by the need for welfare and a programme of 'social justice' on the other. The chapter:

- asks 'what is criminology?'
- reflects upon what 'criminal justice' is;
- questions the historical and contemporary alignment of criminology with a criminal justice system (CJS) defined narrowly as nothing but the police, courts, Crown Prosecution Service (CPS) and prisons;
- explores the contemporary shift in focus from 'crime' to 'antisocial behaviour' as illustrative of a broader trend in blurring the boundaries between welfare and control, between regulating public and private life, and between criminal and social 'justice';
- suggests that the relationship between criminology and social policy is not just an academic conversation, to be undertaken across the divide of problems constituted within parallel but separate domains, but involves us directly by colluding in the depiction and sanctioning of comparable forms of trouble as *either* criminal *or* social problems;
- argues that just as criminology scrutinises the processes of criminalisation, it is also about seizing and envisaging its opposite, namely decriminalisation.

### Drug users and social security benefits

In February 2008 the government set out a series of proposals as part of a ten-year drugs strategy. The Home Office press release included the statement that 'The strategy will use opportunities presented by the benefits system to provide a more personalised approach so that drug users receive tailored support, such as training, and, in return, are required to attend drug treatment sessions. The aim is to strike the right balance of responsibility and support so that drug users stay off illegal substances for the benefit of them, their families and their communities. So, as a first step, if you are a known drug user receiving benefits, you will be required to attend an assessment by a specialist treatment provider.'

It went on to state that the government would explore the case 'for a new regime for drug users to provide more personalised support than the Incapacity Benefit or Jobseeker's Allowance regimes, which in return for benefit payments puts responsibility on claimants to move successfully through treatment into employment' (**http://press.homeoffice.gov. uk/press-releases/drugs** – accessed 2 June 2008).

However, attempts to tie such conditions to benefit entitlement are controversial. The Department for Work and Pensions specify that a first non-attendance will result in the loss of two weeks' benefits, a second would lose four weeks' benefits, and a third would result in loss of benefits for twenty-six weeks, the financial implications of which are clear. The government claimed that the changes were to encourage drugs users to complete their treatment, with 50,000 people who claim Incapacity Benefit or Jobseeker's Allowance having 'drug abuse' as their primary diagnosis for why they cannot work. However, critics argued that cutting benefits for those who fail to turn up for treatment might lead to an increase in crime as people might resort to other criminal activity in order to fund their habit.

Over recent years debates about 'crime' and 'criminal justice' have been informed by input from criminologists. The topic has also been increasingly studied within higher education. But it is not always clear what criminology is, what its subject matter consists of, or its relationship with closely related fields including, notably, social policy. As a starting point it might be said that criminology is all about 'trouble'; it is the criminologist's stock in trade. As Hulsman (1986) points out, when confronted by signs of trouble, by 'events' that disrupt everyday expectations, we are called upon to deal with these, to do something. And criminologists have been all too eager to answer such calls. In the early 1980s, such responses were captured by a series of titles such as *What is to be done about Law and Order* (Lea and Young, 1984), and any number of similar attempts to consider a programme of 'realistic' action appropriate for different 'social' problems. For crime is essentially a social problem, a distinctive way of capturing forms of trouble and dealing or, more often perhaps, failing to deal with them. To say that crime is a social problem is not to imply that we all agree what kind of a problem – the intensity of debates about the nature of the 'crime problem' is enough to put paid to notions of consensus – but merely to register that it *can* be presented as a problem for 'society', for the 'public', for the social domain.

It is here that lies the essential connection between criminology and social policy. Put simply, if, and it is a big if, 'drugs', for example, are defined as 'trouble', and thus require some sort of 'social' response, what sort of 'policies' are appropriate, effective, fair and just? Do we 'criminalise' the problem, and embark upon an all-out 'war on drugs' using the full machinery of **criminalisation**: longer prison sentences for drug dealers; targeting 'drug barons'; enhanced police powers; and international cooperation through law enforcement; 'rebalanced' criminal justice systems, and such like? Do we embrace a policy of education, information, harm reduction, campaigns, needle exchange schemes, incentives, and raised awareness of 'sensible' drinking and so on? Or, do we try both, through, for example, 'compulsory' treatment programmes as highlighted at the start of this chapter? To borrow a fashionable phrase from the current political agenda, there are choices to be made here: we can choose how to deal with 'troubles' and we have a range of options from which to formulate 'policy'. However, how we choose to deal with such troubles can also play a key role in entrenching forms of trouble as different sorts of social problems, more or less serious, incorrigible or malleable.

Both criminology and social policy play parallel and interconnecting roles in constituting and analysing forms of trouble in different and interchangeable spheres. To bowdlerise Garland (1985), it can be a stark choice – punishment *or* welfare. This is posed most visibly at the so-called 'deep' end of the criminal justice system, where an analysis of some states in the USA suggests that, other things being equal, expenditure on punishment and welfare are interchangeable: states with high expenditure on prisons spend comparatively less on welfare and vice versa. Punishment and welfare are deployed as alternative strategies, and this can be summarised as a 'penal–welfare complex'. In some circumstances this constitutes a form of zero-sum, so that increased spending on prisons is matched by savings on welfare and vice versa; and, in turn, this perhaps illustrates the potency of choice. However, any such choices are likely to be influenced by the virulence of 'law and order' debates and the political litmus test of which political party is toughest on crime. Wilkins (1990) even goes as far as to suggest that the prison population reflects not the crime rate, but the amount of testosterone coursing through such debates. In 2008 Lord Phillips, the Lord Chief Justice, echoed these sentiments: 'The reaction of Government to what they see as media pressure in relation to sentences can produce changes in legislation designed to counter what they see to be public opinion' (cited in Dyer, 2008). Allied to this political question, social policy and criminology are tasked both to analyse the process and practice of any such policy decisions, and, because both have always had a deeply pragmatic hinterland, to inform, contribute and even influence such choices that might have the power to determine whether individuals end up in prison or on a welfare programme.

## What is criminology?

This question engenders endless debate and to some extent it can be resolved quickly: criminology is delimited by those arguments that contest what it is! Put simply, those people who argue about its 'true' nature set the boundaries of what is, can and ought to be 'criminology'. However, in reality, attempting to agree on a definition of criminology is not easy. Indeed, it can be seen as a conceptual variation on the popular question of 'does prison work?' The answer to that depends upon the corollary 'for whom', prisoners or society, and the subsequent infinite regress of 'what is society?' Muncie (2001), for example, identifies around ten different definitions of 'what is crime' in current debates about criminology, a kaleidoscope that extends from so-called 'black letter law' ('a crime is a crime is a crime'), through to any violation of human rights anywhere in the world, or to the somewhat bizarrely named '**zemiological**' imperative.

It is instructive to start with David Garland, who has spent a lifetime attempting to secure the historical and conceptual pedigree of criminology. For him criminology is not '. . . everything that has ever been said or thought or done about law-breakers' (Garland, 1997, p. 17). Instead, Garland states:

> I take criminology to be a specific genre of discourse and inquiry about crime - a genre which has developed in the modern period and which can be distinguished from other ways of talking and thinking about criminal conduct.
>
> Garland (1997, p. 11)

He goes on to say that: scientific *claims* distinguish it from moral/legal thought; a focus on crime and dependence upon criminal law distinguish it from social science which it otherwise resembles; and further, criminology is divided into a *governmental* project (loosely defined by the problem of governing troublesome populations) and a *lombrosian* project (loosely named after Lombroso the founder of the Italian **positivist** school and the search for the holy grail of criminology – the cause(s) of crime).

For Garland, criminology is constructed historically by the claim to be 'scientific' and a distinctive focus on the criminal law. It is further driven by the quest for an essential 'criminality' which is at the back of all 'crime', and it is this that 'science' seeks to discover. At heart is a belief that there are deep-seated causes at work that conspire to produce criminality in our midst, and the use of science by men and women of goodwill and adequate resource will reveal these to the policy maker who can then set about eliminating, or at the very least substantially reducing, crime. There are powerful arguments put forward by Garland and by Foucault (1977) which, in different ways, highlight the emergent purpose of criminology – whether it be to address the problem of unrest, trouble or 'antisociality', or to act as an alibi for the 'modernist' project of transforming criminals back into citizens. Whatever their historical merits, such conceptions are deeply contested and raise major questions. For example, if it is claimed that criminality has a genetic base, how far could or should we go in establishing programmes to breed out crime – compulsory sterilization perhaps? And can and should criminology be dictated to by a criminal law which varies historically, geographically and culturally in time and space?

Alternatively, criminology could be described as a place occupied by a number of passing scholars from different academic disciplines. From this perspective criminology is not an academic subject or discipline in its own right but is instead 'interdisciplinary', with a number of different subject specialists gathering around to examine and muse upon the 'crime problem'. Downes and Rock (1982) argue that criminology is centred on a terrain defined empirically by:

- the presence of crime and criminals;
- the state and the criminal law;
- the police, courts and prisons;
- victims and bystanders;
- reform, deterrence, treatment and punishment.

From this perspective criminology is therefore defined by the coherence of what it does, rather than how it does it. 'It is what Downes once called a "rendezvous subject" – a subject where people from different theoretical backgrounds and with very different purposes meet and sometimes fail to understand one another' (Rock, 1988: xii). Thus criminology could be seen as nothing more than an assembly of sociological, psychological, economic and legal musings conveniently badged as criminology. It is distinguished from Garland's dismissive characterisation as everything that has ever been said or written upon law-breakers by the 'academic' credentials of the writers and talkers.

> Downes and Rock (1981) argue that what amounts to criminology is better understood as the residues of knowledge left behind by the occasional visits of scholars emanating from a master discipline. Such scholars, they say, may develop, for a time, an interest in the area of crime/deviance; these scholars research and write about it, but in the context of a framework of knowledge which comes from their 'home' or master discipline, whatever it may be: sociology or psychology, for example. These scholars then move on; but they leave behind a residue of knowledge, and over time, criminology is portrayed as being built up out of the accretion of these residues, but not as having a stable core itself.           Young (1992, p. 425)

Finally, we could conceive of criminology as a vacuum. As Smart puts it, 'The thing that criminology cannot do is *deconstruct crime*. It cannot locate rape or child sexual abuse in the domain of sexuality, or theft in the domain of economic activity or drug use in the domain of health. To do so would be to abandon criminology to sociology' (Smart, 1990, p. 77). This echoes an earlier critique of criminology emanating from Hirst (1975), amongst others, in that if you are to analyse crime properly you cannot view it one-dimensionally in terms of its sometimes arbitrary label as a crime, but have to examine it in terms of a broader range of economic, social, psychological actions/relations in order to gain a fuller picture. To put it another way, not only is the shoplifter but one aspect of a real person with an extended biography, they are also only one part of an economic chain involving legitimate retailing at one end and an illegal market of disposal of goods at the other (Hobbs, 1998), what Ruggiero (2000) refers to as the 'Bazaar'. As MacIntosh (1973) puts it, 'all crime is organised' – even the ram raider requires a target, a plan and a network for the disposal of illegal goods. To isolate the criminal or his (sometimes her) criminality is doomed to failure. Destined to reproduce the inexplicable as monstrous we are condemned to recycle the vacuously futile outrage that constitutes the staple diet of the tabloid press.

 *Controversy and debate*

### Responsibility for murder?

In his analysis of murder in Britain, Dorling (2004) identifies the complexity in unravelling the numerous interconnected (and not necessarily 'criminological') issues surrounding an act of 'crime' and the challenges of such contextualisation for policy makers:

Behind the man with the knife is the man who sold him the knife, the man who did not give him a job, the man who decided that his school did not need funding, the man who closed down the branch plant where he could have worked, the man who decided to reduce benefit levels so that a black economy grew . . . Those who perpetrated the social violence that was done to the lives of young men starting some twenty years ago are the prime suspects for most of the murders in Britain.

Dorling (2004, p. 191)

Dorling's acknowledgement that murder is predominately committed by young males within the least affluent areas of the country, and that the same men suffer from the highest rates of suicide, reinforces further the problem of delineating distinctive types of 'trouble' that belong to different disciplinary trails, and raises particular questions about the criminal's responsibility for his/her actions.

The difficulty in distilling individual criminal agency from the soup of criminality also echoes Hobbs (1998). In similar vein, Norrie makes much of the *social process* of attribution: 'Causal agency can only be artificially located in individuals in abstraction from their place in social relations, structures and belief systems, and therefore the work of location must ultimately be carried out by a fiat based upon non-individualistic, socio-political criteria' (Norrie, 1991, p. 39). In other words, the popular image of the criminal as the loner, the sole and absolute author of his or her own criminality, can only be achieved by doing violence to the fact that we all belong somewhere, to some place and to some bodies. The legal subject is indeed the true 'fiction'.

A good example would be the attribution of criminal responsibility to Peter Sutcliffe, 'the Yorkshire Ripper', at his trial despite compelling evidence concerning his mental state and its subsequent acceptance in terms of his psychiatric referral post sentence (see Prinns, 1995). If he were not to be held 'responsible' for his killing, who or what is?

A similar point can be made where killing occurs in a corporate context through the breach of health and safety laws, and the resultant attention to the possibility of reform of the law on 'corporate manslaughter/corporate killing'. Consider who was 'responsible' for the Hatfield rail crash in 2000, caused by damage to a rail and leaving four people dead and over a hundred injured.

Given these arguments, to what extent, if at all, is it possible to render criminals the 'authors of their own misfortune'? And, if we cannot attribute responsibility to an individual (or individuals) for someone's death, does this mean that this 'killing' was not 'criminal'?

## Beyond criminology?

There are, inevitably, a variety of ways in which some writers seek to move beyond these debates. One of these is effectively a rendition of 'positivist' method, designed to replace the arbitrary concept of 'crime' with something that has more purchase in the real world – deviance, rule breaking in general, or the 'actively antisocial' (see Schwendinger, 1975; also Eysenck and Gudjonsson, 1989). This is based on the idea that collecting together those who break rules, or deviate in some way from the normal, constitutes a more coherent group or object for study and thus can generate more meaningful hypotheses or worthwhile scientific theories. This is clearly very different from the idea that the criminal law can and must dictate what criminologists study, but raises major issues around who defines or labels such activities and groups.

From a rather different perspective Hulsman (1986) argues that crime has no 'ontological reality', by which he means that not only do criminals have nothing in common, but neither does crime itself. There is no real connection or shared essential criminality between the council tax rebel, perjurers, money launderers and corporate killers, other than their contingent and occasional outlaw status accorded through the criminal law. In similar vein, the so-called '**dark figure of crime**' ensures that only a fraction of potential criminals ever get to be loaded into the criminal file and thus cannot express the 'real' characteristics of the criminal (Coleman and Moynihan, 1996). This latter view arguably supports Sutherland's (1949) call for a general inclusive theory of crime that avoids the 'one-dimensional' depiction of crime as solely related to disadvantage or pathology rather than the advantage and greed more often associated with **corporate** and **white collar criminality** (Hagan, 1994).

Whether there is an underlying unity to crime, criminality and criminology is sharply contested by those who would seek to replace the concept of crime with the much more inclusive one of harm and construct a new study of 'zemiology', or, as a colleague more accurately calls it, 'harmology'. In this analysis the 'policies' we adopt, discard, borrow and replace, in order to grapple with the problem of crime, are a far more coherent subject for study than the 'presumed' common characteristics of convicted criminals.

The crucial question remains, however: is there something distinctive about the process of criminalisation that is worthy of systematic and coherent study by, for example, self-styled criminologists, or should such issues be subordinated to the more general analysis of troubles, conflicts and conflict resolution? Or, to put it another, more concrete way, is there a fundamental difference between the way in which, for example, 'organisational misconduct' is approached from a 'criminological' standpoint rather than from a sociology of organisations or a legal or a policy approach? Are the core questions asked by each essentially different? This poses questions about the nature of the relationship between criminology and other approaches, most notably, for present purposes, that of social policy.

## What is 'criminal justice'?

All of this returns us to the basic question: how do we deal with 'trouble'? Why are some troubles rounded up by the police, dispatched to the Crown Prosecution Service to be filtered out or referred to the courts, and thence, after **due process**, recorded in terms of guilt or innocence and suitably punished or discharged? Why are some troubles dealt with by this process, but not others? We know that it is not always the most harmful forms of misconduct that reach the Criminal Justice System (CJS). Over time, vast swathes of recognisably harmful conduct including war 'crimes', genocide, ethnic cleansing, corporate killing, corporate theft, swindling and corruption have proven relatively immune from systematic criminalisation. Box, amongst others, puts it down to power: 'Criminal law categories are artful, creative constructs designed to criminalise only some victimizing behaviours, usually those more frequently committed by the relatively powerless and to exclude others, usually those frequently committed by the powerful against subordinates' (Box, 1983, p. 7). In reality, it more often involves troubles that are *avoidable*, are *proscribed* in some form, and are *punishable*, at least in theory. Some troubles are dealt with elsewhere by some other agency, such as the Health and Safety Executive or the General Medical Council; some are dealt with as something else, such as 'failure to maintain a safe environment' or violation of section 33, subsection 1(a) of the 1974 Health and Safety at Work Act, and that carries the very important consequence that any resultant killing is 'legally irrelevant'. To a degree, criminology itself has been complicit in such a process, in its restrictive conception of criminal justice to nothing but police, courts, the CPS and prisons (Slapper, 1999), its neo-classical conception of crime as a violation of a presumed minimal social contract perpetrated by idealised individuals (Jones, 1982; Wells, 2001), and, until recently, the marginalisation of 'organisational crimes' from the scope of criminology (Schrager and Short, 1978).

This is a double-edged sword in that it involves two-way traffic between a narrowly defined conception of the CJS in terms of police, prosecution, courts and prisons, and what could be called 'other agencies', charged with adjudicating and imposing sanctions in relation to misconduct and or conflict.

One approach therefore would be an **abolitionist** plea to deal with all forms of trouble as far as possible outwith the bureaucratic distortion of the CJS (Hulsman, 1986; Bianchi, 1994). This would involve a substantially reduced role for criminalisation. However, while there may be a consistent abolitionist instinct, too often the approach taken can be somewhat schizophrenic, combining calls for increased criminalisation of, for example, corporate killing or crimes of violence against women, on the one side, with diversion and informal dispute resolution of 'more conventional' conflicts on the other. Clark summarises the potential results nicely: 'Presidents, congressmen and corporation bosses on long-term prison sentences for tax frauds, illegal profiteering and war mongering, while petty thieves freely wander the streets attending occasional and voluntary therapy classes' (Clark, 1978, p. 53).

This is a reminder of the need to avoid a one-dimensional portrait of the 'crime problem', in favour of an inclusive approach to the analysis of the theory and practice of **criminalisation**, and the focus upon exactly how, where, when and why harms, wrongs and punishability are brought into the eclipse of crime.

Equally, the debate about so-called '**victimless crimes**' at the very least challenges any privileged relationship between harm and crime, in that the two do not map on to each other or even on occasion overlap at all. This plays into the conception that crime is nothing but an instrument of control and criminologists are the handmaidens of repression, a view that can be challenged in that criminology has always had a deep-seated critical impetus, albeit often subdued (for example, see Young, 1992). But it is not just about power in the narrow sense; it concerns the role of criminology, and in turn social policy, in constructing troubles as distinctive complexes involving discrete kinds of crime or social problems in the first place and thus their role in reproducing the most suitable agendas for their attempted resolution.

To explore the foundational role of criminology in relation to the criminalisaton of trouble we shall draw on Garland and Young. In their view penality (which is more than just punishment and includes a complex of ideas and practices in which punishment is embedded) has a core determining role in the construction of crime. Not only does this acknowledge an explicit link to Durkheim's prioritisation of punishment in any stand-off with crime, but also echoes Sutherland's insistence that punishability, or the potential capacity to punish, determines both criminality and criminological relevance (see Briefing 14.1).

## Briefing 14.1
### Which comes first, crime, criminality or punishment?

Of course, if one begins by asserting the existence of 'crime' or 'anti-social behaviour', then we can grant that this might necessitate - and in that sense 'determine' - some kind of regulatory or penal response.

But the possibility of that response, and its precise nature, form and content would *not* be determined in all its aspects by the 'crime problem', nor would its social functions and effects be necessarily confined to the space of crime and its control. [In other words, to say that 'something must be done', does not tell us what.]

In any case, there is no need to grant the primacy of crime, either logically or historically. We might argue just as readily that *penality defines and determines criminality*:

● in specifying the *types* of behaviour which are to *count* as crimes (through the criminal law);
● in identifying those *actual* behaviours which fall into these categories (through the courts);
● and in producing a social knowledge of the official significance and character of criminality (as moral, medical or legal fact).

Garland and Young (1983, p. 21) additional emphasis, bullets and brackets

Criminology is clearly involved in the production of social knowledge and, for Garland at least, penality is in turn the harbinger of criminology itself. This is a difficult place to be, in that criminology is at once implicated in the constitution of criminality, and also in the analysis of the process and practice of criminalisation. If nothing else, this underlines the sheer amount of work that goes into the social construction, depiction and analysis of troubles as crime, and perhaps constitutes a legitimate claim for this to be the bedrock of any distinctive criminology.

## What do we mean by 'criminal'?

In conventional terms the criminal justice system (CJS) comprises those institutions that deal with the problem of crime – the police, courts, prisons and so on. This raises the very question of what is crime? We have already seen that there are many different and competing definitions of crime to choose from, that crime and harm are not synonymous, and that the police, courts and prisons do not have a monopoly on troubles that are potentially crimes and that there are many more different regulatory 'police forces' at work outside the formal CJS (Kagan, 1984; Slapper, 1999). And yet it is difficult (or indeed impossible) to define 'crime' without at least some reference to the criminal justice system. Without 'crime' there would be no work for the criminal justice system, and yet without some formal system of justice, no behaviour could be described as 'crime'. Erickson (1966) would describe this as the true 'function' of the CJS – to produce criminals – but this begs the question, why? It also belies the complexity of the agencies involved in the process of 'criminalisation'.

It is the *prospect* of criminalisation which defines a particular behaviour as criminal. No matter how socially unacceptable behaviour might be, it is not a crime until a 'law' has been socially and politically constructed to prohibit it. Such constructions do not normally occur overnight; and not all legal instruments are criminal. For example, breach of contract is illegal, but it breaches only civil contract law, not a criminal code. What is distinctive then about the criminal law? How does it differ from the civil law? Two conventional differences are evident:

1  In a criminal trial, there is punishment attached to the prohibition, whilst in civil law the court will only order the defendant to put right the wrong done, for example to fulfil a contract or pay compensation for losses incurred. In contrast, the criminal courts have the right to impose punishment where a crime is committed. This is often justified in terms of deterrent effect – the individual (and perhaps others) will be deterred from committing crime in the future – but it can also be seen as a form of retribution.

2  Given the potential severity of the consequences (that is, punishment through loss of liberty) in a modern criminal trial, the case is brought by the state, not by the aggrieved individual or 'victim'. The case is taken out of the hands of the parties involved (such as the perpetrator of an assault and the victim) and the state's resources are used in the prosecution of the charge. The evidence must prove 'beyond reasonable doubt' that the offence was committed, compared to the civil standard of proof merely 'on the balance of probabilities' (that it was more likely than unlikely).

This may seem quite straightforward, but the demarcation of civil and criminal spheres is relatively recent in historical terms and is compromised further by the existence of 'punitive' or treble damages, penal enforcement of injunctions and so on, in relation to 'civil' or 'administrative' cases. This will become apparent in our discussion of Anti-social Behaviour Orders (ASBOs) below. In addition the parallel use of punitive measures in other domains involving adjudication, from medicine through law, accountancy, football, motor racing and higher education, seriously compromises any view that the criminal law has any monopoly on punishment and, by extension, 'crime'.

Thus if the only defining aspect of criminal behaviour is the creation of a criminal law prohibiting that behaviour, this would suggest that there is little distinctive about it at all. And this returns us to the problem of 'criminality' and what is coherent or uniform about crime that makes it a worthy object of study. Or, to revisit Hulsman (1986), what is the ontological reality of crime? How do we know what to criminalise if no behaviour is inherently criminal? We may agree that violence, killing and cheating are not very nice, but these activities are not spontaneously criminal, and there are all too many examples of 'legitimate' uses of 'reasonable force' in contemporary society.

Thought provoker:

### Eric Cantona

When he was a Manchester United footballer, Cantona was effectively disciplined and punished three times for the 'same' substantial 'offence', namely the now infamous kung fu-style kick that he aimed at a spectator he claimed was racially abusing him. He was suspended by his club, banned from playing football by the FA and sentenced to community service by the criminal court.

To what extent does this constitute 'triple jeopardy' (being tried for the same offence thrice)? If it does, is this a contradiction of a fundamental principle of justice?

## From crime to deviance and back?

In trying to focus on the question of why certain behaviours are condemned in such a way by the criminal law, the concept of **deviance** may provide a useful substitute for crime. Deviance can be defined as behaviour which deviates from social norms – from socially acceptable codes of conduct. Thus, whilst it is claimed that criminal acts can be clearly defined by the criminal law, deviant behaviour is both more ambiguous and more general. Indeed it is fluid and flexible, changing over time and without any necessary connection to changes in criminal law. It has been argued that due to this ambiguity 'deviance, like beauty, is in the eye of the beholder' (Simmons, 1969, p. 4) and what is deviant to one social group may be 'normal' to another. But its generality does at least imply a more socially inclusive object of attention, rule breaking *per se*, and thus a potential escape route from the contingent nature of criminal law.

The **labelling** or social reaction perspective is often invoked in any discussion of crime and deviance. Becker, in his classic 1963 text, *Outsiders*, provides an account of the ways in which behaviour is labelled as deviant and thus subject to control:

> . . . *social groups create deviance by making the rules whose infraction constitutes deviance*, and by applying those rules to particular people and labelling those as outsiders. From this point of view, deviance is *not* a quality of the act the person commits, but rather a consequence of the application by others of rules and sanctions to an 'offender'. The deviant is one to whom that label has been successfully applied; deviant behavior is behavior that people so label.
>
> Becker (1963, p. 9)

This approach directly questioned the taken for granted concept of crime, and allowed further exploration of how and why such labels were applied, and in particular how they became incorporated into the criminal law. In essence it addressed the question of whose or which conception of deviance becomes enshrined in the criminal law.

'Whose side are we on?' (Becker, 1967) became a clarion call, and conflict theorists identified class struggle as a key factor in the labelling process. Quinney (1970) argued that developed societies lack consensus over the values to be defended by that society. Conflict is therefore inevitable. However, it is those groups who have greater levels of power who are able to defend their values more effectively, and to label others who conflict with such values as 'deviant' or 'criminal'. Indeed Chambliss (1975) noted that the criminal law is not arbitrary and neutral. It does not reflect the interests of all members of that society equally. Rather, it is constructed in the interests of the powerful/wealthy in order to maintain their dominant political and economic position. Indeed, the criminal law can be argued to be structured in such a way that it defends the structures of capitalism as a whole and justifies the coercion and control of any individual who might threaten that.

Sumner (1990) goes further than a conspiracy approach to criminal law, and its alleged determining role in the construction of crime, by referring to those 'labels' such as 'criminal', 'vandal', 'pervert' or 'prostitute' as 'social censures'. This highlights the amount of work that goes into processes akin to criminalisation – they are not 'mere labels' – and further evidences the complex way in which troubles can be fashioned as particular types of problem and, in some circumstances, criminalised. For Sumner, deviance implies some abnormality within the individual who is subject to the label (as they are seen as deviating from social norms). By contrast, the concept of social censure focuses on the processes by which such categories of behaviour are denounced. The object of attention shifts from crime (or deviance) to denunciation, from crime to control:

> Their general function is to signify, denounce and regulate, not to explain. Their typical consequence is not an adequate account of a social conflict but rather the distinguishing of 'offenders' from 'non-offenders', the creation of resentment in their targets, or the cessation of the offensive matter. They mark off the deviant, the pathological, the dangerous and the criminal from the normal and the good. They say 'stop' and are tied to a desire to control, prevent or punish.
>
> Sumner (1990, p. 27)

Sumner argues that such censures cannot be justified in terms of pure self-interest and are therefore framed in widely accepted moral principles or ideologies, for example in condemning idleness, promiscuity or violence. Although they are presented as neutral 'descriptions' they are, according to Sumner, 'organized slanders in what is essentially a political or moral conflict' (Sumner, 1990, p. 17). Whilst class distinctions played an important role in explaining such censures, for Sumner this was too narrow. Gender and race, for example, are equally important factors in determining these organised denunciations. In fact any explanation of social censures must take account of the political economy of the society and the historical and cultural contexts in which they develop. Censures are unstable forms, they are 'the outcome of relationships between people in conflict' (Sumner, 1990, p. 18) and are therefore constantly subject to contestation.

The content of criminal law is clearly not inevitable or predetermined and this can be illustrated by simple international comparison (Nelken, 1994; Pakes, 2004). For example, behaviour which is socially and culturally acceptable, or even approved of, in one country (such as drinking alcohol in the UK) is subject to intense censure and regulation in another (for example, in Saudi Arabia).

**Thought provoker**

### A teddy bear named Muhammad

In 2007 British schoolteacher Gillian Gibbons was convicted of insulting Islam after allowing the children in her class in Khartoum, Sudan, to name a teddy bear Muhammad. She was sentenced to 15 days in prison followed by deportation from Sudan, a judgement that prompted demonstrations by thousands of protestors, calling for her to receive the death penalty.

This example illustrates not only the fact that criminal law is culturally constructed, reflecting the values of different societies, but that 'seriousness', and therefore 'proportionality', of response is also culturally produced.

If we are to seek solace in a simple view that the CJS deals with crime, and crime is that which is dealt with by the CJS, then we are destined to disappear in a vortex of circularity. We shall see whether the analysis of categories of denunciation signals a way out of this impasse and whether it provides a bridge between criminology and policy in a more detailed analysis of **ASBOs** below.

## What do we mean by 'justice'?

At first glance the concept of 'justice' appears straightforward, even if crime is ambiguous and the idea of a system questionable, surely the middle term in the CJS, justice, is more secure? We are familiar with it through its daily use in media headlines and government policy initiatives. Even within this context, however, there are differing intentions and interpretations behind the word 'justice', and it is more difficult to define what it is than how or indeed why it should be achieved. John Stuart Mill argued that 'Justice is a name for certain classes of moral rules, which concern the essentials of human well being more nearly, and therefore of more absolute obligation, than any other rules for the guidance of life' (quoted in Hudson, 2001, p. 145). Yet this still does not help us in identifying what such rules might be, and implies a great deal of social agreement on what the 'essentials of human well being' might entail: for example, does justice require the criminalisation of trouble? And does justice require a commitment to real equality? (see also Chapter 4).

In particular, three starkly different conceptions of 'justice' can be identified. Whilst the first two can be identified in relation to 'criminal justice', the third offers a more complex challenge to policy makers.

### Justice as due process

Justice can be described as fairness and neutrality in the application of those sets of rules which govern our society. Applying those rules equally to every member of that society through a fixed and certain process produces 'justice' in this sense. Within the criminal law, principles of 'due process' act as legally binding obstacles to the arbitrariness and excesses of state power, and provide a number of 'rights' which protect the suspect or defendant. For example, the defendant's rights to legal representation or to a jury trial (for some offences) offer such protection, as do prohibitions on the kind of evidence which may be used or the circumstances in which an individual might be searched. This is often described as formal justice as it exists on the level of formal procedure.

However, a number of now infamous cases have called into question the extent to which due process is carried out in practice rather than merely espoused as policy. Consider the case of Stefan Kiszko, jailed in 1976 for the murder of eleven-year-old Lesley Molseed. He was released 16 years later after DNA evidence taken from the victim's clothing proved that he could not have been the attacker. Serious questions were raised about the ways in which Kiszko's confession was extracted by police and their failure to disclose crucial forensic evidence. However, no legal charges were brought against the officers involved. Stefan Kiszko died within two years of his release and following further investigation Ronald Castree was convicted of the killing in November 2007.

## Justice as retribution

Even where criminal justice procedures do appear to adhere to due process principles and reflect notions of formal justice, there are frequently criticisms of the outcomes reached by such processes. Most commonly these centre on demands for 'tougher' sentencing in order to reflect the seriousness of the case and the trauma experienced by the victim. Limits on judicial discretion in sentencing may be an attempt at increasing formal justice, but are viewed with suspicion by a public who do not see substantive justice being done.

The tabloid press in particular can be seen to support campaigns for 'justice' in the name of the victims. The *Sun* newspaper demanded 'Justice For James' following the murder of James Bulger in 1993 by two ten-year-old boys, and successfully petitioned the Home Secretary to increase the minimum sentencing tariffs given to the two children convicted. This is a clear example of how 'justice' in this second sense challenges the neutrality of formal justice and due process and seeks a more substantive criminal justice reflecting the desire for retribution – an eye for an eye; a tooth for a tooth. Bottoms (1995) goes so far as to describe it as 'popular punitiveness' and Zimring and Hawkins (1991) note the impact of political attempts to meet the apparently insatiable demand for more punishment.

However, this raises the additional problem of proportionality. That the punishment must fit the crime may sound simple, but what does it mean? How do you measure 'desert', or determine how punitive sanctions should be, and indeed what are the limits to proportionality from one day to three years in prison or one week to 600 years?

## Justice as social justice

The term 'social justice' was developed in the nineteenth century but has become particularly popular in contemporary political debate through numerous government initiatives and increasing concern with social exclusion. However, it still lacks clear definition and what constitutes social justice can to some extent still be rather subjective (see Chapter 4).

Knepper (2007) argues that discussion of social justice principles have historically and contemporarily been couched within three vocabularies: the vocabulary of rights, the vocabulary of need, and the vocabulary of membership.

For Knepper, the vocabulary of rights has grown out of political and economic liberalism in which the free market economy is defended as a fair means of distributing resources. Civil and political rights are therefore proposed as a means of ensuring the individual's participation in this economic system. However, this produces a greater concern with equality of *opportunity* than with equality of *outcome* and this is where we may once again identify a gap between formal justice and substantive justice.

In contrast to the economic liberalism of rights-based vocabularies, socialist critiques of the inequalities inherent in capitalism led to a focus on meeting the needs of the individual. They thus saw social justice as providing a minimum standard of living, regardless of class position, in order to meet basic human needs.

Whilst Knepper identifies the roots of the vocabulary of membership within nineteenth-century religious discourse, it has clear contemporary relevance to debates about communitarianism, and in relation to the current political drive to encourage greater levels of community involvement and social capital in order to tackle social exclusion and the promotion of citizenship as a means of increasing social cohesion.

The question remains, however, whether social justice, in this sense, can be achieved within the remit of criminal justice. The extent to which criminal justice processes provide substantive justice or merely reinforce existing inequalities of rights, needs and membership, and therefore reproduce social injustice, must be considered. In simple terms, at one level it can be argued that the law does treat everyone as if they are equal, and that is the power and attraction of legal ideology; the problem is that if we are not all actually equal, then to treat us as if we are may be to further inequality. In terms of outcome, should the CJS be fuelled by the fundamental idea of not unduly impeding individual liberty, or the rather different ideal of not contributing to further inequality? Not only must we address the issue of choice – between 'punishment and welfare' – or between different constructions of social problems or troubles, thus highlighting the distinctive domains of social policy and criminology, but in making such choices we are forced into a consideration of these overlapping policy domains. In addressing the questions of why, what and how troubles are turned into crimes, we have to consider the opposite, namely how crimes could be reclassified as troubles or conflicts and dealt with elsewhere. In this manner the abolitionist instincts and the process of criminalisation are united as two sides of the same coin and in their opposition perhaps provide an object worthy of analysis. The study of **antisocial behaviour** provides a useful focal point for the exploration of these themes and illustrates the recent trend in utilising non-criminal mechanisms for exerting control over merely 'deviant' behaviour.

## Antisocial behaviour, 'justice' and criminalisation

### How antisocial is 'antisocial behaviour'?

The term 'antisocial behaviour' has become synonymous with 'trouble', and it is remarkable the speed with which the term has entered our vocabulary and taken on a life of its own. However, defining what behaviour *is* 'antisocial' is a rather more difficult task. In the same way that deviance is in the eye of the beholder, so that which is 'antisocial' is defined by the reaction of others and therefore relative to time and place. The Crime and Disorder Act 1998 defined antisocial behaviour as that which 'caused or was likely to cause harassment, alarm or distress to one or more persons not of the same household as himself'. This appears deliberately vague, with one MP, in a now much-quoted statement in the House of Commons, likening antisocial behaviour to an elephant on the doorstep, in that it is 'easier to recognise than to define' (cited in Rutherford, 2000, and MacDonald, 2006).

How does this rather partial and imprecise definition relate to the kind of 'trouble' which is commonly perceived as being 'antisocial behaviour', and thus subject to control through an 'Anti-social Behaviour Order' (ASBO) or other such measure? It would appear that a whole spectrum of actions or omissions might at some point cause people to become harassed, alarmed or distressed, and yet the problem of 'antisocial behaviour' has been constructed within a very narrow and restricted agenda. Consider the following:

1 cutbacks in funding to maternity services lead to staff shortages and women spending long periods of time during labour unattended by a midwife, potentially suffering pain and becoming distressed;

2 vehicles persistently changing lanes on the motorway without indication, alarming the drivers around them;

3 cold callers from companies supplying double glazing, time share apartments, or gas and electricity telephoning private homes on a regular basis.

These are not incidents of 'antisocial behaviour' as we would normally understand the phrase and yet, potentially could, and perhaps should, fall within the broad ambit of the legislation.

What kind of problem, then, becomes labelled as antisocial? Who is it a problem for? And which *people* are deemed problematic?

### Problem youth?

Predominantly, discussion of antisocial behaviour has centred on more pervasive concerns about 'youth'. The ubiquitous image of the 'hoodie' has become a trademark for antisocial behaviour and the hoodie bearer is assumed to have 'trouble' on their mind. This concern about youthful deviance is fuelled by media reporting which claims that our young people are committing more crime than ever before, are engaging in binge drinking and heavy use of drugs, and have lost 'respect' for themselves and others. Yet these concerns are not new. Each generation of young people is rebuked by the older generations for their alternative values (or indeed lack of them) and comparisons to a nostalgic vision of the past are perhaps inevitable. Pearson (1983) describes this as the 'perpetual novelty of youth' and traces such anxieties back through the Victorian period and into the Middle Ages. Youthful deviance is from this perspective a constant feature of social life and is more the consequence of the disapproving reactions of others than the malicious intention of the young. The current attacks on antisocial behaviour are in danger of drawing greater numbers of juveniles into the 'criminal justice system' for relatively minor deviance which, in another era, would have been dealt with informally within local networks. As Martin Spragg, Head of the Youth Offending Service, put it, 'In Devon alone there were 367 referral orders last year. We are drowning in these things. And well over half were for three month orders for very, very trivial offences' (cited in Morris, 2007). This further underlines the central factor of choice: how we choose to construct, analyse and deal with differing forms of 'trouble' – whether as 'crimes', or as other types of social or personal problems.

The 'trouble' labelled so often as antisocial behaviour is also frequently focused on particular places, not just particular people. Areas of less affluent housing may provide challenges for young people in particular. Lack of garden space and small rooms inside may lead children and young people to be ejected into public places and, consequently, working-class youth have always found entertainment in public spaces. Burney describes public space as 'a contested area in which adults are asked to assume that young people have lesser rights' (Burney, 2005, p. 74). The provision of greater powers to local police in 'designated areas' allows the imposition of a 9 p.m. curfew and enables young people in groups to be 'dispersed' and taken home by the police. Such legislation is based on the assumption that young people have no right to be congregating in public, and that such behaviour inevitably leads to 'trouble'. It further assumes that 'home' is the safest place for children to be, yet for many children this may be far from the truth.

With registered landlords given the right to apply to the court for an ASBO, those in rented accommodation and social housing especially have become subject to greater levels of control. There is increasing pressure for landlords to evict tenants behaving in an 'antisocial' manner in order to meet the duty of care they have to other residents of the accommodation. Garside (2005) expresses serious concern that such an approach may do more harm than good. He cites research by Hunter and Nixon into 67 case files relating to nuisance from 10 landlords, which found that two-thirds of those individuals labelled as engaging in 'antisocial behaviour' had 'some form of vulnerability', including mental health problems, physical disability and being a victim of physical or sexual abuse. This clearly locates the problem of 'antisocial behaviour' within a broader spectrum of social problems and harms, which may provide a more complex challenge to correct.

The British Institute for Brain Injured Children (2005) claims that 35 per cent of youths receiving ASBOs have a diagnosed mental health disorder or an accepted learning difficulty. Examples of ASBOs given to children with neurological conditions include a 15-year-old with Tourette's syndrome issued with an ASBO with a condition that he does not swear in public, and a 13-year-old autistic boy who was issued an ASBO preventing him from jumping on his trampoline in the garden because the neighbours did not like the noises he made. This reinforces the concern that antisocial behaviour is not simply a social problem inflicted upon the surrounding community, but is also a symptom of social problems experienced by that community and by particular individuals more intensely.

Yet the problem is frequently constructed as troublesome youth in problematic communities, where people have lost respect for one another and are unable or unwilling to take responsibility for themselves or for their children. Whilst this imagery is strongly evident in media reporting, it is further exploited by politicians as an effective and dramatic political tool which appears to reflect Tony Blair's (and Gordon Brown's) now notorious claim to be 'tough on crime, tough on the causes of crime'. Identifying troublesome gangs of youths as a 'cause' of crime, is a neat alternative to tackling the more difficult 'causes' of crime which become conflated with issues of poverty, inequality and marginalisation.

## Communities and 'justice': crime control or social control?

Strengthening communities has become a cornerstone for government policy on antisocial behaviour. The ministerial foreword of the 2003 White Paper *Respect and Responsibility: Taking a Stand Against Anti-Social Behaviour* begins by stating that:

> As a society, our rights as individuals are based on the sense of responsibility we have towards others and to our families and communities. This means respecting each other's property, respecting the streets and public places we share and respecting our neighbours' right to live free from harassment and distress . . . This responsibility starts in the family, where parents are accountable for the actions of their children and set the standards they are to live by. It extends to neighbours who should not have to endure noise nuisance. It continues into local communities where people take pride in the appearance of estates and do not tolerate vandalism, litter or yobbish behaviour.                    Home Office (2003, p. 3)

To some extent the concerns over problematic communities and antisocial behaviour have arisen out of the victim movement. One key objective of the 1998 Crime and Disorder Act was to close what had become known as the 'justice gap', where members of communities were unable to seek justice through the criminal justice system for the persistent nuisance that they may have endured due to the non-criminal nature of such nuisance behaviour. Noisy neighbours outside your home in the early hours may not be perceived as serious enough to warrant a criminal conviction, but where that noise features on a nightly basis, it becomes more harmful and potentially distressing. The intention of the ASBO is that everybody should have the right to enjoy a 'quiet life' (Labour Party, 1995). Unfortunately, this idealistic phrase does little to answer the question of 'how quiet?' Given the differing sensibilities and expectations of members of a single community, the definition provided in the legislation is ineffective in clarifying expected standards of behaviour and acceptable levels of noise. Nor should it attempt to do so, as such clarity is conventionally seen as the preserve of the criminal law, and the definition of antisocial behaviour is clearly intended to cover a much wider ambit.

However, the ASBO does not just tackle behaviour which is non criminal. It is also presumed to be effective in dealing with criminal actions, and the creeping use of the ASBO in addressing crime is an issue of concern. The ASBO is what might be termed a hybrid order, in that it is initially a civil order, rather like an injunction, demanding that the individual refrain from that behaviour. Only upon breach of the terms of the order does the criminal law come into operation and a punishment can then be imposed up to a maximum of five years' imprisonment. For policy makers and enforcement agencies mechanisms such as ASBOs can offer a number of advantages.

There appears to have been a growing tendency to issue an ASBO against an individual for their criminal behaviour where insufficient evidence is available to achieve a criminal conviction. As noted earlier, standard of proof in civil law is significantly lower than the criminal standard, requiring only that the acts are proven on the balance of probabilities – that it is more likely than not, rather than beyond reasonable doubt. This clearly offers less protection for the defendant. Furthermore, the civil court follows different rules of evidence, with hearsay evidence in particular being permitted. This allows for a witness statement to be read by another, rather than requiring the witness to testify in court. For those complainants who feel intimidated and harassed by certain individuals within the community, this offers an opportunity to tackle the behaviour without the need to testify. However, it also potentially allows neighbour disputes based on rumour and personal vendetta to be given legal status, and again restricts the protections available to the defendant.

A number of behaviours which are to some extent covered by the criminal law are now sometimes dealt with through the use of ASBOs as a matter of choice. MacDonald (2006) notes the use of ASBOs against a number of prostitutes to deter them from soliciting in public places. However, the terms attached to such an order and the subsequent punishment for breach can be unhelpful in tackling this social problem. Orders are often issued preventing the woman from going to a certain part of the town, but this may simply moves the problem elsewhere, and there are clearly concerns for the welfare of such vulnerable young women who go 'off the radar'. Even more unhelpfully, one woman was issued with an ASBO preventing her from carrying condoms (Garside, 2005). Given that breach of an order can lead to a five-year jail term, this would appear to make a mockery of attempts in the Criminal Justice Act 1992 to remove the use of imprisonment as a punishment for soliciting, as it was seen as perpetuating a spiral of even greater social marginalisation. The potential five-year jail term may be a significantly greater punishment than is warranted by the criminal act itself, particularly where the breach is of a condition which is relatively trivial.

That there may be a systemic advantage over the usual criminal trial is evident, particularly for a system with targets to meet and budgets to keep to. ASBO-style legislation has now been introduced to tackle organised crime, with powers to freeze assets when an order is granted and clearly evading the need for witnesses to testify. Similarly, for environmental offences, such as fly tipping, where evidence can be thin on the ground, the Environment Agency can apply for an ASBO to be issued in order to prohibit further offences with the support of greater punishment for breach.

The most widely used ASBO, however, is the criminal ASBO or **CRASBO**, introduced by the Police Reform Act 2002, which is given after conviction in order to deter future offending behaviour. The offender therefore receives his (or her) punishment *and* is prohibited from engaging in a range of activities linked to the offending behaviour. Again, the conditions attached can be particularly restrictive, going much further than merely desisting from the behaviour for which the offender was convicted, and incorporating a broader range of actions which may even increase the individual's risk of offending in some way. For example, one persistent burglar was sentenced to $4\frac{1}{2}$ years' imprisonment, but was also prevented from entering any hotel, guest house or bed and breakfast in the Greater London area for 10 years. Breach of this condition would result in his return to prison.

## Blurring boundaries: no crime, no criminology?

Brown (2004) has argued that we should not understand attempts to control antisocial behaviour as increasing social control, but rather as an illustration of the *failure* of a particular type of social control, and that they indicate 'the creation of a new domain of professional power and knowledge' (Brown, 2004, p. 203). Brown utilises Stan Cohen's classic 1985 text, *Visions of Social Control*, which identifies the ways in which systems of deviancy control blur boundaries. She argues that current trends in the management of antisocial behaviour, rather than crime, represent a blurring of boundaries in a number of ways:

1 Between rule-breaking and law-breaking – as is evident from the rather vague and subjective definition of antisocial behaviour, this new form of control dispenses with any formal need to identify the commission of a criminal offence. Merely deviant behaviour will suffice.

2 Between public and private – the scope of the ASBO allows intrusion into the home under the guise of ensuring a 'quiet life' (Labour Party, 1995) for neighbours and the community. How tidy you keep your garden or how loud you play your music (or indeed what genre of music you play) therefore become matters of public concern.

3 Around the edges of formal systems of control – control is no longer just a matter for criminal justice agencies, but is exerted by community organisations, local authorities and social housing agencies. The process of control thus 'penetrates the family, school and neighbourhood, all of which are employed in discipline and normalization' (Brown, 2004, p. 204). Furthermore, Rodger (2006) highlights the increasing popularity of calls for welfare support to be withheld from antisocial families, thus marking a significant shift in the role of the welfare state as an agent of discipline and illustrating the ways in which the social policy agenda is 'increasingly, being re-framed in terms of the management of problem populations' (Rodger, 2006, p. 124).

For our purposes, then, the exploration of the ASBO and similar mechanisms for the control of so-called 'antisocial behaviour' are illustrative of a number of key themes.

First, criminology and social policy are not, and never have been, discrete and separate areas of investigation. Both share a degree of common ground, and could do more to exchange analytical and conceptual frameworks, and the exploration of this possibility for choice is illuminating in itself.

Second, 'crime' may not be a distinctly different phenomenon from other social problems. Its distinctiveness is a result primarily of its social construction as a particular kind of 'trouble', with characteristically 'punitive' solutions provided by specialist regulatory agencies. The manner of 'crime's' social construction is perhaps the only distinctively *criminological* feature of criminology!

Third, social and welfare organisations are not inherently benign, and are capable of acting as controlling or coercive bodies, exerting discipline and ensuring conformity (see also, for example, Chapters 9 and 10). Equally, the distribution of welfare is not immune from the temptations of 'organised slander'; witness the potent impact upon the qualification of need by the concepts of 'lifestyle abuse' or the deployment of the phrase 'authors of their own misfortune' in decisions concerning eligibility.

Finally, crime (or indeed antisocial behaviour) strategies cannot be separated from other public services, in spite of political rhetoric that applauds spending on the criminal justice system and seeks to minimise investment on youth, welfare or healthcare. Indeed, as Burney has identified, such 'social' spending sometimes appears justifiable in the current climate only if it can be perceived as having a tangible impact upon antisocial behaviour:

> Because 'anti-social behaviour' resonates in the public mind it increasingly provides a lever which can be used to activate local politicians, council officials and police resources. As anti-social behaviour strategies, action teams and designated officers become the norm, so do many normal functions of local government – street cleaning, tenancy management, truancy prevention – become validated through the stamp of anti-social behaviour reduction.
>
> Burney (2005, p. 12)

The ASBO is a reflection of a new **managerialism** in criminal justice grounded in multi-agency cooperation. Here, principle and ideology become subsumed by pragmatism and the management of 'trouble', of whatever sort that trouble might be. Moreover, new agencies of control, such as the Home Office Antisocial Neighbour Nuisance Expert Panel, remove the distinction between criminal justice and social welfare organisations and are premised on the need for coercion and convergence, for example in tackling *both* social exclusion *and* antisocial behaviour (Rodger, 2006).

## Controversy and debate

### Family intervention projects

'Will neighbours from hell be thrown into sin bins?' asked Graeme Wilson of *The Daily Mail* on 10 October 2005. He reports:

Problem families could be sent to high-security 'sin bins' as part of the Government's latest crusade against anti-social behaviour, it has emerged.

Ministers are considering draconian powers which would see so-called neighbours from hell removed from their homes and placed in special units monitored by private security guards and CCTV.

Contrast this image with the information on these 'Family Intervention Projects' from the Home Office Respect Task Force:

In some communities there are a small number of highly problematic families that account for a disproportionate amount of antisocial behaviour. They are well known to many service providers and enforcement agencies. Some families have up to twenty different organisations involved with them.

Family intervention projects work to turn around the behaviour of families and reduce their impact on their community. In so doing, they also bring stability to families' lives, prevent homelessness and improve opportunities for children. They combine intensive support with focused challenge – a twin-track approach. For these projects, it is not a question of either/or – support and enforcement are systematically linked to provide families with the incentive to change.

There are *three distinct levels of intervention* which are used according to a family's needs and the impact their behaviour is having on the community. Different levels of intervention may be used at different times as circumstances and behaviour change.

Most projects provide an *outreach service* for families who are responsible for antisocial behaviour in their home, and who are at risk of being evicted. However, services can also be provided in *units* managed by the family intervention project but dispersed in the community. At the most intensive level, families who require supervision and support on a 24-hour basis stay in *a core residential unit*. Upon satisfactory completion of a programme, the family can move into a managed property.

These schemes have impressive results – for more than four out of five (85 per cent) families, complaints about antisocial behaviour ceased or reduced and in nine out of ten (92 per cent), the risk to local communities was assessed as having either reduced or ceased completely by the time families left the project. In addition, for four out of five families, there was no further possession action taken against their homes and significant improvements in school attendance were found.

Because family intervention projects differ in the services they provide, so do the costs. The average costs range from around £8,000 per family for schemes which provide outreach services for families in their homes or living in managed properties, to around £15,000 for schemes which include the more intensive services (in a core residential unit). It has been estimated that the costs to society of a family with severe problems could be £250,000–350,000 in a single year without this intervention.

*Source*: Adapted from: Respect Task Force, **www.respect.gov.uk/members/article.aspx?**

Can such family intervention projects offer 'justice' and, if so, what kind and for whom? Are such projects an appropriate area of study for criminology? Are 'high-security sin bins' effectively prisons?

# Conclusion

This chapter started with a consideration of 'trouble' and will end in the same fashion. The example of ASBOs illustrates perfectly not only the intersection of different strategies of intervention but also the involvement of 'discrete' forms of knowledge – criminology and social policy. Just as its ambiguous criminal status did not prevent whole generations of criminologists immersing themselves in the problem of 'youth', so too will it be a rare example indeed of a criminologist that will shy away from delivering a 'what works verdict' upon the ASBO. Not only does the ASBO extend the purchase of the 'dispersal of social control' thesis, but it also extends the remit of criminology into areas where some would not dare to stray, given the lack of protective cover afforded by the security blanket of the concept of 'crime'. But is this simply an example of conventional forms of welfare being 'turned' into explicit mechanisms of control through 'creeping criminalisation' and an allied accusation of 'criminological imperialism'? Or does it focus much more sharply the role of 'criminalisation' as a two-way process of criminalisation and decriminalisation? The fact that there are alternative ways of dealing with trouble, ways that engage social provision and social justice as strategies to meet human needs, ways that are not just coercive mechanisms of social control and exclusion, means that any given 'solution' to trouble could be otherwise. There is nothing intrinsic to certain forms of trouble that announces their status as crimes, nor is there anything inherent in other forms of trouble that corrals these as 'social' problems. If this is correct, then the only secure and distinctive basis for a definite 'criminological' enterprise lies in the analysis of the practice of criminalising trouble. If criminology is about policing the boundaries of such troubles then it is also about border exchange and the realisation of a commonality to human troubles and the consequences and complicity of involvement therein. Both criminology and social policy are, or should be, gatekeepers of their own troubles, in charge of what they identify, research and resolve rather than being servile to the criminal law or passing political whim and that way lies the challenge of genuine academic freedom.

## Summary

In analysing the relationships between crime, criminalisation and criminology, and the links with social policy, this chapter has argued that:

- The criminal justice system is not, and never has been, comprised solely by the police, Crown Prosecution Service, courts and prisons. There are any number of additional police 'forces', systems of adjudication, and means of dispensing justice and applying sanctions.

- There are forces of convergence between the formal CJS and these other forms of social control, as evident in ASBOs, drug treatment programmes, family intervention programmes and CCTV, to name but a few.

- This directs our attention to questions about the appropriate relationship between criminalisation and decriminalisation as a two-way process that extends from abolitionism on the one side to the more robust application and enforcement of, for example, the Health and Safety at Work Act and laws on corporate killing on the other.

- Criminology is best defined in terms of the focus on criminalisation as the most coherent rationale for its analytical endeavour.

- As such, it is appropriate to engage with the parallel and duplicate rendition of problems as trouble, crime, and so on, by both criminology and social policy.

## Discussion and review topics

1 Does the criminalisation of trouble meet a basic human need, and are there alternative ways of meeting any such needs?

2 To what extent is criminology bound to the study of 'exclusion' whereas social policy is tied to that of 'inclusion'?

3 Is it possible for the criminalisation of trouble to reflect principles of social justice?

4 What do you understand by the term 'antisocial behaviour', and can we see 'labelling' or 'social censures' at work here?

## Further reading

Burney, E. (2005) *Making People Behave: Anti-social behaviour, politics and policy*, Willan, Cullompton. A useful exploration of the contemporary obsession with antisocial behaviour and the impact of the ASBO and other similar legislative instruments of control.

Downes, D. and Rock, P. (2007) *Understanding Deviance* (5th edn), Oxford University Press, Oxford. A detailed account of sociological explanations of deviance, with a particularly pertinent chapter on Deviance Theories and Social Policy, identifying the challenges which such theoretical perspectives pose for policy makers.

Hillyard, P., Pantazis, C., Tombs, S. and Gordon, D. (eds) (2004) *Beyond Criminology: Taking Harm Seriously*, Pluto, London. A critical text which assesses the limitations of criminology with its narrow focus on 'crime' and advances an agenda for the identification of social harms as an alternative which may require a more innovative approach to achieving 'justice'.

Knepper, P. (2007) *Criminology and Social Policy*, Sage, London. Explores the relationship between the two disciplines, in assessing the contribution of criminology in addressing social problems, and the role of social policy in tackling crime.

McLaughlin, E. and Muncie, J. (eds) (2006) *The Sage Dictionary of Criminology* (2nd edn), Sage, London. A key point of reference for many students in relation to crime and criminology, this dictionary brings together definitions and evaluations of key theoretical perspectives on crime, deviance and justice, provided by academics and practitioners.

Newburn, T. (2007) *Criminology*, Willan, Cullompton. A comprehensive but highly readable textbook, incorporating developments in criminological theory as well as criminal justice practice.

## Some useful websites

www.crimeandjustice.org.uk – website for the Centre for Crime and Justice Studies, with links to other excellent sources of information and analysis, including the Harm and Society project, *Criminal Justice Matters* magazine, and *British Journal of Criminology*.

www.homeoffice.gov.uk – an invaluable source of information about current government policy on crime, antisocial behaviour and policing strategies. With links to research findings and policy documents, such as the Respect Action Plan, this is a good way to keep up to date with developments in the law and the political response to crime.

www.corporateaccountability.org – the Centre for Corporate Accountability is a charity which promotes worker and public safety, and which has been particularly active in campaigning for greater levels of accountability for deaths in the workplace. Their website provides clarification of legal judgements in this area and the impact of recent legislative change, statistical data relating to workplace death and injury and links to the Centre's research and briefing documents.

**www.nacro.org.uk** – NACRO is a charity that aims to reduce crime. The NACRO website provides information on the work of the organisation and access to its publications.

**www.statewatch.org/asbo/ASBOwatch.html** – 'ASBOwatch' monitors the use of antisocial behaviour orders and this website provides some useful legal information and evaluation of the use of the ASBO. Of particular interest is the database of ASBOs with unusual or particularly restrictive conditions, with links provided to original news reports on the individual cases.

# References

Becker, H. (1963) *Outsiders: Studies in the sociology of deviance*, Free Press, New York.

Becker, H. (1967) 'Whose side are we on?' *Social Problems,* Vol. 14, No. 3, pp. 239–47.

Bianchi, H. (1994) 'Abolition: Assensus and Sanctuary', in A. Duff and D. Garland (eds) *A Reader on Punishment*, OUP, Oxford.

Bottoms, A. (1995) 'The philosophy and politics of punishment and sentencing: The politics of sentencing reform', in C. Clarkson and R. Morgan (eds) *The Politics of Sentencing Reform*, OUP, Oxford.

Box, S. (1983) *Power, Crime and Mystification*, Tavistock, London.

British Institute for Brain Injured Children (2005) *Ain't Misbehavin': Young people with learning and communication difficulties and anti-social behaviour*, BIBIC, Bridgwater.

Brown, A. (2004) 'Anti-social Behaviour, Crime Control and Social Control', *The Howard Journal*, Vol. 43, No. 2, pp. 203–11.

Burney, E. (2005) *Making People Behave: Anti-social behaviour, politics and policy*, Willan, Cullompton.

Chambliss, W. (1975) 'Towards a Political Economy of Crime', in J. Muncie, E. McLaughlin, and M. Langan (eds) (1996) *Criminological Perspectives*, SAGE/OU, London.

Clark, D. (1978) 'Marxism, Justice and the Justice Model', *Contemporary Crises*, Vol. 2, No. 1, pp. 27–62.

Cohen, S. (1985) *Visions of Social Control: Crime, punishment and classification*, Polity, Cambridge.

Coleman and Moynihan, J. (1996) *Understanding Crime Data: Haunted by the Dark Figure*, OUP, Buckingham.

Ditton, J. (1979) *Controlology: Beyond the New Criminology*, MacMillan, London.

Dorling, D. (2004) 'Prime Suspect: Murder in Britain', in P. Hillyard, S. Tombs, and D. Gordon (eds) *Beyond Criminology: Taking Harm Seriously*, Pluto Press, London.

Downes and Rock (1982) *Understanding Deviance*, OUP, Oxford.

Dyer, C. (2008) 'Senior judge criticises "politicised" prisons policy', *Guardian*, 3 April 2008.

Erickson, K.T. (1966) *Wayward Puritans*, John Wiley, New York.

Eysenck, H. and Gudjonsson, G. (1989) *The Causes and Cures of Criminality*, Plenum Press, New York.

Foucault, M. (1977) *Discipline and Punish*, Allen Lane, London.

Garland, D. (1985) *Punishment and Welfare*, Gower, London.

Garland, D. (1997) 'Of Crimes and Criminals: The Development of Criminology in Britain', in M. Maguire, R. Morgan, and R. Reiner (Eds) *The Oxford Handbook of Criminology*, OUP, Oxford.

Garland, D. and Young, P. (eds) (1983) *The Power to Punish*, Heinemann, London.

Garside, R. (2005) 'Are Anti-social Behaviour Strategies Anti-social? *Whitehall and Westminster World*, 22 March 2005.

Hagan, J., (1994) *Crime and Disrepute*, Pine Forge Press, USA.

Hirst, P. (1975) 'Marx and Engels on Law, Crime and Morality', in I. Taylor, P. Walton, and J. Young (eds) *Critical Criminology*, RKP, London.

Hobbs, D. (1998) 'Glocal Organised Crime', in V. Ruggiero, N. South, and I. Taylor (eds) *The New European Criminology: Crime and Social Order in Europe*, Routledge, New York.

Home Office (2003) *Respect and Responsibility: Taking a stand against anti-social behaviour*, Home Office, London.

Hudson, B. (2001) 'Punishment, Rights and Difference: Defending justice in the risk society', in K. Stenson and R.R. Sullivan (eds) *Crime, Risk and Justice: The politics of crime control in liberal democracies*, Willan, Cullompton.

Hulsman, L. (1986) 'Critical criminology and the concept of crime', *Contemporary Crises*, Vol. 10, No. 1, pp. 63–80.

Jones, K. (1982) *Law and Economy: The legal Regulation of Corporate Capital*, Academic Press, London.

Kagan, R. (1984) 'On Regulatory Inspectorates and Police', in K. Hawkins and J. Thomas (eds) *Enforcing Regulation*, Kluwer, Nihjoff, Boston.

Knepper, P. (2007) *Criminology and Social Policy*, Sage, London.

Kuhn, T.S. (1969) *The Structure of Scientific Revolutions*, University of Chicago Press, Chicago.

Labour Party (1995) *A Quiet Life: Tough Action on Criminal Neighbours*, Labour Party, London.

Lea, J. and Young, J. (1984) *What is to be done about Law and Order?* Penguin, Harmondsworth.

MacDonald, S. (2006) 'A Suicidal Woman, Roaming Pigs and a Noisy Trampolinist: Refining the ASBO's definition of Anti-Social Behaviour', *Modern Law Review*, Vol. 69, No. 2, pp. 183–213.

MacIntosh, M. (1973) *The Organisation of Crime*, MacMillan, London.

Morris, S. (2007) 'Young taken to court for very trivial reasons', *Guardian*, 10 October 2007.

Muncie, J. (2001) 'The construction and deconstruction of crime', in E. McLaughlin and J. Muncie (eds) *The Problem of Crime*, Sage, London.

Nelken, D. (1994) 'Whom Can You Trust? The Future of Comparative Criminology', in D. Nelken (ed.) *The Futures of Criminology*, Sage, London.

Norrie, A. (1991) 'A critique of Criminal Causation', in *Modern Law Review,* Vol. 54, p. 685.

Pakes, F. (2004) *Comparative Criminal Justice*, Willan, Cullompton.

Pearson, G. (1983) *Hooligan: A history of respectable fears*, Macmillan, London.

Prinns, H. (1995) *Offenders, Deviants and Patients*, Routledge, London.

Quinney, R. (1970) *The Social Reality of Crime*, MA, Boston.

Respect Task Force (2007) *What is a family intervention project?* **www.respect.gov.uk/members/ article.aspx**? (accessed 25 November 2007).

Rock, P. (ed.) (1988) *A History of British Criminology*, OUP, Oxford.

Rodger, J.J. (2006) 'Antisocial families and withholding welfare support', *Critical Social Policy*, Vol. 26, No. 1, pp. 121–43.

Ruggiero, V. (2000) *Crime and Markets: Essays in anti-criminology*, OUP, Oxford.

Rutherford, A. (2000) 'An elephant on the doorstep: Criminal policy without crime in New Labour's Britain', in P. Green and A. Rutherford (eds) *Criminal Policy in Transition*, Hart Publishing, Oxford.

Schrager, L. and Short, J. (1978) 'Toward a sociology of organizational crime', in *Social Problems*, Vol. 25, pp. 407–19.

Schwendinger, H. and J. (1975) 'Defenders of order or Guardians of Human Rights', in, I. Taylor, P. Walton, and J. Young (eds) *Critical Criminology*, RKP, London.

Simmons, J.L. (1969) *Deviants*, Glendessary Press, Berkeley.

Slapper, G. (1999) *Blood in the bank: Social and legal aspects of deaths at work*, Ashgate, Aldershot.

Slapper, G. and Tombs, S. (1999) *Corporate Crime,* Essex, Longman.

Smart, C. (1990) 'Feminist Approaches to Criminology or Postmodern Woman Meets Atavistic Man', in J. Muncie, E. McLaughlin, and M. Lagan (eds) (1996) *Criminological Perspectives*, SAGE/OU, London.

Sumner, C. (1990) *Censure, Politics and Criminal Justice*, Open University Press, Milton Keynes.

Sumner, C. (1994) *The Sociology of Deviance: An Obituary*, Open University Press, Buckingham.

Sutherland, E. (1949) *White Collar Crime*, Reinhart & Winston, New York, Holt.

Tappan, P. (1947) 'Who is the Criminal', in *American Sociological Review*, Vol. 12, pp. 96–102.

Taylor-Gooby, P. (2005) *Attitudes to Social Justice*, IPPR, London.

Wells, C. (1994/2001) *Corporations and Criminal Responsibility*, OUP, Oxford.

Wilkins, L. (1990) *Punishment, Crime and Market Forces*, Dartmouth, Aldershot.

Young, P. (1992) 'The Importance of Utopias in Criminological Thought', *British Journal of Criminology*, Vol. 32, No. 4.

Zimring, F. and Hawkins, G. (1991) *The Scale of Imprisonment,* UOCP, Chicago.

# 15

# Health policy

Hugh Bochel

## Chapter overview

For many people the National Health Service has epitomised the post-war welfare state. The idea of universal healthcare, available free at the point of use and funded from general taxation has become generally accepted within the United Kingdom (although there has also been an acceptance of a role for the private sector for those who wish, and can afford, to avail themselves of such provision). Yet there remain very important debates over the direction and shape of health policy, some of which have been highlighted in media and political debates in recent years, whilst others, arguably also of great significance, have received much less attention.

This chapter provides an overview of health policy, drawing upon past and current developments through:

- a consideration of the creation and development of the National Health Service over the first thirty years of its existence;
- examination of attempts to reform the pattern of provision by the Conservative governments from 1979 to 1997;
- attention to New Labour's initiatives including increased funding for the NHS, a more central role for primary care and approaches to inequalities in health.

## Spotlight on the issues
### Reforming the NHS

Reforms to the National Health Service have frequently proved controversial for governments, as illustrated by the following example.

### WARNING OVER 'POLYCLINICS' PROPOSAL

#### Lord Ara Darzi was commissioned to carry out a wholesale review of the NHS

**Government plans for so-called polyclinics could waste hundreds of millions of pounds and undermine the GP system, a doctor's leader has warned.**

The large health centres bringing together several GPs and specialists and opening for extended hours were a high-profile feature of Lord Darzi's interim report on the NHS last year and it is thought his final report in June could propose rolling them out across England.

But they have met opposition from GPs who fear they will damage the relationship between individual patients and their family doctor and bring in competition for NHS work from multinational private medicine companies.

Health minister Lord Darzi, commissioned by Prime Minister Gordon Brown to carry out a wholesale review of the NHS, told BBC1 Breakfast: 'Most patients love their GP, but I think we need to support that fantastic relationship between a patient and a doctor.

'Most practices now are on average four, five or six GPs practising together under a single roof.

'I have no doubt in the future we are going to see a critical mass of general practitioners working together rather than what we used to see in the past, which were practices with a single-handed clinician.'

But the deputy chairman of the British Medical Association's GPs' committee, Dr Richard Vautrey, said the Government was trying to force a 'London-centric' model on to the whole country, when it was not appropriate to less densely populated areas.

GPs were already moving gradually towards larger practices and longer opening hours in areas where they found it was needed, he said.

Dr Vautrey told BBC Radio 4's Today programme: 'This is a Government plan that is potentially going to waste hundreds of millions of pounds of scarce NHS resources, creating very large health centres that many areas of the country simply don't need or want.

'The Government are imposing this centralised plan on to everyone whether they need it or not.'

*Source: Daily Express*, 16 February 2008.

The NHS is one part of the welfare state that receives considerable support from the public, and at the same time there are many powerful interests with significant stakes in the service. Proposals for change will almost inevitably impact negatively on some groups, whether users or professionals, and can frequently be portrayed as damaging to one aspect or another of the work of the NHS. The excerpt above serves to illustrate the difficulty for any government seeking to reform the National Health Service.

Health and healthcare are clearly important as, over time, they affect everyone. The provision of healthcare has long been seen as one of the principal functions of the welfare state, and the National Health Service has equally been viewed as important by public opinion. Yet from the 1980s the form and shape of the NHS, the cost of healthcare and the ways in which healthcare should be delivered have been prominent features of social policy among successive governments. In many respects this can be seen as nothing new, as from the earliest forms of state involvement in health in the mid-nineteenth century in the form of the **public health** acts there have been debates over the role of the state, private and not-for-profit sectors, and equally over how healthcare should be accessed and paid for. However, given some of the fundamental questions that have been asked about the role, function and structures, and even the viability of the welfare state, over the past thirty years, the centrality of health policy to that debate means that health and healthcare remain central to the considerations of governments and the public.

## The growth of state involvement in health policy

Chapter 5 outlined the growing role of the state in relation to welfare from the nineteenth century, and illustrated that the roots of health policy can be traced back to this period. During the nineteenth century the state began to be involved in health issues, largely in connection with the introduction of public health legislation that was designed to reduce the threat of infectious diseases, such as cholera. The passage of the Public Health Act 1848 is often associated with the work of Edwin Chadwick, Secretary to the Poor Law Commission and his supporters. This Act provided the basis for local government to play a role in the provision of adequate water supplies and sewerage systems, but while some local authorities were enthusiastic about and active in making such provision, others were less positive and chose to take little or no action. The 1872 Public Health Act created sanitary authorities, which had a responsibility to provide public health services; and the Public Health Act 1875 brought together existing legislation and established a framework which underpinned the development of public health for the next fifty years (Baggott, 2000).

Government involvement in health took another step forward with the National Insurance Act 1911. Introduced despite opposition from large parts of the medical profession, who feared both state control of their work and negative financial consequences for themselves, this Act provided income during sickness and unemployment and free care from General Practitioners for some groups of workers earning under £160 per annum. To make the Act palatable to doctors the Liberal government agreed that payment should be based on the number of people on a doctor's list – the capitation system – rather than as a salary, thus preserving GPs' independence. In addition, it was agreed that the system should be administered by panels, including the insurance companies and friendly societies that had previously played a significant role in providing cover against ill health, rather than by local authorities. Over the next thirty years this provision grew and by the mid 1940s about half of the British population was covered by insurance under the Act, whilst around two-thirds of GPs were involved (Ham, 2004). However, in many respects this system had significant limitations. For example, it was only the insured workers who were covered, not their families, and it was only GP services, and not hospital care, that was provided by the scheme. There was still significant scope, therefore, for new demands for healthcare.

In addition to private provision, both public and voluntary hospitals were playing a part in healthcare at this time. Public hospital provision in the UK had developed out of the workhouses provided under the Poor Law, whilst there were parallel developments in the voluntary hospital system that grew out of provision by religious organisations and, later, charitable giving by the rich. However, during the nineteenth century, with the growth of medicine as a science, voluntary hospitals became more selective, giving greater attention to the needs of people with acute illnesses at the expense of those who had chronic illnesses or infectious diseases. As a result the workhouses were often providing for those who the voluntary hospitals would not accept. However, the 1867 Metropolitan Poor Act and the 1868 Poor Law Amendment Act allowed for the provision of infirmaries separate from workhouses, and effectively provided recognition that the state had a responsibility to provide hospital care for poor people. The 1929 Local Government Act arguably moved a step closer to allowing for the development of a national health service of some sort, transferring workhouses and infirmaries to local authorities, with the intention that this provision could develop into a local authority hospital service. In addition, since 1845, local authorities had been required to develop hospitals (asylums) for people with mental health problems and people with learning difficulties. By the start of the Second World War local authorities were therefore responsible for a range of hospital provision, and these were brought together with the voluntary hospitals as part of the Emergency Medical Service, providing a framework for the coordination of hospital care during the War.

In addition to these developments, between the First and Second World Wars a number of reports had highlighted problems with existing provision of healthcare, including the need for greater planning and coordination, and had made suggestions for change. The publication of the Beveridge Report on Social Insurance and Allied Services in 1942 made the case for the reform of the social security system together with the creation of a national health service and provided added momentum for change. In 1944 the coalition government published a White Paper proposing a national health service, and the election of a Labour government in 1945 made the establishment of a national health service almost certain. The necessary legislation was passed in the 1946 National Health Service Act. In the creation of the NHS local authorities lost control of their hospitals, which, with the voluntary hospitals, were placed under one central administrative system.

## Health policy 1948–1979

As is widely known, the National Health Service came into being on 5 July 1948 with the aim of providing comprehensive health services to all, free at the point of use and financed through general taxation. These principles have remained largely unchallenged in the period since then, whilst the NHS has also remained popular with the public.

However, the first decades of existence were not unproblematic for the NHS. There had been a general assumption at the time of its creation that the services and care provided would reduce the overall level of ill health, and that as a result expenditure would level off and even decline. Yet this pattern never emerged, and within years of coming into being the NHS was requiring additional expenditure. Prescription charges and a fee for dental treatment were introduced in 1952 in response to the high levels of demand. Whilst expenditure on the NHS therefore increased, the 1950s also saw a degree of consolidation and rationalisation, particularly of hospital services, and expenditure on capital was limited, amounting to only £100 million in the entire decade, with no new hospitals being built (Ham, 2004). However, the 1962 Hospital Plan provided for a major increase in capital expenditure, based upon District General Hospitals, each providing services for the great majority of illnesses, serving populations of around 125,000. The 1960s also saw the first significant steps towards **community care**, rather than care in large institutions, following the 1959 Mental Health Act (see Chapter 12).

There were some suggestions in the 1960s that some of the problems that had emerged in the NHS could be tackled through structural change, and the Labour government of the late 1960s produced two Green Papers considering this. The Conservative government that followed took these ideas a step further in the National Health Service Act 1973, which produced a new structure that came into operation in 1974, intended to achieve three main aims (Ham, 2004): to unify health services by bringing them together under one authority (although GPs remained as independent contractors); to improve coordination between health authorities and local government services including through the introduction of matching boundaries; and to introduce better management. However, the new structure (consisting in England of 14 Regional Health Authorities and 90 Area Health Authorities) came under almost immediate criticism and amongst the recommendations of the Royal Commission on the Health Service, which was established in 1976 and reported in 1979, was that the number of tiers of authority should be reduced.

## Health policy 1979-1997

However, whilst the Royal Commission had been established by a Labour government, it was a Conservative government headed by Margaret Thatcher that was to act upon the report, and, as noted in Chapter 6, this government was much less sympathetic to state provision of welfare and to high levels of public expenditure. In the early 1980s the NHS was again reorganised, this time creating 192 District Health Authorities in England, which in most cases were no longer coterminous with local government boundaries. As with the 1974 changes, general practitioners remained outside the mainstream health authority structure, with Family Practitioner Committees overseeing these services. Changes were also made in Northern Ireland, Scotland and Wales.

However, ideological pressures within the Conservative government were mounting for change that would go beyond concerns with effective structures. As with other elements of the welfare state (and indeed the wider public sector) some on the New Right were seeking more radical reforms including, for almost the first time in mainstream politics, some calls for the replacement of the NHS with private health insurance. However, even after the Conservatives won the 1983 general election their concerns continued to focus upon the management of the health service, and in particular upon attempts to make it more efficient and businesslike, including through learning from the private sector. A report in 1983 by Roy Griffiths (then managing director of the Sainsbury's supermarket chain) recommended the introduction of general managers at all levels of the NHS, both to improve the quality of management and to take greater control from hospital doctors. This was a significant change as, until this point, doctors had arguably exercised considerable control over the service; yet now they were increasingly drawn into the management of limited resources. In a further change recommended by Griffiths, the government created an NHS Management Board and a Health Services Supervisory Board to strengthen central NHS management. Given the nature of these changes, and those that were to follow, it has sometimes been argued that these changes saw the start of a significant shift of power away from doctors and towards managers.

## NHS funding and internal markets

Whilst not adopting the approach supported by some on the New Right in seeking to replace the NHS with private health insurance, the Conservatives did try to encourage market forces within the health service. Alan Enthoven, an American academic, had suggested that forms of markets could be created within health services by encouraging those providing services to compete for patients, and had argued that this would drive up standards and increase accountability (Enthoven, 1985). At the same time, there was evidence of significant funding problems for the NHS, with authoritative reports by the Kings Fund (1988) and the Social Services Select Committee (1986, 1988) highlighting such concerns. In the winter of 1987 it became apparent that many health authorities were finding it difficult to keep expenditure within limits, wards were being closed to save money, and parts of the medical profession, including the presidents of three Royal Colleges, were claiming that the NHS was in need of additional finances. Following considerable media coverage and political debate, in the short term the government provided an additional £100 million of funding, but the Prime Minister, Margaret Thatcher, also established a small committee, chaired by herself, to review the future of the NHS. Although the review was conducted in private, and organisations such as the British Medical Association were not called to give evidence, and despite speculation that the government would seek to use the review to introduce far-reaching changes to the NHS, in reality there was little appetite for truly radical reform, particularly in the face of continued public support for the NHS. Instead the idea of introducing internal markets emerged as a major strand of the White Paper *Working for Patients* (Department of Health, 1989).

The White Paper stated that it was the government's intention to preserve the basic principles on which the NHS had been founded, and within it the emphasis lay heavily on means of improving the delivery of health services through a separation of purchaser and provider responsibilities, the creation of **NHS trusts** and **GP fundholders**, and a series of internal markets where purchasers would be able to buy services from different providers, building on Enthoven's ideas. However, the White Paper also announced other additional changes: the concern with management remained significant, with the creation of the NHS Management Executive and a Policy Board to replace the NHS Management Board and the Supervisory Board, with attempts to strengthen the managerial role of health authorities and the new Family Health Services Authorities (which replaced the Family Practitioner Committees); in an attempt to make doctors more accountable for their performance general managers were to be given a greater role in the management of clinical activity, whilst audit was to become, for the first time, a routine part of clinical work in hospitals and general practice.

Also in 1989 the government published a White Paper, *Caring for People*, which built on a second report by Sir Roy Griffiths, this time on the future of community care. Although having a very different emphasis from *Working for Patients*, this White Paper required local authorities to play the lead role in community care, but in collaboration with the NHS and other voluntary and private sector bodies (see also Chapter 12).

These changes were introduced in the NHS and Community Care Act 1990, and the internal market began to develop from 1991 as the number of NHS trusts and GP fundholders began to increase. However, the success of the reforms was questionable, with supporters and opponents being able to interpret the available evidence in different ways. Conservative Ministers argued that waiting times for hospital treatment were being reduced and that the number of patients being treated was increasing and that these showed that the NHS was becoming more efficient and responsive; however, others suggested that these changes derived at least in part from the increased funding that the NHS was receiving. Similarly, the conclusions of academics and others were mixed, with Le Grand and his colleagues, for example, concluding that the reforms had made relatively little difference, either positive or negative (Le Grand *et al.*, 1998).

## Public health measures

Where public health and health improvement were concerned, in 1980 the Conservative government found themselves confronted by the Black Report (1980) on *Inequalities in Health*, which examined inequalities in health and produced a number of recommendations to reduce social class inequalities in health, including increasing child benefits and improving housing conditions. However, the government did not find the analysis or recommendations to its liking and little action was taken.

The 1980s also saw the spread of HIV/AIDS and the consequent development of policies that sought to combat this. The principle method used was to seek to encourage people, as individuals, to change their behaviour and lifestyle. This approach also underpinned much of the other preventative work of the time, including campaigns aimed at reducing smoking and alcohol misuse. By the

1990s the government had progressed to the production of a White Paper, *The Health of the Nation* (Department of Health, 1992), which set targets for health improvement in five key areas: coronary heart disease and stroke; cancer; mental health; HIV/AIDS and sexual health; and accidents. Whilst many welcomed the strategy, it was also widely criticised, including over the worth of the targets (variously seen as too ambitious or as likely to be met on the continuation of current trends even if no action were taken), a perceived unwillingness to tackle the tobacco and alcohol industries (with, for example, no progress made in banning tobacco advertising), and a failure to take social inequalities and deprivation into account (see Baggott, 2000).

The Conservative governments also sought to involve GPs and dentists more in preventative work, including through the introduction of new contracts in 1990. Those for GPs included requirements for health checks for new patients and those aged 75 or over, whilst targets were introduced for vaccinations, immunisations and screening for cervical cancer, and encouragement was given for additional health promotion work. Similarly, the new contracts for dentists also sought to stress the requirement for preventative work as well as restorative treatments.

## Private health provision

Since 1948 the National Health Service has been the dominant provider of healthcare in the UK, but private provision has continued to play a significant role. For many, private healthcare can be extremely expensive and for that reason much treatment is paid for by private health insurance, for which there are a number of providers, including specialists such as BUPA and general insurers such as Norwich Union. From the 1970s the number of people covered by private health insurance has almost tripled, reaching nearly 7 million in 2000 (Office of National Statistics, 2002), although the bulk of this rise took place during the 1970s and 1980s and the first half of the 1990s saw little change.

However, private health insurers are also affected by the cost of paying for healthcare and as a result face pressure to keep costs down. For this reason the range of services provided is frequently limited whilst providers seek to reduce their potential exposure to those who might be likely to make the heaviest financial demands, such as people with long-term chronic health problems. The main advantages to patients are therefore likely to be avoiding NHS waiting times and higher standards of services such as food and accommodation.

## Health policy since 1997

On coming to power Labour faced a number of challenges in relation to health policy. Many of these have been outlined earlier in this chapter, but they included: the perpetual dilemma of how to adequately fund the National Health Service; what to do about the internal market introduced by the Conservatives; how to make best use of primary health services, provided by general practitioners; and evidence of continued and growing social class inequalities in morbidity and mortality. By December 1997 the government had produced a White Paper, *The new NHS: modern, dependable* (Department of Health, 1997) (Briefing 15.1), which reflected the government's desire for modernisation but at the same time took a pragmatic approach to what was already in place.

## Briefing 15.1
### The new NHS: modern, dependable

The 1997 White Paper set out six principles to guide changes. These were to:

- renew the NHS as a genuinely *national* service;
- make the delivery of healthcare against these new national standards a matter of *local* responsibility;
- get the NHS to work in *partnership*;
- improve *efficiency* so that every pound in the NHS is spent to maximise the care for patients;
- shift the focus on to quality of care so that *excellence* is guaranteed to all patients;
- rebuild *public confidence* in the NHS.

*Source*: Department of Health (1997) *The new NHS: modern, dependable*, Stationery Office, London (emphases in original).

## NHS funding

Whilst the funding of the NHS has been a problem for almost all governments since 1948, by the 1990s issues such as waiting lists, winter bed shortages in hospitals, and rationing of services were bringing this to the fore again. Labour's commitment, prior to the 1997 general election, to abide by the Conservatives' plans for public expenditure for two years, made it impossible for the government to make radical changes to funding the NHS. However, following the **Comprehensive Spending Review**, in 1999 the government undertook to increase spending on the NHS by £21 billion over the next three years, an annual increase of 4.7 per cent in real terms (see Figure 15.1). Despite this increase, NHS funding remained an issue, including at the 2001 general election, and in the 2002 budget the Chancellor, Gordon Brown, announced a further rise in NHS spending of an average of 7.4 per cent a year in real terms for five years, with the total amount going on the health service planned to increase from £72.1 billion in 2003–4 to £105.6 billion in 2007–8. This was intended, over the period, to bring the proportion of GDP spent on the NHS to more than the average EU expenditure on healthcare (Table 15.1 shows expenditure on health in selected countries). However, even a report commissioned by the Treasury, published in 2002, suggested that there remained a number of factors, including public expectations, developments in medical technology and demographic change, which would continue to put pressure on healthcare resources and expenditure, meaning that there will be a need for further increases in expenditure over the next twenty years (Wanless, 2002).

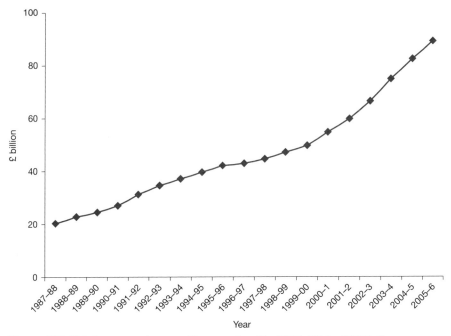

**Figure 15.1** Total managed expenditure on health, 1987-88 to 2005-6

*Source*: HM Treasury (2007) *Public Expenditure Statistical Analyses 2007*, HM Treasury, London (Table 4.2).

**Table 15.1** Total expenditure on health as a percentage of GDP, selected countries

|  | *1997* | *2001* | *2006* |
|---|---|---|---|
| Australia | 8.2 | 8.9 | 9.6 |
| Canada | 8.9 | 9.4 | 9.9 |
| Denmark | 8.2 | 8.6 | 8.9 |
| France | 9.2 | 9.3 | 10.5 |
| Germany | 10.2 | 10.4 | 10.6 |
| Ireland | 6.3 | 6.8 | 7.1 |
| Italy | 7.5 | 8.2 | 8.7 |
| Japan | 6.9 | 7.8 | 8.0 |
| Spain | 7.3 | 7.2 | 8.1 |
| Sweden | 8.1 | 8.7 | 9.1 |
| Switzerland | 10.2 | 10.9 | 11.6 |
| United Kingdom | 6.8 | 7.5 | 8.1 |
| United States | 13.1 | 14.0 | 15.3 |

*Source*: OECD (2006) *OECD Health Data 2006*, OECD, Paris.

Despite the apparent large increases in expenditure on the NHS under Labour, the financing of the service has continued to be a challenge. Whilst the explanations for this can be complex and interpreted in different ways, it is possible to identify a number of possible contributory factors. There is the growing demand for healthcare, which means that there is constant pressure for more provision, a factor which is reinforced by the growing ageing population. In addition, salaries for many NHS staff have grown significantly, with some increases, particularly for doctors, costing more than the government had anticipated. And further, much healthcare continues to be provided in hospitals, when it is likely that some forms of treatment could be provided more cheaply by community services. To all of these, critics would add that the large sums of additional expenditure pumped into the health service have frequently gone on increased pay, or larger numbers of managers, rather than patient care. The consequences of such difficulties in funding became apparent during the 2005/6 financial year, when a major problem emerged in relation to hospital and Primary Care Trust (PCT) deficits, meaning that the service ended the financial year with a £512 million deficit. In response, the Secretary of State for Health, Patricia Hewitt, demanded that the NHS move into surplus in the 2006/7 financial year. As with past budgetary crises, responses to the government's demands led to cutbacks in services to patients in some areas and to reductions in staffing, with the politically unpalatable headlines about delays for operations and health staff losing their jobs. Nevertheless, the 2006/7 year did see the NHS return to surplus, although there were concerns expressed by some about the further impact of the tight budgetary constraints.

 Thought provoker

### The Wanless review and the funding of healthcare

In 2002–03, total NHS spending in the UK is expected to be around £68 billion, or 6.5 per cent of GDP. Including private expenditure on health, the figure is likely to be around 7.7 per cent of GDP.

Under the different scenarios considered, the Review estimates that UK NHS spending will rise to between 9.4 and 11.3 per cent of GDP in 2022–23 to deliver the high quality health service which the Report describes.

On the simple assumption that private health expenditure remains constant at its present level of around 1.2 per cent of GDP, this would raise total UK health spending to between 10.6 and 12.5 per cent of national income in 20 years' time.     Wanless (2002, pp. 76-7)

In what ways, other than general taxation, might the provision of healthcare be funded? What would be the advantages and disadvantages of those approaches?

One of the controversial aspects of Labour's approach to the financing of the NHS has been the use of the **Private Finance Initiative** (PFI) to fund a programme of new hospital building. Given the Labour Party's traditional hostility to privatisation, and particularly the long-standing commitment to a health service free at the point of use and funded from general taxation, the PFI was viewed suspiciously by many of the party's MPs and supporters, whilst others were sceptical about the value for money offered, particularly over the long term. Nevertheless the government saw this as central to its plans for the NHS and pushed ahead with it.

*Controversy and debate*

### The Private Finance Initiative

The Private Finance Initiative was introduced by the Conservative Chancellor Norman Lamont in 1992. The form of PFI that has been most relevant to the NHS is where a private contractor designs, finances, builds, and potentially even operates, a facility such as a hospital. A public sector body may then pay the private contractor agreed payments for the use of the facility over the contract period. When the contract comes to an end the facility can revert to either the private contractor or the public sector, depending upon the agreement.

PFI has been widely used under Labour, particularly for hospitals and schools, and by October 2006 the Department of Health had approved 84 PFI deals in England each worth more than £10 million, which were either completed or where work had started on site, with a total cost of more than £8.5 billion. In contrast the equivalent value of traditionally public funded capital expenditure was around £1.2 billion (Department of Health, 2006).

Critics of PFI have argued, for example, that it is a form of privatisation, that it commits the NHS to a hospital-based system for the long term (with most contracts being for around 30 years), that it contributes to the profits of private sector companies, and that the costs are high, putting pressure on NHS budgets.

Supporters have contended that the use of PFI has allowed the speedy completion of projects and that this helps to offset the costs, and that it has enabled the replacement of old facilities and the development of new ones at a rate that would not have been possible using the public sector alone.

Since 1997 the bulk of major hospital building schemes have been undertaken under PFI, with supporters claiming that it has allowed a significant improvement of NHS buildings more rapidly than would have been possible under traditional public sector funding mechanisms. In contrast, critics have highlighted problems ranging from the poor quality of some buildings, through what are sometimes argued to be higher costs to NHS bodies being tied into such deals for twenty to thirty years, a period over which their priorities may change significantly.

## Reforming primary care

As with many other areas of policy Labour placed great emphasis on some of its key ideas, including the notions of 'modernisation' and using 'what works', reflecting debates of the time around the 'Third Way'. Given Labour's opposition to the internal market prior to 1997 it had been anticipated that they would reverse the policy. In practice the new government accepted many of the reforms, although they did abolish the GP fundholding scheme. However, even in this area they sought to establish some of the principles of fundholding through the creation of primary care groups (PCGs) (Ham, 2004) that included all of the GPs in an area, covering populations of up to around 250,000 people. PCGs were also clearly seen by the

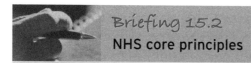

## Briefing 15.2
## NHS core principles

1  The NHS will provide a universal service for all based on clinical need, not ability to pay
2  The NHS will provide a comprehensive range of services
3  The NHS will shape its services around the needs and preferences of individual patients, their families and their carers
4  The NHS will respond to different needs of different populations
5  The NHS will work continuously to improve quality services and to minimise errors
6  The NHS will support and value its staff
7  Public funds for healthcare will be devoted solely to NHS patients
8  The NHS will work together with others to ensure a seamless service for patients
9  The NHS will help keep people healthy and work to reduce health inequalities
10 The NHS will respect the confidentiality of individual patients and provide open access to information about services, treatment and performance.

*Source*: Department of Health (2000) *The NHS Plan*, London, The Stationery Office.

government as a means of integrating provision, with GPs, community nurses and other professionals working together to reduce the fragmentation and gaps in services that had existed under previous organisational models. The intention of this change was that PCGs would be responsible to district health authorities, which in turn would take a strategic approach to identifying health needs and the planning of appropriate provision. These were to be set out in Health Improvement Programmes, to be produced by each health authority but taking into account local interests. However, the new process went further, allowing some PCGs to make a transition to primary care trusts (PCTs), independent of health authorities and able to provide a full range of community services and to commission hospital services. The emphasis on primary care created by the growth in the number of PCTs was further encouraged in *The NHS Plan* (Department of Health, 2000) which, from April 2002 transformed PCGs into PCTs (there were over 300 in England by early 2004, but the figure had fallen to 152 by the middle of 2007) and made these the main bodies responsible for the planning and delivery of primary care, overseen by 10 Strategic Health Authorities. These changes were significant, with PCTs spending more than three-quarters of the NHS budget, compared with the 15 per cent that had been held by GP fundholders during the 1990s.

The steady shift towards a health service led by primary care that had begun under the Conservatives was therefore continuing under Labour. Further echoes of some of the Conservatives' policies emerged when, from 2000, the Labour government also sought to drive reform through the use of market-type mechanisms, including choice for consumers and competition among providers, with the latter extending to the purchase of services from private and not-for-profit organisations.

In 2006, the White Paper *Our health, our care, our say: A new direction for community services* restated the government's desire to provide more services outside hospitals, to continue a shift to prevention, to give greater choice to users, and to ensure greater integration with social care (see Chapter 12).

**Thought provoker**

### Rationing of healthcare

The BMA believes that while the NHS should provide a comprehensive range of services, priority setting and, hence, rationing is inevitable, if we are to retain an equitable approach within limited resources.

This needs to be acknowledged by politicians so that the right environment will exist for politicians, health professionals and the public to debate and decide upon a process to define a list of 'core' services that will be nationally available. The approach should be national and explicit, setting priorities for the whole service. It should provide an ongoing mechanism to review and change priorities in the NHS, which must include an effective way of incorporating public and patient views.                    BMA (2007, p. 45)

What mechanisms have been used to ration healthcare since the creation of the NHS? Who should decide what services and groups should be priorities?

## Structural change

### Foundation trusts

Other than the increased use of the private sector, both through the private finance initiative discussed above and the use of private health providers to deliver services, one of the most politically controversial elements of Labour's approach to the NHS was the creation of foundation trusts. This development differed from previous reorganisations of the health service through the establishment in England of, initially, 'foundation hospitals'. In the first phase, hospital trusts that had achieved 3-star performance ratings were invited to apply for foundation hospital trust status, a form of 'earned autonomy', with freedom from central control and the ability to borrow money from private sources. Foundation hospitals were to be locally controlled, intended to provide greater accountability to local people, with public and staff forming a membership that would elect representatives to the board. Members collectively own the trust, roughly along the lines of a co-operative society, although if a trust were to fail control would pass back to the Department of Health. Foundation trusts therefore remain part of the NHS. The government's stated intention was that foundation hospitals should be free to choose the services that best suit their local community without pressure from the NHS or Whitehall bureaucracies. However, opponents expressed concerns over a number of issues, including the danger of a 'two-tier' health service, for whilst the intention was that by 2008 all hospital trusts should have the opportunity to gain foundation status, the first foundation hospitals would be able to provide better services and take the best staff, whilst lower-status hospitals might not have the chance to recover. Others feared the danger of a return to the internal markets of the 1990s, a lack of genuine democracy, and creeping privatisation. Nevertheless, the government achieved a narrow majority for its legislation in a vote in the House of Commons in 2003 and 25 NHS trusts applied to be in the first wave of foundation trusts. By 2007 the number of foundation trusts had risen to 67, with the government continuing to encourage all NHS trusts to apply for this status. However, there continued to be pressure for further change, including greater independence for the NHS from Ministers, with calls from a number of organisations for such a move.

## Other reforms

As with preceding governments, Labour found the level of demand for healthcare a major challenge. One response was the apparently straightforward means of increasing funding as discussed above, although it is clear that such increases frequently take years to have an impact in terms of any significant improvement in the availability of services to patients, and this was certainly the case under Labour, with frequent questions over the length of time taken to achieve improvements, and, indeed, over where the increased funding was going, with accusations that too much of it was being diverted to pay for managers rather than patient care. A second, more targeted response emerged from the 1997 manifesto commitments to reduce waiting lists, with the 1997 to 2001 government establishing a waiting list initiative including setting targets for a reduction in the number of people on waiting lists. However, in 2001 the waiting list initiative was ended, at least in part as a result of the pressure on NHS staff and concerns that simple non-urgent operations were being prioritised to reduce waiting lists rather than more urgent but more time-consuming treatments. Instead the government announced that it was to seek to reduce waiting times for operations to six months by 2005, a target which it broadly achieved, and which was followed by a target that by the end of 2008 no patient would have to wait more than 18 months from a GP referral to hospital admission. The introduction of NHS Direct, a 24-hour telephone, online and television-based service, was another attempt to channel demand in the first instance, encouraging the public to move away from the traditional reliance upon a visit to a doctor. By 2005–6 NHS Direct was handling around 2 million patient contacts per month, although there were some concerns expressed that it was continuing to refer on too many cases, rather than dealing with them itself.

Labour also sought to move towards a more even 'national' level of provision in some respects, including creating the National Institute for Health and Clinical Excellence (NICE) and the Healthcare Commission. NICE was established in 1999 to provide patients, health professionals and the public with authoritative, robust and reliable guidance on 'best practice' across health technologies (including medicines, medical devices, diagnostic techniques, and procedures) and the clinical management of specific conditions. Among its responsibilities is to make recommendations to the government on the cost-effectiveness and affordability of treatments. The Healthcare Commission came into being in 2004, taking over much of the role of what had been the Commission for Health Improvement, as the independent body responsible for assessing and reporting on the performance of both NHS and independent providers of healthcare in England, and with a more limited remit in Wales, where its concern is primarily with national reviews that cover both England and Wales. In England the Healthcare Commission plays a number of roles including registering and inspecting providers, producing annual ratings for each NHS trust, investigating serious service failures, making information available about the quality of healthcare to individuals and to the government. The Commission is also responsible for monitoring and reviewing (sometimes with other agencies) the implementation of standards set out in National Service Frameworks in England and Wales. These National Service Frameworks set out national standards, or benchmarks, for particular services or care groups (such as coronary heart disease or older people), involve strategies for achieving these targets, and set out milestones against which progress can be measured. The introduction of these bodies and their activities has impacted on health professionals by identifying NHS organisations and professionals as responsible for both the quality and the consistency of clinical decisions.

However, at the same time, Labour, particularly from 2004, has emphasised the importance of choice for users of the NHS. Klein (2005) has noted that whilst in part this was a response to political calculations in the run-up to the 2005 general election, this also reflects the argument, also seen under the Conservatives, that providing choice for users is an important means of encouraging efficiency and quality, 'a weapon against provider dominance' (p. 59). This is based on the belief that given choice, consumers will gravitate to providers that offer good-quality services efficiently, that these providers will benefit from the higher demand, and that in response other providers will have to become more efficient and provide better services. However, not everyone concurs that choice has this effect, or even that consumers of health services desire such choice.

## Inequalities in health

Health inequalities remain significant in the United Kingdom, with factors such as social class, gender and ethnicity being influential in determining patterns of health, morbidity and mortality (for example, males in social class I have a life expectancy of 78.5 years, and this falls with each social class category to 71.1 years for social class V) (see Figure 15.2 for an illustration of socio-economic, cultural and environmental conditions that can impact on inequalities in health). The perceived failure of the preceding Conservative government to accept and seek to

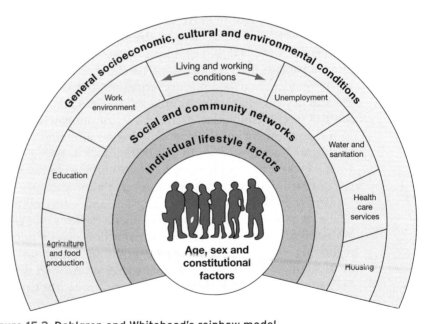

**Figure 15.2 Dahlgren and Whitehead's rainbow model**

*Source*: Dahlgren, G. and Whitehead, M. (1991) *Policies and Strategies to Promote Social Equity in Health*, Institute for Future Studies, Stockholm.

tackle structural causes of ill health meant that the New Labour government faced demands to produce a new approach to promoting public health. The publication of the Acheson Report (Acheson, 1998) further added to the focus on this, noting not only that there remained major differences in mortality and morbidity across social classes, and that there are a range of other significant socio-economic factors affecting health, including income, education, housing and ethnicity, but that in some areas health inequalities had actually widened since the Black Report. The report made a number of recommendations relating to reducing inequalities in relation to areas such as income and poverty, education, housing and environment and nutrition, and across social groups, including gender, age and ethnicity.

The Labour government's initial approach to health improvement was set out with the publication of the Green Paper for England, *Our Healthier Nation* (Department of Health, 1998a), which placed greater emphasis on economic, environmental and social causes of ill health than had *The Health of the Nation*. The new document set out four key areas and targets for 2010: for cancer, to reduce the death rate among people under 75 by at least a fifth; for coronary heart disease and stroke, to reduce the death rate in people under 75 by at least two-fifths; to reduce the death rate from accidents by at least a fifth, and serious injury from accidents by at least a tenth; and for mental illness, to reduce the death rate from suicide and undetermined injury by at least a fifth. Whilst the Green Paper was generally welcomed, some noted that there was an emphasis on reducing mortality, rather than morbidity; others were concerned with the failure to set national targets for reducing health inequalities.

The government also prioritised smoking and drug use as areas for action. In 1998 the government published *Smoking Kills. A White Paper on Tobacco* (Department of Health, 1998b) which set out its intentions to reduce smoking among children and young people, to help adults, and particularly the most disadvantaged, to give up smoking, and to offer particular support to pregnant women. By 2003 the government had introduced a variety of measures designed to help achieve its aims, although some critics believed that further actions, such as banning smoking in public places or curtailing the availability of tobacco, were necessary, and during 2006 and 2007 smoking bans were introduced across the United Kingdom. Where drugs were concerned, in 1998 the government appointed Keith Hellawell as National Anti Drugs Unit Coordinator (or 'drugs czar') to coordinate action across government as a whole to reduce drugs misuse. He was responsible for the production of a ten-year strategy designed to achieve this but resigned in 2002 on the same day that the government announced its intention to downgrade cannabis from a Class B to a Class C drug, although an updated strategy was produced later that year. In 2007 the government established the UK Drug Policy Commission to provide independent analysis of drug policy. A report produced for the Commission provided mixed evidence on the working of the government's strategy, suggesting that attempts to restrict the availability of drugs through tougher enforcement were failing and that while there had been a significant increase in the numbers entering treatment programmes the impact of these was likely to be limited as many users went untreated while others relapsed, although some aspects of criminal behaviour and illnesses, particularly HIV, linked to drug use were being reduced (Reuter and Stevens, 2007).

Labour also sought to give health authorities a leading role in their attempts to reduce health inequalities, requiring them to assess the health needs of their local populations and to develop strategies for meeting those needs, working with PCTs, local authorities and other local interests. This emphasis on collaboration and partnership across organisations is reflected in another strand of Labour policy designed to help tackle health inequalities. A number of Health Action Zones were established in 1998 and 1999 to identify and meet health needs in certain deprived areas, receiving additional funding for a number of years and expected to both involve a wide range of local stakeholders and take innovative approaches to achieving their objectives. However, from 2001 there was a change in emphasis within the Department of Health and HAZs became much less central to the government's approach and were effectively scaled back.

In the run-up to the 2002 Comprehensive Spending Review the government asked Derek Wanless, former chief executive of NatWest, to do a review of future health trends, in part to inform decisions about the long-term financial and resources needs of the NHS, and in 2003 Wanless was asked to undertake further work, particularly on public health. Work for this review reinforced existing evidence that health inequalities remain substantial with Wanless highlighting some of those relating to class, gender, ethnicity and geographic location (see, for example, Figures 15.3 and 15.4), but also the influence of social and environmental factors such as housing conditions, sanitation and education, lifestyle factors such as smoking, diet and the level of physical activity (see, for example, Table 15.2),

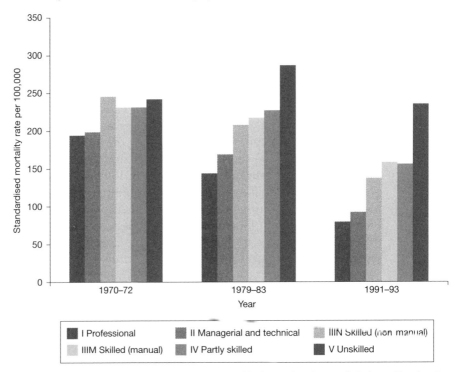

**Figure 15.3** Coronary heart disease mortality in males, by social class, England and Wales

*Source*: Health Inequalities Decennial Supplement, ONS in *Wanless Report*, 2003.

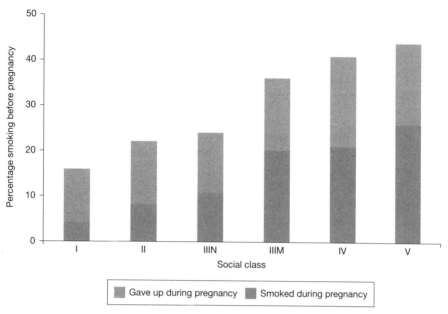

**Figure 15.4** Smoking during pregnancy by social class, UK, 2000

*Source*: Infant Feeding Survey, DoH, 2000, in *Wanless Report*, 2003.

**Table 15.2** Lifestyle determinants of observed morbidity and mortality

| Health problem | Determinants |
| --- | --- |
| Low birth weight and prematurity | Smoking, alcohol abuse, drug abuse, access to quality healthcare |
| Accidents/injuries | Alcohol abuse, drug abuse, environmental, access to quality emergency care |
| Neuropsychiatric | Alcohol abuse, drug abuse |
| Cancers | Smoking, nutrition, obesity, exercise, alcohol abuse, access to quality healthcare |
| Circulatory disease | Smoking, alcohol abuse, nutrition, obesity, exercise, access to quality healthcare |
| Infections | Nutrition, food and water safety, drug abuse, sexual behaviours, travel, access to quality healthcare |
| Asthma and other respiratory problems | Environmental conditions, smoking, access to quality healthcare |

*Source*: European Commission (2003) *The Health Status of the European Union: Narrowing the Health Gap*, European Commission, Brussels.

and the effectiveness of healthcare interventions (Wanless, 2003). It also noted the importance of such inequalities for the lifetimes of individuals and for future generations:

The impact of socio-economic inequalities on health is evident throughout the life course and between generations. For example, babies born to poorer families are more likely to be born prematurely, are at greater risk of dying in infancy, and have a greater likelihood of poverty, impaired development and chronic disease in later life. This sets up an inter-generational cycle of health inequalities. Research shows that low birth weight is closely associated with death in infancy, and with coronary heart disease, diabetes and hypertension in later life. Lower birth weight and father's social class can both increase the risk of dying of CHD [Coronary Heart Disease] over and above the impact of the individual's income and social class.

Wanless (2003, p. 34)

In his final report in 2004 Wanless made a number of recommendations including the use of economic instruments (such as the tax system) in relation to public health, reiterating the need for collaboration between PCTs, local authorities and other partners on identifying local needs and shared local objectives, pointing out the lack of a single accessible source of advice, and producing an annual report on the state of people's health both nationally and locally. In November 2004 the government produced a White Paper, *Choosing Health*, which set out a number of proposals, such as regulating smoking in public places and improving school meals, which were put into action in the following years. However, as with previous initiatives, *Choosing Health* remained vulnerable to criticisms, from some that it reflected a 'nanny' state, telling people what is good for them, and from others that in emphasising individual choice it failed to recognise the ways in which such choices are limited.

Overall, it is apparent that under Labour the emphasis on individuals improving their own health remains, as during the Conservatives' years in government, through changing lifestyles and making choices about healthy and unhealthy behaviours. But, at the same time there has come a renewed awareness that there are health problems associated with factors such as low educational standards, poor housing conditions, poverty and unemployment, and that there are links between social inequality and inequalities in health. However, the strength and relationships of these factors is not always clear, and this in turn means that determining the appropriate policy response to health inequalities remains problematic.

## Private health provision

As noted earlier, during the 1970s and 1980s there was a significant increase in the number of people covered by private health insurance. However, following Labour's return to government in 1997 private health provision scarcely emerged as an issue. It is also worth noting that despite the growth in private health since the 1980s, the proportion of expenditure on healthcare that comes from the public purse in the UK remains significantly higher in the UK (86.3 per cent in 2004, up from 82.2 per cent in 2001) than in many other countries, for example France 78.4 in 2004 (compared with 76.0 per cent in 2001), Germany 76.9 per cent in 2004 (74.9 per cent in 2001), Italy 75.1 per cent in 2004 (75.3 per cent in 2001) and the USA 44.7 in 2004 (44.8 in 2001); indeed, following recent increases the proportion of expenditure on healthcare in the UK that comes from the public sector is actually higher than it was in 1960 (85.2 per cent) (OECD, 2006).

Despite the apparent dominance of NHS provision, however, expenditure on private healthcare remains significant. Although there are other forms of spending on private health, such as for over-the-counter treatments, NHS user charges (such as for dentistry and prescriptions), and payments for private operations, for most people the most obvious form is private medical insurance. After a period of stability during the 1990s the number of people with private health insurance rose by 5 per cent between 1999 and 2000, although this was due to cover paid for by companies, as the number of individual subscribers actually fell at the same time (Office of National Statistics, 2002). A number of social divisions are reflected in the take-up of private medical insurance, and Wallis (2004) draws on evidence from the British Household Panel Survey to show that men are more likely to be covered than women, that people with higher incomes are much more likely to be covered than those with lower incomes, and that people aged up to 34 and over 75 are less likely to be covered than those aged between 35 and 74 (younger people may feel to be less in need of health care, while older people are likely to face the constraints of higher premiums), while those who report their health as poor are less likely to have private medical insurance than those who report their health as good. There are also significant geographical differences, with London, the south and the south-west having the higher levels of private medical insurance coverage and Wales and Scotland the lowest.

It is also worth noting that critics of the Labour government have identified what they see as a variety of forms of 'privatisation' of healthcare, ranging from the use of the Private Finance Initiative, discussed earlier in this chapter, through the outsourcing of primary care services to the private sector and to social enterprises and the use of Independent Sector Treatment Centres (of which there were 24 in mid 2007), and the tendering of a range of other services.

## Devolution

The future development of health policy was also affected by Labour's delivery of its commitment to devolution for Scotland and Wales, and the creation of the Northern Ireland Assembly. As with some other aspects of social policy, health policy and the organisation of the NHS have always differed between the component parts of the United Kingdom, but the devolved administrations in Scotland and Wales were each given powers over the NHS in their countries and as a result there have been quite different approaches and emphases in recent years. Simply considering this in structural terms, in Scotland the government has its own Department for Health and Community care, which oversees the work of 15 area health boards. In an attempt to encourage integration of service delivery the Department is also responsible for some other aspects of social policy, and in particular for community care. Similarly, the Welsh Cabinet has a member responsible for Health and Social Services, including the NHS in Wales, with 22 health boards having been created with boundaries that are coterminous with local authorities. In Northern Ireland health and social care have long been overseen by integrated health and social services boards. One result of devolution, as has been noted elsewhere in this book, is that it has brought with it more potential for much greater diversity of approaches to the provision of healthcare, and even over the relatively short period of time since the devolved administrations came into being in

1999 it is possible to identify significant departures across the four governments (for example, introduction of foundation hospitals only in England, the abolition of prescription charges in Wales from April 2007, and the decision in Scotland in 2000 to provide free personal care for older people (see also Chapter 12)), a situation that is likely to increase as they come under the control of different political parties. At the same time, there is the possibility of good practice to spread from one part of the United Kingdom to another, and for measures adopted in by one administration to lead to greater pressure for similar measures in another, as was arguably the case when Scotland banned smoking in public places from March 2006, followed by Wales and Northern Ireland in April 2007, and finally England in July 2007.

## Conclusion

The provision of healthcare and the role of the National Health Service remain central issues in the United Kingdom, yet, despite the commitment of all of the major political parties to the NHS, there remain a range of challenges, particularly in relation to the funding of the service. After years of stagnating funding New Labour has significantly increased the level of resources devoted to the NHS, but while there have been some improvements, such as a general reduction in waiting times for hospital treatments it is far from clear that these have yet resulted in the major steps forward that the government had hoped for. There also continued to be disagreement about the way in which the NHS should be structured, with major questions over how it can be made to be more responsive to the needs of individuals.

Inequalities in health remain an area of concern, with socio-economic and environmental factors being major influences on the well-being of individuals and groups, as well as on the ability to access services.

## Summary

This chapter has outlined the development of health policy in Britain and has examined some of the major issues around healthcare and health promotion including:

- Continued significant reforms of the NHS throughout its existence, and particularly from the 1970s onwards, with governments seeking to improve efficiency, management, accountability and responsiveness, as well as to control expenditure.

- The perennial problem of meeting demand for healthcare, and in particular the level of funding for the National Health Service, with governments having sought to tackle this in a variety of ways, with New Labour having made significant financial commitments from 1999 onwards to bring spending to more than the EU average.

- Although the NHS dominates health expenditure in the UK there remains a significant private sector, accounting for more than 15 per cent of expenditure and with around 7 million people covered by private health insurance.

- The role of primary care, with successive governments seeking to shift the emphasis of healthcare away from hospital-based provision to primary care, initially under the Conservatives through new contracts for GPs and dentists and the creation of GP fundholders, and then under Labour through Primary Care Trusts.

- Evidence of the persistence, and even widening, of health inequalities, including those grounded in economic, environmental and social factors. The White Paper *Our Healthier Nation* saw shifts towards some recognition of the importance of these factors and established targets for the reduction of the death rate in four key areas. However, the 2004 Wanless Report again highlighted these and despite the White Paper *Choosing Health*, critics continued to question the government's emphasis on reducing mortality rather than morbidity, its commitment to reducing health inequalities and its willingness to tackle producer interests such as the alcohol and tobacco industries.

## Discussion and review topics

1 How true is it that the National Health Service is really a 'national treatment service'?

2 Since 1997 the level of funding for the NHS has increased significantly. How successful has this been in improving the availability and quality of provision?

3 What are the strengths and weaknesses of the arguments for and against the use of private investment in the National Health Service?

4 Inequalities in health remain a significant problem in the United Kingdom. Why have governments found it so difficult to tackle these?

## Further reading

Baggott, R. (2004) *Health and Health Care in Britain*, Palgrave, Basingstoke. This book gives a good overview of contemporary health policy.

Baggott, R. (2007) *Understanding Health Policy*, Policy Press, Bristol. A useful introduction to how health policy is made and implemented and it relates many of the ideas from Chapter 3 to this topic.

Ham, C. (2004) *Health Policy in Britain*, Palgrave, Basingstoke. The fifth edition of this useful work which provides a thorough coverage of many aspects of health policy.

Wanless, D. (2003) *Securing Good Health for the Whole Population: Population Health Trends*, HM Treasury, London. An analysis of health inequalities and future health trends undertaken to inform Wanless's final report to HM Treasury in 2004.

## Some useful websites

www.dh.gov.uk – provides information on the work of the Department of Health, policies, publications and a wide range of statistics.

www.hsj.co.uk – the website of the *Health Service Journal* includes up-to-date articles on a variety of health policy and health management topics.

**www.kingsfund.org.uk** – the King's Fund website not only provides access to information and publications on the Fund's own work, but also has links to a large number of other organisations.

**www.nhs.uk** – this is the official gateway to the websites of NHS organisations in England (see also **www.n-i.nhs.uk**, **www.show.scot.nhs.uk** and **www.wales.nhs.uk**).

**www.oecd.org** – the Organisation for Economic Cooperation and Development provides a range of information on health (and other subject areas) that allows comparisons between its member states.

## References

Acheson, D. (1998) *Independent Inquiry into Inequalities of Health: Report*, Stationery Office, London.

Allen, G. (2001) *House of Commons Library Research Paper 01/117: The Private Finance Initiative*, House of Commons, London.

Baggott, R. (2000) *Public Health: Policy and Politics*, Palgrave, Basingstoke.

Black Report (1980) *Inequalities in Health*, Department of Health and Social Security, London.

British Medical Association (2007) *A Rational Way Forward for the NHS in England*, BMA, London.

Department of Health (1989) *Working for Patients*, HMSO, London.

Department of Health (1992) *The Health of the Nation*, Stationery Office, London.

Department of Health (1997) *The new NHS: modern, dependable*, Cm 3807, Stationery Office, London.

Department of Health (1998a) *Our Healthier Nation*, Stationery Office, London.

Department of Health (1998b) *Smoking Kills. A White Paper on Tobacco*, Stationery Office, London.

Department of Health (2000) *The NHS Plan: A plan for investment, a plan for reform*, Cm 4818-1, Stationery Office, London.

Department of Health (2006) 'Progress of new hospital schemes approved to go ahead', Department of Health, London, **www.dh.gov.uk/en/Procurementandproposals/Publicprivatepartnership/Privatefinanceinitiative/index.htm**, accessed 19 June 2007.

Enthoven, A. (1985) *Reflections on the Management of the NHS*, Nuffield Provincial Hospitals Trust, London.

Ham, C. (2004) *Health Policy in Britain*, Palgrave Macmillan, Basingstoke.

King's Fund Institute (1988) *Health Finance: Assessing the Option*, King's Fund Institute, London.

Klein, R. (2005) 'Transforming the NHS: The story in 2004', in M. Powell, L. Bauld, and K. Clarke (eds) *Social Policy Review 17*, Policy Press, Bristol.

Le Grand, J., Mays, N. and Mulligan, J. (eds) (1998) *Learning from the NHS Internal Market*, King's Fund, London.

OECD (2006) *OECD Health Data 2006*, OECD, Paris.

Office of National Statistics (2002) *Social Trends 32*, Stationery Office, London.

Reuter, P. and Stevens, A. (2007) *An Analysis of UK Drug Policy*, UK Drug Policy Commission, London.

Social Services Select Committee (1986) *Public Expenditure on the Social Services*, HMSO, London.

Social Services Select Committee (1988) *Resourcing the National Health Service*, HMSO, London.

Wallis, G. (2004) 'The demand for private medical insurance', *Economic Trends 606*, Office for National Statistics, London, pp. 46–56.

Wanless, D. (2002) *Securing our Future Health: Taking a Long-Term View*, HM Treasury, London.

Wanless, D. (2004) *Securing Good Health for the Whole Population*, Stationery Office, London.

# 16

# Housing

Brian Lund

## Chapter overview

In contrast to education and healthcare, ability to pay has always been the main criterion for distributing houses. Nonetheless, during the twentieth century, the recognition that many people could not afford 'adequate' accommodation helped to stimulate state intervention in the housing market. State involvement reached its zenith in the mid 1970s but, since the early 1980s, state action has been concentrated on promoting home ownership, mitigating the extreme outcomes of the housing market and, since 2003, on attempting to stimulate housing supply.

This chapter will examine:

- the reasons why the state has intervened in the housing market;
- why and how the state was 'rolled back' from housing provision in the 1980s and 1990s;
- the nature of the tenure structure in the United Kingdom;
- the relationships between housing policy, social exclusion, homelessness and neighbourhood deprivation;
- the impact of devolution on housing policies;
- the links between housing and community care;
- the relationships between housing and the ecosystem;
- the impact of the housing system on inequality.

## Spotlight on the issues
### Causes of homelessness

Each local authority in England has to submit returns to the Department for Communities and Local Government giving the number of households living in the temporary accommodation because the household is 'statutorily homeless'. In 1997 44,870 such households were living in temporary accommodation but, by 2005, the number had soared to 101,020. Many would claim that this increase in homelessness was a consequence of the failure to match housing supply – especially 'affordable' housing supply – to housing demand. However, in 2005 New Labour promised a 'new approach to tackling homelessness which focused on people's personal problems rather than just structural bricks and mortar causes' (Office of the Deputy Prime Minister, 2005b: 13). This concentration on the 'personal problems' of homeless people rather than the 'structural' impact of the housing market reflects a long-standing debate on housing problems that is echoed in this chapter. Are housing problems caused by the operations of the housing market or by the personal problems of those who experience difficulties in securing adequate housing?

Clearly housing is a very important and emotive issue, with direct relevance for almost everybody, and problems with housing, whether viewed as arising from personal or structural reasons, can be significant challenges for individuals and for governments. Recent years, for example, have seen significant swings in the housing market, and these generate winners and losers. The level and impact of state intervention in the housing market and the role of governments in responding to housing problems is, unsurprisingly, one of the themes of this chapter.

## State intervention in the housing market

In the nineteenth century, the ideas of 'classical' economists such as Adam Smith influenced thinking about 'the housing issue'. They believed that housing was a **commodity** with no intrinsic merit: a dwelling's value is its exchange price as determined by the interaction between supply and demand. Consumers have different views about how much to spend on housing and different preferences about the style, location and amenities of the dwellings they want to occupy. Thus the free market should determine its supply and distribution.

The '**laissez-faire**' approach was revived in the 1960s by 'neo-classical' economists who asserted that state intervention in the housing market during the twentieth century had generated more problems than it had solved (Hayek, 1960; Pennance, 1969). 'Neo-classical' economists, sometimes called the '**New Right**', are prepared to allow only two exceptions to the general maxim that the state should 'leave to be'. These are to take action to remedy '**externalities**' – the effects of a use decision by one set of parties on others whose interests are not taken into account in the transaction – and to permit an income subsidy to the poor to enable them to afford a minimum housing standard supplied by the private sector. However, other economists claim that extensive state intervention in the housing market is necessary because housing has special characteristics that, taken together, indicate that a free housing market would operate inefficiently and produce hardship. They maintain that housing supply is unresponsive to changes in demand because land is an absolute scarce resource made scarcer by planning controls, the existing housing stock is immobile and there is a long production time in constructing new dwellings (LeGrand, Popper and Robinson 1984; Glennerster, 2003). Moreover, houses are expensive relative to average incomes, so, in a free market, those on low incomes would be unable to afford the decent homes necessary for full participation in civic life.

## Regulation and 'nuisance' removal

In the nineteenth century, as part of its developing role in promoting public health by eliminating 'externalities', local government acquired powers to regulate building standards, control overcrowding and remove the 'nuisances' of individual unfit dwellings and 'slum' areas that were perceived as threats to public health and public order. However, local government's role in providing new homes was strictly limited. It was not until the Housing of the Working Classes Act 1890 that local authorities obtained a clear power to build homes and then only on condition that they did not make a loss on any scheme. Subsidised housing was regarded as the domain of the voluntary, housing association sector, the 'subsidy' being donations from wealthy benefactors or a 'philanthropic' agreement to limit the return on investment to 5 per cent.

## Subsidised council housing and rent control

A specific housing issue, distinct from concerns about the 'slum' threat and the impact of inadequate water supply and poor sanitation on public health, started to emerge at the end of the nineteenth century. The 1891 census included questions on the number of people and rooms in a dwelling and this allowed the housing shortage to be quantified. Government inquiries indicated that clearing slums without replacement new homes at 'affordable' rents had compounded overcrowding (Royal Commission on the Housing of the Working Classes, 1885) and the emerging labour movement questioned whether market capitalism had the capacity to supply the dwellings necessary to overcome the housing shortage.

A range of solutions to 'the housing question' were on offer at the turn of the century. Octavia Hill's belief in managing both people and dwellings retained many followers. She thought that tenants contributed to their poor housing conditions by ill-disciplined behaviour and her housing administration system was to combine managing reconditioned older property with reforming the characters of her tenants. This was to be achieved through the personal influence of a housing worker making regular home visits and applying sanctions and incentives to promote good behaviour. Subsidised local authority housing had some supporters, but many trade unionists regarded subsidies as a 'dole', unsuited to the 'independent' working man. The land issue was at the heart of the most radical proposals. In *Garden Cities of Tomorrow* (1902) Ebenezer Howard argued that cheap land in rural areas could be used to build garden cities where citizens could enjoy the benefits of both town and country. The 'New Liberalism' and the Labour movement concentrated on land taxation, asserting that taxing land at its site value would prevent land hoarding and, by depressing the price of land, make houses cheaper. However, New Towns and land taxation had little impact on the solutions to the 'housing problem' adopted at the end of the First World War.

The First World War was a watershed in British housing policy. With house building terminated until the war was over, even the most ardent free market economist could not argue that supply would meet demand. Rent increases in Clydeside prompted rent strikes and, in 1915, the government responded by freezing rents and giving tenants **security of tenure**. The Conservatives, in office for most of the interwar period, attempted to back-out of **rent control** gradually. New building for rent was decontrolled soon after the end of the war and, by 1939, dwellings with a high rateable value had been decontrolled and houses with middle range rateable values became decontrolled on vacant possession. Low-value houses – about 44 per cent of the total rented stock – remained controlled.

Rent control helped to promote subsidised state housing. If rents were to be controlled at below market level how could the private sector supply sufficient homes when it had failed even under free market conditions? The Housing and Town Planning Act 1919 introduced a central state subsidy to local authorities to encourage them to build houses. Such subsidies to housing 'producers' remained a central pillar of housing policy for 60 years with the central government using subsidy variations to direct local authorities to build either for 'general' needs to increase the overall housing stock or for the 'specific' needs arising from slum clearance and severe overcrowding. Building for 'general needs' was dominant from 1919 to 1933 and 1945 to 1955 whereas slum clearance received priority from 1933 to 1939 and from 1955 to 1979. Dwellings designed for 'general' needs were usually of good quality but those erected for former slum dwellers were often flats with poor amenities.

## Other forms of state intervention in the housing market

Subsidised council housing and rent control were the main mechanisms of housing policy but the state also intervened in the housing market in other ways. In 1955 the Minister for Housing and Local Government urged all local authorities to protect any land acquired around their towns and cities by the formal designation of clearly defined green belts under the powers contained in the Town and Country Planning Act 1947. Such green belts were intended to check the unrestricted sprawl of the built-up areas and to safeguard the surrounding countryside. There were major slum clearance 'drives' in the 1930s, 1950s, 1960s and 1970s. Mandatory improvement grants for basic amenities and tax concessions, especially tax relief on mortgage interest, stimulated home ownership. The idea of improvement areas, first used by local authorities under the Housing Act 1930, was revived in the 1970s. This neighbourhood-based housing action was aimed at encouraging property owners to invest in improvement in the knowledge that their neighbours would also invest. Such simultaneous action would boost the area's image and thereby stimulate further investment.

 Thought provoker

A traditional concern of housing policy has been to establish and promote minimum housing standards. However, establishing such minimum standards is difficult. Try to define:

(a) homelessness

(b) overcrowding

(c) a house unfit for human habitation.

## Conservative housing policy, 1979-1997: state to market: market to state

### Local authority housing

Between 1915 and 1979 state intervention in the housing market helped to transform the United Kingdom tenure structure (Figure 16.1). Until the mid 1970s, the Conservative Party adopted a pragmatic approach to council housing. In contrast to the Labour Party, which supported extensive council building for 'general needs', the Conservatives were willing to subsidise high density housing within the conurbations for those displaced by slum clearance but were prepared to assist local authorities to build homes for 'general needs' only in times when housing was extremely scarce. By the mid 1970s a 'New Right' critique of council housing had developed that claimed:

- a local authority monopoly of rented accommodation for families produced inefficient management;

- subsidies create a 'featherbedded', 'dependent' tenant: in 1979 Margaret Thatcher, in replying to a tenant who had complained about the condition of her property, said:

  > I hope you will not think me too blunt if I say that it may well be that your council accommodation is unsatisfactory but considering the fact you have been unable to buy your own accommodation you are lucky to have been given something which the rest of us are paying for out of our taxes.        (Quoted in *The Times*, 9 April 1979)

- subsidised council housing, let at below market rent levels, prevented the development of a flourishing private landlord sector because tenants expected rents to be lower than the levels necessary to attract investors to supply private rented accommodation;

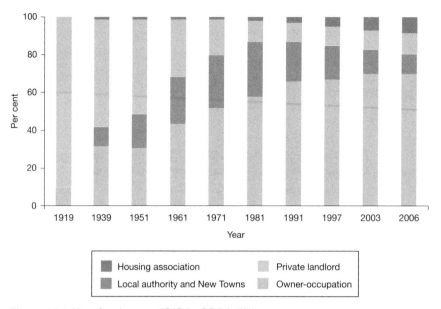

**Figure 16.1 Housing tenure, 1919 to 2006 (UK)**

*Source*: Based on Holmans (2000) and Department for Communities and Local Government (2007a),
www.communities.gov.uk/documents/housing/xls/table-101.

- local authority housing, let at 'sub-market' rents, allowed low-income groups to live in expensive areas and thereby created an unlimited demand for council housing (Hayek, 1960).

The right to buy was the flagship of Conservative housing policy (Figure 16.2). Selling council houses was not a new idea but the Housing Act 1980 gave local authority tenants a statutory right to buy at a substantial discount. The Housing Act 1988 and the Local Government and Housing Act 1989 marked further steps to eclipse council housing. This legislation gave the government the power to control the rents set by individual local authorities and allowed council tenants to choose to transfer their dwellings to another landlord. It also permitted the government to establish Housing Action Trusts that would take ownership of a council estate from a local authority, renovate the dwellings, and then sell them to 'alternative' landlords. However, tenants showed little interest in choosing an 'alternative' landlord and Housing Action Trusts gained modest momentum only when tenants were allowed to return to their local authority when their estate had been improved. Unexpectedly, the main mechanism by which the council housing stock was reduced, other than the right to buy, was voluntary transfer, with some local authorities willingly transferring their dwellings to a housing association, often specially created to facilitate stock transfer. By 1997 the proportion of households renting from a local authority had declined to 17 per cent and the sector was becoming increasingly 'residualised' with higher proportions of tenants without work and with a low income (Hills, 2007).

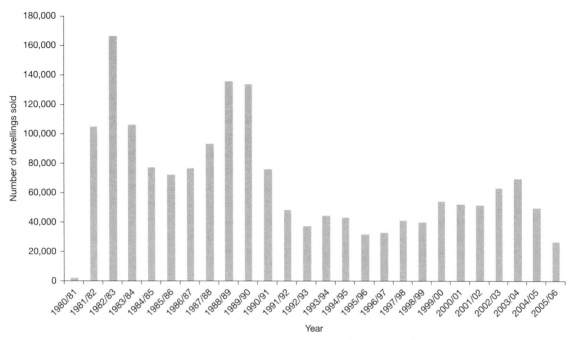

**Figure 16.2** Right to buy sales, England: 1980/81 to 2005/6

*Source*: Department for Communities and Local Government (2007b), www.communities.gov.uk/pub/231/Table670_id1502231.xls.

## Consumer and producer subsidies

Historically, the state has subsidised housing by giving grants to producers (local authorities and, since 1974, housing associations). These organisations usually used their subsidies to reduce the general rent levels charged to tenants. In contrast, consumer subsidies go directly to tenants. Housing Benefit is now the major form of consumer subsidy. Between 1979 and 1996 producer subsidies were reduced and some of the savings were directed towards Housing Benefit which also became more selective. In 1986 the 'taper' – the rate Housing Benefit is reduced for each pound of income above a set threshold – was increased from 29 per cent to 65 per cent (Hills, 1992) with the result that Housing Benefit now makes a major contribution to the 'poverty trap' – the work disincentives involved in a loss of benefits because of a decision to enter the workforce or work longer. In addition, the cuts in producer subsidies in the 1980s and early 1990s pushed rents upwards. The aim was to create a level playing field in rented accommodation with Housing Benefit 'taking the strain' for low-income households. Nicholas Ridley, the Minister responsible for housing at the time, explained the reform:

> Absurdly low rents and a monopoly position in providing rented housing allowed some coun-
> cils to make their tenants entirely dependent upon them . . . I saw the solution as being to pro-
> vide housing benefit on a sufficiently generous scale to enable all tenants to be in a position

to pay their rents, and at the same time to bring rents up towards market levels. This would put all classes of landlords - councils, housing associations and private, landlords - into the same competitive position.

Ridley (1992, pp. 87-8)

## Private landlords

In 1914 nine out of every ten households were rented from a private landlord. By 1979 this had been reduced to one in ten – a consequence of rent control, unfavourable tax treatment compared to home ownership and slum clearance programmes. In the 1980s the Conservatives attempted to revive private landlordism by removing rent controls on new private sector lettings, ending long-term security of tenure, introducing new tax concessions and allowing housing associations to manage property on behalf of private landlords. These measures helped to halt the decline of the private landlord sector and its share of the housing stock increased by 1 per cent between 1987 and 1997.

## Housing associations

After the First World War, **housing associations**, voluntary organisations concerned with providing rented accommodation on a not-for-profit basis, were eclipsed by local authorities but, in the 1960s and the 1970s, Conservative and Labour governments started to provide loans and grants to foster the development of housing associations as vehicles for renovating older property and building new homes. The Housing Act 1988 changed the nature of housing associations. Renamed 'registered social landlords', they were to have more in common with private landlords than local authorities. Their properties were to be let within the same legal framework as private landlords, they would borrow a larger share of their capital from the financial markets and a higher proportion of their revenue would come from higher rents supported by Housing Benefit. Suitably transformed, the registered social landlord sector expanded rapidly in the 1990s. By 1997, registered social landlords owned 5 per cent of the housing stock and had become involved in promoting low-cost home ownership schemes.

## Home ownership

Margaret Thatcher's respect for market economics was matched by her commitment to home ownership. The Conservatives promoted owner occupation by discounts on the market value of dwellings sold under the right to buy, the continuance of tax relief on mortgage interest and direct subsidies to registered social landlords to promote low-cost home ownership schemes. However, the early 1990s were difficult years for home owners. House prices increased rapidly in the mid 1980s but subsequent increases in interest rates and a recession meant that more people were unable to meet their mortgage commitments. House prices fell, leaving many homeowners with 'negative equity' – a debt greater than the current value of their dwelling.

## New Labour and housing policy

### 'Social housing'

Traditionally the Labour Party has supported council housing, but New Labour's 1997 manifesto promised only to promote 'a three-way partnership between the public, private and housing association sectors to promote good social housing' (Labour Party, 1997, p. 26). The term '**social housing**' – used to describe housing let at below market levels and allocated, at least in part, according to 'need' – was adopted by New Labour to blur the distinction between registered social landlords and local authorities and to promote stock transfer from local government. Very few new council houses have been built under New Labour and, until recently, housing production by registered social landlords has been low (see Figure 16.3). However, the Green Paper *Homes for the future: more affordable, more sustainable* (Department for Communities and Local Government, 2007d) announced that, by 2010–11, 'social housing' supply would increase to 45,000 per annum through additional government finance, encouraging housing associations to use their assets and allowing local government to have a larger role in house-building via local housing companies, arm's length management organisations and direct building.

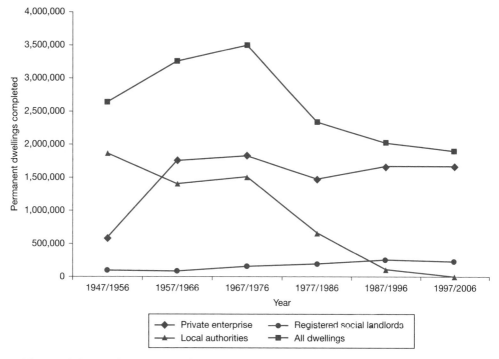

**Figure 16.3** Housing construction 1947 to 2006 (ten-year cycles) United Kingdom

*Source*: Department for Communities and Local Government (2007c), www.communities.gov.uk/pub/57/ Table241_id1156057.xls.

361

### Stock transfer and decent homes

New Labour promoted stock transfer by linking it to the achievement of 'decent' homes. A target was set to ensure that all 'social housing' met the decent homes standard by 2010. In order to be 'decent' a home should be warm, weatherproof and have 'reasonably modern facilities' defined mainly in terms of the age of the bathroom and the kitchen. Meeting this standard would require local authorities to allocate substantial resources to council housing, but central government applied tight constraints on local authority borrowing and rent levels. This meant that local authorities had to investigate three avenues for securing extra resources set out by central government, all of which brought additional central government assistance. A few selected the Private Finance Initiative, more preferred an arm's length management organisation and many opted for partial or full stock transfer to a registered social landlord.

Despite tenant resistance in some areas, 459,578 dwellings were transferred from local government between 2001 and 2006 (Department for Communities and Local Government, 2007e). This stock transfer has contributed to a fall in the number of 'social' sector homes failing to meet the decent homes standard – down by over a million since 1996 (Department for Communities and Local Government, 2007f).

### Choice-based lettings

In 2004 a policy objective that all local authorities should be running a choice-based lettings system by 2010 was set, and registered social landlords were encouraged to join such schemes. Choice-based lettings usually involve allocating 'currency' in the form of priority bandings and then advertising vacant properties on websites or local newspapers. Prospective tenants 'bid' for a property and, if unsuccessful, are informed of their relative priority for a particular property type in a particular area. Choice-based lettings mimic the market, with 'consumers' learning about supply and demand in the social rented market.

## Private landlords

Between 1997 and 2005 347,000 dwellings were added to the private landlord sector, far more than in the eighteen years of Conservative governance. In part this expansion reflected New Labour's friendly approach to private landlords thereby securing the necessary political consensus for long-term investment. The 2000 housing Green Paper outlined a role for private renting and set out New Labour's welcoming attitude:

> A healthy private rented sector provides additional housing choices for people who do not want to, or are not ready to, buy their own homes. It is a particularly important resource for younger households. Through its flexibility and speed of access, it can also help to oil the wheels of the housing and labour markets . . . We therefore want the sector to grow and prosper . . .
>
> Department of the Environment, Transport and the Regions/Department of Social Security, 2000, sections 5:1 and 5:2

Although New Labour's 1997 manifesto had promised private landlord tenants 'protection where most needed' by 'a proper system of licensing by local authorities which will benefit tenants and responsible landlords alike', this did not become law until the 2004 Housing Act. When the legislation was implemented, apart from the introduction in 2007 of mandatory Tenancy Deposit Protection Schemes, the regulation was 'light touch' and targeted on landlords operating in 'stress' areas and dwellings in multiple occupation.

'Buy-to-let' was the principal driver in the growth of private landlordism. In 1996 a consortium of mortgage lenders launched 'buy-to-let' loans, lending to private landlords on terms close to those offered to owner occupiers. The number of buy-to-let loans outstanding had reached 938,500 by 2007, up from 28,700 in 1998 and between 2004 and 2006 the number of dwellings rented from private landlords increased faster than owner-occupation – 236,000 compared to 181,000 (Department for Communities and Local Government, 2007g).

## Home ownership

House prices started to increase in 1994 and a decline in interest rates allowed the Conservatives to withdraw some of the tax relief on mortgage interest in order to reduce the **Public Sector Borrowing Requirement**. New Labour completed the process of withdrawing tax relief on mortgage interest but, despite this subsidy loss and increases in Stamp Duty Tax, house prices increased rapidly.

Concerns about the 'affordability' of home ownership, especially for first-time buyers, promoted three policy initiatives. New Labour attempted to improve the efficiency of the housing transfer process by starting to introduce 'Home Information Packs' giving potential buyers information on the characteristics of the house they are intending to buy. Various low-cost home ownership initiatives, mainly directed at 'key workers' in areas where house prices were exceptionally high, were reformulated under the 'Homebuy' label to provide a range of avenues into home ownership via equity sharing. However the main policy initiative was an attempt to stimulate housing construction that, in England, had slumped to a post-war low of 129,992 in 2001/2.

*Sustainable Communities: Building for the future* (Office of the Deputy Prime Minister, 2003) identified a housing shortage in the south-east where housing construction was well below government targets. Investment in four 'growth areas' (the Thames Gateway, Ashford, Milton Keynes–South Midlands and the London–Stansted–Cambridge corridor) was announced and Kate Barker was appointed to examine ways to deliver stability in the housing market and meet our future housing needs. Her report (Barker, 2004) recommended a step change in housing supply to be achieved by reforming the planning system, setting national and regional affordability targets that, if unmet, would trigger land release and an examination of a planning–gain supplement to capture some of the enhanced value resulting from planning permission.

The Green Paper *Homes for the future: more affordable, more sustainable* (Department for Communities and Local Government, 2007d) summarised the government's plans to expand housing supply and thereby make housing more affordable. It stated that overall housing supply needed to be increased because the latest (2004-based) household projections showed that the number of households was projected to grow by 223,000 a year until 2026 and housing supply had not kept pace with household formation. As a consequence 'house prices have doubled in real terms over the last 10 years' (Department for Communities and Local Government, 2007d, p. 17). Moreover:

> On average, lower quartile house prices are now more than seven times lower quartile earnings . . . [and] rising house prices create pressure for first-time buyers. Nearly 40% of first-time buyers under 30 now depend on help from family or friends to get them started on the housing ladder. In London an assisted young first-time buyer had an average deposit of £57,000 compared to £12,500 for unassisted young first-time buyers.
>
> Department for Communities and Local Government, 2007d, p. 19

To meet the shortfall, housing supply is scheduled to increase over time to 240,000 in 2016 and then continue at about 240,000 per annum until 2020. Two million additional homes are planned by 2016, three million by 2020. The mechanisms by which overall housing supply will be pushed to 240,000 by 2016 include five new 'eco-towns' and continuing infrastructure finance to both existing 'growth areas' (with a new one in the north) and 'growth points'. Surplus government sites will be allocated for housing and local authorities will be encouraged to allocate land by a Housing and Planning Delivery Grant plus a threat that, if a local authority does not allocate sufficient land for a rolling five-year house-building programme, developers will find it easy to obtain planning permission. Existing low-cost home ownership schemes will be boosted by offering a 17.5 per cent government equity loan which can be used with any lender.

## Sustainable homes

The ecological dimension of 'sustainable homes' relates to housing 'which meets the needs of the present without compromising the ability of future generations to meet their own needs' (World Commission on the Environment and Development, 1988). Carbon dioxide emissions from the domestic housing sector contribute around 27 per cent of the total carbon dioxide output in the UK and, in addition, there are associated concerns such as 'urban sprawl' and the wasteful use of water.

The policy, pursued since the late 1990s, of building at higher densities on **brownfield** sites contributes to sustainability by reducing the loss of 'green fields' and minimising the overall 'ecological footprint' of residents by concentrating their activities. However, prompted by the development of 'an overwhelming body of scientific evidence that indicates that climate change is a serious and urgent issue' (Department for Communities and Local Government, 2007h, p. 4) and criticisms that its proposals to boost housing supply neglected the environment (Friends of the Earth, 2005, House of Commons Environmental Audit Committee, 2006), New Labour has gradually developed a policy on housing and the environment. Initially a 'Code for Sustainable Homes' measuring the sustainability of a home against key design categories – voluntary for the private sector but mandatory for housing associations – was issued, but the Green Paper *Homes for the Future: more affordable, more sustainable* (Department for Communities and Local Government, 2007d) proposed a phased enhancement of the building regulations so that, by 2016, all new homes will be 'zero carbon', defined as 'over a year, the net carbon emissions from all energy use in the home would be zero' (Department for Communities and Local Government, 2007h, p. 4).

In addition the Green Paper announced that new zero carbon homes would be exempt from stamp duty and five eco-towns would be created. Eco-towns will be new small towns of at least 5–20,000 homes which will have a mixed community consisting of a variety of tenures and house sizes. They will be 'places with a separate identity but with good links to surrounding towns and cities in terms of jobs, transport and services' and 'the development as a whole will achieve zero carbon' and 'be an exemplar in at least one area of environmental technology' (Department for Communities and Local Government, 2007i, p. 4).

With regard to existing homes the 'decent homes' standard for the social sector that includes energy efficiency measures and the 'Warm Front' grants to the over 60s have helped to protect the environment. Home Information Packs, with their Energy Efficiency Certificates are designed to make home owners more energy conscious but, overall, there is a dearth of fiscal incentives to mitigate the ecological impact of existing homes.

## Controversy and debate

There is a political consensus that housing production in the United Kingdom needs to be substantially increased to keep pace with the estimated 223,000 per annum new households that will form up to 2026, slow down house price inflation and make an impact on homelessness, overcrowding and local authority housing waiting lists - up by 600,000 between 2001 and 2006. But where are these new homes to be built? From the late 1990s it has been government policy to concentrate building on 'brownfield' (previously developed) sites to help boost city economies and reduce the pressure on 'greenfield' locations. In 2006 72 per cent of new development was on 'brownfield' sites compared to 56 per cent in 1997. However, the policy has had it downsides. Densities have increased from 25 per hectare in 1997 to 40 in 2005 (112 in London) meaning that far more flats and smaller houses with tiny gardens - unsuitable for families - have been built. Moreover, whereas some districts have a good supply of 'brownfield' land, other areas - where people can find work and want to live - have a shortage. Does this mean that in order to meet the demand for affordable 'family' homes, close to where well paid work is available, we need to release more greenfield sites perhaps by changing the boundaries of established green belts? Kate Barker thought so. In her review of land use planning she said:

If more land is likely to be required for development, the question arises of where it would be most environmentally sustainable to develop . . . the land that can be developed with the least likely environmental or wider social impact is low-value agricultural land with little landscape quality and limited public access. This will also often be near towns and cities. In part this is because urban fringe land is often run-down due to its location. But it is also because encouraging development away from major towns and cities has the effect of increasing average commuting distances, thereby increasing carbon emissions, as currently occurs when commuters 'jump' the green belt. Much of this land currently falls within green belt classification . . . However, the green belt now covers almost 13 per cent of England, and in light of the discussion above,

▶

regional and local planning bodies should review their green belt boundaries to ensure they remain relevant and appropriate and so ensure that planned development takes place in the most suitable location.

Barker (2006, p. 9)

However, the idea of releasing more greenfield sites and amending the green belts has met with strong opposition. Max Hastings, President of the Campaign to Protect Rural England, expressed the core of the argument against 'greenfield' development:

. . . when 72 per cent of forecast growth in households is for single occupancies, it is surely sensible to build only limited numbers of four-bedroom detached houses . . .

Politicians of all parties have become fixated with a belief that housing in this country is uniquely expensive. In reality, British spending on housing as a proportion of total household consumption is around the mid-mark for Europe, and well below that of Sweden, Germany and France. Our house-price inflation in 2004-5 was significantly less than that of many countries.

Following the 2004 Barker Report, the CPRE commissioned extensive independent research. This exposed the great myth on which the government's dash for development and assault on the planning system is based: that high house prices are the consequence of a development land famine. Prices in Australia and the US - countries with infinite space - have risen pretty much in line with ours, for the same reasons: low interest rates, rising incomes and falling enthusiasm for equity investments.

Hastings (2006)

What might the arguments be for and against building on certain sites within existing green belt boundaries?

## Housing Benefit

Lower unemployment and eligibility restrictions introduced by the Conservatives restrained the cost of Housing Benefit but expenditure was still over £11 billion in 2001. At first, New Labour concentrated on improving the administration of the existing scheme but, in 2002, the Department for Work and Pensions announced that a flat-rate, standard local housing allowance paid directly to the tenants would be introduced in the deregulated private rented sector. This reform would give 'a new deal for tenants' because:

Tenants who rent a property at below the standard allowance or who move to a cheaper property in their local area, or who negotiate to keep the rent below the standard allowance, will be able to keep the difference - putting the decision in their hands.

Department for Work and Pensions (2002, p. 4)

The standard local housing allowance was tested in nine 'pathfinder' areas and under the 2007 Welfare Reform Act, the government intends to roll out a national scheme – less generous than that piloted in the 'pathfinder' areas – phasing it in to new tenants. The 2004 Budget statement announced that a standard local allowance would be extended to social tenants 'when conditions were right' but a final decision on such an extension has been delayed (Department for Work and Pensions, 2006a).

**?** Thought provoker

As part of its agenda to reduce 'antisocial behaviour' New Labour suggested that tenants involved in such behaviour should lose their entitlement to Housing Benefit (Secretary of State for Work and Pensions, 2003). Later this proposal was modified to be available only in eight pilot schemes and applied only when a household had been evicted for antisocial behaviour and had subsequently refused to engage with the rehabilitation services offered. Why do you think that the original proposal was modified?

## Housing and social exclusion

The Social Exclusion Unit was established in 1998. It defined social exclusion as 'a shorthand term for what can happen when people or areas suffer from a combination of linked problems such as unemployment, poor skills, low incomes, poor housing, high crime environments, bad health and family breakdown' (Social Exclusion Unit, 2002). Two of its first three reports focused on housing.

### Neighbourhood renewal

The Social Exclusion Unit's report *Bringing Britain Together: A National Strategy for Neighbourhood Renewal* (1998a) concentrated on 'deprived neighbourhoods' rather than the 'problem council estates' that had been the focus of Conservative initiatives such as the Priority Estates Project and Estate Action. It stated:

> Poor neighbourhoods are not a pure housing problem. They are not all the same kind of design, they don't all consist of rented or council housing, and they are not all in towns and cities.
> Social Exclusion Unit (1998a, para. 1.2)

Several thousand poor neighbourhoods in England were identified, characterised by multiple problems coexisting in the same area. The Social Exclusion Unit attributed the failure of earlier programmes to a lack of 'joined-up' thinking and action, too many initiatives, a dearth of resident participation and a concentration on 'bricks and mortar' rather than on people. 'New Deal for Communities' was aimed at rectifying these perceived defects. It promised long-term funding for 39 'pathfinder' authorities to tackle high levels of crime, educational underachievement, poor health, and housing and the physical environment in an intensive and coordinated way with a high level of community involvement in identifying problems and devising solutions. New Deal for Communities was supplemented by other area-based initiatives including the Neighbourhood Renewal Fund (Social Exclusion Unit, 2001). This fund emphasised the importance of **local strategic partnerships** – bringing together local authorities, other public services, residents and private, voluntary and community sector organisations – and the idea of a manager to coordinate mainstream services at a neighbourhood level.

## Housing market renewal

The *Sustainable Communities Plan* (Office of the Deputy Prime Minister, 2003) identified a 'low-demand' problem in certain parts of the north and the Midlands and a Market Renewal Fund was established to which nine 'pathfinder' agencies had access. These 'pathfinders' covered about 60 per cent of the identified low-demand stock and the broad programme objective was to revitalise failing local housing markets by 'radical and sustained action to replace obsolete housing with modern sustainable accommodation, through demolition and new building or refurbishment' (Office of the Deputy Prime Minister, 2003, p. 5).

 *Controversy and debate*

### Are New Labour's Neighbourhood Renewal policies working?

*Progress on twenty 'unpopular' estates, 1980-2005: Turning the tide?* (Tunstall and Coulter, 2006), a report from the team that has tracked the progress of 20 council estates in England subject to various special initiatives since 1980, concluded that, although significant gaps remained on all measures and the gap on economic inactivity has increased, the differences between the estates and their local authorities and the national average had narrowed on a range of measures, for example employment, popularity and educational performance.

New Deal for Communities has struggled to make an impact. Many schemes found it difficult to generate community consensus around an action programme (Knutt, 2003) and the New Deal for Communities National Evaluation reported that there had been virtually no change in the proportion of residents wanting to move; 42 per cent of residents had little trust in NDC; 43 per cent thought that NDC has not improved their area and the programme had influenced only an extra 2 per cent into thinking that 'neighbours look out for each other' – disappointing given the NDC focused on fostering 'community spirit' (Department for Communities and Local Government, 2006a). However, New Deal for Communities, alongside other initiatives, has made an impact of the incidence of crime and the fear of crime in deprived neighbourhoods (Page, 2006).

The Market Renewal Initiative has been controversial with claims that, in certain areas, it is breaking up established communities and replacing affordable housing with more expensive stock. Low demand has been significantly reduced but whether this reflects the impact of the Market Renewal Initiative or overall change in the housing market is difficult to determine.

New Labour regards each specific initiative as interacting with other area-based programmes to produce an overall 'area effect' and hence it is inappropriate to rely only on specific programme evaluations. Given that New Labour's declared target is to narrow the gap between England's most deprived neighbourhoods and the rest of the country this benchmark is an apt criterion for measuring success. Unfortunately, there is a dearth of neighbourhood level statistics suitable for long-term outcome measurement. Thus, in its evaluation of success, New Labour relied on local authority-level indicators comparing the 88 most deprived local government areas with the rest of England (see Table 16.1).

**Table 16.1** The gap between deprived areas and the England average

| | Gap between deprived areas and England average ( − reduction, + increase) |
|---|---|
| Employment | −0.3 |
| Teenage conceptions | −1.0 |
| Female life expectancy | +0.1 |
| Male life expectancy | +0.1 |
| Vehicle crime | −1.3 |
| Robberies | −0.1 |
| Burglaries | −2.2 |
| Key Stage 2: Level 4 Maths | −3.3 |
| Key Stage 2: Level 4 English | −2.2 |
| GCSEs | −1.8 |

*Source*: Office of the Deputy Prime Minister (2005a) *Making it happen in neighbourhoods: The national strategy for neighbourhood renewal – four years on*, London, ODPM.

What has been the impact of New Labour's Neighbourhood Renewal Initiatives?

## Rough sleeping

In the late 1980s far more people, especially young people, were seen sleeping on the streets of London and other large cities across the UK. A new term, 'rough sleepers', entered the discourse on housing policy. The 'roughness' of the rough sleepers was seen as a threat to law and order. As Margaret Thatcher explained: 'Crowds of drunken, dirty, often abusive and sometimes violent men must not be allowed to turn central areas of the capital into no-go areas for ordinary citizens' (Thatcher, 1995, p. 603).

Initially the government's response to the increased visibility of single homelessness was to cut Housing Benefit so that it did not 'add to the already too evident lure of the big city for young people' (Thatcher, 1995, p. 603). However, the number of rough sleepers continued to increase and, in 1990, a Rough Sleepers Initiative was introduced aimed at contacting people sleeping rough in London, offering an emergency hostel place and then a 'move on' to permanent accommodation. This initiative reduced the number of people sleeping rough but street homelessness remained a highly visible problem throughout the 1990s.

New Labour's 1997 manifesto declared 'there is no more powerful symbol of Tory neglect in our society today than young people without homes living rough on the streets' (Labour Party, 1997, p. 26). A report by the Social Exclusion Unit estimated that, in June 1998, 1,850 people were sleeping rough in England. It stressed the 'personal troubles' of rough sleepers, pointing out, for example, that there was a high incidence of mental illness, alcohol problems and drug misuse among older rough sleepers. Many had experienced 'institutional' life with 50 per cent having been in prison, between 25 and 33 per cent in local authority care and 20 per cent in the armed forces (Social Exclusion Unit, 1998b).

A target was set to reduce the number of rough sleepers by two-thirds by 2002. A programme was introduced with the aim of encouraging rough sleepers to 'come in out of the cold'. Once in centres and free from the street homelessness culture they would be helped to find homes and jobs and overcome any drug or alcohol dependency. A Rough Sleeping Unit was set up to promote 'joined-up thinking', the Ministry of Defence was asked to review its discharge policies for members of the armed forces and the Home Office was required to examine how ex-prisoners are helped to find accommodation.

In late 2001 the government announced that it had reduced the number of rough sleepers in England to 532 – a notable achievement despite the doubts expressed about the accuracy of the count (White, 2001). Aided by the *The Homelessness (Priority Need for Accommodation) (England) Order 2002*, which extended the duties of local authorities to offer temporary accommodation to children aged 16 to 17, young people who had been in care and those vulnerable because of an 'institutionalised background', the number of rough sleepers counted in the national statistics remained below 600 between 2001 and 2006.

## Statutory homelessness

The National Assistance Act 1948 placed a duty on local authorities to provide 'temporary accommodation for persons in urgent need thereof, being need arising in circumstances that could not reasonably have been foreseen'. The duty to supply temporary accommodation fell on local authority welfare departments (the forerunners of social services departments), not housing departments. As was revealed in the television drama/documentary *Cathy Come Home*, first broadcast in 1966, most welfare departments interpreted their duties in a restricted way. They offered very poor accommodation for a limited period, separated partners and sometimes took the children of the homeless parents into local authority care. The Housing (Homeless Persons) Act 1977 was an attempt to ameliorate the circumstances of homeless families. The Act defined homelessness in terms of having no legal right to occupy accommodation. If a person accepted as homeless was in priority need, not intentionally homeless and had a local connection then the local housing authority had a duty to supply temporary accommodation while the local authority arranged permanent, secure accommodation. Despite restrictions on the obligations imposed on local authorities – people without children, for example, were not in 'priority need' unless 'vulnerable' because of age, mental illness/handicap or physical disability' – recorded homelessness soared in the 1980s. The Conservative government attributed the increase to the 'perverse incentives' inherent in the Housing (Homeless Persons) Act

1977. It asserted that, because legislation placed duties on local authorities to house the homeless families, then 'inevitably this makes the homelessness route seem a more attractive way into subsidised housing for those wishing to be re-housed' (Department of the Environment, 1994, p. 3). Thus, under the Housing Act 1996, local authorities became obliged to provide temporary accommodation only when satisfied that other suitable accommodation was not available. More-over, the allocation of local authority dwellings was divorced from the duty to provide accommodation for homeless people. Authorities had to offer dwellings only in accordance with guidelines incorporated in the Act. Homelessness was not included as a category of need for which 'reasonable preference' had to be given in allocating 'social housing' although homeless people might receive priority under other categories.

In opposition, New Labour condemned the Housing Act 1996. Its 1997 mani-festo promised to 'place a new duty on local authorities to protect those who are homeless through no fault of their own and are in priority need' (Labour Party, 1997, p. 23). However, significant change to the Housing Act 1996 had to wait until New Labour's second term. The Homelessness Act 2002 imposed a duty on local authorities to develop a homelessness strategy, abolished the two-year limit on the provision of temporary housing and made it unlawful for local authorities to discharge their duties simply by offering an assured shorthold tenancy in the private rented sector.

By 2005 statutory homelessness, as measured by the number of households in temporary accommodation, had reached record levels – a consequence of patterns of migration, increased household formation rates, low overall supply relative to demand reflected in the escalation in house prices and a reduction in the avail-ability of 'social housing' lettings – between 1996/7 and 2004/5 the number of let-tings available to social landlords in England declined from 561,000 to 354,000 (Wilcox, 2006). The government's response to the accelerating 'headline' home-lessness statistic was to restrict the terms on which tenants could buy their coun-cil houses, producing a scarp decline in right to buy sales, and promote a 'new approach to tackling homelessness which focused on people's personal problems rather than just structural bricks and mortar causes' (Office of the Deputy Prime Minister, 2005b, p. 13). Local authorities were encouraged to prevent homeless-ness by providing people with the ways and means to address their housing and other needs in order to avoid homelessness. A target was set to reduce the use of temporary accommodation by 50 per cent by 2010 and new 'Best Value' perform-ance indicators were introduced aimed at stimulating local authorities into adopt-ing a preventative approach. Local authorities introduced a number of schemes in response to the call to prevent homelessness applications. These included: inter-views prior to a formal homelessness assessment – often called 'housing options' – from which ways of dealing with an accommodation problem, other than desig-nation as homeless, might emerge; mediation with landlords/friends and rela-tives; tenancy support and 'sanctuary' schemes, often in the form of a safe room to offer protection from a violent partner. These schemes were remarkably suc-cessful in reducing the number of households in temporary accommodation (see Figure 16.4).

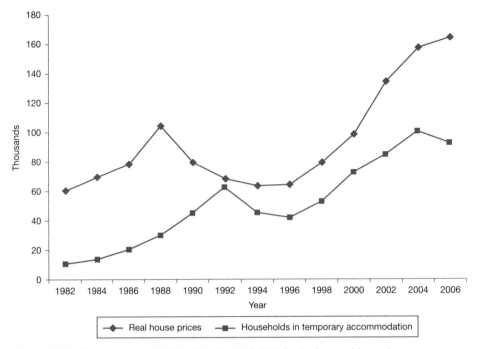

**Figure 16.4** House prices deflated by the Retail Price Index and homelessness, 1982-2006

*Source*: Based on Nationwide Building Society (2007), **www.nationwide.co.uk/hpi/historical/Jan_2007.pdf**; and Department for Communities and Local Government (2007j), **www.communities.gov.uk/pub/308/ Table623_id1156308.xls**.

# Devolution

In 1999, housing was included in the areas of responsibility devolved to the Scottish Parliament. The Scottish Parliament has legislative powers but limited tax-raising capacity and Housing Benefit, an important element of housing policy, is reserved for Westminster. The National Assembly for Wales, established in 1999, was granted neither primary legislative powers nor the right to vary taxation but could vary secondary legislation and was given responsibility for supervising the Welsh Office, a task previously undertaken by the Secretary of State for Wales. The Northern Ireland Assembly was established in 1998 as part of the Belfast Agreement but was suspended in 2002 when the Secretary of State for Northern Ireland resumed direct control of housing policy via the Northern Ireland Housing Executive.

Although there have been significant differences in other social policy domains, devolution has had only limited impact on housing policy. Scotland was granted the most power to develop a distinct path but has tended to follow England's policy bearing, albeit expressed in different terminology. Thus, for example, the 2006 Housing (Scotland) Act introduced 'purchasers' information packs', analogous to the English 'home information packs' plus a tenancy deposit scheme, similar to the system in England introduced under the 2004 Housing Act. Scotland's 'Home-stake' replicates England's 'Homebuy' and the Scottish Executive promoted stock transfer but with the Scottish Housing Quality Standard used as the benchmark for assessing investment requirements. The most significant policy divergence relates to homelessness. In Scotland the definition of priority need is broader than that in England and Wales and those not in priority need have been given entitlement to temporary accommodation as a prelude to the scheduled 2012 abolition of the 'priority need' obstacle to securing permanent accommodation. Moreover, in discussing responses to homelessness, the tone of the Scottish Executive (now known as the Scottish Government) is more liberal than the stance adopted by the Department for Communities and Local Government and, in Scotland, less emphasis is placed on preventing homelessness applications. However, as yet, the main outcome of the Scottish approach to homelessness has been an increase in its recorded incidence: the number of households in temporary accommodation has increased by 21 per cent between 2005 and 2007 (Scottish Government, 2007a).

Mullins and Murie (2006, p. 10) conclude their discussion of devolution by stating 'it seems unlikely that devolution will exert a sufficiently strong influence to overwhelm the nationalizing, unifying and converging forces of national economic management, global markets and housing developers' approaches to design and marketing'. Overall, it seems that housing policies in England, Scotland, Wales and Northern Ireland remain broadly similar. This is unsurprising given the dominance of New Labour in England, Scotland and Wales and, after 2002, the return of direct rule in Northern Ireland. The impact of devolution – 'politics' or 'structural determinants' – will be clearer when the devolved governments have significantly different political compositions to that of Westminster. The restoration of the Northern Ireland Assembly in 2007 and the minority Scottish Nationalist Party government in Scotland will provide interesting testing grounds.

## Housing and community care

Whilst this book contains a chapter devoted to adult health and social care (Chapter 12), the role of housing in community care is worthy of consideration here (the term '**community care**' is subject to a variety of interpretations but, since the late 1950s, community care policy has been directed to delivering care and support to the person's own home rather than in the 'institutional' settings of hospitals, residential care homes, nursing homes and hostels). Given this objective, then, the quality of the accommodation available to people with care and support requirements is an important dimension of community care.

### Housing quality

In the past, mandatory grants have been available to assist householders to improve their dwellings to a standard above the statutory definition of unfitness. Such mandatory grants became discretionary in the late 1990s and the Department for Communities and Local Government now attempts to steer the resources available for private sector improvement to the most 'vulnerable' households. A 'vulnerable' household has been defined as:

> one that receives one or more of a number of income-related or disability benefits. These benefits are: income support, housing benefit, council tax benefit, disabled persons tax credit, income based job seekers allowance, working families tax credit, attendance allowance, disability living allowance, industrial injuries, disablement benefit, war disablement pension.
>
> Department for Communities and Local Government, 2007k

An 'expectation' has been set that the 57 per cent of vulnerable households living in 'decent' private sector homes in 2001 would be increased to 65 per cent by 2006, 70 per cent by 2010 and 75 per cent by 2020 and that 'local authority power to provide assistance for repairs and improvements will be one of key vehicles for delivering these increases' (Department for Communities and Local Government, 2007k). The modest 'expectation' for 2006 was achieved with 66.1 per cent of vulnerable households living in decent homes in 2005. None the less, over 1 million vulnerable households in the private sector live in 'non-decent' houses and the homes of 48.3 per cent of vulnerable households (360,000) in the private landlord sector are not 'decent' (Department for Communities and Local Government, 2007k).

## Supported housing

Good 'social landlords' can provide considerable help to people with special requirements through their everyday housing management activities. Nevertheless, some people may require additional assistance and, in the past, such aid was provided in supported housing. Help was linked to 'bricks and mortar' provision, in the belief that clustering of people with support needs would lead to more effective and efficient support.

In the 1980s and 1990s supported housing schemes developed in a haphazard manner. Social services departments, health authorities, the probation service and housing associations used a variety of funding streams to meet the growing need for 'accommodation with support' arising, in part, from the closure of larger institutions. The creative use of funding packages from a variety of sources – the Audit Commission (1998, p. 93) identified 25 funding mechanisms – helped to promote a form of 'community care'. However, concern was expressed at the possible motives underlying some of the projects (the 'shunting' of long-term costs to other authorities and on to Housing Benefit) and whether the pattern of provision was in line with need. The government's immediate response to these issues was to urge health, social services and housing to cooperate in assessment and in commissioning supported housing. In addition, 'floating support' (help unconnected to a specific 'special needs' housing scheme) was promoted. In 1999, following the publication of the consultation paper *Supporting People – A New Policy and Funding Framework for Support Services* (Department of Social Security, 1998), the government announced that fiscal incentives would be introduced to promote planning and cooperation. In 2003 funding streams for housing-linked support were united in a single pot distributed by local government.

## Adapted properties

Disabled Facilities Grants for home adaptations are available to help frail elderly people and people with a physical or sensory impairment to live in their own homes. It is a statutory entitlement but subject to a means test – except for children who require home adaptations – and a maximum payment. Although central government funding for Disabled Facilities Grant more than doubled between 1997 and 2006 and local authorities have made significant contributions from their own resources there are long waiting lists for grants – the outcome of an ageing population and the increasing number of children with severe disabilities (Department for Communities and Local Government, 2006b).

## Lifetime homes

The idea of 'lifetime homes', developed by the Joseph Rowntree Foundation, is that all dwellings should be built to design standards to make them convenient and accessible for all sections of the population. This will then make it easier for people with disabilities to live in and to visit ordinary houses in ordinary streets and has the potential to save money on future adaptations. In 1999 some of the lifetime homes design features were incorporated into the Building Regulations and the Housing Corporation demands standards close to lifetime home norms as a condition for assisting registered social landlords to develop new homes.

## Conclusion

Despite the 'roller-coaster' housing market and the complex impact of state intervention, it is possible to identify broad categories of 'winners' and 'losers' in the housing system. Land owners have made substantial gains as the cost of residential development land has increased rapidly – up, for example, from £731,168 per hectare in 1994 to £3,590,419 per hectare in 2006 (Department for Communities and Local Government, 2007l). Home owners, as a broad category, have also benefited because over the long term house prices have increased faster than general inflation.

Amongst the losers have been many 'social housing' renters who have not benefited from the right to buy and who have found themselves in an increasingly 'residualised' sector with, in some places, associated 'neighbourhood' problems. Some home owners have also lost ground. With 70 per cent of households now home owners, the tenure covers a broad range of circumstances with house prices rising or falling at different rates in different locations. Home owners in 'low-demand' areas have found that the value of their properties have not kept pace with overall price increases, placing restrictions on their opportunities to move up the housing market.

There is a generational dimension to the 'winners' and 'losers' in the housing market. According to a report by the International Longevity Centre (2007) young people are tumbling into debt to get a foothold on the housing ladder, reducing their spending on pensions and postponing starting a family. The report shows that mortgage debt for 20- to 29-year-olds more than doubled between 1995 and 2005. In contrast, a person who retired at 65 in 1995 has seen their wealth increase by £90,000, with the biggest gainers being people in middle age who have benefited from the same increases in housing wealth as the old but have also enjoyed real wage increases.

However, there are other dimensions to housing opportunities. Gender has an impact, with, for example, only 27 per cent of female single parents in Scotland being owner-occupiers (Scottish Government, 2007b). Ethnicity also influences housing outcomes. There is, for example, a five percentage point difference between minority ethnic households and white households living in 'non-decent homes' and, although patterns in migration and clustering vary by ethnic group and locality, in England 68 per cent of minority ethnic groups live in a deprived area compared to 20 per cent overall (Department for Work and Pensions, 2006b).

Despite its neglect in the recent analysis of housing outcomes, social class continues to have an impact. Tenure follows the social class gradient with 86 per cent of 'higher professionals and managers' being home owners compared to 62 per cent of people with 'routine' occupations (Department for Communities and Local Government, 2007m). Different house values in different locations has helped to produce a situation where, according to Thomas and Dorling (2007), an average child in the wealthiest 10 per cent of neighbourhoods could expect to inherit at least 40 times as much cash as a typical child in the poorest 10 per cent.

## Summary

It is possible to identify five broad stages in the evolution of housing policy:

- During the nineteenth century insanitary housing became regarded as a social problem because of its 'external' impact on the moral and physical condition of the nation state.
- The second stage was manifest in the identification of an overall housing shortage and the attempt to stimulate housing construction by central state subsidies to local authorities to encourage them to build homes for rent as an addition to building for home ownership. Private renting declined in this period.
- In the third stage the scale of the housing shortage prompted the expansion of both local authority housing and home ownership by state subsidies to housing production and consumption. Private sector renting continued to decline and a 'third arm' to housing supply – housing associations – emerged.
- During the fourth stage a belief in market forces prompted a state withdrawal from direct intervention but supply constraints in the form of planning controls meant that supply did not match demand.
- And from 2003 a fifth stage in housing policy has emerged, characterised by state action to promote housing supply in the context of promoting choice and intervention to mitigate the extreme consequences of the housing market.

# Discussion and review topics

1 How did tenure pattern change during the twentieth century? Explain these changes.

2 What is the current role of private landlords in housing provision?

3 How can housing policy contribute to promoting social inclusion?

4 How has New Labour promoted choice in housing?

5 Examine the relationships between housing and the ecosystem

## Further reading

Hills, J. (2007) *Ends and Means: The future roles of social housing in England*, CASE Report 34, http://sticerd.lse.ac.uk/dps/case/cr/CASEreport34.pdf. An independent report for the Secretary of State for Communities and Local Government which considers the role of social housing.

Holmes, C. (2006) *A New Vision for Housing*, Routledge, London. This book outlines what the author sees as mistakes in the development of social housing and sets out a vision for the future.

Lund, B. (2006) *Understanding Housing Policy*, Policy Press, Bristol. A thorough coverage of housing policy including discussion of policy problems, policy responses and a range of theoretical perspectives.

Mullins, D. and Murie, A. (2006) *Housing Policy in the UK*, Palgrave Macmillan, London. An accessible and informative overview of housing policy.

## Some useful websites

www.communities.gov.uk – in 2006 the housing responsibilities of the Office of the Deputy Prime Minister were transferred to the Department for Communities and Local Government. Its website contains policy documents and a statistical section.

www.scotland.gov.uk/Topics/Housing/Housing, www.dsdni.gov.uk/index/hsdiv-housing.htm, http://new.wales.gov.uk/topics/housingandcommunity/housing/?lang=en – information on housing policies in Scotland, Northern Ireland and Wales can be found at the websites of their respective administrations.

www.ukhousingreview.org.uk – a treasure-trove of statistics related to housing, compiled by Steve Wilcox.

http://housingpolicy.moonfruit.com – the Housing Policy website contains updates on the material in Brian Lund's *Understanding Housing Policy* and includes links to over 150 websites concerned with housing policy.

## References

Audit Commission (1998) *Home Alone: The Role of Housing in Community Care*, Audit Commission, London.

Barker, K. (2004) *Review of Housing Supply: Delivering Stability: Securing our Future Housing Needs, Final Report-Recommendations*, HM Treasury, www.hm-treasury.gov.uk/consultations_and_legislation/barker/consult_barker_index.cfm.

377

Barker, K. (2006) *Review of Land Use Planning: Final Report – Recommendations,* ***www. hmtreasury.gov.uk/independent_reviews/barker_review_land_use_planning/barkerreview_land_use_planning_index.cfm.***

Department for Communities and Local Government (2006a) *New Deal for Communities National Evaluation: An Overview of Change Data Research Report 33,* **www.neighbourhood.gov.uk/ publications.asp?did=1898.**

Department for Communities and Local Government (2006b) *Disabled Facilities Grant Programme: The Government's proposals to improve programme delivery,* **www.communities.gov.uk/pub/ 650/ DisabledFacilitiesGrantProgrammeTheGovernmentsproposalstoimproveprogrammedelivey_id15 05650.pdf.**

Department for Communities and Local Government (2007a) *Dwelling Stock by Tenure (United Kingdom),* **www.communities.gov.uk/pub/7/Table101_id1156007.xls.**

Department for Communities and Local Government (2007b) *Social Housing Sales,* **www.communities.gov.uk/documents/housing/xls/table-648http.**

Department for Communities and Local Government (2007c) *Housebuilding: Permanent Buildings Completed,* **www.communities.gov.uk/pub/57/Table241_id1156057.xls.**

Department for Communities and Local Government (2007d) *Homes for the future: more affordable, more sustainable,* Cm 7191, Stationery Office, London.

Department for Communities and Local Government (2007e) *Completed Local Authority LSVTs,* **www.communities.gov.uk/pub/566/CompletedLSVTs_id1152566.xls.**

Department for Communities and Local Government (2007f) *English House Condition Survey 2005 Headline Report: Decent Homes and Decent Places,* **www.communities.gov.uk/pub/983/ EnglishHouseConditionSurveyHeadlineReport2005_id1508983.doc.**

Department for Communities and Local Government (2007g) *Dwelling Stock by Tenure: England, historical series,* **www.communities.gov.uk/pub/10/Table104_id1156010.xls.**

Department for Communities and Local Government (2007h) *Building a Greener Future: Policy Statement,* **www.communities.gov.uk/publications/planningandbuilding/building-a-greener.**

Department for Communities and Local Government (2007i) *Eco-towns Prospectus,* **www.communities.gov.uk/documents/housing/doc/Eco-towns.**

Department for Communities and Local Government (2007j) *Households in temporary accommodation arranged by local authorities (England),* **www.communities.gov.uk/pub/308/ Table623_id1156308.xls.**

Department for Communities and Local Government (2007k) *Policy on Private Sector Housing Renewal,* **www.communities.gov.uk/index.asp?id=1152774.**

Department for Communities and Local Government (2007l) *Average valuations of residential land with outline planning permission (England),* **www.communities.gov.uk/documents/housing/xls/141389.**

Department for Communities and Local Government (2007m) *Socio-economic classification by household reference person by tenure,* **www.communities.gov.uk/documents/housing/xls/144302.**

Department for Work and Pensions (2002) *Building Choice and Responsibility: A Radical Agenda for Housing Benefit,* Stationery Office, London.

Department for Work and Pensions (2006a) *A New Deal for Welfare: Empowering people to work,* Cm 6730, Stationery Office, London.

Department for Work and Pensions (2006b) *Opportunity for all, sixth annual report,* **www.dwp.gov.uk/ofa/reports/2004/chapter2-6.asp.**

Department of the Environment (1994) *Access to Local Authority and Housing Association Tenancies: A Consultation Paper,* Department of the Environment, London.

Department of the Environment, Transport and the Regions/Department of Social Security (2000) *Quality and Choice: A Decent Home for All, The Housing Green Paper,* Stationery Office, London.

Department of Social Security (1998) *Supporting People – A New Policy and Funding Framework for Support Services*, Department of Social Security.

Friends of the Earth (2005) *Housing: Building a Sustainable Future*, Friends of the Earth, London.

Glennerster, H. (2003) *Understanding the Finance of Welfare: What Welfare Costs and How to Pay for It*, Policy Press, Bristol.

Hastings, M. (2006) 'Call me a Nimby, but it's madness to concrete vast tracts of countryside: the alliance of Cameron and Brown in favour of a development free-for-all is misguided – and deeply pernicious', *Guardian*, Tuesday 4 July 2006.

Hayek, F.A. (1960) *The Constitution of Liberty*, Routledge, London.

Hills, J. (1992) *Unravelling Housing Finance: Subsidies, Benefits, Taxation*, Clarendon Press, Oxford.

Hills, J. (2007) *Ends and Means: The future roles of social housing in England*, CASE Report 34, **http://sticerd.lse.ac.uk/dps/case/cr/CASEreport34.pdf**.

Holmans, A.E. (2000) 'Housing', in A.H. Halsey and J. Webb, *Twentieth-century British Social Trends*, Palgrave Macmillan, Basingstoke.

House of Commons Environmental Audit Committee (2006) *Sustainable Housing: A Follow-up Report: Fifth Report of the Session 2005–06*, **www.publications.parliament.uk/pa/cm200506/cmselect/cmenvaud/779/77902.htm**.

Howard, E. (1902) *Garden Cities of Tomorrow*, Faber, London.

International Longevity Centre (2007) *Asset Accumulation in Focus: The Challenges Ahead*, International Longevity Centre, London.

Knutt, E. (2003) 'It was never meant to be like this', *Housing Today*, 13 June.

Labour Party (1997) *New Labour Because Britain Deserves Better*, Labour Party, London.

Le Grand, J., Popper, C. and Robinson, R. (1984) *The Economics of Social Problems*, Macmillan, Basingstoke.

Mullins, D. and Murie, A. (2006) *Housing Policy in the UK*, Palgrave Macmillan, London.

Office of the Deputy Prime Minister (2003) *Sustainable Communities: Building for the future*, ODPM, London.

Office of the Deputy Prime Minister (2005a) *Making it happen in neighbourhoods: The national strategy for neighbourhood renewal – four years on*, ODPM, London.

Office of the Deputy Prime Minister (2005b) *Sustainable Communities: Settled Homes; Changing Lives*, **www.communities.gov.uk/index.asp?id=1163057**.

Page, D. (2006) *Respect and renewal: A Study of neighbourhood social regeneration*, Joseph Rowntree Foundation, York.

Pennance, F.G. (1969) *Housing Market Analysis and Policy*, Hobart Paper No. 48, Institute of Economic Affairs, London.

Ridley, N. (1992) *'My Style of Government': The Thatcher Years*, Fontana, London.

Royal Commission on the Housing of the Working Classes (1885) *Reports and Minutes of Evidence*, HMSO, London.

Scottish Government (2007a) *Operation of the Homeless Persons Legislation in Scotland: National and Local Analyses 2005-6*, **www.scotland.gov.uk/Publications/2005/11/0193147/31478**.

Scottish Government (2007b) *Housing and Equality*, **www.scotland.gov.uk/Publications/2006/11/20102424/13**.

Secretary of State for Work and Pensions (2003) *Housing Benefit Sanctions and Anti-social Behaviour*, **www.dwp.gov.uk/housingbenefit/consultations/hb.pdf**.

Social Exclusion Unit (1998a) *Bringing Britain Together: A National Strategy for Neighbourhood Renewal*, Stationery Office, London.

Social Exclusion Unit (1998b) *Rough Sleeping*, Stationery Office, London.

Social Exclusion Unit (2001) *A New Commitment to Neighbourhood Renewal: National Strategy Action Plan*, Stationery Office, London.

Social Exclusion Unit (2002) *What is social exclusion?* **www.socialexclusionunit.gov.uk**.

Thatcher, M. (1995) *The Downing Street Years*, HarperCollins, London.

Thomas, B. and Dorling, D. (2007) *Identity in Britain: A Cradle-to-Grave Atlas*, Policy Press, London.

Tunstall, R. and Coulter, A. (2006) *Progress on twenty 'unpopular' estates, 1980–2005: Turning the tide?* Policy Press, Bristol.

White, G. (2001) 'Charity questions rough sleepers cut', *Housing Today*, 6 December.

Wilcox, S. (2006) *UK Housing Review 2006/2007*, Chartered Institute of Housing/Council of Mortgage Lenders /Joseph Rowntree Foundation, York.

World Commission on the Environment and Development (1988) *Our Common Future*, Oxford University Press, Oxford.

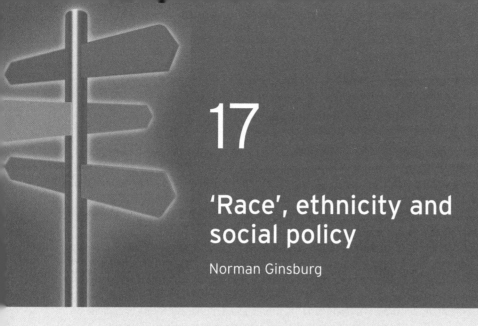

# 17

# 'Race', ethnicity and social policy

Norman Ginsburg

## Chapter overview

Issues around race and racism have become increasingly pervasive within social policy in Britain, as England in particular has become a multi-racial and multi-ethnic society over the decades since the Second World War. Yet the issues raised by this, and the struggles and discourses they generate, are often hidden from public gaze or, when they do come to the surface, they are sensationalised and distorted, particularly by the tabloids. There is wide-spread discomfort about discussing these matters because racism is often deeply embedded and racial inequalities are seemingly so intractable. Policy discourse conducted within the public services, the political realm and the media often lurches from complacent denial to panic and back again. Britain is sometimes portrayed as a bastion of anti-discrimination measures and good race relations compared to 'Europe'. Yet consider, for example, the number of black people in prison, the extent of racial violence, the underachievement of black boys in school, hysteria about 'bogus' asylum seekers scrounging off the welfare state and about alleged self-segregation by Muslims – the persistence of such issues and discourses suggests a society struggling to cope with racism and racial inequalities.

This chapter considers some of the most prominent aspects of recent policy making and discourse, namely:

- the operationalisation of the concepts of **'race', ethnicity** and race relations, and the relationship between them;
- arguably the centrepiece of policy – racialised immigration and refugee policy, through which the state has signalled the inferior status of people of minority ethnic origin in the welfare state;
- the economic status of minority ethnic groups in the labour market, particularly the persistence of income inequalities, and the role and impact of anti-discrimination measures in mitigating racial injustice;
- Issues and policy developments in four areas of social policy – policing, schooling, housing and mental health – which have been particularly important and intense arenas of oppression and challenges thereto.

### Spotlight on the issues
### 'Race' and psychiatric care

Over recent decades there have been a series of cases of abuse of black patients in psychiatric care, the most notorious perhaps being the case of David 'Rocky' Bennett. He died at a secure psychiatric unit in Norwich in 1998 after being severely restrained for a prolonged period of time. Eventually the health authority commissioned an inquiry chaired by a judge, John Blofeld, whose report appeared in 2003 (Blofeld, 2003). He said that there was a 'festering abscess' of institutional racism in the NHS, and made a number of important recommendations, including a three-minute time limit on pinning patients to the floor and the appointment of an 'ethnicity tsar' to lead reform. Neither of these recommendations has been implemented. This is a good illustration of the making and implementation of contemporary British social policy in the field of 'race' and ethnicity. It shows that, under pressure from minority ethnic users, public authority is capable of making a critical and progressive anti-racist response, but that progress is slow and implementation in practice continues to be resisted.

Despite anti-discrimination legislation having been in place for more than four decades, '**race**' and 'racism' remain important challenges in British society, and not least for social policy. This chapter considers some of the policy approaches and decisions taken by governments, the impacts that these have had, and the outcomes for different groups within society.

## 'Race', ethnicity and race relations

It is essential to examine briefly a few of the key concepts involved both in the public discourse and in social scientific understanding of this topic. Here we are obviously and immediately confronted by a huge conundrum. 'Race' does not exist as an essential difference among human beings, yet it continues to be widely used to denote differences in physical appearance, differences of 'skin, hair and bone'. Over the centuries white Europeans used notions of racial hierarchy and superiority to bolster their imperialist ambitions and regimes. This means that the moment we use notions of 'race' and 'anti-racism' we are unavoidably embracing ideas of essential difference and hierarchy. In order to distance themselves from that embrace, social scientists in recent years have often put the word 'race' in inverted commas, to signify that it is a social construction, which must be continually subject to critical reflection. The terms 'ethnicity' and 'ethnic group' have came to the fore in the second half of the twentieth century, as the idea of 'race' became discredited by its exposure as scientifically bogus and by its role in Nazi ideology. Membership of an ethnic group suggests an identity socially constructed around descent and/or culture. Obviously in everyday usage there is much blurring and inconsistency in the use of the terms 'race' and 'ethnicity'. Prejudice and discrimination on the basis of ethnic identity is commonly described as racism or racial discrimination, because there is no such word as 'ethnicism', which is particularly confusing. Hence the 'race relations' legislation in the UK covers discrimination on 'grounds of race, colour, nationality (including citizenship), or ethnic or national origin' and has been successfully used by members of the UK's old, national ethnicities (Scots, Welsh, Irish, English). The legislation steers clear of defining 'race' and ethnicity, but the mere fact that such a wide range of identities is covered by 'race relations' indicates the enduring, if constantly shifting, ambit of the idea of 'race' in social policy. In contemporary British discourse the phrase 'ethnic minorities' is most commonly used as a coded term to describe non-whites. Social scientists refer to 'minority ethnic groups' to point up that there is a white 'ethnic majority'. Public services sometimes use the category 'black and minority ethnic' (BME) in recognition of black identity as a political and cultural force. 'Black' is used to describe people of black African and African-Caribbean descent, while 'black' is often used as a generic term for non-white people or people of colour.

Explicit operationalisation of the ideas of 'race' and ethnicity in British social policy emerged in the second half of the twentieth century in the wake of the great postcolonial migration. But it was embedded in the origins of the modern welfare state as it developed out of the Poor Law. The first immigration legislation (the Aliens Order, 1905, which sought to exclude Jews fleeing ethnic cleansing in Eastern Europe) went alongside the development of national insurance and public education, healthcare and family welfare services for the indigenous population. This occurred amidst a panic about the unfitness of British troops fighting Dutch farmers and Africans for control of southern Africa. This was the era of 'social imperialism' when it was realised that the world's foremost imperial power had to attend to the breeding, education and welfare of its own people not only to survive but to cement their sense of collective superiority over others. The linkage between welfare policy and national ethnic identity was strengthened after the First World War with the promise of 'homes fit for heroes to live in' (council housing) and, again, after the Second World War, with the construction of a more fully fledged national welfare state and social rights of citizenship. Eligibility for these rights was founded on membership of the national community, a British ethnic identity which reached its peak strength during and after the Second World War. Both the British and English ethnic identity (which the English have in the past largely seen as synonymous) embrace a peculiarly insular and disdainful attitude towards 'bloody foreigners' as a whole, laced with ethnic and racial stereotypes as appropriate (Winder, 2004). This is reflected in continuing and widespread hostility towards asylum seekers, refugees, immigrants and even the EU, which is, in turn, reflected in social policy.

The watershed 'event' in shaping the complex relationship between 'race', ethnicity and social policy in contemporary Britain was the great postcolonial migration of people of colour from the late 1940s to early 1970s, coinciding with the flowering of the classic welfare state. The latter was part of the post-war 'class settlement', but it was not envisaged that it would be accessible to immigrants, initially in particular for housing. Hence there began a long and continuing struggle to establish the social rights of the then 'new' minority ethnic groups in the face of direct and institutionalised racism. There was a particular ambiguity towards the black and Asian postcolonial migrants in British social policy. It formally bestowed British citizenship on them under the British Nationality Act 1948 and actively recruited staff for the public services in the former colonies, while in practice making them second-class citizens and deterring immigration. Governments in the 1950s and 1960s tried to juggle the needs of the economy for migrant workers, including the welfare state itself (most notably doctors, nurses and ancillary workers for the NHS), with virulent hostility to their presence in many quarters. The boom/bust economy from the late 1950s generated bouts of unemployment, which contributed to the spread of explicit racism into mainstream politics, Labour as well as Conservative. This 'movement' is often known as Powellism (Weight, 2002; Rattansi, 2007), after the maverick Conservative politician Enoch Powell, who advocated forced repatriation of postcolonial migrants to prevent 'rivers of blood'. Thus 'race relations' came on to the policy agenda.

'Race relations' (or 'community relations'), as it emerged in the 1960s, has a rich meaning in British social policy. It is explicitly two sided – strong, racialised immigration control combined with measures to integrate settled minorities. Hence it is about the managed exclusion of racialised others and the management of those who have got under the wire, as it were. The former was achieved with a series of racist immigration acts from 1962 to 1971, which all but prevented migration by people of colour from the former colonies. The latter is encapsulated in the words of the Labour Home Secretary in 1966, Roy Jenkins, as 'equal opportunity accompanied by cultural diversity in an atmosphere of mutual tolerance'. In policy terms this 'liberal' consensus generated fairly soft anti-discrimination legislation to deter more explicit forms of racism, and a laissez-faire approach to cultural diversity, an arm's length **multiculturalism**. A Conservative Home Secretary in 1971, Reginald Maudling, outlined the policy consensus very bluntly: 'The main purpose of immigration policy . . . is a contribution to peace and harmony . . . If we are to get progress in community relations, we must give assurance to the people, who were already here before the large wave of immigration, that this will be the end and that there will be no further large-scale immigration. Unless we can give that assurance, we cannot effectively set about improving community relations' (quoted in MacDonald, 1983, pp. 16–17).

This two-sided policy consensus has been sorely tested over the decades by pressure from many and varied quarters. In the late 1970s the far right made a big push for repatriation of black and Asian settlers, accompanied by increased police harassment and violence against black and Asian young people. This was fiercely resisted on the streets and in local politics. In the early 1980s very high levels of youth unemployment and more police brutality contributed to the inner-city uprisings of 1981. The policy response was to tone down quietly some of the pressure on minority communities. The ten years or so from the mid 1970s to the mid 1980s saw a crucial turning of the tide against exclusionary and segregationist sentiment, and the emergence of black British and British Asian as respected identities. Above all it established firmly in the white majority's minds that black British and British Asian people were here to stay and that, like it or not, Britain is a multiracial society.

Another big moment came in the early 2000s, when the far right coordinated attacks on Pakistani communities in some northern towns in the run-up to the

May 2001 general election, which provoked strong resistance. Politicians and the media rushed to blame the Pakistani community, hundreds of whom were subsequently convicted of violent offences, unlike any of their white foes. 9/11 and the 7/7 London bombings in July 2005 added significantly to anti-Muslim feeling, directed in Britain largely against those of Pakistani origin who form by far the largest Muslim community. Suddenly in the wake of such events these communities were identified by politicians, intellectuals and policy makers across the mainstream as self-segregated, as living 'parallel lives', and as having failed to integrate into British society. The truth is almost the exact opposite – it was local segregationist policy making in housing and education, accompanied by 'white flight' from urban neighbourhoods and industrial decline, which contributed substantially to the social exclusion of the Muslim communities of the northern towns. Kundnani (2007) argues that the aftermath of 2001 has led to 'the end of tolerance' and of liberal, laissez-faire multiculturalism with the move towards a more authoritarian **integrationism** directed at Muslim communities across the land. It is certainly true that 'the Muslim community' has effectively become 'an ethnicity rather than a group sharing a religion' (Kundnani, 2007, p. 126) and that a new discourse in local policy making has rapidly emerged built upon the idea of 'community cohesion'. The concepts of 'parallel lives' and 'community cohesion' first came to prominence in Cantle (2001), a report for the government on the events in the northern towns in 2001. The view of Cantle (2005), seemingly very much shared by New Labour, is that central and local government should pursue a much more interventionist, normative strategy towards the integration of those minorities leading 'parallel lives', essentially a coded reference to Muslim communities and groups. The government's Commission on Integration and Cohesion (CIC, 2007) came up with a large number of policy recommendations including more funding for voluntary groups promoting integration and for classes in English for non-English speakers, restricting the translation of council documents into foreign languages, and, most controversially, an end to funding for voluntary organisations representing a single ethnic or religious identity. The government accepted most of the recommendations, but implementation will be fraught, not least because this cultural integrationism does little to address social exclusion in employment, education and housing.

One of the effects of the 'settlement' of the 1980s was the recognition of the social significance of the minority ethnic communities by social policy makers, symbolised by the inclusion of a question about ethnic identity in the 1991 population census. If the 'equal opportunities' element of the liberal consensus was to have any credibility, then ethnic inequalities and the particular needs of different ethnic communities had to be officially quantified. Public and private organisations had begun collecting ethnic data routinely in the 1980s using various classifications. The only source of quantitative socio-economic data on a national basis had been the large surveys by the Policy Studies Institute (PSI, formerly Political and Economic Planning), roughly every ten years from the 1960s through the 1990s. The ethnic classification in the census is similar (but not identical) to that of PSI and other organisations. It is very much shaped by the postcolonial migration and the labels most commonly used by the host community. Hence in 2001 there were five principal categories – White, Mixed, Asian, Black and Chinese/Other. Table 17.1

Table 17.1 Population of England by ethnic group, census, April 2001

| | Numbers (000s) | % |
|---|---|---|
| **White** | 44,679 | 90.9 |
| British | 42,747 | 87.0 |
| Irish | 624 | 1.3 |
| Other | 1,308 | 2.7 |
| **Mixed** | 643 | 1.3 |
| White and black Caribbean | 231 | 0.5 |
| White and black African | 76 | 0.2 |
| White and Asian | 184 | 0.4 |
| Other mixed | 151 | 0.3 |
| **Asian or Asian British/Scottish** | 2,248 | 4.6 |
| Indian | 1,209 | 2.1 |
| Pakistani | 707 | 1.4 |
| Bangladeshi | 275 | 0.6 |
| Other Asian | 238 | 0.5 |
| **Black or black British/Scottish** | 1,133 | 2.3 |
| Black Caribbean | 561 | 1.1 |
| Black African | 476 | 1.0 |
| Black Other | 95 | 0.2 |
| **Chinese or other ethnic groups** | 435 | 0.9 |
| Chinese | 221 | 0.5 |
| Any other ethnic group | 215 | 0.4 |
| **All ethnic groups** | 49,139 | 100.0 |

*Source*: ONS, 2005 (Table 1.17).

gives the results of the 2001 census for England, with 90.9 per cent of the population describing themselves as white – Wales and Scotland were both 98 per cent white, Northern Ireland 99 per cent. There are obvious inconsistencies in the mix of racial and ethnic categories, even more so in the limited number of sub-categories which bring in national identity. Respondents were invited to tick one of 16 categories. Inevitably this census classification cannot capture the ethnic diversity of more recent settlers and the **racialisation** of Muslims with origins in the Indian sub-continent. The 'White' category is sub-divided into British, Irish or Any Other, not specifying other intra-UK national identities nor, for example, Jews and gypsies. Recent national data on educational inequalities has included gypsies as a category, who are very significantly failed by the schools system.

## Immigration and refugee policy

Racialised control of immigration lies at the heart of social policy in the UK because it is the means by which the state discriminates as to who has the right to be resident, even temporarily, within its borders. This inevitably has racial and ethnic dimensions, because many if not most of the people wanting to reside in

Britain are not of white European origin, whether they are economic migrants or asylum seekers. Hence immigration controls can be described as an example of structural racism, a consequence of the global structure of inequality between the predominantly white rich countries and the predominantly non-white poor countries. But it can also be conceived as an example of **institutional racism** (institutionalised within the state itself) whereby people of colour and distinct ethnic difference are treated adversely compared to whites. By the early 1970s Britain had closed the door to non-white economic migrants from the former colonies, except for spouses and relatives of those already settled, itself a major site of conflict ever since. It would be difficult to underestimate the impact and the message conveyed by the 1962–71 immigration legislation; it officially recognised and legitimated Powellite racism, and it made non-white postcolonial migrants and their families settled in Britain feel permanently insecure and of second-class status.

 ## Thought provoker

Perhaps the most blatant examples of discrimination in immigration policy concern family reunion, affecting particularly people of Asian and Caribbean origin whose relatives have already settled. From the early 1970s British immigration policy 'assumed that South Asian marriages were a sham, contracted solely to gain entry to Britain, unless proved otherwise' (Wilson, 2006, p. 77). This meant that families, particularly women, were subjected to rigorous investigation and interrogation, amounting to a form of psychological humiliation and even torture in some cases. Most notoriously in the mid 1970s virginity tests were performed on fiancés and wives at Heathrow airport and elsewhere. In the early 1980s policy was enshrined in three rules. Under the 'primary purpose rule' applicants for entry had to prove that their primary intention in getting married was not to settle in the UK. This was a severe constraint on the tradition of arranged marriage. The 'one year rule' required that those coming to the UK to join spouses had to stay in the marriage for at least one year. After that year, an application for permanent leave to remain in the UK could be made, but only if supported by both spouses. This has had the effect of trapping some women in violent and abusive marriages (Joshi, 2003; Wilson, 2006). The 'no recourse to public funds rule' means that people coming to the UK have no social rights within the welfare state, denying access to benefits, social housing and even women's refuges. This can leave women completely bereft of support should they flee an abusive relationship. The 'primary purpose rule' was modified under the New Labour government in the late 1990s, ushering in a renewed campaign by Asian women's groups to achieve greater protection for women. This has achieved some important concessions but policy continues to leave women at great risk, not least if they are eventually deported to countries like Pakistan. The situation has been complicated further in the 2000s by government drives against 'forced marriages' and 'honour killings' which have been infected by anti-Muslim racism. As Wilson (2006, pp. 86-95) and Siddiqui (2003) conclude, the rights and protection of women have been subjugated to heavy-handed attempts to regulate South Asian patriarchy.

Britain's economic stagnation and recurrent high levels of unemployment through to the mid 1990s meant that economic migration remained at a low level. Up to around 1993, very few of the growing numbers of asylum seekers and refugees arriving in Western Europe were allowed to enter the UK. Both of these situations changed in the mid 1990s – an economic boom lasting for more than a decade produced an unprecedented demand for labour and Britain could no longer sustain its rejection of asylum seekers in the face of EU and human rights pressures. The latter issue dominated the policy discourse from the mid 1990s to mid 2000s, as the government busily responded to xenophobic and racist hostility to refugees and asylum seekers across wide swathes of British society, pumped up by the popular press. Paralleling in some ways the development of immigration control in the 1960s, no less than six acts of parliament between 1993 and 2006 have ratcheted up the legal and administrative means to deter refugees from seeking asylum in the UK, to deny those already here access to employment and the welfare state, and to incarcerate them prior to deportation as quickly as possible. Much of the hostility to asylum seekers is couched in terms of their real motives being to scrounge off the welfare state. Hence the legislation has steadily sought to deny them the social rights which the welfare state proclaims as universal. The 1993 Asylum and Immigration Appeals Act withdrew asylum seekers' access to social rented housing tenancy. The 1996 Immigration and Asylum Act ended their right to social security benefits unless they had children, and replaced them with vouchers. The 1999 Asylum and Immigration Act created a separate welfare regime for asylum seekers and their families, run by a new agency – the National Asylum Support Service (NASS)–providing voucher support at levels significantly less than the official poverty line. The 1999 Act also introduced compulsory dispersal which took people away from the informal support of their ethnic communities and often left them isolated on bleak housing estates in hostile, poor white communities. These features of the 1999 Act were an unmitigated disaster creating destitution and desperation, and exposure to racist violence, which was in a few cases murderous. The 2002 Nationality, Immigration and Asylum Act partially abandoned dispersal and vouchers in favour of warehousing in prison-like residential centres with their own education and healthcare provisions. This signalled a move towards physically excluding asylum seekers from normal life in the community. Asylum Acts in 2004 and 2006 further tightened the monitoring of asylum seekers and speeded detention and removal by the withdrawal of legal rights. Throughout, these measures have been challenged in the courts (sometimes successfully), with refugee organisations, other NGO's and minority communities themselves leading the resistance and trying to fill the gap left by the withdrawal of the welfare state. Riots, serious fires and mass escapes at detention centres have demonstrated a different form of resistance.

While asylum seekers and refugees were the focus of most media attention and policy making in this period, at the same time there took place another important shift in policy on migrant workers or 'economic migration'. The New Labour government proclaimed a shift towards 'managed migration' in the context of growing shortages of labour across almost all occupations from dentists, teachers and social workers to farming, catering, hotels, elder and childcare, and construction. The management of labour migration is not new in itself; the postcolonial migration of the 1950s and 1960s was managed covertly as employers (both public and private) were permitted to recruit in the former colonies under government surveillance. Although primary immigration was formally ended from the 1970s through the 1990s, there were government schemes and quotas to facilitate recruitment abroad to fill specific niches and to encourage wealthy people to settle in Britain. Nevertheless the economic boom since the mid 1990s has generated a new large-scale inward migration of workers, arriving in very diverse circumstances ranging from the victims of traffickers and unscrupulous gangmasters to skilled, self-organised craftspeople and graduates. The key point about this migration in relation to 'race' and ethnicity is that the 'legal' migrants have been largely white people from the new member states of the EU in central Europe, while the undocumented have come from outside the EU and are non-white or ethnically distinct.

The new migration has therefore been managed to exclude differentially people from outside Fortress Europe, and to make permanent settlement much more difficult for them. So, the era of managed migration has witnessed an extremely racialised process. This has allowed the New Labour government to be much more open about the benefits of immigration than previous regimes. A watershed was reached in 2002 in the White Paper *Secure Borders, Safe Haven* when the Home Secretary, David Blunkett, acknowledged rather wearily 'the inevitable reality' of migration in the era of economic globalisation and 'the significant benefits' it brings, backed up by a Home Office research study (Home Office, 2001). Britain's first five-year strategy for asylum and immigration, published in 2005, was principally concerned with meeting the specific needs of business for migrant workers, primarily from the EU, and to minimise and control more strictly recruitment from elsewhere (Home Office, 2005). For the latter there is a simpler system for granting work permits, with just five types of 'work and study routes' (as opposed to eighty prior to 2005); skilled workers have to have a clear job offer, and low-skilled workers can only be recruited to a temporary and specific project. The unspoken assumption throughout is that the new migrants should not be encouraged to settle. Hence managed migration does not extend to social provision being made for their welfare. Local education, healthcare, housing and social services experience extra demands on their limited resources without extra funding, as, inevitably, many of the new migrants will settle on at least a semi-permanent basis. This fuels anti-immigrant sentiment, and increases support for the far right.

## Poverty and the labour market

Perhaps the most pressing racial and ethnic inequalities which should be addressed by social policy are those surrounding incomes and jobs. A recent thorough review of the data by Platt (2007) found substantially higher than average poverty rates for all the major non-white ethnic groups, particularly among people of Bangladeshi, Pakistani and black African origin. These differences have persisted over recent decades and are experienced as much by children as by older people: 'Bangladeshis were identified as having the greatest poverty for most measures. Poverty for this group also appeared to be severer and more long lasting than that experienced by other groups' (Platt, 2007, p. x). While much of this entrenched poverty can be explained in terms of poor education and employment opportunities, the bedrock of social policy in the form of the pensions, benefits and tax credits system has also differentially failed minority ethnic groups, who 'both experience more limited entitlement to certain benefits (through, for example, interrupted contributions records) and are less likely to claim various forms of benefit to which they are entitled' (Platt, 2007, p. 100).

 ## Thought provoker

Berthoud (2000) used government *Labour Force Survey* data from 1985-1995 on young men in their 20s and 30s to estimate the 'ethnic penalty' they experienced in the labour market. He isolated the effect of educational factors (i.e. qualifications differences) and of other factors (age of migration, local economic environment, family structures). Even setting aside these factors, the net ethnic penalties remained very substantial, particularly for African Caribbeans, black Africans, Pakistanis and Bangladeshis (see Table 17.2). This suggests that discriminatory processes in the labour market are deeply entrenched. Particularly striking here are the black Africans who, despite being relatively well qualified educationally (reducing their disadvantage by £30 a week), suffered the highest ethnic penalty of all. Heath and Cheung (2006) present data which demonstrate the persistence into the twenty-first century of ethnic penalties in earnings and in access to professional and managerial jobs.

**Table 17.2 Estimates of disadvantage in terms of earning power (£ per week)**

| | Average earnings per week | Attributable to education | Attributable to other factors | Net penalty |
|---|---|---|---|---|
| White | £332 | | | |
| Caribbean | £217 | £11 | £24 | £81 |
| African | £216 | −£30 | £14 | £132 |
| Indian | £327 | −£8 | −£10 | £23 |
| Pakistani/Bangladeshi | £182 | £24 | −£3 | £129 |

*Source:* Berthoud, 2000 (Table 14).

The most obvious measure of the disadvantaged position of minority ethnic groups is the difference in their employment rates compared to whites – the proportion of adults in paid employment. Clark and Drinkwater (2007) reviewed the available data comparing 1991 with 2001. There was a significant narrowing of the differences, particularly for the most disadvantaged groups, but the gap still remained substantial. Black Caribbean men failed to share in the growth in employment rates, and for some minority ethnic women the gap actually widened. Between 1991 and 2001 unemployment rates for minority ethnic men fell less than for whites. With the economy booming in 2001, black Caribbean and Bangladeshi men recorded unemployment rates of 16.8 per cent and 20.3 per cent respectively, compared to 5.7 per cent for white British men (see also Chapter 10).

There are many complex social, structural and biographical factors involved in maintaining the persistent disadvantages of minority ethnic groups in the labour market, but direct discrimination by employers and employees is certainly of serious significance. Heath and Cheung (2006, p. 67), reporting to the Department for Work and Pensions, concluded that their evidence 'on continued ethnic penalties, on the rates of job refusals reported by members of ethnic minorities, and on the levels of prejudice reported by white managers and employers, all suggest that discrimination continues to be a major problem and is unlikely to disappear of its own accord without new and effective interventions . . . directed at firms and employers'. The same conclusion is reached by Clark and Drinkwater (2007).

## Anti-discrimination

The centrepiece of official anti-racist policy is the Race Relations Act 1976, strengthened and extended by the Race Relations (Amendment) Act 2000. The 1976 Act enabled individuals to seek legal redress against direct discrimination; it established the Commission for Racial Equality (CRE) as the public agency promoting anti-discrimination with legal powers to challenge indirect (or institutional) racism; and it obliged local authorities to 'promote good race relations'. The impact of the legislation and the associated measures has been modest as the data above suggest, but certainly not insignificant. If the Acts did not exist, the situation would undoubtedly be a lot worse. Individuals mostly use the legislation to pursue claims of discrimination in employment. In 2006–7 3,780 claims of race discrimination were taken up by employment tribunals, but only 95 cases ended in compensation awards, with a median award of £7,000 (ETS, 2007). Complainants are not eligible for legal aid and bringing a case to the tribunal is extremely stressful: 31 per cent of claims were withdrawn, presumably under pressure from the employer, and 38 per cent were settled by negotiation. Successful complainants usually have the backing of their trade union or the CRE. Compared to the US the prospects of individual success in pursuing individual claims of employment discrimination and the level of compensation are much less. The situation in the UK has changed little over many years, contributing to the widespread cynicism about the effectiveness of individuals' legal rights to pursue anti-discrimination claims.

The CRE pursued a quiet strategy of behind the scenes negotiation with employers and organisations to persuade and cajole them into adopting more conscious and explicit anti-discrimination measures, as laid out, for example, in their Code of Practice on Employment. The Code is not legally obligatory, but it is used by employment tribunals to try to bring employers into line. In recent years the CRE advocated the virtues of 'diversity management' and the 'business case' for positive action on equal opportunities (see Wrench, 2005). The CRE was severely limited by its modest funding and its vulnerability to ridicule by the tabloid media, underpinned by right wing hostility to the 'race relations industry' as a whole. This was particularly true during the 1980s, when there was a constant threat to its existence under the Thatcher governments. The CRE did over fifty 'formal investigations' into organisations where systematic, institutionalised discrimination has come to light. Many of these have led to the issuing of a 'non-discrimination notice' to try to ensure that the organisation implements the

CRE's recommendations. In 1984 a 'non-discrimination notice' was served on the London Borough of Hackney, after a CRE investigation (CRE, 1984) revealed indirect discrimination in the allocation of council housing. This process served as a benchmark for more equitable local authority housing allocation throughout the country thereafter. In 2003 the CRE published a major investigation into the prison service, documenting entrenched racism therein (CRE, 2003). The prison service agreed to implement an action plan under CRE supervision, but in 2005 the CRE announced that 'major questions remain over the effectiveness of this work' (CRE, 2005, p. 11). In such front-line challenges to institutionalised racism the CRE clearly had very limited power to achieve change.

## Controversy and debate

A new phase in anti-discrimination policy began in the wake of the Macpherson (1999) Inquiry into the death of Stephen Lawrence, the victim of a racist murder in 1993 (see below). The performance of the police was understood as the outcome of institutional racism which Macpherson (1999: para 6.34) defined as:

The collective failure of an organisation to provide an appropriate and professional service to people because of their colour, culture, or ethnic origin. It can be seen or detected in processes, attitudes and behaviour which amount to discrimination through unwitting prejudice, ignorance, thoughtlessness and racist stereotyping which disadvantage minority ethnic people.

This is a distinct and controversial definition of institutional racism, because in the second sentence it focuses on individual behaviour rather than the policies of an organisation and the accompanying managerial and workplace cultures. The notion of 'unwitting prejudice' is particularly confusing because it seems to absolve individuals but only partially (see Rattansi, 2007, pp. 132–40).

In the wake of public concern about the Stephen Lawrence case, not least from the black community, the government, somewhat hesitantly, enacted the Race Relations (Amendment) Act 2000, which lifted the scandalous exemption from the 1976 Act of important public bodies, notably the police and prison services, and required most publicly funded services, not just local authorities, to produce Race Equality Plans covering both users and employees to challenge institutional racism. This inaugurated the 'Macpherson process' across the welfare state and the public services, involving much more ethnic monitoring of employment within and use of services, and the setting of targets for specific improvements. As yet, no adequate assessment of the impact of race equality planning is possible, but there is obviously a danger that the process remains a bureaucratic, managerial exercise, as the political force behind the Macpherson Inquiry wanes.

The most recent shift in official race equality policy was the incorporation of the CRE into the new Commission for Equality and Human Rights (CEHR) in 2007. The CEHR is responsible for all the 'equalities' recognised by EU legislation, namely age, disability, gender, religion or belief, sexual orientation or transgender status, as well as race. The CRE and the anti-racist movement opposed this change as a potential dilution of public commitment to the cause and signi-fying a loss of public identity for anti-discrimination work. Thus far there is little discernible difference between the CRE and the CEHR in their anti-race discrimi-nation work.

## Policing

From the 1960s to the 1980s the media and policy 'conversation' and the practice of the police and criminal justice system (PCJS) stereotyped black young men as a particular threat on the streets, which had to be met with a tough law and order response from the police, the courts and the prisons. When the police response is unjust or disproportionate as it often has been, the discourse suggested and con-tinues to suggest that it was a price worth paying. There was and is no evidence that black youth are any more criminal than white youth in poor neighbour-hoods with high levels of street crime. Public disorder and protest are fuelled both by police brutality and by police inaction against racist violence. The 'sus' law (routine stop and search of black youth on the street on suspicion of whatever) was always a major focus of conflict (Hall *et al.*, 1978; Rowe, 2004). Within the PCJS there has been an attitude of internal colonialist policing, control and repression in which visible minorities have been treated as particularly threatening and dangerous. This seems to have been embedded within the canteen cultures (the everyday, subcultural assumptions) of the police, courts and prison services. Black and Asian youth get the most pressure because their presence on the streets has represented a visible form of defiance and resistance to these processes. The Scarman (1981) report on 'disorders' in Brixton (essentially arising out of increased police brutality against black youth) suggested that there was no institu-tional racism in the Metropolitan Police, just a few bad apples, but that the disor-ders were fuelled by a genuine sense of social injustice. The latter issue was largely ignored by the Thatcher government.

The Stephen Lawrence case and the Macpherson Inquiry (SLMI) exposed these processes to critical, public scrutiny. Stephen, a black British teenager, was murdered in April 1993; after a collapsed trial in 1996, an inquest took place in February 1997, exposing police incompetence. The *Daily Mail* then named five white youths as the murderers, a cataclysmic event. In May 1997 the New Labour government was elected, anxious to repay some of their debts to black and Asian voters. In July 1997 the Macpherson Inquiry was announced, and its Report in February 1999 exposed professional incompetence, institutional racism and 'fail-ure of leadership at senior levels' in the police response to the murder. Institutional racism was exemplified in the lax approach by the police to the investigation, the fobbing off treatment of Stephen's family, and the web of suspicion cast over his companion Duwayne Brooks. There was strong evidence of racial stereotyping. The Macpherson Report made over 70 recommendations, largely concerned with police procedures and accountability, which have formally been implemented. They include a new, explicit definition of racial incidents; new procedures and practice at serious incidents; improved family liaison and handling of victims and witnesses; much more race awareness training; the establishment of the Independent Police Complaints Commission and the Metropolitan Police Authority bringing significantly increased lay scrutiny of policing in London.

## Controversy and debate

A study for the Home Office of the impact of the Stephen Lawrence case and Macpherson on policing conducted in 2002–4 found much activity and anxiety within the police, but also confusion and anger around the notion of institutional racism, widely misunderstood as labelling all police officers as racist. The study (Foster, Newburn and Souhami, 2005) found continuing mistrust and expectation of discrimination among minority ethnic communities, particularly young people. The police have been 'weathering the storm'; the managerial, public face signifies reform and a change of culture, but on the ground the changes are not so dramatic. A review of SLMI by criminologists (Rowe, 2007, p. xvii) concluded that 'while police officers might have stopped being overtly racist, a more widespread understanding of diversity has not been embedded within the service' and that the 'reconstruction of the police as an anti-racist service' has stopped short. SLMI is far from having achieved fundamental institutional change. Racial violence is still far from effectively policed; stop and search, and deaths in police custody continue to be much more likely for visible minorities; the criminal justice system beyond the police remains largely unaffected by SLMI. Legislation in related areas (freedom of information, refugees and asylum seekers, prevention of terrorism) strengthen institutional racism. In other words, the processes uncovered during SLMI and prior to that by decades of struggle and of solid sociological research still seem to persist.

## Schooling

Two big issues have been recurrently prominent in policy discussion around schooling since the postcolonial migration in the 1950s and 1960s, namely 'underachievement' and 'segregation and multiculturalism'. The former is focused on adverse outcomes for black pupils, while the latter is focused on the situation affecting some Muslim Asian communities. We will deal with each in turn.

'Underachievement' covers a number of linked issues. Black pupils leave school with lesser qualifications than whites and Asians, and they are much more likely to be suspended or expelled from school. Over more than four decades black parents have struggled to get their voices heard, sometimes with some impact at the local level, but at the national level, until recently, they have been fobbed off. In 1971 a famous pamphlet discussed *How the West Indian Child is Made Educationally Subnormal in the British School System* (Coard, 1971). The subsequent pressure on the Labour government in the late 1970s produced two useful reports by Rampton (1981) and Swann (1985), but by the time they surfaced, the Thatcher government was in power and they were shelved. Rampton and Swann drew particular attention to the problem of teachers' low and stereotyped expectations of black pupils and the small numbers of black teachers in schools to act as role models.

Until 2003 governments did not collect ethnic data on any of these issues, so that activists had to fall back on local data and campaigning. The advent of New Labour at last brought some purposeful recognition of the issues with the publication of national data and the allocation of grant funding for initiatives in schools to try to remedy the situation. The data confirm that pupils of Indian, Chinese, Irish and mixed white–Asian origin perform consistently better than average across all stages of schooling, while pupils of Gypsy/Roma, Irish traveller, black, Pakistani and Bangladeshi origin perform significantly worse than average (DfES, 2006). Table 17.3 gives a snapshot of different groups' achievement using the most widely used benchmark criterion.

**Table 17.3** Percentage of pupils reaching the school-leaving age of 16 achieving 5+ A*–C GCSE passes including English and Maths, 2005

| White | 43 | Indian | 57 | Pakistani | 33 |
|---|---|---|---|---|---|
| Black Caribbean | 27 | Black African | 35 | Bangladeshi | 35 |
| Black other | 28 | Chinese | 69 | National average | 43 |

*Source*: DfES, 2006 (Table 8).

Clearly there are many economic and cultural factors at work here beyond black–white racism, but the situation of black pupils is exacerbated by their being much more likely to be suspended or excluded from school. In 2003–4 the proportion of black Caribbean pupils permanently excluded from state schools was three times that for white British pupils (DfES, 2006, Figure 44). Research by Gillborn (1990), in particular, has demonstrated the workings of a teacher subculture which frequently has stereotyped expectations of black pupils as non-academic and as a threat to authority in the classroom: 'when teachers are asked to identify pupils with promise, black pupils are often under-represented. They are perceived as lacking in motivation or having a bad attitude or having highly inflated opinions of themselves. When a black pupil hands his homework in on time and does it well and is studious in class it is not noticed' (Gillborn, 2002). Increased academic competition between schools in the wake of the Education Reform Act 1988 has probably intensified these processes. The proportion of teachers not self-identified as white British was around 10 per cent in 2006, compared to around 20 per cent of pupils, though a substantial number of teachers do not respond to the ethnic question. The proportion of black Caribbean teachers is around half the proportion of black Caribbean pupils.

After 1997 under renewed pressure from black parents the New Labour government tried to use the authority of OfSTED, the schools inspectorate, to bring black underachievement, suspensions and so on, under managerial and public scrutiny. OfSTED (1999) reported on a sample of 48 schools which demonstrated a great diversity of practice, both good and bad. The government launched the Ethnic Minority Achievement Grant (EMAG) in 1999 with £155 million per year aimed at raising standards for all minority ethnic groups 'at risk of underachieving'. However, a report on EMAG found it 'was increasingly being used to meet the initial needs of newly-arrived asylum seekers, giving less flexibility to focus on raising achievement of British-born minority ethnic pupils' (DfES, 2003, para 4.5). In 2003 the government launched

*Aiming High*, a series of projects to tackle underachievement, including an African Caribbean Achievement Project, funding and supporting schools in developing a 'whole school' strategy. Evaluation of a pilot programme in 30 schools suggests some modest success, but with a long way to go (Tikly *et al.*, 2006).

A number of interrelated aspects of multiculturalism in schools have become national policy issues over the decades. In the 1960s there was much concern about the **integration** of the children of immigrants into the school system, particularly through language teaching. Some extra resources were allocated to schools with significant numbers of African Caribbean and Asian pupils, and there was some experimentation with 'bussing' secondary school students to prevent 'segregated' schools – those with a predominance of non-white pupils. In the 1970s and 1980 there was much conflict around shifting the curriculum and school culture away from monocultural, traditional approaches towards having both multicultural and anti-racist content (Troyna, 1993). In 1985 in Bradford a prominent headteacher, Ray Honeyford, lost his job for staunchly resisting the multicultural and anti-racist momentum. Despite the personal support of the Prime Minister, Mrs Thatcher, he had lost that of white and Asian parents (Todd, 1991). In Dewsbury in 1987 white parents withdrew their children from a school with an Asian majority, demanding an alternative choice. Eventually in 1992 the High Court ruled that 'local education authorities must comply with parents' wishes to transfer a child to another school, even if the request is motivated by racial factors' (Law, 1996, p. 170). But these events were exceptional, as schools adapted to the development of a consciously multicultural and multiethnic society, moving away to some extent from a completely monocultural curriculum and avoiding extreme segregation, with the exception of some northern towns. Johnston, Wilson and Burgess (2004) found that across England, attendance at predominantly mono-ethnic schools is only the norm for white pupils.

The disturbances in the northern towns in 2001 and the increased concern about Islamism in the 2000s has generated much increased anxiety about the integration of pupils and teachers from Muslim communities of Pakistani and Bangladeshi origin. There are several schools in the northern towns whose pupils are either over 90 per cent Asian or over 90 per cent white, where their representation in the town as a whole is roughly two-thirds white, one-third Asian (Burgess, Lupton and Wilson, 2005). The government has made it a duty of schools and education authorities to promote 'community cohesion', using funding to encourage collaboration between such schools. At the same time the government also favours the development of more faith schools, including Muslim state schools, which seems to give rather different signals. A number of individual cases have exposed an ongoing conflict over the role and presence of aspects of Muslim culture in schools, focused unsurprisingly around gender issues. In March 2006 a secondary school pupil, Shabina Begum, lost a case in the House of Lords concerned with the wearing of the jiljab, having won her case in lower courts. In November 2006 teaching assistant Aishah Azmi was sacked for refusing to remove her veil in school if a man was present, though she was awarded compensation for the bungling of the case by the school and LEA. In contrast to the banning of the veil in French schools, Britain is arguably stumbling towards difficult and unstable compromises with religion in general, and Islam in particular, in schools.

# Housing

The postcolonial immigrants of the 1950s and 1960s faced a housing policy regime which firmly excluded them, while priority was given to the housing needs of the white British in the forms of council housing and subsidies to mortgaged owner occupation. Racialised minorities were largely excluded from council housing by institutionalised discrimination in access to waiting lists and in allocation of tenancies. They were excluded from mainstream owner occupation by the conservative, discretionary lending policies of the building societies. Hence they had to fall back on informal borrowing for low-cost ownership or on private renting, often enduring very poor and overcrowded conditions. In the 1970s and 1980s this began to change as, to some extent, access to both council housing and housing association tenancies and to mainstream mortgages was opened up.

The contemporary pattern of housing tenure in Table 17.4 shows some of the diversity of housing experiences across the major ethnic groups. The Pakistani community comes closest to the tenure distribution of the white British majority, but the average quality and value of owner-occupied homes differs very considerably between the two groups. The table shows that social housing, rented both from councils and from housing associations, now houses proportionately much more of the black Caribbean, black African and Bangladeshi communities than the white British. Fifty-three per cent of the Bangladeshi community are in social housing, much of it in London where the costs of home ownership are prohibitive. In this respect the welfare state is making a significant contribution to the welfare of one of the poorest minority ethnic communities. Communities with higher proportions of relative newcomers, black Africans and Chinese, are much more likely to be in the private rented sector, which remains the reception tenure with the poorest housing conditions on average. The very high proportion of Chinese in private renting runs against the stereotype of their living above successful self-owned businesses, and suggests considerable housing need unmet by social housing provision. The Indian community, with a much higher proportion of economically successful households in middle-class occupations, has an even higher proportion of owner occupation than the white British.

Table 17.4 Housing tenure, percentage by ethnic group, England 2006

|  | Owner-occupation | Council rent | Housing Association rent | Private rent |
|---|---|---|---|---|
| White British | 73 | 10 | 7 | 10 |
| Black Caribbean | 46 | 24 | 19 | 11 |
| Black African | 26 | 27 | 16 | 30 |
| Indian | 75 | 5 | 5 | 16 |
| Pakistani | 68 | 11 | 6 | 16 |
| Bangladeshi | 39 | 38 | 15 | 9 |
| Chinese | 54 | 1 | 4 | 38 |

Source: DCLG, 2007 (Table 1.16).

Access to social rented housing in the 1980s, particularly for the black Caribbean, black African and Bangladeshi communities, was not achieved without much struggle and self-organisation. Efforts to undermine racialised access and allocation polices, institutionalised in both the council and housing association sectors, took many years. The allocation of social housing and of housing regeneration funds has always raised profoundly difficult issues for local policy making, just as much in the 2000s as in previous decades and perhaps more so because of more limited public spending on housing. A recent study of the Bangladeshi and white communities in London's East End (Dench, Gavron and Young, 2006) illustrates this very starkly. While recounting the robust survival of the Bangladeshi community against all the odds, it also tells of widespread resentment among white families that their housing needs have, they believe, been given a lower priority than those of the Bangladeshis. The older generation of white people want their sons and daughters to be allocated housing in the neighbourhood to keep kith and kin close together, not least to facilitate informal caring for elders and children. For a number of years the boroughs in some neighbourhoods had an allocation policy to match this aspiration, but that was seen to discriminate against Bangladeshis and more recent newcomers who had more pressing housing needs. This sense of injustice among low-income white families raises a 'moral dilemma' about the role of the welfare state and the allocation of scarce resources, which lies at the heart of recent support for the BNP in East London, the northern towns and beyond.

It remains the case that BME tenants are generally living in poorer-quality social housing in relation to their needs (Robinson, 2002). The formation of BME housing associations to address the pressing need for rented housing, particularly in London, has been a very important and positive development (Harrison, 2002). The increasingly vocalised demand for social rented housing from minority ethnic communities in the 1980s and 1990s coincided with a sharp decline in the supply of social rented housing with the end of new council housebuilding and around a third of existing council housing being sold to tenants under the 'right to buy'. So while racist barriers in access to social housing were coming down, new barriers were being erected in the form of reduced supply, perhaps an example of institutional racism or an ethnic penalty at the level of government policy.

Parallel processes also occurred from the late 1980s in the owner-occupied sector. The phased withdrawal of subsidies to home owners through mortgage tax relief and of assistance with mortgage costs for home owners claiming Income Support coincided with an accelerated growth of mortgaged home ownership among minority ethnic groups. The withdrawal of these forms of assistance to low-income households has differentially affected minority ethnic groups because of their relatively adverse socio-economic circumstances, and can be considered as another form of institutionalised discrimination or ethnic penalty in housing. Data on the proportion of minority ethnic households experiencing mortgage default, arrears and repossession are not available, but it is probable that they are significantly higher than average. Direct and indirect discrimination by mortgage lenders and estate agents was exposed in the 1970s and 1980s by social scientists and the CRE (see Sarre *et al.*, 1989). However, these institutions are not required to do ethnic monitoring, so it is impossible to assess the extent of institutional racism in the sector today (Phillips, 2002).

Despite these ethnic penalties in housing policy, the established minority ethnic groups have shared in the general improvement in housing conditions and in access to home ownership, while also continuing to experience relatively adverse housing conditions and homelessness. The lack of priority accorded to such issues is illustrated perhaps by the content of the government's report on *Housing in England 2005/06* (DCLG, 2007, Table 1.15) which cites only 'over-crowding' as a parameter of housing need in relation to ethnicity, and then simply compares white with BME households. This reveals that 10.4 per cent of BME households were overcrowded compared to 1.8 per cent of white households. A report for the government on minority ethnic homelessness suggests that 'minority ethnic households are around three times more likely to become statutorily homeless than are the majority' (ODPM, 2005, p. 5).

## Mental health

Mental illness and mental healthcare have been and remain an arena of conflict with and resistance to established policy and practice for Britain's minority ethnic communities, especially the African Caribbean community. For the latter there have been two linked 'headline' issues, consistently since the 1970s: the frequent diagnosis of schizophrenia and high rates of compulsory admission and treatment, particularly for African Caribbean young men. According to Nazroo (1997, p. 3) 'hospital-based research in Britain over the past three decades has consistently shown elevated rates of schizophrenia among African Caribbeans compared with the white population'. It was not until 2005 that the NHS published ethnic data on mental health patients. The rate of admission for black Caribbean and for mixed white and black Caribbean people in 2006 was over four times that for white British people (CHAI, 2007, Table 6). There are also much higher levels of compulsory detention in hospital from these ethnic groups under referrals from the police and the courts (CHAI, 2007, Appendix B, Table 5). Differential and racialised policing thus extends into the mental health field.

Nazroo and others have suggested that there are serious doubts about the widespread assumption that psychotic disorders are more common among the African Caribbean community, because all the studies have been based on hospital admissions, often involving short-term crises, perhaps misdiagnosed as schizophrenia. Nazroo (1997, p. 82) found 'no evidence . . . to suggest that Caribbean men had higher rates of psychosis than white men'. Nazroo also surveyed experience of neurotic disorders among different ethnic groups and found a much higher rate of depression among African Caribbeans compared to whites; yet African Caribbeans were less likely to receive medication from GPs for depression. Nazroo's survey confirmed earlier findings that Asians reported generally lower rates of neurotic disorder to GPs than whites, though this may be an underestimate due to inadequate diagnosis. There is certainly evidence that suicide, attempted suicide, self-harm and depression are considerably higher than average among Asian young women (Wilson, 2006). The situation of Asian women reflects the intense and violent pressures they sometimes face when confronting patriarchal attitudes and culture. Asian women's organisations such as Southall Black Sisters (Siddiqui and Patel, 2003) see many women with mental health problems arising from abuse by spouses and other male relatives. If and when they get access to NHS services, drugs and electro-convulsive therapy (ECT) hardly get to the root of their problems. Burman, Chantler and Batsleer (2002) detail how service responses to Asian women who attempt suicide or self-harm need to change radically to develop gender-sensitive and culturally appropriate practices.

The biggest issue, which has a considerable 'race' dimension and has dominated national policy making, is public safety, generated by fears that the closure of mental hospitals and shortages of resources in psychiatric units has led to the release of 'dangerous' patients into the community, compounded by a particular fear of 'black dangerousness'. The mid 1990s saw a panic over this issue in the wake of the case of a young black man with a history of mental illness, Christopher Clunis. In 1993, Clunis killed an innocent stranger (Jonathan Zito) on a station platform in north London; he had not taken his medication (Neal, 1996; Fernando, 1998). Concerns about patients, who for whatever reason fail to take medication, encouraged the government to propose compulsory treatment in the community. This led to 'hasty enactment of legislative and administrative measures . . . aimed at preventing severely mentally ill people from harming members of the public' with even more emphasis in practice 'on the role and on the regular administration of anti-psychotic medication' (Littlewood and Lipsedge, 1997, p. 255). Compulsory treatment in the community (in people's homes and in GP's surgeries) has been stoutly resisted by the Mental Health Alliance of more than 60 charities, professional bodies and user groups. After almost a decade of failure to get parliamentary approval, the government finally got through the Mental Health Act 2007 including Community Treatment Orders. Such measures obviously affect black people differentially.

The great majority of users of mental health services are not, of course, a danger to others. The treatment of people labelled as schizophrenic now involves only short stays in hospital during crises and is predominantly managed by the administration of psychotropic drugs. Such treatment creates a 'nomadic lifestyle' combined with the physical side-effects of the drugs, which often denies effective citizenship to the user. Medication often makes it very difficult to hold down a job, to maintain a home, a family and relationships. There are strong parallels with the situation of Asian women here. A major research report (SCMH, 2002) described 'the circles of fear' that surround the engagement of African and African Caribbean service users. The latter make 'a clear association . . . between the mental health services as part of a coercive "system" and the criminal justice system in terms of regulation and control', while mental health workers 'are clearly afraid to talk openly about issues concerned with race and culture that affect their practice' (SCMH, 2002, p. 4).

Manifestations of institutional racism in psychiatric diagnosis and treatment have been challenged over recent decades in many different contexts, by users, patients' families and anti-racist activists. The David Bennett campaign (see the start of this chapter) was led by his sister, paralleling the role of Stephen Lawrence's parents. Alongside these external pressures, there has been an ongoing struggle within 'institutional psychiatry' and the mental health services, not only to develop anti-racist awareness but also more appropriate, transcultural forms of practice. Fernando (2003) describes a range of local projects addressing these issues within both the statutory sector and the black voluntary sector. The NHS and the government responded to these pressures with an unprecedented series of policy responses addressing mental health needs and inequalities faced by minority ethnic communities (NIMHE, 2003; DoH, 2004; DoH, 2005).

## Conclusion

Social policies have played a central role in both maintaining and mitigating the processes involved. The challenge to discrimination and to differentially inferior treatment of minority ethnic groups has been led by the postcolonial migrant communities themselves, whose presence is firmly established both within the political sphere and within the professional and managerial realms of the public services. The 2000s has witnessed the growth of a new dimension of racism directed against British Asian Muslims, officially reflected in concerns about their alleged self-segregation and failure to integrate, something which had been fostered by local policy regimes and racism in previous decades. The New Labour era since 1997 has seen a wider acceptance and understanding of the notion of indirect discrimination or institutional racism. This has translated into a managerial, regulatory form of anti-discrimination practice, focused largely on the public services, whose impact seems likely to be quite limited. The racialised dimension of immigration policy has, if anything, been strengthened by the anti-asylum seeker panic and the new economic migration from Central and Eastern Europe. In the arenas of policing, schooling, housing and mental health discussed here, social science and minority ethnic activism have generated much better evidence and understanding of the complex processes involved. Hopefully this will contribute to more effective policy and practices for the future.

## Summary

This review of policy in a number of key areas suggests that racial and ethnic inequalities and injustices remain a prominent feature of British society and, hence, of its welfare state. It has been suggested that:

- The definitions of 'race' and ethnicity in contemporary British social policy have been shaped by the diverse politics (racist, liberal and anti-racist) generated by the postcolonial migration and more recently by the racialisation of the Muslim community.

- Since the 1960s racialised immigration control has been legitimated by anti-discrimination measures.

- Issues around migrant family settlement have been a constant arena of injustice, particularly affecting women.

- Since the mid 1990s policy and legislation on asylum seekers and refugees has ratcheted up their isolation and exclusion within British society, including their access to the welfare state.
- There are persistent ethnic penalties in the labour market, resulting in quantifiable disadvantages in earning power, particularly affecting people of black Caribbean, black African, Pakistani and Bangladeshi origin.
- Liberal anti-discrimination policy and legislation has had some success in mitigating more overt forms of discrimination. It has been strengthened in the 2000s by the use of managerial, regulatory processes in the public services.
- There has been a protracted series of important challenges to institutional racism in the police service, culminating in the post-Macpherson processes.
- Black pupils' underachievement in schools remains a prominent issue which central government has finally taken up with the prospect of some success.
- Minority ethnic groups' access to decent, affordable housing has improved compared to earlier decades, but is constrained by the shortage of social rented housing and by racialised income inequalities.
- Issues around adverse or inappropriate treatment of black and Asian people with mental health problems have come to greater prominence in recent years, shedding light on institutionalised discrimination and eliciting some positive policy responses.

## Discussion and review topics

1 How useful is the concept of institutional racism in understanding and challenging processes at work in particular areas of social policy?

2 To what extent, if any, has British immigration policy shifted from its racist antecedents in the 1960s?

3 How and why are ethnic groups categorised within British social policy?

4 What are the strengths and weaknesses of anti-discrimination legislation and policies in the UK?

## Further reading

Bhavnani, R., Mirza, H. and Meetoo, V. (2005) *Tackling the Roots of Racism*, Policy Press, Bristol. A thorough review of key issues, putting effective anti-racism at the forefront and holding up law and policy to critical scrutiny.

Kundnani, A. (2007) *The End of Tolerance: Racism in 21st Century Britain*, Pluto Press, London. A radical perspective putting policy in the context of the new, global wave of racism after multiculturalism.

Pilkington, A. (2003) *Racial Disadvantage and Ethnic Diversity in Britain*, Palgrave Macmillan, Basingstoke. Discusses a wide range of topics with a useful emphasis on cultural, geographical and labour market aspects.

Rattansi, A. (2007) *Racism – A Very Short Introduction*, Oxford University Press, Oxford. Lengthier than the title suggests, this unpacks this complex concept with great clarity and care, with plenty of focus on contemporary policy and discourse.

Sales, R. (2007) *Understanding Immigration and Refugee Policy*, Policy Press, Bristol. An accessible yet detailed account of this central issue, giving appropriate attention to both explanations and experiences.

## Some useful websites

www.equalityhumanrights.com – Commission for Equality and Human Rights – publications of the old Commission for Racial Equality are archived here, alongside the CEHR's more recent material on law, policy and current debates.

www.irr.org.uk – Institute of Race Relations – invaluable archive of critical analysis, data, commentary and articles on a wide range of issues, British, European and global.

www.guardian.co.uk/racism – *The Guardian* – archive of the newspaper's articles on race in Britain.

www.blink.org.uk – Black Information Link – up-to-the-minute source of information and further links on issues concerning black and minority ethnic communities.

www.refugeecouncil.org.uk – Refugee Council – campaigning and research material, advocating the needs and rights of asylum seekers.

www.ihrc.org – Islamic Human Rights Commission – a UK site delivering intelligent discussion and analysis of the issues surrounding the rise of Islamism and anti-Muslimism in the wider context of anti-racism and human rights.

## References

Berthoud, R. (2000) 'Ethnic employment penalties in Britain', *Journal of Ethnic and Migration Studies* Vol. 26, No. 3, pp. 389–416.

Blofeld, J. (2003) *Independent Inquiry into the Death of David Bennett*, Norfolk, Suffolk and Cambridgeshire Strategic Health Authority, Norwich, www.blink.org.uk.

Burgess, S., Lupton, D. and Wilson, R. (2005) *Parallel lives? Ethnic segregation in Schools and Neighbourhoods*, Centre for the Analysis of Social Exclusion, Paper 101, London School of Economics, London, http://sticerd.lse.ac.uk/case.

Burman, E., Chantler, K. and Batsleer, J. (2002) 'Service responses to South Asian women who attempt suicide or self-harm: Challenges for service commissioning and delivery', *Critical Social Policy,* Vol. 22, No. 4, pp. 641–68.

Cantle, T. (2001) *Community Cohesion: A Report of the Independent Review Team*, Home Office, London, www.communities.gov.uk.

Cantle, T. (2005) *Community Cohesion: A New Framework for Race and Diversity*, Palgrave Macmillan, Basingstoke.

CHAI (2007) *Count Me In: Results of the 2006 National Census of Inpatients in Mental Health and Learning Disability Services in England and Wales,* Commission for Healthcare Audit and Inspection, London, www.healthcarecommission.org.uk.

CIC (2007) *Our Shared Future*, Commission on Integration and Cohesion, London, www.integrationandcohesion.org.uk.

Clark, K. and Drinkwater, S. (2007) *Ethnic Minorities in the Labour Market: Dynamics and Diversity,* Policy Press, Bristol, www.jrf.org.uk.

Coard, B. (1971) *How the West Indian Child is Made Educationally Subnormal in the British School System*, New Beacon Books, London.

CRE (1984) *Race and Council Housing In Hackney*, Commission for Racial Equality, London.

CRE (2003) *Racial Equality in Prisons,* Part 2, Commission for Racial Equality, London, **www.equalityhumanrights.com**.

CRE (2005) *CRE Submission to Phase II of the Zahid Mubarek Inquiry*, Commission for Racial Equality, London, **www.equalityhumanrights.com**.

DCLG (2007) *Housing in England 2005/06*, Department for Communities and Local Government, London, **www.communities.gov.uk**.

Dench, G., Gavron, H. and Young, M. (2006) *The New East End: Kinship, Race and Conflict*, Profile Books, London.

DfES (2003) *Aiming High: Raising the Achievement of Minority Ethnic Pupils*, Department for Education and Skills, London, **www.dfes.gov.uk**.

DfES (2006) *Ethnicity and Education: The Evidence on Minority Ethnic Pupils Aged 5-16*, Department for Education and Skills, London, **www.dfes.gov.uk**.

DoH (2004) *Celebrating Our Cultures: Guidelines for Mental Health Promotion with Black and Minority Communities*, Department of Health, London, **www.dh.gov.uk**.

DoH (2005) *Delivering race equality in mental health care – An action plan for reform inside and outside services and the Government's response to the independent inquiry into the death of David Bennett*, Department of Health, London, **www.dh.gov.uk**.

ETS (2007) *Annual Statistics 2006-7*, Employment Tribunal Service, Department of Trade and Industry, London, **www.employmenttribunals.gov.uk**.

Fernando, S. (1998) *Forensic Psychiatry, Race and Culture*, Routledge, London.

Fernando, S. (2003) *Cultural Diversity, Mental Health and Psychiatry*, Brunner Routledge, Hove.

Foster, J., Newburn, T. and Souhami, A. (2005) *Assessing the Impact of the Stephen Lawrence Inquiry*, Home Office Research Study 294, Home Office Research, Development and Statistics Directorate, London, **www.homeoffice.gov.uk**.

Gillborn, D. (1990) *Race, Ethnicity and Education*, Unwin Hyman, London.

Gillborn, D. (2002) *Education and Institutional Racism*, reported by Berliner, W. 'The Race is Over', *The Guardian (Education)*, 12 March, p. 5.

Hall, S., Critcher, C., Jefferson, T., Clarke, J. and Roberts, T. (1978) *Policing the Crisis,* Macmillan, Basingstoke.

Harrison, M. (2002) 'Black and minority ethnic housing associations', in P. Somerville and A. Steele, (eds) *'Race', Housing and Social Exclusion*, Jessica Kingsley, London, pp. 114-29.

Heath, A. and Cheung, S.Y. (2006) *Ethnic Penalties in the Labour Market: Employers and Discrimination*, Department for Work and Pensions Research Report 341, London, **www.dwp.gov.uk**.

Home Office (2001) *Migration: An Economic and Social Analysis,* Research Development and Statistics Directorate, Occasional Paper 67, London, **www.homeoffice.gov.uk**.

Home Office (2005) *Controlling Our Borders: Making Immigration Work for Britain,* **www.homeoffice.gov.uk**.

Johnston, R., Wilson, D. and Burgess, S. (2004) 'School segregation in multiethnic England', *Ethnicities*, Vol. 4, No. 2, pp. 237-65.

Joshi, P. (2003) 'Jumping through hoops: Immigration and domestic violence', in R. Gupta, (ed.) *From Homebreakers to Jailbreakers*, Zed Press, London, pp. 132-59.

Kundnani, A. (2007) *The End of Tolerance: Racism in 21st Century Britain*, Pluto Press, London.

Law, I. (1996) *Racism, Ethnicity and Social Policy*, Prentice Hall, Hemel Hempstead.

Littlewood, R. and Lipsedge, R. (1997) *Aliens and Alienists: Ethnic Minorities and Psychiatry*, Routledge, London.

MacDonald, I. (1983) *Immigration Law and Practice in the UK*, Butterworths, London.

Macpherson Report (1999) *The Stephen Lawrence Inquiry*, CM 4262-1, Stationery Office, London, **www.archive.official-documents.co.uk/document/cm42/4262/4262.htm**.

Nazroo, J. (1997) *Ethnicity and Mental Health*, Policy Studies Institute, London.

Neal, S. (1998) 'Embodying black madness, embodying white femininity: Populist (re)presentations and public policy – the case of Christopher Clunis and Jayne Zito', *Sociological Research Online*, Vol. 3, No. 4, **www.socresonline.org.uk**.

NIMHE (2003) *Inside Outside: Improving Mental Health Services for Black and Minority Ethnic Communities*, National Institute for Mental Health, London.

ODPM (2005) *Causes of Homelessness in Ethnic Minority Communities*, Office of the Deputy Prime Minister, London, **www.nimhe.org.uk**.

OfSTED (1999) *Raising the Attainment of Minority Ethnic Pupils: School and LEA Responses*, Office for Standards in Education, Report HMI 170, London, **www.ofsted.gov.uk**.

ONS (2005) *Focus on People and Migration: 2005*, **www.statistics.gov.uk**.

Platt, L. (2007) *Poverty and Ethnicity in the UK*, Policy Press, Bristol, **www.jrf.org.uk**.

Phillips, D. (2002) 'Housing achievements, diversity and constraints', in P. Somerville, and A. Steele, (eds) *'Race', Housing and Social Exclusion*, Jessica Kingsley, London, pp. 25–46.

Rampton Report (1981) *West Indian Children in Our Schools*, HMSO, London.

Rattansi, A. (2007) *Racism: A Very Short Introduction*, Oxford University Press, Oxford.

Robinson, D. (2002) 'Missing the target? Discrimination and exclusion in the allocation of social housing', in P. Somerville and A. Steele (eds) *'Race', Housing and Social Exclusion*, Jessica Kingsley, London, pp. 94–113.

Rowe, M. (2004) *Policing, Race and Racism*, Willan, Cullompton.

Rowe, M. (2007) 'Introduction: Policing and racism in the limelight', in M. Rowe (ed.) *Policing Beyond Macpherson*, Willan, Cullompton, pp. xi–xxiv.

Sarre, P., Phillips, D. and Skellington, R. (1989) *Ethnic Minority Housing: Explanations and Practices*, Avebury, Aldershot.

Scarman Report (1981) *The Brixton Disorders*, HMSO and Penguin Books, London.

SCMH (2002) *An Executive Briefing on 'Breaking the Circles of Fear'*, Briefing 17, Sainsbury Centre for Mental Health, London, **www.scmh.org.uk**.

Siddiqui, H. (2003) '"It was written in her kismet": Forced marriage', in R. Gupta (ed.) *From Homebreakers to Jailbreakers*, Zed Press, London, pp. 67–91.

Siddiqui, H. and Patel, M. (2003) 'Sad, mad or angry? Mental illness and domestic violence', in R. Gupta (ed.) *From Homebreakers to Jailbreakers*, Zed Press, London, pp. 109–131.

Swann Report (1985) *Education For All: The Education of Children from Ethnic Minority Groups*, HMSO, London.

Tikly, L., Haynes, J., Caballero, C., Hill, J. and Gillborn, D. (2006) *Evaluation of Aiming High: African Caribbean Achievement Project*, DfES Research Report 801, Department for Education and Skills, London, **www.dfes.gov.uk**.

Todd, R. (1991) *Education in a Multicultural Society*, Cassell, London.

Troyna, B. (1993) *Racism and Education*, Open University Press, Buckingham.

Weight, R. (2002) *Patriots: National Identity in Britain 1940-2000*, Pan Macmillan, London.

Wilson, A. (2006) *Dreams, Questions, Struggles: South Asian Women in Britain*, Pluto Press, London.

Winder, R. (2004) *Bloody Foreigners: The Story of Immigration to Britain*, Little Brown, London.

Wrench, J. (2005) 'Diversity management can be bad for you', *Race and Class*, Vol. 46, No. 3, pp. 73–84.

# 18

# Exploring the boundaries of social policy

Catherine Bochel

## Chapter overview

Over the last twenty years it has become increasingly apparent that social policy analyses have a much wider relevance than had previously been generally recognised. The example given below provides a perspective on social exclusion in the context of food issues.

This chapter will consider why it is that issues that were not previously regarded as being within the domain of social policy are now seen as having relevance to social policy issues and concerns.

Traditionally social policy has primarily been concerned with areas such as health, housing, education and the personal social services, as covered elsewhere in this book (see also Chapter 1), but with the continued development of the subject of social policy, combined with changes in society, it is now possible to argue that the scope of analysis of social policy can appropriately and usefully be broadened. Authors such as Cahill (1994 and 2002), Fitzpatrick (2002) and Huby (2001) have highlighted the relationship between 'new' and 'traditional' social policy concerns, and the resonance that studying these can have. This chapter therefore:

- examines the development of the subject and the extension of social policy analyses to areas other than the traditional concerns;
- focuses upon issues of food, the environment and sustainability, transport and travel, ICT, and new forms of money to illustrate links with key social policy ideas;
- considers the implications of these for social policy and society.

## Spotlight on the issues
### Obesity and inequality

This obesity debate is full of humbug and denial. Fat is a class issue, but few like to admit that most of the seriously obese are poor. This is not about the nanny state telling Boris Johnson to keep off the claret in his club. It's about people like us telling people down there in the underclass to eat up their greens. Health professionals say 'we' must take more exercise and stop eating fast food, but mostly they really mean 'them'.

It's an old story – trace it back to the poor laws. The middle classes like to worry about the morals, health and drag on public expenditure of the poor. Horrendous projections of what obesity will cost the NHS naturally worry taxpayers forking out to fill hospital beds with poor fat folk.

True, many of us middle classes are overweight, but most of the dangerously obese – the 22% with a body mass index in the red zone – are to be found carless on council estates and not in the leafy suburbs where kids are driven to school in supertanker 4×4s. It is poor children at most risk of swelling up like balloons, in danger of losing limbs and eyesight to diabetes as they grow up. It's wrong to talk about 'fat cats' when the privileged are usually thin and sleek with bodies well-exercised by gyms and personal trainers on diets of radicchio and sparkling water.

Kinder experts look for sympathetic reasons why the poor are fat and unhealthy. Fresh fruit and vegetables are so expensive, they say. There is no transport to get from estates to the good food shops. Poor women are too hard-pressed to have time to cook proper family meals, so they snack. It's hard for poor children to exercise in dangerous concrete jungles, with no cars to take them to ballet and judo lessons . . .

So why are the poor getting dangerously fat? They are mainly a little better off and food has got cheaper . . . fat means poor and out of control. People who feel they have no control over their own lives give up. What's there to struggle and make sacrifices for? No job, no prospects, no point. A little of what you fancy compensates for life's big disappointments. So drinking and smoking and eating the wrong things become small treats in desolate lives. Being out of control becomes a mindset ever harder to climb out of. No job becomes no status, no hope and, rapidly, unemployable semi-despair, whatever the job market out there . . .

It is inequality and disrespect that makes people fat: obesity took off 25 years ago, up 400% in the years when inequality has exploded. People are only getting thinner when they are included in things that are worth staying thin for. Offer self-esteem, respect, jobs or some social status and the pounds would start to fall away . . .

*Source*: Polly Toynbee, 'Inequality is fattening' (selected extracts), *The Guardian*, Friday 28 May 2004.

Whilst at one stage it was possible to crudely characterise the study of social policy as largely concerned with five main areas of service delivery – education, health, housing, the personal social services and social security – the contents of the remainder of this book make clear that the subject has developed significantly. This chapter demonstrates that the application of social policy to new areas continues to develop, and that many of the analyses that have developed from social policy are applicable across many aspects of life.

## New and traditional social policy concerns

Briefing 18.1 sets out some of the new and old social policy concerns in order to illustrate the scope and permeability of the boundaries of social policy. It is important to recognise that these areas of interest are effectively a web of interconnecting policy concerns, impacting not only on one another, but also on issues such as social exclusion, lifestyle and quality of life, which in turn can be linked to topics such as the role of big business, globalisation and the world economy (see Chapter 21).

To illustrate the complexity of this we can consider the role of transport. Good public transport can be important to people without private transport, such as those on low incomes, people in isolated rural communities, and to people in congested cities, in enabling access to work and facilities. Transport therefore facilitates the workings of the economy in transporting people, services and goods. Conversely, poor or non-existent public transport may have negative health impacts on individuals and families in respect of limiting possibilities of employment, and hence affecting the level of income (in turn restricting possibilities for consuming food and other goods), reduced possibilities for socialising and poorer access to facilities such as GP surgeries, dental provision or crèches, and is likely to be detrimental for the economy, reducing governments' income from taxes and therefore their ability to provide services.

Clearly, social policy analysts also have to recognise that there is a possibility (or even a likelihood) that inequalities in these areas may replicate and/or reinforce existing social divisions. There may also be some role for government in monitoring or seeking solutions to such problems. Therefore, alongside a consideration of the effects of these issues on individuals and families, we also need to examine the wider policy context and consider how governments are responding to these issues. The role of other bodies such as the media and pressure groups may also be worthy of consideration.

*Briefing 18.1*
### Developing social policy concerns

| *Late 20th and 21st century concerns* | *Traditional concerns* |
|---|---|
| Food | Health |
| Environment and sustainability | Housing |
| Transport and travel | Education |
| ICT | Personal social services |
| Work | Social security |
| New forms of money | Employment |
| Leisure | |

# Setting the context: the changing nature of social policy

As outlined in Chapter 1, the subject of social policy has not always existed as we know it today, and has developed in a number of different ways over the years. However, it is possible to argue that for a considerable period the study of social policy and administration was based on the traditional welfare state and tended to focus around subjects such as health, housing, poverty, education, the personal social services, employment and social security. Much of this was set in the context of the post-war consensus, over a period stretching from 1945 to the 1970s, when the major political parties were in broad agreement over many aspects of the welfare state, such as the maintenance of full employment, funding of the NHS and a basic standard of social security provision, despite differences in political ideology.

This consensus came to an end in the mid to late 1970s and rapid change began to take place. A new language of politics and social policy emerged, centred on 'Thatcherism'. Emphasis, which had previously been on collective provision, now shifted towards the individual, underpinned by New Right ideology with its desire for reduced state intervention and greater individual responsibility, which in New Right terms justified a cutback in collective provision to tackle concerns around inequality and social exclusion. During this period much emphasis was placed on the restructuring of the welfare state. New terminology and 'buzz words' appeared – choice, participation, cost, efficiency, and effectiveness all became major parts of the language of government. Those who had previously been seen as 'service users' were now viewed as 'consumers' who were to have a say in the operation and delivery of services. This period saw the introduction of privatisation, internal markets such as those in the NHS and education, the use of performance measures and standards, a centralisation of power and the reform and residualisation of local government.

Change continued after 1997 under the Labour government. The 'Third Way' was adopted by some as an argument for a mix of market and state provision in welfare, albeit in a very different sense from that of the post-war consensus, and there was arguably a greater recognition of the structural causes of poverty, inequality and social exclusion, but at the same time individuals were expected to recognise that they had duties and responsibilities to society in return for social rights and services. These issues are all dealt with in greater depth elsewhere in this book.

Alongside these developments changes have been taking place in the global economy. Food policy, one of the areas with which this chapter is concerned, is no longer just about local or national policy; increasingly it is about European and global policy. It concerns powerful lobbies, such as the food industry, that use their contacts in government to help shape policy and steer regulations in the direction that food retailers and manufacturers find most beneficial. On the other side are the interests of the consumers, who are usually much less powerful. Multinational and transnational companies, and the ways in which they operate, impact on transport, the environment, work and many of the issues that can be associated with a broader interpretation of social policy.

Inequalities have become accentuated between those at the top, who are highly paid, and those at the bottom, who are not. Inequalities are further heightened by the consumerist nature of society today. Through the media we are constantly bombarded with products and images that we are encouraged to believe we 'need'. Local services and facilities such as shops, health centres and various welfare services are declining in preference to centralised facilities. These tend to require travel, costing money, causing environmental damage and increasing the risk that those who are poor or who do not have access to a car or good local transport facilities may be excluded. A further consequence of the consumer society we live in is the massive amount of waste we produce through our consumption.

These areas impact on social policy concerns and therefore need to be taken seriously by governments and consideration given to policies and approaches that might help to minimise any new inequalities that might arise from them. The remainder of this chapter considers a range of very different concerns that reflect the broader boundaries of social policy and which have been explored by social policy analysts: food, the environment and sustainability, transport and travel, information and communication technology, and new forms of money. Given the potentially huge debates around these issues the discussion here is inevitably limited and focuses on particular aspects of these debates.

## Food

Food is regularly headline news on the television and in the newspapers, be it over concerns with GM foods, intensive farming methods, the use of fertilizers and pesticides, antibiotics and growth-promoting agents, scares over carcinogenic dye in food products, or problems such as BSE, listeria and salmonella. The role of the media has helped to create a climate of public awareness and concern, which in turn has helped keep food on the agenda. For example, in recent years, one of the reasons that food has been in the public eye has been because of concern over the growing number of people who are obese. In early 2004 the Royal College of Physicians, the Royal College of Paediatrics and Child Health, and the Faculty of Public Health published a report, *Storing up Problems: The Medical Case for a Slimmer Nation*, which suggested that more than half of the UK population is either overweight or obese, and that if current trends were to continue, at least one-third of adults, one-fifth of boys and one-third of girls would be obese by 2020. Figure 18.1 illustrates obesity as measured by body mass index (BMI) for age 16+ in England in 2005. This shows that obesity tends to rise with age in both sexes. For example, 8 per cent of men aged 16–24 were obese compared to 29 per cent of men aged 55–64 and 12 per cent of women aged 16–24 were obese compared to 34 per cent aged 65–74. This trend continues until age 75 and over when levels fall (Central Statistical Office, 2007, p. 92). However, despite the recent emphasis on BMI-based health risk categories, there is not universal agreement that this is necessarily the best measure of judging obesity amongst all age groups. Research carried out by the London School of Hygiene and Tropical Medicine found that waist–hip ratio was a better indicator of mortality risk in older people (London School of Hygiene and Tropical Medicine, 8 August 2006).

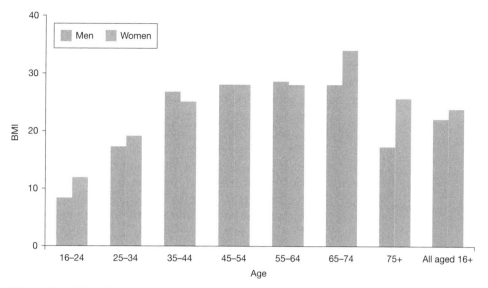

**Figure 18.1** Obesity as measured by BMI, England, 2005

*Source*: Adapted from Central Statistical Office, 2007, p. 93.

In 2001 the National Audit Office found that obesity was costing the NHS at least £500 million a year and the economy £2 billion. So here food can be seen to impact upon health, and poor health in turn impacts on the economy. This also raises implications for the role of education in tackling the link between poor health and diet, as well as over the food given to schoolchildren, as discussed later.

There are other concerns over diet and nutrition. Fewer people now cook their own meals, either using the numerous fast food outlets or relying on the rapidly growing market for ready meals. This means that we have less control over the nutritional content of our food. Ready meals and food from fast food outlets are often high in fats, salt and sugar. Furthermore, everyday foodstuffs often contain large amounts of additives and flavourings. This leads some to argue that there should be a role for government in regulating food manufacturers and retailers to ensure that the food we eat is safe. Others, such as Boris Johnson (Mayor of London and former Conservative MP for Henley), argue that diet and related issues should remain a matter for individual choice and that governments should not interfere. Johnson famously questioned Jamie Oliver's healthy school meals campaign, asking 'Why shouldn't [parents] push pies through the railings?' (*The Guardian*, 17 July 2007, p. 11). However, diet is a public health issue and to suggest that what we eat is purely a matter of personal responsibility merely reinforces existing inequalities in this area. People on low incomes may not be able to afford fresh fruit and vegetables, they may lack transport facilities to get to good food stores, and are more likely to suffer from diet-related diseases. However, this does not necessarily mean that they have a worse diet than the rest of the population. In fact findings from the Food Standards Agency in 2007 found that people on low incomes actually have similar diets to the rest of the population, suggesting that the population as a whole could eat more healthily.

Issues associated with diet are compounded by the dominance of the large supermarket chains and major food producers in the supply of food to the consumer, and this has a whole range of social policy impacts. In general, smaller local stores are unable to compete on price or the range of goods available in supermarkets and risk being forced out of the market. The supermarket then becomes the main supplier of food to consumers in the area. By relying on a small number of producers, they are able to influence the choices available to the consumer, but the supermarkets' primary concerns might be about the shelf-life or appearance of food, rather than with its taste or quality.

In addition, pricing policies within supermarkets often mean that fresh, 'healthy' food is more expensive than less healthy options. People on low incomes may find supermarkets expensive, and those without a car, or those without access to good public transport, perhaps in outlying rural areas, may find that it is difficult to get to them. Thus, as noted above, income affects choice of food and this in turn impacts on diet and health. The dominance of a few large food producers and retailers may therefore create hardship for groups such as low-income families, older people, disabled people and homeless people. In these ways food moves on to the social policy agenda alongside some of the more traditional concerns of the subject.

## Food interests

In the UK there are powerful bodies which represent the interests of food manufacturers and retailers, notably the British Retail Consortium and the Food and Drink Federation, which act as pressure groups (see Chapter 3) and which are skilled in lobbying government and shaping the food agenda to promote the interests of the food industry. As governments have sought to improve food safety and related health issues, lobbying has become intense. The Food Standards Agency was set up by the government in 2000 to act as a watchdog for consumer interests and public health in relation to food because of concerns that the interests of consumers have been neglected by policy makers because of the dominance of producer interests. The issue of food labelling has been particularly controversial. The Health Select Committee's Report on Obesity (2004) recommended that the Government introduce a 'traffic light' system for labelling foods, with red for high energy foods, amber for medium, and green for low, in order for consumers to see more easily what was in food products and to help tackle obesity in the population. The aim was that the food industry would work with the Food Standards Agency and introduce a single standard coding system in order for consumers to easily see which foods could contribute to a healthy diet. However, a coalition of major food and drink producers campaigned against this and argued for their own labelling scheme detailing the percentage of 'guideline daily amounts' of fat, salt and sugar contained in food products, with the result that there are now two labelling systems in operation. Opponents of the coalition of food and drink producers' scheme argue that by adopting the traffic light system, they would lose sales as much of the food would be shown to have high levels of sugar, salt and fat.

The interests of the major food and drink producers and TV and advertising industry came under the media spotlight when, as part of the government's drive towards healthier eating in 2006, Ofcom announced a ban on junk food advertising around all children's programming that have 'particular appeal' to under 16-year-olds. The major food and drink producers and the TV and advertising industry were concerned about loss of sales and advertising revenue, whilst health campaigners concerns were that people have healthy choices of food and know whether they are making healthy choices. Food is a controversial topic. We can see that there are push and pull factors at play here. The different food interest groups each have their own agendas and are constantly lobbying and working to achieve their aims which are likely to be different from those of other food interest groups.

Pressures do not operate solely at national level, but are occurring in Europe and globally, with one example of the latter being the accusation in early 2004 that the United States was trying to sabotage the World Health Organisation's guidelines designed to curb rising obesity and disease, which could be damaging to its food and drink corporations. However, the big corporations are not always successful in getting their way. For example, the multinational company Monsanto had to abandon its worldwide **genetically modified** (GM) wheat project following pressure from US and Canadian farmers who feared the introduction of GM wheat would lead to the collapse of their markets in Europe and Japan, where consumers had shown much greater resistance to GM food. Within the European Union the Common Agricultural Policy has also been a major factor affecting food production and policy, providing subsidies to producers (which generally benefit larger farms and encourage more intensive methods of agriculture), rather than, for example, encouraging measures that are good for the environment.

It is important to recognise that there are a number of different interests at work in relation to food production, distribution and safety. On the one hand there are the food and drink corporations that are often able to influence the agenda of governments through effective lobbying; and on the other there are consumers and health organisations. However, the reality is that (as is the case in many areas of social policy) these groups have differing levels of power and ability to influence the agenda and political decisions, and that at present manufacturers and retailers can often have more influence than consumers.

## Government policy

Following the Second World War, British governments generally sought to increase the amount of food being produced and to keep the costs of food down for consumers. For much of the post-war period, food safety policy was concerned with ensuring that health legislation and regulations were enforced, rather than with a broader view of the consumer interest or public health. However, following a number of food safety crises, including **BSE**, the Labour government established a Foods Standards Agency in 2000, and a new Department of the Environment, Food and Rural Affairs in 2001, in an attempt to shift some of the emphasis back to wider food safety issues and to give a greater voice to consumers.

However, food is also important at a more micro level. Until 1992, when the White Paper *Health of the Nation* was published, the Conservative governments had largely pursued an individualistic approach to food policy in which the individual consumer was responsible for their own health and diet through their food choices. This publication marked an important change in government policy so that, as Lang notes, there was 'a shift in policy from the denial of food poverty to an exploration of coping strategies' (Lang, 1997, p. 223). Now the relationship between diet and income was recognised, hailing a shift towards a more structural approach in terms of government policy, and a Nutritional Task Force was established to consider issues such as catering education and school meals. From 1997 the Labour governments aimed to build on this structural approach and to strike 'a new balance – a third way – linking individual and wider action . . .' (DOH, 1999, para. 1.27). The White Paper *Saving Lives: Our Healthier Nation* recognised the importance of a combination of physical activity and a balanced healthy diet. The Department of Health therefore sought to focus on matters such as the links between cancer, heart disease and diet and the health benefits of eating five portions of fruit and vegetables a day. A variety of 'healthy eating' initiatives, such as the National Fruit Scheme aimed at schoolchildren, were promoted, which sought to provide a free piece of a fruit a day for every child under the age of 6 from 2004. This structural approach can also be seen in the *Government Response to the Health Select Committee's Report on Obesity* (2004) which sets out a list of recommendations to tackle obesity which involve government working with schools, organisations and individuals in what was previously seen to be a personal area of food choice and diet. For example, the Health Select Committee recommended that government intervene in the National Curriculum to ensure that children gain practical cooking skills to enable them to make healthy choices; that schools in England implement a 'whole school approach to healthy eating and drinking' (*Government Response to the Health Select Committee's Report on Obesity*, 2004, p. 7) as part of the National Healthy Schools Programme.

Alongside this, celebrity chef Jamie Oliver ran a campaign in the media highlighting the poor nutritional content of school meals, which further acted as a catalyst for policy change. The Labour government agreed to provide £280 million to improve the situation. In addition, in September 2005 the Education Secretary announced that junk food was to be banned in schools, including a ban on slot machines selling chocolate bars and fizzy drinks.

Whilst the government might claim to have taken actions in relation to food safety, and to some extent in relation to food quality, critics are still able to argue that this has been insufficient. In particular, they can suggest that the individualistic perspective remains largely dominant (as is also sometimes said to be the case with regard to wider issues of public health, as discussed in Chapter 15) and that the interests of the food producers often dominate at the expense of those of consumers.

 Thought provoker

### The link between individual action and costs to the welfare state

As individuals we all make lifestyle choices. What to eat and drink, how much exercise to take, whether to smoke and so on. Our actions impact directly on our health but also have wider implications for the welfare state and how its resources are used.

- Should obese individuals who take no action to reduce their body weight be denied treatments on the NHS?

- Smokers cost the NHS an estimated £1.5 billion a year in tackling smoking-related diseases. Should smokers be compelled to give up smoking before they can receive NHS treatment or else have to pay for the treatment they receive?

- Binge drinking, especially amongst young people is a growing concern. Taxes on alcohol could be increased in order to discourage people from drinking to excess. Would this work? Is it fair? What might be the benefits to the individual and to the welfare state?

Food is clearly an important social policy issue. It has impacts on diet and on health. Government and the food industry have a responsibility in enabling individuals to make healthier choices. In particular government can intervene to regulate food manufacturing and retailing in order to help reduce inequalities in this area. In the past governments have pursued a policy of leaving food to the free market and have been unwilling to challenge the dominance of the food producers and retailers. This has suited big business, which has a major influence in food policy. More recently government has started to pursue a more structural approach, but the extent to which governments are willing to challenge the major food interests and to force change remains to be seen.

## Controversy and debate

### Wider actions and responsibilities

Food manufacturers and retailers have an enormous amount of power over the range of food available to us and the nutritional content of that food. They operate in the interests of profit and rarely take into account impacts on the individual or the wider environment. This has costs to the taxpayer and directly to individuals. For example, transporting products long distances via planes and HGVs causes pollution, with consequent impact on health, which might be a cost to the NHS, and damage to roads, which the taxpayers have to pay to repair.

- To what extent should governments encourage the large food corporations to take more responsibility for their actions? How might they do this?

- Why might governments not wish to challenge the power of the major food interests?

- Which groups are likely to suffer most from policies which fail to challenge the power of the large food corporations?

- Consumers are exercising choice when they purchase products from supermarkets. They are buying goods in a free market system. Should they take more responsibility for their choices, and what might help them do this?

# The environment and sustainability

> Climate change is about social justice, it is inter-generational, it is a global issue and it is about risk. If you are not serious about social justice you cannot tackle the climate change problem, because at the heart of the log jam in achieving an international deal is the social justice issue. David Miliband, Environment Secretary, *The Guardian*, 11 December 2006, p. 12

The Brundtland Commission, established in 1987 by the United Nations Commission on Environment and Development, developed a definition of sustainability that is about 'meeting the needs of the present without compromising the ability of future generations to meet their own needs' (Brundtland, 1987, p. 43). This concern with sustainability has gathered pace in recent years as governments have begun to take on board the importance of 'green' issues and as attention has been paid to their implications for social policy. Neglect of such issues in the past has led to damage to the natural environment, pollution, and land being stripped of its natural resources.

Britain annually generates around 30 million tonnes of rubbish, most of which is buried or burned. Much of this comes from the unnecessary packaging of consumer goods. Because producers do not have to take into account the cost of disposal of packing when they set the price of the finished goods, there is no incentive for them to cut down on unnecessary packaging. This is an example of what economists call 'market failure', where prices fail to reflect full social costs.

Figure 18.2 illustrates that the UK has one of the lowest household recycling rates in Europe at around 19 per cent, whilst some countries such as Belgium, Austria and the Netherlands appear to achieve much higher levels. Along with Portugal the UK sends around three-quarters of its municipal waste to landfill. Only Greece

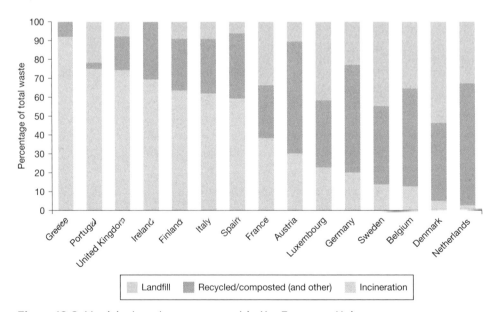

**Figure 18.2 Municipal waste management in the European Union**
*Source*: www.defra.gov.uk/environment/statistics/waste/kf/wrkf08.htm.

sends more, with over 90 per cent going to landfill. But how does this affect social policy and why should it be of concern to all of us? It is important to reduce the amount of biodegradable waste sent to landfill because it decays to produce methane, a greenhouse gas which contributes to climate change. This affects our quality of life in a variety of ways, including pollution of the environment, the quality of the food that we eat, our health, and our very existence. However, policies to address environmental issues often have costs attached to them and these impact differentially on groups within society. If people are charged for how much waste they put in their bins, for refrigerator disposal, vehicle recycling and disposal, then the burden falls most on the least well off in our society, who are most likely not to be able to afford these costs. Thus strategies which promote charging may serve only to exacerbate and reinforce existing inequalities. This may also lead to increased dumping of waste thereby contributing to environmental pollution with consequent impacts on health of the population.

Climate change is a serious problem which affects us all. Emissions of greenhouse gases, such as carbon dioxide ($CO_2$) are changing the world's climate. Over 40 per cent of $CO_2$ emissions in the UK come from our actions as individuals, for example, heating our homes, using electricity to power lighting and appliances, such as washing machines, fridges, tumble dryers, computers, televisions, mobile phone chargers etc. Driving vehicles and making plane journeys are also a source of individuals' $CO_2$ emissions.

Carbon trading is potentially a way of reducing carbon emissions. The idea behind this is that a global emissions limit would be set, then emissions rights would be divided equally across the population. Each individual would be given a carbon allowance or carbon credits which would be used up when, for example, buying airline tickets, paying home energy bills, purchasing fuel and so on. People who do not use all their carbon credits would be able to sell these to those with a high carbon lifestyle. Over time, the level of the emissions limit could be reduced in line with international agreements.

 *Thought provoker*

## Carbon footprints

We each have a 'carbon footprint'. This is a measure of how much $CO_2$ we each create and how much we are contributing to climate change.

- Calculate your carbon footprint and then decide which measures you are going to take to reduce it. See **http://actonco2.direct.gov.uk/index.html**.
- What difference can your action make?
- How feasible are carbon trading schemes?
- Who or which groups will benefit most from the introduction of carbon trading schemes?
- What measures should there be to prevent individuals and companies from using more than their carbon allowance?

But, as with the issue of food, there are a range of different interests at play and this needs to be set in a global context since the actions or inactions of individual nations impact on all nations and their populations.

In 1994 most countries joined an international treaty – the United Nations Framework Convention on Climate Change (UNFCCC) – to consider what could be done to address global warming. The 1997 **Kyoto Protocol** on greenhouse emissions was an addition to this treaty approved by a number of nations, although not by the United States, a major polluter, which refused to endorse it and adopted the stance that big business had no responsibility to tackle climate change. In the United Kingdom the government signed up to the Protocol, and is on track to meet its internationally agreed target for reducing greenhouse gases by 2008–2012. However, since the Kyoto Protocol events in the United States, such as flooding in New Orleans and individual states and businesses committing themselves to carbon reductions, has pushed climate change slowly up the United States political agenda. After considerable lobbying from EU leaders at the G8 Heiligendamm Summit in June 2007, the United States promised to '"seriously consider" a proposal that would result in a 50% cut in carbon emissions by 2050', and pledged the US to a '"substantial" cut in greenhouse gasses – but only if China and India do the same' (*The Guardian*, 8 June 2007, p. 1).

As with the issue of food, there are push and pull factors at play. Different countries and organisations have different agendas and it is likely to be the least powerful that lose out. Huby puts this well when she says that 'it is useful to recognise that the people benefiting most from environmentally damaging activities are not usually the people who would benefit most from policies to alleviate them. The latter tend to be people living on low incomes and those for whom age, disability, gender or race means that they lack the means, resources or power to avoid or ameliorate the effects of living in a degraded environment' (2001, p. 298).

*Source*: www.CartoonStock.com.

## Government policy

We have seen how the UK government is a player in the global arena in respect of trying to reduce the effects of climate change, notably through the 1997 Kyoto Protocol and the 2007 G8 Summit but what is it doing within the UK to tackle environmental issues and minimise the effects on social policy? It has taken a range of different approaches emanating from global, EU and local levels. Agenda 21 emerged from an **Earth Summit** in Rio in 1992; this aimed to promote environmental and sustainable development through a 'global action programme' across all participating countries. Local Agenda 21 (LA21) in turn emerged from this, based on the idea that because of their range of responsibilities local authorities were best placed to incorporate environmental issues into their policies and practice. Cahill notes that 'Undoubtedly, the most active and enthusiastic response to Rio in the UK came from those local authorities who adopted Agenda 21. UK local authorities have been among the pace-setters in the drive towards local sustainability' (2002, p. 22). Since its inception the UK government has continued to build on LA21 by, *inter alia*, encouraging local authorities to set up recycling schemes in their areas. LA21 has now been superseded by the statutory duty, under the Local Government Act 2000 to produce community strategies 'for promoting or improving the economic, social and environmental well-being of their areas, and contributing to the achievement of sustainable development in the United Kingdom' (Local Government Act 2000, Part I, 4(1)).

England, Scotland and Wales each set their own targets for waste recycling. England has targets for the recycling and composting of household waste of at least 40 per cent by 2010, 45 per cent by 2015 and 50 per cent by 2020 (DEFRA, 2007). Scotland met its 2006 target of composting and recycling 25 per cent of municipal waste by 2006 and has a new target of 55 per cent by 2020 (Scottish Executive, 2003). Wales exceeded the Assembly Government's municipal recycling target for 2003–4 of 15 per cent and has introduced a new target of 40 per cent recycling and composting by 2009–2010 (Welsh Assembly Government, 2002).

At national level the Stern Review was commissioned by the government in 2005 to look into the economics of climate change. This underlined the need to act now in order to 'avoid the worst impacts of climate change' (Stern Report, 2007, p. vi). It also drew attention to the differential impacts – 'The most vulnerable – the poorest countries and populations – will suffer earliest and most, even though they have contributed least to the causes of climate change' (Stern Report, 2007, p. vii). Again, this draws attention to the inequalities created by the impacts of climate change and underlines the importance of government policies to reduce these.

Much UK environmental policy originates from the EU and Britain has played a proactive role in shaping this, as noted previously. However, not all EU directives have been implemented by the government and this raises a problem that although the government is willing to set targets for recycling waste it does not necessarily set up the structures to enable EU directives to be met. This can result in further pollution of the environment through, for example, the illegal dumping of waste including cars and fridges as well as household rubbish with consequent effects on the areas we live in and on the health of the population.

The environment and sustainability are important issues which the government is now beginning to address, although not to the satisfaction of all. Whilst this is to be welcomed, it is important that the relatively new emphasis on 'green issues' is not seen in isolation but is integrated into all areas of policy making at both local and national level, including areas such as transport (see below), food, education and health.

## Transport and travel

Transport has consequences for many areas of relevance to social policy including the economy, the environment, food and social life. These in turn impact upon issues such as quality of life, inclusion and exclusion. Good transport systems for passengers and freight are vital for the workings of the economy. Road, rail, water and air transport are key to transporting goods not only from one part of the country to another but also from destinations around the globe. Globalisation has created new opportunities for business in the opening up of worldwide markets (see Chapter 21). For example, supermarkets source their produce from around the globe, enabling the consumer to purchase many types of fruit and vegetables all year round regardless of the season. For individuals, travel to distant destinations provides the opportunity to experience other cultures and broaden our knowledge of the world. This has been aided by the growth in ICT (discussed later in this chapter), which has enabled communication between people on opposite sides of the world to take place at the touch of a button, reducing distances of both time and space.

However, whilst opportunities may have been created, there are also downsides to the revolution in transportation and travel. The volume of traffic on our roads has increased, causing pollution, road damage, traffic congestion, noise, increasing the chances of accidents and having consequent effects on the health of people who live on or near to busy traffic routes. Many of these are clearly issues of concern to social policy analysts. If we have access to good transport systems then this has the potential to benefit our work and social lives. However, this is frequently skewed. For example, in 2004 one in four households in Great Britain did not have access to a car. Access to a car varied according to income group: whilst 90 per cent of households in the highest fifth of the income distribution in Great Britain had access to at least one car in 2005, this compares with only 47 per cent of households in the lowest fifth of the income distribution (Central Statistical Office, 2007, pp. 163–4).

Not surprisingly, not having access to a car increases reliance on public transport, and certain groups, including people living in the most deprived areas of the country, are forced to rely on public transport. For people who do not own a car, or who do not have access to good public transport, the effects can be damaging. Access to jobs and facilities may be restricted, with consequent effects on people's economic and social life. Research for the Social Exclusion Unit suggested that both the lack of transport and the cost of transport can be barriers to getting a job and has been linked to young people dropping out of college (SEU, 2003). The research also found that people who are reliant on public transport often experience problems attending their local hospital and that access to local supermarkets can be difficult. These issues have consequences for the range of facilities available in communities and for those who live there. If there are few shops, those which do exist may be more expensive and offer less choice, little by way of library facilities may discourage learning, and difficulties in accessing leisure facilities may make it hard to encourage participation in sport, with consequent negative impacts on health and well-being and opportunities for social life. The research also highlighted the disproportionate effects of transport policy on different groups in society. For example, traffic pollution may put children, pregnant women and those with respiratory illnesses at risk. In poor neighbourhoods this is more likely to trigger asthma attacks and exacerbate existing medical conditions. The health impacts of traffic pollution are further compounded by the likelihood of accidents. Grayling *et al.* show that 'children in the ten per cent most deprived wards were more than three times as likely to be pedestrian casualties as their counterparts in the ten per cent least deprived wards . . .' (2002, p. 6), highlighting the link between poverty and child deaths on the road.

So transport is not just about travelling, it is clearly much more than this. Poor transport is a contributor to social exclusion, 'it restricts access to activities that enhance people's life chances, such as learning, healthcare, work, and food shopping' (SEU, 2002, p. i) and 'deprived communities also suffer the worst effects of road traffic through pollution and pedestrian accidents' (SEU, 2003, p. 13). These are all reasons why transport is of concern to social policy analysts in the twenty-first century and why it is an issue for government to address.

## Transport/travel interests

Car manufacturers, road haulage firms, and fuel companies all have a major interest in a transport policy that favours road users. Big businesses, supermarket chains and others also seek to influence policy in a way that will benefit them. There are also a variety of other pressure groups, such as those that seek to represent pedestrians, and which campaign on environmental concerns and other issues such as health. As with the issues of food and the environment, discussed above, these interest groups have different agendas and varied abilities to lobby government, which is affected by factors such as the amount of power they each wield, public opinion and the role of the media.

## Transport policy

Transport policy is multifaceted, serving economic, social and environmental goals. It has the potential to affect social exclusion and inclusion and to impact upon the quality of life in communities. The 1998 White Paper *A new deal for transport* (DETR, 1998) recognised much of this in setting out a framework to promote healthy lifestyles by encouraging walking and cycling, and in acknowledging the threat to health through accidents, traffic noise, vibration and pollution. *Transport 2010: The 10 Year Plan* (DETR, 2000) built on the White Paper, setting targets in relation to road safety to reduce the number of people killed or seriously injured in road accidents. It also discussed measures to contribute towards meeting the target from the Kyoto Protocol to reduce greenhouse gas emissions. From this perspective we can see at least an element of 'joined up' government in the linking of environmental, transport and health issues.

The government aimed to implement the ten-year plan through a partnership with the private sector and local government and investment of £180 billion. However, Figure 18.3 illustrates that public spending on transport benefits the rich more than the poor. Just under 40 per cent of benefits go to the richest 20 per cent of households, whilst only 12 per cent of benefits go to the bottom fifth of households. Much of the investment is going into roads and railways with less money for footpaths and bus services and this benefits richer people because they tend to make longer journeys, mainly by car and rail. Poorer people lose out because they tend to make fewer journeys, mostly on foot and by bus.

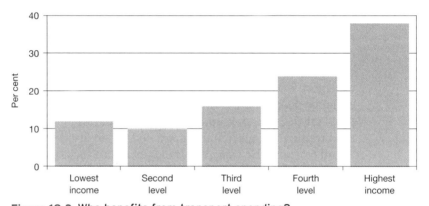

**Figure 18.3** Who benefits from transport spending?

*Source*: Redrawn from *The Guardian* 21.5.02. Copyright © The Guardian.

From another perspective, the Department for Transport recognises that good transport can help to reduce social exclusion and is undertaking a range of initiatives to this end. These include:

- Providing cheaper bus fares for elderly and disabled people.
- Targeting resources at improving transport links for socially excluded people in urban areas.
- Enhancing the role of community transport in providing a more flexible, demand-responsive public transport service.
- Encouraging access through better information on transport services.
- Making accessibility for disabled people a condition of public investment in transport.
- Reducing crime and the fear of crime wherever it occurs in the transport system.
- Introducing measures to reduce child pedestrian casualties in disadvantaged communities.
- National concessionary fares scheme for older and disabled people in England, providing free off-peak travel on buses anywhere in the country.
- Factoring social exclusion into local transport planning.

*Source*: www.dft.gov.uk/pgr/inclusion/se/socialexclusion.

However, whilst such measures are a start and have the potential to improve access to services and facilities for some groups, there is clearly room for further measures, such as the extension of concessionary fares to other groups in society, to improve access to work, education and libraries, hospitals, food stores and leisure facilities. This is particularly important given evidence from the Office of National Statistics in 2007, which found that bus fares had risen by 52.9 per cent over the last decade. Given that this is the mode of transport which many socially excluded groups are reliant on, it demonstrates the importance of government intervening in this area in order to try to reduce inequalities.

Perhaps one of the biggest question marks over Labour's transport policies has been its attitude to the car. In the early years of the government it emphasised an integrated transport policy, but it later, perhaps fearing being seen as 'anti-car', played down measures such as road-pricing by shifting much of the onus for these on to local authorities (although the then Mayor of London, Ken Livingston, did introduce such a charging scheme and a number of other cities have been considering the idea). In 2007 Labour introduced a draft Local Transport Bill which aimed to tackle congestion and improve public transport. The Bill set out plans to reform existing legislation relating to road pricing schemes in order to give local authorities the power to develop their own pricing schemes if they chose to do so. These were seen as a precursor to a possible UK-wide network.

## Information and communication technology

The growth of new technology has impacted enormously on areas such as work, money, leisure, travel, communication, consumption and the environment. This has led to a blurring of the boundaries between our public and private lives as the development of mobile phones, digital technology, the Internet and wireless networks are transforming the ways in which we work and use our leisure time.

Access to a huge range of information is available at the press of a button. Through the Internet we can download documents, search for specific information, access market information on customers, and market products to a worldwide audience. As consumers we can search for products and select the supplier that offers the product at the cheapest price, often below the price in shops. With the growth of cable networks and satellite broadcasters numerous TV channels can be brought into our homes, increasing the choice available to the consumer. We can now select from dedicated channels for films, cartoons, sport, history, cookery, shopping, chat shows and so on. Technology can also bring social policy issues into peoples' lives. We can sit at home and watch debates on homelessness and poverty and sometimes participate by phoning in, texting, or through TVs or PCs. We can choose to watch or listen to programmes that have previously been broadcast, for example by downloading podcasts at a time that suits us. We can see debates on programmes such as *Newsnight* on current issues with professionals, politicians and others. Soap operas dramatise social policy issues such as teenage pregnancy, drug and alcohol addiction, and so on. These can help raise consciousness around social policy issues and people can learn about what is going on in the world and how the actions of others impact on people's lives.

423

Modern methods of communication such as mobile phones and email have reduced both real time and space. We can be in almost constant contact for work or leisure. We can work from home and on the train, and can bring the world into our personal space. We can communicate with customers, family and friends from across the other side of the world via technology that enables us to see one another whilst we speak. Communication has become faster and the divide between the public and private worlds of the individual has become blurred. In the welfare state sector technology has the potential to make life easier for both professionals and consumers of services. Recent years have seen major attempts by government to provide services online, with initiatives ranging from those such as NHS Direct to online payment of council bills. It has also been suggested that the appropriate use of ICTs could help reduce social exclusion, for example in raising skill levels for employment, developing, individuals' self-esteem, and providing networks to bring communities together (Policy Action Team 15, 2000).

There are however a range of possible negative impacts of this revolution in ICT. For example, one of the main contributors to exclusion from this ICT revolution is cost. To take advantage of much of this choice we have to pay. If you can afford a computer and then to pay for access to the Internet and for the running costs of mobile phones then you can be part of this growth in new technology and the opportunities it brings. However, those who cannot afford to pay may be disadvantaged and excluded from access to knowledge. The Policy Action Team 15 (2000) report noted, for example, that those in deprived neighbourhoods and in lower socio-economic groups have lower use of PCs and the Internet than was the case for the UK as a whole. Similarly, research by Pilling, Barrett and Floyd (2004) showed that many disabled users required assistive devices (aids, equipment, adaptations) to access a computer or the Internet, and that the cost of such devices was also a problem for some respondents. There is therefore a danger that existing social divisions may be replicated or reinforced through new developments in ICT.

We have considered above some of the potential new technologies have to both reduce and widen the digital divide with consequent impacts on social inequality, but what evidence is there to support either view? *Inclusion Through Innovation: Tackling Social Exclusion Through New Technologies* (ODPM, 2005) challenges the view that new technology is widening inequalities. It cites examples such as the NHS Direct telephone service, which is available to all regardless of whether they are registered with a GP or not. This facilitates access to health services for people who might normally be excluded from them because they are not registered with a GP. Other examples include homeless people who, by leaving a mobile phone number on job applications, avoid the stigma of not having a permanent address. Access to information for people who are socially excluded is vital. Websites such as *Homeless UK* and *UK refuges online* list hostel, refuge, advice and support services for homeless people and women experiencing domestic violence across the UK. Such information can be accessed via a mobile phone or through a computer. Individuals do not need to own a computer since they are available in a variety of places such as libraries, drop-in centres, community centres, Internet cafés etc. Both central and local government provide Internet portals to enable people to identify services that are available through 'Directgov' and the 'Local Directgov' programme. The national charity *StartHere* provides a one-stop-shop electronic information service which is available on PCs, digital TV, kiosks and mobile phones, providing information on employment, housing, health and social issues. In addition, some welfare services now make greater use of ICT, for example Jobcentre Plus and the Pensions Service now encourage clients to make new claims over the telephone, whilst a small number of benefits such as Child Benefit and Carers Allowance can now be claimed online.

However, all the above presumes that people have access to new forms of technology and want to engage with it. Cost is still a barrier and research confirms that 'People living in households in the highest income decile group are seven times more likely to have home access to the Internet than those in the lowest decile group' (ODPM, 2005, p. 20). Davies (2005), citing the government's 'Wired Up Communities' experiment, which was completed in 2003, draws attention to the lack of interest in digital technology. As part of this project 12,000 disadvantaged homes were supplied with Internet access. One of the findings was that the majority had little interest in using it. Davies also suggested that it was a myth that disadvantaged people had the most to gain from digital technology, because it was the 'middle class suburbs' that made 'the best local use of the internet, through portals and discussion boards' (Davies, 2005). This has implications for educational achievement and access to life opportunities. Access to technology also has clear links with new forms of money, which is considered later in this chapter.

The growth in new technology has also raised other issues. For example, one challenge is associated with the regulation of information – there are issues around balance of coverage, access for independent producers, content and appropriateness. One element of these developments has also raised new health concerns, with mobile phones and masts having been linked by some to concerns over cancer. And there are concerns over data protection, privacy and civil liberties, with some expressing fears over the amount of data that is collected by the state and other organisations, and the uses to which this may be put. The loss by HM Revenue and Customs in 2007 of discs containing the bank details, addresses and telephone numbers of 25 million Child Benefit claimants has served to highlight concerns over the security of personal data.

## Government policy

In November 1996 the Green Paper *government.direct* (Cabinet Office, 1996) was published, providing a prospectus for the electronic delivery of government services. It envisaged the introduction of direct, electronic one-stop access to public services, to be available 24 hours a day, 7 days a week, in the manner of 'direct' banking or insurance services. This was embraced by the incoming Labour government and the White Paper *Modernising Government* (Cabinet Office, 1999) confirmed the central place of electronic government in the government's plans and promised that all government services would be available electronically by 2005.

*Connecting the UK: The Digital Strategy* was published in 2005, setting out a variety of measures to reduce social exclusion. These included:

- Giving all learners their own virtual learning space where they can store and access their work.

- The aim to give secondary school pupils the opportunity to access ICT at home.

- To establish by 2008 universal access to advanced public services delivered through and powered by information technology.

*Source:* Adapted from Cabinet Office and DTI, 2005, p. 6.

The publication in 2007 of *Transformational Government: Enabled by Technology* is part of the government's digital strategy. This outlines some of the initiatives taking place, including an investment of over £500 million for ICT in schools in 2005/6. All schools now have broadband access and are linked to the National Education Network. Computers for Pupils, a £60 million initiative to install ICT in the homes of around 100,000 of the most disadvantaged pupils in England, was launched in 2006; and MyGuide, an initiative that aimed to make the Internet more accessible for groups of people who currently do not use it, was piloted in 2006.

The government's electronic strategy has the potential to create positive outcomes for many. But a key issue that remains for social policy is that of access for individuals and groups to this ICT revolution, particularly those on low incomes.

## New forms of money

This chapter has illustrated some of the many different ways in which 'old' and 'new' social policy concerns can be linked. One final example is Pahl's (1999, 2001) work on the use of 'new forms of money' and the 'electronic economy'. We now live in a world where cash has been replaced by credit cards, smart cards and Internet banking and where benefits are paid into bank accounts instead of 'real money' (Pahl, 2001, p. 17). However, not everyone has equal access to this world of new money. Research published by the Financial Services Authority 'has shown that around 1.5 million (7%) households in Britain do not have any mainstream financial products at all. In addition a further 4.4 million (20%) are on the margins of financial services and have either one or two financial products only – usually bank or building society accounts . . .' (Kempson, 2000, p. 21). Cruickshank (2000, p. 227, cited in Pahl, 2001, pp. 23–4) draws attention to class differences in access to financial services and illustrates that nearly all those in social classes A and B hold a current account compared to only around half of those in social class E. It is also the case that when low-income households borrow money they often have to pay more for it because they are seen as a greater risk. Not only are they disadvantaged to start with because they are poor, but they often resort to money lenders and loan sharks because they find it hard to get credit through banks etc. and then they may end up paying extortionate rates of interest.

'Those more likely to be without personal finance services are concentrated both geographically and among certain groups of people such as lone parents, those on low wages, ethnic minorities, people with disabilities and the unemployed' (Financial Services Authority, 2000, **www.fsa.gov.uk/library/communication/pr/2000/093.shtml**).

Pahl has noted that 'There are clear patterns of exclusion from the electronic economy, which reflect education, income, employment status, gender and age.

Those who are 'credit rich' tend also to be 'information rich' and 'work rich'; those who are 'credit poor' tend also to be 'information poor' and 'work poor' (1999, p. viii). 'Those who are poor, unemployed or elderly are less likely to use credit cards than those who are in employment; and, except when they are in full-time employment, women are less likely to use credit cards than men' (1999, p. 69) (see Table 18.1).

**Table 18.1** Percentages of individuals using a credit card to make a purchase, by household employment categories

| Household employment categories | Credit card used to make a purchase | | | |
|---|---|---|---|---|
| | Men | | Women | |
| | % | No. | % | No. |
| Both full time | 42 | 350 | 41 | 349 |
| Full time/part time | 42 | 356 | 35 | 304 |
| Full time/no paid job | 37 | 256 | 25 | 170 |
| Woman main earner | 24 | 66 | 23 | 63 |
| Both retired | 21 | 174 | 14 | 119 |
| Both unemployed | 6 | 9 | 7 | 12 |
| All | 33 | 1221 | 28 | 1017 |

Total number = 3676 couples

*Source*: Pahl, 1999, p. 32.

People who suffer financial exclusion may be in need of more affordable credit. Some schemes do exist to help provide this and credit unions are one example. These are not-for-profit, co-operative financial institutions which are founded on the principle of self-help. Collard and Kempson (2005) have undertaken research into more affordable credit for low-income households and suggest that one possible way forward might be to work in partnership with banks on a range of regional community-based loan schemes, including larger and more professionally run credit unions.

There are also a range of alternative 'forms of new money' aimed at helping to reduce financial exclusion and to encourage inclusion. These include 'Time Dollars' in the United States and Local Exchange Trading Schemes (LETS) which operate in many countries including the UK. Individual schemes differ, but the general principle is that individuals belong to a network and earn credits or 'time dollars' by undertaking work such as carpentry, cutting hair, painting or child-care for another person. They can then spend those credits on buying goods or services from someone else in the network. This enables them to work and earn without the need for cash. It is estimated that there are about 300 LETS schemes in the UK involving around 30,000 people.

Financial exclusion has a range of implications for social policy. Alternative forms of 'credit', although increasing, are still limited, and without access to the full range of financial services one has to question whether one can truly partici-pate as a citizen in society today.

## Conclusion

This chapter has demonstrated how the subject of social policy has broadened out beyond the traditional areas such as health, housing, education and social services, to new areas, such as food, transport, the environment and sustainability, ICT and new forms of money.

In the past it was recognised that inequalities existed in the traditional areas and therefore it was appropriate that governments should intervene to try to address these. However, it is now accepted that inequalities also exist in the new areas and thus it is legitimate for governments to also try to tackle these.

Above all, the chapter illustrates the ways in which all these areas impact on one another. The environment impacts on health, which affects quality of life and well-being. Transport creates pollution, which in turn affects the environment and health. Poor health affects the ability to participate in society, whether this is contributing to the economy by working or taking part in sport and leisure activities. Good transport also provides access to work and facilities, and can enhance life chances and opportunities, whilst poor transport links can contribute to isolation and reduced opportunities for work and leisure. Lack of employment may result in financial exclusion, which affects the ability to purchase goods and services. Together these can create a web of social exclusion.

Whilst individuals can work to ameliorate the impact of the above to some degree, there is also a role for governments in helping reduce inequality in these areas and in encouraging big business to take a more socially responsible attitude to the provision of goods and services.

## Summary

This chapter has sought to examine and explain the relevance of social policy beyond the traditional boundaries and concerns of the subject.

In this chapter a number of issues have been highlighted:

- The constantly changing and permeable barriers of the subject of social policy, with economic, social, political and technological developments combining to produce both new areas of study for social policy analysts and new impacts on existing areas of social policy concerns.

- That social policy ideas and analyses continue to be relevant to new economic and social developments, so that each of the topics examined in this chapter - food, the environment and sustainability, transport and travel, ICT and new forms of money - is amenable to social policy analysis and to considerations of issues such as inequality, equity, exclusion and inclusion, as well as to other social policy concerns such as the appropriate roles of public and private sectors and the means of policy formulation, implementation and evaluation.

- There is a danger that existing social inequalities and divisions will be replicated and reinforced - the chapter has illustrated that in relation to each of the areas studied there is evidence that groups that have traditionally been the focus of social policy are in danger of losing out and being further excluded by recent developments, and there is a need for analysts and policy makers to be aware of this and that action, including potential government intervention, may be necessary to ensure that greater social exclusion does not result.

## Discussion and review topics

1 Why is food important for social policy?

2 To what extent are 'green issues' compatible with traditional social policy concerns?

3 What might a transport system that emphasised accessibility and inclusion look like?

4 Will the government's emphasis upon the use of ICT to deliver services reduce or exacerbate social inequalities?

5 How is inequality affected by access to new forms of money?

## Further reading

**Cahill, M.** (2002) *The Environment and Social Policy*, Routledge, London. This book explores the relationship between environmental concerns (including housing and urban development, food and work) and social policy and the role of governments with regard to these.

**Collard, S. and Kempson, E.** (2005) *Affordable Credit: The Way Forward*, Policy Press, Bristol. This study examines the scope for widening access to more affordable credit and looks at ways of developing sustainable provision.

**Grayling, T., Hallam, K., Graham, D., Anderson, R. and Glaister, S.** (2002) *Streets Ahead: Safe and liveable streets for children*, IPPR, London. Dealing with child pedestrian accidents, this booklet highlights the links between deprivation and high casualty rates.

**Lucas, K.** (ed.) (2004) *Running on Empty: Transport, Social Exclusion and Environmental Justice*, Policy Press, Bristol. Considers the social effects of 'transport poverty' and transport policy.

**Pahl, J.** (1999) *Invisible Money – Family finances in the electronic economy*, Policy Press, Bristol. A report on a study that examines the ways in which men and women use new forms of money and which highlights the potential for greater polarisation and inequality.

**Policy Action Team 15** (2000) *Closing the Digital Divide: Information and Communication Technologies in Deprived Areas*, Social Exclusion Unit, London. This report (also available through the Social Exclusion Unit's website, listed below) examines the importance and potential role of ICTs in relation to helping people who live in deprived neighbourhoods.

## Some useful websites

**www.dft.gov.uk** – the Department of Transport's website gives access to government policy and other documents in transport and related issues.

www.foodstandards.gov.uk – the site of the Food Standards Agency, which provides advice and information to government and consumers about food safety, including nutrition and diet.

www.jrf.org.uk – the Joseph Rowntree Foundation funds a wide variety of research and publishes the results on a range of social policy issues. Its website gives access to some of the results and recommendations as well as providing links to other organisations.

www.nacab.org.uk – the National Association of Citizens Advice Bureaux provide a variety of publications including research, policy issues and advice to consumers on this site.

www.cabinetoffice.gov.uk/social_exclusion_task_force – holds a range of publications by the Task Force and the Social Exclusion Unit that deal with some of the issues dealt with in this chapter together with many others.

# References

Brundtland Commission (1987) *Our Common Future*, Oxford University Press, Oxford.

Cabinet Office and DTI (2005) *Connecting the UK: The Digital Strategy*. Available at www.strategy.gov.uk/downloads/work_areas/digital_strategy/report/pdf/digital_strategy.pdf.

Cabinet Office (2007) *Transformational Government: Enabled by Technology. Annual Report 2006*, The Stationery Office, London.

Cabinet Office (1996) *government.direct*, The Stationery Office, London.

Cabinet Office (1999) *Modernising Government*, The Stationery Office, London.

Cahill, M. (1994) *The New Social Policy*, Blackwell, Oxford.

Cahill, M. (2002) *The Environment and Social Policy*, Routledge, London.

Central Statistical Office (2007) *Social Trends 37*, The Stationery Office, London.

Collard, S. and Kempson, E. (2005) *Affordable Credit: The Way Forward*, Policy Press, Bristol.

Cruickshank, D. (2000) *Competition in UK banking: A report to the Chancellor of the Exchequer*, The Stationery Office, London.

Davies, W. (2005) 'Don't assume that improving IT alone will breach the digital divide', *The Times*. Available at http://ippr.org.uk/articles/index/asp?id=508.

Department for Environment, Food and Rural Affairs (2007) *Waste Strategy for England 2007*, The Stationery Office, London.

Department of Health (1999) *Saving Lives: Our Healthier Nation*, The Stationery Office, London.

Department of Health (1992) *The Health of the Nation*, The Stationery Office, London.

Department of the Environment, Transport and the Regions (1998) *A New Deal for Transport: Better for Everyone: The Government's White Paper on the Future of Transport*, The Stationery Office, London.

Department of the Environment, Transport and the Regions (2000) *Transport 2010: The 10 Year Plan*, The Stationery Office, London.

Financial Services Authority (2000), www.fsa.gov.uk/library/communication/pr/2000/093.shtml.

Fitzpatrick, T. (2002) *Environmental Issues and Social Welfare*, Blackwell, Oxford.

*Government Response to the Health Select Committee's Report on Obesity*, 2004.

Grayling, T., Hallam, K., Graham, D., Anderson, R. and Glaister, S. (2002) *Streets Ahead: Safe and liveable streets for children*, IPPR, London.

Health Committee (2004) *Obesity*, third report of session 2003/4, House of Commons, London.

Huby, M. (2001) 'Food and the Environment', in M. May, E. Brunsdon, and R. Page (eds) *Understanding Social Problems: Issues in Social Policy*, Blackwell, Oxford.

Kempson, E. (2000) *In or Out? Financial Exclusion: A literature and research review*, PFRC, University of Bristol, Bristol.

Lang, T. (1997) 'Dividing up the cake: Food as social exclusion', in A. Walker and C. Walker (eds) *Britain Divided: The Growth of Social Exclusion in the 1980s and 1990s*, Child Poverty Action Group, London.

London School of Hygiene and Tropical Medicine, 'Waist-hip ratio should replace body mass index as indicator of mortality risk in older people', Press Release, 8 August 2006.

ODPM (2005) *Inclusion Through Innovation: Tackling Social Exclusion Through New Technologies*, ODPM/Social Exclusion Unit, London.

Pahl, J. (2001) 'Couples and their money: theory and practice in personal finances', in R. Sykes, C. Bochel, and N. Ellison (eds) *Social Policy Review 13, Developments and Debates: 2000-2001*, Policy Press, Bristol.

Pahl, J. (1999) *Invisible Money – Family finances in the electronic economy*, Policy Press, Bristol.

Pilling, D., Barrett, P. and Floyd, M. (2004) *Disabled People and the Internet: Experiences, Barriers and Opportunities*, Joseph Rowntree Foundation, York.

Policy Action Team 15 (2000) *Closing the Digital Divide: Information and Communication Technologies in Deprived Areas*, Social Exclusion Unit, London.

Royal College of Physicians, Royal College of Paediatrics and Child Health and Faculty of Public Health (2004) *Storing up Problems: The Medical Case for a Slimmer Nation*, Royal College of Physicians, London.

Scottish Executive (2003) *The National Waste Plan 2003*, Scottish Executive, Edinburgh.

Social Exclusion Unit (2003) *Making the Connections: Final Report on Transport and Social Exclusion*, Social Exclusion Unit, London.

Social Exclusion Unit (2002) *Making the Connections: Transport and Social Exclusion – Interim Findings from the Social Exclusion Unit*, Social Exclusion Unit, London.

Stern, N. (2007) *The Economics of Climate Change: The Stern Review*, Cambridge University Press, Cambridge.

Toynbee, P. (2004) 'Inequality is fattening', *The Guardian*, 28 May.

'Chavs, losers, addicts and frankfurter buses', *The Guardian*, 17 July 2007.

'Strings attached to Bush climate pledge', *The Guardian*, 8 June 2007.

'We nearly threw it away. We must be more radical', *The Guardian*, 11 December 2006.

Welsh Assembly Government (2002) *Wise about Waste: The National Waste Strategy for Wales*, Welsh Assembly, Cardiff.

www.defra.gov.uk/environment/statistics/waste/kf/wrkf08.htm.

http://actonco2.direct.gov.uk/Index.html.

www.dft.gov.uk/pgr/inclusion/se/socialexclusion.

# Part IV

## EUROPEAN AND INTERNATIONAL DEVELOPMENTS

# 19

# European welfare states and European Union social policy

Rob Sykes

## Chapter overview

This chapter deals with the character and roles of European Union (EU) social policy in the context of the problems confronting European welfare states. Social policy is usually understood and analysed in terms of national boundaries and national policies. The EU, however, is a body linking together its national member states in a variety of ways, and affecting these states through a variety of policy making and policy delivery processes including some, though not yet all, aspects of what is usually regarded as social policy. In order to explain how the EU may be affecting social policy in the member states, this chapter reviews not only the development and current character of its specifically *social* policy initiatives (and this in itself is complicated by the way in which social policy is regarded within the EU), but also sets these social policy initiatives in the context of the EU's main economic policies. Some analysts argue, indeed, that EU social policy is very much the 'poor relation' of the more developed and significant economic policies it has developed, such as the Single Market and the Single Currency (the euro). Others argue that although primacy may have been given by the EU to economic issues and policies in the past, EU social policy has now developed to become a (relatively) independent area of EU policy making which increasingly affects the member states of the EU.

Different EU bodies, such as the Commission, the Council and the European Parliament, are involved in making EU policy alongside the governments of the member states. Does this then mean that EU policy, including EU social policy, is becoming 'transnational' - are we approaching a European welfare state? Having looked at the development and current character of EU social policy and how policy is made, the chapter concludes by discussing possible futures for EU social policy, including such important developments as the EU Declaration on Human Rights, the enlargement of EU membership in June 2004, and the proposed Treaty of Lisbon.

The chapter therefore considers:

- patterns of similarity and difference in European welfare states;
- the development of the EU's *social dimension* - from common market to European Union;
- social policy making in the EU;
- EU social policy now and in the future.

## Spotlight on the issues
## Europe: pensions crisis in a greying continent

Italy's state pension scheme faces bankruptcy within the next decade unless some radical reforms are enacted soon. Italy's state pension fund will shortly have to pay out to retirees more than it receives each year in contributions from an ever decreasing national workforce.

In France the public debt stands at 67 per cent of GDP – five times its level in 1980. However, when gross pension liabilities are included the public debt rises to 120 per cent. One in four people is employed by the public sector, and there are simply not enough people working to fund the pensions of those who are retired.

Germany has one of the lowest birth rates in Europe and, at the same time, people are living longer. The German parliament has voted to raise the retirement age from 65 to 67 to help reduce pension costs. Trade unionists and others have demonstrated against these changes, and some politicians have argued that the changes will actually lead to higher unemployment and pensioner poverty.

In the UK the age at which Britons can claim the state pension will rise gradually from 65 to 68 over the next three decades as the government struggles to cope with an ageing population and rising pension costs. People now live longer but save less for their pensions, and the state pension system is increasingly unable to cope.

If we look to the East of Europe, the crisis is even worse. In Hungary there is a mixture of low fertility rates and relatively high death rates: the country is set to lose 8 per cent of its population between 2000 and 2025. Only 60 per cent of working-age Hungarians actually work. There is a state pension scheme but this is inadequate to the extent that early retiring police and armed forces workers have been told to expect nothing from the scheme. The retirement age will also steadily increase as in Western European countries.

Clearly the pensions crisis is a major social policy issue confronting all European countries as its inhabitants get older, fewer children are born, relatively fewer workers are paying taxes upon which welfare benefits including pensions are based, and pension schemes fail to cope. If this is the case, what is the European Union (EU), to which all the above states belong, seeking to do about providing a possible trans-European response to the pensions crisis? The answer is, essentially, nothing. As we shall see in the chapter that follows, despite the fact that the various European countries share a number of economic and social welfare problems only some of those problems are dealt with at the EU level. The EU is fundamentally concerned with issues surrounding the single European market and although it has a social policy dimension, many areas, including pensions, are expressly excluded from the EU's intervention except in terms of sharing information about the dimensions of the problem and different governments' approaches to coping with it.

# Patterns of similarity and difference in European welfare states

This section reviews some of the patterns of similarity and difference in the nature of social policy issues or problems confronted by different European Union welfare states. This provides a background to help understand how and why the EU's social dimension has been developed, and the ongoing issues for EU social policy. The best and most available source for statistical and other descriptive material about the comparative information referred to here is the European Union's own statistical service, *Eurostat* (see Briefing 19.1: Accessing EU information)

## A greying and less familial Europe?

As the 'baby-boomers' born after the Second World War reach retirement age there will be growing numbers of people in the elderly age groups. Whilst at present people aged 65 and over represent about 16 per cent of the total population across the EU, those below 15 represent 17 per cent. However, by 2010 these ratios will become 18 per cent and 16 per cent. The most dramatic increase will occur in the number of 'very old' people (aged over 80), which will rise by almost 50 per cent over the next 15 years. Although the accession states joining the EU in 2004 currently have a younger age structure than existing member states (those 65+: 13 per cent; those less than 15 years: 19 per cent), the overall effect on the age structure of the EU will be both small and temporary. In the medium to long term, acceding states will also tend to reinforce the population decline of the EU. Given the low fertility levels, the proportion of children in the population is rapidly declining and by 2020 the share of older people will approach EU-15 levels.

These rising old age **dependency rates** are important for a number of reasons. First, there is the question of whether older people have adequate financial support, especially as they are now likely to live longer than in the past. The so-called 'pensions crisis' does not only affect those who are currently approaching retirement

## Briefing 19.1
### Accessing EU information

The best and easiest way to EU information is via its website, *Europa*. The main address for this website is **http://europa.eu.int**. Within this site the official, legal texts such as treaties and directives can be found, but so too can a whole range of other useful material on the EU social and other policies, its institutions and so on. Statistical and allied materials can be found via the *Eurostat* site within *Europa*, most of it for free. For further information on this and other sources on the EU refer to the *Further reading* section at the end of this chapter.

age, however, but has serious implications for those now starting or into their work careers. All this is happening at a time when the proportions of people in work and paying taxes for welfare services are also declining. Put simply, a fundamental question confronting all EU member states is, 'Who will pay for pensions in the future?' Turning to non-financial factors, clearly older people are likely to need health and other forms of care more than younger people. If services are not provided through state welfare systems then there are two alternatives for the care of older people: the market or the family. With regard to the latter, care of the elderly, and for that matter other 'welfare' provision through families, is being challenged by developments in family and household structures across the EU. Typically, there are fewer and later marriages, and also more marital breakdowns. In 2001, there were only 5 marriages per 1,000 inhabitants in the EU-15 compared with almost 8 in 1970. The divorce rate for marriages in 1960 was 15 per cent, whereas for marriages entered into in 1980 the figure almost doubled to 28 per cent. The trend in the EU is towards smaller households, with more people living alone at all ages.

These are overall statistics; in some of the EU states these issues are more pressing since the age dependency ratios, for example, are even higher than these averages. Table 19.1 indicates the old age dependency ratios both for the EU overall and the 15 member states). As can be seen from these figures, the issues of old age dependency are set to become particularly acute in Germany (D), Greece (EL) and Italy (I), whilst Ireland (IRL) will have the lowest ratio.

All letters and corresponding country names used in Tables 19.1, 19.2 and 19.3 are appended at the end of the chapter.

## Unemployment

Unemployment is a continuing area of concern for the EU and all member states. In 2001, the total number of unemployed people in the EU stood at 12.8 million or 7.4 per cent of the labour force. This is the lowest rate since 1992. Looking at the trend in unemployment in 1994 there was a peak rate of 10.5 per cent for the EU-15. The rates in Denmark, Spain, Portugal, Finland and the United Kingdom fell by more than 40 per cent during the period from 1994 to 2001, and in Ireland and the Netherlands, the 2001 rates are just one-third of the 1994 rates. The countries

**Table 19.1** EU age dependency ratios

*Old age dependency ratio (population aged 65 and over as a percentage of the working-age population (15–64) on 1 January)*

|  | EU15 | B | DK | D | EL | E | F | IRL | I | L | NL | A | P | FIN | S | UK |
|---|---|---|---|---|---|---|---|---|---|---|---|---|---|---|---|---|
| 1990 | 21.6 | 22.1 | 23.2 | 21.6 | 20.4 | 20.2 | 21.1 | 10.0 | 21.6 | 19.3 | 18.6 | 22.1 | 20.0 | 19.8 | 27.7 | 24.0 |
| 1995 | 23.0 | 23.8 | 22.7 | 22.5 | 22.8 | 22.3 | 23.0 | 17.8 | 24.1 | 20.6 | 19.3 | 22.4 | 21.6 | 21.1 | 27.4 | 24.3 |
| 2000 | 24.3 | 25.5 | 22.2 | 23.9 | 25.6 | 24.6 | 24.6 | 16.8 | 26.6 | 21.4 | 20.0 | 22.9 | 23.8 | 22.2 | 26.9 | 23.9 |
| 2001 | : | 25.7 | 22.2 | 24.5 | : | 24.7 | 24.8 | 16.6 | 27.1 | 21.5 | 20.1 | 22.9 | 24.2 | 22.4 | 26.8 | : |
| 2010 | 27.3 | 26.7 | 24.6 | 30.3 | 29.2 | 26.8 | 25.5 | 17.3 | 31.3 | 23.6 | 22.3 | 26.3 | 24.5 | 24.9 | 28.1 | 24.2 |

*Source*: Eurostat – Demographic Statistics © European Communities, 1995–2008.

**Table 19.2 EU unemployment rates**

*Unemployment rate (total unemployed individuals as a share of total active population. Harmonised series)*

|  | EU-15 | B | DK | D | EL | E | F | IRL | I | L | NL | A | P | FIN | S | UK |
|---|---|---|---|---|---|---|---|---|---|---|---|---|---|---|---|---|
| 2001 Total | 7.4 | 6.6 | 4.3 | 7.7 | 10.5 | 10.6 | 8.6 | 3.8 | 9.4 | 2.0 | 2.4 | 3.6 | 4.1 | 9.1 | 4.9 | 5.0 |
| 2001 Men | 6.4 | 6.0 | 3.8 | 7.7 | 7.0 | 7.5 | 7.0 | 3.9 | 7.3 | 1.7 | 1.9 | 3.0 | 3.2 | 8.6 | 5.2 | 5.5 |
| 2001 Women | 8.5 | 7.4 | 4.9 | 7.8 | 15.6 | 15.4 | 10.3 | 3.7 | 12.9 | 2.4 | 3.0 | 4.3 | 5.1 | 9.7 | 4.5 | 4.4 |
| 2000 Total | 7.8 | 6.9 | 4.4 | 7.8 | 11.1 | 11.3 | 9.3 | 4.2 | 10.4 | 2.3 | 2.8 | 3.7 | 4.1 | 9.8 | 5.8 | 5.4 |
| 1994 Total | 10.5 | 9.8 | 7.7 | 8.2 | 8.9 | 19.8 | 11.8 | 14.3 | 11.0 | 3.2 | 6.8 | 3.8 | 6.9 | 16.6 | 9.4 | 9.4 |
| Unemployment, 2001 (1000) | 12861 | 286 | 123 | 3073 | 457 | 1892 | 2221 | 68 | 2248 | 4 | 198 | 137 | 212 | 238 | 225 | 1485 |

*Source*: Eurostat – Unemployment rates (ILO definition) © European Communities, 1995–2008.

with the highest unemployment continued to be Spain and Greece. Women are more likely than men to be unemployed in the EU, and the female unemployment rate (8.7 per cent) was still more than two points higher than the male unemployment rate (6.4 per cent) in 2001. Table 19.2 illustrates the patterns of national variation.

However, these national unemployment rates conceal significant regional differences within countries: in Germany between the west (low) and east (high), in Italy between the north (low) and the south (high), and in the UK between the north (high) and south (low). In 2000 in Germany, the unemployment rate ranged from less than half the national average of 7.9 per cent in Oberbayern (3.1 per cent) to 16.9 per cent in Dessau and Halle in Sachsen-Anhalt. Similarly, while many regions in the north of Italy were largely unaffected by unemployment, between 21 and 25 per cent of the workforce in the southern regions of Campania, Calabria and Sicily was unemployed. In the UK, Merseyside (13.2 per cent), in particular, has high unemployment compared with the south-east (2.2 per cent).

Regional differences in unemployment are even more pronounced among young people (under 25 years of age). Dytiki Macedonia and Sterea Ellada in Greece and parts of Andalucia in Spain all recorded youth unemployment rates of 40 per cent or more in 2001 and several regions in southern Italy have rates of 50 per cent or more.

As if these rates of unemployment were not sufficiently problematic from an overall welfare viewpoint, what is even more worrying is the fact that a significant proportion of the unemployment in the EU is long term, i.e. of twelve months or longer duration. In fact, just under half (44 per cent) of the unemployed in the EU have been out of work for this period or longer. Once again the rates of long-term unemployment vary across the EU: in Denmark, the Netherlands and Austria less than 1 per cent of the unemployed were affected, but in Greece, Spain and Italy the rates are 5 per cent. Interestingly, the gender breakdown of long-term unemployment shows that whilst in general there is a greater likelihood of being in this category if you are a woman (3.9 per cent) than a man (2.8 per cent), in both the UK and Ireland the pattern is reversed, with men being almost twice as likely as women to be out of work for long periods. Once again, it is when we look at youth unemployment that the worst picture is revealed. The period of six months or more is used for measuring long-term unemployment amongst young people, and on this basis, though it had reduced from a level of 13.1 per cent in 1994, the level was still 6.9 per cent in 2001. Greek and Italian young people are particularly likely to be long-term unemployed (18 per cent and 20 per cent respectively).

## Poverty and social exclusion

People living in households which are poor and/or where one or more adult is unemployed are also more likely to be suffering from some form of sickness or ill-health, to be educated to a lower level, and in general to suffer from exclusion from the full range of social, economic and cultural activities in their society. Two very simple measures of the pattern of relative wealth and poverty are the distribution of income by head and between different groups in a society. The usual indicator used in the EU to indicate a basic measure of wealth and poverty is the distribution of a country's **Gross Domestic Product** per head. Table 19.3 indicates what the pattern of GDP per capita is across the EU.

What this simplistic measure shows is that in some countries, notably Greece, Spain, and Portugal, the level of GDP per head is significantly below the EU average, and people in these countries may thus be regarded as 'poorer' than their counterparts in the rest of the EU. Although these measures are used as a basis for certain EU intervention programmes on a regional basis, notably the Structural Funds, it is obvious that not all citizens of a given country *do* get an equal portion of the national GDP. Some groups, the 'rich', in each country get more than their proportional 'share', and some, the 'poor', much less. The distribution of income between different groups of the population varies in different EU countries (all of the following figures in this section refer to 1999). The top 20 per cent, or quintile, of the population received 4.6 times as much of the total income as the bottom 20 per cent of the population of the EU as a whole. This pattern of inequality is generally higher in the southern and non-continental countries: Portugal was the highest with the top quintile getting 6.4 times what the bottom quintile received, but Greece, Spain, Ireland, Italy and the UK were also above the EU average. Those countries with the least unequal distribution between top and bottom income quintiles were Denmark and Sweden (3.2), followed by Finland (3.4), Germany (3.6) and the Netherlands and Austria (3.7). In general, the member states with higher levels of inequality tend to have a lower level of average income (although the UK has both above-average income and above-average inequality).

It is also possible to map the likelihood of being in poverty against other factors such as patterns of employment and unemployment in a household, the age of household members, whether the household is headed by a lone parent, and so on. Certain household types display higher than average levels of being at risk of

Table 19.3 GDP per head (Index EU-15 = 100, in PPS)

|  | EU 15 | Euro 12 | B | DK | D | EL | E | F | IRL | I | L | NL | A | P | FIN | S | UK |
|---|---|---|---|---|---|---|---|---|---|---|---|---|---|---|---|---|---|
| **1995** | 100 | 101 | 113 | 118 | 110 | 66 | 78 | 104 | 94 | 104 | 172 | 110 | 111 | 70 | 97 | 103 | 97 |
| **2001** | 100 | 100 | 106 | 119 | 104 | 67 | 83 | 100 | 119 | 105 | 191 | 112 | 112 | 74 | 103 | 100 | 100 |

poverty: single parents with dependent children (38 per cent), young people living alone (32 per cent), old people living alone (24 per cent) and women living alone (24 per cent). Couples with three or more dependent children were also at high risk (25 per cent).

Again, the overall picture varies country by country. More than 50 per cent of single parents in Spain and the UK could be classified as having a 'low income' in 1999. Levels were also high (around 40 per cent) in Portugal, the Netherlands, Ireland and Germany. Over 30 per cent of households with more than three children in Portugal, the UK, Italy, Spain and Luxembourg had a 'low income'. Over 50 per cent of young people (under 30) living alone had a 'low income' in Denmark and Finland. Levels were also above the EU average (32 per cent) in Germany, France, the Netherlands, Sweden and the United Kingdom. More than 60 per cent of old people living alone (aged over 65) had a 'low income' in Ireland. Rates were also high (over 50 per cent) in Portugal and Denmark compared with an EU average of 24 per cent. Women (compared with men) and children (compared with adults) are also more likely to be poor.

These patterns illustrate that the range of 'welfare problems' found in individual EU countries are broadly shared across all the member states. Thus it is not surprising that as the European Community, as it was once known, and more recently the EU, as the body which links together the member states economically and politically, should consider providing some sort of social policy to deal with these problems. Even if, as we shall see in the next section, it has primarily developed alongside, and to a large extent as a corollary to, economic developments, it is nevertheless the case that a significant range of what could broadly be described as EU social policy has been developed. What is more, in the period since the establishment of the Single European Market the development of what the EU often refers to as its 'social dimension' has developed more rapidly. One of the reasons for this is that EU social policy has been seen to be a necessary support for developments such as the Single Market – put crudely, without schemes such as the Structural Funds the effects of creating and extending the Single Market would have consigned poorer countries to worsening conditions for many of their citizens, and increasing affluence for others. These 'regional disparities', as they are known, have been increasingly regarded by leading figures within the European Commission, such as Jacques Delors (President of the European Commission from 1985 to 1994), and also by some, but not all, heads of government in the member states as at best socially and ethically unfair, and at worst liable to create tensions which could challenge the achievement of a truly European Single Market. This approach to the development of EU social policy has sometimes been referred to as 'negative integration': in other words, social policy development across the EU which is primarily driven by the negative economic and political consequences if it did not occur.

What these patterns also clearly show is that there is considerable amount of national and regional variation in the various welfare issues we have considered. Whilst unemployment, for example, has been a continuing issue across all the EU member states, as we have seen, its level and other characteristics vary considerably both between EU countries and in the different parts of countries. What this suggests is that any EU intervention to deal with unemployment must not only seek to deal with it as a trans-EU problem, but also as a problem which affects some EU citizens more than others and in different ways. The same may be said about issues of old age dependency, poverty and social exclusion, and other areas we have not yet considered such as education, health policy, disability, housing and other urban issues. In short, the problems of social policy for the EU are not simply those of the member states multiplied by 15 or 25. Since the EU is now increasingly acting as a unified political and economic entity within a regional and global environment then it is also increasingly being expected to intervene to help deal with the various social welfare problems its citizens face. The EU might even be said to be causing some of its own welfare problems as, for example, it has sought to rationalise (reduce the size of) certain industries such as coal, and iron and steel. Whether it can or should intervene as some sort of 'European welfare state' over and above the national member states, or whether it should do it alongside these member states in some sort of partnership is an ongoing debate to which we shall return. However, what is clear is that social welfare is now established as a key object of EU concern and intervention. What is more, as the EU enlarges these problems and the need for intervention are likely to increase, as we shall discuss at the end of this chapter.

## The development of the EU's 'social dimension' – from common market to European Union

Though this section is concerned with the development of EU social policy since the 1950s to date, it is by no means a comprehensive historical account of all the social policy related activities that occurred during this time. It simply attempts to indicate the key developments, mainly focusing on the most recent period from the 1990s, and to give an overall feel for the nature of EU social policy as opposed to the social policy activities of the UK and other nation states. As you will see, there are definite characteristics and limits to what passes for social policy in the EU, though its role in this area is of increasing importance for both the member states and, arguably, the rest of Europe, and even non-European countries.

Article 2 of the Treaty on European Union states that the first objective of the EU is:

> to promote economic and social progress and a high level of employment and to achieve balanced and sustainable development, in particular through the creation of an area without internal frontiers, through the strengthening of economic and social cohesion and through the establishment of economic and monetary union . . .
>
> Consolidated Version of the Treaty on European Union, 2002

This rather vague statement usefully sets the context for any understanding of:

(a) what EU social policy is; and

(b) how it has developed since the start of the European Economic Community (EEC) in the 1950s, and forerunner of the European Union, up to today.

First, it clearly links economic and social policy; second, it employs a key phrase, 'economic and social cohesion', which recurs throughout the development of EU social policy; and third, it refers to economic and monetary union and the common market (this is what 'an area without internal frontiers' really refers to) as the context for social and economic policy interventions. We shall return to how we may characterise current EU social policy later, but first let us see how the so-called 'social dimension' has developed since the 1950s.

## From common market to Single Market: the 1950s to the 1980s

In the Treaty of Rome (Article 2) that established the European Community of six member states (see Briefing 19.2) we find the first statement of its 'social dimension':

> a harmonious development of economic activities, a continuous and balanced expansion, an increase in stability, an accelerated raising of the standard of living and closer relations between the States belonging to it.

This statement set the tone for the EEC's social strategy for much of its early development. Thus in the period from 1958 to 1974 the EEC's approach to social policy was, essentially, to neglect it whilst focusing on economic and political matters. It is not until 1974 with the adoption of the first Social Action Programme (SAP) that we see what was increasingly referred to as the European Community (EC) was beginning to take a more active role in the promotion of a 'social dimension'. The forty or so initiatives of the first SAP were still focused upon labour market and employment-related issues. The three major objectives were:

- full and better employment;

- improved living and working conditions;

- worker participation.

### Briefing 19.2
### The stages of EU enlargement

| | |
|---|---|
| 1952 | The founding states: Belgium, France, Germany, Italy, Luxembourg, the Netherlands |
| 1973 | Denmark, Ireland, the United Kingdom |
| 1981 | Greece |
| 1986 | Portugal and Spain |
| 1995 | Austria, Finland, Sweden |
| 2004 | Cyprus, the Czech Republic, Estonia, Hungary, Latvia, Lithuania, Malta, Poland, the Slovak Republic, and Slovenia |

Following the SAP's adoption, however, there was a significant surge of activity by the EC in the areas of education and training, health and safety at work, workers' and women's rights and poverty.

It was in the 1980s that the idea of a 'social space' (*éspace social*), to complement the 'economic space', of the EC was first mooted as a central feature of the restructuring of the Community after its most recent enlargement and as it moved towards the establishment of a Single Market. The idea was taken up and promoted most vigorously by Jacques Delors, the European Commission's President from 1985. Delors saw the idea of a social space as a necessary complement to the completion of the internal market. He also saw the development of a social space alongside the Single European Market (SEM) as a way of moving the EU forward from the deadlock it had reached over the social dimension. The most important piece of EC legislation for both economic and social policy to come out of this period was the Single European Act (SEA). The SEA linked various social policy 'flanking measures', as they were called, to the completion of the Single Market and it thus represents a quite conscious attempt to complement EC economic policy with some form of EC social policy. The most important of these measures was what came from this point forward known as the Structural Funds (see Briefing 19.3).

The complementarity between EU economic and social policy becomes even more apparent when one considers the next significant development, the Social Charter. The Community Charter of the Fundamental Social Rights of Workers, adopted in 1989 by eleven of the twelve member states (with the UK as the exception), was accompanied by a second Action Programme of some 47 separate initiatives. It is important to note three important features of Social Charter insofar as they consolidate certain key developments of previous EC social policy developments and also prefigure subsequent developments. The first feature is that the Charter is a charter of *workers'* rights. Although the term 'citizen' had originally been used in its drafting, a number of member states, not least the UK again,

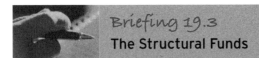

Briefing 19.3
**The Structural Funds**

There are four components of the EU's Structural Funds:

1  the European Regional Development Funds (ERDF), designed to promote economic and social cohesion within the EU through the reduction of imbalances between regions or social groups;

2  the European Social Fund (ESF), designed to provide the main financial support for the EU's strategic employment policy objectives;

3  the European Agricultural Guidance and Guarantee Fund (EAGGF – Guidance Section), designed to help the structural reform of the agriculture sector and to the development of rural areas;

4  the Financial Instrument for Fisheries Guidance (FIFG), designed to help the structural reform of the fisheries sector.

objected to this form of words. This reflects both the previous and subsequent focus of EC/EU social policy upon labour market concerns rather than, as in the case of the Council of Europe's Social Charter, a broader concern with matters such as social and medical assistance as part of broader perception of social rights and social policy. The second feature is that the Social Charter is not a binding document and leaves the relevant decisions and implementation to member states. The third feature is the non-involvement of the UK. Each of these characteristics has echoes in subsequent EC/EU social policy.

## The EU's economic and social policies in the 1990s

The 1990s saw considerable political, economic and, to a lesser extent, social policy development. The signing in 1992 of the Treaty on European Union at Maastricht in the Netherlands (usually referred to as the Maastricht Treaty for obvious reasons) was a major step forward for the member states in that it established a new form of organisation linking them together in a form unlike anything else, politically or economically, in the world. In legal terms the European Union became a combination of three elements, or 'pillars'.

 Thought provoker

**The first pillar** – the European Community – comprising the arrangements of the EC, ECSC and Euratom Treaties (the founding treaties), i.e. union citizenship, Community policies, economic and monetary union, etc.
**The second pillar** – the common foreign and security policy.
**The third pillar** – policing and judicial cooperation on criminal matters.

Given the three pillars, how easy is it to understand why opponents of further integration feel uneasy about attempts to develop the social dimension of the EU?

The pillar with a major social policy remit continues to be the European Community, however, and this is why in extracts from Treaties you will see that it is the 'Community', not 'the European Union', that is referred to.

The creation of the European Union brought with it significant development in social policy terms. The link between the proposals made on social policy as part of the Treaty on European Union and the preceding Social Charter is quite explicit. The principles of the Charter provide the basis for the Agreement on Social Policy which was appended to the Maastricht Treaty and signed by all the member states except the UK. Thus the Agreement called for upward harmonisation of living and working conditions, improved health and safety at work, the promotion of 'social dialogue' between management and labour at the European level, and equal pay for women and men. It also extended the EU's competence in the areas of education and vocational training.

Despite the at times heated debate which surrounded the discussions and final ratification of it in some of the member states, such as the UK and Denmark, the Agreement on Social Policy reached at Maastricht still represented more of a continuation of previous trends than a shift to a new level of social policy intervention by the EU. The significant difference between the Maastricht Agreement and earlier EC social policy provision is that the eleven signatories could take decisions which would be binding in some ways upon the member states, rather than being what were often referred to in EC jargon as 'solemn declarations'. Although it was never attempted, there was the possibility that the eleven signatories could have made social policy decisions under these arrangements that would have affected the UK as an EU member state, even though the UK had not signed up to the Agreement.

Following the creation of the European Union, in the mid 1990s two major White Papers set out its economic and social policy objectives for the longer term. They indicate the way in which the EU moved to a more strategic approach to both policy areas in response to continuing economic problems in the EU such as high unemployment, to the prospect of a single currency, to the enlargement of the Union by the addition of new member states, and to the continuing issues of social and economic imbalances across the EU.

The central proposition of the White Paper on economic policy, *Growth, Competitiveness, Employment* (*GCE*), was that ways should be found of reducing unemployment and increasing employment opportunities through radical changes in the EU economy. However, what was needed above all was an economy characterised by solidarity: '. . . solidarity between those who have jobs and those who do not; solidarity between the generations; solidarity between the richer and poorer regions; and solidarity, lastly and most importantly, in the fight against social exclusion' (p. 15). This statement indicates the clear link drawn between the EU's economic and social policy objectives.

The major proposals in GCE were essentially a continuation of the supply-side initiatives of the type which characterised the Structural Funds. Thus, there were proposals for lifelong education and training provision with each country aiming towards universally accessible advanced vocational training. Government expenditure on the unemployed should be shifted to 'active measures' to promote employment.

The other White Paper, *European Social Policy – A Way Forward for the Union* (*ESP*), suggested that though levels of social solidarity in the EU had been higher than in either the US or Japan in the past, '. . . such solidarity has been mainly passive. It is devoted to maintaining the incomes of large groups in society – by providing cash benefits through the redistribution of income, shouldered by an ever declining active population – without preparing them sufficiently to contribute to economic activity' (p. 4). Now, however, 'The accent has to be shifted from the objective of assistance to the objective of employment generation.' The key to both social and economic integration was employment: 'Continuing social progress can be built only on economic prosperity, and therefore on the competitiveness of the European economy'.

Both the White Paper and the Action Programme which complemented it argued that, rather than more EU social policy legislation, there should be consolidation and encouragement of the various national systems to move towards the common goals identified in the White Paper. The Structural Funds, and in particular the European Social Fund, were identified as the main Union instrument for promoting cohesion.

The next major development in the 1990s was the preparation and signing of the new Treaty of the EU, the Amsterdam Treaty, which was designed to streamline the decision-making processes of the Union in preparation for enlargement, and to allow EU policies to be developed without unnecessary delays caused by the individual member states. In both these regards the Amsterdam Treaty has been judged subsequently as a significant disappointment, if not a complete failure. Positive moves were made in some areas, such as EU citizenship rights, and the allowing of a greater role for the European Parliament in decision making. But the major questions of institutional reform were either fudged or simply postponed for later decision. Yet in the areas of social policy and the EU's broader socio-economic interventions it may be thought that the Amsterdam Treaty was somewhat more successful. The UK was finally brought back fully into the EU fold by agreeing to the incorporation of the Agreement on Social Policy signed by the other eleven member states at Maastricht. The Agreement has now become an integral part (Title VIII) of the new Treaty (all the following references to the Amsterdam Treaty are to the version that can be found on the Europa website at **http://europa.eu.int/eur-lex/en/treaties/dat/amsterdam.html**). The new Article B at the very start of the new Treaty certainly appeared to commit the EU unequivocally to:

> promote economic and social progress and a high level of employment and to achieve balanced and sustainable development . . . through the strengthening of economic and social cohesion . . .

There was also a new Community task (Article 2) which seemed to set social policy concerns right at the heart of the EU's project, albeit in economistic terms:

> to promote throughout the Community a harmonious, balanced and sustainable development of economic activities, a high level of employment and of social protection, equality between men and women, sustainable and non-inflationary growth, a high degree of competitiveness and convergence of economic performance, a high level of protection and improvement of the quality of the environment, the raising of the standard of living and quality of life, and economic and social cohesion and solidarity among Member-states.

Yet perhaps the most significant part of the Treaty from a social policy perspective was the new chapter (3) on employment since, as we have already seen, employment policy has become the central focus of the EU's social dimension. Under this chapter the member states agreed to develop coordinated strategy for employment, and to regard promoting employment as a matter of common concern. Furthermore, the Community itself was committed to support the member states and, if necessary, complement their actions on employment.

## Current issues and developments

So where does EU social policy stand at the start of the twenty-first century? All the treaties and other decisions we have reviewed above, alongside a whole raft of other measures, such as Action Programmes and Observatories, mean that the social dimension of the EU has now become a much more developed and significant part of the overall activities of the EU. One only has to look at the Europa website to discover that the range of interventions listed under the Directorate of Employment and Social Affairs now covers a very wide range of fields. These include: pensions and other forms of social protection; the European Social Fund; equal opportunities between women and men; anti-discrimination and fundamental social rights; health and safety; disability issues; social inclusion. These areas are in addition to a whole host of interventions focusing on the employment field. If we look beyond the Employment and Social Affairs Directorate, we find a range of social policy-related activities which are the responsibility of the Directorate for Regional Policy including the Regional Development Fund, the Cohesion Fund and the Solidarity Fund. EU education and training policy falls within the remit of the Directorate General for Education and Culture. Although at present comparatively less developed than the other areas of EU social policy, there is now a growing range of activities in the area of public health such as smoking and communicable diseases such as SARS, and also food safety interventions. These areas fall within the remit of the Directorate General for Health and Consumer Protection. In short, the EU has come a long way from the very limited social policy activity of earlier years.

## Social policy making in the EU

In order to make sense of EU social policy making and its impact on the member states it is necessary to have some idea of the key decision-making bodies of the EU. It is also important to understand how the basic processes of policy making involve these bodies in different ways. This applies not only to *policy making*, but also to *policy delivery* in the member states. In addition to the EU's own major policy-making bodies there are the different national governments and their sub-national administrative systems (such as regional and local government bodies) which together carry out the policies. A term which has often been used to describe the EU policy-making process both for social policy and for other policy areas is *multi-level governance*. This refers to the fact that social policy making within the EU involves a variety of bodies: formal EU institutions and consultative bodies; national governments and sub-national organisations; politicians and full-time officials at both national and EU level; policy communities, and so on. All of these bodies may be involved in the policy-making process within the EU in different ways on different policies and at sub-national, national and transnational (European) levels. In this section we shall outline the key policy-making bodies for social policy, their roles, and what multi-level governance looks like in the social policy context.

### The key EU social policy-making bodies

The key bodies in terms of EU social policy making are:

- the European Commission;
- the Council of the European Union and the European Council;
- the European Parliament.

However, alongside these four bodies there are some other EU bodies that have a role in social policy development and delivery. Two of the most important are the European Economic and Social Committee and the Committee of the Regions.

## The Commission

The European Commission represents the whole EU and has four main roles:

1 to propose legislation to Parliament and the Council;
2 to manage and implement EU policies and the budget;
3 to enforce European law (jointly with the Court of Justice);
4 to represent the European Union on the international stage, for example by negotiating agreements between the EU and other countries.

When the term the 'Commission' is used it can refer to two different but related aspects of the overall institution. The first is as the twenty men and women Commissioners appointed by the member states and the European Parliament who head up the different sections of the institution and take decisions. The second is as the institution itself and the permanent staff who work in its various offices and component agencies. Currently the part of the Commission which has the main responsibility for what most would recognise as social policy is called the Directorate General (DG) for Employment and Social Affairs. The Commissioner responsible for this DG is currently Stavros Dimas, but the person with day-to-day control is known as the Director General who is at present Odile Quintin. If one looks at the Europa website for the DG for Employment and Social Affairs (**http://europa.eu.int/ comm/employment_social/index_en.html**) one finds a range of social policy-related information ranging from the most recent strategic statement of the EU's social policy (the Social Policy Agenda), through material about the EU's employment strategies and policies, information on the European Social Fund, health and safety at work, social inclusion, social protection and much more. To get an idea of both the range and the character of EU social policy one could do worse than look through the various links and content on this site. However, the DG for Employment and Social Affiars is not the only one with some sort of social policy role. Policies relating to the Structural Funds, the Cohesion Fund and the Solidarity Fund are all managed through the DG for Regional Policy. There are clear social policy links between the work of this DG and that for Employment and Social Affairs. Once again this DG's website provides a very wide range of information on its activities (**http://europa.eu.int/comm/regional_policy/index_en.htm**).

## The Council of the European Union and the European Council

These two bodies have been grouped together because whilst they are separate entities they are very much linked. What is more, and not least since the EU itself often refers to both bodies as 'the Council' it is very easy to get confused between them. There is even another, non-EU international organisation called the Council of Europe just to confuse us still further. Let us first look at the Council of the European Union (to which we shall refer as 'the Council') then the European Council.

Formally, the Council is the EU's main decision-making body. It represents the member states, and its meetings are attended by one minister from each of the EU's national governments. Which ministers attend depends on what subjects are on the agenda and there are nine different Council configurations depending on the policy areas. These include Economic and Financial Affairs; Education, Youth and Culture; Justice and Home Affairs; Agriculture and Fisheries; and one which deals with Employment, Social Policy, Health and Consumer Affairs. Each minister acts on behalf of and commits his/her government to the decisions of the Council. Thus the Council has amongst its responsibilities the role of passing European laws: in many areas it makes policy and laws along with the European Parliament. Within this body decisions are made on the basis of what is known as *qualified majority voting* (QMV). This means that the countries with the larger populations, such as the UK, Germany and France get more votes than the less-populous countries, such as Luxembourg and Ireland (see Briefing 19.4). The number of votes is not strictly proportional, however, since the smaller countries get more votes than population proportionality alone would justify. The idea behind the system of QMV is that individual countries cannot veto decision making in the policy areas where this system applies, and also that the bigger countries alone cannot force through legislation against the wishes of the smaller countries. Under the Treaty of Lisbon the system of QMV will be simplified and will be applied to more areas of policy. This is a highly contentious point, not least with regard to certain aspects of social and economic policy, and we shall return to this in the last section of the chapter.

The European Council is made up of the heads of state of the member states and its principal role is described in Article 4 of the Treaty on European Union as follows: 'The European Council shall provide the Union with the necessary impetus

## Briefing 19.4
### Qualified majority voting

Until 1 May 2004 countries each had the following votes:

| | |
|---|---|
| Germany, France, Italy, the UK | 10 |
| Spain | 8 |
| Belgium, Greece, the Netherlands, Portugal | 5 |
| Austria, Sweden | 4 |
| Denmark, Ireland, Finland | 3 |
| Luxembourg | 2 |

A majority of 62 of the 87 votes was required.

If the Treaty of Lisbon is ratified a new system of QMV will be introduced based on a principle of 'double majority'. Decisions in the Council of Ministers will need the support of 55 per cent of the member states (currently 15 of the 27 EU countries) representing a minimum of 65 per cent of the EU's population. To make it impossible for a small number of the most populous member states preventing a decision being adopted, a blocking minority must comprise at least four member states.

for its development and shall define the general political guidelines thereof'. What this means in practice is that, although the European Council does not *legally* exist as an EU institution, it is nevertheless a major decision-making body within it. At present the Presidency of the Council rotates every six months between the 15 member states so that each country can be said to be able to provide a particular lead or focus for the EU's work during that period. (There are proposals to change this arrangement under the new Constitution.) The meetings of the European Council provide the major 'set-piece' events that punctuate the EU's yearly activities, and it is usually these events that receive the media coverage we see on our televisions and in newspapers. The probable reason for this is that these meetings provide crucial decision-points when the EU as a whole agrees (or sometimes does not agree!) major policy developments.

### The European Parliament

The European Parliament (EP) is directly elected by the citizens of the EU member states. The members (MEPs) sit in broad party groupings, not in national blocks. As a whole the EP is thus supposed to make its decisions on an EU-wide, not an inter-governmental basis.

Parliament has three main roles:

1 It shares with the Council the power to make policies and laws.

2 It is expected to exercise democratic supervision over all EU institutions, and in particular the Commission. It has the power to approve or reject the nomination of Commissioners, and it has the right to censure the Commission as a whole.

3 It shares with the Council authority over the EU budget and can therefore influence EU spending. At the end of the procedure, it adopts or rejects the budget in its entirety.

The most common procedure for adopting (i.e. passing) EU legislation is 'co-decision'. This places the European Parliament and the Council on an equal footing and the laws passed using this procedure are joint acts of the Council and Parliament. It applies to legislation in a wide range of fields. On a range of other proposals Parliament must only be consulted, and its approval is required for certain important political or institutional decisions. Parliament also provides impetus for new legislation by examining the Commission's annual work programme, considering what new laws would be appropriate and asking the Commission to put forward proposals. In this sense it could be argued that the EP has a policy-formation role as well as a policy-making role. In practice, however, the European Council and the Commission are much more influential in the policy-formulation role.

So how do these bodies link together in terms of social policy making? Although there are three main forms of decision making in the EU – co-decision, consultation and assent – the most common and increasingly used method is co-decision. In the co-decision procedure, Parliament and the Council share legislative power. The Commission sends its proposal to both institutions. They each read and discuss it twice in succession. If they cannot agree on it, it is put before a 'conciliation committee', composed of equal numbers of Council and Parliament representatives. Commission representatives also attend the committee meetings and contribute to the discussion. Once the committee has reached an agreement, the agreed text is then sent to Parliament and the Council for a third reading, so that they can finally adopt it as law.

 Controversy and debate

### 'Democratic deficit' and the EU

The European Union is sometimes accused of having a 'democratic deficit', with policy making having a lack of democratic accountability and control. This can be identified at two levels:

- The European Parliament (EP) is directly elected every four years by voters in the member states, but it is arguably the least important of the major European bodies. This weakness is in part because the EP's main powers are in relation to the European Commission, yet it is from the Council of Ministers that most initiatives emerge. The EP does have the ability to reject the budget, or nominees to the Commission, but is able to do so only as a whole, not selectively. The EP spends little time in full legislative session in Strasbourg, and undertakes much of its work in committees in Brussels, whilst the main secretariat is located in Luxembourg. Whilst the EP can claim democratic legitimacy through elections, the Council of Ministers is also able to claim that its members, representing national governments, also owe their position to popular election.

- Within the United Kingdom, the Westminster Parliament also has limited ability to scrutinise and affect EU policy. Both the House of Commons and the House of Lords have select committees that examine around 1,500 European documents a year on behalf of Parliament, with the work of the two committees generally complementing each other. However, there is clearly a great deal of work that could be done here, and the bulk of it is scrutiny, with Parliament rarely able to influence EU policy.

With the gradual shift of control in many policy areas from national governments to the European level, and with EU policy having an expanding effect on member states, including aspects of social policy, the 'democratic deficit' is seen by many as problematic.

The areas covered by the co-decision procedure include the major areas of social policy for the EU such as: social security for migrant workers; social exclusion; equal opportunities and equal treatment; implementing decisions regarding the European Social Fund; education; vocational training; health and the European Regional Development Fund. Despite this formal statement, however, the analyst of policy making in the EU needs to look at *specific* policies at *particular* times to see how different levels of the system operate together. It is almost impossible to provide a general statement about how this operates for all areas of policy, even for the area of social policy. When discussing social policy, however, and in particular issues such as pensions, unemployment benefits and other forms of social protection it is quite clear that the member states have jealously guarded their right to make policy in these areas with only limited intervention from the EU. Politically and financially these areas of welfare provision are highly contentious and the EU now accepts that its role in these areas should be that of information collector, monitor and reporter of good practice which the different member states may choose to take account of in their own countries in their own ways. In this regard the EU and the member states are applying two key principles of EU policy making: subsidiarity and proportionality. The term subsidiarity is used in the EU to refer to the principle that the EU should act as a body which complements rather than supersedes its member states' authority. Or, to put it in the EU's own terms: 'the Union does not take action (except on matters for which it alone is responsible) unless EU action is more effective than action taken at national, regional or local level'. The idea of proportionality complements subsidiarity and refers to the principle that EU action should only occur to the extent that is necessary to meet its treaty and other obligations. In practice, what this sometimes means is that social policy initiatives are developed 'indirectly' or via a previous EU decision or provision that may not seem, at first sight, to be completely relevant. An example of this is the way in which equal opportunities legislation affecting men and women has been progressed not through statements and policy proposals expressing the ethical, social or political case for equal opportunities, but rather about the need to provide a level playing field in employment and in more general economic terms across the EU. Thus some of the legislation about equal opportunities refers to the need for women workers to be treated equally across the EU to prevent certain countries or employers taking advantage of their competitors by employing cheaper female labour, whilst some draws upon health and safety in the workplace provisions. The outcomes have, arguably, become significant for men and women beyond the workplace but they have had to be developed within the framework and principles of policy making all the same.

## EU social policy now and in the future

The EU now has a considerable range of social policy interventions that may be argued to affect not only the welfare states that are EU members, but also other welfare states in the rest of Europe. The reason why its social policy may be said to extend beyond the member states is that the model of social policy that is increasingly being developed within the EU has economic as well as social and political implications for the other countries in Europe. Their governments and their citizens are part of an increasingly interlinked economic network within which welfare provisions are a crucial factor. Indeed, in the developing global economy the EU 'social model' might be said to have significance beyond the boundaries of Europe. So what is the current character of this social model in the EU? How can we summarise the character and content of EU social policy at present, and what can we say about its future possible development?

## EU social policy summarised

As we have argued above, the EU now has a range of social policy interventions and social policy responsibilities as part of its activities. A useful summary of the overall picture can be found in the EU's Social Policy Agenda. This agenda identifies the following main features:

- the European Employment Strategy;
- improving working conditions and standards;
- social inclusion and social protection;
- equality of women and men.

Thus we might summarise the overall character of the EU's social policy as being predominantly focused upon the labour market and work-related provisions, even where many of these provisions actually extend beyond the workplace in practice. To UK eyes this may seem unusual, but the link between social policy and employment has been a central feature of many of the other European welfare states almost since the inception of their modern welfare systems. To this extent, it may be the case that EU social policy is already encouraging a convergence around work and employment conditions as the focus for social policy provision in the future development of welfare provision across the EU. As the three major studies by Geyer (2000), Hantrais (2000) and Kleinmann (2002) of EU social policy provision all clearly indicate, social policy in the EU continues to have extremely strong links to the EU's economic project. Yet some have argued that this character may be changing somewhat both as a result of the spread of the EU's intervention beyond workplace issues – for example ethnic and racial discrimination, public health, and human rights – and that it may possibly be developing the character of a more broadly based welfare system. Threlfall (2002), for example, has argued that the range of EU social policy intervention is now so broad that it is difficult to argue that its previous focus on labour market concerns can now be said to characterise its social policy interventions as a whole. What is more, she argues, the EU's Charter of Fundamental Rights already suggests a possible shift to a more citizen (rather than worker) based approach to welfare. Currently the Charter is no more than a 'solemn proclamation', though each member state is a signatory to it. The Charter does not create any new power or task for the EU, but it does state that member states are expected to 'respect the rights, observe the principles and promote the application thereof . . .' when implementing EU law (European Commission, undated). From a social policy perspective there are a number of very significant clauses in the Charter which, were it to become something which was enforceable in law across the EU, would have some very significant impact. For example, Article 34 entitled 'Social security and social assistance' contains the following clauses:

1 The Union recognizes and respects the entitlement to social security benefits and social services providing protection in cases of maternity, illness, industrial accidents, dependency, or old age, and in the case of loss of employment . . .

2 Everyone residing and moving legally within the European Union is entitled to social security benefits and social advantages . . .

3 In order to combat social exclusion and poverty, the Union recognizes and respects the right to social and housing assistance . . .

In Article 35 the Charter refers to the right to preventative healthcare and the right to medical treatment. Elsewhere in the Charter reference is made to a right to education (Article 14), the prohibition of discrimination on the grounds of race, sex, religion, birth disability, and so on (Article 21), that equality between men and women must be ensured in all areas, including employment and pay (Article 22), and to the right of children to have access to 'such protection and care as is necessary for their well-being' (Article 23). Were such provisions to become subject to legal enforcement as, for example, Human Rights legislation now is in Britain, then one can imagine that this might lead further along the path towards a trans-EU welfare regime rather more integrated than the mix of different national welfare regimes that currently prevails. Some, who regard this prospect with alarm (for example the Conservative Party and other Euro-sceptics in the UK), fear that the proposed move to an EU Constitution would have precisely this effect. The Constitution is associated with the enlargement of the EU by the addition of ten new members on 1 May 2004, and to that we now turn.

The ten new member states are primarily from the former Soviet bloc – Estonia, Latvia, Lithuania, Poland, Hungary, Slovakia, Slovenia, and the Czech Republic – plus two others from the south – Cyprus and Malta. Together these countries added 74 million people to make a new EU total population of 455 million. However, the combined GDP of the ten new member states represents only 5 per cent of the total GDP of the EU-15 and, as Table 19.4 shows, the GDP of the new members is considerably below that of the EU average in almost all cases. In the Czech Republic, for example, it was only 57 per cent of the average for the EU-15 states in 2001, whereas in Latvia it is only 33 per cent.

So what are the implications of these facts for social policy in the EU following enlargement? In the first place, it is quite clear from the already-stated policy of the European Commission that one of the first priorities in the period immediately after accession of these ten new countries is to bring their economies closer to the level of the rest of the EU. What this will mean in terms of direct EU intervention is that the Structural Funds that have previously been targeted at certain regions and countries within the EU-15 are now to be targeted on the new member states. Given only a very small increase in the amount of these Funds that has been agreed by the member states, the clear outcome will be that some will get less in order that the new states may get more.

In order to join the EU the new member states were supposed to have achieved certain standards in terms of their welfare provision. Yet it is clear that the ex-Soviet bloc states have witnessed an almost total collapse of their social

Table 19.4 GDP per head in the May 2004 accession states (Index EU-15 = 100)

| | Cyprus | Czech Republic | Estonia | Hungary | Latvia | Lithuania | Malta | Poland | Slovak Republic | Slovenia |
|---|---|---|---|---|---|---|---|---|---|---|
| 1995 | 83 | 62 | 34 | 46 | 25 | 32 | 53 | 34 | 46 | 63 |
| 2001 | 77 | 57 | 42 | 51 | 33 | 38 | : | 40 | 48 | 69 |

policy provisions at the same time that they have moved into the capitalist economic mainstream. What is more, as various studies indicate (see, for example, Ferge, 2001) these countries have established economic and social policies that are much closer to the neo-liberal approach of the United States than to the mixed economies of welfare prevalent in the rest of the EU states. This means that problems of unemployment, poverty and social exclusion, as well as housing and social care provision, welfare provision for children, and a whole host of other provisions, are poorly catered for or not at all in some of the new member states. Some politicians in the Western European member states fear that, as a result, significant numbers of people from Eastern European countries will migrate to the west in search of work and a better standard of life, putting further pressure on the welfare systems of countries such as the UK, The Netherlands and others. Others argue that, given the ageing population and other factors discussed at the beginning of this chapter, the boost to the labour markets of the Western EU economies offered by younger and certain skilled migrants can only be beneficial to the receiving economies. There is clearly a political disagreement that will continue to develop in coming years as to which, if either, of these scenarios becomes reality. One thing seems clear, however, and that is that the EU is set to change dramatically in the early years of the twenty-first century, and EU social policy seems set to become one of the most contentious areas of development as both member states and the EU overall struggle to respond to these changes. It would certainly not be accurate to say that there is a 'European welfare state' within the EU at present. Social policy is still very much the preserve of the individual member states, albeit within the context of a broad EU strategy that is very much focused on employment as the key to welfare. Yet a broad 'social model' could be said to exist which marks off the EU from other welfare systems in other parts of the world. The future of this model could be seen to be under threat from a variety of pressures such as economic globalisation, demographic change and the simple problems of scale and differentiation between 455 million people. One analyst has, however, suggested that the enlargement process itself may prove to be one of the most damaging threats to this 'social model'. Vaughan-Whitehead (2003) argues that the move towards neo-liberal economic and social policies in the new states, a reduction of some social provisions in the existing member states and a similar 'modernisation' of the EU's social provisions, plus a move towards global markets and the seen imperative of making economies more flexible and competitive 'may well lead to a progressive collapse of social policy in an enlarged EU' (2003, p. 530). This may prove to be too pessimistic a judgement, but change rather than continuity in EU social policy now seems the more likely prospect.

## Conclusion

This chapter has shown that there has been a slow but continuous expansion of the 'social dimension' of the European Union, a situation which has arguably been given greater importance by the view that social policy is necessary to support the

Single Market, so that the EU now undertakes a wide range of social policy related activities. However, the policy-making mechanisms of the EU have not necessarily developed in a similar fashion, and whilst the Council of the European Union and the European Council have significant power, the role of the European Parliament remains limited, and its influence over EU social policy is slight. The accession of new member states in 2004 has resulted in even greater imbalances within the EU in terms of, for example, unemployment, poverty and levels of social provision, meaning that pressures on and for EU social policy continue to evolve.

## Summary

As we saw in the first section of this chapter, the EU countries share a broad range of characteristics (associated with unemployment, poverty and an ageing population, for example) that generate social policy concerns both for the national governments and, arguably, for the EU itself:

● Although these social policy 'problems' are broadly shared, their intensity and significance in some countries and regions are much greater than in others. Unemployment problems, for example, are much worse in the south than in the north of the EU, and since the May 2004 accession are even more problematic within most of the Eastern European countries. This regional variation in social policy problems across the EU is a characteristic feature in the context for EU intervention.

● In the section on the development of EU social policy we saw that economic targets and economic policy have been predominant. Current policies have a distinctly 'economic' focus and refer largely to labour market and employment-related issues. Thus, they do not have the full range that they may have in individual member states – they do not, for example, include policies on social care or housing. Nevertheless, the accumulated legislation and other forms of social policy intervention at the EU level are now extensive. There is no 'European welfare state' but there is now a significant body of EU social policy.

● With regard to the most recent developments the chapter has argued that further change is likely. In the first place, the significance of the EU Charter of Fundamental Rights may mean that EU social policy changes character from an economic focus to one more linked to citizens' rights. Second, the accession of the Central and Eastern European states is likely to provide a significantly increased social policy 'burden' on the EU which could mean that it has to undertake a fundamental restructuring of these policies for the whole EU.

## Discussion and review topics

1 What are the main patterns of similarity and difference in the socio-economic characteristics of European Union countries?

2 What are the key principles of EU 'social policies'?

**3** To what extent is social policy within the EU member states being affected by their membership of the European Union?

**4** Given the variations in the social and economic characteristics of the EU member states, is any sort of unified EU social policy possible for the future?

## Further reading

**Cousins, M.** (2005) *European welfare states: A comparative perspective*, Sage, London. This book discusses the development of European Union social policy including detailed examination of five states.

**Hantrais, L.** (2007) *Social policy in the European Union*, Palgrave Macmillan, Basingstoke. Examines European social policy as it relates to national policy making and implementation.

**Kleinmann, M.** (2002) *A European welfare state?* Palgrave Macmillan, Basingstoke. This book covers the role of economic integration and its implications for the scope and aims of social policy.

**McCormick, R.** (2005) *Understanding the European Union: A concise introduction,* Palgrave Macmillan, Basingstoke. One of a very large number of books about the European Union, its institutions, politics and policies; this is a useful starting point.

*The Journal of European Social Policy* – a journal focused specifically on European social policy.

## Some useful websites

http://europa.eu.int – the European Union's website portal EUROPA provides links to an enormous amount of information about the EU – its history, its institutions, its policies, even its laws. On EU social policy itself go to the EUROPA portal, select the 'EN' icon (for English language version), then select 'Employment and social affairs' from amongst the various Activities listed. This will provide most of the information on EU social policy, but you could also usefully click on the 'Education, training and youth', 'Public health', and the 'Regional policy' activity links too.

http://europa.eu.int/comm/eurostat – for information about the socio-economic situation in the various EU member states the Eurostat web pages provide a welter of information, most of it free to view and much of it free to download. From the Eurostat home page select the 'EN' icon (for English language version), then click on the 'Themes' button, and then select the 'Population and social conditions' link.

## References

European Commission (undated) *Charter of Fundamental Rights Homepage* (**http://europa.eu.int/comm/justice_home/unit/charte/index_en.html**).

European Commission (2003) *The social situation in the European Union 2003,* European Commission/Eurostat, Brussels.

Ferge, Z. (2001) 'Welfare and "ill-fare" systems in Central-Eastern Europe', in R. Sykes, B. Palier and P.M. Prior (eds) *Globalization and European welfare states: Challenges and change,* Palgrave, Basingstoke.

Geyer, R. (2000) *Exploring European social policy,* Polity, Cambridge.

Hantrais, L. (2000) *Social policy in the European Union* (2nd edn), Palgrave Macmillan, Basingstoke.

Kleinmann, M. (2002) *A European welfare state?* Palgrave Macmillan, Basingstoke.

Threlfall, M. (2002) 'The European Union's social policy focus: From labour to welfare and constitutionalised rights?' in R. Sykes, C. Bochel and N. Ellison (eds) *Social Policy Review 14*, pp. 171–94, Social Policy Association/Policy Press, Bristol.

Vaughan-Whitehead, D. (2003) *EU enlargement versus Social Europe? The uncertain future of the European Social Model*, Edward Elgar, Cheltenham.

Letter abbreviations and corresponding country names used in EU Tables for EU-15:

| | | | | | |
|---|---|---|---|---|---|
| A | Austria | EL | Greece | L | Luxembourg |
| B | Belgium | F | France | NL | Netherlands |
| D | Germany | FIN | Finland | P | Portugal |
| DK | Denmark | I | Italy | S | Sweden |
| E | Spain | IRL | Ireland (Eire) | UK | United Kingdom |

# 20

# A comparative view of social policy

Rob Sykes

## Chapter overview

This chapter discusses the ways in which the similarities and differences in social policy in different countries might be compared and explained. The comparative approach to the study of social policy has developed considerably in recent years, yet it is fraught with difficulties – just how do you compare different countries' policies when there are different ideas of what 'social policy' and 'social welfare' are, different approaches to the organisation and delivery of social policy, and when there are different mixes of social policy roles for governments, private providers, the family, and so on? Some even argue that whole-country comparison of welfare policies is simply not possible, precisely because each country has a complex mix of history, welfare systems and welfare ideas that make their particular social policy system essentially different from others. Whilst accepting that there are problems with cross-national social policy comparison, others argue that it is a worthwhile and even necessary dimension of social policy analysis as we all become part of an increasingly globalised and interlinked world. So just what is involved in a comparative approach to analysing social policy, how can we overcome the difficulties briefly outlined above, and what does a comparative approach have to offer that a purely national approach does not? These are the central issues that run through this chapter. The main focus of the discussion in the chapter is on the comparative perspective, rather than actual comparisons between different national welfare systems since this would be impractical in one chapter. However, the second part of the chapter uses a number of brief 'snapshots' focused on welfare in different countries that will both give a flavour of the patterns of similarity and difference between different national welfare systems, and link back to the earlier theoretical discussion.

The chapter looks at:

- the issue of defining social policy and social welfare for comparative purposes;
- approaches to comparing social policy: theoretical models and analytical issues;
- applying the models: some comparative social policy 'snapshots'.

## Comparative social statistics

| | National income per capita (current prices in US dollars) | Social expenditure (% GDP) | Public healthcare expenditure (% GDP) | Unemploy- ment rate (% of labour force) | Poverty rate (% of population with income less than 50% of national average in 2000) | Human Develop- ment Index ranking |
|---|---|---|---|---|---|---|
| Australia | 26,438 | 17.9 | 6.2 | 5.2 | 11.2 | 3 |
| France | 25,056 | 28.7 | 8.3 | 9.9 | 7.0 | 10 |
| Germany | 24,215 | 27.6 | 8.5 | 11.3 | 9.8 | 22 |
| Greece | 19,768 | 21.3 | 5.3 | 9.8 | 13.5 | 24 |
| Ireland | 26,616 | 15.9 | 5.7 | 4.3 | 15.4 | 5 |
| Japan | 26,617 | 17.7 | 6.5 | 4.6 | 15.3 | 8 |
| Korea | 17,837 | 5.7 | 2.9 | 3.9 | n.a. | 26 |
| Mexico | 9,320 | 6.8 | 3.0 | 3.6 | 20.3 | 52 |
| Slovakia | 10,692 | 17.3 | 5.2 | 16.2 | n.a. | 42 |
| Sweden | 26,883 | 31.3 | 7.7 | 7.8 | 5.3 | 6 |
| Turkey | 7,004 | 13.2 | 5.5 | 10.5 | 15.9 | 84 |
| United Kingdom | 28,030 | 20.1 | 7.1 | 4.6 | 11.4 | 16 |
| USA | 34,681 | 16.2 | 6.9 | 5.1 | 17.1 | 12 |

Source: OECD, *Society at a Glance: OECD Social Indicators – 2006 Edition (Poverty rates: 2005 edition)*;
UNDP, *Human Development Report, 2007/2008.*

Before we begin to engage in the debates about what comparative social policy is all about, let us first get an idea of the social and economic context for social policy in differ-ent parts of the world. The table above provides us with a range of information on thirteen states, but these need contextualisation and interpretation. On their own they may not provide us with sufficient understanding of what is happening in each state to enable us to make meaningful comparisons.

The concern of this chapter is therefore to provide a consideration of comparison in social policy, including what it is that we seek to compare, and how we set about making compar-isons, particularly through the use of the type of framework provided by the idea of wel-fare regimes.

## Comparing social statistics

In the 'Spotlight on the issues' a selection of comparative social statistics is presented. What do these figures tell us about the different countries that might help us to compare their social policies? In the past some analysts suggested that there was a degree of correlation between how 'rich' a country was and its provision of welfare services: the richer the country, the more likely it was to have a developed welfare system. Yet the figures here present a somewhat unclear picture on this. Some of those 'richer' countries with the higher rates of national income per head, such as Sweden, France and Germany, do indeed have high levels of social expenditure (spending on welfare services), at roughly 30 per cent of **Gross Domestic Product** (GDP). Yet other 'richer' countries have much lower social expenditure levels: for example, the 'richest' country listed, the United States, spends only 16.2 per cent of GDP on social expenditure, the UK spends only 20 per cent, Australia 17.9 per cent and Japan 17.7 per cent. If we look at a country with a much lower level of national income per head, Slovakia, we see that it has a social expenditure level comparable to these much richer countries at 17.3 per cent of GDP. So there is not a clear and consistent level of social expenditure related to the richness of a country measured in national income per head. What if we look at one important area of social policy, healthcare, and see what these statistics indicate for comparison? To some extent there seems to be a correlation between how much countries spend on social expenditure overall and what they spend on healthcare: for example, high spenders such as Sweden, France and Germany are also amongst the highest spenders as a proportion of GDP on healthcare. Low spenders overall, such as Mexico (6.8 per cent) and (South) Korea (5.7 per cent), also spend lower proportions on healthcare (3 per cent and 2.9 per cent). Yet both the USA and the UK also spend relatively large proportions of GDP on healthcare though their social expenditure levels are lower than comparably richer countries. However, Turkey, with a lower social expenditure level of 13.2 per cent of GDP spends 5.5 per cent of GDP on healthcare, which is not much less proportionally than a rich country such as Australia (6.2 per cent). Once again the patterns of similarity and difference here are not simple but rather complex and confused. If we look at the columns on unemployment rates and poverty rates we might expect to see that countries with higher unemployment rates also have high poverty rates. Some do: Turkey and Greece both have higher unemployment rates matched by high poverty rates. Yet a number of richer countries with low unemployment rates actually have higher poverty rates: Ireland, Japan, the UK and, with the highest poverty rate of all the countries shown at 17.1 per cent, the USA.

So the picture derived from such simple statistical comparisons that we might expect to show some sorts of pattern relating to the context for and spending on social policy programmes is, in fact, rather confusing. When we then relate these statistics to the United Nations Development Programme's (UNDP) **Human Development Index** the pattern is even more confused. For example, Australia ranks very near the top of the rankings at number 3, but has comparatively high levels of poverty and middling levels of social expenditure. Greece spends some 21.3 per cent of GDP on social expenditure and ranks at 24 in the HDI; however, Korea is only two rankings below Greece at 26, but spends only 5.7 per cent of GDP on social expenditure.

What lessons might we draw from this simple exercise for the purposes of comparing social policies cross-nationally? The first is that simple statistical exercises such as this are of limited use in identifying accurate and useful patterns of similarity and difference in social policy provision in different countries. Second, although we have taken these figures as some sort of indicator of social policy issues (unemployment, poverty, healthcare), there is nothing in them that helps us to identify the way in which these issues figure within the broader pattern of social policy provision, or indeed the way in which the dominant philosophies of welfare are in these different countries. In short, if we are to compare social policy cross-nationally we need first to be clear *what* it is we are comparing, and what sorts of information and data we use in order to undertake such comparison. The next section deals with the first of these topics – just what are we comparing?

## What are we comparing? Defining social policy and social welfare

It may seem strange to ask this question so late in a book on social policy. However, before we can compare effectively, we need to recognise that assumptions we hold about the 'normal' ways in which social policy is organised and delivered are in turn based on assumptions about what social policy is, and these are usually based on our own national knowledge and practices. Yet these assumptions may well prove to be misleading when looking at social policy in other countries. Perhaps the most common assumption is that social policy is something organised and carried out exclusively by some or other level of government – in short, when we talk of welfare we are talking of a welfare state. Another assumption is that the field of social policy is composed of a number of areas of state activities specifically focused on welfare outcomes, for example on personal and family income, healthcare, pensions, housing, education and personal social care. But are these assumptions justified?

To clarify the issue of what social policy is, it is helpful to rephrase the term social policy as *social welfare* provision. The term *welfare* may mean many things, but if we take it as essentially to do with human well-being then it soon becomes clear that our well-being is constituted in a variety of ways and can be contributed to, or indeed reduced, in a variety of ways also. Our well-being ranges from the meeting of basic needs, such as sustenance, shelter and health, to much more complex individual and social needs, such as the need for social interaction and individual fulfilment. Doyal and Gough's work, *A Theory of Human Need* (1991), focuses on these central questions that lie at the heart of understanding what well-being and welfare are. Or we should rather say, what welfare and well-being *might be* since, as they and other welfare theorists point out, what constitutes human needs, and in turn what constitutes individual or social welfare, is disputed between different groups of people, different societies and in different periods of time. In, say, nineteenth-century England, the idea that all children between certain ages should have had access to free schooling would have seemed simply ridiculous because, at that time, the notion of universal free education as part of a welfare provision simply did not constitute part of the current social or political thinking about social well-being. If we now switch our focus from historical comparison to cross-national comparison, we can see that in certain countries today the provision of free education to all children also does not form a part of the current social or political thinking about social well-being, even though such provision is enshrined in welfare provisions in other parts of the world. These two rather simplistic historical and cross-national examples simply illustrate that what social welfare is, and indeed how such welfare needs might be met, need to be understood in the context of the current understandings of welfare in different periods and different social and political contexts. Just as we need to understand how 'welfare' was thought of in different historical periods, if we are to be able to properly understand the social policy provisions that were made, or not made, at these times, we also need to understand how 'welfare' is understood in different countries if we are to understand their social policy provisions and to be able properly to compare them with those in other countries.

Having 'opened up' the idea of social policy to encompass welfare, we might usefully consider the following question: 'Who or what might deliver social welfare in a given society?' Once we pose the question in this way it becomes clear that a wide range of agencies, organisations and people might be involved in some way in welfare provision, and not just the state. Our welfare can depend upon our families, both immediate and extended (for example, parents 'educating' their children, grandparents or aunts undertaking childcare), upon friends and local communities and, of course, ourselves, in terms of (income from) work to pay for healthcare, housing, pensions and so on. In addition to these sources of welfare support, none of which, of course, is specifically designed to deliver 'social policy', we may add other agencies where welfare provision forms part of their wider roles in society. These might include churches and other religious groups, charities, trades unions, employers, in the form of welfare benefits in addition to wages and salaries (such as dental care or housing assistance), and voluntary organisations of various sorts. Add to these various commercial for-profit welfare providers, such as private hospitals and schools, childcare agencies and so on, and it begins to become clear that the state is but one, albeit in many countries a major, provider of welfare. Even with regard to the state there can be a range of different forms in which it might be involved ranging from central government regulation and provision, through regional government, to local government. In addition there may be government agencies or near-government agencies (**Quangos**) that deliver and administer social policy within remits provided by the government.

 Thought provoker

The Organisation for Economic Cooperation and Development classification social expenditure includes 13 categories (OECD, 2003), one of which is 'health'.

What expenditures might be counted as being on 'health', and where, for example, might a distinction be made between 'health' spending and that on 'services for the elderly and disabled'?

What does this tell us about the challenges of undertaking comparative analyses?

However, governments also pursue other policies that may have welfare dimensions to them, even if this is not the main, intended function. If we consider economic policies focusing on employment levels or taxation, and criminal justice policies, it becomes clear that these policies may have outcomes that in various ways may be said to affect the welfare of citizens in different national contexts.

In sum, the question as to who or what delivers social policy in a given country is not an easy one to answer without examining the specifics of what the dominant approach to welfare/social policy is, and what form the 'welfare mix' of different agencies is at a given time. Thus, if we wish to compare social policies in different countries this suggests that we need not only to describe what forms social policy takes in these countries, and to identify similarities and differences between the countries, but also to have some framework for making sense of these similarities and differences. This framework needs on the one hand to recognise that different countries 'do' social policy in different ways, which in turn relate to different welfare ideologies, whilst on the other hand the framework should allow meaningful comparison to be made that does not simply collapse into saying that 'Country A does it like this, and Country B does it like that'. In other words, we need a framework for cross-national comparison of social policy that both recognises the specificities of different national practice and welfare ideas, and allows patterns of similarity and difference to be identified and explained. In the next section of this chapter we consider the general issue of comparative approaches in social policy, and then look at the key frameworks that exist.

## Approaches to comparing social policy

### General issues

There are various ways in which we might compare a country's social policy. Comparison might consider social policy in different periods in a country's history, it might compare social policy similarities and differences within a country, and comparison might consider social policy in one country with that in others. It is this last that we are focusing on here. Then we might break social policy down into its different elements for comparison. Here we might separately or together consider the *origins* of social policy (welfare ideas and ideologies), we might consider the *content* of social policies, and finally we might consider the *outcomes* of policies. Some studies, usually those which focus on only a limited number of countries and which also tend to focus on a specific area of social policy in the different countries (such as housing or pensions), break down the framework of comparison into detailed elements. These studies tend to focus on a small number of countries and usually upon one area of policy given the complexity and range of factors to be compared.

More recently, academic comparative cross-national studies that wish to compare a larger range of countries have tended to adopt a less detailed framework that commonly focuses on the national approach to welfare set within the political economy of the country in question, the dominant welfare philosophy, the main features of national welfare provision, and the main welfare outputs and out-comes. Often these studies comprise a selection of individual country 'portraits' where the real cross-national comparison is left for the reader to perform (for example, Alcock and Craig, 2001). However, some of these 'macro' studies seek to apply some sort of comparison across national boundaries, usually by grouping similar types of welfare system together (Esping-Andersen, 1996; Sykes *et al.,* 2001). In order to provide some sort of framework for such comparison countries are usu-ally grouped together into similar families or types. This idea of grouping together similar welfare systems is most developed by using the idea of *welfare regimes.* The idea of welfare regimes owes much to Esping-Andersen, whose work has dominat-ed recent cross-national comparative social policy debates. The framework devel-oped by Esping-Andersen in his *Three worlds of welfare capitalism* (1990) has generated a considerable amount of debate and criticism, yet it is fair to say that it provides a reference point for most, if not all, subsequent comparative social policy frameworks, and it is thus important to understand what it says.

## The Esping-Andersen welfare state regime approach

Esping-Andersen suggests that welfare provisions and the form of welfare regime in different countries reflect not simply some sort of 'natural' development as industrial societies mature, but rather the result of political struggles in particular involving organised labour movements (trades unions), political parties and the state. Welfare provision may thus be seen as political in at least two senses: (a) that it results from political pressure and bargaining between governments and citizens; and (b) that it represents a cost that capitalism needs to pay in order to secure social and political peace. What is more, he argues, welfare systems actively affect the system of social stratification in a given society – they may, for example, operate to deliver some degree of redistribution of resources, or they may alterna-tively reinforce existing inequalities in the labour market and elsewhere. The key to understanding the three different welfare regime types and their potential for affecting society is via the notion of *decommodification*, that is the degree to which welfare provision is relatively independent of a person's position in the labour market, and of that person's ability to pay for his or her welfare. Each regime type also represents a typically different welfare mix between the three major welfare providers: the family, the state and the market. His three welfare state regimes, Liberal, Conservative–Corporatist and Social Democratic, are summarised in Briefing 20.1.

Esping-Andersen suggests that these three types of welfare state regime may be used to help recognise groups or 'families' of countries where the welfare systems and ideas are broadly similar. It must be stressed, however, that the regime types are just that: they are theoretical constructs or 'ideal types' that the analyst may use to help make sense of the complex real patterns of similarity and difference that exist in the welfare provisions of different countries. No one country's wel-fare system or welfare ideas corresponds to these typifications – they are a guide to comparison, not a substitute for it. In the *Liberal* welfare state regime type the em-phasis is on social insurance provided through the market. The range of welfare

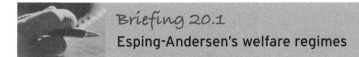

**Briefing 20.1**
**Esping-Andersen's welfare regimes**

**Liberal** – low decommodification: strong role for the market and the family; relatively minimal state welfare provision.

**Conservative–Corporatist** – medium decommodification: the state has major role in welfare alongside the labour market and the role of the family.

**Social Democratic** – high decommodification: welfare mainly provided through the state, minimal role for family and market.

provision delivered by the state is otherwise very limited. There is a high use of means tests to establish both access to and levels of welfare benefits. Overall the levels of welfare benefits are low in relation to the proportion of income the recipient would otherwise receive (the replacement ratio) and forms of social insurance are 'modest'. Overall, state welfare provision is largely oriented to the poor in these countries, i.e. working-class people with low incomes who are or become dependent on the state. Benefits are limited in amount, access and duration and are stigmatised because the dominant welfare philosophy is based on the assumption that high benefits reduce incentives to work. Private schemes are encouraged for those wanting more than minimum cover, and sometimes these private schemes are actively subsidised by government. Esping-Andersen argues that such regimes are highly stratified and differentiated – there are and continue to be significant gaps between rich and poor. What is more, the overall welfare of citizens living in such regimes is significantly affected by their ability to pay for it privately through private health schemes, private housing and private pensions, for example. So, he argues, there is minimisation of decommodification effects in such systems. The Liberal regime 'effectively contains the realm of social rights, and erects an order of stratification that is a blend of relative equality of poverty among state-welfare recipients, market-differentiated welfare among the majorities, and a class-political dualism between the two' (1990, p. 27). Esping-Andersen suggests that the welfare states in countries such as the USA, Canada, Australia, New Zealand and, more recently, the UK might be best understood in terms of this regime type (see Briefings 20.5 and 20.6 on the UK and USA below).

Turning to the *Conservative–Corporatist* regime type, Esping-Andersen points out that in countries falling within this group, corporatist arrangements are pronounced. By the term corporatism we mean that the government, employers' federations and the leading trades union organisations collaborate in setting and delivering key public policies, such as welfare and economic policy. State welfare in this type of regime is used to maintain and even reinforce existing class and status differentials. The purpose of this is to encourage social and political stability and continued loyalty to the government. This approach relates to earlier political strategy of state-building in the nineteenth century in countries such as Germany, often referred to as 'Bismarckian' welfare strategy (see the section on German welfare below). In Conservative regimes it is the state (rather than the market, as in the

Liberal regimes) that is the dominant provider of welfare. However, the state's welfare role is not to increase redistribution or equalisation of status groups in society through its actions.

Welfare thinking was typically shaped by the (Catholic) church, and there remains a commitment in both welfare ideology and practice to traditional patterns of familyhood and the roles of men and women in both the labour market and the domestic sector. Women are discouraged from participation in the labour market, and non-working wives excluded from benefits. Day care, family services and the like are relatively underdeveloped in such regimes. Whilst the state has a major welfare role, it is designed to intervene only where the family cannot resolve welfare problems. Austria, Germany, France and Italy and a number of other northern European countries may be grouped together with reference to this type of welfare regime according to Esping-Andersen (see welfare snapshot of Germany (Briefing 20.4) below).

Esping-Andersen's third regime type is the *Social Democratic*. Welfare in these regimes is characterised by the principle of universalism – all citizens are in principle eligible to receive all welfare benefits provided by the state, regardless of ability to pay. The market as a welfare provider is relatively insignificant in such systems and so decommodification also extends to the middle classes not just to the poor or the working class. There is a tendency to encourage equality across classes based on high standards of welfare provision rather than being based on minimum standards. Thus services and benefits have to be provided which are acceptable to middle-class groups whilst working-class people get access to the same benefits. Attitudes to the family contrast with those of the other two regimes, in that the state takes on and socialises many traditional family responsibilities, such as support for children and older people. Women are actively encouraged to participate in the paid labour market. Full employment is central to this sort of regime because it provides income support and makes it possible to pay the costs of welfare. Esping-Andersen groups the following welfare states in terms of the Social Democratic regime type: Norway, Sweden, Finland and Denmark (see welfare snapshot of Sweden below).

## Controversy and debate

Few comprehend the full scope of the problems with the Swedish welfare state.

First, unemployment is not at all low. The official rate stands around 6 percent, which is just above normal for a market economy. But according to the trade unions . . . the real – and hidden – level of unemployment rises above 20 percent. Out of a population of nine million people, over one and a half million healthy Swedes have chosen not to enter the labour market and live on welfare instead . . . Companies do not dare to hire new staff; because of labour legislation, it is impossible to get rid of them. There is no doubt that this is a major reason for Sweden's mass unemployment.

And second, while Sweden's growth (around 3 percent) is above the European average, it is still relatively low. If Sweden were a state in America today, it would be the fifth poorest. Even more, the total tax pressure is 63 percent. In that perspective, perhaps it is not surprising that not a single largescale enterprise – like IKEA or Ericsson – has been created in Sweden since 1970.

Are these the trademarks of the world's most successful society? I think not, and there is even more: ten percent of Swedish students leave compulsory school without complete grades, and one third of the students in upper secondary school drop out. And the universal health care system – widely celebrated abroad for its 'fairness' – is an equally dismal story. The wait between a first doctor's appointment and an operation may be as long as a year or more, which in some cases is enough time for the patient to die . . .

. . . Sweden's immigration model, which bears much resemblance to the French model, is unsuccessful for a host of reasons. Multiculturalism has been allowed to grow strong enough to challenge the welfare state, and this multiculturalism is in no way related to the natural symbiosis of lifestyles that come into existence when people live together . . . Instead of putting immigrants to work and assimilating them to Sweden's democratic values, they are placed in economically destitute suburbs. It is in these suburbs that immigrants begin hating freedom and start dreaming up ways to set cities ablaze.

As chilling as the news may be to the European Left, the Swedish welfare society is no longer a success.

Wennström, J. (2005) 'The Awful Truth About Sweden', 22nd IEA Current Controversies Paper, Institute of Economic Affairs, London.

## Criticisms and extensions of the Esping-Andersen approach

### Too few regimes

One of the most obvious criticisms of Esping-Andersen's model is that it is simply too limited in having only three regime types. Some who raise this criticism appear to miss Esping-Andersen's point that the three regime types are not meant to exhaust the range of actual differences between real welfare systems around the world, but are rather meant as ideal types to help group together similar sorts of system for the purposes of comparison. Nevertheless, a number of writers have argued that even as ideal types the three regimes are inadequate. Some, for example Ferrara (1996), have argued that grouping countries such as Italy, Spain and Portugal with the Conservative–Corporatist welfare systems of northern European countries such as Germany and Austria is misleading. Ferrara argues that the welfare systems in these southern welfare systems actually combine elements of the Social-Democratic regime type, in terms of access to welfare, welfare funding and welfare ideology, along with a strong emphasis on occupational roles when it comes to income transfers. They thus form an additional *southern* welfare state regime to add to Esping-Andersen's three.

A similar sort of criticism, but focused on Australia and New Zealand, is that of Castles and Mitchell (1992) who argue that the welfare systems of these two countries represent a significantly different type of welfare regime from the Conservative type.

With reference to East Asian countries' welfare systems, such as those of Japan, South Korea and Hong Kong, a number of writers have argued that Esping-Andersen's regime types simply do not 'fit' the welfare systems of these countries. One argument is that the dominant welfare ideologies of these countries include beliefs relating to Confucian religious ideas and the role of the family that were simply not envisaged in Esping-Andersen's focus on what are essentially 'Western' welfare states (see welfare snapshot of Hong Kong below (Briefing 20.6)).

### Silences on gender and 'race'

The final group of criticisms relate to two distinct gaps or 'silences' in Esping-Andersen's approach to developing the three regime types – namely the absence of gender and 'race' considerations. Various writers have pointed out that his model makes little or no reference to the role of gender in the ideology, organisation or delivery of welfare. This is important, it is argued, precisely because Esping-Andersen focuses on the notion of 'decommodification' in developing his three types, but fails to recognise the role of women in the domestic sphere, which is seen as a necessary basis for the commodification of work and welfare. Men and women have different experiences of the labour market which in turn relate to their different experiences of family life – welfare states are thus 'gendered'. The significance of 'race' with reference to immigration, citizenship and the labour market has been important especially, but not only, in post-war European welfare systems. Popular political ideologies have often identified 'immigrants' as being in some way unworthy of welfare benefits, despite the fact that many of these so-called immigrants are in fact long-term residents of the countries in question (for example, Germany, the UK, France) and in many cases are involved in working in the welfare services such as healthcare. Evidence indicates that such 'racialised' groups often find themselves excluded from or have difficulty in gaining access to welfare benefits despite the fact that they tend to be concentrated in the poorer and more excluded social groups. In sum, the argument is that *welfare states are racially-structured*, yet Esping-Andersen does not consider this dimension.

## Beyond the advanced welfare states: Gough's model of welfare regimes

The attention of comparativists has more recently turned to making sense of welfare in the less-developed countries of the world. A major contribution to this developing area of comparative social policy is the work of Gough and Wood and their associates (2004). Essentially, Gough argues that the 'welfare state regime' approach is less applicable to the less-developed, the developing and the transitional societies of the South and the East, namely most of the countries in Africa, Asia and Latin America. Gough and his colleagues attempt to bring together a concern with cross-national comparison of social policy and an interest in these less-developed countries' welfare provisions as well as those of the more developed welfare systems of the world. The central idea is that of welfare regime rather than welfare *state* regime: 'Welfare *state* regimes refer to the family of social arrangements and welfare outcomes found in the OECD world of welfare states Welfare regime is a more generic term, referring to the entire set of institutional arrangements, policies and practices affecting welfare outcomes and stratification effects in diverse social contexts' (2004, p. 24). Gough and his colleagues argue that in addition to welfare state regimes found predominantly in the Western capitalist countries there are two further sorts of regime: *informal security regimes* and *insecurity regimes*. In the informal security regimes people rely heavily on the family to meet their security needs, the state is only weakly differentiated from other systems of power in society based on caste, ethnicity, kinship groups and so on, and poorer people commonly rely on more powerful 'patrons', and there are only weakly developed and usually informal sets of welfare rights. Insecurity regimes are, as the title suggests, characterised by high levels of social, economic and political insecurity for their inhabitants. Not only are there few or no formal institutions to protect people from these insecurities, there are also no informal mechanisms either. Countries where such regimes exist are essentially unstable politically, and the governments that do operate there find themselves weakened by corruption and weak politicians, and confronted by the power of local warlords and other more or less illegal power groups. Such countries are heavily dependent on external aid and other international agencies.

Gough suggests a breakdown of countries in addition to the welfare states of the OECD countries, summarised in Briefing 20.2.

### Briefing 20.2
### Gough's additional welfare regimes

1 *Actual or potential welfare state regimes*: much of Central Europe and some of Eastern Europe; southern Latin America, Kenya, Algeria, Tunisia and Thailand.

2 *More effective informal security regimes*: Southeast Asia, Sri Lanka, the rest of Latin America, and parts of the Middle East.

3 *Less effective informal security regimes*: South Asia excluding Sri Lanka but probably including India, and some countries in sub-Saharan Africa.

4 *Externally dependent insecurity regimes*: most of sub-Saharan Africa.

*Source*: Gough, in Gough and Wood, 2004.

## Applying the models: comparative social policy 'snapshots'

The purpose of this section is primarily to indicate patterns of similarity and difference between different national welfare systems and to throw some empirical 'light' back on the previous discussion in the chapter. Each snapshot begins with a Briefing box containing key facts of relevance to the social policy of the country or system being summarised. There is then a very brief summary of each country's social policy system in terms of:

- the political and economic context for social policy development;
- the dominant welfare ideology;
- reference to the Esping-Andersen theoretical model.

At the end of the snapshots section there is a summary that suggests some issues for comparative analysis arising from these summaries that links back to the rest of the chapter.

## Sweden

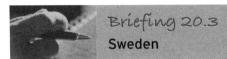

### Briefing 20.3
### Sweden

**People**

Population: 9,031,088

Population age groups:

  0-14 years: 16.4%

  15-64 years: 65.7%

  65 years and over: 17.9%

Infant mortality rate: 2.76 deaths/1,000 live births

Life expectancy at birth: 80.63 years

**Economy**

GDP (Purchasing Power Parity (PPP)): US $290.1 billion

GDP per capita (PPP): US $32,200

Unemployment rate: 5.6%

Household income or consumption by percentage share:

  Lowest 10%: 3.6%

  Highest 10%: 22.2%

Distribution of family income by Gini coefficient: 0.25

Part of European Union common market but NOT member of Euro zone

**Politics**

Government form: formally a constitutional monarchy (Kingdom of Sweden - Konungariket Sverige); actually a parliamentary democracy

Administrative structure: central government plus 21 counties (Lan)

Policy making and administration: primarily central government, some devolved authority to counties and municipal governments for administration

Member of European Union

*Source:* Adapted from *CIA World Factbook 2007*, plus UNDP *Human Development Report, 2007/2008*.

### Political and economic context

Sweden is often regarded as an example of the successful combination of an extensive and expensive welfare state with a successful capitalist economy with low unemployment and a high quality of life for its citizens. Whilst the costs of providing this welfare system are high in terms of personal and corporate taxation, the provisions in a very wide range of welfare services are also of high quality. For most of the post-war period Keynesian economic management methods have been used by governments to ensure high levels of employment and thus the possibility of high taxation returns from those employed and their employers. The success of the welfare state has meant that the welfare roles of the family and private welfare providers are rather limited in Sweden, certainly when compared to many other welfare systems in other parts of the world. Whilst this 'success story' image has been largely accurate for much of the period since the Second World War, Sweden has experienced considerable economic problems in recent years that have led to a number of questions being raised about its high costs of state welfare. Unemployment levels rose in the 1990s to levels that had been unseen since 1945, and the global economic environment impacted adversely on the Swedish economy in the early years of the twenty-first century. Sweden is a member of the European Union and is thus subject to its policies regarding the single economic market, and other areas of policy such as social policy too. It has chosen not to join the single currency, the Euro zone, however.

The politics of Sweden have been dominated for most of the post-war period by the Swedish social democratic party, the SAP, but this domination has been increasingly challenged in more recent years by parties from the right which have targeted the welfare state and high levels of taxation as being central to Sweden's economic problems. Some of these parties have also targeted Sweden's membership of the EU and the levels of inward migration which, they say, are encouraged by the promise of access to jobs and high levels of welfare provision. Despite these challenges, for the moment at least the Swedish welfare state created in the early post-war period has remained largely intact, even if some benefit amounts and periods of benefit have been reduced. The Swedish welfare state has been retrenched rather than restructured.

## Welfare ideology

The ideas underpinning the welfare regime in Sweden are a mixture of populist and socialist elements that have been promoted by the SAP. The populist ideas relate to notions that all Swedes, regardless of their socio-economic status, have essentially shared interests, rather like members of a single family. Thus politics and welfare should focus on cooperation, compromise and coalition. The socialist elements of Swedish welfare ideology relate to notions of solidarity, meaning that there should be limits to competition and inequality. In welfare terms this is expressed in the provision of universal benefits paid to all, at the same, high rates. In the development of the Swedish welfare system after 1945 Keynesian approaches to managing the economy so as to keep employment levels high were used in combination with this welfare ideology. Swedish governments have now moved away from such forms of economic management, but the welfare ideas are still largely intact. In this they are broadly comparable with similar ideas in other Scandinavian welfare states.

## What type of welfare regime?

Sweden is usually regarded as the archetypal example of the *Social Democratic regime* type in Esping-Andersen's typology. Yet there are aspects of social policy in Sweden that do not 'fit' this typology, such as some aspects of the pensions system. Furthermore, the financial and political pressures from within (and the impact of globalisation from 'outside') for change in the Swedish welfare regime may mean that some sort of shift occurs in the regime in future years.

## Germany

### Briefing 20.4
### Germany

**People**

Population: 82,400,996

Population age groups:

0-14 years: 13.9%

15-64 years: 66.3%

65 years and over: 19.8%

Infant mortality rate: 4.08 deaths/1,000 live births

Life expectancy at birth: 78.95 years

**Economy**

GDP (Purchasing Power Parity PPP): US $2.632 trillion

GDP per capita (PPP): US $31,900

Unemployment rate: 7.1%

**NB:** This is the International Labor Organization's estimated rate for international comparisons. Germany's Federal Employment Office estimated a seasonally adjusted rate of 10.8% (2006 est.)

Household income or consumption by percentage share:

Lowest 10%: 3.2%

Highest 10%: 22.1%

Distribution of family income by GINI coefficient: 0.28

Part of European Union common market and member of Euro currency zone

**Politics**

Government form: federal republic (formal name: Federal Republic of Germany - Bundesrepublik Deutschland)

Administrative structure: central (federal) government plus 16 states (Länder)

**NB:** Germany divided into four zones of occupation (UK, US, USSR, and later, France) in 1945 following the Second World War; Federal Republic of Germany (FRG or West Germany) established 1949 and included the former UK, US, and French zones. German Democratic Republic (GDR or East Germany) established 1949 and included the former USSR zone. Reunification of West Germany and East Germany took place 1990.

Policy making and administration: divided between central and state governments

Member of European Union

*Source: Adapted from CIA World Factbook 2007, plus UNDP Human Development Report, 2007/2008.*

## Political and economic context

The Federal Republic of Germany was created in 1949 following the Second World War and was based on a written constitution, the Basic Law, which allocates roles and responsibilities to the various levels of government. Some of these roles, including social policy roles, are devolved to the constituent states, or länder, as well as to the central state. Although in recent years the social democratic party, the SPD, has come to the fore in government, for much of the period of post-war development of the German welfare state governments were dominated by two essentially conservative parties, the CDU and the CSU. All parties have, however, broadly supported the idea of the social market economy that underpins the German welfare regime. The development of the German welfare system was closely related to its economic upturns and downturns. To this we must add the impact of the reunification of Germany to incorporate the five länder that from 1949 had been part of East Germany, the Soviet state. Thus the period of rapid economic growth between the end of the war and the 1960s, was matched by the inception and development of the German welfare state system. However, the period was still one of considerable economic hardship for many German people, with high levels of unemployment and the economic and welfare situation was further complicated by the high numbers of refugees from East Germany. Since the German welfare system is very much based on the citizen's role in the labour market, whilst some were beginning to benefit, many were not, and the next period in the 1960s and 1970s saw many protests and strikes, the focus of which was often welfare provision. As a result this period saw further extensions of welfare rights and reforms to the welfare system in which trades unions, the leading employer federations and the government worked together in a corporatist fashion. The 1970s saw Germany confronting the same sort of economic problems as most other capitalist countries, and it responded by making cuts in public expenditure that significantly affected welfare provision in the 1970s and 1980s.

After 1990 the German welfare state was confronted by what to do with the inhabitants of the ex-Soviet German states who had not, of course, made any contributions to the Federal German welfare system, but who suffered from high rates of unemployment and other forms of welfare need. Essentially these citizens gained full access to the German welfare state but at enormous financial cost to the German economy.

Since the 1990s the German economy has seen itself struggling in global economic markets and it has continued to experience high levels of unemployment.

## Welfare ideology

In the constitution the concept of the 'social state' (*sozialstaat*) expresses the link between the roles of the state, the rest of society and the market that in turn provides the basis of the German welfare regime. Essentially the state is committed to providing some form of income and employment security. This role is supposed to be reinforced by trades and other private associations, whilst the family and individuals have the responsibility for their own support. The corresponding idea of the social market economy is that the state should be subsidiary to the market: social and economic policy should not interfere with the market, including income and wealth distribution. These ideas can be seen to be expressed in the compulsory social insurance schemes based on occupational status. Families, assumed to be led by a male bread-winner, have responsibility for their own welfare – the state intervenes only in last resort.

### Applying the models

Germany was regarded by Esping-Andersen as the welfare regime closest to the Conservative–Corporatist type. However, women's roles have significantly increased in the paid labour market in more recent years, and this has put pressure on the existing system of, for example, childcare and welfare benefits such as pensions. Furthermore, the rather rigid labour market has come under increasing pressure as the German economy seeks to compete in the global marketplace. German governments have tried to make the labour market more flexible in recent years, and also to restructure the pensions system in response to financial pressures and a rapidly ageing population. Similarly, the impact of reunification and the changing roles of women have put pressure on the dominant German welfare ideology of the social state. It remains to be seen whether German government strategies will be as successful as, say, the British government's under Mrs Thatcher were in restructuring welfare towards a more liberal type of provision (see the UK, below).

## United Kingdom

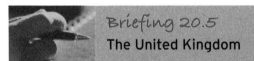

### Briefing 20.5
### The United Kingdom

**People**

Population: 60,776,238

Population age groups:

   0-14 years: 17.2%
   15-64 years: 67%
   65 years and over: 15.8%

Infant mortality rate: 5.01 deaths/1,000 live births

Life expectancy at birth: 78.7 years

**Economy**

GDP (Purchasing Power Parity PPP): US $1.928 trillion

GDP per capita (PPP): US $31,800

Unemployment rate: 2.9%

Household income or consumption by percentage share:

   Lowest 10%: 2.1%
   Highest 10%: 28.5%

Distribution of family income by GINI coefficient: 0.36

Part of European Union common market but NOT member of Euro zone

## Politics

Government form: formally a constitutional monarchy (United Kingdom of Great Britain and Northern Ireland; Great Britain includes England, Scotland, and Wales); actually a parliamentary democracy

Administrative structure: central government plus varying structures in different parts of the UK

*England*: 34 two-tier counties, 32 London boroughs and 1 City of London or Greater London, 36 metropolitan counties, 46 unitary authorities

*Northern Ireland:* Northern Ireland Executive plus 26 district council areas

*Scotland:* Scottish Government plus 32 unitary authorities

*Wales:* Welsh Assembly Government plus 22 unitary authorities

Policy making and administration: primarily central government but growing significance of devolved authorities in Scotland and Wales, plus various *executive agencies* responsible to central government departments

Member of European Union

*Source*: Adapted from *CIA World Factbook 2007*, plus UNDP *Human Development Report, 2007/2008*.

## Political and economic context

The modern British welfare state was established in the years immediately following the Second World War. The welfare system created was based on a mix of Keynesian economic policy, plus welfare provision in areas such as education, health, pensions and housing based on principles outlined in the 1942 Beveridge Report social policy. Both major political parties broadly supported the development of the welfare state on this basis, and in the period between the 1940s and the 1970s under governments led by both the Conservative and the Labour parties, there was a broad consensus about welfare principles and programmes. However, in the 1960s a number of academic and other studies pointed out that the welfare state was having little impact on poverty, and indeed that there were a number of groups, such as women and ethnic minorities, who in practice fell outside the supposedly universal provision of welfare for all citizens. Some attempts were made to broaden the base of welfare provision, but the welfare system suffered criticism and pressure from various pressure groups and simultaneously to experience financial problems as costs grew.

The second major phase of welfare state development in Britain saw a growing crisis in the overall economy and growing pressure to reduce welfare costs. With the advent of the first of the Thatcher governments in 1979 a major political project to restructure both the economy and the welfare system was set in train that ultimately changed both the policy base and the welfare ideas that characterised the UK's welfare regime. Under the various Conservative governments, and somewhat differently under the Blair Labour governments, there has been a shift away from the universalist system of welfare that characterised the system until the 1970s, towards a much more targeted and work-related welfare system. Crudely put, if the British welfare state was similar to that of Sweden in its earlier years, it is now more similar to that of the United States.

Also, in recent years with the devolution of authority in various policy areas, including some parts of social policy, to separate Welsh, Scottish and Northern Irish bodies, the 'national' character of the British welfare state has become much more confused and dislocated than it once was.

### Welfare ideology

Ginsburg (1992) has usefully characterised the nature of post-war welfare ideology as 'Liberal Collectivism'. The ideas of Keynes on managing a capitalist economy, plus those of Beveridge about welfare free at the point of delivery but based on contributions within a free market form the liberal component. But these ideas were nevertheless combined in the early post-war years at least with collectivist notions relating to the proper role of the state in providing welfare directly, with universal access and with common national standards.

However, this welfare ideology has changed. First, the Thatcher governments engaged in an attack on the notion of public provision as expensive, wasteful and essentially uneconomic, whilst at the same time extolling the virtues of private providers where the consumer could choose. These ideas were linked to the neo-liberal arguments of American writers such as Milton Friedman. Though less antagonistic to public provision, the subsequent Blair governments continued to shift the arguments of what welfare provision should be towards ideas of a welfare mix of private, state and voluntary provision. In the New Labour welfare vision, jobs rather than state provision of benefits are the best way to secure welfare for both individuals and society.

### Applying the models

One of the most interesting features of UK social policy from a comparative perspective is that unlike most other developed welfare regimes it has been significantly restructured in the period since 1945. From Esping-Andersen's perspective it has moved from the Social Democratic family welfare states such as Sweden and the other Scandinavian countries, and now might best be analysed in terms of the Liberal welfare regime type, like the US, Australia and Canada.

## The United States of America

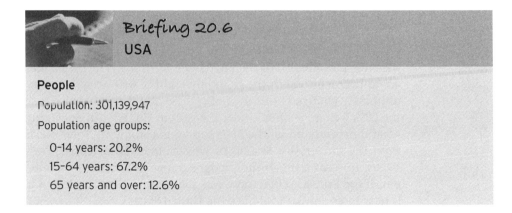

### Briefing 20.6
### USA

**People**

Population: 301,139,947

Population age groups:

  0-14 years: 20.2%

  15-64 years: 67.2%

  65 years and over: 12.6%

Infant mortality rate: 6.37 deaths/1,000 live births

Life expectancy at birth: 78 years

## Economy

GDP (Purchasing Power Parity PPP): US $13.06 trillion

GDP per capita (PPP): $43,800

Unemployment rate: 4.8%

Household income or consumption by percentage share:

   Lowest 10%: 1.9%

   Highest 10%: 29.9%

Distribution of family income by GINI coefficient: 0.45

## Politics

Government form: constitution-based federal republic (United States of America)

Administrative structure: central (federal) government plus 50 states

Policy making and administration: divided between central government and state governments

*Source*: Adapted from *CIA World Factbook 2007*, plus UNDP *Human Development Report, 2007/2008*.

## Political and economic context

Although, like Germany, the United States of America is a federal political system, unlike Germany it has little in the way central government organised, delivered and funded welfare programmes. Indeed, we might ask whether the US has a welfare state at all. There are major variations across the US in terms of how welfare is organised and delivered, and what the entitlement rules and interpretation are in different states. The United States is thus not just a low welfare spending country; there is also limited range of state provision at either federal or individual state levels, and there is a major role for the market – private providers – in welfare provision.

There have been three major periods in the political economy of welfare provision in the US. The first was in the 1930s and associated with the New Deal, a government programme designed to rescue an American economy that had been ravaged by the Depression, and to secure some sort of reconstruction of American society. In the latter case it was not only responding to pressures from unemployed and other workers and farmers, but also to the capitalists who ran the economy. Essentially the New Deal was a programme of massive public works, plus the development of a more systematic welfare system across the US. The welfare initiatives were very much based on contributory, in other words insurance, principles. A key distinction was developed between social insurance that was intended only to cover certain 'involuntary' risks, not for all welfare problems, and public assistance that was intended primarily as a short-term, means-tested form of benefit or 'handouts' for those who were without other forms of support. This distinction and the associated stigma attached to the latter has continued to characterise US welfare provision since then.

The second period of welfare development was during the 1960s, primarily associated with the government's Great Society programme. This saw a considerable expansion of federal government welfare expenditure, increases in eligibility to cover more people, and a move to welfare services rather than benefits in areas such as health and housing provision. However, social security provision remained the central feature of the government's welfare approach.

The third period of welfare development has been the so-called 'welfare backlash' from the 1980s – a mix of criticism of the whole notion of federal government welfare provision orchestrated by New Right conservatives such as Milton Friedman and Charles Murray, plus significant cuts in welfare provision.

### Welfare ideology

Ginsburg (1992) identifies two elements of US welfare ideology: voluntarism and liberalism. He suggests that there are two elements to this form of voluntarism: (a) individuals and the (patriarchal) family should be responsible for their own welfare, and (b) public welfare intervention should restore not replace individual and family self-sufficiency. However, these ideas have often been combined with (American) liberal ideas, where the term means not conservatism as in 'neo-liberal' but the acceptance of social policy interventions to meet social needs as identified by various pressure and client groups.

This characteristic welfare ideology has found itself expressed in the character of US welfare provision where there is a split between the 'deserving' and the 'undeserving' (for example, those who have paid insurance contributions and those who have not); between targeted and means-tested short-term benefits ('handouts') where the recipients are stigmatised, and insurance-based social security; and between social insurance and public assistance.

### Applying the models

The USA is taken as the archetypal example of a Liberal welfare state in the Esping-Andersen typology of welfare regimes. Whilst there have been periods of increased government spending and involvement in welfare, in the United States most welfare outcomes depend on a mix of individual and family roles and responsibilities, plus a heavy dose of market provision where 'you get what you pay for'.

## Hong Kong

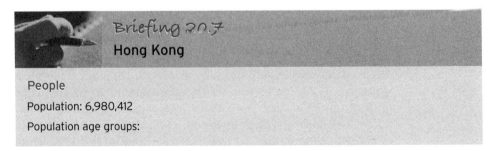

*Briefing 20.7*
**Hong Kong**

People
Population: 6,980,412
Population age groups:

0-14 years: 13%

15-64 years: 74%

65 years and over: 12.9%

Infant mortality rate: 2.94 deaths/1,000 live births

Life expectancy at birth: 81.68 years

Economy

GDP (Purchasing Power Parity PPP): US $259.1 billion

GDP per capita (PPP): US $37,300

Unemployment rate: 4.9%

Household income or consumption by percentage share: *not available*

Distribution of family income by GINI coefficient: 0.52

Politics

Government form: Special Administrative Region (SAR) of China

Administrative structure: devolved authority from central Chinese government

Policy making and administration: Hong Kong Legislative Council plus government departments of Hong Kong SAR

NB: Hong Kong was a colony of the UK from 1841. It became the Hong Kong Special Administrative Region (SAR) of China in 1997. In this agreement, China has promised that, under its 'one country, two systems' formula, China's socialist economic system will not be imposed on Hong Kong and that Hong Kong will enjoy a high degree of autonomy in all matters except foreign and defense affairs for the next 50 years.

*Source*: Adapted from *CIA World Factbook 2007*, plus UNDP *Human Development Report, 2007/2008*.

## Political and economic context

In July 1997 Hong Kong reverted to being a part of China after having been a British colony since 1841. Hong Kong has an important position in the global economy, and also a social, economic and political/administrative structure that supports this economy, and which Hong Kong citizens understand and broadly support. To radically change Hong Kong to make it more like the socio-economic and political system prevailing in mainland China would weaken its economic strength, and indeed risk major social and political unrest in Hong Kong. Hence the Chinese government has alighted on the notion of 'one country, two systems', allowing Hong Kong broadly to continue as it has, at least for the time being. In order to understand Hong Kong's political economy of welfare we therefore need to look at developments in the period up to 1997.

There was hardly any systematic government provision of welfare services in Hong Kong until after the Second World War, and such provision as there was for ordinary people and vulnerable groups came via charities, missionaries and churches. However, after the war spending on social welfare grew significantly, so that by the end of the 1960s it represented some 40 per cent of all government expenditure. Nevertheless the programmes were still inadequate to satisfy demand in the areas of housing, health, education and social services. The colonial authorities were motivated less by a desire to really address the welfare needs of the local population, and more by an interest in curbing costs whilst avoiding social unrest. Ideas of citizenship, justice and inequality were never mentioned with regard to welfare for the indigenous population.

It was not until the 1970s, under the colonial governorship of MacLehose, that Hong Kong saw an expansion of welfare services to add to those already provided in the areas of public housing, education and public assistance. Expenditure on education grew by nearly five times between 1970 and 1980, and that on health, housing and social welfare by around five, eight and seventeen times respectively. Free primary education was introduced in 1971, massive increases in public housing were made, and those people who could receive public assistance were significantly increased in numbers. Both the quantity and indeed the quality of welfare provision improved markedly in the 1970s. Universally available services became the norm in the areas of education and medical care and, arguably, the notion of welfare rights began to develop alongside more traditional ideas of individual responsibility and family care.

However, the 1980s and 1990s saw a move towards 'marketisation' of welfare provision. Although the overall scale of provision was not reduced, further growth was limited. Furthermore, the ideas of 'those who can pay should pay' and 'those whom use it should pay for it' came to dominate government statements and policy developments on welfare. A shift to private provision, charging for some services and targeting was developed. In the 1990s the emphasis continued on marketisation and there was a focus on introducing commercial management principles into culture and practices of welfare management. Nevertheless, by 1997, when Hong Kong reverted to China, over half of government expenditure was on welfare services of various sorts. Thus, whilst in many senses Hong Kong has a free market economy, it is not a place that has little or no state welfare provision, a residual welfare state; rather, it has a well-developed public welfare system that runs alongside market and family provision.

## Welfare ideology

As already noted, the notion of social rights to welfare is only a very recent aspect of welfare ideology in Hong Kong and even now these ideas must compete with those of free market capitalism and indeed notions of individual and family responsibility that have a particularly Asian meaning. Hong Kong is sometimes described as having a Confucian welfare ideology, which is a reference to the ideas of Confucius, a Chinese philosopher, whose ideas are said to imbue the moral and political beliefs of a number of South East Asian societies. Essentially these ideas revolve around the notion of obligation to family, clan and, by extension, government. Ideas of rights to welfare are deemed to be secondary to those of responsibility to family and indeed the rest of society. These ideas were manipulated by the colonial powers and, it appears, are being resuscitated by the new Chinese government as it attempts to refocus welfare in Hong Kong. Whilst of course there are similar ideas about family roles and responsibilities in Europe and elsewhere that inform welfare ideologies there, the character and significance of such Confucian values and their use by governments is often seen by comparative analysts as something that sets Hong Kong and other South East Asian welfare regimes apart from Western welfare systems.

## Applying the models

As we have seen above, the Esping-Andersen typology seems to have some sort of explanatory utility for comparing the welfare regimes of developed Western capitalist systems, even if that typology has limitations and the experience of these systems is changing. When, however, we turn to Hong Kong the usefulness of the typology is highly questionable. Hong Kong does not seem to fit to any of the ideal types, and indeed it seems to combine elements of all three – it has some aspects that seem to correspond to the decommodified character of Social Democratic regimes, some that are essentially Conservative in character with regard to family roles, and some that have the character of residualised, Liberal provision. Some have suggested (for example Walker and Wong, 2005) that the Esping-Andersen typology is simply inadequate for comparative purposes if we wish to consider Hong Kong and countries such as Japan, South Korea, China and Taiwan.

## Conclusion

In this section we have briefly reviewed five different welfare systems or regimes. Whilst this review provides no more than snapshots of the different systems it does at least put some flesh on the bones of the analytical and theoretical issues about comparison dealt with in the first section. Furthermore, the snapshots indicate the variety of ways in which social policies, their organisation and delivery, and associated welfare ideas are all part of a complex national and regional political economy. Patterns of similarity have also become apparent, for example between the United States and the UK welfare systems. The usefulness, and limitations, of the Esping-Andersen regime typology has been referred to. What these snapshots also indicate is that in order to truly compare social policy cross-nationally a range of empirical material needs to be collated that allows adequate description of the relevant social policy patterns in the chosen state. However, this simply describes and does not, on its own, lead to comparison. For this to begin patterns of similarity and difference need to be identified.

## Summary

Having identified such patterns of similarity and difference, true comparison then needs to try to answer the question 'Why?' – if country A organises and delivers its social policies like this, and country B like this, then what are the patterns of similarity and difference between them and what accounts for these patterns? It is when we seek to identify patterns of similarity and difference and, most importantly, when we seek to answer the question 'Why do these patterns exist?' that we need to refer to some sort of theoretically-informed framework:

● Even simple comparative descriptions such as those outlined above in the country briefings throw up questions worthy of investigation. For example, what, if any, correlation is there between the welfare regimes in each of our countries and factors such as: GDP per capita; the age breakdown of the population and the proportion of elderly people in particular; the distribution of family income between richer and poorer groups expressed by the GINI index; the unemployment rate?

- How far do the different forms of government and administration outlined in different regimes interlock with the ways in which social policy is organised and delivered? Even where there are similar government forms, such as the federal state in Germany and the USA, this does not necessarily correspond to the same patterns of welfare provision. Also, how far is the pattern of devolved government in the UK creating more than one welfare regime? In what sense does membership of the European Union affect the national welfare state regimes of its member states? Turning to one of the criticisms of the Esping-Andersen model outlined above, we might also ask how the dimensions of gender and 'race' interact with other factors in the welfare regimes of the countries outlined.

- Even if the exercise of simply describing welfare systems in different countries is in itself interesting, it is only the first step to effective comparison. Comparing social policies needs a theoretically-informed framework to support analysis as well as description. Ultimately, however, though cross-national social policy comparison may be fraught with empirical, technical and conceptual difficulties, and it may throw up more questions than can be answered, it is an exciting and fascinating exercise that provides us with a better understanding of our own welfare system and of others in an increasingly globalised world.

## Discussion and review topics

1  When we compare social policies cross-nationally just what are we comparing?

2  What is meant by the term *decommodification* and why is the term useful for understanding the different roles of the family, the government and private providers in delivering welfare?

3  What is a social welfare *regime*?

4  If each national welfare state is different, how can we compare social policies cross-nationally?

### Further reading

**Alcock, P. and Craig, G.** (eds) *International social policy*, Palgrave Macmillan, Basingstoke. This book provides coverage of developments in welfare provision in twelve states.

**Hill, M.** (2006) *Social policy in the modern world,* Blackwell, Oxford. Rather than taking a country approach this examines five areas of social policy together with a range of social divisions.

**May, M.** (2008) 'The role of comparative study', in P. Alcock, A. Erskine and M. May (eds) *The student's companion to social policy*, Blackwell/SPA, Oxford. A succinct discussion of the part that comparative analysis can play in the study of social policy.

**Sykes, R., Palier, B. and Prior, P.M.** (eds) (2001) *Globalization and European welfare states*, Palgrave Macmillan, Basingstoke. This book focuses on globalisation and social policy, primarily within the European context.

A number of journals also provide very useful comparative social policy articles, especially *Global social policy*, the *Journal of European social policy*, and special issues of *Social policy and administration*.

## Some useful websites

**www.globalwelfarelibrary.org** – the E-library for global welfare. This is a collection of online resources for international and comparative policy analysis, research and teaching.

**www.intute.ac.uk/socialsciences/socialwelfare** – the INTUTE information portal for the social sciences/social welfare: from this page use the search facility to look for comparative materials.

**www.oecd.org/home** – the Organisation for Economic Cooperation and Development is very useful as a source of statistical and other data about the social policy in the most advanced economies, plus some information on a selection of other countries.

**www.cia.gov/library/publications/the-world-factbook/index.html** – the *CIA World Factbook*. Despite (or perhaps because of) its links with the interests of the United States government, this site provides a very convenient and accessible resource of comparative information on almost all countries in the world.

Here is a list of government information portals for the main countries considered in the social policy snapshots. For information on social policy try typing 'social policy' or 'social welfare' into each site's search facility.

**www.bundesregierung.de/Webs/Breg/EN/Homepage/home.html** (in English) – German government portal.

**www.gov.hk/en/residents** – Hong Kong SAR government portal.

**www.sweden.gov.se** (in English) – Swedish government portal.

**www.direct.gov.uk/Homepage/fs/en** – UK Direct government portal.

**www.firstgov.gov** – USA government portal.

## References

Alcock, P. and Craig, G. (eds) *International social policy*, Palgrave Macmillan, Basingstoke.

Castles, F. and Mitchell, D. (1992) 'Identifying welfare state regimes: The link between politics, instruments and outcomes', in *Governance*, Vol. 5, No. 1, pp. 1-26.

*CIA World Factbook* (no date) web publication at: **www.cia.gov/library/publications/the-world-factbook/index.html**.

Doyal, L. and Gough, I. (1991) *A theory of human need*, Macmillan, Basingstoke.

Esping-Andersen, G. (1990) *Three worlds of welfare capitalism*, Polity, Cambridge.

Esping-Andersen, G. (1996) *Welfare states in transition*, UNRISD/Sage, London.

Ferrara, F. (1996) 'The "southern model" of welfare in social Europe', in *Journal of European Social Policy*, Vol. 6, No. 1, pp. 17-37.

Ginsburg, N. (1992) *Divisions of welfare*, Sage, London.

Gough, I. and Wood, G. (eds) (2004) *Insecurity and welfare regimes in Asia, Africa and Latin America: Social policy in development contexts*, Cambridge University Press, Cambridge.

OECD (2003) *1980-1998: 20 Years of Social Expenditure, The OECD Database*, OECD, Paris.

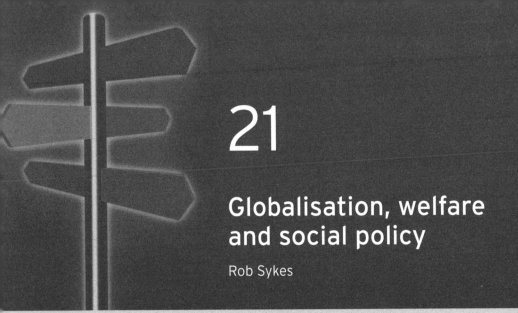

# 21

# Globalisation, welfare and social policy

Rob Sykes

## Chapter overview

This chapter deals with one of the great controversies of current times: the development of globalisation in various forms throughout the world, and its effects upon our lives: socially, politically and economically.

The controversy is not simply about what globalisation *is*, however. It is also about whether globalisation is a 'good' or a 'bad' thing. The key issue that is contested is one which is central to our interest in welfare and social policy: does globalisation improve or worsen the welfare of the peoples of the world? As we shall explain, there are those who argue from either side, but can they both be right? The chapter examines some of the major questions around this debate before going on to consider how globalisation is implicated in the changing activities on national welfare states around the world.

The key topics of this chapter are:

- what *is* globalisation? Contested ideas – contested reality?
- the variety of globalisation processes – social, political and economic;
- globalisation and welfare state change;
- globalisation and the future of welfare.

**Spotlight on the issues**

## IT and outsourcing – globalisation and its contradictions

A news story from 2007 reveals the curious and contradictory nature of globalisation and its effects. The story (see the BBC News website at **http://news.bbc.co.uk/1/hi/ business/ 6288247.stm**) refers to a young American student living in California who used an Internet e-tutoring service for help with her maths and English. The service was based not in the USA but in Bangalore, India. It cost a fraction of what a US-based e-tutoring service would cost ($2.50 per hour rather than $40 per hour) and helped the student gain top marks in all her classes.

Bangalore is the centre of India's IT industry, which is enjoying unprecedented growth as foreign multinationals rush to outsource their back-office functions to India. More than 500 major international companies have IT operations in Bangalore alone. Among the household names are Hewlett-Packard, Dell, IBM and Accenture. India's IT sector employs 1.3 million people directly, and 3 million indirectly – and 40 per cent of the IT sector is concentrated in Bangalore. Bangalore also has the highest average income in India, and the jobs are plentiful. Clearly the global market for IT services is benefiting Bangalore and the Indian economy, and, at least for those working in this sector, it is having beneficial effects.

Now let us turn to the USA, a country that has been in the forefront of IT development in the past. Also on the BBC News website there are stories from IT professionals based in the UK and US who have, effectively, lost out to Indian IT workers either as a result of the latter being able to provide cheaper services, such as the e-tutoring service above, or because their own companies have outsourced work to other countries such as India. One US IT professional tells the tale of how, despite being recognised as excellent in his area of IT, he has nevertheless seen work that he had previously developed being outsourced to either Indian or Chinese IT workers. As he points out (**http://news.bbc.co.uk/ 1/hi/ talking_point/6341923.stm**) 'In each case, I was expected to train my replacement, and in each case, they were a lot less qualified than me'. But these workers are paid much less than those in the US or UK, work much longer hours and, as this worker and others researching the field have pointed out, this manner of working is actually generating welfare and health problems for these Indian IT workers and their families.

There is much talk, and considerable debate and disagreement, about what globalisation is (or even whether it does exist) and its impacts on individuals and on states. As this chapter will show, globalisation is a multifaceted and sometimes contradictory set of processes and we need to keep this in mind when looking at the links between welfare and globalisation.

## Considering globalisation

If we examine the story outlined above, it has a number of points that can help us understand the phenomenon known as globalisation:

● First, the development of international economic connections now means that production, goods and services are increasingly developed and delivered in a global network. You are just as likely to find that your shoes were made in China, your electricity supplier is French-owned, and your customer services come from people living in India as to discover that any of these things are made or delivered from your home country.

- Second, it is often argued that it is mainly the cheaper, unskilled work that is going from the older industrial countries of the North to the developing countries of the South, but it is also the case, as we see here, that certain quite advanced service sector jobs are now also 'going South'. What does this mean for the future employment patterns of people in both these regions of the global economy?

- Third, global economic patterns are uneven and constantly changing. Jobs are not all gradually going from the developed Northern countries to the underdeveloped South, nor is it the case, whatever we see in Bangalore, that the people of countries such as India all have access to jobs, let alone well-paid ones.

- Finally, in terms of the overall welfare effects of these global economic changes, again there is a mixed pattern. Certainly many unskilled and semi-skilled workers in the US and Europe have lost their jobs in industries such as steel-making, car production and other areas of manufacturing. In many cases these workers remain unemployed for long periods of time, with obvious consequences for the economic and broader welfare of themselves and their families. Where developed welfare systems exist, these people are, to some extent, protected from the full effects of unemployment. However, these welfare systems are finding it more and more difficult to continue to provide benefits, as the numbers of unemployed people increases or does not decline. But what about the welfare of the workers where the jobs go – in India, China and other similar countries? Most of these countries have either rudimentary or less-developed welfare systems than are found in the North. The development of IT work in India, and massive developments in heavy industry and manufacturing in China, for example, clearly benefits the workers who get jobs in these industries. But most Indian and Chinese workers do not get such jobs. They continue to exist on incomes and with resources that are but a fraction of the normal wage or salary of those in the North. Plus, those over-worked people in the Bangalore IT sector and the many workers in unsafe and polluted environments in Chinese factories and cities can expect little or no organised state welfare provision to help them.

## What is globalisation? Contested ideas – contested reality?

What is globalisation? As Briefing 21.1 suggests, the answer to this question is by no means undisputed. The term has been used to refer to a bewildering variety of phenomena: from the spread of worldwide financial linkages, to the growing power of multinational corporations able effectively to control national and international economic activities; from the spread of the 'Coca Cola culture' and 'Mac-Donaldization', as both economic and social developments, to the growth of worldwide television, telecommunications and the Internet; from the growing

**Briefing 21.1**
## Globalisation

Global capitalism, driven by the TNCs [Trans National Corporations], organized politically through the transnational capitalist class, and fuelled by the culture-ideology of consumerism, is the most potent force for change in the world today.                    Sklair (2002)

. . . global economic integration has supported poverty reduction and should not be reversed . . .
                                                                            Collier and Dollar (2001)

'Globalization' is a big idea resting on slim foundations.                    Weiss (1997)

. . . globalization, as conceived by the more extreme globalizers, is largely a myth.
                                                                        Hirst and Thompson (1999)

influence of international organisations, such as the International Monetary Fund and the European Union, to the 'shrinking' of the world through air travel and mass tourism; from the growth of a high-cost, consumer culture with recognised world brands such as Nike and Microsoft to the increasing impoverishment of millions, especially those living in the poorer countries of the world. We could extend this list almost endlessly – some see globalisation as evident in almost every aspect of our lives.

But the question is not just about what constitutes globalisation: it is also about what effects it is having on our lives. Some, commonly termed 'anti-globalists', are critical of what is happening, suggesting that unfettered globalisation is detrimental to the economic, political and cultural interests of most ordinary people. This, essentially, is the position of those who demonstrate at meetings of the major governments, such as the G8 summits and European Union summits. On the other hand, 'globalists', such as the World Bank, the US government and other major governments in the West, accept that globalisation is a fact of life in the contemporary world, but argue that properly managed it can, and indeed does, benefit people in both the richer and poorer countries of the world.

Then there are those who are sceptical of the claims that globalisation already exists, cannot be avoided, and already conditions the lives of all in the contemporary world, whether for good or ill. For these, often academic, writers, much of the discussion surrounding globalisation, and many of the claims about its impact on our lives, are essentially hype and exaggeration, and for this reason should be seen more as myth than reality.

In the context of this fundamental dispute both about whether globalisation even exists, as well as debates about the forms it takes and the impacts it may have, we clearly need to unravel the competing positions somewhat more before we can move on to consider globalisation's importance with regard to social policy. The central point here is this: *globalisation is both a contested concept and a contested reality*. Not only are there disagreements about how globalisation should be understood, theorised and analysed, but there are also disagreements about what actually constitutes globalisation in economic and/or social and/or political senses. What this means for anybody trying to make sense of globalisation is that s/he needs to be constantly aware that both general discussions of globalisation and accounts of the relationship between globalisation and other areas of social and economic life, such as welfare policies or, say, the European Union, are intrinsically disputable. To provide a focal example of this sort of contestation, there are those who argue that globalisation (ultimately) reduces world poverty and inequality (for example, the World Bank and most Western governments), and those who argue that it makes world poverty and inequality worse (such as the various groups of anti-global demonstrators, and a number of governments in Africa, Asia and Latin America). This dispute is both about how globalisation does or does not increase poverty and inequality, and about the evidence marshalled by each side to prove its point. The debate between Wade and Wolf, 'Are global inequality and poverty getting worse?' (2002) is a good example of this sort of argument.

Whilst debates about globalisation – just like debates about democracy, political power, social class and so on – will continue to be characterised by conceptual and evidential dispute, it is already possible at least to separate out the different ways in which 'globalisation' is used, and the different sorts of evidence which would be needed to test out these competing approaches. This is vital if we are to be clear about the possible links between globalisation and social policy. So let us unpack still further what has been suggested about the character of globalisation in terms of its social, political and economic forms. Then we can see how these different elements are combined in arguments about globalisation and welfare and, indeed, suggest which of these approaches seem to provide the most useful framework for understanding what is happening in recent social policy developments.

## The variety of globalisation processes – social, political and economic

As the previous paragraphs indicate, most arguments about the development of globalisation are either challenged or disputed by alternative readings. Borrowing from Held and McGrew (2002), we can recognise two broad groups: the 'globalisers' and the 'sceptics'. The first group is composed of those who argue that globalisation processes are already developed or are developing rapidly across the world. The second group are those who doubt that an overall system of globalisation has developed, and suggest that many of the assertions made by the globalisers are either overstated and/or are less different from previous circumstances than the globalisers are prepared to admit. For reasons of space and emphasis, we shall not consider the arguments of the 'sceptics' in any detail in the following sections, focusing rather on the main assertions of the 'globalisers' so that we can then consider how far these assertions are borne out in the case of globalisation and social policy later. As will become apparent, however, many, if not most, of the assertions made by the globalisers are challengeable.

## Social and cultural globalisation

Giddens (1990, 1991), Harvey (1989) and Robertson (1992) have each suggested that not only are individuals, localities and nations now more effectively linked, but that the world now is (or appears to be) shrunk and compressed: we are living in a 'global village'; there has been a shrinking of 'time–space distanciation'. Here the role of the Internet, cable and satellite TV, cell phones and suchlike are cited as examples of the ways in which more and more people are able to experience life outside their own local and national contexts and even to partake of almost instantaneous communication with other people living thousands of miles away.

It is not simply the role of information and communication technologies and other technologies which are considered: rather there is a concern with how social and cultural life has more generally been affected by and indeed affects globalisation processes. So it is both the consciousness of and responses to globalisation which such theorists concern themselves with. Some argue that a global awareness now exists for many people living around the world – we are all now, or so it is argued, 'global citizens'. This may mean that distinctions such as nationality, ethnicity, class and gender are becoming less and less relevant. What is more, flows of migrant groups, tourists and refugees alongside the free flow of ideas, information, images and cultural products are all said to be contributing to forms of cultural globalisation. Indeed, for some a 'global culture' already (incipiently) exists, even if its supposedly 'global' character has a very Western/US form.

## Political globalisation

In the field of politics and international relations much is made of the connection between economic changes and their consequences for national and international politics. It is often argued that the autonomy and authority of sovereign nation states is now challenged if not superseded through globalisation processes. Constraints imposed by international economic forces in a 'globalised' environment, and in particular by transnational corporations (TNCs) and **intergovernmental organisations** (IGOs) such as the World Bank and the World Trade Organisation (WTO), have, according to some, emasculated states as policy makers and as sovereign authorities within their national boundaries. The number of international organisations, all of whom may be said to affect or even supersede the authority of nation states, is now very large. As Figure 21.1 shows, these organisations operate in the fields of economic intervention, security, welfare and the environment.

Another dimension of the globalisation of politics is the way in which issues are increasingly perceived as global in character and thus requiring global solutions. In this sense, political globalisation refers to the argument that social, economic and environmental issues are now essentially transnational and worldwide in both their significance and resolution. Environmental issues, such as global warming, pollution and the development of genetically modified (GM) crops, do not recognise or remain within national boundaries. Accordingly, governments, transnational companies (TNCs), **non-governmental organisations** (NGOs), trades unions and even community groups and other social movements are increasingly

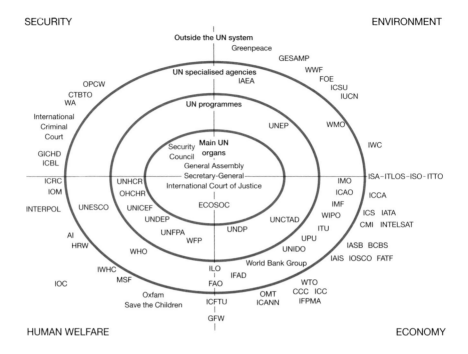

SECURITY                                                    ENVIRONMENT

Outside the UN system
Greenpeace
GESAMP
WWF
UN specialised agencies        FOE
OPCW                        IAEA              ICSU
CTBTO                                          IUCN
WA
International               UN programmes
Criminal                                          WMO
Court                              UNEP
IWC
GICHD                    Security   Main UN
ICBL                     Council    organs
General Assembly
ICRC          UNHCR    Secretary-General              IMO    ISA–ITLOS–ISO–ITTO
IOM           OHCHR   International Court of Justice   ICAO   ICCA
INTERPOL   UNESCO   UNICEF            ECOSOC      IMF
UNDEP                      UNCTAD   WIPO   ICS  IATA
AI              UNFPA          UNDP         ITU   CMI  INTELSAT
HRW        WHO      WFP                  UPU
WHO                          UNIDO   IASB  BCBS
IWHC                 ILO    World Bank Group  IAIS IOSCO FATF
IOC     MSF         IFAD
FAO                    WTO
Oxfam                    OMT   CCC  ICC
Save the Children   ICFTU   ICANN   IFPMA
GFW

HUMAN WELFARE                                          ECONOMY

| Key to abbreviations | | IMF | International Monetary Fund |
|---|---|---|---|
| AI | Amnesty International | IMO | International Maritime Organization |
| BCBS | Basel Committee on Banking Supervision | INTELSAT | International Telecommunications Satellites |
| CCC | Customs Cooperation Council | | Organization |
| CMI | Comité Maritime International | INTERPOL | International Criminal Police Organization |
| CTBTO | Comprehensive Nuclear-Test-Ban Treaty | IOC | International Olympic Committee |
| | Organization (not yet operational) | IOM | International Organization for Migration |
| ECOSOC | UN Economic and Social Council | IOSCO | International Organization of Securities Commissions |
| FAO | Food and Agriculture Organization | ISA | International Seabed Authority |
| FATF | Financial Action Task Force | ISO | International Organization for Standardization |
| FOE | Friends of the Earth | ITLOS | International Tribunal for the Law of the Sea |
| GESAMP | Joint Group of Experts on the Scientific | ITTO | International Tropical Timber Organization |
| | Aspects of Marine Environmental Protection | ITU | International Telecommunication Union |
| GFW | Global Fund for Women | IUCN | World Conservation Union |
| GICHD | Geneva International Centre for Humanitarian | IWC | International Whaling Commission |
| | Demining | IWHC | International Women's Health Coalition |
| HRW | Human Rights Watch | MSF | Médecins Sans Frontières |
| IAEA | International Atomic Energy Agency | OHCHR | Office of the High Commissioner for Human Rights |
| IAIS | International Association of Insurance | OMT | World Tourism Organization |
| | Supervisors | OPCW | Organization for the Prohibition of Chemical Weapons |
| IASB | International Accounting Standards Board | UNCTAD | UN Conference on Trade and Development |
| IATA | International Association of Transport Airlines | UNDCP | UN Drug Control Programme |
| ICANN | Internet Corporation for Assigned Names and | UNDP | UN Development Programme |
| | Numbers | UNEP | UN Environment Programme |
| ICAO | International Civil Aviation Organization | UNESCO | UN Educational. Scientific and Cultural Organization |
| ICBL | International Campaign to Ban Landmines | UNFPA | UN Population Fund |
| ICC | International Chamber of Commerce | UNHCR | UN High Commissioner for Refugees |
| ICCA | International Council of Chemical | UNICEF | UN Children's Fund |
| | Associations | UNIDO | UN Industrial Development Organization |
| ICFTU | International Confederation of Free Trade | UPU | Universal Postal Union |
| | Unions | WA | Wassenaar Arrangement on Export Controls for |
| ICRC | International Committee of the Red Cross | | Conventional Arms and Dual-Use Goods and |
| ICS | International Chamber of Shipping | | Technologies |
| ICSU | International Council for Science | WFP | World Food Programme |
| IFAD | International Fund for Agricultural | WHO | World Health Organization |
| | Development | WIPO | World Intellectual Property Organization |
| IFPMA | International Federation of Pharmaceutical | WMO | World Meteorological Organization |
| | Manufacturers Associations | WTO | World Trade Organization |
| ILO | International Labour Organization | WWF | Worldwide Fund for Nature |

**Figure 21.1 Organisational infrastructure of global governance: a UN-centric view**

*Source*: Koenig-Archibugi (2002), pp. 64–5.

directing political action to the global or international arena. This is certainly, though not exclusively, the case with anti-globalisation protesters who, in turn, have increasingly set the agenda for discussion if not the resolution of issues such as the indebtedness of developing countries and global poverty.

## Economic globalisation

Arguments suggesting various forms of economic globalisation are by far the most numerous and common. They are also those most frequently linked to arguments about globalisation and social policy so we shall concentrate on these at greater length than the arguments about social and political globalisation.

We are constantly told that governments and individual firms have to cope with the pressures of global economic competition and the problems associated with the interlinkage of the different economies of the world. Not only are we subject, we are told, to a world capitalist economy which is increasingly competitive, increasingly dominated by large firms and/or trading blocs, and within which national economies are less and less open to control by national agents such as governments, but also this world economy is now so interdependent that changes in one part affect other parts, with fundamental consequences which can be good or bad. Some say the nature of the global economy, based on free markets and increasing trade etc. is essentially beneficial for all; others say that the system is unequal and benefits the developed economies most, generating a bigger and bigger gap between rich and poor both between countries (rich and poor nations) and within countries.

Those who argue for a global economy point to the unprecedented scale of world economic interaction. National economies, they argue, are enmeshed in what are now global patterns of production and exchange unlike any previous period. International economic integration is also at new levels both within and between different regions or economic blocs such as the USA, Japan and the EU. Ohmae (1990) is credited with suggesting that there is now a 'borderless world', where national boundaries are now essentially irrelevant to what is, in essence, already a global economy.

According to this view, the current phase of economic globalisation is different from earlier internationalisation of the world's economies because now the system is essentially open – there are no trade barriers and tariffs – and integrated – even the most marginal economies are in some senses integrated in the world capitalist economy. There has been a parallel process of economic regionalisation in areas such as the Single European Market (a central feature of the European Community/EU) and the North American Free Trade Agreement (NAFTA). This form of regionalisation is an 'open' form of linkage, however, involving the liberalisation of national economies rather than protectionism. As such, the modern economic regionalisation process has been both a response to and a facilitator of economic globalisation.

Although most economic flows are between the developed economies of the OECD (Organisation for Economic Cooperation and Development) member states, the share of world trade and investment flows have increased for developing

493

countries too. If we look at long-term statistics we can see how the volume of world merchandise trade has increased very significantly in recent decades as compared with earlier periods of international trading (see Table 21.1).

**Table 21.1** Export-GDP ratios, 1870–1998

| | Merchandise exports as % of GDP (1990 prices) | | | | | |
|---|---|---|---|---|---|---|
| | *1870* | *1913* | *1929* | *1950* | *1973* | *1998* |
| France | 4.9 | 7.8 | 8.6 | 7.6 | 15.2 | 28.7 |
| Germany | 9.5 | 16.1 | 12.8 | 6.2 | 23.8 | 38.9 |
| Japan | 0.2 | 2.4 | 3.5 | 2.2 | 7.7 | 13.4 |
| UK | 12.2 | 17.5 | 13.3 | 11.3 | 14.0 | 25.0 |
| United States | 2.5 | 3.7 | 3.6 | 3.0 | 4.9 | 10.1 |
| World | 4.6 | 7.9 | 9.0 | 5.5 | 10.5 | 17.2 |

*Source*: Maddison (2000), cited in Held and McGrew (2002).

Who or what are the agents of this globalising economy if it is not national economies or states? Multinational corporations (MNCs) and/or transnational corporations (TNCs) are the central actors in the globalising economy (see Briefing 21.2 on MNCs and TNCs).

## *Briefing 21.2*
## Multinational corporations and transnational corporations

What is the difference between an MNC and a TNC? It is commonly suggested that MNCs have a clear national base, although they operate in more than one country. TNCs, on the other hand, operate without any clear national 'home'. Thus a transnational corporation would produce and market its goods or services on a truly international scale.

Spatially, it is argued that these patterns of economic globalisation are creating changes in labour markets and the patterns of division of labour around the world. The deindustrialisation of the northern economies can be linked to increasing relocation of manufacturing activities to other regions, such as Latin America, East Asia and Eastern Europe, as MNCs and others restructure production to the least expensive sites. A new and more complex New International Division of Labour (NIDL) is developing, and new patterns of wealth and inequality are developing to go with it (see Figure 21.2).

## Summary: the key features of globalisation?

Clearly there is a very wide range of arguments about the various forms and dimensions of globalisation processes, and we have only touched on a very small sample of these here. From this rather bewildering array of ideas we can, however,

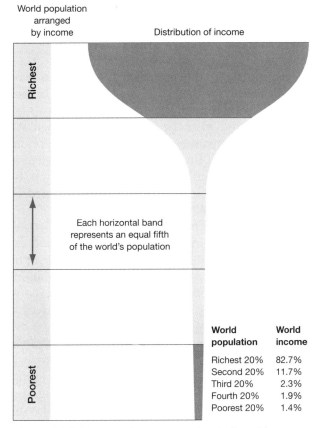

World population
arranged
by income

Distribution of income

Richest

Each horizontal band
represents an equal fifth
of the world's population

Poorest

| World population | World income |
|---|---|
| Richest 20% | 82.7% |
| Second 20% | 11.7% |
| Third 20% | 2.3% |
| Fourth 20% | 1.9% |
| Poorest 20% | 1.4% |

**Figure 21.2** Wade's 'champagne glass' of world income distribution

*Source*: After Wade (2001).

*Note*: National Incomes are converted into US dollars at market exchange rates.

identify some key features and potential effects of globalisation from the point of view of social policy analysis.

The first and foremost notion is that globalization involves an increasing inter-connectedness between states, peoples and regions across the world. Increasingly, a range of social, economic and political processes operate at global rather than na-tional or other local levels. What is more, these processes are occurring with increas-ing frequency and intensity at the global level – we communicate more frequently through email, telephone and fax across countries and regions; global financial transactions are now increasing in both volume and frequency; international or-ganisations such as the EU and the WTO come up with more and more decisions and policies which affect both nation states and their citizens. Third, time and space have become compressed· world travel whether for business or leisure purposes is now more common and more frequent than ever before; SARS and AIDS became global health crises almost immediately they were discovered. There really are senses in which the world has now become smaller: we are now economically, physically and culturally 'closer together'. Through telecommunications, the spread of satellite television and other communications media people are now more aware of the rest of the world and how developments in one part of it can affect their own lives. In short, these various aspects of globalisation may be said to link together the local and the global to such an extent that '. . . the impact of distant events is magnified while even the most local developments may come to have enormous global consequences. In this sense, the boundaries between domestic matters and global affairs may be blurred' (Held *et al.*, 1999: 15).

If this summarises the key features of globalisation as a set of processes in overall terms, what can be said about the key economic, political and social dimensions in terms of their potential impact on governments as social policy makers? Though social issues are important – migration, health risks, world poverty – the main ways in which governments are affected by globalisation are in terms of economic and political challenges.

It may be said that the main problems of economic policy making are now at an international rather than a national level: exchange and interest rates, the prices of oil and other raw materials, the state of health of the world economy are all matters beyond the exclusive control of national governments. What is more, national governments must make policy decisions which broadly meet the criteria of other public and private economic players, such as MNCs, the OECD, the WTO and credit agencies. If they do not, they risk losing credibility, MNCs may choose not to invest, and private speculators can attack national currencies. Even national taxation levels can be seen as a factor influencing the world markets, such that overall, governments will try to keep taxes low so as to make their economies as competitive as possible. Alongside tax policy, governments have generally sought to **deregulate** their financial systems as a result of pressures from the private sector and international bodies such as the WTO. Indeed, these international groups – WTO, G8, EU, NAFTA, etc. – all heavily influence and constrain the economic policies of national governments nowadays. All in all, the key principle in attempts by national governments to meet the various economic challenges posed by globalisation has been to maximise competitiveness. Government politicians of every persuasion consistently argue to their electorates that various policy initiatives, whether in the economic or the social fields, are necessitated by the pressures of globalisation and the requirement for the nation's economy to be competitive.

If we look at these economic constraints overall they may appear to suggest that the scope for national governments to manage their own economies, and by extension the rest of their societies, is increasingly curtailed by the pressures of economic globalisation. This question of government autonomy or, as some writers would prefer to put it, of government sovereignty, is of course fundamental to an understanding of the political challenges posed by globalisation. Some argue that the nation state has now become almost an irrelevance in the age of the global economy: '. . . in terms of the global economy, nation states have become little more than bit actors' (Ohmae, 1996: 12). Yet most writers on globalisation and politics now argue that globalisation actually needs the state almost as much as states have to operate within the context of global political circumstances. It may well be that, as Hirst and Thompson argue, national governments are having to function 'less as sovereign entities and more as components of an international quasi-polity' (1999: 257), but others have persuasively argued that the notion of a completely powerless state in the face of globalisation is a myth. It is a myth which, to some extent, may be seen as a useful fiction to serve the interests of national politicians since it shifts the blame for unpopular policy decisions away from them and to the impersonal forces of 'globalisation'. This important ideological dimension of globalisation cannot be underestimated – the very fact that it has been necessary here to try to clarify and demystify the character of globalisation is a testament to the powerful use of a vague and unspecific use of the term by politicians all over the world. Nevertheless, it is clear that international bodies such as the EU, the IMF and the World Bank do now play an important role in policy debates and policy initiatives, although it is still national state governments which make policy in almost all areas.

To sum up, globalisation is not a unified 'thing' but rather a range of processes that may affect different countries and different peoples in different ways around the world. In order to consider how it is implicated in welfare issues and social policy developments we now need to move on to consider some of the major theoretical approaches to globalisation and welfare.

## Controversy and debate

### Can we make poverty history?

One of the most controversial dimensions of an already highly contentious debate about globalisation and its effects is the argument about whether globalisation is improving or worsening the position of the world's poor people.

On the one hand there are the various members of different 'anti-globalisation' groups – such as the World Development Movement, Oxfam and the Global Justice Movement – who in various ways criticise the way in which the world's economy is managed and dominated by multinational corporations, the rich nations of the North, and what they see as 'their' agents, such as the World Trade Organisation and the World Bank. The essential criticism here is that trade and the management of the overall global economy is done on the basis that it prioritises the interests of the dominant capitalist economies and forces the economies, and societies, of the weaker economies in Africa, Asia and Latin America into subservience. What is more, they argue, these same processes do little to improve the position of poorer people in the richer countries either.

On the other hand, there are the governments of the North, and international organisations such as the World Bank and the WTO, who argue that globalisation represents both an unavoidable and ultimately beneficial development in the world economy for all countries and their citizens. Whilst they accept that currently there is widespread poverty in various parts of the world, they also argue that protecting the economies of, for example, the African and Asian economies is neither efficient for the world economy, nor does it benefit the people of such regions. Put simply, the more efficient and competitive the world is, and the less restrictions there are on world trade, then the more this will benefit all countries and citizens. Nevertheless, the World Bank, for example, does also have a commitment to eradicating world poverty, and programmes designed to assist in reducing poverty, at the same time as it promotes free trade and open competition in world markets.

Unfortunately, the most vocal supporters of each side of this argument tend to talk past each other, and the rest of us are often left confused as to what is actually true and what is not in terms of globalisation's effects on poverty. One example of a more considered and academically-informed discussion of these issues is that between Wolf and Wade (2002) that is freely available from its original source, *Prospect* magazine, via the Internet (see references).

Another dimension of this controversy is the issue of whether poverty can in fact be reduced or 'made history', if globalisation is indeed unavoidable as a feature of the world's economy and politics. A fundamental issue for national governments and international agencies, as well as bodies such as Oxfam, is how far even the most well-intentioned anti-poverty strategies can actually reduce poverty, let alone get rid of it altogether, assuming, of course, that such strategies and commitments existed. Then the issue shifts away from a concern with globalisation in itself towards a more fundamental concern with the character of the world's economics and politics. Can poverty be made history in a capitalist world economy?

## Globalisation and welfare state change

In this section we shall look at some theoretical perspectives which are useful for analysing the link between globalisation and social policy, followed by an assessment of the usefulness of such perspectives for understanding what actually seems to be happening in the world of globalisation and welfare state change.

### Theories and perspectives

It is possible to identify a number of different perspectives on the relationship between globalisation and welfare. For clarity we will focus on just four here, then consider how far they seem to make sense of what is happening in the real world (see Figure 21.3).

Let us unpack each of these perspectives further.

### Perspective 1: Globalisation has a significant impact on welfare states through the increasing dominance of the (market) economy

In this perspective the view of globalisation and welfare is closest to the apocalyptic version of the globalisation thesis summarised above. Among this group are those who argue that globalisation has a strong impact because internationalisation of the world economy implies the demise of nation state autonomy, a reduction of national governments' policy options (especially those of social democratic governments) and a weakening of labour movements. Others explain that globalisation has an effect on welfare states in the sense that the expansion of trade is responsible for unemployment and rising inequality, which creates (new?) problems for the welfare states. Trade and technological change both create a significant decline in

**1 Globalisation causes welfare retrenchment through capitalism's dominance**

- Internationalisation of the world economy implies the demise of nation state autonomy, a reduction of national governments policy option s and a weakening of labour movements – the main foundations of the national welfare state are fundamentally weakened
- The development of global capitalism is responsible for unemployment and rising inequality, creating worsening problems for the welfare states
- Both international trade and technological change create a significant decline in demand for unskilled, semi-skilled and traditionally skilled workers
- The need for national economies to compete in world market exerts pressure for reduction in social expenditure by governments and private firms
- All the above create pressures to shift from social democratic and collectivist to neo-liberal and individualist welfare ideologies – overall retrenchment and decline of welfare states

**2 Globalisation has little effect upon welfare states**

- Changes in the world economy are less widespread, smaller and more gradual than the full-blown globalisation thesis suggests
- Even if globalisation has occurred, welfare states remain compatible with this process – globalised economies need to provide some sort of social welfare and political counterbalance to the effects of economic change
- The 'threat of globalisation' is more an ideological ploy of national governments wishing to restructure welfare than an unchallengeable economic force
- Welfare states are changing, but due to factors other than globalisation (for example, population ageing, technology, changes in family structures and new risks)

**3 Globalisation's effects on welfare states are mediated by national politics**

- External global forces are impacting on national welfare state changes
- Certain types of welfare state are more compatible with economic competitiveness than others, and can adapt better than others to the new environment
- Worldwide competitive economic environment means that high-wage national economies will lose jobs to low(er)-wage countries unless checked
- Particular character of the previous political and institutional arrangements (the form of welfare state) in different countries will heavily affect responses to global challenges
- Thus, different welfare states will change in different ways in responding to globalisation – not simply welfare retrenchment or decline – and the support of different constituencies (unions, politicians, voters, and so on) will ensure continuation of welfare state in some form

**4 Welfare states generated globalisation and limit its future development**

- Globalisation is largely a by-product of the development of democratic welfare states in the advanced economies
- The guaranteeing of social rights within these welfare states allowed for the development of deregulation of national economies and the liberalisation and re-regulation of the international economy – 'globalisation'
- 'Globalisation' was an unintended consequence of national governmental social policy initiatives that were pursued for other motives
- National rather than international bodies remain the key decision makers in economic policy as well as welfare policy
- The future relationship between globalisation and national welfare states depends on the decisions of national governments

**Figure 21.3** Four perspectives on globalisation and welfare states

demand for the unskilled, semi-skilled and traditionally skilled workers for whom the traditional welfare states were designed.

Mishra (1999) provides an example of this perspective. For Mishra, the major effect of globalisation is the decline of the nation state in terms of its autonomy. Mishra makes seven propositions regarding globalisation and welfare:

1 globalisation undermines the ability of national governments to pursue full employment and economic growth;

2 globalisation results in increasing inequality in wages and working conditions;

3 globalisation exerts downward pressure on systems of social protection and social expenditure;

4 globalisation weakens the ideological underpinnings of social protection;

5 globalisation weakens the basis of social partnership and tripartism;

6 globalisation virtually excludes the option of left-of-centre policy options for national governments; and

7 the logic of globalisation conflicts with the 'logic' of national community and democratic politics (1999: 15).

Mishra argues that globalisation has empowered and privileged neo-liberal economics as a transnational force beyond the control of nation states and governments. Thus globalisation 'must be understood as an economic as well as a political and ideological phenomenon', and 'is without doubt now the essential context of the welfare state' (1999: 15).

### Perspective 2: Globalisation has relatively little impact on welfare states

Various writers have argued that globalisation has no significant impact on welfare states. Some claim that there is no such thing as globalisation since trade is at the same level as it was at the beginning of this century, and that the changes in the world economy are far less widespread, smaller and more gradual than the full-blown globalisation thesis suggests.

Others argue that, even if globalisation has occurred, welfare states remain compatible with this process, and that it may even be a necessary feature of globalised economies to provide some sort of social welfare and political counterbalance to the effects of economic change. Such writers argue that the erosion of welfare state is due more to the ideological projects of governments seeking to restructure than to the impact of economic globalisation processes.

For others in this theoretical camp, the argument is that, whilst welfare states *are* changing, the cause is not globalisation: national welfare states are challenged by domestic factors (demography, technology, changes in family structures, new risks) rather than by globalisation. Pierson (1998, 2000) asserts that the welfare state, rather than facing fundamental retrenchment and decline, is likely to be sustained in almost all countries in the future. This is not to say that there are not pressures on welfare states. These are likely to lead to renegotiation, restructuring and modernisation, but not to dismantling of welfare states. What Pierson calls the 'irresistible forces' playing upon welfare states are domestic forces, in particular the changed economies of advanced societies, the consequences of the 'maturation' of welfare states, and demographic change. Globalisation as an exogenous set of forces is, at best, of secondary significance.

Pierson argues that three processes are largely responsible for the pressures on welfare states and are essentially unrelated to globalisation:

1  Advanced economies have witnessed a shift from manufacturing to services as their dominant sector along with slower economic growth. The low productivity associated with service employment means that such economies have a fundamental and growing fiscal problem in paying for welfare.

2  Such economies have, nevertheless, seen a tremendous expansion in the coverage and complexity of welfare state commitments because welfare states have come to 'maturity'. These present serious budgetary problems, plus a loss of policy flexibility.

3  The changing demographic balance, coupled with the growth of welfare programme commitments, presents two sorts of problems for welfare states. The first is that as the elderly increase as a proportion of the population, there is a corresponding reduction in the proportion in work, and thus in the fiscal base for welfare provision. Second, the increasing numbers of elderly people have direct effects in two areas of welfare provision where costs are thus likely to increase significantly: pensions and healthcare.

## Perspective 3: Globalisation is having an effect on welfare states, but these effects are mediated through (national) institutional structures and policy responses

Proponents of this perspective argue that certain types of welfare state are more compatible with competitiveness than others, and can adapt better than others to the new environment. Different welfare states are thus differently affected by globalisation. Esping-Andersen and his associates (1996), provide an account of the relationship between the global economy and welfare states that illustrates this approach. Esping-Andersen concludes that a nation's economic growth now appears to require economic openness, involving greater competition and vulnerability to international trade, finance and capital movements. Consequently, national governments are more constrained in their economic and other related policies: ' . . . Keynesianism, let alone social democracy, in one country is accordingly no more an option. It may even be that governments' freedom to design discrete social policies has eroded . . . ' (1996: 256). This worldwide competitive economic environment means that high-wage national economies will lose jobs to low(er)-wage countries.

So far there are similarities between this perspective and Perspective 1, but Esping-Andersen's analysis leads to quite different conclusions. First, he argues that Keynesianism in one country was, in any case, something of a myth: ' . . . the most advanced welfare states tended to develop in the most open economies . . . the more residualistic welfare states in countries with relatively protected domestic economies . . . ' (1996: 257). Second, he argues that, in terms of labour costs, the real pressure from globalisation for advanced economies is on their low-skilled and labour-intensive mass production economic sectors: 'The most acute globalization problem that Europe and North America face may, indeed, be that the market for unskilled labour has become international' (1996: 258). Esping-Andersen's key point here is that in responding to the dilemmas created by globalisation, different national systems can and do respond in different ways.

Alongside the economic pressures, welfare states also face two other crises, according to Esping-Andersen. The first is the change for advanced welfare states from provision for the working classes to provision for all. The crisis rests in the fact that the principles upon which such universal provision might be made no longer command broad consensus. The other crisis concerns the fact that neither the egalitarianism of the 'Swedish model' nor the targeted approach of the 'US model' (see Chapter 20) seem, for different reasons, to support the sort of human capital improvement which contemporary economies require. In the first case, the system provides disincentives to work and to improve skills and education, whereas the second generates poverty traps and also disincentives to work.

Esping-Andersen concludes that 'the welfare state is here to stay . . . The fact of the matter is that the alignment of political forces conspires just about everywhere to maintain the existing principles of the welfare state' (1996: 265). Within the advanced economies, though perhaps less so in the embryonic welfare states, existing political alignments of clients, welfare state workers, trades unions, political parties, and so on, imply that welfare state change will be limited and slow, even in the face of global economic changes and challenges. The particular character of the previous political and institutional arrangements in different countries will also heavily affect change. Accordingly, responses to globalisation and other pressures on welfare states are also likely to be differentiated.

### Perspective 4: Welfare states generated globalisation and limit its future development

The fourth perspective, represented by Rieger and Leibfried, argues that welfare states provided the vital precondition for the development of post-war economic liberalisation, or what is more commonly known as 'economic globalisation', and continue to constrain globalisation now. They argue that a range of policies focused on citizens' 'social rights' were developed in the Western European nations in the 1950s and 1960s as part of the social democratic governments' attempts to regulate their economies to form a sort of welfare capitalism. In other words, these welfare measures actually helped free-market capitalism to develop internationally. Unlike earlier periods of the development of international trade, welfare states are now able to lessen the social effects of free trade in terms of unemployment and lowering of incomes of certain groups. What is more, the role of national governments making decisions that are still domestically focused continues to be at the heart of global economic developments – the roles of bodies such as the WTO and the IMF are still much less important for global economic and political decision making than national governments. Thus globalisation is not some sort of inevitable and all-powerful process that governments and people have to respond to: 'Instead of speaking of an independent, globalized economy, it makes more sense to proceed from the assumption of an international system of interdependent national economies. Globalized conditions are made up of processes that develop out of individual national economies' (Rieger and Leibfried, 2003: 21). National governments now have a threefold challenge: to reform their welfare state policies without alienating the various groups who have a stake in the status quo (welfare recipients, welfare workers, and so on), to manage the socio-economic effects of globalisation in their countries, and to maintain global market conditions. Whether each government can do this, and the ways in which they do it, are open questions, according to this view.

## Applying the perspectives

How close to real developments are these competing perspectives? In relation to the first perspective, there is in fact little evidence of a direct and essentially similar impact by globalisation on the world's welfare states or of overall retrenchment along similar lines. Changes which have occurred, though they may have been indirectly related to globalisation, have rather been mediated through national governmental policies and institutions, a process that has led to quite different outcomes.

There are similar problems with the second perspective, which links changes in welfare states solely to domestic factors. Whilst the significance of factors such as population ageing and the increasing cost of welfare systems should not be undervalued, it is clear that external factors, some or which were related to globalisation, have been part of the reason for changes in welfare states.

The third perspective seems to match the experiences of welfare states better than either of the previous two. Esping-Andersen argues that existing institutional arrangements and welfare commitments constrain change in response to economic globalisation in 'path-dependent' ways. This 'path dependency' idea suggests that different types of welfare state regime will respond in type-similar ways. Thus what he calls Liberal welfare states (primarily the Anglo-Saxon welfare states such the UK, the USA, and New Zealand) have responded in one, broad sort of way whilst Social Democratic welfare states (the Nordic states, such as Sweden, Norway and Denmark) have responded in another.

Perspective 4 goes even further in arguing for variation in welfare state changes: however, it suggests that what happens will not depend on the 'external' impact of globalisation, because globalisation is not a process that is free of national governmental intervention. They argue that what happens will depend more on the actions and policies of national governments, the responses of their national constituencies, and the possibility, for example, that certain countries may decide to retreat from full involvement in the global economy and return to protectionist trade policies to defend both their economic and social constituencies. In essence, we should be prepared for a variety of different responses and policy initiatives or, indeed, for the whole complex interdependent network to collapse.

How might we draw upon these differing perspectives to guide our understanding of what is, or might be going to happen to welfare states in a globalising world? Sykes, Palier and Prior (2001, especially pp. 198–206) argue that globalisation should not be seen as a homogeneous, exogenous force, impacting on nation states causing them to adapt their welfare states, but rather should be seen as a differentiated phenomenon, the character of which is constructed and interpreted differently in different types of welfare system. Furthermore, rather like Rieger and Leibfried, they suggest that the relationship between globalisation and welfare state change should be understood as being two-way and reciprocal, not unidirectional. Drawing together the arguments of the four perspectives and using Sykes *et al.*'s suggestions we could suggest the following features as being characteristic of the links between globalisation and welfare states:

1 Welfare state changes have occurred that can be linked with globalisation.

2 There are differences between countries both in terms of their responses to globalisation and in terms of the forms that globalisation may take in different countries. A major pattern of differences may be expected between the more advanced and the less developed economies of the world in both these senses.

3 National politics and policies matter, so they are likely to have had a significant effect on how globalisation is perceived and responded to in different countries.

4 Globalisation may not only have created problems for welfare states, especially pressure for cuts and retrenchment, but it may also have provided opportunities taken by certain governments to develop new social policies which are actually beneficial to their citizens.

## Globalisation and the future of welfare

So how might we expect the relationship between globalisation and welfare to develop in the future? To begin with, we can argue that the major players in setting and delivering social policies will continue to be nation state governments. Though there are clearly significant economic and political constraints on governments posed by globalisation in its various guises, it is clear that only national governments currently command the authority and support of their citizens to deliver various forms of welfare provision. Furthermore, given the 'path-dependent' character of such policies and their associated organisational and ideological underpinnings, it is unlikely that all welfare states will gradually converge around one form in the near, or even quite distant, future. The British, French and Chinese welfare systems, for example, are embedded in different political strategies and decisions, different systems for delivering education, health etc., and different ideas about, for example, 'welfare', 'citizenship' and 'poverty'. However, in contradistinction to this argument, it should be noted that Deacon has argued recently that, especially with regard to less economically developed and more politically dependent states in Africa, Asia and Latin America, it is more the international agencies than the national states that are in control of the processes of welfare change (Deacon, 2007).

We can recognise a drift by welfare states around the world to a more neo-liberal approach to welfare. This approach, both ideologically and practically, prioritises economic competitiveness above welfare provision. Or, at least, it prioritises economic competitiveness above welfare provision that is seen to be excessively expensive and/or counter to the needs of economic flexibility and efficiency. What this means in practice is that social polices around the world are less and less focused on targets of 'equality' or redistribution, less related to ideas of collective as opposed to private and/or market-based provision, and fundamentally related to employment as the central feature of social policy. In this regard the role of the various international organisations such as the WTO, the IMF and the World Bank, as well as regional organisations such as NAFTA and the EU, is proving to be increasingly significant.

Yet an increasing number of academics and others have questioned whether globalisation is inextricably linked with this neo-liberal project. Some have argued for a different approach, a 'socially responsible' globalisation that both permits the benefits of a truly global economy, but also sustains and even develops the welfare of peoples around the world. They argue that capitalism continues to need the provision of some sort of welfare outputs as much in the global era as in the past. Without these provisions, economies, societies and governments around the world will become less and less legitimate in the eyes of their citizens and thus less stable. The worldwide anti-globalisation movement is a clear example of how many people are already challenging the unchecked growth of trade that benefits the rich much more than the poor, the actions of multinational corporations such as Nike and Microsoft in making decisions that appear to supersede or at best ignore national governments, and the environmental and public health costs of uncontrolled industrial development and dangerous work practices.

 **Thought provoker**

This advertisement for an Amnesty International lecture highlights some of the potential issues and challenges, probably unforeseen by many, that might arise from globalisation.

**Speaking Out: The Sigrid Rausing series**

Date: Tue 28 November 2006

**The impact of globalisation on women's human rights**

Whilst globalisation should offer increased opportunities for women to take up their full role in the public sphere and be recognised for their contribution, the reality is often very different. Women may be offered work opportunities but on what terms? With what security? How safe even is it for them to get to and from work? How is their new role received by often more conventional standards of their society? Is privatisation making it even harder for women to access education and health?

Is a globalised, standardised image of women and their role adding to the sexual exploitation and trafficking of women? Globalisation is here to stay – how can we make sure that women benefit from it rather than adding to their exploitation and abuse?

Source: www.amnesty.org.uk/events_details.asp?EventsID=234

## Conclusion

It is clear that there is no consensus on what globalisation is, what may cause it, or what its implications might be. However, globalisation does not at present appear to be developing in a way that helps the poor. Any realistic assessment of progress towards a globalised form of social policy to deal with global welfare issues such as poverty and social exclusion, unemployment and health would have to conclude that fine words have not yet been translated into much significant action. Does this mean that neo-liberal forms of global economic development are likely to continue unchecked, and that the welfare of peoples around the world is likely to be less and less protected and provided by national welfare states to be replaced either by market-based provision or nothing? As with so many issues in the social policy field, we shall have to wait and see.

## Summary

This chapter has examined debates around globalisation and welfare and has argued that:

- Globalisation is essentially contested both as an idea and in terms of what it actually involves economically and/or socially and/or politically.

- Despite this controversy, we may say a central feature of globalisation is that it involves an increasing interconnectedness between states, peoples and regions across the world.

- Increasingly, a range of social, economic and political processes operate at global rather than national or other local levels.

- Most analysts of globalisation suggest that it is its economic characteristics that are primary and that the features of increased international competition, trade and the role of transnational corporations are challenging the power of nation states to make effective policy, not least in the economic policy and social policy fields. At very least, the range of policy options open to national governments have become curtailed by the various features of the global economic context.

- In terms of the links between globalisation and welfare state changes, four perspectives have been outlined:

  1 That globalisation is causing wholesale retrenchment in welfare provision.

  2 That globalisation has little effect on national welfare systems.

  3 That globalisation does have effects, but these do not prevent national governments from still making effective policy choices.

  4 That globalisation was effectively created by nation states and what happens in future will depend on how those states make decisions.

- The chapter then drew upon these perspectives to suggest that the linkage between globalisation processes and welfare state changes should be regarded as a two-way process - globalisation does have the potential to limit policy choices, but the form globalisation takes is also affected by the choices that various national governments, and international organisations such as the EU make.

● In the future the major players in setting and delivering social policies will continue to be nation state governments. Although there are constraints on governments posed by globalisation, only national governments currently command the authority and support of their citizens to deliver various forms of welfare provision. Furthermore, it is unlikely that, as a result of globalisation, all welfare states will gradually converge around one form in the near future.

# Discussion and review topics

1 What is the most important evidence that globalisation is occurring?

2 Which of the four perspectives on globalisation and welfare state changes do you find most persuasive? Why?

3 How might national governments mediate the impact of globalisation on their welfare state systems?

## Further reading

George, V. and Wilding, P. (2002) *Globalization and human welfare*, Palgrave, Basingstoke. Reviews current trends and suggests future developments.

Held, D. and McGrew, A. (2007) *Globalization/Anti-Globalization*, Polity, Cambridge. The best short introduction both to the various dimensions of globalisation and to its disputed character.

Scholte, J.A. (2005) *Globalizations: A critical introduction*, Palgrave, Basingstoke. For a more advanced approach than Held and McGrew.

Sykes, R., Palier, B. and Prior, P.M. (eds) (2001) *Globalization and European welfare states: Challenges and change*, Palgrave, Basingstoke. Focuses on both theories and evidence concerning globalisation and social policy within a specifically European context.

Yeates, N. (2001) *Globalization and social policy*, Sage, London. A longer review of similar issues to those covered here.

## Some useful websites

www.globalwelfare.net – this website provides a range of resources specifically focused on the interests of students, lecturers and researchers with links to other useful websites in the field of globalisation and welfare.

www.protest.net and www.wdm.org.uk – these two websites provide a view of globalisation and its welfare impacts from various broadly 'anti-globalisation' perspectives.

www.ilo.org, www.wto.org and www.worldbank.org – the websites of the International Labour Organisation, the World Trade Organisation and the World Bank, three of the most important international organisations concerned with globalisation and welfare.

# References

Collier, P. and Dollar, D. (2001) *Globalization, growth and poverty*, Oxford University Press/ World Bank, Oxford.

Deacon, B. (2007) *Global social policy and governance*, Sage, London.

Esping-Anderson, G. (1990) *The three worlds of welfare capitalism*, Polity Press, Cambridge.

Esping-Andersen, G. (ed.) (1996) *Welfare states in transition: National adaptations in global economies*, Sage, London.

George, V. and Wilding, P. (2002) *Globalization and human welfare*, Palgrave, Basingstoke.

Giddens, A. (1990) *The consequences of modernity*, Polity, Cambridge.

Giddens, A. (1991) *Modernity and self-identity*, Polity, Cambridge.

Harvey, D. (1989) *The condition of postmodernity*, Blackwell, Oxford.

Held, D. (1996) *Models of democracy*, 2nd edn, Polity, Cambridge.

Held, D. and McGrew, A. (2002) *Globalization/Anti-Globalization*, Polity, Cambridge.

Held, D., McGrew, A., Goldblatt, D. and Perraton, J. (1999) *Global transformations*, Polity, Cambridge.

Hirst, P. and Thompson, G. (1999) *Globalization in question*, 2nd edn, Polity, Cambridge.

Koenig-Archibugi, M. (2002) 'Mapping global governance', in D. Held and A. McGrew (eds) *Governing Globalization*, Polity Press, Cambridge.

Leibfried, S. and Rieger, E. (1998) 'Welfare state limits to globalization', *Politics and Society*, Vol. 26, No. 4, pp. 363–90.

Maddison, A. (2000) *The world economy: A millennial perspective*, OECD, Paris.

Mishra, R. (1999) *Globalization and the welfare state*, Edward Elgar, Cheltenham.

Ohmae, K. (1990) *The borderless world*, Collins, London.

Ohmae, K. (1996) *The end of the nation state*, Free Press, New York.

Pierson, P. (1998) 'Irresistible forces, immovable objects: Post-industrial welfare states confront permanent austerity', *Journal of European Public Policy*, Vol. 5, No. 5, pp. 539–60.

Pierson, P. (2000) *The new politics of the welfare state*, Oxford University Press, Oxford.

Rieger, E. and Leibfried, S. (2003) *Limits to Globalization; Welfare States and the World Economy*, Polity Press, Cambridge.

Robertson, R. (1992) *Globalization: Social theory and global culture*, Sage, London.

Sklair, L. (2002) *Globalization. Capitalism and its alternatives*, Oxford University Press, Oxford.

Sykes, R. (2003) 'Social policy and globalization', in P. Alcock, A. Erskine and M. May (eds) *The student's companion to social policy*, 2nd edn, Blackwell/SPA, Oxford.

Sykes, R., Palier, B. and Prior, P.M. (eds) (2001) *Globalization and European welfare states: Challenges and change*, Palgrave, Basingstoke.

Wade, R. (2001) 'Inequality of world incomes: what should be done?, **www.opendemocracy.net/themes/article.jsp?id=6&articleId=257.**

Weiss, L. (1997) 'Globalization and the Myth of the Powerless State', *New Left Review*, No. 225, pp. 3–27.

Wolf, M., and Wade, R. (2002) 'Are global inequality and poverty getting worse?' *Prospect*, 72, March 2002, 16–21 or via the internet at **www.prospect-magazine.co.uk/article_details.php?id=4982.**

# Part V

## CONCLUSIONS

# 22

# Conclusions

Catherine Bochel

## Chapter overview

This book has outlined some of the many areas of debate in contemporary social policy. This chapter reflects briefly upon:

- trends in social policy since 1997;
- changes that may affect the subject;
- the emergence of a possible new political consensus on social policy.

As outlined in Chapter 1, and repeatedly evident in other chapters throughout this book, social policy is an academic subject that is founded in the social sciences and which relates to other social science and related subjects such as economics, history, politics and sociology. It is a subject which continues to have a major relevance to a range of professions, such as nursing, social work and housing. Yet, at the same time, social policy is also something that goes on in the real world and which affects real people on a daily basis. It is sometimes therefore necessary to take all of these actualities into account when discussing 'social policy'. To some extent this chapter reflects this: its primary purpose is to focus on developments in the real world, but at the same time it seeks to point out a number of areas where the academic subject is concerned, and where the two may come together, to point this out.

Any reading of this volume will have made clear that social policy is continually developing, and that there are inevitably a wide range of interactions with many other policy areas and with economic, political, ideological and social imperatives. Chapters 2, 3 and 4 serve to highlight the ways in which social policy is both affected by and impacts on wide swathes of economic, social and political life. Indeed, during 2008 the links between social policy and other influences were highlighted again, when a shift in the use of agricultural land away from the production of food to biofuels in an attempt to reduce $CO_2$ emissions was blamed for increases in food prices which impacted not only on poorer people in the UK, but particularly on poorer areas of the developing world where food costs make up a far bigger proportion of individuals' expenditure.

Chapter 5 discusses the development of social policy historically, and in particular the ways in which governments increasingly became involved in the provision of welfare services. Building on this, for three-quarters of the twentieth century it was possible to argue that the key social policy development in the United Kingdom was the gradual extension of state welfare and the establishment of a welfare state, closely linked with the rise of organised labour, and in particular the 1945 Labour government, which was strongly influenced by social democratic and democratic socialist thinking, including the Fabian tradition. Following the Second World War there was a broad consensus on the idea of the welfare state, together with a commitment to full employment, and to a mixed economy, managed by governments using Keynesian techniques.

However, by the 1970s this consensus was coming to an end, shaken by a variety of criticisms from different parts of the political spectrum, as outlined in Chapters 6, 7 and 8, and by a recognition that the welfare state had not achieved all that many of its supporters would have wished. Indeed, from 1979, with the election of the Conservative government led by Margaret Thatcher, elements of previously widely accepted social policy were being seriously questioned, with a new emphasis on individualism, selection and the market replacing that on collectivism, universalism and the state. At the same time, within the academic subject of social policy, there was a much greater recognition of the diversity of the subject, with the development of a variety of critiques of past approaches and the incorporation of new ideas from both domestic and comparative approaches to the study of social policy. Many of these changes are reflected in the topics considered in Chapters 9 to 18.

Despite much of the rhetoric, and some significant reforms, after eighteen years of Conservative government, substantial parts of the welfare state remained largely intact, when Labour returned to power in 1997. However, by the late 1990s Labour's approach to social policy was not the same as it had been (see Chapter 7). There was now a much greater commitment to the use of a diversity of forms of provision, from public, private and voluntary sectors, and a view that was expressed from the New Labour government was that what mattered was 'what works', rather than who provides services and benefits. Public opinion, which, as measured by opinion polls and surveys, frequently favours increased expenditure for improved public services (and particularly for services used by the bulk of the population), but does not always match this with a willingness to pay the higher taxes necessary for this, made the government's position more difficult, although it was to some extent aided by the failure of the Conservative Party to offer effective electoral opposition until 2005. In addition, the rising costs of welfare were encouraging governments to seek to control levels of expenditure and to spread the financial burden, whether through reliance upon informal and voluntary provision, or through encouraging people to make provision for themselves and their families, for example through insurance or pensions provision by the private sector.

One of the major questions for the future remains, therefore, how welfare should be paid for. However, equally important is how resources should be used. Questions of government income and expenditure therefore relate strongly to issues around the distribution, and potentially the *re*distribution, of resources. For much of the post-war period there had been a broad commitment, particularly from the political left, to a degree of redistribution from the wealthier in society to the poorer, to be achieved primarily through higher taxes on the former and the provision of benefits and services to the poorer. By the 1990s this had largely been replaced by a desire by New Labour to keep 'middle England' happy and, in particular, to do so by avoiding increases in income tax. Any attempts at redistribution under New Labour would therefore have to be very different from those of the post-war years (see Chapter 9).

One of the other developments under New Labour, although not unique, is an attention to the mechanisms of policy making and implementation, not seen since the 1960s, if then. This helps to remind us of the importance of politics and decision making for social policy. Social policy is not technocratic: it is not simply a question of making minor adjustments to ensure the smooth running of mechanisms. As noted above, there are fundamental decisions to be made that affect society, including how resources are raised and distributed. To these traditional social policy concerns have been added, as has been highlighted, particularly following the introduction of devolved administrations in Northern Ireland, Scotland and Wales since 1997, an awareness of the importance of the mechanisms that are used to make and implement social policy, and there is now the potential for even greater diversity within the United Kingdom. Yet, as has frequently been noted by many commentators, like the Conservatives before them, Labour's apparent desire to devolve some aspects of decision making was matched by a high degree of centralisation and control, again reflected in many chapters of this book.

In addition to its constitutional and governmental reforms, New Labour has also been, importantly for the subject of social policy, a government that has paid some attention to both policy making, and to engagement with academics and academic research. One example of this was the creation of the 'Magenta Book', designed by the Government Chief Social Researcher's Office to provide guidance on policy evaluation and analysis, and which draws heavily upon social policy approaches; another was the publication of *Professional Policy Making for the Twenty First Century* (Cabinet Office, 1999), which set out nine key features of 'good' policy making, and which was followed by a number of related outputs. Academics have, arguably, been drawn into advising government in a way and to an extent that has not been the case for forty years. Nevertheless, some critics might be sceptical of the extent to which any of these have impacted on the government's policies; such questions occur in a number of chapters here.

While the domestic agenda remains important, Chapters 19, 20 and 21 remind us that international developments, including the United Kingdom's membership of the European Union, are also having an impact on social policy. Yet the discussions within these chapters also make clear that the same phenomenon can be interpreted very differently from different analytical or ideological perspectives. In the same way, the realm of social policy has also been broadened by other debates, including those that continue over the boundaries of the subject (Chapter 18), and by the impact of others, including debates over 'risk' (Chapter 4).

Some of these have also been significant for decision makers. Given what it has seen as these uncertainties, New Labour has taken the view that the world is very different, and that rather than providing a range of state welfare services to passive recipient citizens, that approach is neither viable nor necessarily desirable. Rather, supporters of New Labour have argued that the role of governments is to work towards flexibility for governments and their citizens in their interactions with a complex society and economy. Citizens therefore have to take greater responsibility for themselves, with the role of the state becoming primarily that of an enabler, rather than a provider. It may, in some instances, continue to pay for services, but even in those areas there is a greater requirement for individual initiative.

One of the debates that was important in social policy after 1997 was the extent to which the approach to social policy under New Labour has been similar to or distinct from that of the preceding Conservative governments. Some of the discussions in Chapters 9 to 17, in particular, demonstrate that it is possible to consider the answer to that question in different ways. Critics of the Labour government have been able to support their arguments by pointing to a number of examples where there appears to be significant continuity, such as the commitment to a significant role for the private sector in the provision of welfare, the managerialist approach and the continuing use of performance measures and targeting. There have been some apparently quite right-wing policies introduced by New Labour, such as the introduction of fees for higher education and cutbacks in entitlements to some social security benefits. On the other hand, there have been commitments to eradicate child poverty and a major expansion in the provision of childcare, and it has been possible to demonstrate that there has been an increase in expenditure on welfare services, such as education and the National Health Service, which has grown significantly under Labour, and to argue that there has been some redistribution of wealth from the rich to the poor, and in particular the working poor. This leads on to one of the fundamentals of the Labour approach since 1997, the emphasis on work, with 'welfare-to-work' being a central part of their programme, so that people are expected to work where possible, and there should be no reliance on benefits. This can be portrayed as a shift away from a passive to an active welfare state, and can be interpreted either as a move towards governments requiring people to work and blaming and penalising them if they are unable or fail to do so, or as a return to a past position where citizens have both rights and responsibilities, with work being a key obligation for individuals.

Looking beyond the Labour governments since 1997 to the broader political debate, some have argued that within the major political parties there is again something approaching a general consensus on social policy, particularly following the Conservatives' election of David Cameron as leader and the consequent shifts in policy away from the Thatcher legacy. This new consensus could be said to be founded in: a belief that there should be mixture of providers, drawn from across the sectors, but with regulation by the state; some commitment to public provision, but with a significant emphasis on provision by the private sectors, and on encouraging individuals to make provision for themselves; and a greater concern by the state with tackling social problems and exclusion through attempts to create more equal opportunities for individuals, rather than through financial redistribution from the richer to the poorer. However, the extent to which such a consensus actually exists, either within the political parties or the wider public, is unclear. As always in social policy, one of the few certainties is that both the subject that is social policy, and social policies themselves, will continue to change and develop.

## Discussion and review topics

1  Do you agree that there is an emerging political consensus on social policy? What evidence would you use to support or refute such a view?

2  What do you believe should be the balance of welfare provision across informal, public, private and voluntary sectors? Why?

## Reference

Cabinet Office (1999) *Professional Policy Making for the Twenty First Century*, Cabinet Office, London.

# Glossary

**abolitionism** used as shorthand to describe the scrapping of, for example, hanging, prison, or corporal punishment. It is allied also to attempts to substantially limit the use of prison or, more loosely, to move away from the punitive fixation of the criminal justice system towards restorative/restitutive forms of justice

**activation policies** government programmes that intervene in the labour market to help the unemployed find work

**anti-social behaviour** technically defined in the Crime and Disorder Act 1998 as behaviour which has 'caused or was likely to cause harassment, alarm or distress to one or more persons not of the same household'. However, it has come to be understood as a catch-all category for nuisance behaviour, which may or may not be criminal, and which is most commonly associated with youth

**Anti-social Behaviour Orders** a hybrid legal instrument in that it spans both civil and criminal law. Orders are granted in a civil court (rather like an injunction) and impose a number of prohibitive conditions on an individual in order to prevent them from engaging in 'anti-social behaviour'. Breach of these conditions, however, is a criminal offence which is punishable with a maximum of five year's imprisonment

**applied philosophy** seeks to apply philosophical ideas and approaches to real problems and issues

**'Back to basics'** a campaign launched by John Major at the Conservative Party conference in 1993, aimed at raising moral standards, it became focused particularly on lone parenthood.

**British Social Attitudes Survey** a long-running (since 1983) set of annual surveys looking at changes in attitudes within society. Run by the National Centre for Social Research

**brownfield sites** a term loosely used to describe land which has previously been developed, as opposed to greenfield sites which have not

**BSE crisis** in 1996 fears over an epidemic of Bovine Spongiform Encephalopathy and over vCJD (new variant Creutzfeldt-Jakob Disease, the human equivalent of BSE) led to a crisis in British farming, with the slaughter of millions of cattle and the introduction of new regulations on the slaughter and consumption of beef

**Children's Commissioner** following the Children Act 2004, the post of Children's Commissioner for England was appointed to act as an independent voice for children and young people. Scotland, Wales and Northern Ireland each have their own Commissioner

**Children's Fund** focused on developing services that support multi-agency working, the Fund was targeted at 5-13 year-olds and was a key part of the Labour government's strategy to tackle disadvantages and inequalities which derive from child poverty and social exclusion. However, from 2008 these were absorbed into local authority mainstream provision.

**commodity** a good or service regarded as having no intrinsic merit. Its value is its exchange price as determined by the interaction between supply and demand

**community care** a term that can be understood in many different ways, but is generally applicable to a range of policies applied to looking after people with particular needs in the community, including the movement of people from long-stay institutions to living in the community

**Community Charge** in 1989 (in Scotland) and 1990 (in England and Wales) the Conservative government replaced the existing system of local taxation, known as 'rates' with the Community Charge (often known as the Poll Tax), a charge on each member of a household. Following widespread protests and significant problems with collection it was replaced by the Council Tax in 1993

**comprehensive education** a system of state secondary schools designed to ensure that all children receive similar education, thus increasing equality of opportunity

**Comprehensive Spending Review** introduced by Gordon Brown this involves government departments justifying their expenditure plans to the Treasury for a three-year period, rather than the previous annual spending allocations. It also gave the Treasury a greater role in coordinating and controlling government expenditure

**corporate crime** crime committed in some form of organisational context. This highlights the problem of attributing individual human agency to the 'author' of the crime, and thus the problem of exacting appropriate punishment. Recent attempts to upgrade the law on 'corporate killing' testify to some of the problems here. Sutherland uses this interchangeably with white collar crime as a rhetorical challenge to Criminology. See too 'zemiology'

**CRASBO** a criminal ASBO, which the court can impose upon conviction of a criminal offence in addition to the punishment. Conditions of the CRASBO are intended to help prevent re-offending, but extend further than merely desisting from committing the offence in future

**criminalisation** refers to a range of social and criminal justice processes (including policing, prosecution, punishment, penalisation, stigmatisation and blame) through which an individual or group is accorded the 'label' of criminal

**cycle of deprivation thesis** Conservative Minister Keith Joseph, in a speech to the Pre-School Playgoup Association, propounded the view that deprivation was transmitted through the family

**dark figure of crime** refers to the truism that 'recorded crime' is but a fraction of the potential total of activity that *could be* processed as crime. The British Crime Survey, which is a victim survey, goes some way to fleshing this out

**demand-side** stimulation of demand for goods and services

**dependency culture** often used to describe a situation where people are seen to have become passive recipients of welfare, dependent upon benefits

**dependency ratio** dependency rates or ratios focus on the relative sizes of the economically active part of the population and those who are designated as dependent (primarily children and older people). Generally, a lower dependency ratio implies relatively more workers and less requirement to support dependent populations, while a higher dependency ratio suggests that a higher proportion of a population is dependent and a smaller proportion economically active

**deregulation** the process by which governments have sought to reduce and remove regulations on businesses in order to improve the theoretical efficiency of markets. The theory is that deregulation will lead to greater competitiveness and efficiency

**deviance** is used to refer to 'rule breaking behaviour' and, more controversially, to deviations from the normal, that is, pathological states

**due process** a set of procedural rules that should be followed in order to approximate formal justice

**Earth Summit** an attempt to bring together participants, including heads of state and government, national delegates, non-governmental organisations, businesses and other major groups, to focus upon improving people's lives and conserving natural resources

**economic inactivity** refers to people not looking for, or not available for, work

**ethical theory** ideas that seek to provide a framework for consideration of what is ethical

**ethnicity** the identification of individuals as members of a particular group on the basis of their origin in a community, which may be mythical or real, with a historical, territorial, cultural and/or racial basis

**eugenics** can be interpreted as the view that society can be improved through the manipulation of genetic inheritance through reproduction

**Exchange Rate Mechanism** the European Exchange Rate Mechanism is a system which sought to reduce variability between currencies, with currencies fixed but fluctuating within set margins

**externality** a side effect of an activity that affects other parties without being reflected in the price of the good or service involved

**Fabianism** the Fabian Society has existed for more than 150 years. Fabians have believed that the free market system was inappropriate for the solution of social problems and that instead there should be collective provision. Closely linked with the Labour Party and with social democratic and democratic socialist thinking, Fabian ideas were influential in the development of the post-war welfare state

**Fordist** a range of processes associated with industrial mass production, named after Henry Ford's approach in the car industry

**further education** education often provided by further education colleges, sometimes available to children aged 16 to 19, but also aimed at adults. Although often linked to qualifications or careers, it can also be used solely to enhance knowledge and skills

**genetically modified crops** these (GM) crops are from plants that have had their genes modified, for example, to make them more tolerant of particular conditions or resistant to certain herbicides

**Gini coefficient** a measure of inequality ranging from 0 (complete equality) to 1 (one person has all the income or wealth, depending on what is being measured). Sometimes expressed as 0-100 per cent

**globalisation** whilst there are different perspectives, globalisation recognises that a variety of forces are leading to similar cultural, economic, social, political and technical developments around the world

**GP fundholders** as part of the internal market within the health service created by the Conservatives in the 1990s, GP practices were able to opt to receive a budget (become fundholders) with which they could then establish contracts with their chosen providers

**grant maintained schools** schools which opt out of local education authority control, are self-governing and receive their funding directly from central government

**gross domestic product** the total value of goods and services produced by a nation. The GDP includes consumer and government purchases, private domestic investments and net exports of goods and services. It therefore measures national output

**higher education** more specialist provision through universities and colleges of higher education, including undergraduate degrees (BA (Bachelor of Arts), BSc (Bachelor of Sciences), LLB (Bachelor of Laws), etc.), taught postgraduate awards (such as MA and MSc) and research degrees (frequently a PhD, or Doctor of Philosophy)

**housing associations** non-profit making bodies that specialise in housing and plough any surplus into maintaining existing homes and helping to finance new ones. They provide homes to rent and also run low-cost home ownership schemes

**human development index** the HDI provides a composite measure of three dimensions of human development: living a long and healthy life (measured by life expectancy), being educated (measured by adult literacy and enrolment at the primary, secondary and tertiary level) and having a decent standard of living (measured by **purchasing power parity**, PPP, income). Based on this composite measure the countries of the world are ranked in terms of their relative development.

**human genetics** the understanding of human genes and their behaviour, a topic which has received greater attention with the unravelling of the human genome and the development of a greater ability to manipulate DNA

**Independent Sector Treatment Centres** treatment centres owned by the private sector or by social enterprises which are contracted to work within the NHS in England. They generally perform common elective surgery and diagnostic tests

**informal economy** those economic activities conducted mostly outside of the legal and administrative institutions of the formal economy

**institutional racism** processes within an organisation which lead to differentially adverse outcomes for minority ethnic users, going beyond prejudicial behaviour of individuals within the organisation

**intergovernmental organisations** organisations that are generally created by treaties or agreements between states, such as the World Bank; these have a legal status and often have mechanisms for resolving disputes between members

**internal markets** the Conservative governments of 1979–1997 sought to improve the efficiency and responsiveness of services such as health and social care through the introduction of internal markets, based on the separation of the functions of purchasing and providing of services

**integration, integrationism** the notion that members of minority ethnic groups should feel and be seen to be participant in the culture, economy and politics of society as a whole, while having their own particular ethnic identity

**Keynesianism** the economist John Maynard Keynes argued that governments could successfully intervene in the economy to stimulate demand (and therefore to achieve full employment) and to reduce demand (and therefore achieve lower inflation). Keynesianism provided the basis for economic policy in most Western states from 1945 to the 1970s

**Kyoto Protocol** signed in Kyoto in 1997 this committed the industrialised nations to reducing worldwide emissions of greenhouse gases by an average of 5.2 per cent below 1990 levels over the next decade

**labelling theory** a convenient shorthand for the social reaction perspective based on the premise that a situation, if defined as real, will be real in its consequences. The area is contested, but ranges from a focus upon the interaction between the potential deviant and those who so label him/her, through to the idea that if you call someone deviant/criminal this will confirm and reproduce their problem behaviour and thus make things worse. For example, the idea that the criminal justice system is part of the problem of crime in that it makes things worse, and is not necessarily the best solution

**labour intensification** refers to how some people are working harder

**labour market segmentation** a situation in which there are so-called 'insiders', the workers with a protected job requiring high skills, and 'outsiders', who are low-skilled people that are either unemployed or employed with fixed-term, part-time or temporary with little chance to climb the career ladder

**laissez-faire** the economic doctrine that urges abstention by governments from interfering in the workings of the free market

**Lease Lend** a programme that allowed the United States to provide the United Kingdom (and other allies) with material for the Second World War in return for military bases

**liberal feminists** seek the same rights and opportunities for women as for men and focus largely on inequalities caused by prejudice and stereotyping, calling for legislation which outlaws discrimination

**Local Strategic Partnership** a single non-statutory, non executive body, aligned with local authority boundaries, that brings together at a local level the different parts of the public sector as well as the private, business, community and voluntary sectors so that different initiatives and services support each other and work together; they are intended to operate at a level which enables strategic decisions to be taken and is close enough to individual neighbourhoods to allow actions to be determined at community level

**male breadwinner** a model of the family where the husband works (the breadwinner) and earns the family income whilst the wife provides care for the family

**managerialism** an approach to criminal justice which emphasises the management of the system as a whole, with a focus on effective service delivery, efficiency and value for money. It also reflects a concern with identifying and managing 'risk' through the collection of aggregate data on offending and calculation of statistical probabilities.

**means-testing** the testing of a claimant's means in order to assess their entitlement to benefits. Only those whose resources fall below the eligibility level receive the benefits

**multiculturalism** the notion that a multi-ethnic society should respect, protect the rights of and even foster distinct minority ethnic cultures

**National Curriculum** introduced by the Education Reform Act 1988 the National Curriculum specifies what subjects must be taught to children of compulsory school age in virtually all state schools

**nationalisation** taking into public (state) ownership, as happened with major industries such as coal, gas, electricity and iron and steel in the post-war years

**neo-liberalism** a political ideology promoting economic liberalism, partly as a means to political liberty.

**new public management** a phrase used to describe a set of ideas widely implemented by governments, particularly in English-speaking countries, from the 1980s, which emphasised marketisation and drew on private sector practices

**New Right** the ideas of a group of right wing thinkers, often associated with the Thatcher governments. Neo-liberalism and neo-conservatism are were important elements of this political position

**NHS trusts** created by the Conservative government in the 1990s as part of the internal market within the NHS, the trusts run hospitals as self-governing bodies, although their freedoms have been constrained by governments

**Non Governmental Organisations** organisations established by individuals or associations of individuals and non possessing governmental powers; NGOs vary widely in size and influence.

**nursery education** pre-school education for children below the age of formal compulsory education

**occupational pension** a company pension to which both the employer and the employee make contributions

**outdoor relief** following the 1601 Poor Law, this was provision (such as money, food or clothing) given to help individuals avoid poverty without the need to enter an institution

**performance measurement** the use of measures of performance for organisations, such as schools, hospitals or even local authorities, sometimes linked with the use of 'league tables'

**pluralism** a view that believes that power is or should be shared amongst the diverse groups and interests in society, and that political decision-making should reflect bargains and compromises between these groups

**policy transfer** the practice of governments learning from approaches in other states and implementing them in their own jurisdiction

**positivism** often used interchangeably to refer to the 'positive' Italian school of criminology associated with Lombroso, and a particular method based upon observation and the search for the causes of crime. Essentially it is a 'method' characterised by the organising question, why did s/he do it and what can be done to stop them?

**post-Fordist** used to describe a perceived contrast with fordist methods of production, with an emphasis on flexible systems of production and a flexible workforce

**predictive genetic testing** the ability to test or screen using genetic tests which may suggest that individuals are likely to develop one or more particular condition, such as Huntington's disease

**primary education** education from the age of 5 to 11, designed to provide children with basic skills

**Private Finance Initiative** the Private Finance Initiative is a method of injecting private capital into the provision of public services. It can take the form of an agreement between a public body and a private company for the supply of buildings or services over a period of time, often thirty years. The public body sets the standards and pays a fee to the private company for the services provided, such as a hospital or school building, or the repair and improvement of local authority dwellings. Borrowing by the private company does not count as part of the Public Sector Borrowing Requirement

**public health** the health of the population as a whole, initially concerned with issues such as sanitation, but more recently focused on areas around the prevention of illness, such as immunisation

**public schools** independent schools which charge fees, they do not have to teach the National Curriculum

**Public Sector Borrowing Requirement** (PSBR) the difference between Government spending and its income. It is regarded as an important indicator of the Chancellor of the Exchequer's prudence in managing the economy

**public service agreements** established between the Treasury and central government departments, public service agreements set out what the department aims to achieve with a given level of resources

**quangos** although not entirely accurate, the term quasi-autonomous non-governmental organisations (quango) is widely used to describe organisations that are not directly accountable to elected bodies, such as parliament or local government

**race** the identification of individuals as members of a particular group on the basis of some physical difference of 'skin, hair and bone'

**racialisation** a descriptive process in which **race** and/or **ethnicity** is used to categorize people in groups

**radical feminists** see women as a group as oppressed by men as a group, including through male dominance of the state, and tend to call for a radical transformation of all spheres of life, with some calling for political, and in some cases personal, separation from men

**replacement ratio** the ratio of the amount a person could receive in social security benefits out of work relative to the amount they could receive if they were earning

**rent control** state determination of the rents charged by private landlords. The Conservatives attempted to phase out rent control in the 1930s and 1950s. By the 1970s, the major form of rent control was the determination of 'fair' rents by rent officers

**secondary education** education from 11 to the minimum school leaving age of 16, or to 18

**security of tenure** refers to the legal presumption that a tenant should remain in a dwelling unless the landlord can convince a court that there are very good reasons to evict the tenant

**social democracy** this position has historically encompassed both socialism and democracy as essential components. Social democrats see capitalism as capable of transformation and reform through democratic action including the welfare state. However, from the 1980s some social democratic parties have adjusted their positions in response to critiques from the New Right and others

**social exclusion** often used to describe the wider processes and outcomes that prevent people from participating in society and from accessing services

**social housing** defined by the Office of the Deputy Prime Minister as accommodation let at a rent below the market price. The term was invented in the 1980s as a way to blur the distinction between local authority housing and accommodation provided by housing associations;

**social inclusion** a situation where people do not suffer the problems associated with social exclusion

**social mobility** the degree to which an individual's, family's, or group's social status can change throughout the course of their life

**socialist feminists** socialist feminists aspire to an economically just society, with both women and men having the opportunity to fulfil their potential

**standardised attainment tests** (SATs) standard assessment tasks designed to assess the levels of attainment that pupils have achieved in core subjects, as defined by the Secretary of State for Education and Skills

**stealth taxes** taxes where the population are supposedly unaware (or at least are only partially aware) of their existence and function

**subsistence** the minimum required to maintain life, but often used to refer to the lowest level at which benefits should be set

**Sure Start** a programme introduced by the Labour government designed to address the social and health needs of children and families, including the availability of childcare

**tax credits** are used to reduce the amount of taxation paid by subtracting a sum from an individual's tax bill, but where people are not paying tax can lead to a cash payment

**Thatcherism** the ideas and policies of Margaret Thatcher, the British Prime Minister 1979–1990

**think-tanks** arguably a special type of pressure group that often has close (usually informal) links with a particular political party (such as those of the Adam Smith Institute, the Institute for Economic Affairs and the Social Affairs Unit with the Conservatives, particularly from 1979 to 1997, and the Institute for Public Policy Research with Labour)

**Toryism** essentially a form of paternalistic Conservatism, with a better off minority having a responsibility to the poorer majority

**transferable married person's allowance** proposal by the Conservative Party to allow married couples to transfer the personal tax allowance, worth about £20 per week, if one partner was not working

**underclass** often used to denote a class of people dependent on welfare, and in particular state assistance, for survival. It has been associated, by thinkers on the right, with dependency, whilst some on the left have made a link with social exclusion

**victimless crime** crime in which there is no 'obvious' direct victim of the criminal act, but instead the victim may be public morality/decency, or the criminal him/herself, for example, in relation to personal drug use

**welfare dependency** relying on social security benefits for financial support (see also **dependency culture**)

**welfare state** where the state takes responsibility for providing at least minimal levels of economic and social security through the provision of public services (such as education, health, housing and income maintenance)

**welfare to work** policies intended to move those reliant on the state for financial support (welfare) into a position of relative financial independence through paid work

**white-collar crime** may be defined as those offences committed by people of relatively high status in the course of their occupation and so could include (for example) fraud, embezzlement, tax evasion and corporate crimes involving health and safety violations and pollution

**Workers' Education Association** a voluntary movement, founded in the early twentieth century, to support the educational needs of working people

**workfare** the requirement to work, or engage in other work-related activity, in return for welfare

**zemiology** the study of all harmful activity, not just that which is criminalised.

# Index